# The European Past

SECOND EDITION

VOLUME I

## Reappraisals in History from the Renaissance Through Waterloo

**Shepard B. Clough**
*Professor of History, Columbia University*

**Peter Gay**
*Professor of History, Yale University*

**Charles K. Warner**
*Professor of History, University of Kansas*

**John M. Cammett**
*Professor of History, City University of New York*

The Macmillan Company

ACKNOWLEDGMENTS

Lynn Thorndike, "Renaissance or Prenaissance?" from *The Journal of the History of Ideas,* Vol. IV (January 1943), pp. 65-74. Reprinted by permission.

Federico Chabod, "The Concept of the Renaissance," Chapter IV, pp. 159-189. Reprinted by permission of the publishers from Federico Chabod, *Machiavelli and the Renaissance,* Cambridge, Mass.: Harvard University Press, Copyright 1958, by Federico Chabod. Reprinted in Canada by permission of The Bodley Head.

Wilhelm Pauck, "Luther's Faith," From *The Heritage of the Reformation* (rev. ed.; Glencoe, Ill.: The Free Press, 1961), pp. 19-28. Revision of an article in *Religion in Life,* Vol. XVI, No. 1. Copyright 1946 by Stone & Pierce. Reprinted by permission.

Jacques Maritain, "Martin Luther: 'A Monk Who Lacked Humility,'" from *Three Reformers: Luther, Descartes, Rousseau* (Charles Scribner's Sons, 1929), pp. 4-11, 13. Reprinted with the permission of Charles Scribner's Sons from *Three Reformers* by Jacques Maritain.

Philip Hughes, "The Reformation: 'Nothing Less Than Catastrophic.'" Reprinted with permission of The Macmillan Company from *The Reformation in England* by Philip Hughes. First published in 1951. Reprinted in Canada by permission of Burns & Oates, Ltd.

E. G. Schweibert, "The Reformation: 'A Much-Needed One,'" from *Martin Luther and His Times* (St. Louis: Concordia Publishing House, 1950), pp. *1-11*. Reprinted by permission.

Herbert Butterfield, "The Historical Importance of a Theory of Impetus," from *The Origins of Modern Science 1300-1800* (New York: Collier Books, 1951), pp. 1-12. Reprinted by permission of Collier Books, New York, and G. Bell & Sons, Ltd., London.

Leonardo Olschki, "The Search for Truth," from *The Genius of Italy* by Leonardo Olschki (New York: Oxford University Press, 1949), pp. 368-385. Reprinted by permission of Cornell University Press.

Carl L. Becker, "The Laws of Nature and the New History," from *The Heavenly City of the Eighteenth-Century Philosophers* (11th ed., New Haven, Conn.: Yale University Press, 1955), pp. 29-31, 37-41, 67-70, 84-88, and 99-102. Reprinted by permission.

Peter Gay, "Carl Becker's Heavenly City," from *The Political Science Quarterly*, Vol. LXXII (June 1957), pp. 182-199. Reprinted by permission. This paper was delivered in slightly different form at the Sixth Annual Meeting of the New York State Association of European Historians on October 13, 1956, at Colgate University.

R. H. Tawney, "Max Weber: An Evaluation." Selections from *The Protestant Ethic and the Spirit of Capitalism* by Max Weber, translated by Talcott Parsons (Foreword by R. H. Tawney and "The Spirit of Capitalism") are used by permission of Charles Scribner's Sons. Reprinted in Canada by permission of George Allen & Unwin, Ltd.

Max Weber, "The Spirit of Capitalism." Selections from *The Protestant Ethic and the Spirit of Capitalism* by Max Weber, translated by Talcott Parsons (Foreword by R. H. Tawney and "The Spirit of Capitalism") are used by permission of Charles Scribner's Sons. Reprinted in Canada by permission of George Allen & Unwin, Ltd.

V. A. Demant, "The Weber Thesis: Controversy and Consensus," from *Religion and the Decline of Capitalism* by V. A. Demant (London: Faber & Faber, Ltd., 1952), pp. 16-19. Reprinted by permission of Faber & Faber, Ltd.

Earl J. Hamilton, "The Role of Monopoly in the Overseas Expansion and Colonial Trade of Europe Before 1800," from *Papers and Proceedings of The American Economic Association*, supplement to *The American Economic Review*, Vol. XXXVIII (1948), pp. 33-53. Reprinted by permission.

J. H. Parry, "The Expansion of Europe Overseas, 1415-1715," from *Europe and a Wider World* by J. H. Parry, 1949, by permission of Hutchinson's Publishing Group, pp. 7-12, 29-32, 36-37, 39-40, 43, 64-67, 185-194.

H. R. Trevor-Roper, "The General Crisis of the Seventeenth Century," world copyright, The Past & Present Society, Corpus Christi College, Oxford. This article is reprinted by kind permission of the Society from *Past & Present*. This article is included in *Crisis in Europe, 1560-1660*, edited by Trevor Aston, and published by Routledge & Kegan Ltd., and in other editions of this book published by Basic Books, and by Doubleday & Co., Inc., Anchor Books.

Roland Mousnier, J. H. Elliot, and H. R. Trevor-Roper, "Trevor-Roper's 'General Crisis'– Symposium," *world copyright:* The Past & Present Society, Corpus Christi College, Oxford. This article is reprinted by kind permission of the Society from *Past & Present*. This article is included in *Crisis in Europe, 1560-1660*, edited by Trevor Aston, and published by Routledge & Kegan Paul, Ltd., and in other editions of this book published by Basic Books, and by Doubleday & Co. Inc., Anchor Books. Because of a shortage of space, not all contributions in the original Symposium are included here.

R. M. Hartwell, "Interpretations of the Industrial Revolution in England: A Methodological Inquiry," from *The Journal of Economic History*, Vol. XIX (June 1959), pp. 229-249. Reprinted by permission.

E. P. Thompson, "The English Working Class," from *The Making of the English Working Class* by E. P. Thompson. Copyright © 1963 by E. P. Thompson. Reprinted by permission of Pantheon Books, a division of Random House, Inc. and Victor Gollancz Ltd.

Friedrich Meinecke, "Machiavelli," from *Machiavellism, The Doctrine of Raison d'État and Its Place in Modern History* (trans. Douglas Scott) (New Haven, Conn.: Yale University Press, 1957), pp. 29-44. Reprinted by permission.

C. J. Friedrich, "Machiavelli: The State as a Work of Art and Its Rationality," from C. J. Friedrich, *Constitutional Reason of State: The Survival of the Constitutional Order* (Providence, R. I.: Brown University Press, 1957), pp. 15-33. Copyright 1957 by Brown University. Reprinted by permission.

David Ogg, "Louis XIV: The Ruler of France," from *Louis XIV* (London: Oxford University Press, 1933), pp. 102-110, 113-116, 125-132. Reprinted by permission.

Roland Mousnier, "Louis XIV as State-Builder," from *Les XVIᵉ et XVIIᵉ siècles*, Tome IV, Histoire générale des civilizations (Paris: Presses Universitaires de France, 1954), pp. 229-236. Editors' translation. Copyright by Presses Universitaires de France, 1953. Reprinted by permission.

Roland Mousnier, "Some Reflections on Absolutism and Despotism," from R. Mousnier and F. Hartung, "Quelques Problèmes concernant la monarchie absolue," *Relazioni del X Congresso Internazionale di Scienze Storiche* (Florence: G. C. Sansoni, 1955), Vol. IV, pp. 4-12. Editors' translation. Proprietà Letteraria. Reprinted by permission.

J. H. Hexter, "The English Aristocracy, Its Crises, and the English Revolution, 1558-1660," from *The Journal of British Studies*, Vol. VIII, No. 1 (November 1968), pp. 22-24, 52-78, published by the Conference on British Studies at Trinity College, Hartford, Connecticut. Reprinted by permission.

Lawrence Stone, "Postscript to Eight Hundred and Forty-one Pages," from *The Journal of British Studies*, Vol. VIII, No. 1 (November 1968), pp. 79-82, published by the Conference on British Studies at Trinity College, Hartford, Connecticut. Reprinted by permission.

J. H. Hexter, "Postscript to an Awfully Long Review," from *The Journal of British Studies*, Vol IX, No. 1 (November 1969), pp. 45-48, published by the Conference on British Studies of Trinity College, Hartford, Connecticut. Reprinted by permission.

Sir Lewis Namier, "The Biography of Ordinary Men." Reprinted by permission of The Macmillan Company from *Crossroads of Power* by Sir Lewis Namier. Copyright 1962 by Lady Namier. Also reprinted by permission of Hamish Hamilton, Ltd., London.

Herbert Butterfield, "George III and the Namier School." Reprinted by permission of The Macmillan Company from *George III and the Historians* (rev. ed.) by Herbert Butterfield. Copyright 1957, 1959 by Herbert Butterfield. Pp. 202-213.

Jacob M. Price, "Party, Purpose, and Pattern: Sir Lewis Namier and His Critics," from *The Journal of British Studies*, Vol. I (November 1961) pp. 72-93. Reprinted by permission.

Vittorio Lanternari, "Messianism: Its Historical Origin and Morphology," from *History of Religions* (Chicago: University of Chicago Press, 1962), Vol. II, No. 1, pp. 52-72. Reprinted by permission of the publisher and author and by permission of Felice Laudadio, Daedalo Libri, Bari, Italy, publishers of *Occidento e Terzo Mondo,* by Vittorio Lauternari.

E. J. Hobsbawm, "Archaic Forms of Social Agitation," from *Primitive Rebels* (New York: Frederick Praeger, 1963), pp. 1-12, 57-65, 105-107. Reprinted by permission of the publisher, and of the University of Manchester Press, Manchester, England, holder of Canadian rights.

George Rudé, "The Crowd: The Subject and Its Problems," from *The Crowd in History, 1730-1843* (New York: John Wiley & Sons, 1964), pp. 3-6, 214-236, 259-269. Reprinted by permission.

Peter Worsley, Ghita Ionescu, and Maurice Cranston, "To Define Populism: Symposium," from *Governments in Opposition* (London: Government and Opposition, Ltd., at the London School of Economics and Political Science, Spring, 1968), Vol. III, No. 2, pp. 168-179. Printed in the United States by the Johns Hopkins Press. Reprinted by permission *of Government and Opposition.*

Albert Soboul, "Classes and Class Struggles During the French Revolution," from *Science and Society,* Vol. XVII, No. 3 (Summer 1953), pp. 238-257. Copyright 1953 by Science and Society, Incorporated. Reprinted by permission.

Ernest Labrousse, "The Fiscal and Economic Crises at the End of the Ancien Régime," from *La Crise de l'économie française à la fin de l'ancien régime et au début de la Révolution* (Paris: Presses Universitaires de France, 1944), pp. xlii-li. Copyright by Presses Universitaires de France, 1943. Editors' translation. Reprinted by permission.

Jacques Godechot, "'World Revolution' or 'French Revolution,'" from *La grande nation: l'expansion révolutionnaire de la France dans le monde de 1789 à 1799,* 2 vols. (Paris: Aubier, 1956), pp. 15-19. Copyright Éditions Montaigne. Editors' translation. Reprinted by permission.

Georges Lefebvre, "Napoleon," from "Napoléon," *Peuples et Civilisations,* Vol. XIV (4th ed., revised and augmented; Paris: Presses Universitaires de France, 1953), pp. 63-69 and 139-151. [Editors' trans.] Copyright by Presses Universitaires de France, 1936. Translation prepared with the kind permission of Columbia University Press, publishers of an English translation of the entire volume. Reprinted by permission.

Louis Madelin, "Napoleon," from *Histoire du consulat et de l'empire* (Paris: Librairie Hachette, 1937-1954), Vol. III, *De Brumaire à Marengo,* pp. 78-83 and 97; Vol. IV, *Le Consulat,* pp. 169-173, 176-180; Vol. XVI, *Les Cent Jours, Waterloo,* pp. 372-374. [Editors' trans.] Vol. III, Copyright by Librairie Hachette, 1938; Vol. IV, Copyright by Librairie Hachette, 1939; Vol. XVI, Copyright by Librairie Hachette, 1954. Reprinted by permission.

# Preface to the Second Edition

This edition of *The European Past* is informed by the same purpose as the first edition; that is, to present recent evaluations and conflicts in the interpretation of important historical topics. Increasing numbers of both scholars and students, with good reason, have been drawn to the study of modern history. Consequently, changes in this edition are more extensive than is usual in a revision. Some twenty-six selections in the first edition have been deleted, and twenty-eight new essays have been added. The majority of the new ones are recent contributions which have appeared since the publication of the first edition of *The European Past*. Several topics are altogether new; among them are "The Crisis of the Seventeenth Century," "Towards the Origins of Modern Revolution" (Volume I), and "Fascism," "Stanlinism," and "Twentieth-Century Revolutions" (Volume II).

S.B.C.
P.G.
C.K.W.
J.M.C.

# Preface to the First Edition

It has been the object of the editors of this book to introduce new materials and a new approach to the study of European history. Included in these two volumes are historical essays which present revaluations or conflicts of interpretation centered around thirty-two important historical topics.

Sometimes controversies evolve from differences in method; sometimes from fundamental differences in the philosophy of history; sometimes from the selection of different data. In every case, however, the reader is introduced to the frontiers of research in history. He is given a sense of the "sifting and winnowing" involved in historical judgment and provided with an opportunity to make informed judgments of his own.

Controversies or reinterpretations produced by different historical questions have, of course, been used to some degree in other books of readings. But the typical "case study" frequently offers a hodgepodge of primary and secondary materials in such fragmentary form as to vitiate their meaning. The selections presented in this book aim at conveying a sense of depth of the subject being treated.

It will be noticed that the largest part of the selections included here have been published during the last twenty years. All come from the current generation of scholars or their teachers. This choice has been deliberate. The great classic controversies of the last century or the earlier years of this one which fill the pages of some books of readings are not, of course, without interest. But if history is a cumulative study which permits us to know more and more about the past, is not the latest history the best gauge of whatever consensus has been reached on a given issue?

The selections presented here are either articles from scholarly journals, most often reproduced in their original length, or they are meaningful portions of monographs or broader studies. An innovation has been to offer, where possible, an historiographical essay as one of the selections under a particular topic. Where this has not been possible, background information is included in the topic introduction. Several of the essays have been translated expressly for this book.

The editors wish to acknowledge the research assistance of James Friguglietti, the secretarial help of Patricia Cutler Warner, and the translation assistance of Cambridge Editorial Research, Inc.

S. B. C.
P. G.
C. K. W.

# Contents

**INTELLECTUAL CURRENTS**

1.  The Problem of the Renaissance     *3*

    Lynn Thorndike—"Renaissance or Prenaissance?"     *4*
    from *The Journal of the History of Ideas*

    Federico Chabod—"The Concept of the Renaissance"     *11*
    from *Machiavelli and the Renaissance*

2.  The Reformation: Catholic and Protestant Views     *29*

    Wilhelm Pauck—"Luther's Faith"     *31*
    from *The Heritage of the Reformation*

    Jacques Maritain—"Martin Luther: 'A Monk Who Lacked
    Humility' "     *36*
    from *Three Reformers: Luther, Descartes, Rousseau*

    Philip Hughes—"The Reformation: 'Nothing Less than
    Catastrophic'"     *40*
    from *The Reformation in England*

    E. G. Schweibert—"The Reformation: 'A Much-Needed One'"     *45*
    from *Martin Luther and His Times*

3.  The Scientific Revolution: The Problem of the Origins     *51*

    Herbert Butterfield—"The Historical Importance of a Theory
    of Impetus"     *52*
    from *The Origins of Modern Science 1300-1800*

    Leonardo Olschki—"The Search for Truth"     *59*
    from *The Genius of Italy*

4.  The Enlightenment: A Break with the Past?     *70*

    Carl L. Becker—"The Laws of Nature and the New History"     *72*
    from *The Heavenly City of the Eighteenth-Century
    Philosophers*

    Peter Gay—"Carl Becker's Heavenly City"     *78*
    from *The Political Science Quarterly*

## ECONOMIC AND SOCIAL TRANSFORMATIONS

5.  Protestantism and the Rise of Capitalism: Max Weber and His
    Critics                                                                          93

    R. H. Tawney—"Max Weber: An Evaluation"                                           95
    from *The Protestant Ethic and the Spirit of Capitalism* by
    Max Weber; foreward by R. H. Tawney

    Max Weber—"The Spirit of Capitalism"                                            101
    from *The Protestant Ethic and the Spirit of Capitalism*

    V. A. Demant—"The Weber Thesis: Controversy and Consensus                       114
    from *Religion and the Decline of Capitalism*

6.  The Expansion of Europe: The Profit Motive or Missionary Zeal?                  118

    Earl J. Hamilton—"The Role of Monopoly in the Overseas
    Expansion and Colonial Trade of Europe Before 1800"                             119
    from *Papers and Proceedings of the American Economic
    Association*

    J. H. Parry—"The Expansion of Europe Overseas, 1415-1715"                       134
    from *Europe and a Wider World*

7.  The Crisis of the Seventeenth Century                                           149

    H. R. Trevor-Roper—"The General Crisis of the Seventeenth
    Century"                                                                        151
    from *Crisis in Europe 1560-1660*

    Roland Mousnier, J. H. Elliott, H. R. Trevor-Roper—"Trevor-
    Roper's 'General Crisis'"—Symposium                                             174
    from *Crisis in Europe 1560-1660*

8.  The Industrial Revolution: Misery or Well-Being for the Working
    Classes?                                                                        189

    R. M. Hartwell—"Interpretations of the Industrial Revolution
    in England: A Methodological Inquiry"                                           191
    from *The Journal of Economic History*

    E. P. Thompson—"The English Working Class"                                      206
    from *The Making of the English Working Class*

## THE AGE OF STATE BUILDING

9.  Reason of State: The Legacy of Machiavelli                                      237

    Friedrich Meinecke—"Machiavelli"                                                239
    from *Machiavellism, The Doctrine of Raison d' État and
    Its Place in Modern History*

C. J. Friedrich–"Machiavelli: The State as a Work of Art and Its Rationality"    *251*
from *Constitutional Reason of State: The Survival of the Constitutional Order*

10. Louis XIV: Despot or State-Builder?    *261*

David Ogg–"Louis XIV: The Ruler of France"    *262*
from *Louis XIV*

Roland Mousnier–"Louis XIV as State Builder"    *269*
from *Les XVIᵉ et XVIIᵉ siècles, Tome IV, Histoire générale des civilizations*

Roland Mousnier–"Some Reflections on Absolutism and Despotism"    *275*
from *"Quelques Problèmes concernant la monarchie absolue," Relazioni del X Congresso di Scienze Storiche*

11. The Origins of the English Civil War: Socio-Economic Crisis or a Conflict of "Faith and Freedom"    *281*

J. H. Hexter–"The English Aristocracy, Its Crises and the English Revolution, 1558-1660"    *283*
from *The Journal of British Studies*

Lawrence Stone–"Postscript to Eight Hundred and Forty-one Pages"    *303*
from *The Journal of British Studies*

J. H. Hexter–"Postscript to an Awfully Long Review"    *305*
from *The Journal of British Studies*

12. Politics in the Reign of King George III: The Controversy Around Sir Lewis Namier's History    *308*

Sir Lewis Namier–"The Biography of Ordinary Men"    *310*
from *Crossroads of Power*

Herbert Butterfield–"George III and the Namier School"    *313*
from *George III and the Historians*

Jacob M. Price–"Party, Purpose, and Pattern: Sir Lewis Namier and His Critics"    *319*
from *The Journal of British Studies*

**THE AGE OF REVOLUTION**

13. Towards the Origins of Modern Revolutions: Crowds, Millenarianism Populism    *335*

Vittorio Lanternari–"Messianism: Its Historical Origin and Morphology"    *337*
from *History of Religions*

E. J. Hobsbawm—"Archaic Forms of Social Agitation"
  from *Primitive Rebels*                                          *345*

George Rudé—"The Crowd: The Subject and Its Problems"
  from *The Crowd in History 1730-1843*                            *360*

Peter Worsley, Ghita Ionescu, and Maurice Cranston—"To Define
Populism: Symposium"
  from *Governments and Opposition*                                *383*

14.  The Origins of the French Revolution: Three Recent Views      *392*

Albert Soboul—"Classes and Class Struggles During the French
Revolution"
  from *Science and Society*                                       *394*

Ernest Labrousse—"The Fiscal and Economic Crises at the End
of the Ancien Régime"
  from *La Crise de l'économie française à la fin de l'ancien
  régime et au début de la Révolution*                            *406*

Jacques Godechot—"'World Revolution' or 'French Revolution'"       *412*
  from *La grande nation: l'expansion révolutionnaire de la France
  dans le monde de 1789 à 1799*

15.  Napoleon: "An Argument Without End"                           *416*

Georges Lefebvre—"Napoleon"                                        *418*
  from *Napoleon, Peuples et Civilisations*

Louis Madelin—"Napoleon"                                           *428*
  from *Histoire du consulat et de l'empire*

# INTELLECTUAL CURRENTS

# 1 / The Problem of the Renaissance

The Problem of the Renaissance

The Renaissance is an appropriate starting point for a collection of historiographical problems because, as Professor Wallace Ferguson has noted, historians of "every generation since Plutarch" have contributed to the interpretation of the Renaissance.[1] The idea of the Renaissance began with the Italian humanists themselves who declared their own time a rebirth of learning after a dark age and seemed thoroughly established, in the middle of the nineteenth century, with Friedrich Burckhardt's great synthesis which defined the Renaissance as a distinct historical period. In the second quarter of the twentieth century, however, the "revolt of the medievalists" nearly expunged the word *renaissance* from the historical vocabulary.

The first selection presents Professor Lynn Thorndike, one of a group of distinguished medievalists, who, emphasizing historical continuity, finds many of the supposed characteristics of the Renaissance in the Middle Ages[2] and thinks the concept of a Renaissance too synthetic and too arbitrary.

The second selection presents the views of the late Federico Chabod, one of the most versatile of the twentieth century Italian historians. Chabod declares that the alleged continuity of Medieval and Renaissance life is in most respects superficial. This, he asserts, becomes clear when we distinguish practical from intellectual life: Unscrupulous princes have always existed but the conception that "politics is politics and nothing more" is a Renaissance idea. The literature of classical antiquity had always been studied but in the Middle Ages it was mere ornamentation whereas in the Renaissance it represented "the ideal moment of human history." The Renaissance transformed the Medieval notion of a hierarchy of all learning crowned by theology into an insistence on the "autonomy of art, politics, science, and history." Nonetheless, Chabod concedes that the Renaissance world view was fragmentary and incomplete. It never dreamed of asserting the autonomy of economic activity nor of the possibility of a purely rational ethics. Apparently, the "problem of the Renaissance" is that it is both the end of one era and the beginning of another.

[1] See particularly his *The Renaissance in Historical Thought* (Boston: Houghton Mifflin Company, 1948).
[2] Conversely he has also stressed "medievalism" in Renaissance thought. See "The Survival of Medieval Intellectual Interests into Early Modern Times," *Speculum,* Vol. II (April, 1927), pp. 147-159.

# RENAISSANCE OR PRENAISSANCE?

**Lynn Thorndike**

Professor Dana B. Durand has accused me of harboring a personal antipathy to the Renaissance. Whether my motive is personal or rational, objective or subjective, conscious or sub-conscious, it must be confessed that my aversion to the term in question is even more sweeping than Durand perhaps thinks and extends to such catchwords as the Carolingian Renaissance and the twelfth-century renaissance, as well as to the more often mentioned Italian Renaissance of the fifteenth century or somewhere thereabouts. Religion may have its resurrections and revivals, but I have even less faith than Nicodemus in rebirths or restorations of whole periods of human history. I take my stand with the blind writer of Christian hymns, Fanny Crosby, who sang,

> But the bird with the broken pinion never soared so high again;

with William Muldoon who said of former heavy-weight champions,

> They never come back;

with Omar Khayyam who mused,

> The moving finger writes and having writ
> Moves on; nor all your piety nor wit
> May lure it back to cancel half a line
> Nor all your tears wipe out one word of it;

and with a verse from the light opera, Tom Jones,

> Time is not a necromancer;
> Time's a thief and nothing more.

Legacies from the past? Yes. Inheritances from previous periods? Yes. Survivals? Yes. Resemblances to our forebears? Yes. Reformations? Perhaps. Reactions? Unfortunately. But no rebirths and no restorations!

Books and works of art are about all that remains to us of the past. The latter are all too soon sadly altered, and their restoration, whether by some German professor or by a Thorwaldsen or Viollet-le-Duc, only makes them less like what they originally were. Books remain less changed by the lapse of time, but even their text may become corrupt, or the meaning of the very words they use alter in the interim. The humanists of the so-called Italian Renaissance had only a bookish knowledge of antiquity; they failed almost as dismally as have Mussolini and his Fascists to make the reality of ancient Rome live again. If, even in our own day, all the resources of the art of history aided by archaeology can give us only a faint and imperfect idea of the past, how can we expect actual renaissances of it, or recognize them as such, if they were to occur? At the age of sixty I am perhaps more like myself at the age of twenty than I am like anyone else. But I couldn't possibly put myself back into the frame of mind that I had then. I have a dim recollection of it; my present state of mind is an outgrowth of it; that is all. A girl of eighteen, dressed up in the clothes which her grandmother wore

4

when a girl of eighteen, may look more like her grandmother as she was then than her grandmother herself does now. But she will not feel or act as her grandmother felt and acted half a century or more ago. Much more tenuous is the connection between distant historical periods, and much less likely is it that historians can successfully venture upon glittering generalities about them. Who can evoke from the past more than a wraith, a phantasy, a specter, which murmurs, like the ghost in *Hamlet*, "Historian, remember me!"

It is true that history offers examples of human customs which somewhat resemble the conception of a renaissance. For instance, at Tonalamatl in ancient Mexico the recurrence of the year date 2. acatl every 52 years was considered a critical occasion, it being feared that the sun might fail to rise next day and that the evil spirits might destroy the world and mankind. Accordingly, a festival of ceremonial fire-making was held. All the old fires were carefully extinguished and at midnight on the mountain top the high-priest by rubbing sticks together kindled a new fire on the breast of a prisoner who was forthwith sacrificed. The new fire was then distributed to the temples of the surrounding cities and thence to the adjacent peoples. Old garments were thrown away and household dishes and utensils were broken or freshly painted over in token of the new lease of life given to mankind.[1] But this rekindling and renewal was immediate, continuous, and perfunctory. Only a part of one night intervened between the two periods, not centuries of dark ages. There was no intellectual or spiritual rebirth.

We might also adduce the influence upon our notions of revolutions and periods in history of the astrological theory of conjunctions and revolutions of the planets.

But let us turn to the development of the concept of an Italian Renaissance and begin with the translation into Latin of Ptolemy's *Geography* in the first decade of the fifteenth century. Durand is inclined to censure the previous medieval translators for neglecting this work. If they did—for a previous translation may have escaped our notice—it is to be remembered that after all the text in question consists largely of lists of ancient place-names, many of which cannot be identified and located with any assurance and are of purely historical and linguistic interest. Moreover, Ptolemy had made the Mediterranean Sea too short by one-third, whereas one of the medieval *portolani* is more accurate than any other map of the Mediterranean until the eighteenth century. Concerning the Far East, too, and islands in the Atlantic the thirteenth and fourteenth centuries were much better informed than Ptolemy. The translation and subsequent vogue of his *Geography* were therefore in some ways regrettable. Be that as it may, in the dedication of his translation to Pope Alexander V, Jacobus Angelus, who was a booster of his native town of Florence, says:

> This very age of ours, especially in our city of Florence, has sparkled with how many wits, who to their great glory have resuscitated liberal studies which had grown almost torpid.

In the fifth volume of *A History of Magic and Experimental Science* I have given various examples of this notion of a resuscitation of liberal studies becoming stereotyped and being extended to most inappropriate fields, such as astronomy by Moravus and Santritter, chiromancy and physiognomy by Cocles, anatomy by Vesalius, and magic in the case of Antiochus Tibertus. Abstemius depicted Pope Paul III as restoring astrology after it had lain in darkness, disrepute, barbarism and sordid squalor for many centuries past; Pena praised Charles, cardinal of Lorraine, for having

---

[1] Joyce, *Mexican Archaeology* (1914), 74.

resuscitated the prostrate mathematical sciences.[2] Just as the humanists who found
manuscripts of the Latin classics in monasteries represented themselves as discovering
the work in question and rescuing it from neglect and decay, saying nothing of the fact
that the monks had copied it in Carolingian times and preserved it ever since, but
leaving their own manuscripts when they died to some monastery as the safest place in
which to keep them, so publishers who printed a text for the first time, even if it was a
typical product of medieval scholasticism, represented themselves as snatching it from
Gothic filth and dust and mildew and cobwebs and bringing it to the light of fairest
impressions with the text carefully restored to its pristine purity and freed from
barbarisms, when in reality they were very likely using a single inferior manuscript and
neglecting a dozen older and superior versions.

When was the word *Renaissance* first used? Nicolaus Prucknerus or Prugner
approached such usage when, in the preface to his re-edition of the ancient Roman
astrologer, Julius Firmicus Maternus, addressed from Strasbourg on January 28, 1551,
to young King Edward VI of England, he spoke of religion reviving in that realm (*una
cum renascente religione istius regni*). But evidently he was speaking of the Protestant
Reformation. Two years later, however, the French naturalist, Pierre Belon, in the
dedicatory epistle of his *Les observations... de plusieurs singularitez* to François
Cardinal Tournon, assured him that, as a result of his patronage of learning and
education of promising young scholars, it had followed that the minds of men, which
were formerly as it were asleep and sunk in a profound slumber of long-standing
ignorance, had begun to awake, to come forth from the shadows where they had so
long dwelt, and to develop in all sorts of good disciplines a happy and desirable
Renaissance, like plants that, after the rigors of winter, regain their strength with the
sun and sweetness of springtime.[3]

Peter Ramus, in an oration delivered in 1546, made the following vivid contrast
between his own and the preceding century. Suppose, he said, a master of a century
ago should return to life now, what progress he would discover, how astounded he
would be! He would be as surprised as one who, risen from depths of earth, should see
for the first time sun, moon and stars shining bright. For then he heard no one speak
except in a barbarous and inept manner, while now he would hear countless persons of
every age speaking and writing Latin correctly and ornately. Then no one could read
Greek, now men not only read it but understand it thoroughly. He used to hear as
grammarians, poets and orators, Alexander of Villa-Dei, Facetus, the *Graecismus;* in
philosophy, Scotists and followers of Petrus Hispanus; in medicine, the Arabs; in
theology, I know not what upstarts. Now he would hear Terence, Caesar, Virgil,
Cicero, Aristotle, Plato, Galen, Hippocrates, Moses and the prophets, the Apostles and
other true and genuine messengers of the Gospel, and indeed voices in all languages.[4]

[2] *A History of Magic and Experimental Science*, V, 334-335, 52-53, 524, 530, 55, 265, and 304.
[3] Edition of Paris, 1553, printed by Benoist Prevost, rue Prementel: "De la est ensuivy que les esprits des hommes qui auparavant estoyent comme endormis et detenuz assopiz en un profond sommeil d'ancienne ignorance ont commencé à s'esveiller et sortir des tenebres ou si long temps estoyent demeurez ensueliz et en sortant ont iecté hors et tiré en evidence toutes especes de bonnes disciplines lesquelles à luer tant eureuse et desirable renaissance, tout ainsi que les nouvelles plantes après saison de l'hyver reprennent leur vigeur à la chaleur du Soleil et sont consolées de la doulceur du printemps."
[4] For the Latin of the passage, which I have rendered freely, see K. Waddington, *Ramus, sa vie, ses écrits* (1858), 304-305. For a very similar attitude by Giovanni Ferrerio, in an academic dissertation published at Paris in 1539, see *Magic and Experimental Science*, V, 295.

Except for the closing allusions to vernacular translations of the Bible, this passage well expresses the original restricted significance of the Renaissance as a purification of Latin diction and grammar, a revival of Greek, and a return from medieval compilers, commentators and originators to the old classical texts. This was all that the revival of learning meant to the Italian humanists of the quattrocento and to their fellows beyond the Alps, and for them it was enough. The mere thought of it aroused in Ramus a grand and glorious feeling of enthusiasm tempered with complacency. He neither sensed any change in the political and economic set-up nor was aware of any alteration in social and moral values.

As the study and reading of Latin and Greek waned, however—and this was partly because the humanists and classicists had substituted a dead for a living language—fewer and fewer persons could sincerely share in this thrill or impart it to others. Such fervor as the concept of the Renaissance still invoked was largely in the realm of the fine arts, where the term had been applied to the post-Gothic period. It was at this juncture that Michelet called the Renaissance "the discovery of the world and of man," and was followed in this lead by the very influential book of Burckhardt, in which, on what seem too often to be dogmatic or imaginary grounds without sufficient presentation of facts as evidence, the Renaissance was no longer regarded as primarily a rebirth of classical learning and culture but rather as a pre-birth or precursor of present society and of modern civilization—"a period," to quote the *Boston Transcript* (February 27, 1926) concerning Elizabethan England, "that witnessed the birth pangs of most that is worth while in modern civilization and government."

This made a well-calculated appeal to the average reader who is little interested to be told that Erasmus was a great Greek scholar or that Leonardo da Vinci copied from Albert of Saxony, but whose ego is titillated to be told that Leonardo was an individual like himself or that Erasmus's chief claim to fame is that he was the first modern man—the first one like you and me. All this was quite soothing and flattering and did much to compensate for one's inability to read Horace or to quote Euripides. It even had its appeal for professors of modern European history and for teachers of the modern languages. It appears to be the concept of the Renaissance, which such recent advocates thereof or apologists therefor as Wallace K. Ferguson and Hans Baron are concerned to defend, retreating to new standing ground of plausible hypothesis and ingenious conjecture, when some of Burckhardt's old bulwarks are proved to be untenable by new masses of facts concerning either or both the middle ages and the quattrocento. But would it not make things clearer if they ceased to employ the old name, since the old concept has been abandoned, and, instead of talking of the Renaissance, spoke of the period or movement or whatever it is they have in mind as the Prenaissance?

With regard to the work of Burckhardt I may perhaps be permitted a few further comments. Of its six parts, the third on the Revival of Antiquity seems to me scholarly and just, recognizing the defects as well as the merits of the Italian humanists and containing many bits of illuminating detail. But most of the political, social, moral and religious phenomena which he pictures as Renaissance seem almost equally characteristic of Italy at any time from the twelfth to the eighteenth centuries inclusive. The fourth part on the discovery of the world and man uses only popular, not scientific literature, nor may this be dismissed as merely a sin of omission, since elsewhere in the volume are such atrocious misstatements as that few works of Aristotle had been translated into Latin by the fourteenth century. By including such personalities as Frederick II and such authors and literary compositions as Dante and the *Carmina burana* within the Renaissance, Burckhardt freed the movement from the embarrassment of chronological limits and made any differentiation between it and medieval culture well-nigh impossible. At bottom this was a wholesome tendency, equivalent to recognition that there is no dividing line between "medieval" and "renaissance" culture, just as most historical museums have a single section labeled "Middle Ages and Renaissance." In general, Burckhardt devoted so much of his pages and energy to the attempt to trace intangibles, such as personality, imagination, passion, spirit, the popular mind, the feeling for this and that, such and such a sentiment, that his book hardly touches the domain of intellectual history and seems to possess a will-o'-the-wisp sort of character.

The attraction which this kind of writing has for many has been well expressed by Professor Schevill in reviewing another book:

If the modern scientific method, a well co-ordinated plan, and the view-point regarding the character of the social process which obtains among present-day scholars are the indispensable requirements of a good history, it would have to be conceded that Mrs. Taylor's book stands self-condemned. But if there is salvation outside the ruling formulas, if a work may still be history, and good history, when, instead of building up a solid edifice of facts, it occupies itself with the spirit behind the facts in the hope of communicating the color and perfume of a segment of human experience, this book can be confidently recommended not only to the notoriously unscientific lovers of the Renaissance but to those grave and reverend signors, the professional historians themselves.[5]

The trouble is that this kind of writing is almost invariably based upon an insufficient acquaintance with the facts and misinterpretation of them. Of the same genus is another bête-noire of mine, those writers who proclaim that this or that person was far in advance of his time, like Roger Bacon or Leonardo da Vinci.[6] But should you ask them to name a few contemporaries of the person in question who were typical of that time, they would hardly be able to do so.

Was the individual freed and personality enhanced by the Renaissance or Prenaissance? Burckhardt affirmed that with it "man became a spiritual individual and recognized himself as such," whereas "in the middle ages both sides of human consciousness—that which was turned within as that which was turned without—lay dreaming or half awake beneath a common veil."[7] It might be remarked that individualism may be a mark of decline rather than progress. The self-centred sage of the Stoics and Epicureans rang the knell of the Greek city-state. Basil, on the verge of the barbarian invasions, complained that men "for the greater part prefer individual and private life to the union of common life."[8] Carl Neumann held that "true modern individualism has its roots in the strength of the barbarians, in the realism of the barbarians, and in the Christian middle ages."[9] Cunningham believed that the Roman

[5] Review of Rachel Annand Taylor, *Aspects of the Italian Renaissance: American Historical Review*, XXIX (October 1923), 122.
[6] Durand has recognized this antipathy, too, in reviewing my fifth and sixth volumes in *Isis*, XXXIII (June 1942), 691-712, especially 702-703, 704-706.
[7] English translation (1890), 129.
[8] *Hexaemeron*, VIII, 7.
[9] "Byzant. Kultur u. Renais. Kultur," *Historische Zeitschrift*, XCI (1903), 215-232; translated in Munro and Sellery, *Medieval Civilization*, 524-546.

Empire "left little scope for individual aims and tended to check the energy of capitalists and laborers alike," whereas Christianity taught the supreme dignity of man and encouraged the individual and personal responsibility. Moreover, in the thirteenth century there were "fewer barriers to social intercourse than now."[10] According to Schäfer, "So far as public life in the broadest sense, in church and state, city and country, law and society, is concerned, the middle ages are the time of most distinctive individuality and independent personality in volition and action."[11] We may no longer think of the Gothic architects as anonymous, and de Mely discovered hundreds of signatures of miniaturists hidden in the initials and illuminations of medieval manuscripts.[12] No period in the history of philosophy has discussed individuality and its problems more often or more subtly than did the medieval schoolmen. Vittorino da Feltre and other humanist educators may have suited their teaching to the individual pupil; at the medieval university the individual scholar suited himself. The humanists were imitative in their writing, not original. Vitruvius was the Bible of Renaissance architects who came to follow authority far more than their creative Gothic predecessors. For the middle ages loved variety; the Renaissance, uniformity.

Not only has it been demonstrated that the thirteenth and fourteenth centuries were more active and penetrating in natural science that was the quattrocento,[13] but the notion that "appreciation of natural beauty" was "introduced into modern Europe by the Italian Renaissance"[14] must also be abandoned. Burckhardt admitted that medieval literature displayed sympathy with nature, but nevertheless regarded Petrarch's ascent of Mount Ventoux (which is only 6260 feet high) in 1336 as epoch-making. Petrarch represented an old herdsman who had tried in vain to climb it fifty years before as beseeching him to turn back on the ground that he had received only torn clothes and broken bones for his pains and that no one had attempted the ascent since. As a matter of fact, Jean Buridan, the Parisian schoolman, had visited it between 1316 and 1334, had given details as to its altitude, and had waxed enthusiastic as to the Cevennes. So that all Petrarch's account proves is his capacity for story-telling and sentimental ability to make a mountain out of a molehill. Miss Stockmayer, in a book on feeling for nature in Germany in the tenth and eleventh centuries, has noted various ascents and descriptions of mountains from that period. In the closing years of his life archbishop Anno of Cologne climbed his beloved mountain oftener than usual.[15]

As for the feeling for nature in medieval art, let me repeat what I have written elsewhere anent the interest displayed by the students of Albertus Magnus in particular herbs and trees.[16]

[10] *Western Civilization in Its Economic Aspects*, II (1910), 8 ff., 2.
[11] "Zur Beurtheilung des Wormser Concordats," *Philos. u. Hist. Abhandl. d. kgl. preuss. Akad. d. Wiss.* (1905), 94.
[12] F. de Mely, *Les primitifs et leurs signatures: les miniaturistes* (1913).
[13] In addition to the bibliography given by Durand may be noted "Science in the Renaissance," by George Sarton, in *The Civilization of the Renaissance* (Chicago, 1929), 75-95. As Dr. Sarton remarks, "From the scientific point of view the Renaissance was *not* a renaissance."
[14] J. E. Spingarn, *A History of Literary Criticism in the Renaissance* (1899), 226.
[15] Gertrud Stockmayer, *Über Naturgefühl in Deutschland im 10. und 11. Jahrhundert* (1910), 38 ff. For further bibliography on feeling for nature in the Middle Ages, consult Paetow, *Guide to the Study of Medieval History* (rev. ed., 1931), 463, which, however, does not mention B. Q. Morgan, *Nature in Middle High German Lyrics* (1912).
[16] *Magic and Experimental Science*, II, 536-537.

This healthy interest in nature and commendable curiosity concerning real things was not confined to Albert's students nor to "rustic intelligences." One has only to examine the sculpture of the great thirteenth-century cathedrals to see that the craftsmen of the towns were close observers of the world of nature, and that every artist was a naturalist too. In the foliage that twines about the capitals of the columns in the French Gothic cathedrals it is easy to recognize, says M. Mâle, a large number of plants: "the plantain, arum, ranunculus, fern, clover, coladine, hepatica, columbine, cress, parsley, strawberry-plant, ivy, snapdragon, the flower of the broom and the leaf of the oak, a typically French collection of flowers loved from childhood."[17] *Mutatis mutandis*, the same statement could be made concerning the carved vegetation that runs riot in Lincoln cathedral. "The thirteenth-century sculptors sang their *chant de mai*. All the spring delights of the Middle Ages live again in their work—the exhilaration of Palm Sunday, the garlands of flowers, the bouquets fastened on the doors, the strewing of fresh herbs in the chapels, the magical flowers of the feast of Saint John—all the fleeting charm of those old-time springs and summers. The Middle Ages, so often said to have little love for nature, in point of fact gazed at every blade of grass with reverence."[18]

It is not merely love of nature but scientific interest and accuracy that we see revealed in the sculptures of the cathedrals and in the note-book of the thirteenth-century architect, Villard de Honnecourt,[19] with its sketches of insect as well as animal life, of a lobster, two parroquets on a perch, the spirals of a snail's shell, a fly, a dragonfly, and a grasshopper, as well as a bear and a lion from life, and more familiar animals such as the cat and swan. The sculptors of gargoyles and chimeras were not content to reproduce existing animals but showed their command of animal anatomy by creating strange compound and hybrid monsters—one might almost say, evolving new species—which nevertheless have all the verisimilitude of copies from living forms. It was these breeders in stone, these Burbanks of the pencil, these Darwins with the chisel, who knew nature and had studied botany and zoology in a way superior to the scholar who simply pored over the works of Aristotle and Pliny. No wonder that Albert's students were curious about particular things.

Finally, can we accept the altered concept of a Prenaissance as the vestibule to modern times and seed-bed of the modern spirit? Chronologically, perhaps. But, aside from the circumstance that modern times and spirit seem at present to be swiftly shifting, are not our political, economic, charitable, educational and ecclesiastical institutions quite as much an outgrowth from medieval life? Without attempting here to argue this larger question, I would merely recall that medieval men coined the word *modern* and regularly spoke of themselves or the last generations of themselves as such. "Maurus, Matthew, Solomon, Peter, Urso are modern physicians through whom reigns the medicine of Salerno."[20] About 1050 Berengar of Tours was accused of "introducing ancient heresies in modern times";[21] about 1108 Hugh of Fleury wrote his *Historia moderna*. "On all sides they clamor," wrote John of Salisbury in the twelfth century, "what do we care for the sayings or deeds of the ancients? . . . The golden sayings of the ancients pleased their times; now only new ones please our

---

[17] Emile Mâle, *Religious Art in France in the Thirteenth Century*, translated from the third edition by Dora Nussey (1913), 52.

[18] *Ibid.*, 53.

[19] Published in facsimile at London (1859) and Paris (1908).

[20] Epilogue to a *Regimen Salernitanum* in Sloane MS. 554, f. 155, at the British Museum; S. de Renzi, *Collectio Salernitana*, V, 139.

[21] *Soc. Hist. Franc.*, 50 (1884), 75.

times."[22] When in the next century Robertus Anglicus composed his treatise on the quadrant, it was called *Tractatus quadrantis secundum modernos*. But then improvements were made in the quadrant and Robert's work became *Tractatus quandrantis veteris.*[23] Even scholastic philosophy had its *via moderna* as well as *via antiqua.*[24]

The concept of the Italian Renaissance of Prenaissance has in my opinion done a great deal of harm in the past and may continue to do harm in the future. It is too suggestive of a sensational, miraculous, extraordinary, magical, human and intellectual development, like unto the phoenix rising from its ashes after five hundred years. It is contrary to the fact that human nature tends to remain much the same in all times. It has led to a chorus of rhapsodists as to freedom, breadth, soaring ideas, horizons, perspectives, out of fetters and swaddling clothes, and so on. It long discouraged the study of centuries of human development that preceded it, and blinded the French *philosophes* and revolutionists to the value of medieval political and economic institutions. It has kept men in general from recognizing that our life and thought is based more nearly and actually on the middle ages than on distant Greece and Rome, from whom our heritage is more indirect, bookish and sentimental, less institutional, social, religious, even less economic and experimental.

But what is the use of questioning the Renaissance? No one has ever proved its existence; no one has really tried to. So often as one phase of it or conception of it is disproved, or is shown to be equally characteristic of the preceding period, its defenders take up a new position and are just as happy, just as enthusiastic, just as complacent as ever.

> You may break, you may shatter the vase, if you will,
> But the scent of the roses will hang round it still.

Still lingers the sweet perfume of the Renaissance; still hovers about us the blithe spirit of the Prenaissance.

# THE CONCEPT OF THE RENAISSANCE

### Federico Chabod

Wholly at variance with the traditional picture of the Renaissance are the findings and assertions of a considerable number of recent critics.

[22] Hauréau, *Notices et Extraits,* III, 216, quoting the *Entheticus.*
[23] Duhem, *Le sytème du monde* III, 306.
[24] The ancients were the thirteenth-century thinkers before William of Ockham, the moderns his followers. See "modern" in the indices of *Magic and Experimental Science,* II-IV, for other examples of medieval use of the word.

It goes without saying that such critics must have come under the increasingly dominant influence of that historiographical *forma mentis* to which reference has already been made—a *forma mentis* characterized by a passionate belief in the theory of "continuity" and strengthened in its convictions by the results that have followed the deepening of our knowledge of mediaeval life. The last few decades of European scholarship have in fact led to the definite rehabilitation of the life of the Middle Ages, even from the point of view of art and literature (whereas the Romantics' love for the Middle Ages had been confined mainly to the religious and political fields). Indeed, one of the greatest achievements of the art-criticism of recent decades, as Max Dvořák has rightly observed, has been its arrival at a full understanding of the mediaeval art-forms, the mediaeval "style," previously regarded as crude and barbarous and invariably judged in the light of Vasari's classical schemes, which applied to a type of art whose predominance was complete only towards the end of the fifteenth and at the beginning of the sixteenth centuries.

Scholars have come to see how ancient civilization was not entirely swamped by the tide of the barbarian invasions, how instead it bequeathed to the Middle Ages a legacy of juridical standards, economic customs and, moreover, cultural traditions. They have emphasized how, beneath the apparent "religious" uniformity of the period extending from the sixth to the fourteenth centuries, there existed a world distinguished by the complexity of its sentiments and ideas, which cannot easily be reduced to the single common denominator of other-worldly aspirations. They have discovered periods of intellectual and artistic reflorescence even in the centuries that once were known as "the iron age," and they have spoken of a Carolingian renascence and an Ottonian renascence—that is to say of renascences that occurred even before the French renascence of the twelfth century. Finally, they have learned to understand, to love and to appreciate as a powerful expression of art what Vasari had execrated as "an accursed jumble of little tabernacles piled one on top of the other, with innumerable pyramids and spires and ornamental leaves" (*Del la Architettura*, Chapter III), or—referring to painting—"those wild eyes, and bodies poised on tip-toe, and long, tapering hands, and that absence of shadows, and the other monstrous conceits of those Greeks" (*Proemio della II Parte*).

As a result of these new findings the age which preceded the Renaissance no longer appears to have resembled a desert. Instead, it is looked upon as an age rich in variety, stimulated incessantly by multifarious problems, interests and aspirations—a restless age, full of exuberant life. Hence the more positive tone of the question which had already been asked by Emile Gebhart in 1885 (in an article in the *Révue des Deux Mondes* on the French translation of Jacob Burckhardt's work): What in reality are the *points d'attache* between the Renaissance and the Middle Ages—*points d'attache à peine visibles* in *Die Cultur der Renaissance*.

The question is entirely logical and justified. It is obvious that the Renaissance must have inherited, at least in part, some of the tendencies and attitudes of mind of the preceding era on to which the Renaissance was grafted. We must therefore seek out and define the connecting-links between these two periods of history, which once were separated in men's minds by so wide and irreducible a gulf.

But here we find that more than one foreign scholar, having drawn what is generally speaking a somewhat superficial parallel between mediaeval patterns of life and thought and their Renaissance counterparts, has used this first and legitimate inference as a direct stepping-stone to the far more radical assertion that the Renaissance created nothing essentially new, that all its observations on man, nature, history, etc., were already present, in embryo at least, in the thought of the twelfth and thirteenth centuries—that, in short, contrary to the belief that has prevailed for centuries, it does not represent an epoch of decisive importance in the history of mankind.

The tendency to extol the Renaissance as an isolated phenomenon, as a first reflorescence of the humane virtues following the dark ages of barbarism, had first been manifested chiefly by artists and art-critics in the field of art; and it was in this field too that the first positive attempt to deny its originality and importance found expression, at the end of the last century, in the thesis advanced by Courajod, who maintained that "the new art" had been invented by the Flemish artists of the fourteenth century and had originated not, indeed, in Italy but in the Netherlands. Since then, keeping pace with the growing tendency to re-assess the art, thought and culture of the Middle Ages, this tendency to deny the importance of the Renaissance has become steadily more marked. Developing to the utmost limit of possibility a view which had already attained prominence during the last century, the view that it is in twelfth-century France that the real seeds of the Renaissance must be sought (cf. W. Pater, *The Renaissance*), historians speak to-day of a twelfth-century French renascence which, they assert, anticipated all the spiritual achievements of the Italian renascence of the fourteenth and fifteenth centuries. It is asserted that by the thirteenth century European culture was essentially complete, nothing remaining but to exploit what had already been achieved (J. Boulenger, *Le vrai siècle de la Renaissance*, in *Humanisme et Renaissance*, I, 1934, p. 30). And in the opinion of some scholars, of whom Nordström is one, the most that can be said is that the term "Renaissance" can in some measure be justified so far as Italy is concerned, but that it cannot be accepted as applying to Europe, which had already prefected its civilization in the course of a century of evolution north of the Alps (*Moyen Âge et Renaissance*, Paris, 1933, p. 47).

Thus the problem is clearly posed: What should we understand by the term "Renaissance"? In its classical form, in which it is primarily Italian, how far is it original in its basic motifs, and to what extent does it reveal features of its own? Are we confronted with something which, by comparison with mediaeval civilization, is essentially new? Or are we rather confronted merely with a development and a broadening—notable, if we like, but not very original—of motifs of which there were already traces in that vast crucible which was the European civilization of the Middle Ages?

### Preliminary Questions: Facts and Ideas. The Idea of Classical Antiquity in the Middle Ages and the Renaissance

To enable ourselves to solve the problem thus formulated we must first of all purge our minds of a great and gross error into which scholars are all too prone to fall. This error consists in confusing practical life with the life of the mind, the day-to-day activities of man with the rational consciousness which he may or may not have of those activities. It consists in regarding as a single entity what I would call the "physical" life of the individual on the one hand and his thoughts and ideas on the other.

For example, we find Chamard asserting that the love of life in its sensuous and more objective form—wine, women and various kinds of amusement—was in no sense a discovery of the Renaissance. Mediaeval man, far from being bowed down by remose for his sins and devoting all his time to the singing of psalms, was profoundly attached to worldly life with its many and not always pure pleasures. He therefore had no need to look to the Italians of the fifteenth century to initiate him in the delights of love and to imbue him with a taste for agreeable living. *L'amour intense de la vie, l'esprit gaulois et l'esprit courtois* were a legacy bequeathed to the Renaissance by the Middle Ages (*Les origines de la poésie française de la Renaissance*, Paris, 1920, pp. 47, 181). Again, we find Nordström emphasizing that the "devine Hildebert," that is to say Hildebert of Le Mans, who lived in the twelfth century, was, like many of his brethren, an ardent worshipper of women and love, a fact which proves him to have been a child of a new age (*op. cit.*, p.65).[1]

At this point we must make it absolutely clear that when we use the term "Renaissance" to describe a certain very definite phase of European history we are referring to a mobilization of ideas, an artistic, literary and cultural "period" which is first and foremost an "intellectual" reality.

So defined, the Renaissance does not find its expression in practical activity, which is incidental to the existence of the individual—in the gay life of a citizen of Florence, the self-indulgence of a Mantuan gentlewoman, the unrestrained ambition of a *condottiere* or the amorous intrigues of some member of the Court of Naples—but rather in the manner in which human designs and actions conform to an ideal system and are elevated from the plane of mere practical, instinctive activity to the status of a spiritual creed, a programme of life. Ever since the world began men in their everyday life have always obeyed certain instinctive and fundamental passions; and love and ambition, sensuality and the need for amusement, the desire for riches and the yearning for political power are peculiar to men of all ages and countries. Hence, if we had to reconstruct history in the light of such considerations we should be obliged to regard as equal and alike in their significance all the things that have happened from the times of the Egyptians and the Babylonians down to the present day, and history would become a grey blur in which we could no longer distinguish one epoch from another. But this is not so; for when we speak of historical "periods," of the classical world and the mediaeval world, of the Renaissance, of the Age of Enlightenment, of Romanticism, to what are we referring if not to political, moral and cultural ideas and the institutions in which those ideas have found expression—ideas and institutions which characterize individual epochs? The eighteenth-century man loves, studies his personal convenience, is fond of luxury and sings the praises of wine and women no more and no less than did his predecessor of the fourteenth century; but the "manner" in which men sing the praises of love, extol riches and hanker after political power has changed, and it is precisely this "manner" that interests us.

The "manner" is dictated by contemporary thought, and it is to this alone that we must direct our attention.

It is obvious, for instance, that the actions of Heads of States and politicians have

---

[1] [Occasionally we find even so excellent a scholar as Gilson falling into the same error, as when, referring to Héloïse and Abélard, he asks himself the question: "If it is claimed that a Renaissance is only possible in an age of dominating personalities, may we not retort that the age which produced our own hero and heroine is singularly worthy to be so described"—or, again, when he speaks of a "drama of passion, peopled with clerics, monks and nuns" that is "none the less a story of the twelfth century" (*Héloïse et Abélard*, pp. 160 and 178).

Dopsch had earlier maintained that powerful personalities had already existed in the Middle Ages, even going so far as to assert that individualism was one of the chief characteristics of that era (*Wirtschaftsgeist und Individualismus im Früh-Mittelalter*, "Archiv für Kultur-geschichte," XIX, 1928).]

always been determined by political interest. A French scholar, Benoist, has seen fit to examine "Machiavellism" as it was practised before the age of Machiavelli in order to prove that even before the time of the Florentine secretary Heads of States had applied the doctrine which he subsequently formulated in *The Prince* and the *Discourses on the First Ten Books of Titus Livius*. Even in the Middle Ages men like Charlemagne, Otto I and Frederick Barbarossa acted, on isolated occasions, in conformity with the dictates of what were destined to be described after Machiavelli's death as "reasons of state"—in conformity, that is, with the principle that where affairs of state are involved decisions must be based above all on political criteria. But this does not make it any the less true that only when Machiavelli arrives on the scene are we confronted with the theoretical affirmation—complete, clear and brutal—that politics are politics, apart from all other considerations; *only then*, in other words, does a practical truth become a theoretical precept, a law explicitly credited with a universal validity. The horror with which such affirmations have filled even those who on the other hand have been not at all shocked when they have come up against the virtual "Machiavellism" practised from day to day by this or that ruler shows clearly what a profound and real difference there is between a simple fact or practical truth and its postulation as an axiom.

In the same way, it is certain that the Middle Ages were not lacking in human figures of the first magnitude: we do not have to wait for the "virtuous" Italian princes of the Renaissance to provide us with examples of such figures. Men like Charlemagne, Otto I and Philippe Auguste are "personalities" who certainly have nothing to fear from comparison with Gian Galeazzo Visconti, Francesco Sforza and Caesar Borgia. But, as we shall shortly see, the respective ways in which these powerful personalities influenced the thought of their contemporaries and shaped their ideas were entirely different. Completely different, too, is the importance ascribed to each of the two groups by historiographers. This, then, is the problem—not whether or not the Middle Ages produced strong personalities (which at this time of day no one could dream of denying), but whether or not in the general conception of the world the personalities of great men had the same importance and the same function in the Middle Ages as in the Renaissance.

In short, that the mediaeval man also loved women, that he liked a good dinner or costly fabrics or artistic ornaments in his house, that he too experienced a swelling of the heart when he contemplated the burnished blue of an April sky—to-day all this is acknowledged, it is outside the realm of discussion. But what we are concerned to know is whether he ever ventured to set up as an ideal, a theoretical standard of life, that emotion which Leon Battista Alberti for his part idealized half-way through the fifteenth century as "delight in living." This delight in living, in so far as it is an immediate and instinctive sensation, is experienced by the men of every age. The question rather is whether and to what extent, as a conscious, deliberate affirmation of principle, it characterizes the Renaissance as distinct from the Middle Ages.

Having thus rid our minds of this first, gross and dangerous misconception we now have to see whether the qualities hitherto looked upon as peculiar to and typical of Renaissance civilization are in fact nothing but a reproduction of qualities previously possessed by mediaeval civilization.

Those critics who have seen fit to deny or at any rate to minimize the importance of the Renaissance have adopted the following argument. While, they declare, the disciples of Burckhardt maintained that the "discovery of man and of nature" (i.e. individualism and realism in art, literature, the sciences, etc.) was an achievement of the Renaissance, it must on the other hand be recognized that the concepts of realism and individualism are already clearly implied in the literature and thought of the Middle Ages; and while it has been maintained for centuries that the rediscovery of classical antiquity (i.e. Humanism) was a typical achievement of the Italian civilization of the fourteenth and fifteenth centuries, it must be realized that classical antiquity had never suffered an eclipse, that its influence had remained strong even during the early Middle Ages, and that, actually even before the era of Italian Humanism there had been a genuine revival of "Latinity" in twelfth-century France, where we find a species of "humanism" which anticipates the much-vaunted Humanism of fourteenth- and fifteenth-century Italy. This earlier "humanism" produced such men as Hildebert of Le Mans, Pierre de Blois—and above all John of Salisbury; it gave the world the Chartres School, and, a little later, the neo-classical carvings which adorn Rheims Cathedral.

However, as soon as we try to probe more deeply into the question we see that the two periods only resemble each other very superficially, while they differ profoundly in their essential character.

Certainly, the influence of classical culture was extremely strong throughout the Middle Ages. This fact has been established following decades of research, and it can no longer be open to question. In literature, as in philosophy and—at any rate from the twelfth century onwards—even in art, there are frequent and abundant examples of the debt which the men of the Middle Ages owed to classical culture.

In the second or third decade of the ninth century Alginard sketched a portrait of Charlemagne; and we find him turning to Suetonius and taking from the *Lives* of Augustus, Tiberius and Claudius a number of distinctive physical characteristics, calculated to lend majesty and virile beauty to the personage portrayed. We find him assembling them and transforming them into a likeness of the pious Emperor who was crowned by the Pope on Christmas Day in the year 800 A.D. (cf. L. Halphen, *Études critiques sur l'histoire de Charlemagne,* Paris, 1921). This is a single example, but it is enough; and a thorough investigation of the mediaeval chronicles would show that if many of the protraits of eminent personages comply with the *rex iustus* and *rex iniquus* or *tyrannus* formulas of Augustinian and Gregorian memory, in other words with the formulas popularized by the Pseudo-Cyprian in the *De XII abusivis saeculis*, others are based on the models provided by classical historiography, and especially by Suetonius.

It would be superfluous now to allude to the mediaeval cult of Virgil. It would be superfluous to stress how in the *tabulae exemplorum*—those curious books of examples and comparisons, so widely circulated during this period and so necessary to preachers and writers—examples are freely derived not only from the Holy Scriptures but also from the legends of the ancient "pagans," (cf. T. Welter, *L'exemplum dans la littérature religieuse et didactique du moyan âge,* Paris, 1927, pp. 94 *sqq.*). Finally, it would be superfluous to recall the survival of ancient mythology in the form of poetry.

It is very true also that this cult of classical antiquity finds even more enthusiastic champions in the twelfth century. Pierre de Blois—one of those who to-day are given the title of "humanists" born before their time—professes himself to be a devotee of classical Rome, in spite of dogs and pigs; while John of Salisbury in his turn is a declared champion of antiquity. And the artists who, in the thirteenth century, carved what is known as the Visitation group on the main door of Rheims Cathedral were certainly inspired by ancient models, on which they intentionally based their work.

However, as soon as we try to probe more deeply into the so-called "Latinity" of the Middle Ages we perceive how profoundly it differs from the "Latinity" of the fifteenth-century humanists.

Let us consider Hildebert of Lavardin (or Le Mans), perhaps one of the most widely-acclaimed of these "humanists" of the twelfth century; let us read his famous elegy on Rome, which he visited in 1106. Undoubtedly he too was stirred as he contemplated the spectacle of the mighty ruins and the proud remains of the Eternal City; he too was filled with boundless admiration for the men who had been able to create so many and such mighty masterpieces. But his admiration of the past is accompanied by regret for the present. His eulogy is coupled with the assertion that what has been has been and will never return. Hence his cry of desolation:

*Vix scio quae fuerim, vix Romae Roma recordor;*
*vix sinit occasus vel meminisse mei.*

It is a beautiful world—but a world that has gone for ever. *Par tibi, Roma, nihil cum sis prope tota ruina.*

Let us now look at the collected letters of Cola di Rienzo, in which we shall read the proud statement, made in July, 1350, that he, Cola, would think he had achieved nothing if he did not imitate his ancient models with the object of making them live again: "Nichil actum fore putavi, si que legendo didiceram, non aggrederer exercendo" (Cola di Rienzo, *Briefwechsel,* ed. Burdach, Berlin, 1912, p. 204). And we shall find the lofty statement made to the Emperor Charles IV, also in July, 1350, that he, Cola, having from his earliest years derived his mental nourishment from the study of antiquity, had made up his mind—proud aim!—to reconstitute and revive the Roman Empire: "Vos etiam allegastis, quod non absque divino miraculo Romanorum imperium reformaretur. Certe totum hoc ad divinum spectat miraculum, si per virum pauperem ac novum ruenti imperio Romano succurritur, sicut alias ruenti Romane Ecclesie per Franciscum" (*ib.*, p. 209). These notions had already been clearly formulated in the famous decree of 1 August 1347, regarding the sovereignty of the Roman people: "Nos ... volentes et desiderantes ... voluntates, benignitates, et liberalitates antiquorum Romanorum principum ... imitari ..." (*ib.*, p. 101). *Imitatio*: here we find uttered the all-important word that divides the world of Cola from the world of Hildebert of Le Mans. In place of admiration, mingled with regret, for what can never return, we find a determination to act in scrupulous conformity with the teachings of the Ancients. *Legere* becomes *exercere*. And instead of an elegy we have an exhortation to revive the ancient splendours, the glories of Rome.

After Cola di Rienzo comes Coluccio Salutati: "Latent in literis documenta virtutum, latent mores, latent omnia quae scire non est satis, nisi et operibus impleantur"; then Leonardo Bruni, with the "studia quae pertinent ad vitam et mores, quae propterea humanitatis studia nuncupantur, quod hominem perficiunt et exornant"; then, greatest of all, Machiavelli, who never tires of adducing the example of the Romans as a stimulus to better deeds in the present, and makes the "imitation" of ancient wisdom the keystone of his political and military doctrine. Men must imitate the Ancients "in matters calling for strength and vigour, not in those which require delicacy and gentleness"; they must "adopt the true and perfect ways of antiquity, not the false and corrupt" (*The Art of War, I*)—in other words, they must not confine themselves to a purely formal, stylistic and literary imitation, but must revive the "human" [i.e. manly] virtues of the Ancients, superimposing a new world, deeply imbued with political consciousness, patriotism and human sensibility, on the religious world of the Middle Ages, which is responsible for the present "weakness." This is far removed indeed from the nostalgic regrets of Hildebert of Le Mans!

The fact is that the mediaeval spirit, for all its indebtedness to classical authors—poets, historians and philosophers—had never ceased to be dominated essentially by another consideration and by another paramount motif, to wit, the problem of the relationship between God and man and the Christian and Augustinian sense of sin and grace. Hence, classical antiquity had been a mere instrument, a cultural tool placed at the disposal of a spiritual way of life which derived its *raison d'être* from quite a different source. To be sure, we may exploit Virgil, Ovid, Lucan, Statius, Cicero and Quintilian. We may even try to imitate them, superficially. But when all is said and done they are all merely ornaments whose function is to add lustre to a moral and spiritual way of life that is founded on a religious conception of the world and finds active expression in the ecclesiastical and hierarchical organization of society.

Imitation of the classics, then, when it occurs, can only be purely superficial—so much so that even in those writings which most strongly resemble the classics we detect an inspiration profoundly alien from the spirit of the Ancients. Indeed, this is true of the Visitation group at Rheims with its much-vaunted classical form. This group (as has been shrewdly noted by E. Panofsky and F. Saxl, *Classical Mythology in Mediaeval Art*, in "Metropolitan Museum Studies," New York, IV, 1933, pp. 266 *sqq.*), despite its seemingly classical poses, remains profoundly "Gothic" in the spirit that informs it and in the sensibility that it expresses.[2]

As regards the actual cult of *Roma aeterna*, we must draw a clear distinction between classical and pagan Rome, the Rome of the Scipios and the Caesars, and Christian Rome. Indeed, the concept of Rome has about it a complexity and a magnificence that are sometimes unsuspected. Prudentius, we may recall, in his *Peristephanon* extolled the soil of Rome, declaring that it was hallowed by the bones of the Christian martyrs ("Quam dives urbanum solum—sacris sepulcris floreat": *Hymnus in honorem passionis Laurentii*, vv. 543—4); and St. Augustine, in the *De Civitate Dei*, imparted majesty to the conception of the Roman basilicas, before which even the barbarous Visigoths, when in the summer of the year 410 they sacked the city, halted in awe (Book I, Chapters I and VII). Ever since then—ever since the fifth century, in fact—the concept of pagan Rome, a city made great by her military victories and the splendour of her sons, has been associated with, and often eclipsed by, the concept of another Rome—Christian Rome. This other Rome was great because she was the centre of the Catholic world and the home of the successors of Peter. This was the Rome which, as Pope Leo the Great said mid-way through the fifth century, had become, thanks to Peter and Paul, "civitas sacerdotalis et regia, *per sanctam beati Petri sedem caput orbis* effecta." Two ideas, these, which could quite easily be reconciled; and they had indeed been linked together in the imagination of

---

[2] [Such formal qualities are intended to express different ideas and to symbolize Christian themes: "Les idées païennes se dépouillant graduellement de leur expression plastique, les idées chrétiennes sont venues habiter ces formes désaffectées, tout comme le culte chrétien s'installait dans les temples vides." And the Renaissance appears as the "réintégration d'un sujet antique dans une forme antique" (J. Seznec, *La survivance des dieux antiques*, London, 1940, pp. 181–2; and "il est remarquable ... que pendant la période la plus radieuse de la Renaissance les types iconographiques 'transmis' et donc altérés,—soient presque partout abandonnés au profit des types 'retrouvés' dans leur pureté première" (*ib.*, p. 289).]

Prudentius. Yet they could also appear as irreconcilable—witness the eleventh-century fragment *De Sancta Romana Ecclesia*, by Cardinal Humbert a Silva Candida who, about 1053, had clearly contrasted, as being diametrically opposed, Rome "fundata super arenam per Romulum et Remum profana sacerdote et quo nescitur sacrilego editos" and Rome "hedificata super Christum petram per Petrum et Paulum" (in P. E. Schramm, *Kaiser, Rom und Renovatio*, II, Leipzig, 1929, pp. 129 *sqq*.).

If we bear all this in mind we perceive what is the crucial point of the question: ancient Rome had indeed found favour in the eyes of mediaeval man, but *only* in so far as it was compatible with, or rather "served the interests of," Christian Rome. Classical culture had survived merely as a subordinate element. Its function was to provide an aesthetic outlet, a vision of the world, a means by which men might contemplate a life which possessed an organic structure of its own, totally independent of classical influence. Virgil was world-famous in the Middle Ages; but it was not merely Virgil the poet who had prophesied the coming of Christianity: it was Virgil the semi-magician, the Virgil whom Dante himself, who was, all in all, a product of the Middle Ages, chose to guide him on his journey to the after-world. His, then, was a pagan soul in Christian guise; and this is enough to explain the true nature of mediaeval "classicism."

Completely different in meaning and importance is the idealization of classical antiquity in the Italy of the Renaissance, even though it did not necessarily amount to a repudiation of Christian Rome: cf. a characteristic passage from Flavio Biondo, in which Prudentius's vision of Rome as great "sacro martyrum cruore" is reproduced (Garin, *op. cit.*, p. 93). It is not surprising that here too the idealization has sometimes been no more than superficial, assuming an exclusively literary and erudite character, and that in consequence the influence of classical antiquity has become in such cases a liability, to which may be ascribed the Byzantinism of contemporary scholars.

But on the whole, and in its greatest exponents—Cola di Rienzo, Petrarch, Coluccio Salutati and Valla, Ghiberti, Alberti and Machiavelli—the idealization of classical antiquity represented the essential "myth" of which the Renaissance movement, like all great historical movements, stood in need. This movement—originally political and economic, and later cultural and ideological in character—had rocked and convulsed Italy ever since the age of the Communes. It was the *mot d'ordre*, a programme indicating a common line of action to those whose aspirations after new forms of life, more in keeping with the needs of the times, were still confused. Men fixed their gaze on Ancient Greece and Rome in the manner—to quote Machiavelli—of prudent archers, "who, considering that their intended objective is too far off, and knowing the range of their bows, aim much higher than their target, hoping, not that their arrows will reach such a height, but that, by aiming so high, they will attain their objective" (*The Prince*, Chapter VI).

In other words, classical antiquity now became the ideal moment of human history, in which the highest aspirations of mankind were realized. It became the supreme moment, in which men must seek clear and sure guidance to loftier achievements, in literature and the arts as well as in politics and war.

If it does not entirely supersede it (and some, Machiavelli for instance, maintain that it does), this supreme moment at least ranks equally with what mediaeval Christendom had regarded as the only supreme moment, namely the moment of Revelation; and in any event, granted that the latter takes precedence in ultramundane matters, it remains

the "only human pattern from which men can draw their inspiration." This attitude is
very different from that of the "humanists" of the twelfth century.[3]

In the Middle Ages, classical antiquity was purely an ornament, a decorative fringe, a
stylistic pattern. Now, it becomes a *pattern* of life. Hence also it is at last identified
with the will to probe it, to understand it in itself and for itself in all its forms and
aspects, quite apart from the fact that it may act as a useful dispensary of prescriptions
of formulas for the use of writers or preachers who are seeking examples and
resounding phrases with which to dignify their writings or sermons. The fact that
archaeology and philology in the modern sense date only from the Renaissance is in
itself sufficient proof of the difference between the two ages so far as their attitudes to
antiquity are concerned.

It has been pointed out that the question here is one of approach, not one of
material divergence (Faral, *Recherches sur les sources latines des contes et romans
courtois du moyen âge,* Paris, 1913, p. viii); but in the history of the human spirit
what matters is in fact "how," not "how much."

### "Realism and "Individualism" in the Middle Ages and the Renaissance,

Similar considerations must be given to the problem of "realism," as it is called, and
"individualism."

We are urged to note that even mediaeval writers and artists observed living and
corporeal reality with close attention, that even they, far from being perpetually
absorbed in spiritual contemplation of God and the Saints, the Madonna and the
Cherubim, knew how to portray, with an accuracy that was sometimes very crude, the
incidents of everyday life, subjecting to scrutiny now the human body, whose
anatomy they described with a wealth of detail, even if not yet with precision, now
various aspects of nature, both smiling and horrible. We are urged to note that even
they would willingly pause to describe the figures of the protagonists of history,
sometimes, indeed, lingering unduly long over the portrayal of, let us say, Charlemagne
or Henry IV.

Here too, indeed, we can readily perceive that the men of the Middle Ages knew
how to observe with watchful eyes the reality that surrounded them, and that they
loved to portray it in their writings. There are numberless examples of this. Think of
the *Fabliaux*; think of the miracle plays themselves, into which realistic—I was about
to say "veristic"—detail is introduced readily and with great frequency; think of the
chronicles, which abound in realistic details. See, for instance, how a lively and
vivacious chronicler like Liutprand of Cremona describes the death of King Arnulf,
whose body is gnawed by countless tiny worms which suddenly appear on every side
in teeming multitudes, while the doctor stands impotently by (*Antapodosis,* Book I,
Chapter 36). It is immaterial that he is echoing a Biblical story (from the Second Book
of Maccabees), because even in this imitation he reveals a taste for the crudely realistic

[3] [On this twelfth-century practice of turning to Antiquity for isolated motifs and
forms which could be made to serve a present purpose cf. the opinion of Liebeschütz, who
asserts that the men of that age, unlike their Renaissance successors, never regarded "das Ganze
der Antike" as a medium of escape from the present, i.e. as an ideal that would inspire them to
invent and create new forms of life (H. Liebeschütz, *Das zwölfte Jahrhundert und die Antike,*
"Archiv für Kulturgeschichte," XXXV, 1953, p. 271).]

detail. Or consider Acerbo Morena's insistence on the exquisite hands and gleaming white teeth of Frederick Barbarossa and his consort Beatrix (*Historia Friderici I*, ed. Güterbock, p. 170); or the vignettes with which Friar Salimbene da Parma embellishes his chronicle—a beautiful Pisan garden in which graceful youths and girls sing and dance, rare animals from the East, monks who devour with great relish highly-seasoned capons, the strange garb of Friar Benedetto. Or again, to seek examples outside Italy, note how realistically Villehardouin describes the Crusaders' assault on Constantinople, and observe the fidelity of the Sire de Joinville's picture of Louis IX, King of France, dispensing justice in the shade of a great oak, or of his account of the death of his chaplain at Mansourah: "Quant je vi que il vouloit cheoir, je, qui avoie ma cote vestue, sailli de mon lit tout deschaus. . . ."

It would be hard to imagine anything more scrupulously realistic than the minute, accurate and colourful descriptions of human beings inspired by this material "curiosity." Indeed, mediaeval writers and artists often reveal a taste for the horrible and terrifying detail.

But this adherence to sensible reality remains, as always, emotional rather than intellectual in character; it is still instinctive rather than premeditated. Hence it is confined to the detail, the episode. If the detail is "realistic," the general conception is not, inasmuch as the Prime Mover of life and of human history is located outside the world and the destinies of men are invariably determined by the will of God. The sensibility is "human" and "mundane"; but the spirit is nourished by an inner life whose centre lies outside the earthly city and carnal humanity.

A few examples will serve to clarify this statement. In no field, perhaps, is the profound difference between the two forms of "realism" more immediately and easily perceived than in the field of historiography. The mediaeval chronicler does indeed assemble vast quantities of realistic details, and he likes to paint every scene in vivid, flamboyant colours, delighting in a sort of "photographic" naturalism. But afterwards, as from his eyrie he surveys the course of human fortunes, he sees the hand of God as the supreme and universal arbiter. The great Florentine historians of the Renaissance are far less inclined to cap their work with realistic flourishes. They prefer to create a comprehensive picture, continually sustained by a sense of human reality, of the will of those single individuals who, through their interests and passions, alone weave the pattern of universal history. Mediaeval realism is naturalistic and purely descriptive; it is made up of bits and pieces and, we may say, it lacks perspective; and the characteristic of the chronicler or of any mediaeval writer is just this accumulation and juxtaposition of minute details. Look, for example, at Acerbo Morena's description of Frederick Barbarossa, in which the writer lists in mechanical succession all the attributes, physical and moral, of the Emperor—his well-proportioned body, his reddish hair, his white teeth, his beautiful hands, his extreme bellicosity, his daring, his speed of movement, his eloquence, his passion for justice, his devotion to the laws. His qualities are listed one after the other, in such a way that we cannot form a clear and reliable opinion of the man as a whole. Note also how all historians ascribe the same qualities, at any rate the same moral qualities, to nearly all kings. Nothing could be more monotonous than an inspection of the gallery of "portraits" painted by mediaeval historians. It can be subdivided into two distinct categories. On the one hand there are the good kings, conforming to the Augustinian and post-Augustinian pattern and tradition of the king who fears God, reveres the Church, protects the widows and the orphans, etc. On the other, there are the bad kings—violent, cruel, despising God, true personifications of the Antichrist on earth. There are the two types of the *rex iustus* and the *tyrannus,* described, as has been said already, by the Pseudo-Cyprian in the *De XII abusivis saeculis.* If, for instance, we examine the historiography of the age that witnessed the struggle of the Investitures we see how it is based entirely on this a-prioristic system (cf. G. Werdermann, *Heinrich IV, seine Anhänger und seine Gegner im Lichte der augustinischen und eschatologischen Geschichtsauffassung des Mittelalters,* Greifswald, 1918, pp. 9 *sqq.*).

On the other hand, the realism of historians like Machiavelli and Guicciardini is a "conceptual" realism. It may even ignore the realism of a particular detail, it may be less "photographic," precisely because the impressionistic clarity of an isolated detail is far less emphatic and important when it forms part of a picture completely dominated by a sense of human reality. It is enough to compare, for example, Eginhard's description of Charlemagne with Guicciardini's description of Clement VII in his *History of Italy.* The one strives to portray his protagonist by picking out one after the other the various aspects of his personality, the physical in particular (the minuteness with which Alginard describes the person and habiliments of Charlemagne is extraordinary!), but at the same time he is incapable of combining his separate observations into an organic whole. The other furnishes a precise, expert, powerful sketch of the Pontiff's personality, a concentrating exclusively, be it noted, on his character and his spiritual and moral attributes, whereas the physical details are disregarded. Here, then, in a nutshell, is the historian whose conception of a series of events determined purely by human influences is perfectly expressed and epitomized by analysis of the characters and their motives. On the other hand, the mediaeval chronicler's representation of the physical traits of this or that prince is still purely superficial. It serves merely to adorn, to embellish an edifice that was built by another and far more sublime craftsman.

The realistic description of outward physical detail is undertaken by a Machiavelli or a Guicciardini, if at all, only inasmuch as it serves to complete the moral portrait of the man, in other words only inasmuch as it can furnish the writer with material which will help him to integrate his general assessment of the man's personality. Alginard, Liutprand of Cremona and the rest describe physical appearance and moral character without properly connecting the two. Here, on the other hand, is how Machiavelli portrays the Duke of Athens: "This Duke, as his administration proved, was avaricious and cruel. He was wayward in audience, he was haughty in response. In others he looked for servility, not goodwill; and for this reason he desired to be feared rather than loved. Nor was his presence any less odious than his behaviour; for he was short and dark, with a long, sparse beard: so that, all in all, he deserved to be hated . . ." (*Florentine Histories*, Book II, Chap. XXXVII). Here the reference (a very fleeting one, incidentally) to the Duke's physical appearance—"short and dark, with a long, sparse beard"—is only inserted inasmuch as, in the historian's opinion, it completes the moral picture of the man, who is, in a word, odious. We are very far from the attention to physical detail which characterizes Acerbo Morena's description of Frederick Barbarossa.

The distance that has been travelled in the period between the fourteenth and the beginning of the sixteenth centuries, in other words the difference between the "realism" of the high Renaissance and that of a more primitive age, emerges with crystal clarity if we compare Villani's and Machiavelli's explanations of the civil strife in Florence. It should be noted that Machiavelli (in the second book of the *Florentine Histories*) uses Villani as the source from which he derives his information and his facts; but this lends all the more significance to the profound disparity that exists between the comments of the two authors.

It should also be observed that we have selected Villani as a term of comparison—a man, that is to say, who is a typical representative of the Florentine *bourgeoisie,* with his feet firmly planted on the ground; a representative of a calculating, practical *bourgeoisie,* which manages its own affairs with great efficiency, is concerned with harsh realities, eschews vain fancies and dreams, and certainly does not spend its time singing psalms and beating its breast, a prey to the terror inspired by its own sins; a man whose incipient "modernity" has been praised because he bethinks himself in his chronicles not only of political and military events but also of economic factors, because he knows how to give due weight, for example, to the creation of the golden florin, "that excellent coin, made of gold twenty-four carats fine"; a chronicler who describes with great accuracy and much realistic detail the dress worn by the Florentines in the good old days: "And they and their women dressed in thick clothes, and many of the men wore leather jerkins with no outer garments, and caps on their heads, and they all wore long boots. And the Florentine women had shoes without buckles, and the greatest among them wore very tight petticoats of thick scarlet material from Ipro and Camo, fastened with old-fashioned belts, and minever-lined cloaks surmounted by hoods with which they covered their heads . . ." (Book VI, Chapter 69).

Yet this man is still so dominated by typically mediaeval ideas and even superstitions that when he comes to survey the general course of events his realistic grasp of detail deserts him and we witness the re-appearance in human history of God and the devil, who alone pull the strings that control earthly affairs. Already Buondelmonte de' Buondelmonti had, *subsidio diaboli,* broken the pledge he had given to the daughter of the house of Amidei; already he had been slain at the feet of the graven image of Mars, within whose precincts the "enemy of the human generation" was all-powerful. The subsequent party struggles at Pistoia, like the great rift between the Bianchi and the Neri in Florence, were also due to the sins of men and the instigation of the devil: "in consequence of their excessive wealth and the machinations of the devil, anger and enmity were stirred up among them" (Book VIII, Chapter 38). "At the time of which I speak, when our city of Florence was greater and happier than it had ever been . . . the sin of ingratitude and the machinations of the enemy of the human generation transformed the said wealth into a source of pride and corruption, (Book VIII, Chapter 39). As is logical, the writer's contemplation of the course of events culminates in a passionate moral appeal and the historian becomes a preacher: "And let him who reads this note how, as a punishment for our sins, God caused and allowed our city to be visited ere long by all manner of tribulations—floods, famine, hunger, death, defeats, humiliating failures, loss of wealth and substance, bankruptcies among merchants and financial discredit—and finally has led us from freedom into bondage and subjection to tyrannical masters. And so, with God's aid, beloved citizens, present and future, let us correct our faults and foster in our midst love and charity, that we may please the most high God, and that we may not incur the extreme penalty of his wrath, which he reveals to us most clearly in His visible threats" (Book XII, Chapter 3).

This is the climax to which the mediaeval chronicler's descriptive realism has led him. So, at the decisive moment, when we are awaiting his "interpretation" of history, that sense of human "individuality," which had seemed to exist when he was describing the outward appearance of individual men or the idle conversation and multifarious activity of a crowd, comes to nothing.

With Machiavelli, on the other hand, there is no further intervention on the part of God or the devil, the Saints or the "enemy of the human generation." Everything is determined by human agencies—by the conflicting appetites of the *Grandi* and the people or, again, by the "restless spirit" of Messer Corso Donati. Everything is reduced to a purely worldly level. There is no interference from the other world—unless it be a sort of natural, almost mechanical fatality, a note of naturalistic determinism which has nothing to do with the Christian conception of history as expressed by men like St. Augustine and Otto of Freisingen. Note this comment: "Because of his conduct, or else because it comes *naturally* to the Florentines to dislike any state of being and to be divided by any happening." (*Florentine Histories*, Book II, Chapter XXV). Compare this with Villani's lament when he tells "how, *as a punishment for our sins*, God caused and allowed our city to be visited ere long by all manner of tribulations." Or again, observe how Machiavelli regards the "sins" which led to Italy's political ruin not as moral sins, as Friar Gerolamo Savonarola had proclaimed them to be, but as purely political sins, the "sins" of princes (*The Prince*, Chapter XII), and you will have the exact measure of "realism" as it was envisaged at the height of the Renaissance.[4]

We shall be led to similar conclusions if we analyse the "realism" of mediaeval political thought in the light of the realism of a Machiavelli or a Guicciardini. The political writers of the Middle Ages had undoubtedly been concerned to discover and to call attention to rules that were applicable to everyday life, rules that could be put into practice and might prove "useful." Note, for instance, how St. Thomas concerns himself with the actual site on which a city should be built, the salubrity of the air, etc. (*De Regimine Principum*, Book II, Chapter 2).

But sensible and practical observations of this kind are quite unrelated to the realism of Machiavelli, who regards politics as something in which considerations of good and evil, of right and wrong, have no part, and does not permit the State to be embarrassed by any preconceptions or aspirations of an ethical or religious character! And just as other literary men and artists of the Renaissance have clearly perceived how utterly different their world is from the world that preceded it, so too Machiavelli is fully aware of its essential, formidable "novelty." He says so in the plainest terms in Chapter XV of *The Prince*—a chapter which, as has been justly observed, makes us genuinely feel as if we were entering a new world. "But since it is my purpose to write what may be useful to those who need it, I have thought it more fitting to concern myself with the effective reality of things than with speculation. For many have imagined republics and principates which have never been seen or known to exist in reality." The man who seeks to discover this "effective reality" will confine himself to *living* and *being*, without troubling about "how one ought to live," that is to say *how things should be*; and his attitude will reflect exactly that of the historian, who, finding that men and their passions condition his life, seeks in them the immediate "causes" of events and refrains from asking a supernatural Will to explain the ultimate reason for things.

Finally, we are led to precisely the same conclusions when we come to consider art

---

[4] [Cf. the parallel recently drawn between the Chronicles of Utrecht (1481-3) and Machiavelli's *Florentine Histories* by H. Schulte Nordholt, *Het Beeld der Renaissance*, Amsterdam, 1948, pp. 157 *sqq.* A similar comparison might be made between the "realism" of, for example, Froissart or Chastellain on the one hand and that of a Machiavelli or a Guicciardini on the other.]

and its manifestations. Here too there is a difference between naturalistic detail and comprehensive inspiration, between the "sensibility's" adherence to nature and to worldly life and the mystical afflatus from which the "faith" of the artist springs. The mediaeval craftsman creates for the glory of God and seeks to imbue his work with a moral significance, no more and no less than does the chronicler whose purpose in his writings is to exhort men to despise the uncertain and transient things of the world and to eschew pride, or the poet to whom the true and positive virtue of his work consists in its allegorical meaning. He creates—as we read in the "title" of a mosaic in the Church of SS. Cosma and Damiano in Rome—to the end that "the fair house of God may be resplendent with brilliant metals, so that the precious light of faith may shine more brightly." Here are the rules which Theophilus (twelfth century) prescribes for the artist in his treatise *Schedula diversarum artium*: "Do not hesitate, my beloved son, believe with a whole faith that the spirit of God has filled thy heart when thou hast adorned His house with so much richness and variety of ornamentation; and that thou mayest not fear, I will show thee with clear proof that whatever thou mayest study, comprehend or contemplate in art is a gift graciously bestowed upon thee by the Spirit in its seven forms. Through the spirit of wisdom, thou knowest that all created things proceed from God, that without Him there is nothing . . . Spurred on by the promise of these virtues, beloved son, thou hast trustingly entered the house of God and hast beauteously adorned it . . . thou hast revealed to the eyes of the faithful a sort of divine paradise, bright with all manner of flowers, verdant with herbs and leaves, wherewith thou hast exalted the spirits of the Saints according to their deserts; and thou hast succeeded in glorifying the Creator in His Creature, in causing God to be admired in His works" (in L. Venturi, *Il gusto dei primitivi,* Bologna, 1926, pp. 50 and 52-3).

*The glorification of the Creator*—that is the aim of the mediaeval artist; and as for the verdant herbs and the bright flowers, in other words the so-called realistic detail, what purpose have they if not to stir the souls of the faithful by revealing to them a sort of *paradise of God?* This is the theme that reverberates through the writing of St. Francis of Assisi when he glorifies and praises the things of the world, the creature and nature, in which all things bear witness to God and His omnipotence.

On the other hand, the fifteenth-century artist, who is if anything over-conscious of the intrinsic merit of his work, and is convinced that man is capable, unaided, of any miracle, will strive only, according to the precept of Alberti, to ascertain the truth and, on a foundation of precise knowledge, to create a "beautiful," immortal work that will lead men to glorify his name. Let us specifically compare Alberti with Theophilus. Nothing is further from Alberti's purpose to cause God to be admired in His creatures! "The object of painting," he says, is "to earn favour and goodwill and praise"—in other words, the glorification of the painter, whose function is "to represent in line and colour, on a given canvas or wall, a likeness of the visible surfaces of some object, in such a way that the same, when viewed at a certain distance and from a certain position, may appear in perspective and closely resemble the original in shape" (*Della Pittura,* Book II, in *Opere Volgari,* ed. Bonucci, IV, p. 73). In other words, the artist should imitate nature *per se,* not inasmuch as it mirrors the power of God, but inasmuch as it alone can furnish him with happy inspiration. He should imitate it scientifically and exactly—hence he needs to be a man of learning. He must have a perfect knowledge of draughtsmanship. His knowledge of anatomy must be good, his knowledge of perspective very good. We are on the road that leads to Leonardo da Vinci; and we are already witnessing the complete liberation of the artist from every restriction that is not dictated by artistic reason. Henceforth he will be left alone with himself and his dreams; for him the world will become a synthesis of lines and volumes and colours. As has been well said, long before Machiavelli created the hero of politics the world had acclaimed the hero of art, a personage blind to every form of life save that of his own artistic imagination (Venturi, *op. cit.*, p. 101).

And herein lies indeed the essential novelty of the Renaissance. As in art and literature, so in political theory and historiography, its so-called "realism and individualism," by means of a continuous process initiated by Alberti, carried on by Machiavelli and Ariosto, and brought to its logical conclusion by Galileo, lead to the affirmation of the complete autonomy of art, politics, science and history. In other words, they lead to the abandonment of the typically mediaeval conception of the world according to which no branch of human activity could be considered independently of its relationship to life as a whole. The answer to allegory is the well-known precept of "art for art's sake." The two worlds are essentially different.

Art for art's sake, politics for politics' sake, and even, ultimately, science for science's sake—the results of Italian thought might well be summarized in these phrases. Bartolo of Sassoferrato had applied to States the formula *superiorem non recognoscentes* as an indication of their full autonomy; and this formula could very well be applied to forms of cultural activity during the Renaissance. From which it follows that realism, individualism, love of glory and the imitation of ancient culture, which admittedly were sanctioned by the mediaeval world, but only as incidentals serving a loftier purpose, are now freely proposed as ends in themselves.

### *Lack of Coherence and Symmetry in the Renaissance Conception of the World*

This is not intended to imply, however, that the men of the Renaissance made equally original contributions to every sphere of thought, nor that they had an organic, comprehensive conception of the world which could be substituted, immediately and finally, for the previous one.

In certain branches of human activity—for instance, in economic life—definite traces could even now be found of the survival of ancient traditions and ideas. Usually the age of the Renaissance is thought of as that which saw the birth of the capitalist spirit. Yet if the manner in which business was conducted was already seemingly capitalistic, if the financial and commercial structure of Italian economy at least already bore the capitalist stamp, the souls of big business-men continued in fact to be oppressed by cares of a kind unknown to the capitalist of the modern age. It is symptomatic that at a certain moment in their lives, especially—as is logical!—when they were on the point of death, many merchants and financiers were assailed by unexpected qualms of conscience which compelled them to confess their guilt in public and to return, in one form or another, part of their ill-gotten gains. But even more symptomatic is the misgiving which in the second half of the fifteenth century assailed Alessandra Macinghi Strozzi, mother and mother-in-law of merchants and financiers, and hence a woman well-versed in the ways of business, and also Marco Parenti, a silk-merchant who was at the same time a friend of humanists like Cristoforo Landino, Marsilio Ficino, etc. Alessandra Macinghi Strozzi and Marco Parenti (and the year is 1466) consider that it is improper, and indeed *sinful,* to sell Monte di Firenze bonds when their market-price has soared so that they may later redeem them if they happen to depreciate. They regard as *sinful* (and the expression should be noted, for the criticism it implies is no longer economic in character, but purely and simply moral!) what in the modern world has become a normal practice which no one would dream now of condemning! (*Lettere di Alessandra Macinghi Strozzi*, ed. Guasti, Florence, 1877, pp. 573-4.)

Thus in the fifteenth century we are confronted with the survival of a moralistic attitude to economic life which had previously characterized the society depicted by Villani. Villani himself—a merchant and a man of sound practical experience, prompt to celebrate a particular economic event such as the creation of the golden florin—had subsequently been unable, once he had stopped to consider and appraise economic practice in general, to justify his own actions, and had instead allowed himself to be restrained by those very scruples about commerce and finance which the mediaeval mind had fostered as a matter of principle! He who extols Florence, "worthy daughter and creature of Rome," he who celebrates the creation of the golden florin and the opulence of his city, now condemns the luxurious life of the rich, which breeds "softness," while "simple living and poverty" promote "good faith and goodness among them and within their Commune" (Book VI, Chapter 69). Again, at the very moment when he is saluting with heart-felt satisfaction the greatness of Florence and rejoicing in its mansions and villas, which provide a "magnificent spectacle," he is newly and unexpectedly assailed, albeit only for an instant, by a sort of remorse, by the pangs of a conscience that has been suddenly recalled to a sense of Christian humility: "... there was not a citizen, from the highest to the lowest, who had not built or was not building his own large and palatial country property, a sumptuous habitation with beautiful buildings, better by far than those in the city. And in this all *sinned*, and by reason of their extravagance were deemed mad" (Book XI, Chapter 94).

*Sinned*—once again we have a moral stricture on life as it is expressed in action. It is the same expression that will recur to the lips of Alessandra Macinghi Strozzi, an expression that makes us think again of the traditional sins—the sensuality, pride and avarice of Augustinian and Dantesque memory—just as we are reminded of the deadly sins of mediaeval imagination by Villani's stricture on the Peruzzi, in whose banking operations he himself had played an active part: "Lust for gain expressed in a mad scramble for possessions" (Book XI, Chapter 88). In Villani's thinking, as in that of Donna Alessandra, traces persist of a theoretical aversion to all wealth save the fruits of the earth and of husbandry. This aversion was deep-rooted in the Middle Ages. It was based ideally on the Aristotelian precept that money in itself is valueless, and morally on the verse in St. Luke's Gospel: *Mutuum date nihil inde sperantes.*

In the historical and political sphere Machiavelli replaces the God and devil of Villani with man and man alone. But in the sphere of economic thought nothing happens—until the triumph of Calvinism—to change the old attitude, to sweep away men's scruples and perplexities regarding the problem of wealth. And the logical conclusion is reached in 1532, when the Spanish merchants of Antwerp enquired from the Sorbonne whether or not their activities are morally justifiable!

Apart from everything else, this is another very significant example of the profound divergence which, as has already been said, can exist between concrete reality and the life of the mind, between action and its conceptual systematization. The men of the Renaissance, like their mediaeval predecessors, loved wealth, transacted business—and on what a scale!—and built up great concerns on solid foundations. But in their hearts, when they came to consider the great problems of life and death, of earthly activity and the Unknown, they always perceived that there was, to put it mildly, something shady about their conduct. And then they would rush back into the arms of their confessors, seeking forgiveness for that which over so many years had constituted their whole life.

To Alberti's maxim "art for art's sake," to Machiavelli's theory of "politics for politics' sake," there is certainly no corresponding affirmation of principle that can be expressed in the phrase "economic activity for economic activity's sake," or that can be said to contain even the germ of that principle of "production for production's sake" or "making for making's sake" which is characteristic of modern capitalism and which has been so explicitly formulated in the writings of Henry Ford.

But this is not all. When the question arises of fusing the various forms of life into a comprehensive organic unity, then it is that the tone becomes far less certain and the thread is lost.

The excellence of man was extolled all through the fifteenth century. Everyone, from Giannozzo Manetti to Pico della Mirandola, had a little to say about the *dignitas hominis,* while the study of the various aspects and laws of nature was being steadily intensified, especially by artists and art-critics, who adhered rigorously to the principle of "the imitation of nature" (the Ancients were their preceptors, for the precise reason that they had been able to apprehend and reproduce nature). But the more clearly nature is seen in its fullness, as an organic force with its own laws (and not merely as a spectacle rendered agreeable by the greenness of the meadows and the beauties of the house of God), the more pressing becomes the problem of how to reconcile this force with the freedom and excellence of man—and also the problem of how to reconcile man and nature with the divine Will, with the omnipotence of that Providence whose power no one dreams of denying. This latter problem is all the more harassing in that the moral world is always closely bound up with the religious world. Art and politics have at last ceased entirely to serve a supernatural purpose; but ethics have not. The idea of a purely rational ethic, universal in its application and not subject to the dictates of religion—an ethic which (as Hugo Grotius subsequently maintained in the case of natural law) would continue to stand on its solid rational foundation even if, to take an absurd hypothesis, God did not exist—such an idea has not yet been dreamed of. The conception of "how things ought to be" is always closely bound up with the idea of the beyond and the divine ordinances. Its necessary premises and corollaries are the ideas of sin and eternal punishment or eternal bliss.

In their respective fields Alberti and Machiavelli have treated the question of "being" with the utmost realism; but the question of "how things ought to be," even if they consider it at all, is still always bound up with religious precept. The world of morality and the world of religion are one. Ethics finally merges into theology.

Far from having been disposed of, the thorny problem of religion continues to agitate men's minds. Indeed, it reappears in an even more emphatic form at the end of the fifteenth century by reason of the fact that the Italian soul has been plunged into gloom by the tragic happenings of which the peninsula has been the scene. The need to justify the world and existence, nature and creature, will and fortune, and to hold fast to a moral law which seemingly can spring from no other source, brings man back to the idea of God—a transcendent God Who is the Lord of humanity . . .

# 2 / The Reformation: Catholic and Protestant Views

Scholarly work in the field of the Reformation has been immense. From its beginnings in the nineteenth century, it has had, not unexpectedly, a confessional and, at times, a polemical character. Following the lead, however, of such scholars as Gustav von Schmoller, Ernst Troeltsch, and Max Weber—the latter's work is treated in another part of this volume—historians have concentrated increasingly, since the beginning of this century, on the social, political, and economic aspects of the Reformation. Secular interpretations of the Reformation might predominate but for two points. First, the Reformation did have a human agent in Martin Luther, a man of conviction and remarkable character, who introduced a conception of the relationship between God and man radically different from that generally held in his day. And second, this conception and others derived from it led to the disorganization of the unity of Western Christendom. Thus the Reformation cannot be and has not been left to "scientific history" alone. Any comprehensive interpretation of it involves theological as well as historical judgments on the nature of Christian unity and Luther's interpretation of the Scriptures. Therefore, alongside of the work of the social scientists, a vast and painstaking amount of research on the Reformation continues to be done by scholars trained in theology and church history.[1] Although for nearly half a century judgments have become more moderate, and Roman Catholic and Protestant church historians have admired each other's scholarship, their ultimate conclusions parallel their religious convictions. This is reflected in the selections that follow.

The first two deal with Luther's conception of the relationship between God and man. Rev. Wilhelm Pauck, Professor of Church History at the Union Theological Seminary in New York City, points out that while Luther felt himself called to a divine mission, "held and supported by God," he also rejected "personal worth and authority." This, with Luther's call for total dependence on God and his "agonies of faith," seem to imply a sense of deep humility. Yet it is precisely a lack of humility that the distinguished Roman Catholic philosopher Jacques Maritain criticizes in Luther. Central to Maritain's position is the Catholic view that Luther's doctrine of salvation by faith was presumptuous in that it emphasized man's unaided will to salvation at the expense of God's grace normally available through the sacraments.

The third selection is from *The Reformation in England* by Rev. Philip Hughes, one of the most distinguished of Roman Catholic church historians. The fourth is from *Luther and His Times* by a Protestant historian, Prof. E. G. Schweibert. It represents a lifework of Luther research begun under the late Preserved Smith, dean of America's Reformation scholars. Both selections survey, in a general way, the onset of the Reformation. And both offer new insights, such as Hughes's characterization of the

---

[1] For an idea of this work, see Harold J. Grimm, "Luther Research since 1920," *Journal of Modern History*, Vol. XXXII, No. 2 (June 1960), pp. 105-118.

Reformation as "a revolt of clerics against clerics," which is paralleled by Schweibert's interesting enumeration of Luther's early followers. But both writers come to diametrically opposite conclusions. Schweibert, for example, cannot countenance the words *revolt* or *revolution* when applied to the Reformation. And while Hughes finds the Reformation "catastrophic," Schweibert calls it "much-needed."

# LUTHER'S FAITH

**Wilhelm Pauck**

In his sermon on the occasion of Luther's burial on February 22, 1546, Bugenhagen characterized the reformer, his long-time friend and colleague, with the following words: "... he was without doubt the angel of which the Apocalypse speaks in Chapter XIV: 'And I saw an angel flying through the midst of heaven, who had an eternal gospel to preach,' ... the angel who says: 'Fear God, and give glory to him!' These are the two articles of the teaching of Martin Luther, the law and the gospel, by which the whole Scripture is opened and Christ made known as our righteousness and eternal life."

Luther—an angel of God! Such a description suggests that his contemporaries understood his person and work in a religious sense.

## I

Luther himself thought of himself and of his work in the same way. He did not wish to be called a prophet (only once did he speak of himself as "the prophet of the Germans"), but he had the sense of a *divine mission.* In opposition to the defenders of the old faith who called him a heretic, he thought of himself as an *"ecclesiasticus* [churchman] by the grace of God." God had called him, he felt, to use his office of "Doctor of the Holy Scripture" for the reformation of the church according to the gospel. So he wrote: "I have received my doctrine by the grace of God from heaven, and, what is more, I have kept it in the presence of one who can do more with his little finger than a thousand popes, kings, princes, and *doctores* could do." In the same spirit, he once described his mission in the following Pauline way: "If I should want to boast, I should glory in God that I am one of the apostles and evangelists in German lands, even though the devil and all his bishops and tyrants do not want me to be such; for I know that by the grace of God I have taught and still teach faith and truth." Such high claims he justified with the certainty that he was speaking "Christ's word" and not his own. Therefore, he did not hesitate to conclude: "So my mouth must be his whose words it speaks."

Because he knew himself to be an instrument of God and because he felt "more acted upon than acting," he argued that the whole cause of the Reformation could not be measured by human norms. When in his old age he looked back upon the beginnings of the Reformation and contemplated "the very great, heavy care and trouble" which the work of the Reformation had cost him, he exclaimed: "Had I known all in advance, God would have been put to great trouble to bring me to it." Remembering the days of the Diet of Worms, he pondered: "Truly God can drive one mad; I do not know whether now I could be so daring." However, in the midst of the crisis of his trial, he had written: "The die was cast; and so I did not want to do anything else than what I did. I began to put all my trust upon the Spirit who does not carry on a lazy business." Thus he explained that all that took place at the height of the Reformation occurred, not because he had planned it so, but by "divine counsel."

This feeling of being divinely led he expressed best in the following characteristic words: "God has led me on as if I were a horse and he put blinkers on me that I could not see who came running up upon me. . . . A good deed rarely issues from planning wisdom and cleverness; it must all happen in the vagaries of ignorance."

These descriptions of the feeling of being called to a work that he had not chosen for himself are all the more impressive because Luther did not derive any pretensions of personal authority from his sense of mission. He did not wish his own special gifts and abilities to be regarded as extraordinary or authoritative. He resented it that his opponents called his teaching "Lutheran," and he got no satisfaction from the fact that his followers called themselves by his name. "Who is this Luther?" he wrote. "My teaching is not my own, and I have not been crucified for the sake of anyone. . . . Why should it happen to me, miserable, stinking bag of worms that I am, that the children of Christ should be called by my insignificant name? . . . I am and will be nobody's master. With the one church I have in common the teaching of Christ who alone is our master."

When, on one occasion, he wrote: "So say I, Dr. Martin Luther, the unworthy evangelist of our Lord Jesus," he desired to appeal to the authority of Christ, who alone, according to his opinion, should be heard as a prophet. But, at the same time, he wished to be taken seriously in his judgment of himself as an unworthy servant of Christ. He dared to appeal with certainty to God's word, but he also confessed frankly that Christian obedience was a daily task for him and the cause of never-ending efforts. That is why he did not want to justify his right to speak in the name of God by his own Christian attainments. "Let everyone," he wrote, "be responsible for his own feelings. As for me, I regard myself as a Christian. Nevertheless, I know how difficult it has been for me, and still is, to apprehend and to keep this cornerstone [Christ]. But they certainly do me wrong [who call me a Lutheran], for—God strengthen me!—I am a small, poor Lutheran."

No one understands Luther who does not pay attention to the two aspects of his sense of calling: on the one hand, the assertion of being held and supported by God, and, on the other, the rejection of any personal worth and authority.


## II

His *faith* corresponded wholly to the spirit which guided him in his work.

His deepest convictions were determined by his conception of God. God, as he saw him, was the restlessly working, driving power in all that is, the ever-active, creative livingness which lets no creature stand still. God is at work everywhere and in all, also in the godless, even in the devil. The whole universe is his "masquerade in which he hides himself while he rules the world so strangely by making a hubbub." The almighty power of God is nowhere and yet everywhere. Because it moves everything, it is immanent in all; but because it creates everything, it transcends all.

It must be present at all places, even in the smallest leaf of a flower. The reason is this: "It is God who creates, works, and preserves all things by his almighty power and by his right hand, as we confess in the creed. He sends out no delegates or angels when he creates and preserves, but everything is the working of his own divine power. But if he is the creator and preserver, he himself must be present, creating and preserving his creature in its most inward and most outward being. That is why he himself is in the very inwardness and in the very outwardness of every creature, from end to end, below and above it, before and behind it. Nothing can be more present and be more really within all creatures than God himself."

"God is smaller than anything small, bigger than anything big, shorter than anything short, longer than anything long, broader than anything broad, slimmer than anything slim, and so on; he is an inexpressible being, above and beyond all that one can name or think."

This all-comprehending, all-penetrating creativity is the fountain and spring of life and of all good. It is closer to every one of us than any of us are to each other. As it is God's nature to create all from nothing, so he is able "to help the forsaken ones, to justify sinners, to resurrect the dead, and to save the damned."

He is the life of every being. He determines everything. He is present everywhere. But he is impenetrable and inscrutable. In such a way Luther spoke of God—most articulately in his book against Erasmus, *Of the Bondage of the Will,* and in his treatises on the Lord's Supper, called forth by his controversy with Zwingli. There he disclosed his profoundest thoughts on the creative power by which he felt himself driven and overcome. But he had still more to say.

It makes a difference whether you say that God is present or whether you say that he is present for you. But he is there for you, when he adds his word [to his presence] and binds himself, saying: Here you shall find me. When you have the word, you can grasp him and have him and say: Now I have thee, as thou sayest. So it is with the right hand of God; it is everywhere, as no one can deny; but it is also nowhere; therefore you cannot apprehend it anywhere unless it binds and confines itself for your benefit to one place. This happens when it moves and dwells in the humanity of Christ. There you will most certainly find it. Otherwise you must run through all creation from end to end, groping and fumbling about, here and there, without finding it. Although it is really there—it is not there for you.

In Christ, the mysterious, inscrutable Lord of everything has made himself accessible. In him he is comprehensible, because he has revealed himself in him without abandoning his mystery. He is hidden in the humbleness of the child in the manger. In the cross he is not *directly* visible as the victor over hell, death, and the devil. He is abscondite in the message of Christ about the mercy that seeks the sinner. And yet—"Whosoever does not apprehend this man born of Mary, simply cannot apprehend God; even if they should say that they believe in God, creator of heaven and earth, they believe really only in the idol of their heart, for outside of Christ there is no true God." In Christ, men have the "mirror of God's paternal heart." In him, God is a God for them, their God. In Christ, he is really the ever-renewing fountain of all good.

But men do not want to accept this teaching of God, for, so Luther argued, "Man by nature does not want God to be God; he would much rather that he himself were God and that God were not God." Because of his self-sufficiency and selfishness, he is God's enemy. Though, when relying upon himself, he is driven from presumptuous security to despair in himself without being able to extricate himself from this dilemma, he refuses to acknowledge that he is a created being responsible to his creator. This unfaith is his sin. It is incomprehensible to him that he is a creature of God (this is proved by the fact that when he engages in worship, he tends to fashion an idol for himself); but it is utterly unfathomable for him that God should be a Father of sinners. His moral sense rebels against such a thought. If there is a God at all, so he thinks, God is the Lord of the righteous, in whose sight only the worthy ones are acceptable.

Such is man's natural religiousness, according to Luther's opinion. Faith is its opposite. It is the acknowledgment of God's sovereignty and the belief in his accessibility in Christ and his word. Faith meant to Luther simply to have God. "Having God," he wrote in the *Larger Catechism,* "is nothing else than heartily to believe and trust in him; . . . this trusting and believing makes both, God and idol; for these two belong together, faith and God."

This faith, Luther taught, must be seen as the personal act of the believer ("If you believe, you have," he repeated unceasingly), but he knew also that it is the work of the Holy Spirit and, as such, a gift of God. Faith can therefore be an event only if the Christian becomes a new person. It is Christ who forms this new person. "I do not live in my own person, but Christ lives within me. To be sure, I live as a person, but not in myself or for my own person." The person of the believer transcends itself, so to speak. This was the experience of Luther's prophetic religion.

He tried to interpret this experience of faith in many ways, for all his thinking circled around it. "Faith," so he defined, "is the knowledge of things not seen; it is directed to things that are not apparent. In order that faith may occur, it is therefore necessary that all that is believed be hidden."

Faith is a miracle that cannot be understood according to ordinary criteria. Particularly when one has found God merciful, such faith appears as a blindly trusting audacity. "For this is the nature of faith, that it dares trust in God's grace. . . . Faith does not require information, knowledge, or security, but a free surrender and joyful daring upon an unfelt, untried, unknown goodness." From here, Luther came to the remarkable conclusion that all certainty must be founded not upon human experience but upon divine revelation. "Our theology is certain," he said, "because it places us outside of ourselves; I do not need to rely upon my conscience, my senses, and my doing, but I rely upon the divine promise and truth which never deceive."

And yet—faith must be a personal experience in order to be valid. A Christian must have faith by virtue of a personal deed and decision. "You yourself must decide; your neck is at stake. Therefore, unless God says to your own heart: This is God's word, you cannot comprehend it. . . . If you do not feel it, you do not have faith, but the word merely hangs in your ears and floats on your tongue as foam lies on the waters."

### III

In what a terrific tension Luther held his faith! On the one hand, he viewed it with radical seriousness as the work and gift of God who acts upon man from without. On the other hand, he experienced it as a concrete personal decision and commitment. In contemplating this tension, one understands why religion was a perpetual crisis and an unceasing battle for Luther.

This is the meaning of the *tentationes,* the agonies of faith, into which he was drawn again and again. He felt that the merciful God was withdrawing from him. He was overcome by doubts concerning his work, when he questioned whether he should have dared to upset age-old customs and traditions in the church. He felt that, in the light of the human need for security, the ambiguity of divine grace was unbearable. He then sensed the nearness of God, not as love and consolation, but as wrath and damnation. When such thoughts beset him, he felt that he was being attacked by the devil and thrown into a battle for his faith. He attributed such agonies to his psychological propensity to melancholy, but he knew also that he did not understand their true significance by such a psychological interpretation. Indeed, he held these agonies of faith to be unavoidable because he was aware that, from the viewpoint of ordinary human experience, faith was an impossibility.

He overcame these *Anfechtungen* (assaults), as he called them in his own tongue, by appealing to Christ and by relying upon the First Commandment: I am the Lord, thy God; thou shalt have no other gods before me. When he was free again and restored in the faith, he knew more definitely than ever before that the inborn and acquired human certainties and safeguards are nothing ultimately sure and that man deceives himself when he pretends to possess certainty in himself. Thus these agonies appeared to him as a means by which the truth of faith, as a truth from beyond man's reach, was confirmed. A Christian, so he concluded, must be continually in the process of becoming. As he is a forgiven sinner who, despite being forgiven, again and again falls into the sin of unfaith, so he is thrown into agonies of faith until the end of his days, in order that he might test his faith by being compelled to fight for it. So Luther could say of himself: "I did not learn my theology all at once; I have had to brood and ponder over it more and more deeply; my *tentationes* have brought me to it, for one learns only by experience."

He once said that the greatest of these *tentationes* was to know of none at all; for such an attitude appeared to him the height of self-deception. He believed it to be an incontestable fact that every man has a bad conscience in spite of all the masks of self-confidence he wears, for at the bottom of his heart he knows himself to be in the wrong before God. Even though he rebels against the gospel of the forgiveness of God, because faith in this gospel involves the surrender of his self and the undoing of his self-determination, he will nevertheless experience faith as a liberation not only from himself but, particularly, from his bad conscience.

Luther best described the human situation which leads to the agony of faith in the following words. They describe the fright and terror by which one can be seized at the sound of a rustling leaf, and they symbolize all the insecurities of pride from which one can be liberated by faith alone.

So it can happen that conscience feels all misfortune that befalls us as the wrath of God, and that even a mere rustling leaf seems to be God's wrath. . . . There is nothing more worthless and more despised than a dry leaf that lies on the ground; worms crawl over it; it cannot ward off even the smallest speck of dust. . . . But there comes a time when its rustling will scare man and horse, spike and armor, kings and princes, the power of a whole army, and even such spiteful and angry tyrants as cannot be scared either by the fear of hell or by God's wrath and judgment, but only become still prouder and more hardened by such threats. Aren't we fine fellows? We do not fear God's anger but stand stiffly unmoved by it. But we can be scared and frightened by the anger of an impotent dry leaf, and the rustling of such a leaf can make the world too narrow for us and become a wrathful God to us.

### IV

From this analysis of Luther's faith we can conclude that his interpretation of the Christian religion corresponded exactly to his conception of the meaning of his mission in the world. In his faith he related himself only to God in Christ; he did not base it upon the content of his experiences. With respect to his work, he relied upon the almighty Lord of history and not upon his own qualities of leadership, of which he did not think much anyway. In his faith as well as in his work as a reformer, he really believed himself "more acted upon than acting." This way of thinking has nothing whatsoever to do with quietism, of which Luther has often been accused. Rather, it is "prophetic"—through and through. This can be proved by the fact that Luther felt himself called to a most personal, active participation in the work which, as he believed, God performed in the world through him. It was God himself, the ever-active creative power, who, by means of the Reformation, made room in the world for his word, and Luther was drawn into this divine work with his whole person. He felt that God had overpowered him; he did not think that he had thereby been drawn into a heteronomous servitude. He was moved, rather, to commit himself to him who had overpowered him and to co-operate with him. Such was Luther's own conception of his faith. His principles of action were: Do not rely on men, but trust in God. Do not fear men, but fear God. That is why Luther acted on the historical scene without special consideration of political and historical consequences. Whosoever wants "to help the cause of the gospel," he wrote in a letter to Wolfgang Capito, must preach it without fear and regard of men, in order that "the free, pure and plain truth" may assert itself by itself alone.

In explaining the beginnings and the course of the Reformation to the people of Wittenberg after his return from his exile in Wartburg castle, he said: "All I have done is to further, preach, and teach God's word; otherwise I have done nothing. So it came about that while I slept or while I had a glass of beer with my friend Philipp [Melanchthon] and with Amsdorf, the papacy was so weakened as it never was before by the action of any prince or emperor. I have done nothing; the word has done and accomplished everything. . . . I let the word do its work."

These words sound quietistic and politically naïve, but they were spoken by one who, in the name of God, changed the course of history. What Luther meant to express was that his decisions and actions were motivated only by his concern for the word of God, and not by political calculations and predictions. By, and on account of, his faith, he became a reformer. His work, the Reformation, will live as long as this faith finds a response in the hearts of men.


# MARTIN LUTHER: "A MONK WHO LACKED HUMILITY"

**Jacques Maritain**

* * *

Martin Luther, strong summoner of the great undefined powers which lie dormant in the heart of the creature of flesh, was gifted with a nature at once realistic and lyrical, powerful, impulsive, brave and sad, sentimental and morbidly sensitive. Vehement as he was, there yet was in him kindness, generosity, tenderness, and, with all, unbroken pride and peevish vanity. What was lacking in him was force of intellect. If by intelligence we mean capacity to grasp the universal, to discern the essential, to follow with docility the wanderings and refinements of reality, Luther was not intelligent, but limited—stubborn, especially. But he had the understanding of the particular and practical to an amazing degree, and an astute and lively ingenuity, skill to detect error in others, the art of finding a thousand ways out of a difficulty and crushing his opponent—in short, all the resources of what philosophers call the "cogitative," the "particular reason."

He entered religion, if we may accept his own story, as the result of a feeling of terror occasioned, first by the death of one of his friends who was killed in a duel, then by a violent storm in which he nearly died. He was "not so much drawn as carried away," *non tam tractus quam raptus*. He seems to have been exact and perhaps fervent in the early days of his religious life, but he was always anxious and troubled. At a time when the general level of clerical life in Germany had fallen wretchedly low, he had declared for the current of reform, and, as he says, did not let cobwebs grow on his snout when there were abuses to be stormed at. At twenty-five he was professor at the University of Wittenberg; at twenty-nine, doctor of sacred theology; and the duty of teaching, so imprudently given to a man so restless, threw him at once into the acrid atmosphere of human controversy and transferred his zeal into arrogance and presumption. From Scholasticism hastily and imperfectly studied, he had derived nothing but an arsenal of false ideas and vague theological notions, and a disconcerting skill in specious argument.

What he became later must not prevent our imagining what he may first have been as a Catholic, as a religious, sincerely setting all his natural impetuosity to that pursuit of perfection which he had vowed. On the contrary, nothing is more instructive than to try to picture what that young religious may have been. From his own witness and the studies of Denifle and Grisar I note here two things in the inner life of Brother Martin.

First, he seems to have sought in the spiritual life chiefly what authors call sensible consolations, and to have been desperately attached to that experimental savouring of piety, that assurance in feeling, which God sends to souls to draw them to Himself, but takes from them when He wills, and which are only means. For Luther, on the other hand, the whole point was to *feel* himself in a state of grace—as if grace in itself were an object of sensation! Did not the theological thesis that grace is infused into the soul at the very moment when sin is effaced "drive him almost to despair of God, of all that God is, and all that He possesses,"[1] because he did not experience in himself that perfect pureness of grace? Thus in a disturbed and carnal soul a strong mystical homesickness distorted all the teaching of spiritual writers, and turned to a brutal craving to enjoy its own sanctity. Luther tasted of the hidden fruits of Christ's grace; he entered the spiritual garden of the Church; I am even inclined to believe that he went a considerable way; but from the very beginning his inner life was disorientated. The human subject, and that in the highest and most subtle order, became in fact for him of more concern than God.

Then, and as a result of the same vicious disposition, he relied on his own strength alone to attain to Christian virtue and perfection, trusting to his own efforts, his penances, the works of his will, far more than to grace. Thus he practised the very Pelagianism with which he was to charge Catholics, from which he himself was never really to be free. In his spiritual life he was, in practice, a Pharisee relying on his works, as his scrupulous fidgetiness shows—for he had at that time many of the characteristics of the scrupulous: he blamed himself for all the first involuntary impressions of the senses as if they were sins, and strove to reach a holiness which should not betray the least sign of human frailty. . . . Moreover he was at the same time tormented by the pride with which the soul in such a state beholds itself. If the sacrament of penance

---

[1] Sermon of 27th December, 1514. Weim., I, 43, 5-12; IV, 665, 15-22. (Denifle, *Luther et le luthéranisme*, ed. Paquier, 2nd ed., 1913, II, 400, suggests 1515.)

does away his sin, he is at once better than everyone else! "I could not understand, in my madness, how, after I had repented and confessed, it could be right for me to think myself a sinner like others and not to prefer myself above the rest."[2]

Then came the night, that *night of sense* whose darkness is proportioned to the soul's need to be emptied of self. Martin Luther has lost all sensible consolation, he is plunged in a sea of agonies, he sees with that pitiless clearness which God gives in such cases the vanity and perversity filling his human heart; the whole building of perfection which he has tried to raise with his own hands seems to collapse on him, to turn against him in reproach. It might be the night of purification, and the time, perhaps, to choose his eternal destiny. What does he do? Does he forsake himself? Does he cast himself on God? Does he repeat to his troubled heart that great saying of Augustine: "Vis fugere a Deo, fuge in Deum"? He gave up praying and threw himself into activity to escape. He tried to drown his anguish in a sea of toil.

"I need two secretaries," he writes in 1516 to Lang, prior of Erfurt. "I do practically nothing all day long but write letters . . . I am Preacher of the Convent and in the Refectory; I am called daily to preach in the parish, I am Director of Studies and Vicar of the district, and thereby elevenfold Prior;[3] I am responsible for the fish-ponds at Leitzkau; I am agent at Torgau in the suit for Herzberg parish church; I give lectures on St. Paul, I am collecting notes on the Psalter. I rarely have time to recite my Office and say Mass."

Now he had hardly strength to stand against the malignant fevers of nature. "I am," he will admit three years later, "I am but a man prone to let himself be swept off his feet by society, drunkenness, the movements of the flesh . . ." And again in a sermon of the same period on the state of marriage, "What is needed to live in continence is not in me." Is it then that at the decisive moment of his crisis he falls into some grave outward failing? Apparently not. But inwardly he fell; he despaired of grace. When a man begins to know the wounds and wretchedness of the sons of Adam, the serpent whispers in his ear: "Be content to be what you are, spoiled angel, misbegotten creature; your business is to do ill, since your very being is bad." A spiritual temptation preeminently. Luther makes that act of perverse resignation; he gives up the fight; he declares that the fight is impossible. Submerged by sin on all sides, or by what he thinks to be sin, he lets himself go with the tide. And he comes to the practical conclusion: *Concupiscence cannot be conquered.*

So far we have only the classical story, if I may dare to call it so, of the fallen monk. Doubtless; but notice: You think he is crushed? He is on the point of breaking free, under full sail for sanctity. It is now that Luther the reformer appears, that he discovers the Gospel, that the Gospel frees him, that Christian liberty is revealed to him. What does he see in the Gospel and St. Paul? Exactly what we were just taking for a confession of despair: *Concupiscence is unconquerable.* The resignation of the man, the pessimist; abandonment to animality, a preface to the optimistic surrender of Jean-Jacques and the false *sincerity* of unmoral asceticism. Concupiscence Luther identifies with original sin. Original sin is always in us, ineffaceable; it has made us radically bad, corrupt in the very essence of our nature. God commanded the impossible when He gave us His law. But now Christ has paid for us and His justice redeems us. He is just in our stead. Justification is wholly exterior to us and we are still

---

[2] Commentary on Ch. 4 of the *Epistle to the Romans,* Folio 1446, Ficker, II. 109.
[3] In the sense that he had 11 convents to guide.

sin to our very bones: it infuses no new life into us, it simply covers us as with a cloak. There is nothing for us to do to be saved. On the contrary, to want to co-operate with the divine action is a lack of faith, a denial of the Blood of Christ, and damnation.

From henceforth "Heaven opens." Good-bye to torments and remorse! *Absolute uselessness of works; salvation by faith alone,* that is to say, by a burst of hope. *Pecca fortiter et crede firmius.* Sin courageously, believe more firmly than ever and you will be saved.

Now Luther has a doctrine; now he heads a school, is master and prophet; and he can win over to his theology all the greed, all the impatient sensuality, the putrid fermentation, mixed with hopes of reform fed more by humanism and learning than by supernatural faith, in the Germany of his day. His doctrine, clearly, is born chiefly of his own inward experience. We must, no doubt, take account of his reading of St. Augustine, ill understood; of the influence of the conflict between conventual and observant Augustinians which Grisar points out; and especially of the action of the theological stream called Augustinian. But all that is secondary. For that soul, now devastated, it is faith saving without works, no longer theological faith but a merely human impulse of trust, aping in its despair the virtue of faith—it is faith-trust which must now ensure the state of spiritual comfort no longer expected of the perceptible tasting of grace, but none the less always essentially aimed at. What Luther's doctrine especially expresses is Luther's interior states, spiritual adventures, and individual history. Unable to conquer himself, he transforms his necessities into theological truths, and his own actual case into a universal law. And, withal, longing for the moral security and the liberty of the sons of the kingdom, he frees himself—he thinks he frees himself—from all the tortures of his conscience by despairing once for all of all works and casting himself, as he is, on trust in Christ. He is only an inverted Pharisee, a runaway victim of scruples.

The unhappy man thinks he no longer trusts in himself, but in God alone. Yet by refusing to admit that man can share really and within himself in the justice of Jesus Christ and in His grace—which, according to him, is always external to us and cannot produce in us any vital act—he shuts himself up for ever in his self, he withdraws from himself all support but his self, he sets up as a doctrine what had first been nothing but the sin of an individual, he places the centre of his religious life not in God but in man. At the moment when, after the storms let loose by the business of the Indulgences, he raises his self in the world against the Pope and the Church, within himself his interior life is completely overturned.

\* \* \*

But what should be observed here is not the result but the cause. That cause is hidden in Luther's spiritual life, and one might say that that immense disaster for humanity, the Protestant Reformation, was only the effect of an interior trial which turned out badly in a religious who lacked humility. It was in the heights of the spirit that he first fell, that he gave battle and was conquered. The play was staged *in acie mentis,* at the highest point of the soul. Luther says that he saw and defied innumerable demons who threatened him and argued with him. In origin and principle the drama of the Reformation was a spiritual drama, a battle of the soul.

\* \* \*

# THE REFORMATION: "NOTHING LESS THAN CATASTROPHIC"

**Philip Hughes**

\* \* \*

By the time that Henry VIII was first seriously moved to threaten and coerce the pope, and to question whether the pope really possessed the spiritual authority which he claimed, vast tracts in central and northern Germany had already repudiated this; so too had Denmark and Sweden; the movement was spreading, and almost everywhere it was a movement led by princes, and successful for that reason.

But although the century of Henry VIII was a "century of secularisation" rather than a religious century, the Reformation was itself a religious, and indeed a theological, revolution. Like every other theological revolution in the mind of western Europe its starting point was practical rather than speculative. It began indeed with anxieties and doubts about the most practical matter of all. Granted that God exists, that there is a future life, and that this must be, for all men, either an eternity of bliss or an eternity of torment, does man's conduct in this present life bear any relation to the condition in which he will spend eternity? The scandal of the way in which indulgences were frequently preached was unquestionably a factor in the religious malaise of the time. So, too, was the scandal of simony in the high places of the Church; so was the scandal of clerical ignorance and ill living; so was the scandal that, for generations now, all this had been allowed to continue almost unchecked. And these scandals produced that indifference to the fate of ecclesiastics, and their privileges, and their property, which characterised the average Catholic of the generation in which the revolution began. But, about the scandals themselves, the zealous Catholic was no less bitter than the hottest of the reforming zealots, bitter too about the shortcomings of the system. It was not the heretic's determination to make an end of these abuses that now so speedily divided western Europe; nor his repudiation of particular details of the traditional practice: it was something positive on his part, his re-interpretation of the fundamentals of Christianity, the organisation of a new species of Christian religion which not only could not be reconciled with the old, but must either kill the old or die itself. Here was a new way of being a Christian, a new view of God and God's ways with man and man's duty to God, that must produce a new type of European, a new culture; and the starting point of it all, in time, was the anxious speculations of a German religious about his own fate in eternity and the divine answer—as he interpreted it—to the disciple's first question, "Lord, what must I do to be saved?"

The charitable wisdom of God has revealed to men the manner of life whose reward is joy with Him everlasting. But although believing man accepts, without any doubting at all, the truth of that revelation, and through believing knows with certainty the difference between what is good and what is evil, he yet remains free to choose which he will do, and, despite his knowledge, attracted often to what he knows to be evil; and he yields to the attraction. He not only sins, he contracts habits of sinning. And he can do this while still retaining all his old desire to be God's friend, and to be with God in eternity. *Infelix ego*, the words go back to the first days of Christianity, and the natural sentiment is older still, "Who shall deliver me from the body of this death?" What is the way out?

It was upon this theme that Luther brooded for years, impressionable, sentimental, passionate, moody—an artist in the cloister, who should never have been a monk or a friar at all; an orator and man of action, not a contemplative, not a thinker; a man with a mission, and a personality to move the nations. Like all other men Luther had his personal difficulties; he no doubt felt them more than most. Why, if he desired to love God, and God desired his salvation, why did sin continue to attract him and himself continue to fall? Why did God's law continue to be so hard—so impossible, he would say—to observe? Could it be that he was created as one foredoomed to hell, sinning because he could not but sin, and yet damned because God willed him to be damned? Despair seized on him at such thoughts, and he writhed in an agony of hatred of God.

When the events of 1517 suddenly revealed him to the great world outside the Saxon universities Luther, thirty-four years of age, had been for five years lecturing on Holy Scripture at Wittenberg. Whatever his technical competence for this speciality, his general theological formation must be reckoned poor, and it is not remarkable that he was unable to resolve his anxieties from any deep consideration of the content of the great mysteries of Original Sin, Redemption, Grace and Election as the classic theologians, long before his time, had worked this out. That Luther was born in a time when theology was at a low ebb was his greatest misfortune, perhaps, after his precipitate, headlong temperament. Nor was his faulty formation Luther's fault alone, or even Luther's fault at all. The slow movement of the theologian away from philosophy; the destruction of philosophy as a knowledge about reality, that followed wherever Ockham's baneful theories spread—and by Luther's time they largely dominated the whole university world; the sterile wrangling of the various schools of thought among the theologians, and the indifference of these technicians to all outside their texts and their professional occupations; the way in which the theologians "materialised" their business; and finally the movement of the protagonists of *la vie dévote* away from the theologians; all this had, by Luther's time, produced a stumbling block in the ways of Christian life at least as dangerous, though less spectacularly evident, as any scandal of wealth or misconduct, clerical or lay.

Another way of theology was now coming into fashion—to learn the ancient tongues, Greek and Hebrew, and to read the Scriptures in the languages in which they had been written, and from the light thereby thrown on their meaning to re-interpret their message to the world. Not theology in the classical sense, but scholarship, was the hall-mark of this school, which thereby cut across the tangle of disputes which for so long had occupied Thomists and Scotists and Ockhamists, and left aside entirely that examination of the great truths conducted in the spirit, and with the methods, of the great philosophers, of Aristotle especially. The great light, in the world of this new theology was, of course, Erasmus. Luther, as an exponent of Holy Scripture, is of the same school. He did not take the traditional theology to assist him as he pondered the meaning of the great texts on which he lectured, the Psalms, and the Epistle to the Romans, and the Epistle to the Galatians. He had his texts, and his knowledge of the languages; he had St. Augustine, studied in the same spirit, and away from the philosophical-minded theologians who had commented him in earlier centuries; and he had the lively stimulus of his own experiences and his needs. What he got out of it all, as a solution, was somewhat as follows.

Man's present unhappy spiritual state is the result of Adam's sin of disobedience to the divine command not to eat of the forbidden fruit. For that sin affected not Adam only—not merely this first human person, that is to say—but it also affected human nature itself; and its effect on human nature was to corrupt it utterly. No man has, since then, been capable of aught but sin. Whatever his intentions the result, in God's sight, has been evil. And the tendency in man to will what he knows to be evil has, since then, not only been continuous, but a thing impossible to overcome. Man's will is not, in fact, free but enslaved to sin; he is, in this respect, born the slave of the devil. From this pit into which Adam's sin has thus thrown all his posterity, the mercy of God has provided for man an escape: first, God, becoming man, gave His life as a sacrifice of expiation for Adam's sin and for all the mass of human sin since Adam; next, God gave man a means whereby to take hold of the infinite worth of that divine sacrifice, and, possessed of it, to be reconciled with God and free from all the consequences of that hostility to God which sin is.

Luther's first notable divergence from the Catholic teaching was his view that Adam's sin had corrupted human nature *utterly*. His next divergence derived, in part, from his views of what the divine omnipotence could do, and of the nature of things in general. For the school of theology from which Luther derived (like most members of the religious order to which he belonged), men's acts were only good because God chose to consider them good—there was no such thing as an action good in itself. Murder was a crime because God had so declared; God might, equally well, have made murder a duty. What mattered about human conduct was not any inherent quality in the acts—whether of goodness or badness—but their acceptability in God's sight. The sole, and all-important, fact was that God should choose to take the act as good. Here was the way out of the impasse that man could not do any act really good, and that the utter corruption of his nature necessarily entailed this. For, if God should choose to take man's act as good, its own deficiencies were of no consequence whatever.

The same false theological principle was at work in Luther's theory of what happened to sinful man's soul in the process of reconciliation with God. Nothing, he thought, could change the inherent sinfulness of man's nature; not even God could alter the fact that man's acts must continue to be sinful—the scroll remained charged with crime; the merits of Christ imputed to the sinner did not remove the blemish; but they made the soul divinely acceptable, covering it as with a cloak; the forgiveness wrought no change in the soul itself.[1]

Here was Luther's explanation of the riddle why Luther—and all other men—continued to be tempted and to fall, despite all that God has promised and performed for them; here was relief from the tormenting anxiety that sin continued with its ineluctable consequence of ultimate, eternal alienation from God. Given that man has once achieved the necessary reconciliation with God through the merits of Christ, the sins he continues to commit are of no ultimate importance; he is now covered with the cloak of Christ's righteousness; and God is accepting him as good. Once man is reconciled through the saving merits of Christ, his salvation is assured. No act of his can come between him and the eternity of heaven—save one, he must not lose faith. For, what secures to man his participation in the saving merits of Christ, what causes him to appear before God clad in their splendour, making him acceptable

---

[1] The very contrary to St. Thomas's answer given 250 years before; *cf. Summa Theol.*, 1a–2ae, q. 110, a.1, *Utrum gratia ponat aliquid in anima*, in which the very problem whether grace consists in an acceptance of man as just by God is discussed, i.e., in the analysis of the first objection, which concludes, "Ergo per hoc quod homo dicitur gratiam Dei habere, nihil ponitur in anima, sed solum significatur acceptatio divina."

to God, just in God's sight, justified, is man's faith that he is already saved by the sacrifice of Christ. This faith alone is the operative element that secures to man all the rest. Such, in outline, is the famous theory of justification by faith alone, the revolutionary doctrine which, in these years when Wolsey ruled England, was spreading over Europe like a prairie fire.

The theory had this first great attractiveness that, side by side with the innumerable abuses which too often, at that time, disfigured the practice of Catholicism, it seemed spirituality itself, a reaction from a material and mechanical conception of salvation, a reaction which restored to its proper place the divine element in that work. Soon all Europe was talking justification; and in no country did this new presentation fail to affect a minority at least of the Catholic thinkers and theologians. It is against a background of discussions about the nature of divine grace and its operation that the whole history of western Europe proceeds for the next hundred years.

The consequences of Luther's discovery—supposing it to be true—were, from the point of view of religion as all western Europe had always understood and accepted this, nothing less than catastrophic. The whole fabric of organised Christianity, of the Church, of pope, bishops and priests; of sacraments and ritual; of theological speculation and of canon law; of asceticism, the contemplative life, monks, friars, nuns; of prayer itself; of penance in satisfaction for sin; all this was a vast irrelevancy, a distraction it might be, and even a hindrance, to man's salvation. *Porro unum est necessarium,* and the one thing, said the new prophet, was Faith—Faith in the prophet's sense of the word.

Here we may need to remind ourselves of the great fact that the Reformation, as a doctrine of salvation, and this is its essence, is a reaction against decadence. Doubtless it is itself a part of the decadence, a development and a product of that decadence, and shares more than one characteristic of that decadence: it is itself decadent in fact, though not in the intention or the will of the Reformers, who are spiritually sick, rather than vicious, unfortunates rather than wicked men. The decadence against which the Reformation is a reaction is a general thing, and its seat is the soul of Europe. The age is one of increasing material prosperity, of great literary and artistic achievement, of pioneer discovery boldly and intelligently exploited, an age of rapidly advancing civilisation; it is an age, if ever, of "progress" undoubted, and it is an age that is spiritually very sick indeed, and whose sickness seems not to be perceived by the official physicians, or else to be a thing whose nature they do not understand, an illness to whose gravity they are apparently indifferent. The Reform movement is not a reaction against decadent Catholicism—a contraditcion in terms and an impossibility—but against the Catholicism of undoubtedly decadent Catholics who, everywhere, are found as rulers in spirituals and in temporals, and who, in too many places and for far too long, have been the masters giving the law to Israel. And the Reformation is, primarily, and necessarily, a revolt of clerics against clerics.

It is as a thing which is essentially a reaction of this sort that we need to see the activities of Luther and the rest of the vast and varied army that followed him out the Church—not merely out of the actual organisation over which the popes presided as universal primates, but out of the accepted traditional belief as to what kind of a thing the Church, the Church of Christ, is. It is against the very actualities of his own time, against the undoubted facts of the present moment, that Luther is making his protest, and that he must be seen as making it. This is not a reaction—and must not be judged as though it were a reaction—against a christendom characterised by the thought of St. Thomas Aquinas; this had never yet existed. Nor was it a reaction against a christendom characterised by the ideals of St. Francis: this, if it ever existed, had long since passed away, and was no more. It was not a reaction against the christendom characterised by the complementary spiritual genius of St. Ignatius Loyola and St. Francis de Sales: which is ours to-day.

And though the actual christendom against which the reaction was directed was that in which saints like John Fisher and Thomas More were active indeed, it was not Catholics of this sort who characterised it. Dr. Luther, Austin Friar, and professor of Sacred Scripture in christendom's newest university, Mgr. Zwingli, chaplain to the Swiss serving with the papal armies against the King of France, Professor Erasmus, Cardinal Wolsey—these were much more typical figures. It was against Catholicism as presented through the minds of the latest generation of Ockham's disciples that Luther first of all reacted; against the Ockham-begotten insufficiencies of the spiritual direction given him by his own devoted master and superior, John Staupitz; against Catholicism as presented not only in the lives of such ecclesiastical scoundrels as his own bishop, Albrecht of Brandenburg, or of Wolsey in England; not only in the lives of the many local rulers of the Church who were no more than professional lawyers—not canonists, but mere canonists, the achievement of Alexander III and Innocent III and Innocent IV in its last formalist degradation; it was not only against Catholicism here that Luther reacted, but also against Catholicism as caricatured in the practically Pelagian spirituality of some of the brethren of the straiter sect whom he saw around him (and perhaps imagined he saw everywhere else). It is as a reaction against undoubted wrong doing and ignorant wrong believing, against actual and prevalent shortcomings, defects, *vitia* in the system, all of them on such a scale as to seem almost the very system itself, that the Reformation needs to be seen—vices seen everywhere; and the fact of all this wrong doing and wrong believing has gone on for years, it is unheeded by authority, which is seemingly either unaware of what is happening or indifferent to it.

Unless we make the effort to see the Reformation in the very place and time in which it happened, to see what the state of things was which produced the Reformers, the kind of christendom in which they produced the new ideas and the new solutions, we shall never understand even the appearance of what went on all over western Europe in the fifty years that followed the event of 1517. Until we can see the Reformers as they were in their own eyes, in their own intentions—and as they were responsible—we shall never realise not only how it was that the Reformation "got going," but also the full nature of its immensely harmful achievement[2]—what that great construction really was into which the Reformers organised the religious life of a

---

[2] Cf. Newman's verdict: "... Luther found in the Church great moral corruptions countenanced by its highest authorities; he felt them; but instead of meeting them with divine weapons, he used one of his own. He adopted a doctrine original, specious, fascinating, persuasive, powerful against Rome, and wonderfully adapted, as if prophetically, to the genius of the times which were to follow. He found Christians in bondage to their works and observances; he released them by his doctrine of faith; and he left them in bondage to their feelings. He weaned them from seeking assurance of salvation in standing ordinances, at the cost of teaching them that a personal consciousness of it was promised to everyone who believed. For outward signs of grace he substituted inward; for reverence towards the Church, contemplation of self. And thus, whereas he himself held the proper efficacy of the Sacraments, he has led others to disbelieve it; whereas he preached against reliance on self, he introduced it in a more subtle shape; whereas he professed to make the written word all in all, he sacrificed it in its length and breadth to the doctrine which he had wrested from a few texts." *Lectures on the Doctrine of Justification,* Lecture xi, Section 9 (edition of 1873, pp. 339-340).

good third of their own time, thereby necessarily deflecting from its true development the culture of whole worlds in the centuries to come.

*  *  *

## THE REFORMATION: "A MUCH-NEEDED ONE"

**E. G. Schweibert**

*The Need of a New Perspective*

Martin Luther is one of those colossal historical figures over whom the modern world is still sharply divided, even though he died four centuries ago. Evaluations of his life and work range from those which see in him "the evil genius of Germany" to those which would make of him "a plaster saint."

It has been said that no one is really qualified to write on monasticism until he has been a monk; and after he has been a monk, he can no longer write impartially on monasticism. So, too, no one can really understand Martin Luther but a Lutheran; but perhaps no Lutheran can maintain a purely academic approach toward Luther. Yet it is encouraging that such scholars as Holl, Strohl, Scheel, and others have been able to approach Leopold von Ranke's ideal of writing history "as it actually was." This aim is well exemplified in James Harvey Robinson's prefatory remarks to Heinrich Boehmer's *Luther in the Light of Recent Research:* "The author seems to me particularly well qualified by knowledge, temperament and style to give us a fresh and stimulating conception of Luther. He is broadly sympathetic but no hero worshiper. There is no trace of religious partisanship in him. He feels that he can afford to tell all the varied truth without suppression or distortion." To the historian there can be no higher tribute.

Of all the periods in German history none has been more diligently studied than that of the German Reformation. The many sermons, letters, political treatises, and polemical tracts employing German, Latin, and some Greek from Luther's pen appeared in nearly a dozen editions between 1546 and 1883. The related source materials, such as court records, church documents, and so on, which have appeared in print are tremendous. Over three thousand biographies and treatises have been written about Martin Luther and his work, and still they continue to roll from the presses. Little wonder that few biographers of Luther have had the time or patience to digest this mass of often apparently contradictory materials before approaching their subject. The result is that all too frequently, both here and abroad, there has been a tendency to oversimplify the German Reformation. A true evaluation of Luther's contributions to the world would require the combined talents and training of a linguist, political scientist, historian, sociologist, and theologian, scarcely to be found in a single individual.

Nor did Martin Luther bring about the German Reformation singlehandedly. At his side labored twenty-two university professors, many of whom were equally zealous to reform the Church. When Luther became convinced that "justification by faith" was

All footnotes in this selection have been omitted—Ed.

God's plan of salvation, he did not rest until he had won the whole faculty of the University of Wittenberg to this point of view . . . This conversion was accomplished between 1513 and 1518.

When, therefore, Luther nailed his *Ninety-Five Theses* on the door of the Castle Church in Wittenberg, it was not as an isolated individual, but with the firm conviction that the entire university faculty wanted the matter of indulgence abuses clarified so as to establish a common principle of action in their midst. This concerted action by the whole group caused the University of Paris to conclude a few years later that they were dealing not with one "viper, but a whole nest of vipers." The German Reformation was, then, an educational movement centered in the University of Wittenberg.

To be sure, the University was not yet Lutheran in 1517, but remained nominally Roman Catholic until Luther was pronounced a heretic by the Edict of Worms in 1521. After that, all the conservative Catholic princes refused to support a school that kept on its faculty a man condemned by both the Pope and the Emperor. The enrollment dropped tremendously in the next few years, owing to the withdrawal of the Catholic support, leaving only the converts to the reform movement. From this date, therefore, the *Album*, or matriculation book of the University of Wittenberg, became the mirror in which was reflected the spread of Lutheranism in Central Europe.

An examination of this interesting old record in the library at Halle, Germany, reveals that no fewer than 16,292 students enrolled at the University of Wittenberg between 1520 and 1560. Naturally, thousands of them left those halls of learning with their souls on fire for the new reform movement, which they had heard so ably expounded at the feet of Luther and Melanchthon. The location of these students on the map of Europe reveals that, even though most of them came from German lands, many of them came from England, France, Poland, the Scandinavian countries, and the Balkans. Who is to measure the impact to these thousands of Gospel preachers and teachers who returned to their home communities and became apostles of the Lutheran reform? The coming of the Reformation to each region, as reflected in the matriculation at the University of students from that territory, is a fascinating study.

Furthermore, it is significant how intimate was the contact between Luther and important men all over Europe. Any student familiar with his voluminous correspondence will need no further evidence. It is amazing that Luther, a busy professor, town pastor, civic leader, and author, was still able to keep his finger on the pulse of Germany. As for Melanchthon, it is claimed that he knew personally every schoolteacher in Germany who had been trained at Wittenberg.

In the light of these facts the German Reformation must be regarded as a very involved movement, the work not of Martin Luther and a few fellow professors, but of an army of people, some 22,000 students, priests, monks, and laymen carrying the Gospel message to the German people. Each community received the Reformation in its own unique way. In one region the message was brought by a Wittenberg layman; in another by a Catholic priest converted by Luther's writings; in a third by the sermon of some Wittenberg professor; but in every case we find the local conditions varied and the success of the movement in each community was determined by the ability of its leaders and the attitudes of those people to whom the message was brought. Thus the picture becomes almost kaleidoscopic in its confused complexity.

Nor does this new perspective detract from the glory of Luther; rather, it augments his place in the whole movement. In this setting Luther becomes the commander in chief of a vast army, while Melanchthon, Jonas, Amsdorf, Bugenhagen, and others make up his advisory staff. Fundamentally, then, the German Reformation was possible only because of a well-organized educational program that made Wittenberg the nursery of the whole movement.

The University assumed leadership in the church visitations, which so clearly exposed the deplorable conditions of ignorance and wickedness and the necessity for the organization of all types of schools throughout central Europe. In fact, it was the new Lutheranism produced in the parochial schools, the Latin schools, the boys' schools, the girls' schools, and the people's schools that caused the Reformation to triumph. And it was the counter-educational system of the Catholic Jesuits which rewon southern Germany.

If the work of Martin Luther could be reduced solely to the religious aspects of the German Reformation, the writing of his biography would be infinitely simpler. But Luther did not limit himself to the religious aspects of reform. His principle of "justification by faith" included a participation in civic affairs, which he ably expressed in the famous tracts of 1520. In his *Address to the German Nobility* of that year, Luther really became the voice of the Saxon court, appealing to the newly elected Emperor Charles V to reform the Church, since Rome had neglected its duty. In his *Babylonian Captivity of the Church* he expressed a maturity on the subject of indulgences that gave to men like Ulrich von Hutten a new hope that here was a champion of their common cause to liberate Germany from the economic and political bondage of the Roman See. In his statement of "the priesthood of believers," Luther destroyed the whole medieval concept of the divisions of society. In his tract of 1523, *Concerning Government: to What Extent One is Obligated to Obey It,* Luther defined the borderline between Church and State. One cannot, therefore, correctly evaluate Martin Luther's role in the sixteenth-century society without considering the impact of his advice and opinions on the attitudes and convictions of princes, prelates, and laymen.

To explain Luther's tremendous influence, one must consider also the value of the printing press and especially his use of that new medium, the *Flugschrift*, or tract. This new polemical vehicle had been employed in a lighter vein, but no one had thought of using it in the field of religion. Luther realized its possibilities as an inexpensive means of reaching the common man. Printed in the German language and attractively illustrated with woodcuts, it became an effective organ of reform by which he could reply in a few weeks to the attacks of his Roman opponents, or a medium for sermons, theological treatises, and so on, all of which would familiarize the average layman with the Gospel movement. Its extensive use is shown by the fact that between 1517 and 1520 some 370 editions of his writings appeared, selling as many as 300,000 copies. Doubtless this was one of the major reasons why Luther succeeded where Hus had failed. The power of the printing press is shown in the report which Aleander, the papal representative at Worms in 1521, made in his dispatches to Leo X that nine tenths of Germany was shouting "Luther" and the other tenth "Down with Rome!"

This report, however, brings up another aspect of the German Reformation, on which must be sounded a word of warning. Aleander was wrong in assuming that all these enthusiastic supporters of Luther's cause were "Lutheran." It is true that the streets of Worms were crowded to the point where Luther could not pass directly from his quarters to the meetings of the Diet. According to contemporary reports, tremendous crowds greeted the Wittenberg monk on the way to and from Worms. But to assume that all these people held the theological views Luther was teaching at

Wittenberg at the time is very wrong. Most of them were only vaguely conscious of the doctrines at stake, but felt that Luther was the champion of a people long bowed under the yoke of Rome. The common impression with laymen was that Martin Luther was the avowed opponent of the indulgence traffic of John Tetzel and the banking house of the Fuggers. Ulrich von Hutten thought he saw in Luther a powerful ally to liberate Germany from the yoke of Roman bondage, but failed completely to understand the deeper implications of Luther's controversy with the Roman Church. All the German princes, including even his bitter enemy Duke George, agreed with Luther in the belief that it was high time for the Diet to consider and act upon the *Gravamina*, the grievance lists drafted by previous diets from the days of Emperor Maximilian.

In addition, then, to the theological aspects of the Reformation, there were the economic, the political, and the social reforms which Luther's writings seemed to promise. As the reports of Aleander also indicate, many of the princes and even the counselors of the Emperor saw in Luther an opportunity to bring about economic and political changes long since overdue.

## What Was the German Reformation?

Definitions are never too satisfactory; yet it may avoid considerable confusion to clarify certain accepted terminology. Textbook authors have employed several other terms than the older, more accepted usage, "The German Reformation." Some seem to prefer "The Protestant Revolt," others, "The Protestant Revolution." This is not just a matter of preference. Although perhaps not always aware of it, the writers using this terminology imply a definite basic assumption as to what the Reformation really was, and, therefore, these labels should be used with discrimination.

The term *Reformation* dates to a Cistercian monk, Joachim of Flora (d. 1202), who took the expression from the Latin Vulgate. He predicted that a new age was about to come in the Church, the Age of the Holy Ghost, and he made use of such terms as *New Life* and *Reformation, nova vita* and *reformatio*, an idea which was continued by Dante and other Humanists. Humanism, then, through the revival of the classical languages, supplied the media for returning to earlier Christian standards. In such Biblical Humanists as Erasmus, Luther, and Melanchthon there developed a *Heimweh*, a longing for the pure forms of early Christianity.

Furthermore, the term *German Reformation* implies a special definition of the Church. In Roman circles the Church was defined as an outward ecclesiastical organization symbolized by The Papacy. In the new reasoning of Lutheranism there was implied something quite different. The Church was not an outward organization, but the *communio sanctorum*, the communion of saints, which had continued to live in the hearts of true believers, even though in outward forms Rome had drifted far from the original course. His many utterances on the subject reflect Luther's deep concern lest a corrupt outward organization create an environment unwholesome for God's elect. Hence, the word *Reformation* meant to Luther a cleansing of the outward Church of the Papacy, the Canon Law, the sacramental system, Scholasticism, saint worship, indulgences, and many other abuses and a restoration of the pure doctrines of the New Testament.

Nor did Martin Luther regard his undertaking as the establishment of a "New Church." Just six years before his death, Luther wrote a lengthy treatise, *On Councils and Churches*, proving by means of many illustrations from the Church Fathers and the early Ecumenical Councils that he had not founded a new Church, but rather that he had restored the "Early Church," the real Catholic Church, which preceded the Papacy. By comparison he ascertained that it was the Roman Church with its seven sacraments, its pope, and its hairsplitting theology that was new.

The use of the expression *Protestant Revolt*, on the other hand, indicates a quite different basic assumption. It implies that the established Roman Catholic Church is the only true Church and that the founding of any other outward organization is a revolt against the divinely instituted authority. In fact, it implies that all those who revolted are now outside the pale of grace. If that is the intent of the historical writer, the use of this term is quite proper.

The expression *Protestant Revolution* has a similar implication, with more of a secular approach toward the whole movement. It implies little interest in, or understanding of, the deeper theological problems which were troubling the sixteenth-century mind. This reasoning places the center of gravity in economic, political, and sociological forces and assumes that they were more influential in shaping the course of events than theological differences.

Because Luther knew better than anyone else his views and objectives, and because he believed, as stated, that he sought only to cleanse and restore the early Christianity in all its purity, the term *Reformation* is most apropos; and because the birthplace of the movement was Germany, it may appropriately be designated the "German" Reformation.

## The Need for Reform

In the days of Martin Luther it was a common error to consider the papacy as synonymous with the Catholic Church. In fact, Catholic supporters of Rome, like Eck, Latomus, Emser, and Aleander, tried to identify the two in their polemical writings against Luther. Yet it does not follow that all Catholics of this period were of this opinion. As early as the fourteenth century such men as Wyclif, d'Ailly, Hus, Gerson, and a large body of northern Christians had taken issue with those who overemphasized the importance of the Roman hierarchy. The corruption of the Renaissance popes considerably augmented this number.

Previous to the Council of Trent (1545–1563) the Roman Church had no common system of dogma universally accepted by all the members of that body. In fact, the Roman Church might be compared to a huge edifice under whose roof a number of theological systems flourished. With the establishment of the universities there arose new scholars, capable of thinking independently of Rome, around whom developed distinct and challenging schools of thought. In broad outlines, there were the Scholastics, the Mystics, and the Humanists, but more careful examination reveals that even these were often subdivided into separate schools. The followers of St. Thomas and those of William Occam had little in common; yet both were Scholastics. The Mystics all stressed emotion, but the different schools were not all in agreement with the views of Thomas à Kempis; while the Humanists, although all of them wanted to return to some "Golden Age," were far from agreed on what age this should be. Housed, therefore, under the roof of the Roman Church could be found widely divergent points of view. In some of the most fundamental doctrines these various schools expressed opposite points of view. One group believed in the doctrine of

Transubstantiation, another in the Real Presence. In the University of Paris the importance of the Papacy had been minimized ever since the Reform Councils of the fifteenth century. For some time certain Catholic writers had stressed *Sola Scriptura*, the principle of making the Bible the sole guide in matters of faith. Bible reading had been emphasized by the Brethren of the Common Life. Such Biblical Humanists as Erasmus emphasized the need for a revival of Greek, Latin, and Hebrew so that scholars might examine the practices of the Roman Church in the light of early Christianity. There was, then, considerable disagreement among those who regarded themselves as Roman Catholics. In this fact lay one of the fundamental causes of the German Reformation.

It was this world of confusion into which Martin Luther was thrust when he entered the Augustinian monastery at Erfurt in 1505. The result was his tremendous soul struggle over the means of becoming reconciled with an angry and righteous God. After a wider study of the Catholic writings of the Middle Ages, Luther concluded that this was not the Christian Church established by the Apostles. In fact, with Erasmus and others Luther realized that early Christianity had been fundamentally quite different from the existing Roman Church.

The early Christian Church was a perfectly normal growth as the result of the teachings of Jesus and the Apostles. In the footsteps of missionaries like St. Paul and St. Peter, Christian communities sprang up all over the Roman Empire, which extended over an area nearly twice as large as the United States. Since there were no theological seminaries, most of the leaders in these communities were elders, men chosen from among the laymen for their fitness to read and to instruct others. Centers in which were capable leaders naturally lent aid to newer or less-favored communities and gradually assumed leadership of surrounding congregations. To their leader was given the name bishop, or *episcopus*. For some time these bishops were the leaders in this episcopal organization. In the second century, however, the larger communities covering the area of a Roman province were supervised by archbishops, and after the division of the Roman Empire by Emperor Diocletian in the third century the new heads of these vast areas were known as metropolitans. The idea of a papacy is, therefore, not a part of this early simple pattern of the Christian Church.

The simple, informal religion of the early Christians is also reflected in the basilica church, an unpretentious structure which they adapted from the Roman banks to ecclesiastical purposes. In this primitive church there was no railing between the worshipers and the altar, symbolic of the fact that the clergy was not yet regarded as a special order, the custodians of the means of grace. Nor can the historian find any traces of a papacy before the fourth century, and even then only in embryonic form.

From his studies Luther concluded that the real Christian Church was that *communio sanctorum*, or communion of true believers, which had existed from the first and which existed still in spite of the many human encrustations clinging to it. Others before him had arrived at this same conclusion. Some, like Erasmus, lacked the courage of their convictions. Others, like John Hus, died for their beliefs because the world was not ready. In Martin Luther the propitious moment and the qualities of leadership combined to produce the much-needed Reformation.

\*    \*    \*

# 3 /  The Scientific Revolution: The Problem of the Origins

In the Introduction to his book *The Origins of Modern Science* (1949), Herbert Butterfield claims that the Scientific Revolution of the sixteenth and seventeenth centuries "outshines everything since the rise of Christianity and reduces the Renaissance and the Reformation to the rank of mere episodes, mere internal displacements, within the system of medieval Christendom. . . . It looms so large as the real origin both of the modern world and of the modern mentality that our customary periodisation of European history has become an anachronism and an encumbrance."[1] In *Main Currents of Western Thought* (1961), Professor Franklin Le Van Baumer of Yale University writes, "This view can no longer be seriously questioned."[2]

This displacement, by the Scientific Revolution, of the Renaissance as beginning the modern era has focused attention on the origins of the former among the present generation of historians. In the matter of origins, however, there is less of a consensus than on the place of the Scientific Revolution in history. The differences, though, are primarily ones of emphasis rather than interpretation. Thus in the first selection below, Professor Butterfield finds the first stage in the history of the Scientific Revolution in a theory of "impetus" taught by a school of thinkers in fourteenth-century Paris. As a result he tends to deemphasize the originality of Galileo and the Renaissance contribution to the Scientific Revolution. Elsewhere in *The Origins of Modern Science* Butterfield has written:

Ideas may have appeared in new combinations, but we cannot say that essentially new ingredients were introduced into our civilization at the Renaissance. We cannot say that here were intellectual changes calculated to transform the character and structure of our society or civilisation. Even the secularisation of thought which was locally achieved in certain circles at this time was not unprecedented and was a hot-house growth, soon to be overwhelmed by the fanaticism of the Reformation and the Counter-Reformation.[3]

By contrast, the second selection, from Leonardo Olschki's *The Genius of Italy*, definitely emphasizes the Italian humanist setting of the beginnings of the Scientific Revolution. The intellectual climate of humanism and the existence of a practical secular tradition in mathematics attracted Northern scholars to Italy and away from the scholasticism still prevalent in Northern centers of learning. For Olschki, for example, the scientific education of the great Copernicus was definitely Italian and humanistic.

[1] Herbert Butterfield, *The Origins of Modern Science 1300-1800* (London: G. Bell, 1949, p. viii.
[2] Franklin Le Van Baumer, *Main Currents of Western Thought* (New York: Alfred A. Knopf, 1961), p. 249.
[3] *Op. cit.,* p. 162.

# THE HISTORICAL IMPORTANCE OF A THEORY OF IMPETUS

**Herbert Butterfield**

It is one of the paradoxes of the whole story with which we have to deal that the most sensational step leading to the scientific revolution in astronomy was taken long before the discovery of the telescope—even long before the Danish astronomer, Tycho Brahé, in the latter part of the sixteenth century, had shown the great improvement that it was still possible to achieve in observations made with the naked eye. When William Harvey in England opened up new paths for physiology by his study of the action of the heart, he alluded once or twice to his use of a magnifying glass, but he carried out his revolutionary work before any serviceable kind of microscope had become available. With regard to the transformation of the science of mechanics, it is remarkable to what an extent even Galileo discusses the ordinary phenomena of everyday life, conjectures what would happen if a stone were thrown from the mast of a moving ship, or plays with pellets on inclined planes in a manner that had long been customary. In fact, we shall find that in both celestial and terrestrial physics—which hold the strategic place in the whole movement—change is brought about, not by new observations or additional evidence in the first instance, but by transpositions that were taking place inside the minds of the scientists themselves. In this connection it is not irrelevant to note that of all forms of mental activity the most difficult to induce, even in the minds of the young who may be presumed not to have lost their flexibility, is the art of handling the same bundle of data as before, but placing them in a new system of relations with one another by giving them a different framework, all of which virtually means putting on a different kind of thinking-cap for the moment. It is easy to teach anybody a new fact about Richelieu, but it needs light from heaven to enable a teacher to break the old framework in which the student has been accustomed to seeing his Richelieu—the framework which is built up sometimes far too rigidly by the Higher Certificate student, and into which he will fit whatever new information he ever afterwards acquires on this subject. But the supreme paradox of the scientific revolution is the fact that things which we find it easy to instil into boys at school, because we see that they start off on the right foot—things which would strike us as the ordinary natural way of looking at the universe, the obvious way of regarding the behaviour of falling bodies, for example—defeated the greatest intellects for centuries, defeated Leonardo da Vinci and at the marginal point even Galileo, when their minds were wrestling on the very frontiers of human thought with these very problems. Even the great geniuses who broke through the ancient views in some special field of study—Gilbert, Bacon and Harvey, for example—would remain stranded in a species of medievalism when they went outside that chosen field. It required their combined efforts to clear up certain simple things which we should now regard as obvious to any unprejudiced mind, and even easy for a child.

A particular development of ideas which was already taking place in the later middle ages has come to stand as the first chapter in the history of the transition to what we call the scientific revolution. It is a field of thought upon which an expositor can embark only with the greatest trepidation, in view of the vicissitudes of lecturers at the very beginning of modern times. Students of history will remember how the humanists of the Renaissance, Erasmus included, were accustomed to complaining of the boredom—deriding the sophistries and subtleties—of the scholastic lectures which they had to endure at the university. Occasionally they specified the forms of teaching and lecturing to which they most objected, and as they particularly mentioned those discussions of mechanics with which we have now to concern ourselves, it will no doubt be prudent to make the examination of their teaching as brief as possible. It is curious that these despised scholastic disquisitions should now have come to hold a remarkable key-position in the story of the evolution of the modern mind. Perhaps the lack of mathematics, or the failure to think of mathematical ways of formulating things, was partly responsible for what appeared to be verbal subtleties and an excessive straining of language in these men who were almost yearning to find the way to the modern science of mechanics.

Of all the intellectual hurdles which the human mind has been faced with and has overcome in the last fifteen hundred years, the one which seems to me to have been the most amazing in character and the most stupendous in the scope of its consequences is the one relating to the problem of motion—the one which was not quite disposed of by Galileo, though it received a definitive form of settlement shortly after his time in the full revised statement of what every schoolboy learns to call the law of inertia. On this question of motion the Aristotelian teaching, precisely because it carried such an intricate dovetailing of observations and explanations—that is to say, precisely because it was part of a system which was such a colossal intellectual feat in itself—was hard for the human mind to escape from, and gained a strong hold on medieval scholastic thought. Furthermore, it remains as the essential background of the story—it continues to present the presiding issue—until the time of Galileo himself; in other words, until the first half of the seventeenth century. On the Aristotelian theory all heavy terrestrial bodies had a natural motion towards the centre of the universe, which for medieval thinkers was at or near the centre of the earth; but motion in any other direction was violent motion, because it contradicted the ordinary tendency of a body to move to what was regarded as its natural place. Such motion depended on the operation of a mover, and the Aristotelian doctrine of inertia was a doctrine of rest—it was motion, not rest, that always required to be explained. Wherever this motion existed, and however long it existed, something had to be brought in to account for it.

The essential feature of this view was the assertion or the presumption that a body would keep in movement only so long as a mover was actually in contact with it, imparting motion to it all the time. Once the mover ceased to operate, the movement stopped—the body fell straight to earth or dropped suddenly to rest. Further—a point that will seem very heretical to the present day—it was argued that, provided the resistance of the medium through which the body passed remained a constant, the speed of the body would be proportionate to what we should describe as the force consistently being exerted upon it by the mover. A constant force exerted by the mover over a given length of time produced not any acceleration at all, but a uniform motion for the whole period. On the other hand, if there was any variation in the resistance of the medium—the difference between moving in air and moving in water, for example—the speed would vary in inverse proportion to this, provided the other factors remained constant. And if the resistance were reduced to nought, the speed would be infinite; that is to say, if the movement took place in a vacuum, bodies would move from one place to another instantaneously. The absurbity of this was one of the reasons why the Aristotelians regarded a complete void as impossible, and said that God Himself could not make one.

It is astonishing to what a degree not only this theory but its rivals—even the ones which superseded it in the course of the scientific revolution—were based on the ordinary observation of the data available to common sense. And, as writers have clearly pointed out, it is not relevant for us to argue that if the Aristotelians had merely watched the more carefully they would have changed their theory of inertia for the modern one—changed over to the view that bodies tend to continue either at rest or in motion along a straight line until something intervenes to stop them or deflect their course. It was supremely difficult to escape from the Aristotelian doctrine by merely observing things more closely, especially if you had already started off on the left foot and were hampered beforehand with the whole system of interlocking Aristotelian ideas. In fact, the modern law of inertia is not the thing you would discover by mere photographic methods of observation—it required a different kind of thinking-cap, a transposition in the mind of the scientist himself; for we do not actually see ordinary objects continuing their rectilinear motion in that kind of empty space which Aristotle said could not exist, and sailing away to that infinity which also he said could not possibly exist; and we do not in real life have perfectly spherical balls moving on perfectly smooth horizontal planes—the trick lay in the fact that it occurred to Galileo to imagine these. Furthermore, even when men were coming extraordinarily near to what we should call the truth about local motion, they did not clinch the matter—the thing did not come out clear and clean—until they had realised and had made completely conscious to themselves the fact that they were in reality transposing the question into a different realm—they were discussing not real bodies as we actually observe them in the real world, but geometrical bodies moving in a world without resistance and without gravity—moving in that boundless emptiness of Euclidean space which Aristotle had regarded as unthinkable. In the long run, therefore, we have to recognize that here was a problem of a fundamental nature, and it could not be solved by close observation within the framework of the older system of ideas—it required a transposition in the mind.

As often happened with such theories in those days, if not now, the Aristotelian doctrine of motion might seem to correspond in a self-evident manner with most of the data available to common sense, but there were small pockets of fact which did not square with the theory at the first stage of the argument; they were unamenable to the Aristotelian laws at what we should call the ordinary common-sense level. There were one or two anomalies which required a further degree of analysis before they could be satisfactorily adjusted to the system; and perhaps, as some writers have said, the Aristotelian theory came to a brilliant peak in the manner by which it hauled these exceptional cases into the synthesis and established (at a second remove) their conformity with the stated rules. On the argument so far as we have taken it, an arrow ought to have fallen to the ground the moment it lost contact with the bow-string; for neither the bow-string nor anything else could impart a motion which would continue after the direct contact with the original mover had been broken. The Aristotelians explained the continued movement of projectiles by the commotion which the initial movement had produced in the air—especially as the air which was being pushed and compressed in front had to rush round behind to prevent that vacuum which must never be allowed to take place. At this point in the argument there even occurred a serious fault in observation which harassed the writers on physical science for many centuries. It was thought that the rush of air produced an actual initial acceleration in the arrow after it had left the bow-string, and it is curious to note that Leonardo da Vinci and later writers shared this mistake—the artillerymen of the Renaissance were victims of the same error—though there had been people in the later middle ages who had taken care not to commit themselves on this point. The motion of a projectile, since it was caused by a disturbance in the medium itself, was a thing which it was not possible to imagine taking place in a vacuum.

Furthermore, since the Aristotelian commentators held something corresponding to the view that a constant uniform force only produced uniform motion, there was a second serious anomaly to be explained—it was necessary to produce special reasons to account for the fact that falling bodies were observed to move at an accelerating speed. Once again the supporters of the older teaching used the argument from the rush of air, or the increasing pressure, as there was a greater height of atmosphere above, while as the body descended there would be a diminishing column of air below, and therefore a diminishing resistance. Alternatively they used Aristotle's argument that the falling body moved more jubilantly every moment because it found itself nearer home.

From the fourteenth to the seventeenth century, then, this Aristotelian doctrine of motion persisted in the face of recurrent controversy, and it was only in the later stages of that period that the satisfactory alternative emerged, somewhat on the policy of picking up the opposite end of the stick. Once this question was solved in the modern manner, it altered much of one's ordinary thinking about the world and opened the way for a flood of further discoveries and reinterpretations, even in the realm of common sense, before any very elaborate experiments had been embarked upon. It was as though science or human thought had been held up by a barrier until this moment—the waters dammed because of an initial defect in one's attitude to everything in the universe that had any sort of motion—and now the floods were released; change and discovery were bound to come in cascades even if there were no other factors working for a scientific revolution. Indeed, we might say that a change in one's attitude to the movement of things that move was bound to result in so many new analyses of various kinds of motion that it constituted a scientific revolution in itself.

Apart from all this there was one special feature of the problem which made the issue momentous. We have not always brought home to ourselves the peculiar character of that Aristotelian universe in which the things that were in motion had to be accompanied by a mover all the time. A universe constructed on the mechanics of Aristotle had the door half-way open for spirits already; it was a universe in which unseen hands had to be in constant operation, and sublime Intelligences had to roll the planetary spheres around. Alternatively, bodies had to be endowed with souls and aspirations, with a "disposition" to certain kinds of motion, so that matter itself seemed to possess mystical qualities. The modern law of inertia, the modern theory of motion, is the great factor which in the seventeenth century helped to drive the spirits out of the world and opened the way to a universe that ran like a piece of clockwork. Not only so—but the very first men who in the middle ages launched the great attack on the Aristotelian theory were conscious of the fact that this colossal issue was involved in the question. The first of the important figures, Jean Buridan, in the middle of the fourteenth century pointed out that his alternative interpretation would eliminate the need for the Intelligences that turned the celesial spheres. He even noted that the Bible provided no authority for these spiritual agencies—they were demanded by the teaching of the ancient Greeks, not by the Christian religion as such. Not much later than this, Nicholas of Oresme went farther still, and said that on the new alternative theory God might have started off the universe as a kind of clock and left it to run of itself.

Ever since the earlier years of the twentieth century at latest, therefore, a great and growing interest has been taken in that school of thinkers who so far back as the fourteenth century were challenging the Aristotelian explanations of motion, and who put forward an alternative doctrine of "impetus" which—though imperfect in itself—must represent the first stage in the history of the scientific revolution. And if it is imagined that this kind of argument falls into one of the traps which it is always necessary to guard against—picking out from the middle ages mere anticipations and casual analogies to modern ideas—the answer to that objection will be clear to us if we bear in mind the kind of rules that ought to govern historians in such matters. Here we have a case of a consistent body of teaching carried on and developed as a tradition by a school of thinkers particularly in Paris, and still being taught in Paris at the beginning of the sixteenth century. It has a continuous history—we know how this teaching passed into Italy, how it was in general resisted even in the days of the humanists, how Leonardo da Vinci picked it up, however, and how some of what were once considered to be remarkable strokes of modernity, remarkable flashes of genius, in his notebooks, were in reality transcriptions from fourteenth-century Parisian scholastic writers. We know how the teaching gained a foothold in later sixteenth-century Italy, amongst the men who influenced Galileo, how it was misunderstood on occasion—sometimes only partially appropriated—and how the early writings of Galileo on motion belonged precisely to this school of teaching, being based on that doctrine of the "impetus" which it is our purpose to examine. It is even known fairly certainly in what edition Galileo read the works of certain writers belonging to this fourteenth-century Parisian school. Indeed, Galileo could have produced much, though not quite all, that we find in his juvenile works on this particular subject if he had lived in the fourteenth century; and in this field one might very well ask what the world with its Renaissance and so forth had been doing in the meantime. It has been suggested that if printing had been invented two centuries earlier the doctrine of "impetus" would have produced a more rapid general development in the history of science, and would not have needed so long to pass from the stage of Jean Buridan to the stage of Galileo.

If the orthodox doctrine of the middle ages had been based on Aristotle, however, it has to be noted that, both then and during the Renaissance (as well as later still), the attacks on Aristotle—the theory of impetus included—would themselves be based on some ancient thinker. Here we touch on one of the generative factors, not only in the formation of the modern world, but also in the development of the scientific revolution—namely, the discovery of the fact that even Aristotle had not reigned unchallenged in the ancient days—all of which resulted in a healthy friction, resulting in the emergence of important problems which the middle ages had to make up their own minds about, so that men were driven to some kind of examination of the workings of nature themselves, even if only because they had to make up their minds between Aristotle and some rival teacher. It also appears that a religious factor affected the rise of that movement which produced the theory of impetus, and in a curious manner, which one tries in vain to analyse away, a religious taboo operated for once in favour of freedom for scientific hypothesis. In the year 1277 a council of Paris condemned a large number of Aristotelian theses, such as the view that even God could not create a void, or an infinite universe, or a plurality of worlds; and that decision—one in which certain forms of partisanship were involved—was apparently extended by the Archbishop of Canterbury to this country. The regions that came within the orbit of these decisions must have been the seat of a certain anti-Aristotelian bias already; and certainly from this time both Paris and Oxford showed remarkable developments in this direction in the field of what we should call physical science. From this time the discussion of the possibility of the existence of empty space, or of an infinite universe, or of a plurality of worlds makes a remarkable step forward in Paris. And amongst the names concerned in this development are some which figure in the rise of the doctrine of impetus. It has also been pointed out that in the same Parisian tradition there was a tendency towards something in the nature of mathematical physics, though the mathematics of the time were not sufficiently advanced to allow of this being carried very far or to produce anything like the achievement of Galileo in the way of a mathematical approach to scientific problems. We must avoid the temptation, however, to stress unduly the apparent analogies with modern times and the "anticipations" which are so easy to discover in the past—things which often owe a little, no doubt, to the trick-mirrors of the historian. And though it may be useful sometimes, in order to illustrate a point, we must beware of submitting to the fascination of "what might have been."

The people who chiefly concern us, then, are the fourteenth-century writers, Jean Buridan, Albert of Saxony and Nicholas of Oresme, but we are interested in them chiefly as leaders of a tradition which still existed in Paris at the beginning of the sixteenth century. They are important for other things besides their teaching on the subject of impetus, because though the contemporaries of Erasmus laughed at their Parisian lecturers for discussing not only "uniform motion" and "difform motion," but also "uniform difform motion"—all carried to a great degree of subtlety—it transpired in the sixteenth century, when the world was looking for a formula to represent the uniform acceleration of falling bodies, that the solution of the problem had been at their disposal for a long time in the medieval formula for the case of uniformly difform motion. The whole development which we are studying took place amongst people who, in fact, were working upon questions and answers which had been suggested by Aristotle. These people came up against the Aristotelian theory of motion at the very points where we should expect the attack to take place, namely, in connection with the two particularly doubtful questions of the movement of projectiles and the acceleration of falling bodies. If we take a glance at the kind of arguments they used, we are not only watching the kind of critical procedure which would take place even in the middle ages in connection with the current forms of orthodox Aristotelianism, we are really observing the early stages of the great debate on the issues that lay at the heart of the scientific revolution itself. Indeed, the arguments which were employed at this early period often reappeared—with reference to precisely the same instances—even in the major works of Galileo, for they passed into general currency in the course of time. And if they seem simple arguments based on the ordinary phenomena available to common sense, we ought to remember that many of the newer arguments brought forward by Galileo himself at a later stage of the story were really of the same type.

It was the view of this Parisian school that the projectile was carried forward by an actual impetus which it had acquired, and which bodies were capable of acquiring, from the mere fact of being in motion; and this impetus was supposed to be a thing inside the body itself—occasionally it was described as an impetuosity that had been imparted to it; occasionally you see it discussed as though it were itself movement which the body acquired as the result of being in motion; but in any case it made it possible for men to contemplate the continued motion of a body after the contact with the original mover had been lost. It was explained that the impetus lay in the body and continued there, as heat stays in a red-hot poker after it has been taken from the fire; while in the case of falling bodies the effect was described as accidental gravity, an additional gravity which the body acquired as a result of being in motion, so that the acceleration of falling bodies was due to the effects of impetus being continually added to the constant fall due to ordinary weight. A constant force exerted on a body, therefore, produced not uniform motion but a uniform rate of acceleration. It is to be noted, however, that Leonardo da Vinci, like a number of others who accepted the general theory of impetus, failed to follow the Parisian school in the application of their teaching to the acceleration of falling bodies. Whereas the Aristotelians thought that falling bodies rushed more quickly as they got nearer home, the new teaching inverted this, and said that it was rather the distance from the starting-point that mattered. If two bodies fell to earth along the same line BC, the one which had started higher up at A would move more quickly from B to C than the one that started at B, though in this particular part of their course they were both equally distant from the centre of the earth. It followed from the new doctrine that if a cylindrical hole were cut through the earth, passing through the centre, a body, when it reached the centre, would be carried forward on its own impetus for some distance, and indeed would oscillate about the centre for some time—a thing impossible to conceive under the terms of the ancient theory. There was a further point in regard to which the Aristotelians had been unconvincing; for if the continued flight of a projectile were really due not to the thrower but to the rush of air, it was difficult to see why the air should carry a stone so much farther than a ball of feathers—why one should be able to throw the stone the greater distance. The newer school showed that, starting at a given pace, a greater impetus would be communicated to the stone by reason of the density of its material than to a feather; though, of course, a larger body of the same material would not travel farther—a large stone would not be more easy to throw than a small one. Mass was used as the measure of the impetus which corresponded with a given speed.

Since Aristotle found it necessary on occasion to regard the air as a resisting factor, he was open to the charge that one could not then—in the next breath, so to speak—start using the argument that the air was also the actual propellant. The new school said that the air could not be the propellant except in the case of a high wind; and they brought the further objection that if the original perturbation of the air—the rush which occurred when the bow-string started the arrow—had the capacity to repeat itself, pushing the arrow on and on, there could be no reason why it should ever stop; it ought to go on for ever repeating itself, communicating further perturbations to every next region of the atmosphere. Furthermore, a thread tied to a projectile ought to be blown ahead of it, instead of trailing behind. In any case, on the Aristotelian view of the matter it ought to be impossible for an arrow to fly against the wind. Even the apostles of the new theory of impetus, however, regarded a projectile as moving in a straight line until the impetus had exhausted itself, and then making a direct vertical drop to earth. They looked upon this impetus as a thing which gradually weakened and wore itself out, just as a poker grows cold when taken from the fire. Or, said

Galileo, it was like the reverberations which go on in a bell long after it has been struck, but which gradually fade away. Only, in the case of the celestial bodies and the orbs which carried the planets round the sky, the impulse never exhausted itself—the pace of these bodies never slackened since there was no air-resistance to slow them down. Therefore, it could be argued, God might have given these things their initial impetus, and their motion would then continue for ever.

The theory of the impetus did not solve all problems, however, and proved to be only the half-way house to the modern view, which is fairly explicit in Galileo though it received its perfect formulation only in Descartes—the view that a body continues its motion in a straight line until something intervenes to halt or slacken or deflect it. As I have already mentioned, this modern law of inertia is calculated to present itself more easily to the mind when a transposition has taken place—when we see, not real bodies, moving under the restrictions of the real world and clogged by the atmosphere, but geometrical bodies sailing away in empty Euclidean space. Archimedes, whose works were more completely discovered at the Renaissance and became very influential especially after the translation published in 1543, appears to have done something to assist and encourage this habit of mind; and nothing could have been more important than the growing tendency to geometrise or mathematise a problem. Nothing is more effective, after people have long been debating and wrangling and churning the air, than the appearance of a person who draws a line on the blackboard, which with the help of a little geometry solves the whole problem in an instant. In any case, it is possible that Archimedes, who taught people to think of the weight of a thing in water and then its weight in air and finally, therefore, its weight when unencumbered by either, helped to induce some men to pick up the problem of motion from the opposite end to the usual one, and to think of the simplest form of motion as occurring when there was no resisting medium to complicate it. So you assumed the tendency in bodies to continue their existing motion along a straight line, and you set about afterwards to examine the things which might clog or hamper or qualify that motion; whereas Aristotle, assuming that the state of rest was natural and that bodies tended to return to it when left to themselves, had the difficult task of providing an active mover that should operate as long as the body continued to have any movement at all.

On the other hand, it may be true to say that Aristotle, when he thought of motion, had in mind a horse drawing a cart, so that his whole feeling for the problem was spoiled by his preoccupation with a misleading example. The very fact that his teaching on the subject of projectiles was so unsatisfactory may have helped to produce the phenomenon of a later age which, when it thought of motion, had rather the motion of projectiles in mind, and so acquired a different feeling in regard to the whole matter.

# THE SEARCH FOR TRUTH

**Leonardo Olschki**

Science has a twofold aim; the rational interpretation of phenomena and the practical application of its doctrines and notions. For many centuries during the Middle Ages the utilization of theoretical knowledge for practical purposes was the

All footnotes in this selection have been omitted.

main interest and achievement of scientists. Their philosophies constituted the basis
for medical theory and practice, just as their cosmology served mainly to perfect
astrological procedure. Medieval science developed out of the philosophical and
scientific heritage of antiquity, mainly through Arabic mediation and interpretation,
and never shook the speculative foundations of the leading disciplines of medicine and
astrology. During all those centuries truth was vested in authority as represented by
such doctrines as Aristotelianism, or by such leading authors as Pliny, Ptolemy,
Avicenna, and Galen, and finally by educational institutions such as the universities of
Bologna, Padua, and Naples.

The unsurpassed advantage of Aristotelianism was that even in its imperfect,
contradictory, and uncritical form it represented—as it still does, for better or
worse—the most complete system of knowledge ever devised by the human mind, and
was always subject to amendment by abstract reasoning and empirical evidence. The
Aristotelian system was the world itself, reduced to order and clarity, to consistency
and evidence, to human understanding and logical perfection. None of its numerous
interpreters ever attempted to undermine that complete and conclusive organism of
scientific lore. Its authority was intrinsic, arising from its fitness and scope, not merely
from ecclesiastical coercion or unthinking tradition. This is proved by the dominant
position and lasting influence of Aristotelianism in both the Mohammedan and the
Christian spheres of thought and religion long after it had satisfied the intellectual
needs of large sections of the ancient pagan world. As an aggregate of treatises on
single branches of knowledge, it had the consistency of a system and the flexibility of
an encyclopaedic synthesis.

Christian civilization had nothing to substitute for the Greek and Arabic authorities
in such specialized disciplines as medicine, astronomy, and mathematics. In the
medieval schools, those branches of knowledge did not advance by empirical research
or methodical investigations, but expanded through discussion, grew by integration,
and spread through an endless compilation of manuals, encyclopaedias, *specula*, and
*thesauri*. The medieval system of science, learning, and education had one great
advantage over modern systems: it possessed a universal theoretical foundation,
without which satisfactory intellectual activity is impossible. The medieval universities
were professional institutions, as are most American universities in our day, but they
were organized within an intellectual framework of universal doctrines. The scientific
truth taught in schools and books was embedded in a spiritual system of thought and
faith that determined its authority and value. This authority was embodied in the rigid
curriculum of the liberal arts, which represented the static aspect of a culture
conservative in its foundations, methods, and objectives.

The main disadvantage of the medieval scientific system was that its exclusively
intellectual foundation and methods prevented the direct absorption of the empirical
world into that vast organization of thought and knowledge. Hence, the strictly
conservative character of scientific education and literature. Just as the absence of an
ethical code for practical life isolated professional activities from the medieval system
of Christian morals, the empirical world found itself excluded for many centuries from
the system of medieval science and culture. In Italy the tension between scholasticism
and empiricism was greater and more protracted than elsewhere because the country
lacked strong cultural traditions, while it was exceptionally rich in practical, secular
experience. Beyond the Alps the great compilations of Vincent de Beauvais, Guillaume
de Champeaux, Bartholomew the Englishman, Roger Bacon, and various authors
specializing in particular fields of knowledge were kept up to date by the inclusion of

recent accomplishments and discoveries. In Italy compilatory encyclopaedism, represented mainly by Brunetto Latini's *Trésor*, did not achieve comparable importance while the contributions of an empirical character were not at first accorded scientific status and dignity.

The case of Marco Polo's famous book is characteristic of this aspect of Italian civilization. Intended as a "Description of the World" and containing the first systematic report of the countries and peoples of the East, the book, written in 1298, was considered exclusively as light and pleasant reading, not as a source of geographical information. Only toward the middle of the fifteenth century, and probably after the impression made in Florence by the representatives of the Oriental sects participating in the Council, did the leading Italian cosmographer, Paolo Toscanelli, avail himself, still rather furtively, of Marco Polo's information that integrated and corrected the data of Pliny and the newly discovered *Geography* of Ptolemy, first translated into Latin in 1406. Again, it was more than a century before the reports of medieval travelers appeared in G. B. Ramusio's famous collection of *Navigazioni e Viaggi* as contributions to geographical lore equivalent, and sometimes superior, to those of the ancients. The situation is clearly defined by one of the most dramatic episodes in the history of geography. A committee of mathematicians appointed, in 1484, by the king of Portugal rejected Columbus' project "to reach the East by the West," because the scientific geographers of the time were still ignorant of the existence of Cipangu (Japan), Cathay (China), and the Great Khans, and because they had a more correct appreciation of the circumference of the earth than the Genoese navigator and his Florentine counselor Paolo Toscanelli. None of the parties involved in those fateful discussions had any idea of an intermediate continent between Europe and Asia, although the knowledge of more or less fabulous Atlantic islands had been for a long time the subject of tales, poems, and legends.

The characteristic development of medieval mathematics shows the same lack of interest among learned circles in the spread of algebra and other methods of calculation to the Western World. After the pioneering attempts of Leonardo Pisano, around 1200, the Italians perfected, mainly in Florence, a system of commercial arithmetic that reached scientific heights after three centuries of an independent practice in trade and money matters. The basic terms of modern bookkeeping still reveal their Italian and medieval origins. Yet the curriculum of the higher schools did not include calculation in the arithmetic of the *Quadrivium*. The separation of the liberal arts from "mechanical" practice was so radical that advancement in mathematical studies in the late medieval schools, as marked by Prosdocimo de' Beldomandi or Biagio Pelacani, was achieved in connection with music, geometry, and astrology, i.e. in speculative disciplines, as branches of a general intellectual training, rather than in the new fields of arithmetic and algebra practiced for convenience in computation.

The cleavage between the two domains of intellectual activity is illustrated by the dramatic story of the first solution of cubic equations. This step, which marks the beginning of a new epoch in mathematical science, was accomplished by two Italians in 1535. The rules for the solution of that crucial algebraic problem were formulated in obscure verses by a practical engineer, Niccolò Tartaglia, who never enjoyed the advantages of a university training, in competition with a talented adventurer of science and medicine, Girolamo Cardano, whose role in the whole affair is as dubious as everything he undertook in private, public, and scientific life. The achievement is the more impressive and extraordinary because it was attained without the symbols and signs that make modern algebraic practice a matter of routine. To the modern mind the old intuitive and discursive methods of mathematical thinking are almost inconceivable, but the unofficial history of science reveals a succession of genuine mathematical talents at work in the most diversified branches of life, feeling their way through the intricacies of practical problems and the narrows of school education. The trend is shown in the great *Summa de arithmetica, geometria,* and so on, published in 1494 by Leonardo da Vinci's friend and collaborator, Luca Pacioli, a Minorite who devoted his life to the didactic co-ordination of the mathematical sciences in theory and practice and to the popularization of this neglected branch of Italian culture. The works of this industrious Italian mathematician grant a profound insight into the spirit and interests of an era that showed little inclination for scientific innovation and made scanty contributions to the theoretical advancement of the natural sciences.

While the static character of medieval science derived from the general opinion that truth lies in authority, the decline of scientific interests in the humanistic era was brought about by the general feeling that truth resides in beauty. Even scientific talents were attracted by the problems of art rather than by those of pure science, as the activity of many artists from L. B. Alberti to Piero della Francesca and Leonardo da Vinci eloquently shows. For half a century Luca Pacioli, the mathematician, was the center of that large circle of experimenting, calculating, and speculating artists and engineers. As has already been described, it was in that spiritual environment that the geometrization of space was developed as an aesthetic canon, a scientific method, and a philosophical intuition entirely independent of the doctrines and teachings of the schools. The mathematical perspective elaborated as a branch of geometry and as a system of optics far transcended artistic requirements and became an experimental science embracing the cosmic mysteries of light and space, and the philosophical problems of reality and truth.

The geometrization of space attained by the arts and their theorists was the empirical, theoretical, and natural premise for the three-dimensional perception of physical phenomena in rest and motion. Only in such a geometrical medium was a quantitative consideration of kinetic and dynamic phenomena truly scientific, that is, accessible to exact measurements and observations. Artists and engineers became so convinced of the universal value of mathematics for the explanation of mechanical and natural happenings that their greatest master, Leonardo da Vinci, could "find proportions not only in numbers and measures but also in sounds, weight, time, and situation, whatever their magnitude." He had the feeling that "mechanics is the paradise of the mathematical sciences" and that the universal order was geometrical, realizing in its proportions precision and beauty in measurable perfection.

The belief that the world was divinely organized according to "measure, number, and weight," was an old one, consecrated in an impressive passage in the "Wisdom of Solomon," where the world stands before God "as the turning of the scale." Yet neither Christian wisdom nor Aristotelian scholasticism ever elaborated this Pythagorean vision mathematically. There is little trace in Italian school philosophy of the substitution of quantitative for qualitative conceptions of physics, as sporadically attempted by Parisian philosophers of the fourteenth century in the wake of Ockhamist suggestions. Even the Platonic revival of the Italian humanists did not promote a mathematical approach to the problems of motion and natural philosophy. The ontological concept of a natural appetite causing the general and individual phenomena of movement made a mathematical explanation superfluous or unsuitable. Therefore there are even fewer contributions to physical science in humanistic literature than in the works and discussions of contemporary scholasticism.

Yet it is a striking fact that the outstanding mathematicians and astronomers of the humanistic era, such as Georg Peurbach, Nicolaus Cusanus, and Johann Müller Regiomontanus, did not join the schools of Paris, Oxford, and Salamanca, where a long tradition of scientific studies had centralized the intellectual life of Europe and the medieval cosmology was taught by renowned professors. Nor, unlike Martin Behaim, the geographer, did those German scholars migrate to Portugal, where Henry the Navigator and King John had grouped the best specialists in their particular fields of science. The leading German mathematicians all went to Italy, although the lack of special schools of cosmography and science would at first sight make this seem surprising. What those famous foreigners sought in the Italian cultural sphere was not a direct contribution to the studies in which they were masters, but rather the inspiration, the intellectual support, and congenial interest which they later helped to create in their own country after years of personal contact with Italian cultural pioneers. What linked Nicolaus Cusanus with the Italian humanists was their unconventional approach to the problem of philosophy and science. In extending his speculations far beyond the scholastic sphere, the German prelate was linked by a sort of spiritual affinity with the humanists, who opposed to the authority of the school a veneration for the doctrines and wisdom of the ancients. Despite the wide range of his mystical and scientific speculation, Nicolaus Cusanus created no resolute system, but, like his Italian humanistic friends, he left behind him a number of intuitions, anticipations, and beginnings that made him the leading figure in the philosophical and scientific renewal of his era.

For the same reason the accomplishments of Regiomontanus in the more specialized fields of mathematics and astronomy belong to the Italian cultural sphere. His determined criticism of the Ptolemaic cosmology was grounded, to be sure, in the glaring discrepancies between astronomical calculations and current observations of the heavenly bodies. But instead of confining himself to corrections based on improved mathematical techniques, astronomical instruments, and planetary tables, as others had done even in his day, he went so far as to express his doubts about the validity of the Ptolemaic cosmology as a whole and of the geocentric system in particular. To support this critical attitude he found in Italy scholars indirectly acquainted with the various astronomical and cosmographical theories of the ancients, handed down in Greek and Latin texts which had been unknown to former generations of scientists. The names and ideas of Aristarchus of Samos, Hipparchus, and Eudoxus had a new meaning to men familiar with Lucretius and Archimedes, Plato and Vitruvius, Cicero and the Greek scientific authors brought to light by the Italian humanists. Premature death deterred Regiomontanus from undertaking a thorough revision of the cosmological system that had become unequal to the practical requirements of astronomers and navigators as well as the intellectual curiosity of the contemporary mind.

That great undertaking was the work of Nicolaus Copernicus, whose treatise on *The Revolutions of the Heavenly Bodies* (1543) marks the overturn of all the scientific and philosophical conceptions commonly accepted until his day. For an independent spirit untouched by the chauvinistic and racial madness of our time the question whether Copernicus was a Pole or a German, a Prussian or a "Sarmatian," is entirely irrelevant. For a modern scientist educated in the spirit and methods of general relativity, the question of the objective value of the geocentric or the heliocentric system has lost much of its interest and significance. What remains is the historical problem of the formation of the Copernican mind and the evolution of his structural vision of the universe. It cannot be doubted that the scientific education of this great man was

Italian and humanistic. Beginning in 1496, he attended the universities of Bologna, Ferrara, and Padua.

It is improbable that he was particularly attracted by the fame of Italian astronomers, such as Paolo Toscanelli in Florence, Giovanni Bianchini in Ferrara, or Domenico Maria Novara in Bologna. It was the general humanistic revival of antiquity that primarily fascinated the intellectual youth of Europe and started the periodic invasion of Italy by foreign scholars that lasted until the end of the eighteenth century. Men interested in the mathematical sciences were able to profit both by the advanced methods of calculation of the Italian *abacisti* and by the geometrical Platonism of the artists and scholars united in the cult and speculations of the "divine proportion." Albrecht Dürer, the greatest of German painters, was in Venice while Copernicus was studying at Italian universities. Both were equally inspired by the scientific *genius loci* that found its expression in mathematical interests and artistic achievements.

It was that spiritual aura rather than any specific technical or practical problems that encouraged the development of the Copernican theory. The theoretical inadequacy and practical deficiencies of the Ptolemaic system were not the principal reasons for its abandonment by some daring spirits and able astronomers of that epoch. The reform of the calendar, promoted by several popes, and more precise astronomic and geodetic measurements, were accomplished within the old cosmological system. Almost a century after the arrival of Copernicus in Italy, the Dane, Tycho Brahe, considerably augmented the astronomic knowledge of his contemporaries without renouncing the traditional geocentric system. The first planetary tables calculated after the publication of Copernicus' great work, in 1543, show little improvement over the old ones. Nor can his heliocentric system be considered a practical simplification as compared to the Ptolemaic and Aristotelian cosmology, since it attributes three movements to the earth, implying a new complexity of mathematical relations.

The innermost causes underlying the new cosmological vision were neither mystical and speculative, like those of Nicolaus Cusanus, nor practical and technical like those of Regiomontanus, but essentially rational and aesthetic, synthesized by a great scientific enthusiasm. To a critical mind the daily rotation of the firmament around the earth had always been inconceivable, even conceding that divine power could move that immeasurable, although finite, cosmic structure with an incalculable velocity. Moreover, in the words of Copernicus, the apparent irregularities in the movements of the planets were so striking and difficult to explain because they disturbed the harmony of the universe and the symmetry of its parts. The geocentric system that tried to reconcile all the apparent incongruities of the "world machine" appeared to him as if "somebody had brought together from different places hands, feet, a head, and other limbs, all very fine in themselves, but not wrought in correct proportions for the same body, so that, if recomposed, they would form a monster rather than a human being."

As his whole book shows, Copernicus rejected the old cosmological system with the same distaste that prompted the Italian humanists to turn away from the amorphous, inartistic, and abstract system of scholastic thought. Again truth was sought in beauty, and perfection attained in formal qualities of structure and style. The aesthetic and scientific temper of contemporary Italy is evident in every aspect of the work. It is written in the typical humanistic style, with a profusion of Latin and Greek quotations, and much solicitude for polished eloquence and rhythmic elegance. The conclusion is summed up in a solemn peroration praising the sun in poetical terms as master of the universe and the perfect work of a divine architect.

Intrinsically the system appears as the geometrical embodiment of a cosmic harmony. It is the product of a free scientific imagination and not of astronomical observations. The movement of the earth and planets around the sun is not caused by metaphysical influences, but by their spherical form, which determines their circular motion in the cosmic space limited by the motionless sphere of the fixed stars. In that form the Copernican vision is a courageous attempt to reconstruct in a geometrical order the system of Aristarchus of Samos and of the so-called Pythagorean cosmologists mentioned in the treatise and very much discussed in the circles of the scientific-minded humanists of that era. Actually, the Copernican system is only one of several attempts undertaken by contemporary humanists in Italy to revive the ancient cosmological doctrines opposed to the Ptolemaic concepts and criticized by Aristotle. In Aristotle's book *On Heaven,* which was a standard work of philosophical and scientific culture, Italy was indicated as the country in which the Pythagorean tradition was kept alive by influential groups of scholars and enthusiasts. The Italian humanists, to whom that famous passage had always been familiar, seem to have cultivated that old tradition as a sort of cultural heritage.

While Copernicus, after almost ten years in Italy, was composing his book, the Veronese physician, poet, and scientist, Girolamo Fracastoro, was at work on an elaborate treatise reconstructing the homocentric system of Eudoxus in which the planets rotated in concentric spheres around different axes. Fracastoro surpassed Copernicus in his attempts to make astronomical observations with a rudimentary telescope, the first mentioned in the history of science. At the same time, around 1520, Celio Calcagnini, a learned and widely traveled scholar from Ferrara, vied with Fracastoro in reconstructing a Pythagorean cosmology that claimed to meet the scientific requirements of a general system of the world and also to satisfy the demands of practical astronomy. The notebooks of Leonardo da Vinci reflect his interest in the same problems before they were taken up in systematic discussions and calculations aiming at a reform of the dominant cosmological views. Several dilettanti joined in devising corrections of the old theories and new explanations of planetary anomalies. Some of those amateur astronomers were popular vernacular writers ignored by the history of science but no less symptomatic for the general scientific trends. They confirm what is indirectly known about the great popularity of astronomy in the Italian society of the Copernican era.

In Florence, around 1550, the heliocentric system was under constant discussion. It was already customary for the Italian nobility to complement their literary curriculum with a private study of astronomy and mathematics, under specially appointed masters. The scientific fervor became even greater than the philosophical curiosity that once prompted some citizens of Florence to write letters to Marsilio Ficino asking for clarification of metaphysical and moral problems. Women did not want to be inferior to men in that intellectual conquest of the skies. In 1539, before the work of Copernicus was printed, the learned and noble Allessandro Piccolomini of Siena ceased to praise his beloved Laudomia with the usual garland of nicely finished sonnets and wrote for her and the educated ladies of Italy a pleasant introduction to astronomy and cosmology, the first of the genre of polished books on science characterized by such masterpieces as Fontenelle's *Pluralité des mondes* and Algarotti's *Newtonianism for Ladies* (1733). The Italian intellectual nobility seem to have tired of courtly discussions on Platonic love, literary topics, and amorous casuistry. They had given up the dangerous reexamination of theological and dogmatical problems. The spiritual interests of the privileged classes and of large sections of the population turned to questions of science and natural philosophy.

Just as in Petrarca's time, these intellectual pastimes found a leading center in Venice, where they were favored by active publishers and booksellers, by the presence of Paduan professors, and by a conditional tolerance of the civilian authorities toward scientific studies. One of the palaces on the Grand Canal, in which scientific-minded patricians, scholars, ladies, and amateurs gathered for their discussions, became the scene of Galileo's dialogues on the principal systems of the world and the new principles and methods of physical investigation. It was, indeed, through these circles, called "academies" and designated by odd names, strange emblems, and precious devices, that scientific interests became widespread among the cultivated public.

The reasons for the evolution of intellectual interests from the pure humanities to astronomy and cosmology were manifold. Purely scientific curiosity concurred with practical experience in directing the public favor toward the skies and a systematic knowledge of natural phenomena. The old conceptions consecrated by a long literary tradition and scholastic education were shaken by the wide geographical experience acquired in the epoch of discoveries and colonial expansion. In the astronomic field, the appearance of Halley's comet, in 1456, and its observation by Toscanelli and his contemporaries inaugurated the discussions on the sublunar or celestial course of the comets that were to endure for nearly two centuries. The appearance of the so-called "new stars" or *novae,* in 1572 and 1604, the systematic investigation of the southern sky, the problem of longitudes and latitudes, and, above all, the reform of the calendar drew the curiosity of numerous Italians to celestial phenomena and astronomical studies.

This general participation in a specific branch of knowledge can be compared with the popularity acquired by the physical sciences after the discovery of electricity, Montgolfier's balloons, the steam engine, Einstein's relativity, or the atomic bomb. In all these cases and in many more, questions connected with scientific views and methods inaccessible to the layman became topics of public interest, instrumental in determining cultural predilections and intellectual developments. It was probably a unique instance in the sociology of science, before or since, when in 1516, the Florentine republic ordered posted up in all public places a printed invitation to the inhabitants of its territory to express their views on the reform of the calendar decreed shortly before by the Lateran council. Every person in the town and countryside received a printed booklet instructing him in the astronomical questions involved in the papal initiative.

Such examples of scientific democracy are, of course, rare in Italy and unknown in other countries. They presuppose a high cultural level and a spirit of intellectual co-operation such as had existed until that time mainly in the field of the fine arts. The *Divina Commedia* had contributed immensely to the popularization of cosmographical views, since the poem had been publicly commented upon in churches and learned circles. The increasing vogue of cosmography is attested by the great success of Gregorio Dati's *Sfera,* a poem in popular stanzas written shortly after 1400 and followed by a scientific vernacular literature in verse and prose. The phenomena of magnetism became a renewed object of speculation and observation after Columbus' discovery of the declination of the magnetic needle during his first Atlantic crossing.

But what really lay at the root of Italian interest in astronomy was the Italian's intense passion for the practice and technique of astrology. If Pope Paul III, the very man who instituted the Holy Office and accepted the dedication of the work of Copernicus, never appointed a consistory without having one of his astrologers calculate a favorable "conjuncture," it should not seem surprising that every high prelate, potentate, nobleman, layman, professional, and physician regulated his life and activity by horoscopes, which many of them had learned to cast by themselves. In the sixteenth century astrology had become a public preoccupation rather than a profession, and involved a general familiarity with celestial phenomena and a skill in mathematical operations inconceivable in our era of planetaria and calculating machines. The religious scruples against this widespread astrological practice were easily overcome by the conventional opinion that the free human will is able to counteract bad astral influences when they are scientifically revealed in horoscopes and conjunctures. And since the theory and practice of astrology were an essential element of the medical curriculum, the universities were more advanced in the fields of cosmology, astronomy, and mathematics than in any other branch of professional education.

All these branches of science enjoyed comparative neutrality and independence in a period when intellectual interests and activities were becoming increasingly limited. No objections were expressed to the Copernican or other cosmological systems, to astrological practice or natural investigations. After the departure of Vesalius for Switzerland and Flanders in 1542, the medical sciences developed freely in Italian universities, especially in the activity and writings of leading anatomists, such as Bartolomeo Eustachio, Gabriele Fallopio, and Realdo Colombo, the man who, in 1556, dissected the body of Ignatius of Loyola in Rome, and published a detailed report on his findings. This professional immunity attracted many talents to science and technology and made Italy a country of naturalists, physicians, mechanics, and mathematicians, while all trends of philosophical and literary thought had to seek more favorable conditions abroad. But as soon as all those technical disciplines and professional abilities evolved into an autonomous natural philosophy and determined a new methodological approach to the fundamental problems of science and knowledge, the scientific thought and the spiritual organization of the country found themselves crippled and misled by the same limitations that brought moral apathy and intellectual disintegration to all other creative activities of Italian society.

That fateful evolution which deprived Italy of scientific leadership and destroyed so much of her intellectual energies took place as soon as a few daring spirits transcended the limits of specialized disciplines and ventured—as Giordano Bruno said—"to understand the whole truth." This philosophical task was assumed by science immediately after the death of the Neapolitan thinker on the Roman pyre had ended all efforts toward a speculative and purely human solution of the riddles of the world. The free endeavors and achievements of an era rich in scientific talents and interests had widely shaken people's faith in authority as a source of truth. The idea that truth is a child of time—*Veritas filia temporis*—had become so popular that it was expressed and represented in many forms, as a motto, an emblem, and an allegory. The scientific fervor that fostered that vague feeling of optimism and progress also weakened the enthusiasm of the generations that had searched for truth in beauty as an image of the cosmic proportions of a metaphysical harmony.

Giordano Bruno destroyed that harmony with the "heroic furor" that led his impetuous speculative imagination to demolish not only the Aristotelian, Ptolemaic, and scholastic cosmology, but also the limited universe of Copernicus and the geometrical foundations on which it was built. He substituted the idea of an infinite universe for the awkward machinery of a world regulated by a mathematical system of human invention and limited by the insufficiency of human knowledge and imagination. Yet the logical shortcomings and intrinsic deficiencies of Bruno's doctrines contributed as much as his punishment to nullifying their influence on Italian intellectual life. He was in fact denounced by one of those scientific-minded Venetian noblemen who expected from the philospher a substantial insight into the secrets of the world and received instead volcanic outbursts of a blasphemous Neapolitan eloquence. The time was past when poetical fiction, mythological allegories, and striking metaphors could satisfy the intellectual interests of unconventional spirits and experienced men.

After the success of the Counter-Reformation, the problems of science, which more than anything else attracted the general curiosity and creative ingenuity of the Italians, had to be solved by scientific procedures and reasoning compatible with the abundance of mathematical talents characteristic of those generations. The free expansion of scientific interests had developed a belief in the identity of truth and certitude, independent of authority and beauty, that is, of religious and aesthetic concerns. The concept, substantiated in Galileo's method and discoveries, marks the turn in the evolution of science and thought from the medieval to the modern. Leonardo da Vinci had a vague feeling of that identity when he strove to find a common principle for art and science. The engineers, architects, and mechanics who observed natural phenomena for professional reasons, though in a scientific mood—such as Tartaglia, Cardano, Guidobaldo del Monte, Benedetti, and some of the best representatives of a *magia naturale*—inherited and confirmed the opinion that the truth can be found through a rigorous methodical procedure of measuring, counting, and weighing, but not by a purely speculative co-ordination or a scholarly classification of facts and data. The thinking of that new generation of speculative empiricists was dominated by the conviction that truth lies in scientific exactness.

In considering the phenomena of motion and concussion, of falling or floating bodies, there was as little agreement among the theorists of mechanics as there was among astronomers and cosmologists in interpreting the structure of the universe and the movements of the heavenly bodies. The ontological distinction between the "natural" circular motion of the planets and the "violent" and accidental rectilinear motion assigned to our earthly sphere prevented the formulation of a coherent system of physical knowledge and of a consistent methodological procedure equally valid for the qualitative and quantitative interpretation of natural phenomena. Moreover, as long as the Copernican and other cosmological systems rested on speculative assumptions and mathematical expedients, they were open to discussion and, so to speak, were a matter of taste. In case of conflicts between orthodox philosphy and new doctrines, the customary escape of double truth granted the able dialecticians in universities and "academies" enough protection against the risks that Bruno, in a defiant attitude of intellectual self-assurance, had accepted.

After 1609, when Galileo's telescope revealed the satellites of Jupiter, the structure of the moon, the sun-spots, the anomalies of Saturn, the phases of Venus, and hitherto unknown astronomical phenomena, the era of conjectural and controversial discussions was closed and no loophole left for the captious expedient of double truth. Galileo had discovered the physical unity of the universe and the methodological unity of science based, as he taught, on "directed experience and necessary demonstrations." That new insight into the secrets of nature abolished forever the concept of immutable, ingenerable, and incorruptible celestial spheres turned around the earth by angelical intelligences and opposed to the sublunar region of rest and corruption. In place of that limited, speculative, dualistic cosmology and an orderly world of geometrical perfection, a new universe was disclosed to the minds and eyes of men.

They were taught to consider their homely planet as a globe moving in an infinite space with all the stars and planets, and moved by the same laws that explain all measurable and calculable phenomena of motion in heaven and earth.

These laws established that the velocity of falling bodies is independent of their mass or weight and proportional to time, and that the distance traveled is proportional to the square of the time consumed in the fall. These simple notions arrived at by experiment and induction constitute the foundation of modern mechanics, and initiated the greatest of intellectual revolutions. That quantitative approach to the phenomena of motion is at once empirical, speculative, and mathematical. It abolished the customary distinction between bodies naturally heavy or light and introduced for the first time into physical speculation the two basic concepts of a new natural philosophy: namely, the principle of inertia, implying that bodies preserve their state of rest or motion indefinitely if not affected by external conditions; secondly, the assumption that "matter is unalterable, i.e. always the same, and because of its eternal and necessary character it is possible to produce demonstrations of it no less straight and neat than those of mathematics."

While the idea of inertia is in Galileo's mind a cosmic vision and an abstract reality of a purely physical nature, the unalterable character of matter justifies, and even requires, a mathematical procedure in the interpretation of natural phenomena. The interdependence of matter and mathematics determines the interdependence, if not the identity, of physics and mathematics, and consequently the submission of natural philosophy and scientific knowledge to the intuitive and inexorable veracity of the methods, principles, and conclusions of physics. Truth does not lie in the perfection of geometrical proportions, but in exact observations, correct calculations, and proper experiments. This new search for truth makes formal considerations useless, syllogistic deductions senseless, and analogical explanations meaningless. The structure of the universe, the contemplation of the wonders of nature, and the penetration of the divine mind are open now to all men who adapt their minds to sound scientific thought and submit their philosophy and cosmology to purposeful observation and experiment. Nature is like a book always open before our eyes and understandable to everybody able to spell out the mathematical language in which it is written. Celestial mechanics are only an aspect of the general rules that explain the fall or floating of bodies, the inclined plane, the movement of the pendulum, and the different forms and variations of motion. On that basis the heliocentric hypothesis was transformed into a problem of mechanics and could be considered as a part of mathematical and experimental science. With that Galileo inaugurated a new method of thinking that obliged his scientific contemporaries to substitute for a finite image of the world and a coherent system of accepted knowledge his independent "new sciences" that represented only the first step in a new and slow conquest of the universe by the human mind.

\* \* \*

# 4 / The Enlightenment: A Break with the Past?

The philosophe d'Alembert, an editor of the *Encyclopédie*, that monumental epitome of eighteenth-century thought, is said to have claimed that his age would represent a revolutionary epoch in the history of thought because of the new ideas it was nurturing. By 1932, when Carl Becker published *The Heavenly City of the Eighteenth-Century Philosophers*, historians had long granted d'Alembert's claim and given his age the dignity of an epoch called The Enlightenment or Age of Reason. The general view was that in the history of ideas, The Enlightenment represented the turning point into our own age, although The Enlightenment's debt to the Scientific Revolution and the Renaissance was by no means neglected. But when Becker proclaimed in his book "that at every turn the *philosophes* betray their debt to medieval thought" or that "they demolished the Heavenly City of St. Augustine only to rebuild it with more up-to-date materials," he was going back further than conventional scholarship had been prepared to penetrate and taking what might have been a controversial stand. It turned out to be otherwise.

The overwhelmingly favorable reception and continuing influence of Becker's thesis are noted in an essay read by Professor Peter Gay at a symposium held at Colgate University in 1956. The theme of the symposium was "Carl Becker's *Heavenly City* Revisited Twenty-Five Years After"—the symposium itself being further testimony to the endurance of this provocative little book by one of America's great historians. As might have been expected, after twenty-five years there were attackers as well as defenders of the *Heavenly City* at the Colgate meeting.

The attackers concentrated on what they considered obvious faults in Becker's interpretation of the Enlightenment, and the defenders had to concede that there were indeed defects of scholarship in Becker's central thesis and many of his supporting points. But most of the defenders asked in one way or another whether every word in the *Heavenly City* was meant to be taken in "deadly earnest." The *Heavenly City*, after all, was not intended to be a definitive history of the Enlightenment. It remains instead a brilliant, paradoxical essay—questioning rather than defining—which asks us, among other things, to think about the nature of the history of ideas and the possibility of mankind's ever achieving perfection. In the face of such stimulating and meaningful inquiry, so the argument ran, may not too much importance be attached to lapses of scholarship, especially when they were committed a quarter century ago?[1]

The attackers of the *Heavenly City*, while they all conceded Becker's brilliance of expression, answered no to the last question with varying degrees of emphasis, the

---

[1] The foregoing is only an approximate and necessarily simplified paraphrase of a discussion in which more than a dozen scholars offered their views. For a record of the proceedings of the symposium, see Raymond O. Rockwood (ed.), *Carl Becker's Heavenly City Revisited* (Ithaca, N. Y.: Cornell University Press, 1958).

most emphatic no coming from Professor Gay's essay already referred to, which is the second selection reproduced below. In it will be found, along with an explanation of Professor Gay's critical stand, important insights into the character of the Enlightenment, inspired by Professor Gay's refutation of Becker. The first selection consists of excerpts from the *Heavenly City* itself. These include some of the points most criticized by Gay, but because of the extensive quotation of Becker in Gay's essay, the excerpts were chosen primarily to give a sample of Becker's thinking and his polished, witty, and sometimes subtly ironic style. They should give the reader an idea of why, in spite of its defects, *The Heavenly City of the Eighteenth-Century Philosophers* will probably remain a classic work in the field of the history of ideas.

# THE LAWS OF NATURE AND THE NEW HISTORY

Carl L. Becker

\* \* \*

We are accustomed to think of the eighteenth century as essentially modern in its temper. Certainly, the *Philosophes* themselves made a great point of having renounced the superstition and hocus-pocus of medieval Christian thought, and we have usually been willing to take them at their word. Surely, we say, the eighteenth century was pre-eminently the age of reason, surely the *Philosophes* were a skeptical lot, atheists in effect if not by profession, addicted to science and the scientific method, always out to crush the infamous, valiant defenders of liberty, equality, fraternity, freedom of speech, and what you will. All very true. And yet I think the *Philosophes* were nearer the Middle Ages, less emancipated from the preconceptions of medieval Christian thought, than they quite realized or we have commonly supposed. If we have done them more (or is it less?) than justice in giving them a good modern character, the reason is that they speak a familiar language. We read Voltaire more readily than Dante, and follow an argument by Hume more easily than one by Thomas Aquinas. But I think our appreciation is of the surface more than of the fundamentals of their thought. We agree with them more readily when they are witty and cynical than when they are wholly serious. Their negations rather than their affirmations enable us to treat them as kindred spirits.

But, if we examine the foundations of their faith, we find that at every turn the *Philosophes* betray their debt to medieval thought without being aware of it. They denounced Christian philosophy, but rather too much, after the manner of those who are but half emancipated from the "superstitions" they scorn. They had put off the fear of God, but maintained a respectful attitude toward the Deity. They ridiculed the idea that the universe had been created in six days, but still believed it to be a beautifully articulated machine designed by the Supreme Being according to a rational plan as an abiding place for mankind. The Garden of Eden was for them a myth, no doubt, but they looked enviously back to the golden age of Roman virtue, or across the waters to the unspoiled innocence of an Arcadian civilization that flourished in Pennsylvania. They renounced the authority of church and Bible, but exhibited a naïve faith in the authority of nature and reason. They scorned metaphysics, but were proud to be called philosophers. They dismantled heaven, somewhat prematurely it seems, since they retained their faith in the immortality of the soul. They courageously discussed atheism, but not before the servants. They defended toleration valiantly, but could with difficulty tolerate priests. They denied that miracles ever happened, but believed in the perfectibility of the human race. We feel that these Philosophers were at once too credulous and too skeptical. They were the victims of common sense. In spite of their rationalism and their humane sympathies, in spite of their aversion to hocus-pocus and enthusiasm and dim perspectives, in spite of their eager skepticism, their engaging cynicism, their brave youthful blasphemies and talk of hanging the last king in the entrails of the last priest—in spite of all of it, there is more of Christian philosophy in the writings of the *Philosophes* than has yet been dreamt of in our histories.

\* \* \*

I shall attempt to show that the underlying preconceptions of eighteenth-century thought were still, allowance made for certain important alterations in the bias, essentially the same as those of the thirteenth century. I shall attempt to show that the *Philosophes* demolished the Heavenly City of St. Augustine only to rebuild it with more up-to-date materials.

\* \* \*

At this point I ought perhaps to mention the well-known word *enthusiasm*. Do not the writers of the eighteenth century, the early eighteenth century, commonly insist on the just measure, the virtue of keeping cool and not straying beyond the call of common sense? Do they not even become a little heated and scornful when confronted with examples of "enthusiasm"? They do indeed, and there's the rub. To be scornful is not to be detached. The aversion of the Philosophers to enthusiasm did not carry them to the high ground of indifference. Their aversion to enthusiasm was itself an enthusiasm, a mark of their resolute rejection of all that was not evident to the senses, of their commendable passion for opening up and disinfecting all the musty, shuttered closets of the mind. The best case in point, the best and most ironical, is Hume, no less: Hume, the personification of common sense, stiffly priding himself on a Jove-like avoidance of enthusiasm. Who, indeed, was so well suited to be an indifferent observer of the human scene? He had the temperament for it, and his philosophical speculations left him quite without illusion, or should have, since they led him to the conclusion that the ultimate cause of things "has no more regard to good above ill than to heat above cold."[1] But a conclusion which left so little scope for enthusiasm was too much even for Hume. He writes in 1737:

I am at present castrating my work . . . ; that is, endeavouring it shall give as little offence as possible. . . . This is a piece of cowardice. . . . But I was resolved not to be an enthusiast in philosophy, while blaming other enthusiasms.[2]

It seems oversubtle—avoiding enthusiasm to the point of refusing to press a pessimistic argument to its logical conclusion. I think Hume's real reason for soft-pedaling skepticism was the feeling that such negative conclusions were useless. He writes:

A man has but a bad grace who delivers a theory, however true, which . . . leads to a practice dangerous and pernicious. Why rake into those corners of nature, which spread a nuisance all around? . . . Truths which are *pernicious* to society, if any such there be, will yield to errors, which are salutary and *advantageous*.[3]

At all events, in mid career Hume abandoned philosophical speculations for other subjects, such as history and ethics, which could be treated honestly without giving "offense," and from which useful lessons might be drawn. By this devious route the

---

[1] *Dialogues Concerning Natural Religion* (1907), p. 160.
[2] J. H. Burton, *Life and Correspondence of David Hume*, I, 64.
[3] *Essays* (1767), II, 352, 353.

prince of skeptics, who abhorred enthusiasm with a pure passion, found his way into the company of those who might be regarded as having "deserved well of humanity."

In all this Hume is representative of his century. Its characteristic note is not a disillusioned indifference, but the eager didactic impulse to set things right. *Bienfaisance, humanité*—the very words, we are told, are new, coined by the Philosophers to express in secular terms the Christian ideal of service. In this connection one is reminded of that earnest and amiable and rather futile Abbé de Saint-Pierre, the man "at whom every one laughs, and who is alone serious and without laughter."[4] How industriously this priest labored in the secular vineyard of the Lord! How many "projects" he wrote, helpful hints for the improvement of mankind—"Project for Making Roads Passable in Winter," "Project for the Reform of Begging," "Project for Making Dukes and Peers Useful." And then one day, quite suddenly, so he tells us, "there came into my mind a project which by its great beauty struck me with astonishment. It has occupied all my attention for fifteen days."[5] The result we know: *A Project for Making Peace Perpetual in Europe!*

Well, let us join the others and laugh at the Abbé, but does not his *penchant* for projects remind us of Jefferson, does not his passion for improvement recall Poor Richard? Let us laugh at him, by all means, but be well assured that when we do we are laughing at the eighteenth century, at its preoccupation with human welfare, at its *penchant* for projects. Who, indeed, was not, in this bright springtime of the modern world, making or dreaming of projects? What were most of the scientific academies in France doing but discussing, quarreling about, and having a jolly time over the framing of projects? What was the *Encyclopédie*, what was the Revolution itself? Grand projects, surely. What, indeed (the question stares us in the face), was this enlightened eighteenth century doing, what significance had it in the world anyway if not just this: that with earnest purpose, with endless argument and impassioned propaganda and a few not unhappy tears shed in anticipation of posterity's gratitude, it devoted all its energies to sketching the most naïvely simple project ever seen for making dukes and peers useful, for opening all roads available to the pursuit of happiness, for securing the blessings of liberty, equality, and fraternity to all mankind? Maybe this project was less futile than those of the Abbé de Saint-Pierre, maybe it only seems so; but it was at all events inspired by the same ideal—the Christian ideal of service, the humanitarian impulse to set things right.

\* \* \*

A poet in search of peace and epigrams might be permitted to repeat the ancient theologians, but the Philosophers could not do so unless they were willing to renounce their premises or deny the evidence of common sense. The very foundation of the new philosophy was that the existence of God, if there was one, and his goodness, if goodness he could claim, must be inferred from the observable behavior of the world. Following Newton, the Philosophers had all insisted on this to the point of pedantry, and so, even, had the enlightened Christian theologians in their desperate effort to find arguments to convince doubting Thomases. How then could Philosophers say that all was somehow good in God's sight unless they could also say that there was no evil to be observed in the world of nature and man? Yet to say that there was no evil in the

4 Quoted from La Bruyère by Sainte-Beuve, *Lundis*, XV, 257.
5 Drouet, *Abbé de Sainte-Pierre*, p. 108.

world—a world where Lisbon earthquakes occurred, where Bastilles functioned, where crowds still gathered to gloat over the lingering agony of men broken on the wheel—was an insult to common sense. No, whatever Locke may have done, he had done nothing to solve, even if for the unwary he had done much to obscure, the problem of evil in the world.

Before the middle of the century Hume had taken up this world-old problem, had looked at it straight, had examined it attentively round and round about; and then, in his *Dialogues Concerning Natural Religion*, with all the dialectical resources of the new philosophy, with a penetrating insight matched only by the serene urbanity with which he displayed it, had remorselessly exposed the futility of reason to establish either the existence or the goodness of God. "Epicurus's old questions are yet unanswered. Is he [God] willing to prevent evil, but not able? Then he is impotent. Is he able, but not willing? Then he is malevolent. Is he both able and willing? Whence then is evil?"[6] In the end Hume manages to chevy Christian mystics and atheists into the same camp, since they obviously agree on the main point, that reason is totally incompetent to answer ultimate questions; and so he concludes with that masterpiece of irony: "To be a philosophical Sceptic is, in a man of letters, the first and most essential step towards being a sound, believing Christian."[7] To read Hume's *Dialogues* after having read, with sympathetic understanding, the earnest deists and optimistic philosophers of the early century, is to experience a slight chill, a feeling of apprehension. It is as if, at high noon of the Enlightenment, at the hour of the siesta when everything seems so quiet and secure all about, one were suddenly aware of a short, sharp slipping of the foundations, a faint far-off tremor running underneath the solid ground of common sense.

There it was then—the ugly dilemma, emerging from the beautiful premises of the new philosophy: if nature is good, then there is no evil in the world; if there is evil in the world, then nature is so far not good. How will they meet it, the enlightened ones who with so much assurance and complacent wit have set out with the rule of reason to rebuild an unlovely universe according to nature's design? Will they, closing their eyes to the brute facts, maintain that there is no evil in the world? In that case there is nothing for them to set right. Or will they, keeping their eyes open, admit that there is evil in the world? In that case nature fails to provide them with any standard for setting things right. They have followed reason faithfully. Will they follow her to the end? She is pointing in two directions: back toward Christian faith; forward toward atheism. Which way will they choose? It does not really matter much, since in either case she will vanish at last, leaving them to face existence with no other support than hope, or indifference, or despair.

Well, we know what the Philosophers did in this emergency. They found, as we all find when sufficiently hard pressed, that reason is amenable to treatment. They therefore tempered reason with sentiment, reasons of the heart that reason knows not of; or held it in leash by experience, the universal judgment of mankind; or induced it to delay its pronouncements in view of the possibility (which in a pinch might be taken as a fact) that the world was after all neither a completed drama nor a perfected machine, but rather something as yet unfinished, something still in the making.

* * *

The age of reason had scarcely run half its course before the Philosophers were

[6] *Dialogues,* p. 134.
[7] *Ibid.,* p. 191.

admitting the feebleness of reason, putting the ban on flippancy, and turning to the study of useful, that is to say, factual, subjects. In the succeeding decades the trend of interest toward the concrete and the practical, the increasing preoccupation of thinking men with questions of political and social reform, and the rising temperature of the climate of opinion are every year more apparent. The time had gone by when statesmen could afford to "let sleeping dogs lie"; when kings could say with a straight face "I am the state." In these years, when a tide in the affairs of men was carrying them on to disaster, kings were under pressure to declare, with Frederick the Great, "I am the first servant of the state." It was everywhere the fashion, therefore, for rulers to turn benevolent in order to mitigate the despotism that was denied them, and to talk of reforms even if they made none; while young princes, their successors to be, were urged to engage, under the tutorial system established by the Philosophers, in the study of history in order to learn, from the experience of mankind, what was "requisite in a prince charged with the amelioration of society."[8]

The amelioration of society was the very thing Philosophers had most at heart, and surely it was eminently fitting that they should be called in to tutor princes in that benevolent art. It was unfortunate, nevertheless, that their service should be enlisted in this practical task at the very moment when they were becoming aware of the incapacity of abstract reason to negotiate that reconciliation between custom and nature which they had so confidently preached as the proper goal of human effort. It was all very well for the philosophical tutor to say to the young prince: "Religion and morality and politics should be based on natural law, they should be in harmony with the nature of man." The young prince, if he knew his philosophy, might very well reply: "The universe, I am told, is only matter in spontaneous motion, and man a mechanically determined product of nature; so that all things, just as they are—priests as well as philosophers, superstition as well as enlightenment, tyranny and the Inquisition as well as liberty and the *Encyclopédie*—are already in harmony with nature." What then? In that case the Philosopher would no doubt need to ameliorate abstract reason before he could ameliorate society. A society so obviously wrong could never be set right unless some distinction could be drawn between the custom that was naturally good and the custom that was naturally bad.

A distinction between good and bad! Not a novel idea, certainly; on the contrary, a very old, a most Christian idea. Must the Philosophers then fly, as Hume put it, to revealed truth? No, it was scarcely necessary to go as far as that; but it was necessary to execute a strategic retreat from the advanced position occupied by abstract reason, from the notion that nature has "no more regard to good above ill than to heat above cold." Otherwise, the campaign for a regenerated society was surely lost, and the great project for making dukes and peers useful no more than a dream. Rousseau understood this better than anyone else, perhaps because he understood it intuitively, without rationalistic inhibitions; and it was Rousseau who pointed out the lines along which the retreat must be made. Unless Philosophers

prescribe bounds to Nature, monsters, giants, pigmies and chimeras of all kinds might be specifically admitted into nature: every object would be disfigured, and we should have no common model of ourselves. I repeat it, in a picture of human nature, every figure should resemble man. . . . We should *distinguish between the variety in human nature and that which is essential to it.*[9]

[8] Condillac, *Oeuvres* (1798), XXI, 13.
[9] *Eloise* (1810), I, 4.

Thus, the innate ideas which Locke had so politely dismissed by way of the hall door had to be surreptitiously brought back again through the kitchen window: the soul that Cartesian logic had eliminated from the individual had to be rediscovered in humanity. The soul of the individual might be evil, it might be temporary, it might even be an illusion. But the soul of humanity, this something "essential to" human nature, this "common model of ourselves" (and what was this but the old medieval "realism" come to life again?) was surely immortal because permanent and universal. What the Philosophers had to do, therefore, was to go up and down the wide world with the lamp of enlightenment looking, as Montaigne did before them, for "man in general." They had to identify and enumerate and describe the qualities that were common to all men in order to determine what ideas and customs and institutions in their own time were out of harmony with the universal natural order. For the successful conduct of this enterprise, this eighteenth-century search for the Holy Grail, the light of abstract reason had to be supplemented by the light of experience. "Without history," said Priestley, "the advantages of our rational nature must have been rated very low."[10] It goes without saying that the history needed by the Philosophers was a "new history"—the history that would be philosophy teaching by example.

* * *

Obviously, therefore, the chronological order was not essential to the writing of history thus conceived. It might, indeed, be adopted as the most convenient order, and, in fact, we find Hume, Gibbon, Voltaire, and Mably presenting their material more or less in this order. But a philosopher-historian might equally well ignore the chronological order, as Montesquieu and Raynal did, without laying himself open to the charge of being no historian. The method adopted by Montesquieu would seem to be *the* method for the philosopher-historian, the ideal method. For the task of the philosopher-historian, theoretically speaking, was to note the ideas, customs, and institutions of all peoples at all times and in all places, to put them side by side, and to cancel out as it were those that appeared to be merely local or temporary: what remained would be those that were common to humanity. From these common aspects of human experience it would then be possible, if at all, to discover, as Hume put it, the "constant and universal principles of human nature" and on these principles to base a reconstructed society. The ideal method for the philosopher-historian would thus be the comparative method, the strictly objective, inductive, scientific method.

Nevertheless, this ideal method was not employed by the Philosophers, not even by Montesquieu, who made the bravest appearance of doing so. It is, indeed, highly illuminating that those parts of the *Esprit des lois* in which Montesquieu was most successful in applying the comparative and inductive method, those parts in which he was most objective and scientific, were precisely the parts that pleased the Philosophers least. Generally speaking, the *Esprit des lois* left a bad taste in the mouths of the Philosophers because Montesquieu insisted that the "constant and universal principles of human nature" were after all "relative," so that, for example, what was suited to the nature of man in certain climates might very well be unsuited to the nature of man in other climates. The Philosophers felt that Montesquieu was too much enamored of facts as such to treat certain facts as harshly as they deserved, and it shocked them to see him dallying lightly with episodes that were no better than they

---

[10] *Lectures on History and General Policy* (Am. ed., 1803), I, 52.

should be. Voltaire (Voltaire of all people!) criticized Montesquieu for his *levity*, for being more disposed to astonish than to instruct his readers, and thought it monstrous that feudal kings and barons should be called "our fathers." According to Condorcet, Montesquieu would have done better if he had not been "more occupied with finding the reasons for that which is than with seeking that which ought to be."[11] And even Rousseau, who admired Montesquieu more than the others did, finds that he, like Grotius before him, is too much inclined to establish the right by the fact.[12] It is surely a paradox needing explanation that the Philosophers, who professed to study history in order to establish the rights suitable to man's nature on the facts of human experience, should have denounced Montesquieu precisely because he was too much inclined to establish the right by the fact. Is it, then, possible that the Philosophers were not really interested in establishing the rights suitable to man's nature on the facts of human experience? Is it possible that they were engaged in that nefarious medieval enterprise of reconciling the facts of human experience with truths already, in some fashion, revealed to them?

*  *  *

[11] *Oeuvres* (1847), VIII, 188.
[12] *Political Writings of Rousseau* (Vaughan ed.), II, 147.

# CARL BECKER'S HEAVENLY CITY

### Peter Gay

This certainly isn't history. I hope it's philosophy, because if it's not it's probably moonshine:—or would you say the distinction is over subtle?
—Carl Becker, on the flyleaf of *The Heavenly City*, presented to T. V. Smith.[1]

Carl Becker's *The Heavenly City of the Eighteenth-Century Philosophers* was published twenty-five years ago.[2] Its urbane and acidulous dissection of the *philosophes* has had great and lasting influence; few recent books on European intellectual history have been as widely read and as generously received. It is that rare work of scholarship that is also a work of literature—a masterpiece of persuasion that has done more to shape the current image of the Enlightenment than any other book. Despite the skepticism of some professional historians, its witty formulations have been accepted by a generation of students and borrowed in textbook after textbook.[3]

When Becker delivered his lectures at Yale Law School in 1931, and when he slightly revised them for publication, he seems to have thought of them as a *jeu d'esprit*, a collection of aphorisms and paradoxes meant to stimulate and (I suspect) to shock his

[1] Quoted by Charlotte Watkins Smith, *Carl Becker: On History and the Climate of Opinion* (Ithaca, 1956), p. 212.
[2] New Haven, 1932.
[3] The reviews of the *Heavenly City* were almost unanimous in their praise. One notable exception was the perceptive review by Ira O. Wade in the *Journal of Modern History*, Vol. V, No. 2, June 1933, pp. 233-235. One amusing exception was "J.A.L." in *America*, who complained, "There is a great deal about atmosphere and climate in this little book. After reading it, one feels that the professor is living in a fog." *America*, Vol. XLVIII, No. 15, January 14, 1933, p. 365.

audience.[4] But, as the Latin tag warns, the fate of books depends upon the capacities of the reader. And the worldly fate of the *Heavenly City* has been success—unexcelled, uninterrupted, and, I believe, unwarranted success. When it was first published, Charles Beard greeted it as a classic;[5] today, the *Heavenly City* is in its tenth printing; it appears prominently in bibliographies on the eighteenth century, and many a student reads no other book on the *philosophes*. It is indeed time that the book be subjected to a careful analysis.

## I

"Before estimating a book it is well to read its title with care," Becker suggests, and the title of this book briefly states its central theme: the *philosophes* destroyed less well than they knew.[6] They were believers in their most skeptical moods, Christians in their most anti-Christian diatribes:

In spite of their rationalism and their humane sympathies, in spite of their aversion to hocus-pocus and enthusiasm and dim perspectives, in spite of their eager skepticism, their engaging cynicism, their brave youthful blasphemies and talk of hanging the last king in the entrails of the last priest—in spite of all of it, there is more of Christian philosophy in the writings of the *Philosophes* than has yet been dreamt of in our histories. . . . I shall attempt to show that the *Philosophes* demolished the Heavenly City of St. Augustine only to rebuild it with more up-to-date materials.[7]

Before launching upon this theme, Becker expounds a general assumption about the relation of change to permanence in history. There is change in history: Thomas Aquinas and David Hume both used the word "reason" but meant very different things by it, so that to compare their philosophies by investigating simply what they said about "reason" would do injustice to both. Words persist, but their meanings

---

[4] I have heard the *Heavenly City* defended on the ground that Becker had only wanted to stimulate his auditors, to make them think and to reexamine their presuppositions. This defense amounts to the view that because the contents did not matter, the book could not have been misleading.
[5] In the *American Historical Review*, Vol. XXXVIII, No. 3, April 1933, P. 591 In estimating the influence of the *Heavenly City*, we must remember: first, the abundance of favorable reviews; secondly, the almost complete absence of published criticism (the tributes to Carl Becker by George H. Sabine, Leo Gershoy, and Mrs. Smith do not criticize the *Heavenly City*, and in addition to Mr. Wade's review, the only severe remarks I have discovered are in Walter L. Dorn, *Competition for Empire* [New York and London, 1940], pp. 180, 402); thirdly, the favorable comments on the book in such distinguished and popular textbooks as Leo Gershoy's *From Despotism to Revolution* (New York and London, 1944), in which the *Heavenly City* is recommended as "penetrating and subtle" (p. 329), and Mr. Gershoy's *French Revolution and Napoleon* (New York, 1941), in which he calls Becker's book "four brilliant essays on the *philosophes;* a penetrating analysis of their ideas and ideals" (p. 539). In the widely used text by Crane Brinton, John B. Christopher, and Robert Lee Wolff, *A History of Civilization* (2 vols., New York, 1955), the *Heavenly City* is described as a "charming series of essays, stressing the similarities between the eighteenth-century Age of Reason and the medieval Age of Faith" (II, 92). There are many other examples.
[6] For Becker's remark, see the *Heavenly City*, p. 115. It has been said (and Becker himself said it jokingly) that the *Heavenly City* is not history at all, but a moral tract. If it is not history at all, it should certainly not be recommended as good history.
[7] *Ibid.*, p. 31.

change. But, also, there is permanence in history: no era wholly liberates itself from its antecedents, although its spokesmen may proudly (or perhaps anxiously) proclaim that they have made a complete break. Rhetoric may change while ideas persist. Becker suggests that intellectual historians must reckon with this dialectic of permanence and change, and must be misled neither by spurious novelty nor by spurious persistence.[8]

This historiographical warning is the most valuable idea in the *Heavenly City*; unfortunately, Becker fails to heed it when he elaborates his thesis. He argues that, despite the great change in the climate of opinion between the thirteenth and eighteenth centuries, the two centuries were far more closely related than would immediately appear or would be admitted by the *philosophes*. The *philosophes'* claim to be modern must therefore be discounted:

I know it is the custom to call the thirteenth century an age of faith, and to contrast it with the eighteenth century, which is thought to be preeminently the age of reason. . . . In a very real sense it may be said of the eighteenth century that it was an age of faith as well as of reason, and of the thirteenth century that it was an age of reason as well as of faith.[9]

The overriding fault of the *philosophes* was their naïveté: they "exhibited a naïve faith in the authority of nature and reason."[10]

This is to fall into the trap of what I have called spurious persistence. It is true that the medieval Catholic rationalists, of whom Thomas Aquinas was the most prominent, assigned to reason an important place in their epistemologies. It is also true—and Becker's reminders are valuable—that the *philosophes* depended upon some unexamined premises which, to the extent that they were unexamined, may be called "faith."

But Becker infers far too much from this. Aquinas' rationalism was by no means as characteristic of the thirteenth century as Voltaire's empiricism was of the eighteenth century. Moreover, Becker forgets his own caution that words may be used in many different ways when he argues that "there were, certainly, many differences between Voltaire and St. Thomas, but the two men had much in common for all that. What they had in common was the profound conviction that their beliefs could be reasonably demonstrated."[11] But the point is precisely that the two philosophers differed over what constitutes reasonable demonstration. For Aquinas, reasonable

---

[8] I hope to expand my remarks on what I have here called "spurious persistence" in a forthcoming article dealing with periodization.

[9] *Heavenly City*, p. 8. Becker's use of the term *Climates of Opinion* as the heading to his first chapter suggests, correctly, that he relied heavily on Alfred North Whitehead's *Science and the Modern World*. Becker frequently quotes or paraphrases Whitehead's book without indicating his source—a sign not of unwillingness to give credit, of course, but of Becker's conviction that Whitehead's views are generally known and accepted. Whitehead describes the eighteenth century as "the age of reason, based upon faith" (p. 83) and asserts that "*les philosophes* were not philosophers" (p. 86). They were men who hated "dim perspectives" (*ibid.*). Whitehead, like Becker, appreciated the *Philosophes*: He admired their humaneness, their hatred of cant and cruelty. But like Becker he did not think they were quite first-rate: "If men cannot live on bread alone," he remarks with reference to Voltaire, "still less can they do so on disinfectants" (p. 87). All these formulations reappear in the *Heavenly City*.

[10] *Heavenly City*, p. 30. Becker does say that "Voltaire was an optimist, although not a naive one." *Ibid.*, p. 37.

[11] *Heavenly City*, p. 8.

demonstration was deductive and definitional;[12] Voltaire derided such demonstrations as "metaphysics," as examples of the despised *esprit de système*.

Aquinas and Voltaire both believed that the powers of reason are limited, but they drew sharply different conclusions from this. For Aquinas, that which is inaccessible to human reason concerns the foundations of Christian theology. Where the light of reason does not shine, the lamp of faith supplies illumination. For Voltaire, on the contrary, that which is inaccessible to reason is chimerical. What can never be found ought not to be sought; it is the realm, not of the most sacred, but of the most nonsensical—that is, of "metaphysical"—speculation. Where the light of reason does not shine, man must console himself with that philosophical modesty so characteristic of Voltaire's heroes Newton and Locke. While Aquinas could make categorical statements about the nature of the soul, Voltaire proudly proclaimed his ignorance in such matters. In seeking to show that "the underlying preconceptions of eighteenth-century thought were still, allowance made for certain important alterations in the bias, essentially the same as those of the thirteenth century,"[13] Becker thus unjustifiably plays with the word *reason*.

Becker plays the same verbal game in his assertion that both centuries were centuries of faith. The word *faith* usually serves to describe two rather different psychological processes. Thirteenth-century faith (if I may simplify a complex matter) was submission, not necessarily to what was absurd, but to what was beyond proof and, after a certain point, beyond argument. Failure to have faith (as Voltaire put it facetiously) led to burning in this world and in the next. Eighteenth-century faith in reason, while perhaps often naïve, should be designated by the more neutral term *confidence*. Its affirmations were public, open to examination and refutation. "Faith in reason" meant simply that for the *philosophes* the method of reason (strictly speaking the scientific method of such natural philosophers as Newton) was superior to other methods of gaining knowledge; it was superior to revelation, authority, tradition, because it was more reliable.[14] In Diderot's pornographic novel, *Les Bijoux indiscrets*, there is a charming dream: the dreamer sees himself transported into a building that has no foundations, and whose columns rise into the mists. The crowds walking in and around the building are crippled and deformed old men. It is the land of hypothesis, and the cripples are the makers of systems. But there is a vigorous small child, growing into a giant as the dream progresses, who draws near the fantastic building and destroys it with one blow. That giant is Experiment—no dweller of the heavenly city. Did not the *philosophes*, in their reveries, see themselves as that giant? And did they not include thinkers like Aquinas among the lame makers of systems? To denounce the *philosophes* for having faith in reason may be witty, but the paradox solves no problems in intellectual history.

Near the end of his first chapter, Becker adduces evidence to buttress his thesis. But

---

[12] Becker himself quotes a characteristic specimen of Aquinas' deductive method of arguing, *ibid.*, p. 3. Here and in many other places in the book, Becker provides material for the refutation of his case.

[13] *Heavenly City*, p. 31.

[14] I do not wish to assert that the *philosophes* were always consistent or thoroughgoing empiricists. Rousseau, who showed his respect for empirical knowledge in Books III and IV of the *Contrat social* and in the other late political works, could write in the *Discours sur l'inégalité*, "Let us begin by laying facts aside, since they do not affect the question." But he was seeking to elucidate the foundations of morality, and if he did not ask a factual question he was not, after all, seeking a factual answer.

the evidence is unsatisfactory. It is embodied in a dozen-odd generalizations designed to contrast the anti-Christian ideology of the *Philosophes* with their real beliefs and premises which were Christian or at least greatly indebted to Christianity: "If we examine the foundations of their faith, we find that at every turn the *Philosophes* betray their debt to medieval thought without being aware of it." Becker's generalizations are indefensible, not because they are too general—most generalizations are—but because some of them are inadequately explored, some are misleading, and others are simply wrong.

"They denounced Christian philosophy," Becker begins, "but rather too much, after the manner of those who are but half emancipated from the 'superstitions' they scorn." This sentence contains an important truth: the *philosophes* were venturing into territory that was largely unexplored, or had not been explored for many centuries, and they were often appalled at their own daring. However, the recurring discussions of the need for a social religion for the masses suggests not that the *philosophes* were "but half emancipated from the 'superstitions' they scorn" but, rather, that they were sometimes afraid of the social consequences of their emancipation. It is the substance of their opposition to Christianity, not the shrillness of their attacks upon it, that matters: much of the *philosophes'* vehemence can be explained by what they considered to be their mission. They were determined to expose *l'infâme* loudly, repeatedly, insistently, unsparingly, until that large public which was tepidly Christian had been won over to the new ideas.

"They ridiculed the idea that the universe had been created in six days, but still believed it to be a beautifully articulated machine designed by the Supreme Being according to a rational plan as an abiding place for mankind." True, but why "but"? There is nothing essentially Christian about this idea of "cosmos"—it had been the foundation of Stoic philosophy. There is nothing essentially Christian about this idea of God as architect—the watchmaker argument for the existence of God, a favorite with the *philosophes*, appears prominently in the discourses of Epictetus. The beautifully articulated machine of the *philosophes* is not a Christian but a pagan machine. What is remarkable is not the supposed resemblance of this machine to Christianity, but its always implicit and often explicit repudiation of miracles: God acts through general and uniform laws alone. Here as elsewhere Becker exploits parallels or similarities or correspondences between Christian and *philosophe* thought to claim that the two are identical or that, at the least, the latter is the direct descendant of the former. This has as much logical merit as the assertion that since Calvin was a determinist and Holbach was a determinist, Holbach was a Calvinist.

"The Garden of Eden was for them a myth, no doubt, but they looked enviously back to the golden age of Roman virtue, or across the waters to the unspoiled innocence of an Arcadian civilization that flourished in Pennsylvania." Becker is doubtless right—a mood of nostalgia for the past or for an unspoiled civilization pervaded Enlightenment thought. But this nostalgia is not merely a substitute for the Christian state of innocence: Roman virtue, Tahitian simplicity, Chinese wisdom and Quaker pacifism provide worldly standards. They are standards, moreover, which helped the *philosophes* to evade the censorship in the *ancien régime*. Voltaire's England, Diderot's Tahiti, Montesquieu's Persia are not simply utopias; they are indirect indictments of France.

"They scorned metaphysics, but were proud to be called philosophers." True again, but it is hard to see what this sentence proves. A philosopher is a man who loves knowledge, and when he rejects authority, revelation, system-making, he may argue that in his empiricism he is the only *true* philosopher, while his forerunners had been idle dreamers. This may be a justified or an unjustified claim, but it does not make the *philosophes* Christians.

"They dismantled heaven, somewhat prematurely it seems, since they retained their faith in the immortality of the soul." Damaging if true, but it is largely false. Montesquieu did not believe in the immortality of the soul, nor did Diderot, nor Hume, nor Helvétius, nor Holbach. Voltaire was far from unequivocal about immortality.[15] Rousseau "retained his faith" or rather claimed that he must believe in order to survive: his was a desperate personal need, by no means representative of the *philosophes*.

"They discussed atheism, but not before the servants."[16] This remark is patently derived from an anecdote told about Voltaire: one evening at supper (runs this story of doubtful authenticity) Voltaire interrupted his guests Condorcet and d'Alembert, who were voicing doubts of the existence of God, and sent the servants out of the room. "Continue your attack, gentlemen," Voltaire said after the three *philosophes* were alone. "I do not want my throat cut or my money stolen tonight." Two comments may be made on this anecdote: most of the *philosophes* of the early generation were not atheists, never claimed to be atheists, and only "discussed atheism" in order to refute it. This did not make them Christians, since their deism was a philosophical doctrine more than once removed from Christianity. Moreover, this anecdote does not concern religion as religion but religion as a social policeman. Whether the uneducated masses needed a supernatural religion to keep them under control was much debated in the Enlightenment, but surely this was a most utilitarian, a most un-Christian debate.

## II

In the second chapter of the *Heavenly City*, "The Laws of Nature and of Nature's God," Becker seeks to show that the *philosophes* belonged to the natural law tradition, that natural law is a significant link between the Christian and Enlightenment climates of opinion, but that the *philosophes* failed to recognize this link.

Becker rightly reminds us that the *philosophes* were not cynics; that their negations were far less important than their affirmations; that they were enthusiastic projectors, reformers, moralists; that their confidence in their ability to penetrate into the mysteries of the universe, and to prescribe effective remedies for social ills, was often exaggerated and sometimes naïve. The *philosophes* might not admit it, but their "childlike faith" was fundamentally Christian: the *philosophes* were the "secular bearers of the Protestant and Jansenist tradition"; their programs for peace and brotherhood were inspired by "the Christian ideal of service"; the words they coined—*bienfaisance, humanité*—were meant to "express in secular terms the Christian ideal of service." And this "childlike faith" was shared by nearly all the *philosophes*: "In the eighteenth century the words without which no enlightened person could

[15] He said more than once that while the case for immortality had not been proved, the contrary had not been proved either. I think that Voltaire did not believe that the soul survived the body.

[16] Becker's statements about the *philosophes* in this and the six preceding paragraphs are in the *Heavenly City*, pp. 30-31.

reach a restful conclusion were nature, natural law, first cause, reason. . . ." And again: "Nature and natural law—what magic these words held for the philosophical century!" This was the *philosophes'* true faith in reason: that they could read God's purposes in the book of nature, and that natural law expressed those purposes. "This is the new revelation, and thus at last we enter the secret door to knowledge."[17]

It is difficult to sort out what is true and what is false in this plausible account. I have suggested that the *philosophes* were not free from naïveté, but that is all, I think, that should be conceded. Historians and political theorists know that the natural law tradition is infinitely complex; to draw a map of its growth, its multiple ingredients, its changing modes and varied influence would be like drawing a map of the Nile Delta. Becker does nothing to clarify, and a great deal to confuse, the matter by lumping together, in the same paragraph and sometimes even in the same ironic exclamation, natural law and the appeal to nature. The appeal to nature, as Becker himself tells us with engaging candor, has been employed by most schools of thought. He mentions a most miscellaneous crew of thinkers, from Aristotle and Marcus Aurelius to Calvin, Montaigne, and Pascal. He might have added Burke, the great adversary of the *philosophes*. To say, then, that the *philosophes* appealed to nature is to say that they used this word to embody the standard by which they could judge existing institutions, morals, and forms of government. They were doing what most of their predecessors had done, and what most of their successors would do. What is notable about the Enlightenment, as Ernst Cassirer reminds us, is that "it returns again and again to the persistent problems of philosophy."[18]

The natural law tradition is much narrower than this appeal to nature. Becker's rather superficial discussion of natural law is based on two assumptions, neither of which is tenable. He suggests that natural law is essentially Christian. But natural law had originated with the Stoics and, in a less systematic form, with the Greeks. With the writings of Justus Lipsius and Grotius in the early seventeenth century, natural law was beginning to strip off its Christian associations—witness Grotius' celebrated assertion that nature would be orderly even if God did not exist. Christian natural law, even at its most rationalist in Aquinas' systematic theology, is part of a complex of laws (eternal, divine, natural, and human) all of which depend upon the wisdom of God. Modern natural law is secular, "profane," autonomous.

Moreover, Becker neglects the fact that many *philosophes* were reaching beyond even this secular natural law. Diderot still employed the conception of *droit naturel*, Vattel still carried on the seventeenth-century tradition of the natural lawyers, but other *philosophes*, following out the implications of British empiricism, were rejecting the natural law arguments in favor of utilitarianism. Inevitably there was much

---

[17] *Heavenly City*, pp. 46, 42, 41, 39, 47, and 51.

[18] *The Philosophy of the Enlightenment* (Princeton, 1951), p. 234. Even if we admit for the sake of argument that the *philosophes* had taken the materials of their philosophy from Christianity alone, what matters for the history of ideas is that they transformed these Christian ideas. "Grace was translated into virtue," writes Becker in the *Heavenly City*, p. 49. Is that not a significant translation? The *philosophes* "had only given another form and a new name to the object of worship: having denatured God, they deified nature" (*ibid.*, p. 63). Only? But the fact is that the sources of Enlightenment thought must not be sought in Christianity alone. When Becker writes, "A distinction between good and bad! Not a novel idea, certainly; on the contrary, a very old, a most Christian idea" (*ibid.*, p. 86), he might well have substituted the word *Stoic* for *Christian*. The relation of Stoicism to Enlightenment thought needs further elucidation: Stoicism entered modern philosophy not only directly, through the works of Marcus Aurelius and others, but indirectly, through the Stoic elements in Christian philosophy.

ambivalence and uncertainty concerning natural law in this time of transition.[19] But far from being uniform disciples of any natural law doctrine, the *philosophes* were providing a bridge to nineteenth-century utilitarianism and historicism. Bentham and Hegel are the philosophical heirs of Hume and Turgot: it is this real continuity between the eighteenth and nineteenth centuries that Becker neglects in favor of a fancied continuity between the Enlightenment and Christianity.[20]

Finally, Becker fails to distinguish between natural law as rhetoric and natural law as conviction: while most of the time he does not take the *philosophes* seriously enough, he takes their rhapsodic paeans to natural law too seriously. The *philosophes* were, above all, practical social reformers, and through their rhetoric we can sense their impatience to get to work. When Voltaire affirms that some moral rules are universally accepted, and that this proves the existence of natural law, and when Voltaire says briskly that "a day suffices for a sage to know the duties of man," he seems to be saying to his reader: "You and I know what is wrong in this society; you and I know what evils must be rooted out and what institutions must be changed; to split hairs about the fundamentals of morals is to escape responsibility, to substitute talk for action."[21] Social reform in the first half of the eighteenth century rested on philosophic positions no longer fully convincing even to its most fiery proponents. In overlooking this gap between talk and action, in taking the rhetoric of the *philosophes* as a literal transcription of their deepest convictions, Becker, while claiming to penetrate to fundamentals, only too often confines his analysis to the surface.

What then has become of Becker's thesis that the *philosophes* did not know what they were doing, and were rebuilding the old heavenly city, only with new materials? Without wishing to be paradoxical for the sake of paradox, let me suggest that Becker's formulation turns the truth upside down: the *philosophes* knew exactly what they were doing; they were building a new, earthly city. And in building it they used, along with much new material, some of the old Christian bricks. Far from being less modern than they knew, they were even more modern than they claimed.

### III

Becker's analysis of natural law is unphilosophical; his analysis of the relation of the *philosophes* to history is unhistorical. That does not make it any the less delightful: in the last two chapters Becker catches, with superb wit, a certain mood of the *philosophes*. His deft characterization of Mme. Roland weeping that she was not born a Roman, of Robespierre apostrophizing posterity; his apt quotation from Diderot, *"La postérité pour le philosophe, c'est l'autre monde de l'homme religieux"*—these

[19] Voltaire is perhaps the best example of this ambivalence. He continues to affirm the existence of natural law, but is uneasy with it. As an empiricist, as a disciple of Locke's philosophic "modesty," as a caricaturist of the *esprit de système*, he is driven to doubt the existence of a law in which he would like to believe. He solves the dilemma (unsatisfactorily) by arguing that there is empirical proof for the existence of a universal, uniform law of nature.

[20] Once again Becker can be quoted on the other side of his own argument. He describes eighteenth-century natural law: "Instead of being a construction of deductive logic, [it] is the observed harmonious behavior of material objects." "This," he says truly, "was a new kind of 'law of nature' " (*Heavenly City*, p. 57). But he fails to draw the necessary inferences from these observations.

[21] I do not have sufficient space to justify in detail my contention that Voltaire's advocacy of natural law was chiefly rhetorical. I refer the reader to my study of Voltaire's political ideas, *Voltaire's Politics: The Poet as Realist* (Princeton: Princeton University Press, 1959).

almost convince us that this anti-enthusiastic century was crowded with enthusiasts. As Becker says, the *philosophes'* aversion to enthusiasm was itself an enthusiasm.[22]

But—like Voltaire's Zadig (and, for that matter, like Becker himself) we are compelled to say "but" once again—while Becker's insights into the character of the *philosophes* are valuable, they are marginal rather than central, and Becker places too heavy a load upon his evidence.

Let me summarize his case: the sensationalism of the *philosophes*, first explored by Locke and extended by his disciples, was at first a heady and later a frightening prospect for them. If Locke was right, there was no total depravity. But if nature was good, whence evil? "How then could Philosophers say that all was somehow good in God's sight unless they could also say that there was no evil to be observed in the world of nature and man?" Pure reason confronted the *philosophes* with an "ugly dilemma, emerging from the beautiful premises of the new philosophy," and in order to escape this dilemma they turned from reason to history. "They found . . . that reason is amenable to treatment. They therefore tempered reason with sentiment, reasons of the heart that reason knows not of; or held in leash by experience, the universal judgment of mankind. . . ." Becker professes to observe a change of temper and ascribes it to fear. "The Philosophers *began to* cold-shoulder abstract reason. . . ." "The age of reason had scarcely run half its course before the Philosophers *were admitting* the feebleness of reason, *putting the ban on* flippancy, and *turning to* the study of useful, that is to say, factual, subjects." And Becker claims to see this historical development in the works of some of the leading *philosophes*, above all in Hume: "Hume's *turning away from* speculation to the study of history, economics, and politics was symptomatic of a certain change in the climate of opinion. . . ."[23]

It is doubtless fruitful to divide the Enlightenment into two periods. In the first half of the century, the *philosophes* were an embattled and socially inferior group; in the second half of the century, they were confident that they were winning the contest for public opinion and social prestige. In the first half of the century, the rhetoric of natural law had still been prevalent; in the second half, it was largely supplanted by utilitarianism. But for Becker's division—the shift from pure reason to reason softened by sentiment, from nonhistorical reason to historical reason—there is little convincing evidence. Diderot, in many respects the most representative of the *philosophes*, celebrated the passions in his earliest writings; Vauvenargues, one of Voltaire's favorite writers, warned against separating the intellect from the sentiments; Hume, developing his epistemology in the 1730s, gave the sentiments the precedence over reason.

Similarly, it cannot be shown that the *philosophes* "turned to" history because they were afraid of the implications of their godless rationalism. They wrote history as they wrote everything else: as men of letters they thought of history as a branch of literature. Voltaire wrote history—and very good history—as early as 1727-1728, when he began his *Histoire de Charles XII*, and his other historical masterpieces were conceived and partly written in the 1730s. Nor is there the slightest evidence that the

---

[22] *Heavenly City*, p. 37.
[23] *Heavenly City*, pp. 67, 69, 69-70, 83, and 84, my italics. Becker qualifies his case at one point: "I would not leave the impression that the Philosophers began to cold-shoulder abstract reason merely, or chiefly, because they found a logical dilemma in the path; still less that they embraced the cause of virtue with greater emotional warmth because they could find no ultimate reason for embracing it at all. There may be something in all that—I am inclined to think there is; but I do not wish to make too much of it" (*ibid.*, p. 83). But having said that he does not wish to make too much of it, he proceeds to make too much of it.

*philosophes* became more, rather than less, cautious: indeed, their daring grew with their successes. Deism was characteristic of the first half of the eighteenth century; a far bolder atheism was, if not characteristic, prevalent in the second half.[24]

Why should Becker have discovered a shift in the Enlightenment that did not exist? I suspect that he needed the shift to account for the *philosophes'* solution of their moral dilemma—how to explain evil in the face of an all-good nature. But the dilemma is as imaginary as its solution. Becker does well to remind us that the *philosophes'* contribution to theodicy was unimpressive. Perhaps, if God becomes unimportant it becomes equally unimportant to justify him. The *philosophes* viewed nature as good, but not as omnipotent: Rousseau was not the only one who held that human institutions could deprave man, that goodness could be thwarted, and that the original intentions of God could be perverted.[25] The *philosophes'* affirmation that man is by nature good does not mean that they could not account for the existence of evil, and Becker's case (that to the Enlightenment writers history provided a standard which philosophy had destroyed) falls to the ground.

While Becker rightly rejects the nineteenth-century charge that the Enlightenment was unhistorical, he accepts the charge that Enlightenment history was not "real" history but ideology. The Enlightenment historians

start out, under the banner of objectivity and with a flourish of scholarly trumpets, as if on a voyage of discovery in unknown lands. They start out; but in a very real sense they never pass the frontiers of the eighteenth century, never really enter the country of the past or of distant lands. They cannot afford to leave the battlefield of the present where they are so fully engaged in a life-and-death struggle with Christian philosophy and the infamous things that support it—superstition, intolerance, tyranny.[26]

Becker is equally harsh on nineteenth-century historians. The *philosophes*, he argues, wrote history in order to change society; the nineteenth-century historians wrote

[24] Becker's sketch of the *philosophe*-frightened-by-his-own-temerity-and-afraid-to-undermine-morality is incorrect in many details. Becker makes much of Hume's refusal to publish his masterly and radical *Dialogues Concerning Natural Religion* and attributes this refusal chiefly to the fact that Hume "took no pleasure in being regarded as the cold and finished skeptic, a destroyer of illusions. He was much more ambitious 'to be esteemed a man of virtue than a writer of taste'; and the fact that his history won for him the popularity he craved naturally confirmed him in the belief that it was useless to search into 'those corners of nature that spread a nuisance all around' " (*Heavenly City*, pp. 77-78). But the fact is that Hume was extremely eager to publish the *Dialogues* and had to be strongly dissuaded by his friends, notably Adam Smith. And Adam Smith was not afraid that Hume would destroy morality but that he would get into trouble. In the last year of his life, Hume revised the *Dialogues* once again and changed his will several times to make sure that they would be published after his death (since he was too ill to see them through the press himself) and published without being emasculated. See Norman Kemp Smith, "Introduction," Appendix C, *Hume's Dialogues Concerning Natural Religion* (Edinburgh, 2d ed., 1947), pp. 87-96. Becker's account of the development of Voltaire's philosophy is equally unconvincing.

[25] See Voltaire's little-known story *Songe de Platon*, in which he portrays the world as created by a minor angel who made it as good as he could—which is far from perfect. In their moral and religious writings, the *philosophes* sought to discredit the Christian doctrine of the fall of man, and their use of nature did not deprive them of a standard by which actions and institutions could be judged. It is only in the Marquis de Sade's perverted version of naturalism that we find the notion that nature speaks only in one voice and that everything possible or even imaginable is "natural." This is an interpretation of "natural" that the *philosophes* would not have accepted nor even understood.

[26] *Heavenly City*, p. 105.

history in order to keep society as it was.[27] His criticism of historians is therefore not one-sided. But it implies either that "objective" history is impossible, or that the *philosophes* fell short of writing good history. It was surely the first of these implications that Becker intended to stress, but it is the second that others have stressed in their disparagement of the *philosophes*.

I do not want to enter into the debate on the possibility of objective history here. I only want to point out that the criticism of Enlightenment historians can be overdone. Montesquieu, Voltaire, Hume, Robertson, Gibbon wrote better histories than their present-day reputations would indicate. Becker quotes two juicy morsels: "Mankind are so much the same, in all times and places, that history informs us of nothing new or strange in this particular. Its chief use is only to discover the constant and universal principles of human nature." Thus David Hume. "History is only a pack of tricks we play on the dead." Thus Voltaire, and it is easy to see why this should have been one of Carl Becker's favorite quotations. But if we look at Hume's history of England instead of this pronouncement on history, and if we look at Voltaire's masterpieces instead of this *bon mot* about history, we are impressed by their scrupulous concern for truth, their careful sifting of evidence, their intelligent selection of what is important, their keen sense of drama, their grasp of the fact that a whole civilization is a unit of study. What if Becker had quoted from the opening pages of the *Siècle de Louis XIV*, or from some of Voltaire's and Hume's correspondence about their historical works? These quotations might not have been as amusing or as telling as the words Becker actually quoted, but they might have been far more revealing about eighteenth-century histories.

It is perhaps a reflection of how intent Becker was to debunk Enlightenment historians that he makes a significant mistake. "The Philosophers felt that Montesquieu was too much enamored of facts as such to treat certain facts as harshly as they deserved, and it shocked them to see him dallying lightly with episodes that were no better than they should be. Voltaire (Voltaire of all people!) criticized Montesquieu for his *levity*. . . ." The *Esprit des lois* "left a bad taste in the mouths of the Philosophers because Montesquieu insisted that the 'constant and universal principles of human nature' were after all 'relative.' . . ."[28] The opposite is true: Voltaire and other *philosophes* admired Montesquieu, but criticized him because he a proponent of the *thèse nobiliaire,* a defender of the privileged *parlements.* They criticized him, in a word, because he was a conservative, and not because he was a relativist. Voltaire criticized Montesquieu, too, for being slipshod in his research, for accepting improbable travelers' tales; not for being "too much enamored of facts as such" but for being too little enamored of facts as such. When Voltaire (and why not Voltaire of all people?) accused Montesquieu of levity, he was referring to Montesquieu's gullibility.[29]

*IV*

But it is not mistakes such as these that really disappoint the reader in this charming book; the disappointment is, I think, more profound. The *Heavenly City,* as I have

---

[27] *Ibid..,* pp. 95-97.
[28] *Heavenly City,* pp. 100-101.
[29] For Voltaire's appreciation (inadequate) and criticisms (excessive) of Montesquieu, see *Commentaire sur l'Esprit des lois; Questions sur l'Encyclopédie,* article "Lois, esprit des"; *Pensées sur le gouvernement;* and *L'A.B.C.*

said, begins with a significant truth: history is concerned with the dialectical struggle between persistence and change. The eighteenth century is a century in which this struggle becomes peculiarly dramatic and complex, and the opportunities for fruitful research are great. Becker rightly urges the reader to ask searching questions, but continually suggests the wrong answers. He argues for persistence where there was change, and he argues for one kind of persistence when there was really another.

The *philosophes* lived in an epoch in which the vitality of Christianity was waning, and in which natural science, the centralized state, the development of industrial capitalism imposed the need for a new world view. In building their earthly city, the *philosophes* fashioned their materials from the most varied sources: Christianity, a revived Stoicism and Epicureanism, a pragmatic recognition of the needs of the new state and the new economy. In their battle for liberation from the old standards and in their search for new standards they experienced the difficulties that any individual struggling for autonomy must face. They contradicted themselves, they failed to see all the implications of their ideas, they sometimes used old words to describe new things, they sometimes used rhetoric that was inappropriate to their ideas. All these questions the *Heavenly City* resolves—wrongly, I believe—with the too simple formula of its title.

The failure of the book is all the more paradoxical in view of Becker's own position. His criticisms of the *philosophes* were from the inside; as Leo Gershoy has said, Carl Becker "had always remained a believer at heart. . . . He had rejoined Voltaire and Condorcet and Wells and all the goodly company who wished humanity well."[30] But in his impatience with his intellectual forebears—an impatience which is always so much greater with those whom you admire than with those you detest—he portrayed the *philosophes* as naïve, and as a little fraudulent. Becker was no conservative, but the conservative implications of the *Heavenly City* are plain.

The *Heavenly City* failed in another, and even more paradoxical, way—through its success. Carl Becker dedicated *Everyman His Own Historian* to those who had assisted him in clarifying his ideas, "chiefly by avoiding the error of Hway, a pupil of Confucius. Hway, said Confucius, is of no assistance to me; there is nothing that I say in which he does not delight." In the twenty-five years that the book has been before the public, the error of Hway has not been avoided. It is time we admitted that Carl Becker's critique of the *philosophes,* like Samuel Johnson's critique of Shakespeare, had every virtue save one, the virtue of being right.

---

[30] "Introduction," Carl Becker, *Progress and Power* (New York, 1949), p. xxxvii.

# ECONOMIC AND SOCIAL TRANSFORMATIONS

# 5 / Protestantism and the Rise of Capitalism: Max Weber and His Critics

There is a large literature of economic histories and monographs showing that from the thirteenth century onward, capitalism, although subordinate to other forms of social and economic organization, continually refined its techniques, produced new forms of economic enterprise, and mobilized larger and larger amounts of capital, so that by the beginnings of the Industrial Revolution modern capitalism is already visible in such institutions as factories, joint stock companies, banks of issue, and stock and commodity exchanges.

This period is called "early capitalism" by Werner Sombart, the distinguished German economic historian, to differentiate it from "full capitalism," a period he extends from the middle of the eighteenth century to the outbreak of World War I. In the earlier period, "the economic principles of capitalism are still struggling for recognition; traditionalism and the medieval idea of working merely for a livelihood still predominate." In the later period, the economic principles of capitalism "attain complete control and fashion all economic relationships." Moreover, they "penetrate gradually into other cultural spheres, reaching even those which are only remotely connected with economic life."[1]

The origins of this triumph of capitalism, as Professor R. H. Tawney tells us in the first selection below, have been conventionally explained as due to changes in "the character of the economic environment." For the German sociologist Max Weber, however, with whose work we are primarily concerned here, these origins were to be found in the triumph of a capitalist spirit, or ethos. Following Sombart's periodization and his hypothesis that a spirit of capitalism (which Weber was later to redefine) was an element in the triumph of capitalism, Weber looked at the beginnings of capitalism in the Middle Ages and found the prevalent ethic hostile to it. By the middle of the eighteenth century, however, he noted that capitalism had found a moral climate that was widespread and congenial. The specific historical problem to which Weber addressed himself was to fix the moment of this shift, or to put it another way, to describe the origins of the capitalist ethos. Impressed by the more developed state of capitalism in the Protestant countries, he was led to find the origins of its ethos in the concept of "the calling" taught by the early Protestant reformers, most notably Calvin, and in the interpretation and diffusion of this concept by Calvinist divines of the seventeenth and eighteenth centuries, whose followers were drawn largely from the business and artisan classes.

[1] Werner Sombart, "Capitalism," *Encyclopaedia of the Social Sciences,* Vol. III (New York: The Macmillan Company, 1930), pp. 198, 206.

As the selections presented will show, Weber's thesis has generated a long and lively historical controversy. The first selection, taken from Professor Tawney's foreword to the English translation of Weber's *Die Protestantische Ethik und der Geist des Kapitalismus,* gives a summary of the Weber thesis as well as an evaluation of it after twenty-five years, which reflects some of the corrections Professor Tawney brought to it earlier in his own study. *Religion and the Rise of Capitalism,* itself a landmark in the controversy. The second selection shows Weber at work defining the spirit of capitalism and in the process carefully anticipating attacks on his thesis. The third selection comes from Father V.A. Demant, one of the outstanding students of the roles of religion and capitalism in our present-day society. It gives a convenient summary of the controversy over the Weber thesis and the most recent consensus on it.

# MAX WEBER: AN EVALUATION

### R. H. Tawney

Max Weber . . . was a scholar whose intellectual range was unusually wide, and whose personality made an even deeper impression than his learning on those privileged to know him. He had been trained as a jurist, and, in addition to teaching as a professor at Freiburg, Heidelberg, and Munich, he wrote on subjects so various as ancient agrarian history, the conditions of the rural population of Prussia, the methodology of the social sciences, and the sociology of religion. Nor were his activities exclusively those of the teacher and the student. He travelled widely, was keenly interested in contemporary political and social movements, played a vigorous and disinterested part in the crisis which confronted Germany at the close of the War, and accompanied the German delegation to Versailles in May 1919. He died in Munich in the following year, at the age of fifty-six. Partly as a result of prolonged ill-health, which compelled him for several years to lead the life of an invalid, partly because of his premature death, partly, perhaps, because of the very grandeur of the scale on which he worked, he was unable to give the final revision to many of his writings. His collected works have been published posthumously. The last of them, based on notes taken by his students from lectures given at Munich, has appeared in English under the title of *General Economic History*.[1]

*The Protestant Ethic and the Spirit of Capitalism* was published in the form of two articles in the *Archiv für Sozialwissenschaft und Sozialpolitik* in 1904 and 1905. Together with a subsequent article, which appeared in 1906, on *The Protestant Sects and the Spirit of Capitalism*, they form the first of the studies contained in Weber's *Gesammelte Aufsätze zur Religionssoziologie.* On their first appearance they aroused an interest which extended beyond the ranks of historical specialists, and which caused the numbers of the *Archiv* in which they were published to be sold out with a rapidity not very usual in the case of learned publications. The discussion which they provoked has continued since then with undiminished vigour. For the questions raised by Weber possess a universal significance, and the method of his essay was as important as its conclusions. It not only threw a brilliant light on the particular field which it explored, but suggested a new avenue of approach to a range of problems of permanent interest, which concern, not merely the historian and the economist, but all who reflect on the deeper issues of modern society.

The question which Weber attempts to answer is simple and fundamental. It is that of the psychological conditions which made possible the development of capitalist civilization. Capitalism, in the sense of great individual undertakings, involving the

---

[1] Max Weber, *General Economic History* (trans. Frank H. Knight, Ph.D.) (London: George Allen & Unwin, Ltd., 1927). A bibliography of Weber's writings is printed at the end of the charming and instructive account of him by his widow, Marianna Weber, *Max Weber, Ein Lebensbild* (Tubingen: J. C. B. Mohr, 1926). See also Maurice Halbwachs, "Economistes et historiens: Max Weber, un homme, une oeuvre," in *Annales d'Histoire Économique et Sociale,* January 1929, No. 1.

control of large financial resources, and yielding riches to their masters as a result of speculation, money-lending, commercial enterprise, buccaneering and war, is as old as history. Capitalism, as an economic system, resting on the organization of legally free wage-earners, for the purpose of pecuniary profit, by the owner of capital or his agents, and setting its stamp on every aspect of society, is a modern phenomenon.

All revolutions are declared to be natural and inevitable, once they are successful, and capitalism, as the type of economic system prevailing in Western Europe and America, is clothed to-day with the unquestioned respectability of the triumphant fact. But in its youth it was a pretender, and it was only after centuries of struggle that its title was established. For it involved a code of economic conduct and a system of human relations which were sharply at variance with venerable conventions, with the accepted scheme of social ethics, and with the law, both of the church and of most European states. So questionable an innovation demanded of the pioneers who first experimented with it as much originality, self-confidence, and tenacity of purpose as is required to-day of those who would break from the net that it has woven. What influence nerved them to defy tradition? From what source did they derive the principles to replace it?

The conventional answer to these questions is to deny their premises. The rise of new forms of economic enterprise was the result, it is argued, of changes in the character of the economic environment. It was due to the influx of the precious metals from America in the sixteenth century, to the capital accumulated in extra-European commerce, to the reaction of expanding markets on industrial organisation, to the growth of population, to technological improvements made possible by the progress of natural science. Weber's reply, which is developed at greater length in his *General Economic History* than in the present essay, is that such explanations confuse causes and occasions. Granted that the economic conditions of the sixteenth and seventeenth centuries were, in some respects, though by no means in all, unusually favourable to an advance in economic technique, such conditions had existed from time to time in the past without giving birth to the development of capitalist industry. In many of the regions affected by them no such development took place, nor were those which enjoyed the highest economic civilization necessarily those in which the new order found its most congenial environment. The France of Louis XIV commanded resources which, judged by the standards of the age, were immense, but they were largely dissipated in luxury and war. The America of the eighteenth century was economically primitive, but it is in the maxims of Franklin that the spirit of bourgeois capitalism, which, rather than the grandiose schemes of mercantilist statesmen, was to dominate the future, finds, Weber argues, its naivest and most lucid expression.

To appeal, as an explanation, to the acquisitive instincts, is even less pertinent, for there is little reason to suppose that they have been more powerful during the last few centuries than in earlier ages. "The notion that our rationalistic and capitalistic age is characterised by a stronger economic interest than other periods is childish. The moving spirits of modern capitalism are not possessed of a stronger economic impulse than, for example, an Oriental trader. The unchaining of the economic interest, merely as such, has produced only irrational results: such men as Cortes and Pizarro, who were, perhaps, its strongest embodiment, were far from having an idea of a rationalistic economic life.'[2] The word *rationalism* is used by Weber as a term of art, to describe an economic system based, not on custom or tradition, but on the deliberate and

[2] Weber, *op. cit.*, pp. 355-356.

systematic adjustment of economic means to the attainment of the objective of pecuniary profit. The question is why this temper triumphed over the conventional attitude which had regarded the *appetitus divitiarum infinitus*—the unlimited lust for gain—as anti-social and immoral. His answer is that it was the result of movements which had their source in the religious revolution of the sixteenth century.

Weber wrote as a scholar, not as a propagandist, and there is no trace in his work of the historical animosities which still warp discussions of the effects of the Reformation. Professor Pirenne,[3] in an illuminating essay, has argued that social progress springs from below, and that each new phase of economic development is the creation, not of strata long in possession of wealth and power, but of classes which rise from humble origins to build a new structure on obscure foundations. The thesis of Weber is somewhat similar. The pioneers of the modern economic order were, he argues, *parvenus*, who elbowed their way to success in the teeth of the established aristocracy of land and commerce. The tonic that braced them for the conflict was a new conception of religion, which taught them to regard the pursuit of wealth as, not merely an advantage, but a duty. This conception welded into a disciplined force the still feeble *bourgeoisie*, heightened its energies, and cast a halo of sanctification round its convenient vices. What is significant, in short, is not the strength of the motive of economic self-interest, which is the commonplace of all ages and demands no explanation. It is the change of moral standards which converted a natural frailty into an ornament of the spirit, and canonized as the economic virtues habits which in earlier ages had been denounced as vices. The force which produced it was the creed associated with the name of Calvin. Capitalism was the social counterpart of Calvinist theology.

The central idea to which Weber appeals in confirmation of his theory is expressed in the characteristic phrase "a calling." For Luther, as for most mediaeval theologians, it had normally meant the state of life in which the individual had been set by Heaven, and against which it was impious to rebel. To the Calvinist, Weber argues, the calling is not a condition in which the individual is born, but a strenuous and exacting enterprise to be chosen by himself, and to be pursued with a sense of religious responsibility. Baptized in the bracing, if icy, waters of Calvinist theology, the life of business, once regarded as perilous to the soul—*summe periculosa est emptionis et venditionis negotiatio*—acquires a new sanctity. Labour is not merely an economic means: it is a spiritual end. Covetousness, if a danger to the soul, is a less formidable menace than sloth. So far from there being an inevitable conflict between money-making and piety, they are natural allies, for the virtues incumbent on the elect—diligence, thrift, sobriety, prudence—are the most reliable passport to commercial prosperity. Thus the pursuit of riches, which once had been feared as the enemy of religion, was now welcomed as its ally. The habits and institutions in which that philosophy found expression survived long after the creed which was their parent had expired, or had withdrawn from Europe to more congenial climes. If capitalism begins as the practical idealism of the aspiring *bourgeoisie*, it ends, Weber suggests in his concluding pages, as an orgy of materialism.

In England the great industry grew by gradual increments over a period of centuries, and, since the English class system had long been based on differences of wealth, not of juristic status, there was no violent contrast between the legal foundations of the old order and the new. Hence in England the conception of capitalism as a distinct and

---

[3] Henri Pirenne, *Les Périodes de l'histoire sociale du capitalisme* (Brussels: Hayez, 1914).

peculiar phase of social development has not readily been accepted. It is still possible for writers, who in their youth have borne with equanimity instruction on the meaning of feudalism, to dismiss capitalism as an abstraction of theorists or a catchword of politicians.

The economic history of the Continent has moved by different stages from that of England, and the categories employed by Continental thinkers have accordingly been different. In France, where the site on which the modern economic system was to be erected was levelled by a cataclysm, and in Germany, which passed in the fifty years between 1850 and 1900 through a development that in England had occupied two hundred, there has been little temptation to question that capitalist civilization is a phenomenon differing, not merely in degree, but in kind, from the social order preceding it. It is not surprising, therefore, that its causes and characteristics should have been one of the central themes of historical study in both. The discussion began with the epoch-making work of Marx, who was greater as a sociologist than as an economic theorist, and continues unabated. Its most elaborate monument is Sombart's *Der Moderne Kapitalismus.*

The first edition of Sombart's book appeared in 1902. Weber's articles, of which the first was published two years later, were a study of a single aspect of the same problem. A whole literature[4] has arisen on the subject discussed in them. How does Weber's thesis stand to-day, after a quarter of a century of research and criticism?

The interpretation of religious beliefs and social institutions as different expressions of a common psychological attitude, which Weber elaborated in his *Aufsätze zur Religionssociologie,* is no longer so novel as when he advanced it. Once stated, indeed, it has the air of a platitude. The capacity of human beings to departmentalize themselves is surprising, but it is not unlimited. It is obvious that, in so far as doctrines as to man's place in the universe are held with conviction, they will be reflected in the opinions formed of the nature of the social order most conducive to well-being, and that the habits moulded by the pressure of the economic environment will in turn set their stamp on religion. Nor can Weber's contention be disputed that Calvinism, at least in certain phases of its history, was associated with an attitude to questions of social ethics which contemporaries regarded as peculiarly its own. Its critics attacked it as the sanctimonious ally of commercial sharp practice. Its admirers applauded it as the school of the economic virtues. By the middle of the seventeenth century the

---

[4] See, in particular, the following: E. Troeltsch, *Die Sozialen Lehren der christlichen Kirchen und Gruppen* (1912); F. Rachfahl, "Kalvinismus und Kapitalismus," *Internationale Wochenschrift,* i. III, 1909; B. L. Brentano, *Die Anfänge des Modernen Kapitalismus* (1916) and *Der Wirthschaftende Mensch in der Geschichte* (1911); W. Sombart, *Die Juden und das Wirthschaftsleben* (1911. English trans. *The Jews and Modern Capitalism,* 1913), and *Der Bourgeois* (1913. English trans. *The Quintessence of Modern Capitalism,* 1915); G. v. Schulze-Gaevernitz, "Die Geistesgeschichtlichen Grundlagen der Anglo-Amerikanischen Weltsuprematie. III. Die Wirthschaftsethik des Kapitalismus," in *Archiv für Sozialwissenschaft und Sozialpolitik,* Bd. 61, Heft 2; H. Sée, "Dans quelle mesure Puritains et Juifs ont-ils contribué au progrès du capitalisme moderne?" *Revue Historique,* Vol. CLV, 1927, and *Les Origines du capitalisme moderne* (1926); M. Halbwachs, "Les Origines Puritaines du capitalisme moderne," *Revue d'Histoire et Philosophie Réligieuses,* March-April 1925 and "Économistes et historiens: Max Weber, une vie, une oeuvre," *Annales d'Histoire Économique et Sociale,* No. 1, January 1929; H. Hauser, *Les Débuts du capitalisme moderne* (1927); H. G. Wood, "The Influence of the Reformation on Ideas Concerning Wealth and Property," in *Property, Its Rights and Duties* (1913); Talcott Parsons, "Capitalism in Recent German Literature," *Journal of Political Economy,* December 1928 and February 1929; Frank H. Knight, "Historical and Theoretical Issues in the Problem of Modern Capitalism," *Journal of Economic and Business History,* November 1928; Kemper Fulberton, "Calvinism and Capitalism," *Harvard Theological Review,* July 1928.

contrast between the social conservatism of Catholic Europe and the strenuous enterprise of Calvinist communities had become a commonplace. "There is a kind of natural inaptness," wrote a pamphleteer in 1671, "in the Popish religion to business, whereas, on the contrary, among the Reformed, the greater their zeal, the greater their inclination to trade and industry, as holding idleness unlawful." The influence of Calvinism was frequently adduced as one explanation of the economic prosperity of Holland. The fact that in England the stronghold of Nonconformity was the commercial classes was an argument repeatedly advanced for tolerating Nonconformists.

In emphasizing, therefore, the connection between religious radicalism and economic progress, Weber called attention to an interesting phenomenon, at which previous writers had hinted, but which none had yet examined with the same wealth of learning and philosophical insight. The significance to be ascribed to it, and, in particular, the relation of Calvinist influences to the other forces making for economic innovation, is a different and more difficult question. His essay was confined to the part played by religious movements in creating conditions favourable to the growth of a new type of economic civilization, and he is careful to guard himself against the criticism that he underestimates the importance of the parallel developments in the world of commerce, finance, and industry. It is obvious, however, that, until the latter have been examined, it is not possible to determine the weight to be assigned to the former. It is arguable, at least, that, instead of Calvinism producing the spirit of Capitalism, both would with equal plausibility be regarded as different effects of changes in economic organisation and social structure.

It is the temptation of one who expounds a new and fruitful idea to use it as a key to unlock all doors, and to explain by reference to a single principle phenomena which are, in reality, the result of several converging causes. Weber's essay is not altogether free, perhaps, from the defects of its qualities. It appears occasionally to be somewhat over-subtle in ascribing to intellectual and moral influences developments which were the result of more prosaic and mundane forces, and which appeared, irrespective of the character of religious creeds, wherever external conditions offered them a congenial environment. *Capitalism* itself is an ambiguous, if indispensable, word, and Weber's interpretation of it seems sometimes to be open to the criticism of Professor Sée,[5] that he simplifies and limits its meaning to suit the exigencies of his argument. There was no lack of the "capitalist spirit" in the Venice and Florence of the fourteenth century, or in the Antwerp of the fifteenth. Its development in Holland and England, it might not unreasonably be argued, had less to do with the fact that they, or certain social strata in them, accepted the Calvinist version of the Reformation, than with large economic movements and the social changes produced by them. "Ce que MM. Weber et Troeltsch," writes Professor Pirenne,[6] "prennent pour l'esprit Calviniste, c'est précisément l'esprit des hommes nouveaux que la révolution économique du temps introduit dans la vie des affaires, et qui s'y opposent aux traditionalistes auxquels ils se substituent." Why insist that causation can work in only one direction? Is it not a little artificial to suggest that capitalist enterprise had to wait, as Weber appears to imply, till religious changes had produced a capitalist spirit? Would it not be equally plausible, and equally one-sided, to argue that the religious changes were themselves merely the result of economic movements?

[5] Sée, "Dans quelle mesure Puritains et Juifs ont-ils contribué au progrès du capitalisme moderne?" *op. cit.*

[6] Pirenne, *op. cit.*

If Weber, as was natural in view of his approach to the problem, seems to lay in the present essay somewhat too exclusive an emphasis upon intellectual and ethical forces, his analysis of those forces themselves requires, perhaps, to be supplemented. Brentano's criticism, that the political thought of the Renaissance was as powerful a solvent of conventional restraints as the teaching of Calvin, is not without weight. In England, at any rate, the speculations of business men and economists as to money, prices, and the foreign exchanges, which were occasioned by the recurrent financial crises of the sixteenth century and by the change in the price level, were equally effective in undermining the attitude which Weber called traditionalism. Recent studies of the development of economic thought suggest that the change of opinion on economic ethics ascribed to Calvinism was by no means confined to it, but was part of a general intellectual movement, which was reflected in the outlook of Catholic, as well as Protestant, writers. Nor was the influence of Calvinist teaching itself so uniform in character, or so undeviating in tendency, as might be inferred by the reader of Weber's essay. On the contrary, it varied widely from period to period and country to country, with differences of economic conditions, social tradition, and political environment. It looked to the past as well as to the future. If in some of its phases it was on the side of change, in others it was conservative.

Most of Weber's illustrations of his thesis are drawn from the writings of English Puritans of the latter part of the seventeenth century. It is their teaching which supplies him with the materials for his picture of the pious *bourgeois* conducting his business as a calling to which Providence has summoned the elect. Whether the idea conveyed by the word *calling* is so peculiar to Calvinism as Weber implies is a question for theologians; but the problem, it may be suggested, is considerably more complex than his treatment of it suggests. For three generations of economic development and political agitation lay between these writers and the author of the *Institutes*. The Calvinism which fought the English Civil War, still more the Calvinism which won an uneasy toleration at the Revolution, was not that of its founder.

Calvin's own ideal of social organization is revealed by the system which he erected at Geneva. It had been a theocracy administered by a dictatorship of ministers. In "the most perfect school of Christ ever seen on earth since the day of the Apostles," the rule of life had been an iron collectivism. A godly discipline had been the aim of Knox, of the Reformed Churches in France, and of the fathers of the English Presbyterian Movement; while a strict control of economic enterprise had been the policy first pursued by the saints in New England. The Calvinism, both of England and Holland, in the seventeenth century, had found its way to a different position. It had discovered a compromise in which a juster balance was struck between prosperity and salvation, and, while retaining the theology of the master, it repudiated his scheme of social ethics. Persuaded that "godliness hath the promise of this life, as well as of the life to come," it resisted, with sober intransigence, the interference in matters of business both of the state and of divines. It is this second, individualistic phase of Calvinism, rather than the remorseless rigours of Calvin himself, which may plausibly be held to have affinities with the temper called by Weber "the spirit of Capitalism." The question which needs investigation is that of the causes which produced a change of attitude so convenient to its votaries and so embarrassing to their pastors.

It is a question which raises issues that are not discussed at length in Weber's essay, though, doubtless, he was aware of them. Taking as his theme, not the conduct of Puritan capitalists, but the doctrines of Puritan divines, he pursues a single line of inquiry with masterly ingenuity. His conclusions are illuminating; but they are susceptible, it may perhaps be held, of more than one interpretation. There was action and reaction, and, while Puritanism helped to mould the social order, it was, in its turn, moulded by it. It is instructive to trace, with Weber, the influence of religious ideas on economic development. It is not less important to grasp the effect of the economic arrangements accepted by an age on the opinion which it holds of the province of religion.


# THE SPIRIT OF CAPITALISM

**Max Weber**


In the title of this study is used the somewhat pretentious phrase, the *spirit* of capitalism. What is to be understood by it? The attempt to give anything like a definition of it brings out certain difficulties which are in the very nature of this type of investigation.

If any object can be found to which this term can be applied with any understandable meaning, it can only be an historical individual, i.e., a complex of elements associated in historical reality which we unite into a conceptual whole from the standpoint of their cultural significance.

Such an historical concept, however, since it refers in its content to a phenomenon significant for its unique individuality, cannot be defined according to the formula *genus proximum, differentia specifica,* but it must be gradually put together out of the individual parts which are taken from historical reality to make it up. Thus the final and definitive concept cannot stand at the beginning of the investigation, but must come at the end. We must, in other words, work out in the course of the discussion, as its most important result, the best conceptual formulation of what we here understand by the spirit of capitalism, that is the best from the point of view which interests us here. This point of view (the one of which we shall speak later) is, further, by no means the only possible one from which the historical phenomena we are investigating can be analysed. Other standpoints would, for this as for every historical phenomenon, yield other characteristics as the essential ones. The result is that it is by no means necessary to understand by the spirit of capitalism only what it will come to mean to *us* for the purposes of our analysis. This is a necessary result of the nature of historical concepts which attempt for their methodological purposes not to grasp historical reality in abstract general formulae, but in concrete genetic sets of relations which are inevitably of a specifically unique and individual character.

Thus, if we try to determine the object, the analysis and historical explanation of which we are attempting, it cannot be in the form of a conceptual definition, but at least in the beginning only a provisional description of what is here meant by the spirit of capitalism. Such a description is, however, indispensable in order clearly to understand the object of the investigation. For this purpose we turn to a document of that spirit which contains what we are looking for in almost classical purity, and at the same time has the advantage of being free from all direct relationship to religion, being thus, for our purposes, free of preconceptions.

Remember, that *time* is money. He that can earn ten shillings a day by his labour, and goes abroad, or sits idle, one half of that day, though he spends but sixpence during his diversion or idleness, ought not to reckon *that* the only expense; he has really spent, or rather thrown away, five shillings besides.

Remember, that *credit* is money. If a man lets his money lie in my hands after it is due, he gives me the interest, or so much as I can make of it during that time. This amounts to a considerable sum where a man has good and large credit, and makes good use of it.

Remember, that money is of the prolific, generating nature. Money can beget money, and its offspring can beget more, and so on. Five shillings turned is six, turned again it is seven and threepence, and so on, till it becomes a hundred pounds. The more there is of it, the more it produces every turning, so that the profits rise quicker and quicker. He that kills a breeding-sow, destroys all her offspring to the thousandth generation. He that murders a crown, destroys all that it might have produced, even scores of pounds.

Remember this saying, *The good paymaster is lord of another man's purse.* He that is known to pay punctually and exactly to the time he promises, may at any time, and on any occasion, raise all the money his friends can spare. This is sometimes of great use. After industry and frugality, nothing contributes more to the raising of a young man in the world than punctuality and justice in all his dealings; therefore never keep borrowed money an hour beyond the time you promised, lest a disappointment shut up your friend's purse for ever.

The most trifling actions that affect a man's credit are to be regarded. The sound of your hammer at five in the morning, or eight at night, heard by a creditor, makes him easy six months longer; but if he sees you at a billiard-table, or hears your voice at a tavern, when you should be at work, he sends for his money the next day; demands it, before he can receive it, in a lump.

It shows, besides, that you are mindful of what you owe; it makes you appear a careful as well as an honest man, and that still increases your credit.

Beware of thinking all your own that you possess, and of living accordingly. It is a mistake that many people who have credit fall into. To prevent this, keep an exact account for some time both of your expenses and your income. If you take the pains at first to mention particulars, it will have this good effect: you will discover how wonderfully small, trifling expenses mount up to large sums, and will discern what might have been, and may for the future be saved, without occasioning any great inconvenience.

For six pounds a year you may have the use of one hundred pounds, provided you are a man of known prudence and honesty.

He that spends a groat a day idly, spends idly above six pounds a year, which is the price for the use of one hundred pounds.

He that wastes idly a groat's worth of his time per day, one day with another, wastes the privilege of using one hundred pounds each day.

He that idly loses five shillings' worth of time, loses five shillings, and might as prudently throw five shillings into the sea.

He that loses five shillings, not only loses that sum, but all the advantage that might be made by turning it in dealing, which by the time that a young man becomes old, will amount to a considerable sum of money.

It is Benjamin Franklin who preaches to us in these sentences, the same which Ferdinand Kurnberger satirizes in his clever and malicious *Picture of American Culture* as the supposed confession of faith of the Yankee. That it is the spirit of capitalism which here speaks in characteristic fashion, no one will doubt, however little we may wish to claim that everything which could be understood as pertaining to that spirit is contained in it. Let us pause a moment to consider this passage, the philosophy of which Kurnberger sums up in the words, "They make tallow out of cattle and money out of men." The peculiarity of this philosophy of avarice appears to be the ideal of the honest man of recognized credit, and above all the idea of a duty of the individual toward the increase of his capital, which is assumed as an end in itself. Truly what is here preached is not simply a means of making one's way in the world, but a peculiar ethic. The infraction of its rules is treated not as foolishness but as forgetfulness of duty. That is the essence of the matter. It is not mere business astuteness, that sort of thing is common enough, it is an ethos. *This* is the quality which interests us.

When Jacob Fugger, in speaking to a business associate who had retired and who wanted to persuade him to do the same, since he had made enough money and should let others have a chance, rejected that as pusillanimity and answered that "he [Fugger] thought otherwise, he wanted to make money as long as he could," the spirit of his statement is evidently quite different from that of Franklin. What in the former case was an expression of commercial daring and personal inclination morally neutral, in the latter takes on the character of an ethically coloured maxim for the conduct of life. The concept spirit of capitalism is here used in this specific sense, it is the spirit of modern capitalism. For that we are here dealing only with Western European and American capitalism is obvious from the way in which the problem was stated. Capitalism existed in China, India, Babylon, in the classic world, and in the Middle Ages. But in all these cases, as we shall see, this particular ethos was lacking.

Now, all Franklin's moral attitudes are coloured with utilitarianism. Honesty is useful, because it assures credit; so are punctuality, industry, frugality, and that is the reason they are virtues. A logical deduction from this would be that where, for instance, the appearance of honesty serves the same purpose, that would suffice, and an unnecessary surplus of this virtue would evidently appear to Franklin's eyes as unproductive waste. And as a matter of fact, the story in his autobiography of his conversion to those virtues, or the discussion of the value of a strict maintenance of the appearance of modesty, the assiduous belittlement of one's own deserts in order to gain general recognition later, confirms this impression. According to Franklin, those virtues, like all others, are only in so far virtues as they are actually useful to the individual, and the surrogate of mere appearance is always sufficient when it accomplishes the end in view. It is a conclusion which is inevitable for strict utilitarianism. The impression of many Germans that the virtues professed by Americanism are pure hypocrisy seems to have been confirmed by this striking case. But in fact the matter is not by any means so simple. Benjamin Franklin's own character, as it appears in the really unusual candidness of his autobiography, belies that suspicion. The circumstance that he ascribes his recognition of the utility of virtue to a divine revelation which was intended to lead him in the path of righteousness, shows that something more than mere garnishing for purely egocentric motives is involved.

In fact, the *summum bonum* of this ethic, the earning of more and more money, combined with the strict avoidance of all spontaneous enjoyment of life, is above all completely devoid of any eudaemonistic, not to say hedonistic, admixture. It is thought of so purely as an end in itself, that from the point of view of the happiness of, or utility to, the single individual, it appears entirely transcendental and absolutely irrational. Man is dominated by the making of money, by acquisition as the ultimate purpose of his life. Economic acquisition is no longer subordinated to man as the means for the satisfaction of his material needs. This reversal of what we should call the natural relationship, so irrational from a naive point of view, is evidently as definitely a leading principle of capitalism as it is foreign to all peoples not under capitalistic influence. At the same time it expresses a type of feeling which is closely connected with certain religious ideas. If we thus ask, *why* should "money be made out of men," Benjamin Franklin himself, although he was a colourless deist, answers in his autobiography with a quotation from the Bible, which his strict Calvinistic father drummed into him again and again in his youth: "Seest thou a man diligent in his business? He shall stand before kings" (Prov. XXIII.29). The earning of money within the modern economic order is, so long as it is done legally, the result and the expression of virtue and proficiency in a calling; and this virtue and proficiency are, as it is now not difficult to see, the real Alpha and Omega of Franklin's ethic, as expressed in the passages we have quoted, as well as in all his works without exception.

And in truth this peculiar idea, so familiar to us to-day, but in reality so little a matter of course, of one's duty in a calling, is what is most characteristic of the social ethic of capitalistic culture, and is in a sense the fundamental basis of it. It is an obligation which the individual is supposed to feel and does feel towards the content of his professional activity, no matter in what it consists, in particular no matter whether it appears on the surface as a utilization of his personal powers, or only of his material possessions (as capital).

Of course, this conception has not appeared only under capitalistic conditions. On the contrary, we shall later trace its origins back to a time previous to the advent of capitalism. Still less, naturally, do we maintain that a conscious acceptance of these ethical maxims on the part of the individuals, entrepreneurs or labourers, in modern capitalistic enterprises, is a condition of the further existence of present-day capitalism. The capitalistic economy of the present day is an immense cosmos into which the individual is born, and which presents itself to him, at least as an individual, as an unalterable order of things in which he must live. It forces the individual, in so far as he is involved in the system of market relationships, to conform to capitalistic rules of action. The manufacturer who in the long run acts counter to these norms, will just as inevitably be eliminated from the economic scene as the worker who cannot or will not adapt himself to them will be thrown into the streets without a job.

Thus the capitalism of to-day, which has come to dominate economic life, educates and selects the economic subjects which it needs through a process of economic survival of the fittest. But here one can easily see the limits of the concept of selection as a means of historical explanation. In order that a manner of life so well adapted to the peculiarities of capitalism could be selected at all, i.e., should come to dominate others, it had to originate somewhere, and not in isolated individuals alone, but as a way of life common to whole groups of men. This origin is what really needs explanation. Concerning the doctrine of the more naive historical materialism, that such ideas originate as a reflection or superstructure of economic situations, we shall speak more in detail below. At this point it will suffice for our purpose to call attention to the fact that without doubt, in the country of Benjamin Franklin's birth (Massachusetts), the spirit of capitalism (in the sense we have attached to it) was present before the capitalistic order. There were complaints of a peculiarly calculating sort of profit-seeking in New England, as distinguished from other parts of America, as early as 1632. It is further undoubted that capitalism remained far less developed in some of the neighbouring colonies, the later Southern States of the United States of America, in spite of the fact that these latter were founded by large capitalists for business motives, while the New England colonies were founded by preachers and seminary graduates with the help of small bourgeois, craftsmen and yeomen, for religious reasons. In this case the causal relation is certainly the reverse of that suggested by the materialistic standpoint.

But the origin and history of such ideas is much more complex than the theorists of the superstructure suppose. The spirit of capitalism, in the sense in which we are using the term, had to fight its way to supremacy against a whole world of hostile forces. A state of mind such as that expressed in the passages we have quoted from Franklin, and which called forth the applause of a whole people, would both in ancient times and in the Middle Ages have been proscribed as the lowest sort of avarice and as an attitude entirely lacking in self-respect. It is, in fact, still regularly thus looked upon by all those social groups which are least involved in or adapted to modern capitalistic conditions. This is not wholly because the instinct of acquisition was in those times unknown or undeveloped, as has often been said. Nor because the *auri sacra fames,* the greed for gold, was then, or now, less powerful outside of bourgeois capitalism than within its peculiar sphere, as the illusions of modern romanticists are wont to believe. The difference between the capitalistic and pre-capitalistic spirits is not to be found at this point. The greed of the Chinese Mandarin, the old Roman aristocrat, or the modern peasant can stand up to any comparison. And the *auri sacra fames* of a Neapolitan cab-driver or *barcaiuolo,* and certainly of Asiatic representatives of similar trades, as well as of the craftsmen of southern European or Asiatic countries, is, as anyone can find out for himself, very much more intense, and especially more unscrupulous than that of, say, an Englishman in similar circumstances.

The universal reign of absolute unscrupulousness in the pursuit of selfish interests by the making of money has been a specific characteristic of precisely those countries whose bourgeois-capitalistic development, measured according to Occidental standards, has remained backward. As every employer knows, the lack of *coscienziosità* of the labourers of such countries, for instance Italy as compared with Germany, has been, and to a certain extent still is, one of the principal obstacles to their capitalistic development. Capitalism cannot make use of the labour of those who practise the doctrine of undisciplined *liberum arbitrium,* any more than it can make use of the business man who seems absolutely unscrupulous in his dealings with others, as we can learn from Franklin. Hence the difference does not lie in the degree of development of any impulse to make money. The *auri sacra fames* is as old as the history of man. But we shall see that those who submitted to it without reserve as an uncontrolled impulse, such as the Dutch sea-captain who "would go through hell for gain, even though he scorched his sails," were by no means the representatives of that attitude of mind from which the specifically modern capitalistic spirit as a mass phenomenon is derived, and that is what matters. At all periods of history, wherever it was possible, there has been ruthless acquisition, bound to no ethical norms whatever. Like war and piracy, trade has often been unrestrained in its relations with foreigners and those outside the group. The double ethic has permitted here what was forbidden in dealings among brothers.

Capitalistic acquisition as an adventure has been at home in all types of economic society which have known trade with the use of money and which have offered it opportunities, through *commenda,* farming of taxes, State loans, financing of wars, ducal courts and office-holders. Likewise the inner attitude of the adventurer, which laughs at all ethical limitations, has been universal. Absolute and conscious ruthlessness in acquisition has often stood in the closest connection with the strictest conformity to tradition. Moreover, with the breakdown of tradition and the more or less complete extension of free economic enterprise, even to within the social group, the new thing has not generally been ethically justified and encouraged, but only tolerated as a fact. And this fact has been treated either as ethically indifferent or as reprehensible, but unfortunately unavoidable. This has not only been the normal attitude of all ethical teachings, but, what is more important, also that expressed in the practical action of the average man of pre-capitalistic times, pre-capitalistic in the sense that the rational utilization of capital in a permanent enterprise and the rational capitalistic organization of labour had not yet become dominant forces in the determination of economic activity. Now just this attitude was one of the strongest inner obstacles which the adaptation of men to the conditions of an ordered bourgeois-capitalistic economy has encountered everywhere.

The most important opponent with which the spirit of capitalism, in the sense of a definite standard of life claiming ethical sanction, has had to struggle, was that type of attitude and reaction to a new situation which we may designate as traditionalism. In this case also every attempt at a final definition must be held in abeyance. On the other hand, we must try to make the provisional meaning clear by citing a few cases. We will begin from below, with the labourers.

One of the technical means which the modern employer uses in order to secure the greatest possible amount of work from his men is the device of piece rates. In agriculture, for instance, the gathering of the harvest is a case where the greatest possible intensity of labour is called for, since, the weather being uncertain, the difference between high profit and heavy loss may depend on the speed with which the harvesting can be done. Hence a system of piece-rates is almost universal in this case. And since the interest of the employer in a speeding up of harvesting increases with the increase of the results and the intensity of the work, the attempt has again and again been made, by increasing the piece-rates of the workmen, thereby giving them an opportunity to earn what is for them a very high wage, to interest them in increasing their own efficiency. But a peculiar difficulty has been met with surprising frequency: raising the piece-rates has often had the result that not more but less has been accomplished in the same time, because the worker reacted to the increase not by increasing but by decreasing the amount of his work. A man, for instance, who at the rate of 1 mark per acre mowed 2½ acres per day and earned 2½ marks, when the rate was raised to 1.25 marks per acre mowed, not 3 acres, as he might easily have done, thus earning 3.75 marks, but only 2 acres, so that he could still earn the 2½ marks to which he was accustomed. The opportunity of earning more was less attractive than that of working less. He did not ask: how much can I earn in a day if I do as much work as possible? but: how much must I work in order to earn the wage, 2½ marks, which I earned before and which takes care of my traditional needs? This is an example of what is here meant by traditionalism. A man does not "by nature" wish to earn more and more money, but simply to live as he is accustomed to live and to earn as much as is necessary for that purpose. Wherever modern capitalism has begun its work of increasing the productivity of human labour by increasing its intensity, it has encountered the immensely stubborn resistance of this leading trait of pre-capitalistic labour. And to-day it encounters it the more, the more backward (from a capitalistic point of view) the labouring forces are with which it has to deal.

Another obvious possibility, to return to our example, since the appeal to the acquisitive instinct through higher wage-rates failed, would have been to try the opposite policy, to force the worker by reduction of his wage-rates to work harder to earn the same amount than he did before. Low wages and high profits seem even to-day to a superficial observer to stand in correlation; everything which is paid out in wages seems to involve a corresponding reduction of profits. That road capitalism has taken again and again since its beginning. For centuries it was an article of faith, that low wages were productive, i.e., that they increased the material results of labour so that, as Pieter de la Cour, on this point, as we shall see, quite in the spirit of the old Calvinism, said long ago, the people only work because and so long as they are poor.

But the effectiveness of this apparently so efficient method has its limits. Of course the presence of a surplus population which it can hire cheaply in the labour market is a necessity for the development of capitalism. But though too large a reserve army may in certain cases favour its quantitative expansion, it checks its qualitative development, especially the transition to types of enterprise which make more intensive use of labour. Low wages are by no means identical with cheap labour. From a purely quantitative point of view the efficiency of labour decreases with a wage which is physiologically insufficient, which may in the long run even mean survival of the unfit. The present-day average Silesian mows, when he exerts himself to the full, little more than two-thirds as much land as the better paid and nourished Pomeranian or Mecklenburger, and the Pole, the further East he comes from, accomplishes progressively less than the German. Low wages fail even from a purely business point of view wherever it is a question of producing goods which require any sort of skilled labour, or the use of expensive machinery which is easily damaged, or in general wherever any great amount of sharp attention or of initiative is required. Here low wages do not pay, and their effect is the opposite of what was intended. For not only is a developed sense of responsibility absolutely indispensable, but in general also an attitude which, at least during working hours, is freed from continual calculations of how the customary wage may be earned with a maximum of comfort and a minimum of exertion. Labour must, on the contrary, be performed as if it were an absolute end in itself, a calling. But such an attitude is by no means a product of nature. It cannot be evoked by low wages or high ones alone, but can only be the product of a long and arduous process of education. To-day, capitalism, once in the saddle, can recruit its labouring force in all industrial countries with comparative ease. In the past this was in every case an extremely difficult problem. And even to-day it could probably not get along without the support of a powerful ally along the way, which, as we shall see below, was at hand at the time of its development.

What is meant can again best be explained by means of an example. The type of backward traditional form of labour is to-day very often exemplified by women workers, especially unmarried ones. An almost universal complaint of employers of girls, for instance German girls, is that they are almost entirely unable and unwilling to give up methods of work inherited or once learned in favour of more efficient ones, to adapt themselves to new methods, to learn and to concentrate their intelligence, or even to use it at all. Explanations of the possibility of making work easier, above all more profitable to themselves, generally encounter a complete lack of understanding. Increases of piece-rates are without avail against the stone wall of habit. In general it is otherwise, and that is a point of no little importance from our view-point, only with girls having a specifically religious, especially a Pietistic, background. One often hears, and statistical investigation confirms it, that by far the best chances of economic education are found among this group. The ability of mental concentration, as well as the absolutely essential feeling of obligation to one's job, are here most often combined with a strict economy which calculates the possibility of high earnings, and a cool self-control and frugality which enormously increase performance. This provides the most favourable foundation for the conception of labour as an end in itself, as a calling which is necessary to capitalism: the chances of overcoming traditionalism are greatest on account of the religious upbringing. This observation of present-day capitalism in itself suggests that it is worth while to ask how this connection of adaptability to capitalism with religious factors may have come about in the days of the early development of capitalism. For that they were even then present in much the same form can be inferred from numerous facts. For instance, the dislike and the persecution which Methodist workmen in the eighteenth century met at the hands of their comrades were not solely nor even principally the result of their religious eccentricities. England had seen many of those and more striking ones. It rested rather, as the destruction of their tools, repeatedly mentioned in the reports, suggests, upon their specific willingness to work as we should say to-day.

However, let us again return to the present, and this time to the entrepreneur, in order to clarify the meaning of traditionalism in his case.

Sombart, in his discussions of the genesis of capitalism, has distinguished between the satisfaction of needs and acquisition as the two great leading principles in economic history. In the former case the attainment of the goods necessary to meet personal needs, in the latter a struggle for profit free from the limits set by needs, have been the ends controlling the form and direction of economic activity. What he calls the economy of needs seems at first glance to be identical with what is here described as economic traditionalism. That may be the case if the concept of needs is limited to traditional needs. But if that is not done, a number of economic types which must be considered capitalistic, according to the definition of capital which Sombart gives in another part of his work, would be excluded from the category of acquisitive economy and put into that of needs economy. Enterprises, namely, which are carried on by private entrepreneurs by utilizing capital (money or goods with a money value) to make a profit, purchasing the means of production and selling the product, i.e., undoubted capitalistic enterprises, may at the same time have a traditionalistic character. This has, in the course even of modern economic history, not been merely an occasional case, but rather the rule, with continual interruptions from repeated and increasingly powerful conquests of the capitalistic spirit. To be sure the capitalistic form of an enterprise and the spirit in which it is run generally stand in some sort of adequate relationship to each other, but not in one of necessary interdependence. Nevertheless, we provisionally use the expression spirit of (modern) capitalism to describe that attitude which seeks profit rationally and systematically in the manner which we have illustrated by the example of Benjamin Franklin. This, however, is justified by the historical fact that that attitude of mind has on the one hand found its most suitable expression in capitalistic enterprise, while on the other the enterprise has derived its most suitable motive force from the spirit of capitalism.

But the two may very well occur separately. Benjamin Franklin was filled with the spirit of capitalism at a time when his printing business did not differ in form from any handicraft enterprise. And we shall see that at the beginning of modern times it was by no means the capitalistic entrepreneurs of the commercial aristocracy who were either the sole or the predominant bearers of the attitude we have here called the spirit of capitalism. It was much more the rising strata of the lower industrial middle classes. Even in the nineteenth century its classical representatives were not the elegant gentlemen of Liverpool and Hamburg, with their commercial fortunes handed down for generations, but the self-made parvenus of Manchester and Westphalia, who often rose from very modest circumstances. As early as the sixteenth century the situation was similar; the industries which arose at that time were mostly created by parvenus.

The management, for instance, of a bank, a wholesale export business, a large retail establishment, or of a large putting-out enterprise dealing with goods produced in homes is certainly only possible in the form of a capitalistic enterprise. Nevertheless, they may all be carried on in a traditionalistic spirit. In fact, the business of a large bank of issue cannot be carried on in any other way. The foreign trade of whole epochs has rested on the basis of monopolies and legal privileges of strictly traditional character. In retail trade—and we are not here talking of the small men without capital who are continually crying out for Government aid—the revolution which is making an end of the old traditionalism is still in full swing. It is the same development which broke up the old putting-out system, to which modern domestic labour is related only in form. How this revolution takes place and what is its significance may, in spite of the fact these things are so familiar, be again brought out by a concrete example.

Until about the middle of the past century the life of a putter-out was, at least in many of the branches of the Continental textile industry, what we should to-day consider very comfortable. We may imagine its routine somewhat as follows: The peasants came with their cloth, often (in the case of linen) principally or entirely made from raw material which the peasant himself had produced, to the town in which the putter-out lived, and after a careful, often official, appraisal of the quality, received the customary price for it. The putter-out's customers, for markets any appreciable distance away, were middlemen, who also came to him, generally not yet following samples, but seeking traditional qualities, and bought from his warehouse, or, long before delivery, placed orders which were probably in turn passed on to the peasants. Personal canvassing of customers took place, if at all, only at long intervals. Otherwise correspondence sufficed, though the sending of samples slowly gained ground. The number of business hours was very moderate, perhaps five to six a day, sometimes considerably less; in the rush season, where there was one, more. Earnings were moderate; enough to lead a respectable life and in good times to put away a little. On the whole, relations among competitors were relatively good, with a large degree of agreement on the fundamentals of business. A long daily visit to the tavern, with often plenty to drink, and a congenial circle of friends, made life comfortable and leisurely.

The form of organization was in every respect capitalistic; the entrepreneur's activity was of a purely business character; the use of capital, turned over in the business, was indispensable; and finally, the objective aspect of the economic process, the book-keeping, was rational. But it was traditionalistic business, if one considers the spirit which animated the entrepreneur: the traditional manner of life, the traditional rate of profit, the traditional amount of work, the traditional manner of regulating the relationships with labour, and the essentially traditional circle of customers and the manner of attracting new ones. All these dominated the conduct of the business, were at the basis, one may say, of the *ethos* of this group of business men.

Now at some time this leisureliness was suddenly destroyed, and often entirely without any essential change in the form of organization, such as the transition to a unified factory, to mechanical weaving, and so on. What happened was, on the contrary, often no more than this: some young man from one of the putting-out families went out into the country, carefully chose weavers for his employ, greatly increased the rigour of his supervision of their work, and thus turned them from peasants into labourers. On the other hand, he would begin to change his marketing methods by so far as possible going directly to the final consumer, would take the details into his own hands, would personally solicit customers, visiting them every year, and above all would adapt the quality of the product directly to their needs and wishes. At the same time he began to introduce the principle of low prices and large turnover. There was repeated what everywhere and always is the result of such a process of rationalization: those who would not follow suit had to go out of business. The idyllic state collapsed under the pressure of a bitter competitive struggle, respectable fortunes were made, and not lent out at interest, but always reinvested in the business. The old leisurely and comfortable attitude toward life gave way to a hard frugality in which some participated and came to the top, because they did not wish to consume but to earn, while others who wished to keep on with the old ways were forced to curtail their consumption.

And, what is most important in this connection, it was not generally in such cases a stream of new money invested in the industry which brought about this revolution—in several cases known to me the whole revolutionary process was set in motion with a few thousands of capital borrowed from relations—but the new spirit, the spirit of modern capitalism, had set to work. The question of the motive forces in the expansion of modern capitalism is not in the first instance a question of the origin of the capital sums which were available for capitalistic uses, but, above all, of the development of the spirit of capitalism. Where it appears and is able to work itself out, it produces its own capital and monetary supplies as the means to its ends, but the reverse is not true. Its entry on the scene was not generally peaceful. A flood of mistrust, sometimes of hatred, above all of moral indignation, regularly opposed itself to the first innovator. Often—I know of several cases of the sort—regular legends of mysterious shady spots in his previous life have been produced. It is very easy not to recognize that only an unusually strong character could save an entrepreneur of this new type from the loss of his temperate self-control and from both moral and economic shipwreck. Furthermore, along with clarity of vision and ability to act, it is only by virtue of very definite and highly developed ethical qualities that it has been possible for him to command the absolutely indispensable confidence of his customers and workmen. Nothing else could have given him the strength to overcome the innumerable obstacles, above all the infinitely more intensive work which is demanded of the modern entrepreneur. But these are ethical qualities of quite a different sort from those adapted to the traditionalism of the past.

And, as a rule, it has been neither dare-devil and unscrupulous speculators, economic adventurers such as we meet at all periods of economic history, nor simply great financiers who have carried through this change, outwardly so inconspicuous, but nevertheless so decisive for the penetration of economic life with the new spirit. On the contrary, they were men who had grown up in the hard school of life, calculating and daring at the same time, above all temperate and reliable, shrewd and completely devoted to their business, with strictly bourgeois opinions and principles.

One is tempted to think that these personal moral qualities have not the slightest relation to any ethical maxims, to say nothing of religious ideas, but that the essential relation between them is negative. The ability to free oneself from the common tradition, a sort of liberal enlightenment, seems likely to be the most suitable basis for such a business man's success. And to-day that is generally precisely the case. Any relationship between religious beliefs and conduct is generally absent, and where any exists, at least in Germany, it tends to be of the negative sort. The people filled with the spirit of capitalism to-day tend to be indifferent, if not hostile, to the Church. The thought of the pious boredom of paradise has little attraction for their active natures;

religion appears to them as a means of drawing people away from labour in this world. If you ask them what is the meaning of their restless activity, why they are never satisfied with what they have, thus appearing so senseless to any purely worldly view of life, they would perhaps give the answer, if they know any at all: "to provide for my children and grandchildren." But more often and, since that motive is not peculiar to them, but was just as effective for the traditionalist, more correctly, simply: that business with its continuous work has become a necessary part of their lives. That is in fact the only possible motivation, but it at the same time expresses what is, seen from the view-point of personal happiness, so irrational about this sort of life, where a man exists for the sake of his business, instead of the reverse.

Of course, the desire for the power and recognition which the mere fact of wealth brings plays its part. When the imagination of a whole people has once been turned toward purely quantitative bigness, as in the United States, this romanticism of numbers exercises an irresistible appeal to the poets among business men. Otherwise it is in general not the real leaders, and especially not the permanently successful entrepreneurs, who are taken in by it. In particular, the resort to entailed estates and the nobility, with sons whose conduct at the university and in the officers' corps tries to cover up their social origin, as has been the typical history of German capitalistic parvenu families, is a product of later decadence. The ideal type of the capitalistic entrepreneur, as it has been represented even in Germany by occasional outstanding examples, has no relation to such more or less refined climbers. He avoids ostentation and unnecessary expenditure, as well as conscious enjoyment of his power, and is embarrassed by the outward signs of the social recognition which he receives. His manner of life is, in other words, often, and we shall have to investigate the historical significance of just this important fact, distinguished by a certain ascetic tendency, as appears clearly enough in the sermon of Franklin which we have quoted. It is, namely, by no means exceptional, but rather the rule, for him to have a sort of modesty which is essentially more honest than the reserve which Franklin so shrewdly recommends. He gets nothing out of his wealth for himself, except the irrational sense of having done his job well.

But it is just that which seems to the pre-capitalistic man so incomprehensible and mysterious, so unworthy and contemptible. That anyone should be able to make it the sole purpose of his life-work, to sink into the grave weighed down with a great material load of money and goods, seems to him explicable only as the product of a perverse instinct, the *auri sacra fames*.

At present under our individualistic political, legal, and economic institutions, with the forms of organization and general structure which are peculiar to our economic order, this spirit of capitalism might be understandable, as has been said, purely as a result of adaptation. The capitalistic system so needs this devotion to the calling of making money, it is an attitude toward material goods which is so well suited to that system, so intimately bound up with the conditions of survival in the economic struggle for existence, that there can to-day no longer be any question of a necessary connection of that acquisitive manner of life with any single *Weltanschauung*. In fact, it no longer needs the support of any religious forces, and feels the attempts of religion to influence economic life, in so far as they can still be felt at all, to be as much an unjustified interference as its regulation by the State. In such circumstances men's commercial and social interests do tend to determine their opinions and attitudes. Whoever does not adapt his manner of life to the conditions of capitalistic success must go under, or at least cannot rise. But these are phenomena of a time in which modern capitalism has become dominant and has become emancipated from its old supports. But as it could at one time destroy the old forms of mediaeval regulation of economic life only in alliance with the growing power of the modern State, the same, we may say provisionally, may have been the case in its relations with religious forces. Whether and in what sense that was the case, it is our task to investigate. For that the conception of money-making as an end in itself to which people were bound, as a calling, was contrary to the ethical feelings of whole epochs, it is hardly necessary to prove. The dogma *Deo placere vix potest* which was incorporated into the canon law and applied to the activities of the merchant, and which at that time (like the passage in the gospel about interest) was considered genuine, as well as St. Thomas's characterization of the desire for gain as *turpitudo* (which term even included unavoidable and hence ethically justified profit-making), already contained a high degree of concession on the part of the Catholic doctrine to the financial powers with which the Church had such intimate political relations in the Italian cities, as compared with the much more radically antichrematistic views of comparatively wide circles. But even where the doctrine was still better accommodated to the facts, as for instance with Anthony of Florence, the feeling was never quite overcome, that activity directed to acquisition for its own sake was at bottom a *pudendum* which was to be tolerated only because of the unalterable necessities of life in this world.

Some moralists of that time, especially of the nominalistic school, accepted developed capitalistic business forms as inevitable, and attempted to justify them, especially commerce, as necessary. The *industria* developed in it they were able to regard, though not without contradictions, as a legitimate source of profit, and hence ethically unobjectionable. But the dominant doctrine rejected the spirit of capitalistic acquisition as *turpitudo*, or at least could not give it a positive ethical sanction. An ethical attitude like that of Benjamin Franklin would have been simply unthinkable. This was, above all, the attitude of capitalistic circles themselves. Their life-work was, so long as they clung to the tradition of the Church, at best something morally indifferent. It was tolerated, but was still, even if only on account of the continual danger of collision with the Church's doctrine on usury, somewhat dangerous to salvation. Quite considerable sums, as the sources show, went at the death of rich people to religious institutions as conscience money, at times even back to former debtors as *usura* which had been unjustly taken from them. It was otherwise, along with heritical and other tendencies looked upon with disapproval, only in those parts of the commercial aristocracy which were already emancipated from the tradition. But even sceptics and people indifferent to the Church often reconciled themselves with it by gifts, because it was sort of insurance against the uncertainties of what might come after death, or because (at least according to the very widely held latter view) an external obedience to the commands of the Church was sufficient to insure salvation. Here the either non-moral or immoral character of their action in the opinion of the participants themselves comes clearly to light.

Now, how could activity, which was at best ethically tolerated, turn into a calling in the sense of Benjamin Franklin? The fact to be explained historically is that in the most highly capitalistic centre of that time, in Florence of the fourteenth and fifteenth centuries, the money and capital market of all the great political Powers, this attitude was considered ethically unjustifiable, or at best to be tolerated. But in the backwoods small bourgeois circumstances of Pennsylvania in the eighteenth century, where business threatened for simple lack of money to fall back into barter, where there was hardly a sign of large enterprise, where only the earliest beginnings of banking were to be found, the same thing was considered the essence of moral conduct, even commanded in the name of duty. To speak here of a reflection of material conditions in the ideal superstructure would be patent nonsense. What was the background of ideas which could account for the sort of activity apparently directed toward profit alone as a calling toward which the individual feels himself to have an ethical obligation? For it was this idea which gave the way of life to the new entrepreneur its ethical foundation and justification.

The attempt has been made, particularly by Sombart, in what are often judicious and effective observations, to depict economic rationalism as the salient feature of modern economic life as a whole. Undoubtedly with justification, if by that is meant the extension of the productivity of labour which has, through the subordination of the process of production to scientific points of view, relieved it from its independence upon the natural organic limitations of the human individual. Now this process of rationalization in the field of technique and economic organization undoubtedly determines an important part of the ideals of life of modern bourgeois society. Labour in the service of a rational organization for the provision of humanity with material goods has without doubt always appeared to representatives of the capitalistic spirit as one of the most important purposes of their life-work. It is only necessary, for instance, to read Franklin's account of his efforts in the service of civic improvements in Philadelphia clearly to apprehend this obvious truth. And the joy and pride of having given employment to numerous people, of having had a part in the economic progress of his home town in the sense referring to figures of population and volume of trade which capitalism associated with the word, all these things obviously are part of the specific and undoubtedly idealistic satisfactions in life to modern men of business. Similarly it is one of the fundamental characteristics of an individualistic capitalistic economy that it is rationalized on the basis of rigorous calculation, directed with foresight and caution toward the economic success which is sought in sharp contrast to the hand-to-mouth existence of the peasant, and to the privileged traditionalism of the guild craftsman and of the adventurers' capitalism, oriented to the exploitation of political opportunities and irrational speculation.

It might thus seem that the development of the spirit of capitalism is best understood as part of the development of rationalism as a whole, and could be deduced from the fundamental position of rationalism on the basic problems of life. In the process Protestantism would only have to be considered in so far as it had formed a stage prior to the development of a purely rationalistic philosophy. But any serious attempt to carry this thesis through makes it evident that such a simple way of putting the question will not work, simply because of the fact that the history of rationalism shows a development which by no means follows parallel lines in the various departments of life. The rationalization of private law, for instance, if it is thought of as a logical simplification and rearrangement of the content of the law, was achieved in the highest hitherto known degree in the Roman law of late antiquity. But it remained most backward in some of the countries with the highest degree of economic rationalization, notably in England, where the Renaissance of Roman Law was overcome by the power of the great legal corporations, while it has always retained its supremacy in the Catholic countries of Southern Europe. The worldly rational philosophy of the eighteenth century did not find favour alone or even principally in the countries of highest capitalistic development. The doctrines of Voltaire are even to-day the common property of broad upper, and what is practically more important, middle-class groups in the Romance Catholic countries. Finally, if under practical rationalism is understood the type of attitude which sees and judges the world consciously in terms of the worldly interests of the individual ego, then this view of life was and is the special peculiarity of the peoples of the *liberum arbitrium*, such as the Italians and the French are in very flesh and blood. But we have already convinced ourselves that this is by no means the soil in which that relationship of a man to his calling as a task, which is necessary to capitalism, has pre-eminently grown. In fact, one may—this simple proposition, which is often forgotten, should be placed at the beginning of every study which essays to deal with rationalism—rationalize life from fundamentally different basic points of view and in very different directions. Rationalism is an historical concept which covers a whole world of different things. It will be our task to find out whose intellectual child the particular concrete form of rational thought was, from which the idea of a calling and the devotion to labour in the calling has grown, which is, as we have seen, so irrational from the standpoint of purely eudaemonistic self-interest, but which has been and still is one of the most characteristic elements of our capitalistic culture. We are here particularly interested in the origin of precisely the irrational element which lies in this, as in every conception of a calling.

# THE WEBER THESIS: CONTROVERSY AND CONSENSUS

### V. A. Demant

The publication of *Religion and the Rise of Capitalism* (by R. H. Tawney) inaugurated an enlivened and enlivening debate; it engendered considerable heat which was often more obscuring than enlightening. Mr. Tawney has made his riposte to some of the adverse comment in his preface to the 1937 edition. The debate concentrated mainly upon the effect of the religious changes of early Protestantism on economic habits and theories; it was concerned especially with the views of Max Weber and others about the influences which had formed the climate in which modern commerce, industry and money-making could grow into social dominants. The debate became very much a Catholic-Protestant rivalry, with weapons varying with the position taken up as to whether capitalism was, like the monarchs of *1066 and All That*, a bad or a good thing. Those who thought it was bad, on both sides, spoke as one who should say: "Please, sir, it wasn't me"; or, "I wasn't the only one"; or, "The other boy led me on." Those who thought it was good on balance, said as it were: "Why this scolding? This thing capitalism is an essential step in the human enterprise; Christians should not resist the hand of God in world history but come to terms with it." Some added: "And religious forces reflected the social and economic changes rather than bringing them about"—an emphasis they would have found admitted and documented in Mr. Tawney's own work.[1] Others like R. S. Sleigh, a disciple of Ernest Troeltsch, valiantly took up the position that "the insight of Calvin was not an illusion, for the relation between Christianity and capitalism is not accidental, but organic, intrinsically essential."[2]

---

[1] Especially *Religion and the Rise of Capitalism* n. 32, p. 319. (Pelican ed., p. 283) and Foreword to Max Weber, *The Protestant Ethic* (Eng. tr., 1930).
[2] R. S. Sleigh, *The Sufficiency of Christianity* (London, 1923), p. 160.

The debate, as it could be followed in English writings, has roughly three stages. In 1904 Max Weber had published his researches, part of which was later translated as *The Protestant Ethic and the Spirit of Capitalism*. Therein he deduced that capitalism with its *laissez-faire* doctrine and its conception of economic behaviour as autonomous, owing responsibility only to its own law, along with its justification of business as "a calling" or a religious vocation—that all this derived its warrant from Protestant and especially Puritan sources. Tawney's lectures to a large extent substantiated this thesis and also corrected it. Critics had pointed out that the spirit of capitalism was older than the Reformation. Tawney allows that it is as old as history. But he adds: "It found in certain aspects of later Puritanism a tonic which braced its energies and fortified its already vigorous temper";[3] the main point being that it soon became regarded as a sign of religious seriousness instead of a menace to be suspected. In 1933 appeared a counterblast in Professor H. M. Robertson's *Aspects of the Rise of Economic Individualism: A Criticism of Max Weber and His School*.[4] He claimed that what he regarded as the Weber-Tawney thesis was more of a polemic weapon than a contribution to historic studies. Weber's essay on *Die Protestantische Ethik und der Geist des Kapitalismus* ushered in, says Robertson, as heavy an attack on the capitalist position as the materialist writings of Karl Marx. He adds: "This is not immediately apparent; but even a cursory second glance shows that its general tendency is to undermine the basis of capitalist society." In a more dispassionate vein, Robertson maintains that Weber failed to see that the notion of "calling," the sense of that station to which it shall please God to call us, when used by early Reformers, actually worked against acquisitiveness and in a conservative interest. True enough, but it does not dispose of Weber's question: How does "the calling" come to have the commercial and acquisitive flavour it possessed by the eighteenth century? It was Tawney's main contribution to show how that came about.

Robertson produced plenty of evidence that at least one Catholic force made in the same direction, namely the casuistry which the Jesuits were elaborating to deal with the growing commercial and financial transactions of the time, especially in the matter of interest on money loans. This evidence was used to suggest that the Jesuit theology was too accommodating, that it exemplified the maxim "there is nothing like business"—a charge already made in 1669 by Pirot and repeated by Groethuysen.[5] The Jesuit moralists, claimed Robertson, stripped their doctrine of those checks on gain which might seem hostile to the adolescent bourgeoisie. An answer to this charge was made in 1934 by Father J. Brodrick in his book: *The Economic Morals of the Jesuits*.[6] The nearest thing we have to a summary of the debate is to be found in the work of Aminotore Fanfani of Milan under the title: *Catholicism, Protestantism and Capitalism*, published 1935.[7] As a Catholic and a critic of capitalism he allows that capitalism arose in a Catholic world when the cupidity of some persons, making injustice for others, eventually resulted in the escape of business dealings from non-economic, that is, from ethical and social sanctions. It is true that the capitalist spirit, as defined most acutely in some ways by Werner Sombart, can be found in the ancient and medieval world; it is also true that the earlier Reformers were as uncapitalist in their outlook as their predecessors. But something was happening, and

[3] Tawney, op. cit., p. 226 f. (Pelican ed., p. 204.)
[4] (Cambridge, 1933.)
[5] *Origines de l'Esprit Bourgeois en France*, 2nd ed. (Paris, 1927).
[6] (Oxford, 1934.)
[7] Eng. tr. London, 1935, with a very full Bibliography.

it might be epitomized by these sentences of Weber's: "A state of mind such as that expressed in the passages we have quoted [from Franklin's *Necessary Hints and Advice to a Young Tradesman*] and which called forth the applause of a whole people, would both in ancient times and in the Middle Ages have been proscribed as the lowest sort of avarice and as an attitude entirely lacking in self-respect."[8] He adds at a later point: "Hence the difference does not lie in the degree of development of any impulse to make money,"[9] (as Sombart and Brentano assumed and, in consequence, pushed the origins of the capitalist spirit much further back[10]), but in the removal of "an ethic based on religion which places certain psychological sanctions (not of an economic character) on the maintenance of the attitude prescribed by it, sanctions which, so long as the religious belief remains alive, are highly effective, and which mere wordly wisdom does not have at its disposal."[11]

A sifting of the essentials of the controversy and a reading of the documents, in place of projecting upon writers what a critic feels sure the writer should be saying out of religious or social polemic attitudes, would, it seems, lead to a consensus of this kind:

What became economic individualism had been arrived at before the Reformation, but it was not acknowledged as moral, let alone regarded as a contribution to the general good. The early Reformers were as opposed to capitalist practices as the schoolmen had been. The regions under Protestant influence capitulated first and co-operated in the transition in a way which has never been the case under Catholic influence. And this is not just an idiosyncratic continental opinion. You can find the same judgment in economic historians, like Cunningham who wrote of seventeenth-century changes in government: "The result was an immense development of economic freedom . . . . But this step was purchased at a heavy price . . . . Under these altered conditions no room was left for authoritative insistence on moral, as distinguished from legal, obligations; the success of Puritanism meant the triumph of the new commercial morality which held good among monied men; capitalists had established their right to secure a return for their money, and there was no authority to insist upon any correlative duty when they organized industrial undertakings and obtained control over the means of production."[12]

It would perhaps not be profitable to recapitulate this debate any more fully, or to assess the correctness of explaining economic changes so largely by religious forces, or to apportion praise or blame on this side or that of the religious world. But the issue has to be recalled, if only in order to realize that all this literature is prompted by a very real question: what could possibly have brought about such a radical, unique and extraordinary change in human behavior as that represented by the emergence of economic life as an autonomous activity? Their conclusions will not all stand, but if Tawney and the others had done nothing else but call attention to the revolutionary character of the transition and to the courage it required to break with tradition, they would have put into their debt all who desire to understand the turns of human

---

[8] *The Protestant Ethic and the Spirit of Capitalism* (Eng. tr. 1930), p. 56.
[9] Ibid., p. 57.
[10] Werner Sombart, *Der Moderne Kapitalismus* (Munich, Leipzig, 1902-24); L. Brentano, *Die Anfänge des Modernen Kapitalismus* (Leipzig, 1923).
[11] Weber, op. cit., p. 197, n. 12. For full list of Weber's work, *vide: Bibliography on Max Weber*, by H. Gerth and Hedwig Gerth in *Social Research* (New York), vol. XVI, March 1949.
[12] W. Cunningham, *The Growth of English Industry and Commerce in Modern Times* (Cambridge, 1903), vol. I, p. 206.

history. In order to account for an entirely new relation of economic life to the rest of society they were compelled to seek for an influence so penetrating that they had perforce to look for it in religion, and thereby they started an inquiry which may throw some light upon the significance of changes in the nineteenth and twentieth centuries which, in cardinal though not in all respects, are in the reverse direction to whose we have been glancing at.

# 6 / The Expansion of Europe: The Profit Motive or Missionary Zeal?

From the end of the fifteenth century through the eighteenth, there occurred that extraordinary first expansion of European arms, commerce, and colonists into lands previously little known. Formerly, the dimensions of this phenomenon were lost in narrow political or national histories, where overseas expansion was treated as an appendage of the power struggles of the great states on the European continent or as a formative factor in the development of new nations in the Western Hemisphere.

That the expansion of Europe has emerged as a subject worthy of study in its own right and even as the single most important historical phenomenon during the period in which it occurred is in large part due to the pioneering work, early in this century, of two American historians, William R. Shepherd and Wilbur Cortez Abbot.[1] Since then, the effect of overseas expansion on European economic, social, political, and intellectual life has been increasingly studied.

Among the present generations of historians, one of the outstanding authorities on the economic aspects of the expansion of Europe is Earl J. Hamilton. His *American Treasure and the Price Revolution in Spain* (1934) is a landmark in the field. Spain also is the favored area of the British historian J. H. Parry, but by contrast his chief interest is in what might be called the philosophy of Spanish expansion. *The Spanish Theory of Empire in the Sixteenth Century* (1940) and *The Audiencia of New Galicia in the Sixteenth Century* (1948) are authoritative works that establish the ethical side of the Spanish presence in the New World.

The following selections by these two historians, which cover roughly the same period and areas, reflect well the different interests of their authors. In the first, Hamilton emphasizes the role of monopoly and the profit motive in overseas expansion. In the second, Parry, while he does not deny the importance of commerce and profits, takes pains to point out the missionary aspect of expansion, which he links to the tradition of the Crusades. Of particular interest are the differing portraits of Prince Henry the Navigator offered in the two selections.

---

[1] William R. Shepherd, "The Expansion of Europe," *The Political Science Quarterly,* Vol. XXIV, Nos. 1, 2, 3 (1919). Wilbur Cortez Abbott, *The Expansion of Europe* (New York: Henry Holt and Company, 1918).

# THE ROLE OF MONOPOLY* IN THE OVERSEAS EXPANSION AND COLONIAL TRADE OF EUROPE BEFORE 1800

Earl J. Hamilton

## I. Introduction

The great European empires of classical antiquity included a fringe in Asia and the Mediterranean littoral of Africa, and the crusading nations and trading states of the late Middle Ages acquired tenuous footholds in Asia Minor and on small islands in the eastern Atlantic. But Europe controlled little territory beyond its own boundaries either in ancient or in medieval times. It remained for the enlightened captains and bold sailors of Prince Henry the Navigator to inaugurate, early in the fifteenth century, the great age of discovery, from which both imperialism and the modern world have emerged. From that time until the Napoleonic Wars suspended expansion by absorbing European energies at home, the leading powers of Europe effectively occupied more than a third of the earth's surface and established claims to more than half of it.[1]

Near the end of this period, Adam Smith concluded, after two decades of reflection and a full year in the British Museum reading on colonial questions, that "the utility which has resulted from . . . the establishment of the European colonies in America and the West Indies . . . is not clear and evident. It was not understood at their first establishment, and was not the motive either of that establishment or of the discoveries which gave occasion to it: and the nature, extent, and limits of that utility are not, perhaps, well understood at this day."[2] Smith was contrasting what the motives should have been with what the uneducated public believed them to be. What they really were he thought he understood well enough; namely, to acquire precious metals and to obtain high profits through monopolistic exploitation of colonial markets. One of Smith's main objectives in writing the *Wealth of Nations* was to refute mercantilism by demonstrating the theoretical folly and practical impossibility of an indefinite accumulation of the precious metals. Nevertheless, monopoly overshadows not only treasure but everything else in his learned and illuminating analysis of colonial policies. Although Smith repeatedly pilloried businessmen and the craft guilds

*I use the term *monopoly* as it was defined by H. de B. Gibbins in his *British Commerce and Colonies from Elizabeth to Victoria* (London, 1897, p. 15): "The possession of a monopoly means the possession of the *sole right* to deal in a certain article or to trade with a certain country; and this sole right might be granted either to individuals or to companies, or indeed might be claimed by a nation, as, *e.g.*, when England claimed the sole right to trade with her American colonies, and tried to force them to deal only with her, and forbade them to carry on manufactures on their own account." Under *monopoly* I also include imperfect competition resulting from staple ports, convoyed fleets, royal favoritism, and other governmental or institutional restrictions.
[1] Grover Clark, *The Balance Sheets of Imperialism: Facts and Figures on Colonies* (New York, 1936), p. 5.
[2] *Wealth of Nations* (Cannan ed., London, 1904), Vol. II, p. 60.

for monopolistic practices in England,[3] he did not argue, as has been fashionable in recent decades, that limitation by monopolies of domestic opportunities for investment and employment drove capital and labor into imperialistic ventures.

Focusing our attention upon the foundation and the trade of the five leading colonial empires before 1800—the Portuguese, Spanish, Dutch, French, and English—we shall endeavor to determine the extent to which a desire to attain monoply was a factor in the overseas expansion of Europe. We shall also see to what extent and in what respects the colonial trade, governed by the vague principles of mercantilism throughout the three centuries under review, was monopolistic or competitive.

## II. Portugal

Most writers on mercantilism have neglected Portugal, and its colonial policy has attracted surprisingly little research. The destruction of a large mass of colonial papers in the Torre do Tombo Archives by the earthquake and ensuing fire on November 1, 1755, and the silence of the early chroniclers on such prosaic matters as trade and navigation have deterred many scholars interested in the Portuguese colonial system and seriously handicapped those who have persevered. Consequently, inadequate knowledge may explain the tendency to dismiss the Portuguese empire with the derogatory conclusions that it consisted only of a chain of forts and trading stations, developed no new institutions, set no important precedents, and made no significant contributions to colonial theory. Although precise information and many details are lacking, we know that Portugal discovered the all-water route to the East Indies, established the first contacts with the natives, forged a colossal empire, exclusively controlled the East India trade for almost a century, solved a host of problems before any rival appeared on the scene, and smoothed the paths of Holland, England, and France to trade and empire in the East. Not the least service, or disservice, of Portugal was to furnish other powers a classic example of absolute monopoly in colonial trade.

A key figure in the early overseas expansion of Europe was Prince Henry the Navigator. The conquest of Céuta in 1415 and the expedition he led three years later to repel a Moorish counterattack against this stronghold permanently fixed the attention of Prince Henry upon Africa. The tragic failure of Portuguese arms against Tangier in 1437 convinced him that Portugal's future lay in the utilization of sea power along the western coast of Africa and in the islands of the eastern Atlantic. As an adjunct to his systematic voyages of exploration, Henry began about 1420 to construct the astronomical observatory, naval arsenal, and institute for nautical research on Cape Sagres at what later became known as the *Villa do Infante*. Whether Henry established a formal school of geography remains a disputed issue. But he assembled Christian, Moorish, and Jewish scientists; provided them with excellent facilities; and gave them favorable working conditions. Research in geography, mathematics, and astronomy was pursued intermittently, if not continuously; and the results were applied to nautical instruments, naval architecture, and navigation. Henry's captains went to sea in good vessels and equipped with the best geographic data then known, and their reports at the end of the voyages provided valuable source material for the scientists on shore. Henry pushed his practical and scientific work

[3] See, for example, *op. cit.*, Vol. I, pp. 63-64, 68-69, 148, 426-427, and 435; Vol. II, pp. 19, 146, and 245-246.

forward for four decades, and the Portuguese kings continued it after his death. Great advances in the art and instruments of navigation, marine architecture, and geography resulted. The good ships and skilled mariners in Portugal and southwestern Spain, where Portuguese skills infiltrated, were important factors in the discovery of America and of the all-water route to the East Indies.[4]

The early Portuguese chroniclers pictured Prince Henry as a recluse, who renounced the pleasures of the Court, to live, at least the last two decades of his life, immersed in study, on the sterile promontory of Sagres, motivated only by intellectual curiosity and a zealous desire to turn the flanks of Islam by skirting the western coast of Africa and effecting a union with a fabled Christian potentate somewhere in eastern Africa. His resources were supposedly drawn from the enormous revenues derived from his grand mastership of the Order of Christ, and trade was of strictly secondary importance. The chroniclers regarded Henry's exploits as a prolongation of the crusades.[5] What his ultimate goals were one cannot say. But in his proximate aims and his methods he bore more resemblance to Commodore Vanderbilt than to Saint Francis of Assisi. Recent research has demonstrated that Henry was not a religious zealot devoid of worldly concerns and pecuniary aims but a company promoter, slave trader, and monopolistic exploiter. Through political influence this "ascetic" Prince obtained a monopoly on woad-dyeing in all Portugal, and he controlled the cloth industry in the provinces of Beira and Minho. He had the exclusive right to manufacture and sell white and dark soap in the entire kingdom. In 1440 Henry secured the exclusive privilege of sardine and tuna fishing off the Algarve coast for the Pescaria do Infante, a company ostensibly organized to end the unbearable tolls levied upon fishermen by the owners of vessels and equipment. Yet he claimed one-fifth of the profits for himself. Prince Henry formed a company in 1441 to enjoy a monopoly on trade with the Canary Islands not belonging to Spain. He loaned the company funds of the Order of Christ at 6 per cent and exacted a fifth of the profits for his services as a promoter. Derived from the capture of slaves and the cheap acquisition of produce, the returns amounted to 80 per cent in some years; and apparently Henry levied his toll until his death twenty years later. In 1450 Henry induced the Crown to force the company floated by foreigners the previous decade, to exploit a monopoly on the coral industry, to allow Portuguese subjects, including Henry, of course, to participate in the enterprise.[6]

What interested Prince Henry in Africa, in the beginning, was the gold brought across the Sahara by caravans; after about 1441, the gold dust and the rich slave-raiding territory found on the west African coast; and, finally, the hope of reaching the East Indies by water, thus giving Portugal complete control over the spice trade of all Europe.[7] In view of Henry's acquisitiveness, his unwillingness to permit either foreigners or compatriots to trade or sail along the coast of Africa is not surprising. Until the gold dust and slaves began to pour into Portugal in significant

---

[4] Samuel E. Morison, *Admiral of the Ocean Sea* (Boston, 1942), Vol. I, pp. xl-xli; C. R. Beazley, *Prince Henry the Navigator* (London and New York, 1923 ed.), pp. 160 ff.
[5] Gomes Eannes de Azurara, *Conquests and Discoveries of Henry the Navigator* (Eng. tr., London, 1936), pp. 130-135. *Cf.* C. R. Beazley, *op. cit.*, pp. 157-159; George Young, *Portugal Old and Young* (Oxford, 1917), pp. 98 ff.; W. W. Hunter, *A History of British India* (London, 1899), Vol. I, pp. 72-73 and 90.
[6] M. A. Hedwig Fitzler, "Portugiesische Handelsgesellschaften des 15. und beginnenden 16. Jahrhunderts," *Vierteljahrschrift für Sozial- und Wirtschaftsgeschichte*, Vol. XXV (1932), pp. 213-221 and 231-234.
[7] Paul Leroy-Beaulieu, *De la Colonisation chez les peuples modernes* (Paris, 1874), p. 48.

quantities in the early 1440's, trade and exploration were confined to the one or two vessels a year Henry was ordinarily able to send out. Since the new opportunities exceeded Henry's resources, he organized the First Lagos Company in 1444 and the Second Lagos Company in 1447 for trade and exploration—to promote more trade. In 1449 he set up an affiliate of the Pescaria do Infante to monopolize the fisheries off the African coast. After Henry's death the Second Lagos Company was dissolved, but the trade was not thrown open. For the remainder of the fifteenth century it was farmed out by the Crown as an exclusive privilege to Portuguese companies and subjects. Not until after the papal bulls of Alexander VI and the Treaty of Tordesillas of 1494 had divided the "world" between the two Iberian powers did Portugal concede to Spain the right to fish in west African waters.[8]

When the acquisition of gold and slaves progressed, and the prospects of finding an all-water route to the Indies brightened, as the intrepid explorers pushed down the African coast, Portugal obtained one papal bull after another forbidding all other powers to trade in the new territory and to navigate in the new seas. The reluctance of Protestant countries for almost a century to violate the claims of Portugal and Spain suggests that the bulls were not mere scraps of paper,[9] but the formidable sea power of the Iberian states was doubtless the primary factor in the initial success of exclusion. The valuable prizes in hand, and believed to be in the offing, were strong incentives for Portugal's precedent of rigidly excluding other nations from overseas dominions, followed, with few and generally brief exceptions, by every other colonial power until the nineteenth century. If the rewards of Portuguese discovery and exploration had appeared less valuable, the subsequent pattern of colonial trade might have been more liberal and international relations somewhat less turbulent.

Vasco da Gama returned from his discovery of the Cape of Good Hope route to the East Indies with spices and other oriental products that yielded approximately 6,000 per cent on the entire cost; and Cabral's voyage four years later, which accidentally established the Portuguese claim to Brazil, paid a handsome profit. With such fabulous returns, the Crown was bound to establish the monopolistic system prevailing in the African trade. In the first three quarters of the sixteenth century vessels went to the East Indies only at the expense and the risk of the king. The king sold licenses to private traders and companies to send goods to the Indies and to import oriental products; but he soon began to take the spice trade into his own hands, and by 1520 his monopoly was complete. Portugal endeavored not only to supply Europe with all her spices but to take over the commerce and the carrying trade of India and the East Indies with China, Japan, Africa, and the Near East. How ruthlessly Portugal pursued this aim is shown by a proclamation of 1524 providing that "the penalty to a native captain found in Indian waters without a Portuguese license was death and seizure of his ship and property. The officials took care, before granting the permit, to secure a lion's share in the profits of the voyage."[10] The Portuguese soon realized they could not attain their objectives without seizing political control over key positions. In the first half of the sixteenth century intrigue and the sword gave Portugal such strategic points as Hormuz, Diu, Goa, Malacca, and Macao; and either directly or through

---

[8] Fitzler, "Überblick über die portugiesischen Überseehandelsgesellschaften des 15. bis 18. Jahrhunderts," *Vierteljahrschrift für Sozial- und Wirtschaftsgeschichte,* Vol. XXIV (1931), pp. 283-284; "Portugiesische Handelsgesellschaften des 15. und beginnenden 16. Jahrhunderts," *op. cit.,* pp. 218 and 235-240; Fernand Braudel, "Monnaies et civilizations: de l'or du Soudan à l'argent d'Amérique," *Annales: Économies–Sociétés–Civilizations,* Vol. I (1946), pp. 9-22.
[9] Hunter, *op. cit.,* pp. 84-86 and 186.
[10] Hunter, *op. cit.,* p. 180.

alliances she controlled most of their hinterlands. By establishing or maintaining friendly dynasties or parties in power, the Portuguese dictated many treaties that excluded all alien traders and either exempted the Portuguese from customs duties or granted them lower rates than native merchants paid. Furthermore, the rulers of Calicut, Malabar, Ceylon, and the Moluccas were forced by treaty to sell all the pepper, ginger, cinnamon, cloves, and nutmeg in their kingdoms exclusively to the Portuguese government. Whenever the quantity of any spice was excessive, that is, was greater than would yield the maximum net revenue to the intruding monopolist, the surplus was destroyed on the spot.[11]

For a few years after Magellan's voyage around the world Spain planned to trade with the spice islands via Cape Horn, but Portugal's purchase of the Spanish claim to the Moluccas in 1529 ended his threat. A few French and English interlopers reached the East Indies; but their activities were sporadic and, for the most part, on a small scale.

The only serious violation of the royal monopoly on direct trade with the East Indies was by Portuguese officials. The high prices resulting from the suppression of competition in Portugal and the Indies made smuggling attractive. Since the captains of Portuguese war vessels received less than Dutch sergeants, and other officials were paid accordingly, the temptation to smuggle proved irresistible. Partially to combat this evil, in 1575 the Crown farmed the exclusive right to trade on a twenty-five mile stretch of coast in Cochin-China. Two years later the king began to contract with a company to import spices and deliver them to him at Lisbon at stipulated prices. To another company he farmed the privilege of selling in Lisbon the spices he did not want to market through his factor in the Low Countries. When Philip II succeeded to the Portuguese throne in 1580, he continued to farm the right to import and sell spices and to permit only favorite merchants, willing to pay dearly for royal licenses, to trade with the East Indies. Under the new system spice prices obviously were administered, not competitive; but the corporate monopolists must have been less grasping than their royal predecessor. For in the midst of the Price Revolution, spice prices in Spain dropped precipitately and did not recover the loss for almost half a century.[12] At no time before Portugal lost her supremacy in the East Indies, early in the seventeenth century, did competition govern the purchase or sale of goods either at home or in the colonies.[13]

Portugal attempted to exclude foreigners from the trade with Brazil, but it appears to have been much more open to natives until 1755 than was the East India trade. In 1502 the exclusive privilege of importing Brazil wood was farmed to a company; but the monopoly ended about 1530, when imports from Spanish America rendered it unattractive. From early in the sixteenth century until the middle of the eighteenth century trade with Brazil was confined to fleets that sailed from Lisbon, touched at

[11] Charles de Lannoy and Herman vander Linden, *Histoire de l'expansion coloniale des peuples européens: Portugal et Espagne* (Brussels, 1907), Vol. I, pp. 139-144; Paul Leroy-Beaulieu, *op. cit.,* pp. 48-54; A. H. L. Heeren, *History of the Political System of Europe and Its Colonies* (Eng. tr., Northampton, 1829), Vol. I, pp. 34-39 and 79-80; Hunter, *op. cit.,* pp. 93-174.

[12] Earl J. Hamilton, *American Treasure and the Price Revolution in Spain, 1503-1660* (Cambridge, Mass., 1934), pp. 232-233.

[13] Fitzler, "Überblick über die portugiesischen Überseehandelsgesellschaften des 15. bis 18. Jahrhunderts," *op. cit.,* pp. 285-287; E. P. Cheyney, *European Background of American History* (New York and London, 1904), pp. 131-132; Hunter, *op. cit.,* pp. 175-189; Heeren, *op. cit.,* p. 114; Leroy-Beaulieu, *op. cit.,* pp. 55 ff.; Eli F. Hecksher, *Mercantilism* (Eng. tr., London, 1935), Vol. I, pp. 341-342.

Oporto, and stopped at four leading Brazilian ports. Apparently all Portuguese subjects were free to participate, but we do not know the extent to which formal associations or informal agreements among businessmen or other trading bodies limited competition. By 1750 concentration of the trade in the hands of the Jesuits was so great that the Marquis of Pombal preferred an absolute legal monopoly. Consequently, he divided the trade between the Maranhao Company, chartered in 1755, and the Pernambuco Company, established in 1759. The companies maintained their monopolies on trade with Brazil until there dissolution in 1778 and 1780 respectively. After experimenting with a concession of the diamond mines discovered in 1730, under a strict limitation on the number of workers who might be employed, the Portuguese government adopted drastic measures to curtail smuggling, limit production, maintain prices, and maximize revenues. No building might be erected, and no unauthorized person might reside, within a hundred leagues of the mine. Apparently the supply of diamonds was restricted, but the agriculture and industry extinguished in the blighted area might have been far more productive. Like other colonial powers in America, Portugal restricted or prohibited certain types of industry to protect vested interests at home. To prevent competition with Portuguese wines, olives, and olive oil, no grape vines or olive trees might be planted. The production of raw sugar was encouraged in every possible way, but refineries were banned. Although the Portuguese textile industry languished after the Treaty of Methuen in 1703, only coarse linen and cotton goods to clothe the slaves and poor whites might be produced in Brazil. Early in the nineteenth century skilled spinners who had set up spindles were banished from the colony.[14]

### III. Spain

The high rewards demanded by Columbus in negotiating the contract for his first voyage show that, whatever other incentives he may have had, his economic motivation was strong;[15] and the delay of the Catholic Kings in accepting his terms, after they had accepted his plans, indicates that they shared his concern for the commercial opportunities.[16] The thorough search by Columbus for the precious metals and valuable objects of commerce and the keen interest of Ferdinand and Isabella in what he found point in the same direction.[17] How far it was from the intention of the Spanish monarchs to share the discovery with any other power is shown by their haste in obtaining a papal bull confirming their claims and by the fact

[14] Herman Merivale, *Lectures on Colonization and Colonies*, Vol. I (London, 1841), pp. 51-53; Heeren, *op. cit.*, pp. 81-82, 161-162, 229-230, and 289; de Lannoy and vander Linden, *op. cit.*, pp. 155-170; Leroy-Beaulieu, *op. cit.*, pp. 61-64; Fitzler, "Überblick über die portugiesischen Überseehandelsgesellschaften des 15. bis 18. Jahrhunderts," *op. cit.*, pp. 295-298; "Portugiesische Handelsgesellschaften des 15. und beginnenden 16. Jahrhunderts," *op. cit.*, pp. 241-244.

[15] In his *Kolonien, Kolonialpolitik und Auswanderung* (2nd ed., Leipzig and Heidelberg, 1856, p. 48), Wilhelm Roscher argues that religion strongly motivated not only Columbus but Cortez and Pizarro as well. Roscher recognizes that Columbus wanted money but maintains that it was only as a means toward religious ends. *Cf.* Wilhelm Roscher, *Zur Geschichte der englischen Volkswirtschaftslehre im Sechzehnten und Siebzehnten Jahrhunderts* (n. p., n. d.) pp. 22-23.

[16] Morison, *op. cit.*, pp. 134-139.

[17] According to Adam Smith, an unexcelled judge of the springs of human action, "the pious purpose of converting the natives to Christianity . . . sanctified the injustice" of occupying their territory. "But the hope of finding treasures of gold there, was the sole motive which prompted to undertake it." *Op. cit.*, Vol. II, p. 63.

that from the beginning no Spaniards except Castilians were allowed to trade with the New World. Monopolistic chartered companies developed late and never controlled a major portion of the trade. The only important examples were the exclusive privilege of trading with Venezuela granted the Caracas Company in 1728, and exercised for half a century,[18] and the monopoly on trade with the Philippines given the Philippine Company in 1785. But, as in the case of Portugal, royal regulation, semistate shipping, and the funneling of commerce through staple ports facilitated private monopolies.[19]

The early discovery of gold in the Antilles and the fabulous amounts of silver secured after regular mining by Spaniards began in Mexico and Peru, in an age when treasure was supposed to provide the key to wealth and power, naturally induced one of the most rigid systems of state regulation of colonial trade ever adopted by any country. With infrequent and unimportant exceptions, licenses had to be obtained from, or through, the House of Trade (Casa de la Contratación), established at Seville in 1503 and transferred to Cádiz in 1717, for all vessels, merchants, and emigrants bound for America. All ships had to return to the House of Trade to pass a severe inspection, unload their cargoes, and deliver their gold and silver. In a vain effort to obstruct the leakage of Peruvian treasure into foreign hands, Castile imposed destructive restrictions—limitation of tonnage, absolute prohibitions, and prohibitive duties—upon trade between Buenos Aires and Spain on the one hand and Peru on the other. The economic development of the rich River Plate region was retarded for generations. To prevent bullion from being smuggled into, or captured by, other nations, almost all trade with the New World was confined to two convoyed fleets after the middle of the sixteenth century. The fleets sailed from and returned to the House of Trade once a year when commerce was flourishing and once every three or four years when it was stagnant. The irregular and infrequent sailings from Spain, inevitable under the fleet system, facilitated the inroads of Dutch, French, and English interlopers upon Spanish exclusionism. Arbitrary searches of foreign vessels in Caribbean waters and other vigorous measures of Spain to suppress the contraband trade were a factor in several wars and were the principal cause of the long conflict with England in 1739-50.[20]

Despite the pressure of special interests in Spain, the policy toward the commerce and industry of the American colonies was relatively liberal. Intercolonial trade not considered injurious to Castilian interests, nor likely to facilitate the smuggling of specie out of the realm, was subjected to low duties and suffered few restrictions.[21] No systematic attempts were made to prevent manufactures for domestic con-

[18] Roland D. Hussey, *The Caracas Company, 1728-1784* (Cambridge, Mass., 1934), pp. 35 ff.; Leroy-Beaulieu, *op. cit.*, p. 36.

[19] Gervasio de Artíñano, *Historia del Comercio con las Indias durante el Dominio de los Austrias* (Barcelona, 1917), pp. 51-94; J. H. Parry, *The Spanish Theory of Empire in the Sixteenth Century* (Cambridge, 1940), pp. 3-5 and 39; André E. Sayous, "Partnerships in the Trade between Spain and America and also in the Spanish Colonies in the Sixteenth Century," *Journal of Economic and Business History,* Vol. I (1928-1929), pp. 284 ff.

[20] Earl J. Hamilton, "Spanish Mercantilism before 1700," *Facts and Factors in Economic History* (Cambridge, Mass., 1932), pp. 224-225; J. Piernas Hurtado, *La Casa de la Contratación de las Indias* (Madrid, 1907), pp. 17-55; C. H. Haring, *Trade and Navigation between Spain and the Indies* (Cambridge, Mass., 1918), pp. 21-122; Alfred Caldecott, *English Colonization and Empire* (London, 1891), p. 29; Heeren, *op. cit.,* pp. 288-289; James Mill, *History of British India* (5th ed., London, 1858), Vol. III, p. 36.

[21] The numerous and complicated restrictions on trade between Peru and Central America, Mexico and Central America, and Mexico and the Philippines were designed either to protect Spanish industry or to retain specie in the realm.

sumption, and so long as an industry did not compete with Castile in an external market it remained undisturbed. For example, woolen and silk manufactures, objects of great concern to the mercantilist statesmen and rulers in Spain, were permitted. But in the seventeenth century exports to other colonies were impeded; and the requirement in 1628 of a license from the Council of the Indies to make cloth in America, ostensibly to protect the Indians from exploitation, was designed to protect Castilian industry. Yet Spain was the only country to allow legal operation of refineries in the sugar colonies. At various times the government outlawed the cultivation of saffron, hemp, flax, tobacco, and olives; but at other times the production of hemp and flax was heavily subsidized. The early prohibitions against vineyards in Peru were not enforced; and no attention was paid to the order received by the Mexican Viceroy early in the nineteenth century to have all the vineyards in northern Mexico destroyed, because the Cádiz Guild Merchant had complained that they were disastrously reducing wine imports from Spain.[22]

Until 1785 goods shipped between Spain and the Philippines had to pass over the bad roads and high mountains between the Mexican ports of Veracruz and Acapulco; and the tonnage, value of cargoes, and amounts of specie that might move between New Spain and the Philippines were severely restricted. The members of the Guild Merchant at Mexico City doubtless utilized their opportunity to levy monopolistic toll. For more than two centuries all lawful European imports into Mexico were carried to Veracruz by the New Spain Fleet and those of the entire western coast of South America to Lima via Panama by the Galleons. The restriction of the Mexican and Peruvian commerce to one metropolitan and two colonial ports enabled small groups of traders in the Merchant Guilds at Seville, Cádiz, Mexico City, and Lima to control the volume and dictate the prices of imports and exports in Spain and America. The habilitation of other ports in Spain and America by the so-called "Free Trade Acts" (Libre Comercio) of Charles III and his progressive ministers beginning in 1765 induced some competition. But even in the last years of peace before the outbreak of the wars of the French Revolution, in 1793, ended peacetime trade between Spain and her colonies four-fifths of the American commerce passed through Cádiz. It is highly significant that five of the nine indictments against Spanish rule circulated throughout Hispanic America by the revolutionaries in 1808 concerned monopolistic abuses; and the Cádiz Guild Merchant was bitterly attacked. One of the chief inducements to fight held out by the intellectual leaders in Latin America during the long War of Independence was the promise of fair prices for produce and for imports through the suppression of the Cádiz monopoly.[23]

## IV. Holland

As Spain declined during the seventeenth century, Holland became the foremost nation in the colonial trade, and its United East India Company the leading economic enterprise in Europe. The company was the instrument through which the Dutch

[22] Alexander von Humboldt, *Essai politique sur le royaume de la Nouvelle Espagne* (2nd ed., Paris, 1827), Vol. II, pp. 483-485; J. W. Horrocks, *A Short History of Mercantilism* (New York, n. d.), pp. 100 ff.; Hamilton, "Spanish Mercantilism before 1700," *op. cit.*, pp. 227-228; Merivale, *op. cit.*, pp. 9-14.
[23] Henry C. Morris, *The History of Colonization* (New York, 1900), Vol. I, pp. 261-276 and 295-296; Haring, *op. cit.*, pp. 123 ff.; Leroy-Beaulieu, *op. cit.*, pp. 9-10 and 21-38; Merivale, *op. cit.*, pp. 7-8; Smith, *op. cit.*, Vol. II, pp. 77-78 and 113.

empire in the East was obtained. But there was much less innovation in the Dutch policies than in those of Portugal and rather less than in those of Spain. Furthermore, the original policies remained surprisingly static until the East India Company expired in 1795.[24] Holland was never a major colonial power in the West.

In the Dutch East Indies the flag not only followed the private trader but was firmly planted there by him. When Philip II, in 1594, closed the Lisbon harbor to the Dutch vessels that had been distributing Portuguese spices in northern Europe, in an effort to bring the Dutch rebellion against Spanish rule to an end, the enterprising traders began to sail directly to the East Indies. Commercial success and the disclosure of unsuspected Portuguese weakness in the East induced voyages in rapid succession. In the last five years of the sixteenth century sixty-odd Dutch vessels sailed to the East Indies. The early traders protested that they had to deal with semibarbarous rulers who did not share European conceptions of law and order or of the sanctity of contracts. The Dutch also complained of cutthroat competition with their compatriots in selling European wares and in buying native products. They did lack knowledge of political conditions and of local markets; and owing to the long period of waiting for the returns, the heavy outlay for transportation, and the great and unpredictable risks involved, their capital was pathetically inadequate. To raise funds and end "abuses," in 1602 the traders and other Dutch businessmen formed the United East India Company. Its charter gave it a monopoly on trade and navigation with the East for twenty-one years and authorized it to acquire territory, establish fortresses, and make war and peace within its sphere of operations.[25]

Historians of colonial policy and of the United East India Company agree that almost the only purpose of the Dutch in the East Indies before 1795 was to earn high profits by acquiring and holding a monopoly on spices. I have found no evidence that they ever pretended to Christianize or lift up the natives. In fighting the Portuguese and the native rulers for control over spices, the Dutch adopted the Portuguese tactics of supporting a dynasty or faction and exacting monopolistic privileges after placing it in power. They also copied the Portuguese preference for the spice islands rather than for the mainlands and of trying to attain their commercial objectives by holding a chain of island fortresses. Like the Portuguese, the Dutch early began the practice of destroying surplus spices; that is, the portion of the supply that might depress prices below the point that would maximize their return. But they pushed this nefarious policy much farther. They limited production to certain selected areas, carefully regulated the output, regularly dispatched inspectors to see that the prohibition of production was obeyed, and not only chopped down spice trees but lopped off heads, to leave no producers, when this seemed the only way to enforce compliance.[26]

---

[24] We are told by Professor Clive Day, upon the authority of a leading Dutch historian of the Company, that "it shows no development in its organization or policy. There are marked changes, from one period to another, in the extent of its operations, and in the financial results, but the underlying principles of its actions remain almost the same." *The Policy and Administration of the Dutch in Java* (New York, 1904), p. 39.

[25] O. van Rees, *Geschiedenis der Koloniale Politiek van de Republiek der Vereenigde Nederlanden* (Utrecht, 1868), pp. 1-26; Hecksher, *op. cit.*, pp. 351-360; Leroy-Beaulieu, *op. cit.*, pp. 67-73; Heeren, *op. cit.*, pp. 116-117; H. E. Egerton, "The Transference of Colonial Power to the United Provinces and England," *Cambridge Modern History* (Cambridge, 1934 ed.), Vol. IV, pp. 729-732.

[26] Morris, *op. cit.*, p. 334; Day, *op. cit.*, pp. 88 ff.; Hecksher, *op. cit.*, pp. 360-361; Heeren, *op. cit.*, pp. 118-119; Leroy-Beaulieu, *op. cit.*, pp. 74-82; Merivale, *op. cit.*, pp. 54-55; van Rees, *op. cit.*, pp. 285 ff.; George Edmundson, "Frederick Henry, Prince of Orange," *Cambridge Modern History* (Cambridge, 1934 ed.), Vol. IV, pp. 710-711.

The ridiculous rigidity in the policies of the East India Company, into which it may have been lulled by monopoly and conspicuous success in its first hundred years, was a major factor in its decadence. Even in the most peaceful years of the eighteenth century vessels returning from the Indies had to sail around the Orkneys instead of through the English Channel, as prudence had dictated during the long conflicts with England in the second half of the preceding century. Even after light, fast, and strong English vessels began to compete most effectively in the carrying trade in the East, the Dutch vessels had to incur the heavy and needless expense of passing by Batavia for inspection on each voyage. The monopoly of the East India Company injured not only the natives but the Dutch as well. For example, when the Cromwellian and Stuart Navigation Acts deprived Dutch vessels of their normal cargoes, the Eastern carrying trade might have afforded some relief had it not been closed by the East India Company's monopoly. As in the case of the Portuguese, the chief infringement of the monopoly was by the underpaid officials of the East India Company. But the natives benefited very little from this breach, for the officials arbitrarily set up monopolies of their own and exploited them mercilessly. The murder of English subjects at Amboina in 1623, in defense of the monopoly, embittered relations with England for generations; and more than once Holland went to war to defend the territory or the trade of the East India Company.[27]

Even though rich booty from privateering against Spain, high profits from trading with the Spanish colonies, and a monopoly on trade from Newfoundland to Tierra del Fuego were held out as inducements, private Dutch investors were not attracted by the stock of the Dutch West India Company, organized in 1621. The government had to subscribe for half the shares and to exert the utmost pressure upon financiers to take the balance. Apparently the clever Dutch businessman saw no opportunity to profit by war even against a power at once as weak and as rich in land as was the Spain of Philip IV. The West India Company has been praised by economists for throwing open the trade with Surinam and taxing it lightly instead of exercising its monopoly, as well as for attempting to develop its possessions in the New World. But apparently these policies did not pay. In 1674 the West India Company was dissolved, after having dissipated most of its capital.[28] "Nevertheless, upon the ruins of the defunct institution another was to rise. The States-General, in 1674, licensed the new organization with a capital of 6,000,000 florins. . . . Although active until 1790 it never flourished, and its possessions were few."[29]

## V. France

Of the great colonial powers before 1800, France was the last to enter the field, the least original in its policies, and the least successful in the use of monopolies to open up and maintain colonial commerce. Hence, for my purpose, French experience merits only brief attention.

[27] Day, op. cit., pp. 102-105 and 119-123; Leroy-Beaulieu, op. cit., pp. 77-93; Heeren, op. cit., Vol. II, pp. 108-110, 157-158, and 199-200; Egerton, op. cit., pp. 737 and 745.
[28] Hecksher, op. cit., p. 357; Egerton, op. cit., p. 749; Merivale, op. cit., p. 56; Leroy-Beaulieu, op. cit., pp. 91-92; Cheyney, op. cit., pp. 153-155; Smith, op. cit., Vol. II, pp. 72 and 134-135.
[29] Morris, op. cit., p. 352; H. T. Colenbrander, Koloniale Geschiedenis, Vol. II ('S-Gravenhage, 1925), pp. 1-24.
[30] Die Akkumulation des Kapitals (Leipzig, 1921 ed.), pp. 339 ff.

Since nothing had come from the Company of Sumatra, Java, and Moluccas, chartered in 1600, Henry IV established the first French East India Company in 1604, with exclusive rights to trade, navigate, and colonize in India and the East Indies. Except for 1769-84, trade and navigation with the East under the *ancien régime* remained in the hands of a monopoly. After the vigorous efforts of both Richelieu and Mazarin had utterly failed to vitalize the East India trade, Colbert gave his East India Company, chartered in 1664, the exclusive privilege for fifty years of trading and navigating from the Cape of Good Hope east to the Straits of Magellan, a heavy bounty on imports and exports, a royal guarantee against losses in the first six years, and naval escorts for its vessels at public expense whenever needed. In view of the uncritical acceptance by many liberals and even conservatives of the communist theory of imperialism, repeated with increasing asperity by writers and statesmen from Rosa Luxemburg[30] and Rudolf Hilferding[31] to Lenin and Molotov, one might expect that French capitalists in the age of Louis XIV, the war lord of Europe, were the instigators and eager beneficiaries of these opportunities. But neither financiers, nor overseas traders, nor any other capitalists cared to invest. When venture capital was not forthcoming, Colbert and Louis XIV appealed to the public to buy the East India shares for the glory of God, country, and king—in much the same fashion that the Russian Court was to appeal for funds for the exploitation of the financially unattractive timber concessions along the Yalu River on the eve of the Russo-Japanese war.[32] The royal treasury actually had to put up more than half the money for the French East India Company; and most of the remainder came from public officials, less able than businessmen to resist the formidable pressure to invest, exerted not only by Colbert but by Louis XIV himself. The company lost more than two-thirds of its capital in its first twenty years, and it languished until the brief interval when the organizational skill and inflationary policies of John Law injected life into the East India trade. For about three decades after the collapse of the Mississippi Bubble the monopolistic privileges could not keep the East India Company going without liberal subsidies from the royal treasury. The Seven Years' War stripped the company of most of the territorial gains achieved during the blaze of glory under Dupleix in the middle of the eighteenth century; and in 1769 physiocratic theories, marshalled by Morellet, succeeded in suppressing the monopoly on trade with the East. The flourishing commerce in the brief interval of freedom seemed to vindicate the physiocrats, but in 1785 the monopoly was restored on the ground that cutthroat competition among French traders was ruinously depressing the prices they received and raising those they paid in the East.[33]

Haiti, by far the most important of all the French colonies under the *ancien régime*, was founded by buccaneers and smugglers without the encouragement or even the knowledge of the government. But most of the leading French colonies in the New World were established under patents granting privileges in which a monopoly on trade, in return for the settlement of a certain number of colonists within a limited

[31] "Das Finanzkapital," *Marx-Studien,* Vol. III (Vienna, 1910), pp. 220 ff.

[32] Eugene Staley, *War and the Private Investor* (New York, 1935), pp. 55-62; Lionel Robbins, *The Economic Causes of War* (London, 1939), pp. 47-49. *Cf.* Jacob Viner, "International Finance and Balance of Power Diplomacy, 1880-1914," *The Southwestern Political and Social Science Quarterly,* Vol. IX (1928-1929), pp. 447-451.

[33] Alfred Zimmermann, *Kolonialgeschichtliche Studien* (Oldenburg and Leipzig, 1895), pp. 126 ff.; C. W. Cole, *Colbert and a Century of French Mercantilism* (New York, 1939), Vol. I, pp. 476-524; Hecksher, *op. cit.,* pp. 346-348; Heeren, *op. cit.,* pp. 106-107 and 161; Leroy-Beaulieu, *op. cit.,* pp. 197-201.

period, figured prominently. When the colonial entrepreneurs lost money and their privileges lapsed, a new company was usually formed to exploit them. In the century between Mazarin and John Law the trade of most of the French colonies in America was theoretically controlled by a monopoly most of the time. But Colbert forced the West India Company to allow any French vessel to trade in the sugar colonies upon the payment of duties to the company; and the proximity of Canada to the active traders and accomplished smugglers of New England, together with the great need of the Caribbean islands for Anglo-American provisions and timber, meant that a great many vessels came from other countries as well. One can hardly imagine the descendants of freebooters and free traders or the progenitors of Toussaint l'Ouverture's soldiers in Haiti having much respect for monopolistic privileges at any time. Between 1721 and 1731 the trade of the American colonies was thrown open to all Frenchmen, and apparently it remained open during the remainder of the century. In 1784 the vessels of the United States were permitted to trade with the French possessions in the Caribbean. In the freedom of their trade with all subjects of the motherland, the French colonies probably ranked next to those of England, and in *de facto* trade with the outside world the French colonies probably ranked first. The French colonies also suffered from the fewest restrictions to protect vested interests in the mother country. The only obstructions that seem to have hampered the colonies very much were the prohibition on the erection of new sugar refineries in 1684 and the law of 1698 suppressing the ones already in operation. As a compensation the colonies enjoyed a monopoly on the metropolitan sugar market. The relative economic freedom was doubtless a vital factor in the prosperous agriculture and commerce of Saint Christopher, Martinique, Guadeloupe, and Haiti.[34]

## VI. England

On the whole, England was the leading colonial power in the East and the West before 1800, as well as after. Through monopoly she established her trade and empire in the East, and through promises of monopoly she motivated her early voyages and first successful and unsuccessful colonial ventures in the West. Except for the first half century, when the colonies were few and feeble, England excluded other countries from direct trade and navigation with her American plantations. Since leading historians and economists interested in the history of economic thought have lavished study upon English colonial experience, the policies are too familiar to economic historians to require detailed examination. Hence, it seems safe to assume that the general features are known and to limit our consideration to the salient characteristics and results.

The English East India Company, chartered in 1600, was given a monopoly on trade and navigation in the area between the Cape of Good Hope and the Straits of Magellan not occupied by a friendly power. It was the company, formed and administered by merchants, not the government, that built up the empire in the East—to protect and promote trade. The monopoly of navigation lasted until 1813, but from late in the seventeenth century merchants willing to pay the exorbitant freight rates on the

[34] E. Levasseur, *Histoire du commerce de la France* (Paris, 1911), Vol. I, pp. 481-489; Hereen, *op. cit.,* Vol. I, pp. 220-221 and 284-285; Merivale, *op. cit.,* pp. 57-60; Leroy-Beaulieu, *op. cit.,* pp. 157-190; Cole *op. cit.,* Vol. II, pp. 1-82; Adam Smith, *op. cit.,* Vol. II, pp. 82-83; Sée, *Histoire economique de la France* (Paris, 1939), pp. 245-247.

company's vessels had the right to send a limited tonnage of goods to the East. The energy and ingenuity of traders and the freedom and vigor of thought in England combined to make interloping much commoner than in any other country, and on several occasions the impecunious Crown granted exemptions from the monopoly for particular voyages in return for substantial fees. Opposition to the monopoly by interloping merchants and liberal economists generally enabled the government to exact increasing rewards, ordinarily in the form of loans at less than the going rate of interest, whenever the privileges were renewed. But in 1793 the company secured an extension of its monopoly by demonstrating the enormous profits of recent years and asking whether the objections of mere theorists should delude Parliament into tampering with such a successful enterprise. The "theorists" happened to be interloping merchants as innocent of, and unsympathetic toward, economics as is a typical member of the National Association of Manufacturers. Despite the relatively high and steadily increasing remuneration of the company's employees, it had almost as much difficulty in preventing the abuse of the company and the natives by the petty private monopolies of its servants in the East as did Portugal or Holland. Even as late as the 1760's, the company's Eastern employees dictated the prices they paid for native products and the prices they charged for such imported necessities as salt, tobacco, and betel nuts. Furthermore, they attempted to limit the output of the produce they purchased and to require the natives to buy minimum amounts of what they sold—after the fashion of the seventeenth-century tax farmers in France and Spain who forced the poor to pay for a certain amount of salt whether they used it or not. How prevalent private trading by the company's officers must have been is shown by a minute from Lord Clive on September 19, 1766. He informed the Select Committee that " 'a Governor ought not to be embarrassed with private business. He ought to be free from every occupation in which his judgment can possibley be biased by his interest.' He, therefore, proposed, that the Governor should receive a commission of one and one-eighth per cent upon the revenues; and in return should take a solemn and public oath, and bind himself in a penalty of £150,000 to derive no emolument or advantage from his situation as Governor of Bengal, beyond this commission, with the usual salary and perquisites: and a convenant to this effect was formally executed by him."[35] Nevertheless, to combat private trading, in 1784, servants of the company returning to England were required to give under oath an inventory of their property and rendered liable to imprisonment and the forfeiture of all their wealth for a false statement.[36]

From Henry VII to James I, English patents for voyages of discovery and for colonization generally provided a monopoly of trade as one of the incentives. The companies that established the initial settlements in Virginia and Massachusetts, the first and most important two of the Thirteen Colonies, had either exclusive privileges or the right to tax commerce conducted by others. But these privileges soon lapsed and were not revived. After the first quarter of the seventeenth century no commercial company monopolized trade with the American colonies south of the Hudson Bay region. The Dutch, whose capital is said to have aided in the foundation of the first

[35] Mill, op. cit., p. 301.
[36] Ibid., Vol. I, pp. 17-18, 58-59, and 79-82; Vol. III, pp. 229-234, 255-262, and 287-292; Vol. IV, p. 373; Vol. V, pp. 349-352; and Vol. VI, pp. 1-13 and 252-253; Heeren, op. cit., Vol. I, pp. 119-121; Vol. II, pp. 95-99 and 197-210; Egerton, op. cit., pp. 730-731; Leroy-Beaulieu, op. cit., pp. 150-151; Hecksher, op. cit., p. 409; Adam Smith, op. cit., Vol. II, pp. 135-136; L. S. Sutherland, "The East India Company in Eighteenth-Century Politics," Economic History Review, Vol. XVII (1947), pp. 17-18 and 23-26.

English sugar colonies, soon supplied the shipping and took over a considerable percentage of the trade of the Anglo-American plantations. In 1625 England forbade imports of tobacco in foreign vessels, but frequent repetition of the prohibition suggests that it was not enforced. Amendments to the Navigation Acts beginning about 1663 shifted the colonial trade to English vessels, allowed imports only from England, and required that exports of enumerated articles—for the most part industrial raw materials in short supply—be shipped to England. In compensation for these restrictions the colonies were given a virtual monopoly on the metropolitan market for enumerated articles through prohibitions and prohibitive duties. Particularly after 1699, the manufacture and intercolonial shipment of various manufacturers were banned in order to protect English industries. Adam Smith probably underestimated the efficacy of these restrictions when he dismissed them as "only impertinent badges of slavery," that neither "cramped" nor "restrained" our industry,[37] but the plethora of advertisements of proscribed manufacturers in colonial newspapers indicates that we were "restrained" very little.[38]

In his study of the Navigation Acts, Professor L. A. Harper, who has thoroughly combed the manuscript sources in England and America, concluded that the Acts gave England and the colonies virtual control over the colonial export trade. Through facts and logic he shows that most of the imports came into the Thirteen Colonies in English vessels through legal channels.[39] In his exhaustive study of the records of Thomas and John Hancock, both of whom were notorious smugglers, W. T. Baxter[40] found no evidence that a single foreign vessel participated in trade with the American colonies in the half century prior to the Revolution, when the temptation to smuggle reached its zenith. As Professor Harper has maintained, the Navigation Acts ousted the Dutch from the American trade and gave England the lion's share for several decades. Whether either the colonies or England gained by this diversion is another matter. But there is reason to wonder whether England would not have retained at least as great a proportion of the trade if she had repealed the Navigation Acts at the end of the Seven Years' War.[41] The overwhelming industrial superiority of England over every rival in 1763-75 and the fact that the percentage of American trade obtained by England rose phenomenally in the first quarter-century after the Revolution—in spite of bitter war memories, the loss of commercial connections by English exporters with American importers, and the irritation in this country over our exclusion from legal trade with England's sugar colonies—suggests that a timely repeal of the Navigation Acts and the other restrictions on our economic life might have retained our trade, gained our good

[37] Op. cit., Vol. II, p. 84.
[38] George L. Beer, The Origins of the British Colonial System, 1578-1660 (New York, 1908), pp. 16-17, 142, 220-236 and 239; Leroy-Beaulieu, op. cit., pp. 99-148; Cheyney op. cit., pp. 149-151; Caldecott, op. cit., p. 23; James A. Williamson, A Short History of British Expansion (2nd ed., New York, 1931), pp. 72, 190, and 259-260; H. de B. Gibbins, op. cit., pp. 20-22; Ramsay Muir, The Expansion of Europe (Boston and New York, 1927), pp. 40 ff.; Harry H. Johnston, A History of the Colonization of Africa (Cambridge, 1913), pp. 169-171 and 176; E. F. Slater (ed.), Sir William Alexander and American Colonization (Boston, 1873), p. 244.
[39] The English Navigation Laws (New York, 1939), pp. 43, 239, 244, 246, 253, 262-263, 265, 268, and 270-274.
[40] The House of Hancock (Cambridge, Mass., 1945), p. 297.
[41] Cf. "Citizen Talleyrand," Memoir concerning the Commercial Relations of the United States with England (Eng. tr., Boston, 1809), pp. 9-10; E. A. Benians, "The Beginnings of the New Empire, 1783-1793," The Cambridge History of the British Empire, Vol. II (Cambridge, 1940), p. 13; Klaus E. Knorr, British Colonial Theories, 1570-1850 (Toronto, 1944), pp. 206, 213-219, and 251-253.

will, and possibly averted or delayed the Revolution. But even if the Navigation Acts, not the efficiency of English industry and commerce, did confine the trade of America largely to England, the deleterious effects of the restriction were reduced by the fact that the commerce was not in the hands of a monopolistic company, carried by convoyed fleets at irregular and infrequent intervals, or channeled through a few ports. Adam Smith, who was a keen observer of the American trade in the thriving port of Glasgow and was disposed to see a monopolist wherever he looked, felt that "the number and dispersed situation of the different traders [exporting to America] renders it impossible for them to enter into any general combination" in restraint of trade.[42]

## VII. Conclusions

The leading motive for the discovery of America and the Good-Hope route to the East Indies, which marked the dawn of modern times, was the hope of material gain from the spice trade. It is inconceivable that any country would have willingly shared access to such fabulous riches as the spices of the Eastern seas or the gold and silver of Mexico and Peru. Following the example of the Iberian kings,[43] every other European monarch refused to permit any other power to trade with his colonies before the end of the eighteenth century. Furthermore, staple ports, convoyed fleets, prescribed routes, and special privileges—designed to extend and protect commerce and empire—closed most of the colonies to most of the subjects of most of the colonial powers most of the time.

The Portuguese concessions of monopolies on trade and navigation to companies and court favorites in the days of Prince Henry the Navigator required exploration at a specified rate,[44] and the kings of England and France promised exclusive trading privileges in their early patents for discovery and colonization. Hence, a monopoly on colonial trade was contractually connected with European expansion into the West. The monopoly on trade granted the Dutch, English, and French East India Companies afforded the incentive to commerce and empire in the East.[45] The issuing governments were convinced that without a joint-stock company[46] enjoying an

---

[42] *Op. cit.,* Vol. II, p. 78; Merivale, *op. cit.,* pp. 70-71, 206, and 218; Leroy-Beaulieu, *op. cit.,* pp. 123-124 and 139-140; Heeren, *op. cit.,* Vol. II, pp. 90-93.

[43] On August 14, 1633, a body of men, including the farmers of the customs and colonial merchants, who had been consulted on whether trade with Virginia by foreigners should be permitted, "now urged that the example of Spain be followed, and that strangers be prohibited from trading to the colony." Beer, *op. cit.,* p. 233. *Cf.* Horrocks, *op. cit.,* pp. 99-100; W. C. Abbott, *The Expansion of Europe* (New York, 1918), p. 308.

[44] Morison, *op. cit.,* pp. 43-44.

[45] James Mill, one of the greatest authorities on colonial questions in his, or any other, day, said in his famous essay on "Colonies": "That English law, which establishes the monopoly of the colonies, at least of the transatlantic ones, professes to have in view, not trade so much as defense." The reasoning was that defense depends on the navy, the navy on sailors, and sailors on colonial trade and its monopoly; "therefore, colonies ought to be cultivated, and their trade monopolized" (Supplement to the Fourth, Fifth, and Sixth Editions of the *Encyclopaedia Britannica* [Edinburgh, 1865], Vol. III, p. 270). Mill also asserted that "in the idea of deriving a peculiar advantage from the trade of the colonies is necessarily included the idea of monopoly" (*ibid.,* Vol. III, p. 265).

[46] "The great joint stock companies in the mercantilist period became everywhere something more than mere bearers of trade; they were concerned in fact with purely political expansion. They more than any other institution were responsible for the extension of European hegemony over other continents." Heckscher, *op. cit.,* p. 450.

exclusive privilege of trade and navigation enough capital could not be raised to tide over the long period of waiting for returns, bear the enormous risks, defray the cost of providing and equipping vessels, and "protect" cargoes, merchants, and ships against semibarbarous natives and rulers. Even such an ardent "laissez-fairist" as Jean-Baptiste Say justified monopoly to induce the establishment of trade in "a distant or barbarous area,"[47] just as a patent is granted to reward invention; and Adam Smith had taken a similar position.[48] But both authors insisted that, like a patent, the monopoly should be tolerated for a limited time only. The East India Companies not only held their privileges much longer than was warranted on economic grounds but abused their authority, and petty monopolies by officers and servants on internal trade in the colonies often paralleled the hold of the companies on external commerce.

The monopolistic trading companies depressed the prices of exports and raised those of imports in Europe and the Eastern colonies. In the short run producers suffered, and consumers were permanently oppressed. The high prices paid for imports in colonial and metropolitan markets went to monopolistic middlemen instead of to producers in the exporting countries, who, under perfect competition, could have been expected to increase their output. Factors of production were diverted from their most fruitful use and were underemployed during the transition. In reality the cost of occupying and exploiting backward areas was defrayed by a sort of tax, paid not to the government presumably for the benefit of the body politic, but to a favored group of courtiers and monopolistic traders.[49] The tax was not rational in its amount or incidence; and the poor in the colonies, upon whom a large share of the burden fell, were taxed without representation or even consultation. The monopolistic toll bore no relation to the cost of the "service," but was based on what the traffic would bear.[50]

Without monopoly, there probably would have been no European empire in the East before 1800. Hence, in the final analysis, one's appraisal of the role of monopoly in the expansion to the East depends upon his view as to how well the white man bore his burden. To economic liberals it is gratifying that the American colonies of England and France, where industry and trade enjoyed the greatest freedom, were the ones that achieved the greatest material progress.


# THE EXPANSION OF EUROPE OVERSEAS, 1415-1715

### J. H. Parry

One of the most striking features of the history of the last two hundred years has been the dominant influence exerted by Europeans outside Europe. The "expansion of Europe" was not, of course, deliberately planned, nor was it willingly accepted by non-Europeans, but in the eighteenth and nineteenth centuries it proved

---

[47] *Traité d'économie politique* (Paris, 1803), Vol. I, p. 206.
[48] *Op. cit.*, Vol. II, p. 245.
[49] Popular resentment of the great fortune and questionable ethics of Sir Josiah Child, a prominent mercantilist writer and *the* leading figure in the East India trade, was one of the most powerful weapons against the East India Company when the New Company challenged its privileges. T. B. Macaulay, *History of England* (Leipzig, 1855 ed.), Vol. VI, pp. 247 ff.
[50] *Cf.* W. R. Scott, *The Constitution and Finance of English, Scottish and Irish Joint-Stock Companies to 1720*, Vol. I (Cambridge, 1912), pp. 452 ff.

irresistible; so much so, that the western nations devoted much of their energy to quarrelling over the spoils. The foundations of European dominance were prepared in the fifteenth century, and firmly laid in the sixteenth and seventeenth. In those centuries seafaring Europeans visited almost every part of the world. They met and conquered a great variety of primitive races. They met also many peoples to whom they were themselves barbarians, peoples who were wealthier, more numerous, and to all appearance more powerful than the western invaders. None of these peoples escaped European influence, whether social, religious, commercial or technical. Many of them fell under European rule; and at the same time many of the world's empty spaces were filled by people of European extraction. What were the motives which impelled European nations, from the fifteenth century onward, to embark on a career of overseas expansion? What were the social and technical abilities which gave that expansion such startling success?

In many directions the fifteenth century was for Western Europe a period of contraction, not of expansion. The Chinese Empire was by far the most powerful and most civilized State in the world at that time. It had been governed, at the height of Europe's Middle Age, by a Tartar dynasty whose dominions had included not only China proper, but Mongolia, Turkestan and part of Russia. This Tartar dynasty at one time had shown toleration, even friendliness, towards Christianity. Europeans had visited its Court and Franciscan missionaries had preached within its dominions; but the moment of Christian opportunity had passed in the middle of the fourteenth century, when the rule of the Tartar Khans had been overthrown by a native dynasty, the Mings. Two other great religions, Buddhism and Islam, divided Central Asia between them to the exclusion of Christianity, and communication between Far East and Far West had ceased. South of China, the kingdoms of Indo-China and the East Indian islands, Hindu in origin, by the fifteenth century were falling rapidly under the influence of Islam. In India, civilized and powerful Hindu states were increasingly threatened by Muslim pressure. Nearer to Europe, the Muslim communities of the Near East were falling more and more under the military leadership of the Ottoman Turks, fanatical semi-nomad warriors who were about to engulf the remnants of the Byzantine Empire and to dominate the whole eastern Mediterranean. They took Constantinople in 1453; early in the following century they were to conquer Egypt and Syria, and having overrun the Balkans, were to press along the Danube towards the heart of Central Europe. Islam, and not European Christendom, was the most obviously expanding community in the fifteenth century.

Military and religious rivalry between Christendom and Islam had been a constant feature of European politics throughout the Middle Ages. From the eighth century Arabs and Berbers controlled not only the whole of North Africa, but much European territory as well, in Spain, Portugal and Sicily. This long contact with the Arab world formed part of the education of a rough and primitive Europe. European art and industry owe much to the Arabs. Greek science and learning found their way to mediaeval Europe—in so far as they were known at all—largely through Arabic translations. Even the elaborate conventions of late mediaeval chivalry were to some extent imitated from Arab customs and Arab romances. With all this, however, there was no fusion between the two civilizations. In places where Christian and Muslim lived together on the same soil, a contemptuous toleration might be offered by one race, in return for payment of tribute by the other; but in general the line between Christian and Muslim was clearly drawn and their normal relation was war. So normal and habitual did this war-like relation become that it seemed at times to lose some of war's bitterness and to take on the conventions of the tournament; but some event, some change in the balance of forces always occurred to renew the bitterness. On the one hand, Muslim religious enthusiasm was strengthened from time to time by waves of reinforcement from Central Asia. These waves—of which the Ottoman Turks formed the last and most dangerous—kept the frontiers of Christendom in recurrent fear. On the other hand, the aristocracies of Western Europe, urged on by the Church, sought repeatedly to defend their territories and to recapture lost ground in the Crusades.

The Holy War against Islam was successful in recapturing, in the course of time, all the territories of Southern Europe which had formerly been Christian and Latin-speaking. Outside Europe, the Crusades made little impression upon the body of Islam. The mixture of motives among the Crusaders—religious zeal, personal love of adventure, hope of trade or of plunder, desire for reputation—made for disunity. The European nations never embarked on Crusades as organized states. Even those armies led by kings or by the Emperor in person were bound together only by feudal and personal ties. No kingdom in Western Europe had then an organization capable of administering distant possessions; only the knightly Orders had the organization, and their resources were inadequate. The conquests of the Crusaders—such, for instance, as the Latin states established after the first Crusade—disintegrated of themselves, without needing the pressure of Muslim counter-attack.

The antipathy between Latin and Greek Christians further weakened the crusading movement and diverted it from its main object, the capture of the Holy Places. The fourth Crusade, without seriously harming the Infidel, dealt a crippling blow against the much battered Byzantine Empire. Its chief beneficiaries were the Venetians, firmly established as the carriers of oriental merchandise from the Levant ports to the insatiable markets of Western Europe. With its principal bastion thus weakened, the crusading movement was thrown upon the defensive—an unsuccessful defensive in the face of the advance of the Ottoman Turks in the fourteenth century. It was not the efforts of the Crusaders, but the military successes of a rival conqueror—Timur—further east, which arrested the conquests of the Turkish Sultan Bayezid and granted Europe a short respite at the end of the fourteenth and beginning of the fifteenth centuries. The fall of Constantinople and the conquest of the Balkans by one Asiatic conqueror or another was clearly only a matter of time. The crusading nations of Western Europe had neither the strength, the will nor the unity to prevent it.

Despite the failures and defeats and the ultimate collapse of the crusading movement in the Near East, the idea of the Crusade persisted in all the countries of Europe which were in contact with Muslim peoples. In those countries, crusading was in the blood of most men of gentle birth and adventurous impulses. This was nowhere more true than in Portugal, a poor and small country which owed its national existence to a long Crusade, and in Spain, where the Crusade was still going on. The frustration of the greater Crusade in the Near East led to attempts to find means of attacking Muslim power elsewhere. If not by land, then by sea; if the Infidel were proof against frontal attack, he might be outflanked or taken in the rear; and if the strength of the European Crusaders were inadequate, then alliances might be sought with other Christian princes. Stories were current of powerful though forgotten Christian kingdoms, perhaps in East Africa, perhaps somewhere in Asia. If communications could be established with the East, moreover, by some route outside Turkish control, then the oriental trade which supplied the Turk with much of his wealth might be diverted into Christian channels.

War and trade went hand-in-hand in the later Crusades. Portugal possessed a long ocean seaboard, a considerable fishing and seafaring population, and a powerful commercial class largely emancipated from feudal interference. Portuguese shippers were able and eager to graduate from an Atlantic trade in wine, fish and salt to more widespread and lucrative ventures in slaves, gold and spices. The first and obvious object of Portuguese military and commercial expansion was North-West Africa, where a large and prosperous Muslim community was living almost within hailing distance. Operations began with a seaborne attack on the town and fortress of Ceuta in 1415.

The expedition to Ceuta was a genuine Crusade, though with a limited and temporary object. It was organized by King John I, partly in order to strike a blow against the Moors by sacking one of their principal harbours—the key to the Mediterranean, Azurara called it; partly to give his sons, who were candidates for knighthood, an opportunity to win their spurs in real battle rather than in the artificial fighting of the tournament. The operation was a brilliant success and the fall of Ceuta struck a resounding blow throughout Europe. Its importance lay, not merely in the fact of the capture, but also in the bold decision to hold the place with a Portuguese garrison instead of razing it to the ground. A European state was undertaking, as a State, the defence and the administration of an overseas possession in Muslim territory. Ceuta offered many possibilities: a base for advance into Morocco, or for an attack on Gibraltar, the other great Moorish fortress in the western Mediterranean; the incentive, and probably to some extent the information, needed for the beginning of systematic African exploration and trade. With the capture of Ceuta the crusading movement passed from its mediaeval to its modern phase; from a war against Islam in the Mediterranean basin to a general struggle to carry the Christian faith and European commerce and arms round the world.

The most outstanding figure in the first stages of Portuguese—and indeed of European—overseas expansion was Prince Henry of Portugal, nicknamed by English historians "the Navigator." Prince Henry served with great distinction at Ceuta, not only at the capture in 1415, but also three years later when he relieved the Portuguese garrison from a Moorish counter-attack. He was intimately concerned with the Crusade in both its forms: its older, narrower form of a Mediterranean war against Moor or Turk, and its newer form of a world-wide strategy for the encirclement of Islam, a strategy in which the exploration of the West African coast and the Atlantic islands was only the first move. He is chiefly remembered now as the organizer of African exploration; but for him the African voyages were a new means to an old end. His many-sided character summed up the best of old and new in the changing times in which he lived. He was both recluse and man of affairs; ascetic and generous host; Governor of the knightly Order of Christ, and friend of seamen, merchants, cartographers, instrument makers; a Catholic Christian of deep and orthodox piety, and a patron of much that was new in learning and science. Under such leadership the beginning of European expansion by sea was no sudden break with the past, but the natural outcome of centuries of crusading hope and frustration.

\* \* \*

The capture of Ceuta placed the Portuguese in possession of much information about Africa which was not available to other Europeans. In Ceuta, Prince Henry must have heard of the caravans which crossed the desert to Timbuktu and returned with ivory and gold dust obtained by barter from the negroes of the Niger basin. Probably he learned of the eastern trend of the Guinea coast, giving rise to the hope that Africa was a peninsula, in spite of the teaching of Ptolemy. Possibly also Prince Henry heard through the same channels of the great estuaries of the Senegal and Niger, which might prove to be either straits leading to the Indian Ocean, or else rivers rising in the Mountains of the Moon, the legendary watershed in the centre of Africa which was generally believed to be the source of the Nile.

In 1419, the year after his second expedition to Ceuta, Prince Henry accepted the more or less sinecure office of Governor of the Algarves, the southern-most province of Portugal. He retired from the Court and from politics and began to build his little settlement of Sagres on Cape St. Vincent, the rocky tip of south-west Portugal. Here, overlooking the Atlantic, he held his small court, consisting largely of men who used the sea or were interested in seaborne trade or discovery. Not only sailors, but astronomers, ship-builders, cartographers and instrument-makers, many of them Italians, were invited to visit Sagres, to work at Prince Henry's expense and under his direction. From 1420 the Prince began to send out from the nearby port of Lagos a series of small but regular expeditions to explore the west coast of Africa and eventually to point the way to India.

Although India was known to Europeans only by hearsay, its products were known. According to Azurara's *Chronicle*, Prince Henry was aware of the commercial possibilities of a sea route to the East and longed for an opportunity to convert the teeming populations of India to Christianity. In addition, he hoped to effect a commercial and military junction with the semi-mythical Kingdom of "Prester John." The foundation of fact upon which the Prester John legend rested was no doubt the forgotten Christian empire of Abyssinia, where the Coptic church still maintained a precarious existence, though surrounded by Muslim enemies. If Prester John's kingdom could be found by the Portuguese, the Muslims of North Africa could be encircled by a powerful league of Christian princes. If it proved impossible to sail round Africa, the Portuguese might still find a river or strait in West Africa which would lead them inland to within striking distance of the source of the Nile; they could then sail down the Nile and take the Moors in the rear. If none of these plans proved possible, there remained the fact that caravans from the North African towns were trading with negro tribes on the southern fringe of the great desert; if the Portuguese could make their way by sea to the territories of these negro chiefs they might establish a profitable seaborne trade and make many converts. Finally, in addition to these military, commercial and religious plans, it is probable that Prince Henry was actuated by motives of scientific curiosity; a curiosity which, though characteristic of his family, was shared by comparatively few of his contemporaries but inherited by many of the next generation.

* * *

When the prince found that the discoveries which he organized had considerable commercial value, he secured from his brother the king the sole right to visit and trade with the Guinea coast. At the same time he tried to make the Guinea venture attractive on religious grounds, by obtaining from successive Popes grants of plenary indulgence to all who took part in African exploration; and received also papal confirmation of his own monopoly of the work of converting the African negroes to Christianity. This habit of appealing to the Pope for confirmation of overseas discoveries was an important feature of the diplomacy of the time, and produced awkward complications later, when Spain and other nations entered the field of maritime exploration. It stood Prince Henry in good stead and was an integral part of his policy—the policy of drawing the Portuguese away from Iberian and European politics, and interesting them in activities where their skill as seamen and ship-builders enabled them to outstrip far stronger nations.

Prince Henry used his monopoly generously, and financed foreign as well as Portuguese traders and explorers. The Venetian Cadamosto, for example, made voyages under Prince Henry's license to the Atlantic islands and West Africa as far as the Gambia, in 1455 and 1456. Cadamosto wrote journals which contain vivid descriptions of the places he visited, observations on trade and navigation, and a wealth of entertaining details such as the most convincing early description of a hippopotamus and some useful hints on how to cook ostrich eggs. This garrulity on Cadamosto's part is a welcome change from the silence of his Portuguese contemporaries. The official Portuguese policy was one of secrecy concerning discoveries, and this secrecy grew closer and stricter after Prince Henry's death.

* * *

The development of the spice trade in the fifteenth century was closely bound up with the expansion of Islam, both west and eastward, at the expense both of Christian and Hindu. The Ottoman Turks were terrorizing eastern Europe. Other central Asian peoples were pressing into India. A series of foreign Muslim dynasties had long been established at Delhi, and a string of loosely organized Muslim sultanates ruled the west coast as far south as Goa. Only in the south the wealthy and powerful kingdom of Vijayanagar survived as the principal stronghold of Hindu power. At the same time Islam was expanding by sea. Arab colonists had long controlled the towns and trade of East Africa as far south as Mozambique. Muslim traders were spreading their religion through the East Indies and establishing trading principalities. Petty sultans, often Malay in race, usually Muslim in religion, set up as merchant princes in the principal spice-producing islands. Wherever the European Christians went in the East they found that the Muslims had gone before them, and by 1500 both the production of spices and the trade in spices were largely in Muslim hands.

* * *

A fleet sailed in 1500 under Pero Alvárez Cabral, who upon his arrival at Calicut, quarrelled with the resident Muslim merchants and with the Hindu authorities, and established a factory at the rival port of Cochin, farther down the coast. The third Indies fleet, commanded again by Vasco da Gama, sailed in 1502. This was a powerful and well-armed force, fourteen sail in all, and with it da Gama carried out a heavy bombardment of the town of Calicut, an important event in the history of naval gunnery as well as in that of Indo-European relations. Da Gama also fought and won the first naval pitched battle in the struggle for control in the East, against a fleet equipped by the Malabar Arabs. The Arab fleet, though numerous, apparently had no manoeuvring organization, and its gunnery was poor. It was almost annihilated by a much smaller Portuguese squadron which had been trained to use its guns and to manoeuvre as a squadron.

These early voyages to India demonstrated that a Portuguese fleet, if properly armed and well commanded, could defeat any Asiatic fleet in the open sea. Further proof was provided by the decisive victory of Almeida, the first Portuguese viceroy, over the combined Egyptian and Gujerati fleets off Diu in 1509. It remained true, however, that in fair and open trade the Portuguese could not compete with the Arabs or rely upon the goodwill of the local Hindu rajas. European manufactures were crude and unattractive in Eastern eyes; and the local rulers could not be expected to see, in the tatterdemalion crews living in crowded squalor in their sea-stained ships, the fore-runners of a power which was to conquer half the East. Momentarily dangerous the Europeans might be; but in the eyes of a cultivated Hindu they were mere desperadoes, few in number, barbarous, truculent and dirty. It became clear that in order to profit fully by their monopoly of the Cape route the Portuguese would have to destroy the Arab trade in spices by force of arms at sea. The task of planning and executing this naval war fell to the ablest sea commander of his day, Affonso d'Albuquerque.

The Portuguese plan in the East was never one of mere commercial competition. They never proposed to undersell Arab and Venetian merchants by flooding Europe with cheap spices; nor could they have done so if they had wished. The relation between Portuguese and Arabs from the start was war, embittered by all the circumstances of racial and religious hatred.

When Albuquerque first went out to India in 1503, the Portuguese settlements consisted merely of warehouses where the royal factors and the agents of the Lisbon merchant houses chaffered for spices in the squalor of the water-front bazaars. Every year or every other year, armed fleets sailed from Lisbon to collect the spice cargoes. The tenure of the factories and the continuance of the trade depended on the forbearance of the local rajas. To convert this precarious foothold into an enduring maritime and Christian Empire, the Portuguese needed a permanent fleet in the Indian Ocean. For this, they required a secure naval base with adequate facilities for provisioning and refitting their ships, and a reserve of seafaring men on the spot to replace the appalling losses caused by climate and disease among their ships' companies. In addition, they needed fortresses, supported by mobile cruiser squadrons, commanding the termini and clearing-houses of the Indian Ocean trade routes. They had to change an entirely seaborne interloping commerce based on Lisbon, into a chain of permanent commercial and naval establishments covering the whole of the Middle East. This was the costly and ambitious plan which Albuquerque forced on a parsimonious government, when in 1509 he became governor-general in succession to Almeida.

* * *

Albuquerque never undertook the responsibility and expense of territorial acquisitions unless they contributed directly to the needs of the fleet. In all the ports held by the Portuguese, fortress areas were set apart containing the dockyards, the warehouses, the barracks and the living quarters of the European residents. Captains of ports seldom intervened in administrative matters outside the fortress areas, except in the event of serious risings or riots threatening Portuguese interests. Even at Goa, the Hindu and Muslim communities were necessarily governed mainly through their own headmen. Obviously if the Portuguese had tried, as the Spaniards did, to train their newly conquered subjects in European ways, the attempt would have failed; but even the will was lacking. Few Portuguese governors deviated from a strictly commercial policy. There was plenty of missionary activity, of course; to this day there are in

South India and Ceylon considerable numbers of Christians with Portuguese baptismal names—Catholic Christians, distinct from the much older Nestorian communities. But they are only a fraction of the population. On the whole the Portuguese showed remarkable obtuseness in dealing with native religions. They regarded the Hindu, in the early years at least, as a kind of Christian, and were outraged when he refused to behave as such. The Muslim was always a potential enemy. Albuquerque himself, alone among Portuguese governors, tried to establish peaceful relations with the resident Muslims and to attach them to his person; but even he could not ruin their trade with one hand, and convert them to Christianity with the other.

* * *

The Spanish conquest in America was a genuine crusade, appealing alike to the missionary's zeal for souls and the soldier's desire for military glory and for plunder. Unlike earlier crusades, however, it brought in its train an immense task of imperial government. The *conquistadores* had gone to America at their own expense, endured great hardships, risked their lives and fortunes—such as they were—without help from the Spanish state. Most of them looked forward to a pensioned retirement; some living in Spain upon the labour and the tribute of the conquered races as the Incas and the Aztecs had done before them. Left to themselves, they would probably have settled in loose communities, employing the feudal forms which already were anachronisms in Spain, exploiting the Indians as the needs of the moment dictated, and according verbal homage but little else to the Spanish Crown. Many of the rebel leaders in Peru—in particular, Gonzalo Pizarro—contemplated just such a society, extravagantly loyal in sentiment but in practice virtually independent.

The rulers of Spain never for a moment thought of allowing such a state of affairs to persist. In the late fifteenth and early sixteenth centuries the Crown, with considerable bloodshed and expense, had successfully cut the claws of the great feudal houses, of the knightly orders and of the privileged local corporations. A growing royal absolutism could not tolerate the emergence of a new feudal aristocracy overseas. At the same time royal government was by no means a lawless or unbridled absolutism. The Church and the legal profession were its honoured partners and its most useful servants. The conquest of America touched not only the royal authority, but the royal conscience and the tradition of royal justice.

Discussion of the nature and duties of kingship, in both legal and theological terms, was a commonplace in sixteenth-century Spain. It was an age of vigorous and outspoken political thought, thought which was, for the most part, resolutely opposed to despotism and which placed the law of God and the laws and customs of free peoples above the will of kings. The conquest of a great and simi-barbarous empire obviously presented a difficult problem to the apologists for constitutional kingship. They all admitted—no Catholic could deny—that the bulls issued by Alexander VI in 1493 had given to the Spanish Crown the duty and the sole right of converting the American natives to the Christian faith. If the Indians resisted the preaching of the Gospel, they might lawfully be subdued by force of arms. The duty of civilizing a barbarous people and the fact that the Spaniards were the first Europeans to discover America were valid, though secondary reasons for the conquest. But if the Indians should be reduced by a just conquest, what legal and political rights remained to them? Should their rulers be deposed—if indeed they had legitimate rulers? Should they be "converted" by force? Might they be enslaved, or deprived of land or property? Were they to be subject to Spanish courts of law, civil and ecclesiastical? What claims had the Spanish settlers upon the tribute and labour of the Indians?

Spanish writers differed profoundly in their answers to these questions, and the main ground of difference was the nature of the Indians themselves. The colonists naturally emphasized the apparent idleness of people accustomed to subsistence farming, and the treacherous resentment of a conquered race. They claimed unfettered local lordship based on forced labour and maintained, not without some plausibility, that a paternal feudalism would best serve the interests of the Indians themselves. Many missionaries, on the other hand—in particular the famous Dominican preacher Las Casas—insisted on the purely spiritual nature of the Spanish enterprise. Las Casas's theory of empire rested upon the belief that the Indians, equally with the Spaniards, were the natural subjects of the Spanish Crown, and enjoyed from the moment of entering into the Spanish obedience all the guarantees of liberty and justice provided by the laws of Castille. He maintained that they were capable intellectually of discharging the duties of Spanish subjects and of receiving the faith. He contemplated an ideal empire in which the Indians would live under their own headmen but subject to the authority of benevolent royal officials who would instruct them in European customs and persuade them to abandon barbarous practices. The Church would proceed peacefully with its work of conversion and spiritual ministration. If other Europeans, as private persons, were allowed to reside in the Indies, they would live apart from the Indians and support themselves by their own labour.

Las Casas was no mere theorist, but a devoted missionary who had himself pacified a large and savage tract of country in Central America. In Spain he was a powerful and respected personality. He represented, of course, an extreme view. The opposite view, that of the colonists, also had its defenders, notably Juan Ginés de Sepúlveda, the distinguished scholar and humanist and friend of Erasmus, one of the ablest apologists of European imperialism. Between Sepúlveda and Las Casas, and between the schools and the interests which they represented, there was fierce and acrimonious debate. The importance of such controversies lay in the public interest which they aroused, and in their effect on royal policy. Spanish methods of government, as distinct from methods of conquest, were cautious, legalistic, slow, above all conscientious. They were influenced both by reports of practical experience and by considerations of abstract right. By the middle of the sixteenth century there emerged from the dust of controversy an official policy and an official theory of empire which, despite constant vacillations in matters of detail, were maintained with very fair consistency for over two hundred years.

The Indies were kingdoms of the Crown of Castille, separate from the kingdoms of Spain, and administered through a separate royal council. The Indians were the direct subjects of the Crown, not of the Spanish state or of any individual Spaniards. They were free men, and might not be enslaved unless taken in armed rebellion. Their land and property were their own, and might not be taken from them. Their headmen were to be confirmed in office and employed as minor officials. They were to be subject to Spanish courts of law, and might sue Spaniards and be sued by them; but their own laws were to be respected except where they were clearly barbarous or repugnant to the Spanish laws of the Indies.

The Indians were, of course, to be converted to Christianity as soon as possible and were to be admitted to all the sacraments of the Church. Their conversion was to be free and not forced, and their lapses into heresy were to be dealt with by the ordinary jurisdiction of the bishops, not by the Inquisition.

To meet the claims of the colonists, the Crown granted to deserving conquerors and settlers the right to draw the assessed tributes of specified villages, by way of pension. These grants of *encomienda* involved no jurisdiction or territorial lordship; nor, after the middle of the century, forced labour. They did involve, for the *encomendero,* the obligation of military service and the duty of paying the salaries of the parish clergy. Forced labour was permitted—was indeed found to be indispensable; but under the *mita* or *repartimiento* system, the compulsion was applied by public, not private authority, and official wage-rates were laid down for labour so recruited.

Of course, the decrees enjoining this policy were often obstructed and sometimes openly defied; but that does not detract from the merits of the policy, as a product of sixteenth-century thought and experience. The enforcement of the policy, moreover, though incomplete, was by no means as incompetent as the enemies of Spain pretended.

*  *  *

By the beginning of the eighteenth century European merchants, missionaries and planters had founded permanent settlements in all the continents of the world except Australia and the Antarctic. The nature of these settlements varied greatly; but all alike depended upon a mother country in Europe. None was self-supporting; none yet aspired to independence of the founding state, though some colonies had changed hands as a result of European wars, and many were to change hands in the eighteenth century. In spite of this common dependence, there was a wide diversity between different types of colony. The hold of the European nations upon many of their outposts was still weak. Only a few relatively small areas could be said to be Europeanized, and the most potent factor in determining the nature of a European colony was the character of the native race among whom it was planted.

In some parts of the world Europeans had settled as a permanent resident aristocracy among more primitive, but settled peoples, living by their labour and to a varying extent inter-marrying with them. This was the situation in Spanish and Portuguese America; though the areas under effective European government still covered only a part of the immense regions claimed by Portugal and Spain, and no province was without its Indian "frontier." In the West Indies also, Europeans formed a resident aristocracy, though the primitive labour force there was not native but imported.

In other regions, where the native population was too sparse or too intractable to furnish an adequate labour force, and where negroes could not thrive, Europeans had cleared the land, pushed the natives aside, and formed purely European communities, living largely by their own labour as farmers, fishermen or traders. A thin fringe of settlements of this type stretched along the Atlantic seaboard of North America; settlements with busy towns and harbours looking towards Europe, but with a dangerous forest frontier not far inland. English and French America still lagged far behind Spanish America in population, wealth and cultural attainments, but was growing rapidly in strength and assertiveness.

In the Old World, Europeans had concentrated their efforts upon regions known to produce articles of value, and armed commercial monopoly rather than empire had been their principal object. In West Africa, source of slaves and ivory, the climate prevented them from settling. In most parts of the East they found civilized peoples, powerful and numerous enough to resist the settlement of Europeans as a resident aristocracy. Europeans had invaded the East as crusaders, as armed traders and as pirates. By developing their technical advantages in shipping and armament, by exploiting oriental dissensions, by using force here and diplomacy there, they had secured commercial footholds in many parts of the East; but they were far from ruling as overlords. Except for a few small areas in Malabar and in the East Indian islands, their actual possessions were still confined to forts and trading factories.

With all these qualifications, the spectacle of European world-wide power was already impressive. It was long since the process of expansion had suffered a major set-back. Even the humiliation of the English East India Company at the hands of Aurangzeb had had but little permanent effect upon the fortunes of the English in India. The colonizing peoples of western Europe looked out upon the world with eager and greedy confidence. Their vital technical superiority in ships and guns was increasing. The late seventeenth and early eighteenth centuries saw great improvements in the rig of sea-going ships, notably the introduction of fore-and-aft headsails working on the stays, and a little later the transformation of the cumbersome lateen mizen into the fore-and-aft "spanker." Both the art of navigation and the design of navigators' instruments were advancing rapidly, with the increasing application of scientific knowledge to technical development. The design of guns, it is true, was changing little; but guns were increasing in size, and the iron-founding industry which produced them was developing fast, especially in England. Throughout the eighteenth century the colonizing nations expanded their trade, added to their territory and exported emigrants at an ever-increasing rate. As their acquisitions increased, their determination to dominate certain favoured areas increased also. In no other century in European history was there more constant and more bitter fighting over the possession of colonial territory. The fighting now took the form of full-scale war in Europe and at sea, as well as the familiar quarrels between rival colonizing groups overseas. Disputes over colonial territory and trade had become too serious to lie outside the normal orbit of European diplomacy, as they had done to some extent in former centuries.

The aims and methods of territorial and commercial expansion had changed profoundly in three hundred years. In the East, the original object of European commercial intrusion had been to establish a monopolistic trade to Europe in small quantities of rare and valuable products, such as spices, silk and precious stones. The Portuguese had obtained these cargoes for themselves, and denied them to others, as often by force or threats of force as by peaceful trading. Their commerce was very close to piracy. By the early eighteenth century European traders in the East had developed in addition a much greater bulk of trade with Europe and between eastern countries in commodities which were in high demand without being particularly valuable or rare: cotton cloth, rice and coffee. To maintain monopolies in all these commodities, it was necessary to control their production so as to ensure a steady but exclusive supply. From being a disturbing predatory element in eastern commerce, the European trading companies were becoming settled powers, exacting tribute as well as monopolizing trade, each interested in the maintenance of stable and profitable conditions in its own area. Each group was intensely jealous of other Europeans and was ready to exploit local disputes in order to protect or extend the sphere of its operations.

In the New World the order of development was reversed. Conquest and settlement, not commerce, had been the objects almost from the start. Since resistance was relatively weak, stable European communities ruling considerable tracts of country, with or without native labour, emerged quickly from the initial stage of fighting and treasure-hunting. Once these communities were established, however, their trade with Europe became a vital consideration. By the early eighteenth century the attention of colonizing governments was concentrated mainly upon territories which produced large quantities of exportable raw materials and which provided stable and exclusive markets for the products of their home countries. Colonial administration and colonial wars in the New World as in the Old were more and more coming to serve the ends of commerce to the exclusion of other considerations.

Buccaneering had ceased to be a semi-respectable profession; but the slave trade, which supplied the labour for sugar and tobacco plantations, was in its heyday. Slaves were wanted not only in Spanish and Portuguese America and in the West Indies, but increasingly in the plantations of Virginia, Carolina, Gerogia and Louisiana. The eighteenth-century slave trade, with the warm approval of government, made the port of Liverpool and was an important factor in the commercial predominance of England.

Negro slaves were not the only unwilling emigrants to the New World. With the steady development of industry in England in the eighteenth century, "colonies of settlement" came back into official favour as markets for manufactures, and government approval was assured for any effort made to populate them. In England there was no longer religious persecution or civil strife to drive people overseas; but in other parts of Europe, especially in Ireland and the Palatinate, recurrent famine and war were leaving thousands of families destitute. Labour was needed in the colonies at almost any price. The captains of trans-Atlantic packets used every method from persuasive advertisement to kidnapping to induce these unfortunates to emigrate. The seventeenth-century trickle of non-English emigrants to English America swelled in the early eighteenth century to a torrent. The long line of the Indian frontier, which had been more or less stationary in the later seventeenth century, began to roll steadily back towards the mountains in the early eighteenth.

In these "colonies of settlement," where the natives were relatively few and primitive, European advance was not seriously retarded either by Indian resistance or by any great tenderness for Indian interests. But where the Indians were numerous and docile, the increasing concentration upon commercial objects accompanied and reflected a steady change in the attitude both of Governments and of colonists towards native races. The old crusading spirit in which the expansion movement was conceived had disappeared in the course of the sixteenth century. The holy war against the infidel could appeal in full force only to peoples who had felt themselves seriously threatened by Islam. The plunder and devastation which accompanied the holy war could not be carried on indefinitely against peoples who submitted, however unwillingly, to European government. Conversion by the sword was repudiated in the sixteenth century both by theologians and by conscientious administrators.

In the colonies of the Catholic powers in the sixteenth century the period of crusading war and plunder had been succeeded by a period of deep and thoughtful missionary fervour. In Spanish America above all the Church had striven not only to convert but to teach the Indians, and to recruit and train an educated native priesthood. By the end of the sixteenth century, it is true, the Spanish missionaries' attitude towards the Christian Indian was becoming less optimistic. The ideal of a native priesthood was abandoned, partly through conviction of its hopelessness, partly through social opposition from secular sources. The principle upon which Las Casas had insisted so strongly, that the Indian was potentially the spiritual and intellectual equal of the European, was less emphatically urged in the seventeenth century both by theologians and by those who professed to know the Indian. Nevertheless, the work of spreading the Faith went on in hundreds of Franciscan and Jesuit missions, penetrating into remote regions of the Americas far beyond the limits of ordinary white settlement. In the Portuguese East also, the work of Jesuit missionaries went on steadily, though often discredited by the piracies which their countrymen committed. In Europe the establishment in 1622 of the Propaganda—the Congregation for the Propagation of the Faith—evinced the direct concern of the Papacy in colonial missions, in the training of missionaries, and once again in the creation of native priesthoods.

In the late seventeenth century, despite the efforts of the Propaganda, missionary enterprise began to slacken. The growing weakness of Spanish and Portuguese colonial government and French preoccupation with European affairs together caused a loss of effective support. The general intellectual temper of Europe, also, grew less favourable to missions. In the eighteenth century, a rationalistic humanism, often antagonistic to Christianity, was to sap the religious enthusiasm of educated people throughout western Europe, and the decline of Catholic missionary effort was to be accentuated by the expulsion of the Jesuit order from the territories of France, Portugal and Spain. Moreover, the main initiative in expansion was passing from the Catholic to the Protestant nations of Europe; and though many Dutchmen and Englishmen had carried abroad religious convictions of a most uncompromising kind, they had shown considerably less skill and enthusiasm than their Catholic rivals in missionary enterprise. There were in New England some notable exceptions. Societies were formed quite early in the seventeenth century for evangelizing the North American Indians, but their achievements were comparatively small. The Dutch Calvinists in the East, particularly in Ceylon, made some converts, but mainly from Catholic Christianity; they made little impression upon the vigorous Buddhism of Ceylon, or upon Islam elsewhere. In general it was not to be expected that commercial concerns should spend much money or thought upon missionary work.

The general decline in missionary enthusiasm by the early eighteenth century was accompanied by a corresponding decline in a sense of responsibility for the material well-being of subject races. In Spanish America the alienation of Indian land, which the Hapsburgs had tried to prevent, proceeded rapidly under the Bourbons; peonage—debt-slavery—became more and more frequent; and the Indians were increasingly subjected to a new form of *repartimiento*—the forced sale of unwanted manufactured goods by local officials. The far-reaching reforms which the Bourbons introduced in Spanish colonial government, unlike much of the legislation of former years, was inspired by a desire to rationalize administration and foster trade rather than by concern for Indian interests. In Brazil the damage done by gold- and slave-hunting *bandeiras* went unchecked by government, though not unreproved by missionaries. In most parts of English America the relations between colonial government and Indian tribes in time of peace were mainly concerned with trade and the purchase of land, by treaties whose clauses often contained a studied ambiguity. The Indians were never regarded as subjects, in any close sense, of the English Crown. In the East the Dutch East India Company was imposing a peaceful and relatively tolerant rule upon the limited territories which it governed directly, but at the cost of a systematic and ruthless subordination of all native economic activity to the trading needs of the company.

The idea, so prominent in present-day theories of colonization, that subject races should be trained to govern themselves in European fashion, has never been entirely absent from European thought. Several Spanish writers in the sixteenth century hinted at such a policy, and determined efforts were made to introduce municipal government of the Spanish type into Indian towns. Such theories had been largely abandoned by the early eighteenth century, though they never quite disappeared. John Archdale advocated an extensive scheme of Indian education in Carolina. He believed "that the hand of God was eminently seen in thinning the Indians to make way for the English" but that the survivors should be taught that the English "were once as they were, but were reduced into a civilized state by a Noble and Heroick Nation." Nothing came of such proposals. In Europe as a whole, neither legislation, writings nor speeches in the early eighteenth century showed much evidence of a feeling that the possession of colonies carried with it a duty towards their non-European inhabitants.

The imperialism of eighteenth-century Europe had many ugly characteristics. It was truculent, cynical and greedy. It combined self-satisfaction with an insensitiveness to the sufferings of other peoples, repugnant not only to the best thought of our time, but to that of the sixteenth century also. Of course greed and brutality had marked every stage of the expansion; but in the earlier days there had been a great sense of wonder, a certain humility underlying the truculence, sometimes an anxious searching of conscience. It is difficult to avoid the conclusion that the general European attitude towards non-Europeans had coarsened and hardened with successful expansion. Familiarity had bred contempt.

Successful expansion was to continue throughout the eighteenth and nineteenth centuries. Despite the constant colonial wars of the eighteenth century, despite the successful political revolt of many European colonial communities, the extension of European influence was continuous, and in time a new sense of responsibility developed. In the East, European governments belatedly recognized that trading corporations, left to themselves, could not be expected to administer vast non-European territories either efficiently or justly. In the West, the slave trade was swept away by a strong and surprisingly sudden growth of humanitarian feeling. The nineteenth century saw the development for the first time of widespread missionary enthusiasm among Protestant peoples—enthusiasm which was to take a highly practical turn in medical and educational directions. The foundations of the revival had indeed been laid in the apparently unpropitious years of the eighteenth century. The English Society for the Propagation of the Gospel was founded in 1701, largely for work among negro slaves. The influence of such bodies in that age of rationalism was at first very small, but later in the century the Moravian communities, English Methodism and other revival movements helped to stir public opinion in many parts of Europe. In more recent times missionary societies of all kinds have played an increasingly important part, not only in education and evangelization overseas, but in teaching European peoples a sense of responsibility towards weaker races.

In "trusteeship" Europe has at present a theory and a policy of colonial government to which all colonizing states profess at least a formal adherence. The early eighteenth century had no such common theory; but the ideas upon which "trusteeship" is based are not new. They are all to be found in sixteenth- and seventeenth-century doctrines of natural law. No firmer insistence could be found than that of the great jurist, Vitoria, lecturing at Salamanca in 1532:

These people [The American Indians] are not unintelligent, but primitive; they are incapable of maintaining a civilized State according to the requirements of humanity and law; . . . their government, therefore, should be entrusted to people of intelligence and experience, as though they were children . . . But this interference must be for their welfare and in their interests, not merely for the profit of the Spaniards; for otherwise the Spaniards would be placing their own souls in peril.

It might be argued that Vitoria's distinction was unreal, the expression of a corporate European hypocrisy. The missionary and the honest administrator, however well-intentioned, may be insidious destroyers of the culture of subject peoples and unconscious agents of the greed of the conquerors. This fact did not escape the notice of some of the early Spanish writers; it is mentioned frequently by the great missionary anthropologist, Sahagún, and in many official reports from Spanish America. Nowadays it is a commonplace that the sudden introduction of European law, European habits and European technical devices among people to whom they are unfamiliar may have disastrous results. These misgivings are yet another expression of a sense of imperial responsibility, of a conscious desire among thoughtful Europeans to soften, since they cannot prevent, the impact of one culture upon another, and to offer the best, not the worst, of European civilization to the rest of the world. Vitoria's distinction was a real one. No nation undertakes the labour and expense of colonial expansion without hope of profit; but throughout the whole story of European expansion there has been conflict between an imperialism interested only in profits an imperialism which accepts duties also. The feeling of duty, of responsibility, was relatively weak in the eighteenth century, weaker than it had been in the sixteenth, weaker than it is to-day; but it was never entirely absent. It was the product of a continuous missionary tradition running back to the thirteenth century.

# 7 / The Crisis of the Seventeenth Century

"The middle of the seventeenth century was a period of revolutions in Europe," wrote H. R. Trevor-Roper, thus summarizing the series of convulsions in England, France, the Netherlands, Spain, and Naples. Recognizing that the upheavals varied according to regional and localized causes and characteristics, the author nonetheless detected a broad family resemblance among the issues and participants and concluded that there was a "general crisis" in Europe during this period. That historians have undertaken with increasing frequency to ascertain larger cross-cultural, transnational patterns in the European past—especially with regard to revolutionary or quasirevolutionary phenomena—is an important development in the discipline. Comparative studies have opened many avenues of insight, deepening and broadening understanding of the components of European civilization. The historical perspective that recognizes the international impact of revolution has doubtlessly been sensitized by twentieth-century experience. Extended fruitfully and critically into the past, historical analyses based on a search for common elements among diverse national experiences have produced, for example, the important and provocative idea of a world revolution in the west in the late eighteenth century (see Chapter 13).

Traditionally, the unifying theme describing the sixteenth- and seventeenth-century European upheavals has focused on those international religious tensions which reverberated out of the Reformation and the Counter-Reformation. In the first selection, Professor Trevor-Roper shifts this emphasis to a different plane, identifying a "general crisis" in the late Renaissance that subsumes the religious question. In this crisis, the "Court" and "Country" or the "State" and "Society" angrily faced each other. His case is illustrated most fully by the English civil war of 1640-1660.

The burden of this analysis is borne in the way Trevor-Roper determines the social composition and political commitment of the contending parties within each national crisis. He identifies the Court party as a composite of royal servants, administrators, and fuctionaries—largely, a bureaucratic element dependent on royal appointment, patronage, and finances. He contends that the size and expense of maintaining this establishment began to outstrip the national capacities supporting it, particularly for those nations engaged in the exhausting Thirty Year's War. Consequently, enormous tension resulted between the "Court" and the "Country" at large.

Could reform measures be employed to alleviate this tension? (This question has been raised also about the situation in France just prior to 1789.) Any answer must be tentative: possibly, but reform jeopardized the very status and prestige of the state establishment and would be inconsistent with its survival.

Is Trevor-Roper's analysis of bifurcation in the ruling elites applicable to the continent? With respect to the French *Fronde*, Professor Roland Mousnier discusses his own doubts about the analysis, although he accepts the existence of a midcentury "general crisis." In reading the second selection, it is important to note where

Mousnier alters and where he sustains Trevor-Roper's application of the "general crisis" to France.

In the third selection, Professor J. H. Elliott questions the inclusion of Spain, although, again, Trevor-Roper's perspective is not totally rejected. In the Spanish case, there is the complicating ingredient of an important Church bureaucracy in the service of the State. Elliott asks if the theory, as laid forth by Trevor-Roper, does not export an analysis, valid for England, to the continent?

Finally, a brief response by Trevor-Roper to his critics concludes this section. Does he satisfy the objections which were levelled against his original presentation of the seventeenth-century crisis?

# THE GENERAL CRISIS OF THE SEVENTEENTH CENTURY*

## H. R. Trevor-Roper

The middle of the seventeenth century was a period of revolutions in Europe. These revolutions differed from place to place, and if studied separately, seem to rise out of particular, local causes; but if we look at them together they have so many common features that they appear almost as a general revolution. There is the Puritan revolution in England which fills the twenty years between 1640 and 1660, but whose crisis was between 1648 and 1653. In those years of its crisis there was also the series of revolts known as the Frondes in France, and in 1650 there was a *coup d' état* or palace revolution, which created a new form of government in the United Provinces of the Netherlands. Contemporary with the troubles of England were those of the Spanish Empire. In 1640 there was the revolt of Catalonia, which failed, and the revolt of Portugal, which succeeded; in 1641 there was nearly a revolt of Andalusia too; in 1647 there was the revolt of Naples, the revolt of Masaniello. To contemporary observers it seemed that society itself was in crisis, and that this crisis was general in Europe. "These days are days of shaking . . ." declared an English preacher in 1643, "and this shaking is universal: The Palatinate, Bohemia, Germania, Catalonia, Portugal, Ireland, England."[1] The various countries of Europe seemed merely the separate theatres upon which the same great tragedy was being simultaneously, though in different languages and with local variations, played out.

What was the general cause or character of this crisis? Contemporaries, if they looked beyond mere surface parallels, tended to find deep spiritual reasons. That there was a crisis they felt sure. For a generation they had felt it coming. Ever since 1618 at least there had been talk of the dissolution of society, or of the world; and the undefined sense of gloom of which we are constantly aware in those years was justified sometimes by new interpretations of Scripture, sometimes by new phenomena in the skies. With the discovery of new stars, and particularly with the new comet of 1618, science seemed to support the prophets of disaster. So also did history. It was at this time that cyclical theories of history became fashionable and the decline and fall of nations was predicted, not only from Scripture and the stars, but also from the passage of time and the organic processes of decay. Kingdoms, declared a Puritan preacher in 1643, after touching lightly on the corroborative influence of the comet of 1618, last for a maximum period of 500 or 600 years, "and it is known to all of you how long we have been since the Conquest".[2] From our rationalist heights we might suppose that the new discoveries of science would tend to discredit the apocalyptic vaticinations of Scripture; but in fact this was not so. It is an interesting but undeniable fact that the most advanced scientists of the early sixteenth century

---

* From no. 16 (1959).
[1] Jeremiah Whittaker, Εἰρηνοποιός, *Christ the Settlement of Unsettled Times*, a fast sermon before the House of Commons, 25 Jan. 1642-3.
[2] William Greenhill, ’Αξίνη πρὸς τὴν ‘Ρίζαν, a sermon preached before Parliament, 26 April 1643.

included also the most learned and literal students of Biblical mathematics; and in their hands science and religion converged to pinpoint, between 1640 and 1660, the dissolution of society, the end of the world.[3]

This intellectual background is significant because it shows that the crisis of the mid-seventeenth century did not come by surprise, out of sudden accidents: it was deep-seated and anticipated, if only vaguely anticipated, even before the accidents which launched it. No doubt accidents made revolution longer or deeper here, shorter or more superficial there. No doubt, too, the universality of revolution owed something to mere contagion: the fashion of revolution spreads. But even contagion implies receptivity: a healthy or inoculated body does not catch even a prevailing disease. Therefore, though we may observe accidents and fashions, we still have to ask a deeper question. We must ask what was the general condition of western European society which made it, in the mid-seventeenth century, so universally vulnerable—intellectually as well as physically—to the sudden new epidemic of revolution?

Of course there are some obvious answers. Most obvious of all is the Thirty Years' War, which began in 1618, the year of the comet, and was still raging in the 1640s, the years of revolution. The Thirty Years' War, in the countries affected by it, undoubtedly prepared the ground for revolution. The burden of war taxation, or military oppression, or military defeat, precipitated the revolts in Catalonia, Portugal, Naples. The dislocation of trade, which may have been caused by the Thirty Years' War, led to unemployment and violence in many manufacturing or commercial countries. The destructive passage or billeting of soldiers led to regular peasant mutinies in Germany and France. One need only look at M. Roupnel's study of Burgundy in those years, or at the reports sent to the chancellor Séguier describing the constant risings of the French peasants under the stress of war-taxation, or at the grim etchings of Callot, to realize that the Thirty Years' War was a formidable factor in the making of that discontent which was sometimes mobilized in revolution.[4]

And yet it is not a sufficient explanation. After all, the European wars of 1618–59 were not new phenomena. They were a resumption of the European wars of the sixteenth century, the wars of Charles V against Francis I and Henry II, of Philip II against Elizabeth and Henry of Navarre and the Prince of Orange. Those sixteenth-century wars had ended with the century, in 1598, in 1604, in 1609: in 1618 and 1621 and 1635 they had been resumed, consciously resumed. Philip IV looked back constantly to the example of Philip II, "mi abuelo y mi señor"; Prince Maurice and Prince Frederick Henry to William of Orange, their father; Oliver Cromwell to "Queen Elizabeth of glorious memory." Richelieu and Mazarin sought to reverse the verdict of Câteau Cambrésis in 1559. And yet, in the sixteenth centuries these wars had led to no such revolutions. Moreover, the seventeenth-century revolutions were sometimes independent of the war. The greatest of those revolutions was in England which was safely—some said ignominiously—neutral. In the country which suffered most from the war, Germany, there was no revolution.

---

[3] It is enough here to refer to J. H. Alsted, the great scholar and educationalist of Herborn, who was also "the standard-bearer of millenaries in our age"; to his pupil, the great Bohemian educator, J. A. Comenius; to the English disciple of Bacon, Joseph Mede, the author of *Clavid Apocalyptica;* and to the Scottish mathematician Napier of Merchistoun, who invented logarithms in order to speed up his calculations of the Number of the Beast.

[4] See G. Roupnel, *La Ville et la Campagne au XVIIe Siècle dans le pays dijonnais* (Paris, 1955); Séguier's documents are printed, in French, in the Appendix to B. F. Porshnev, *Narodnie Vosstaniya vo Frantsii pered Frondoi, 1623-48* (Moscow, 1948).

I have said that the sixteenth-century wars had led to no such revolutions. Of course there had been revolutions in the sixteenth century: famous, spectacular revolutions: the religious revolutions of Reformation and Counter-Reformation. But we cannot say that those revolutions had been caused by those wars. Moreover, those revolutions, however spectacular, had in fact been far less profound than the revolutions of the next century. They had led to no such decisive breach in historical continuity. Beneath the customary wars of Habsburg and Valois, beneath the dramatic changes of the Reformation and Counter-Reformation, the sixteenth century goes on, a continuous, unitary century, and society is much the same at the end of it as at the beginning. Philip II succeeds to Charles V, Granvelle to Granvelle, Queen Elizabeth to Henry VII, Cecil to Cecil; even in France Henry IV takes up, after a period of disturbance, the mantle of Henry II. Aristocratic, monarchical society is unbroken: it is even confirmed. Speaking generally, we can say that for all the violence of its religious convulsions, the sixteenth century succeeded in absorbing its strains, its thinkers in swallowing their doubts, and at the end of it, kings and philosophers alike felt satisfied with the best of possible worlds.[5]

How different from this is the seventeenth century! For the seventeenth century did not absorb its revolutions. It is not continuous. It is broken in the middle, irreparably broken, and at the end of it, after the revolutions, men can hardly recognize the beginning. Intellectually, politically, morally, we are in a new age, a new climate. It is as if a series of rainstorms has ended in one final thunderstorm which has cleared the air and changed, permanently, the temperature of Europe. From the end of the fifteenth century until the middle of the seventeenth century we have one climate, the climate of the Renaissance; then, in the middle of the seventeenth century we have the years of change, the years of revolution; and thereafter, for another century and a half we have another, very different climate, the climate of the Enlightenment.

Thus I do not believe that the seventeenth-century revolutions can be explained merely by the background of war, which had also been the background of the previous, unrevolutionary century. If we are to find an explanation, we must look elsewhere. We must look past the background, into the structure of society. For all revolutions, even though they may be occasioned by external causes, and expressed in intellectual form, are made real and formidable by defects of social structure. A firm, elastic, working structure—like that of England in the nineteenth century—is proof against revolution however epidemic abroad. On the other hand a weak or over-rigid social structure, though it may last long in isolation, will collapse quickly if infected. The universality of revolution in the seventeenth century suggests that the European monarchies, which had been strong enough to absorb so many strains in the previous century, had by now developed serious structural weaknesses: weaknesses which the renewal of general war did not cause, but merely exposed and accentuated.

What were the general, structural weaknesses of the western monarchies? Contemporaries who looked at the revolutions of the seventeenth century saw them as political revolutions: as struggles between the two traditional organs of the ancient "mixed monarchy"—the Crown and the Estates. Certainly this was the form they took. In Spain, the Crown, having reduced the Cortes of Castile to insignificance, provoked the Catalan revolution by challenging the Cortes of the Kingdom of Aragon. In France, after the meeting of the Estates General in 1614, Richelieu contrived to

[5] This point—the growing social insensitivity of the sixteenth-century thinkers as monarchical, aristocratic society becomes more self-assured—is made by Fritz Caspari, *Humanism and the Social Order in Tudor England* (Chicago, 1954), pp. 198-204.

discontinue them, and they never met again till 1789; the Parlement of Paris struck back in the Fronde, but only to be defeated by Mazarin and reduced to the insignificance which was afterwards so bluntly rubbed in to it by Louis XIV. In Germany the Emperor challenged and reduced the Electoral college, even though the electors, as individual princes, reduced their own Diets to insignificance. In England the Parliament challenged and defeated the King. At the same time the Kings of Denmark and Sweden, struggling with or within their Diets, ended by establishing a personal monarchy, while the King of Poland, unable to imitate them, became the puppet of his. Altogether, we may say, the universal casualty of the seventeenth century was that Aristotelian concept, so admired in 1600, so utterly extinct in 1700, "mixed monarchy." The position was described summarily by the English political philospher, James Harrington, who, in 1656, diagnosed the general crisis which had produced such violent results in his own country of *Oceana*. "What," he asked, "is become of the Princes of Germany? Blown up. Where are the Estates or the power of the people in France? Blown up. Where is that of the people of Aragon and the rest of the Spanish kingdoms? Blown up. Where is that of the Austrian princes in Switz? Blown up . . . Nor shall any man show a reason that will be holding in prudence why the people of Oceana have blown up their king, but that their kings did not first blow up them."

Now there can be no doubt that politically Harrington was right. The struggle was a struggle for power, for survival, between crowns and estates. But when we have said this, have we really answered our question? If revolution was to break out otherwise than in hopeless rural *jacqueries*, it could only be through the protest of estates, parliaments, cortes, diets; and if it was to be crushed, it could only be through the victory of royal power over such institutions. But to describe the form of a revolution is not to explain its cause, and today we are reluctant to accept constitutional struggles as self-contained or self-explanatory. We look for the forces or interests behind the constitutional claims of either side. What forces, what interests were represented by the revolutionary parties in seventeenth-century Europe—the parties which, though they may not have controlled them (for everyone would agree that there were other forces too) nevertheless gave ultimate social power and significance to the revolts of cortes and diets, estates and parliaments?

Now to this question one answer has already been given and widely accepted. It is the Marxist answer. According to the Marxists, and to some other historians who, though not Marxists, accept their argument, the crisis of the seventeenth century was at bottom a crisis of production, and the motive force behind at least some of the revolutions was the force of the producing bourgeoisie, hampered in their economic activity by the obsolete, wasteful, restrictive, but jealously defended productive system of "feudal" society. According to this view, the crisis of production was general in Europe, but it was only in England that the forces of "capitalism," thanks to their greater development and their representation in parliament, were able to triumph. Consequently while other countries made no immediate advance towards modern capitalism, in England the old structure was shattered and a new form of economic organization was established. Within that organization modern, industrial capitalism could achieve its astonishing results: it was no longer capitalist enterprise "adapted to a generally feudal framework": it was capitalist enterprise, from its newly-won island base, "transforming the world."

This Marxist thesis has been advanced by many able writers, but, in spite of their arguments, I do not believe that it has been proved or even that any solid evidence has been adduced to sustain it. It is of course easy to show that there were economic changes in the seventeenth century, and that, at least in England, industrial capitalism was more developed in 1700 than in 1600; but to do this is not the same as to show either that the economic changes precipitated the revolutions in Europe, or that English capitalism was directly forwarded by the Puritan "victory" of 1640–60. These are hypotheses, which may of course be true; but it is equally possible that they are untrue: that problems of production were irrelevant to the seventeenth-century revolutions generally, and that in England capitalist development was independent of the Puritan revolution, in the sense that it would or could have occurred without that revolution, perhaps even was retarded or interrupted by it. If it is to be shown that the English Puritan revolution was a successful "bourgeois revolution," it is not enough to produce evidence that English capitalism was more advanced in 1700 than in 1600. It must be shown either that the men who made the revolution aimed at such a result, or that those who wished for such a result forwarded the revolution, or that such a result would not have been attained without the revolution. Without such evidence, the thesis remains a mere hypothesis.

Now in fact no advocate of the Marxist theory seems to me to have established any of these necessary links in the argument. Mr. Maurice Dobb, whose *Studies in the Development of Capitalism* may be described as the classic textbook of Marxist history, consistently assumes that the English Puritan revolution was the crucial "break-through" of modern capitalism. It bears, he says, "all the marks of the classic bourgeois revolution": before it, capitalism is cramped and frustrated, never progressing beyond a certain stage, a parasite confined to the interstices of "feudal" society; in it, the "decisive period" of capitalism reaches its "apex"; after it, the bonds are broken and the parasite becomes the master. Similarly, Mr. E. J. Hobsbawm, in his two articles on "The Crisis of the Seventeenth Century",[6] consistently maintains the same thesis. "Had the English Revolution failed," he writes, "as so many other European revolutions in the seventeenth century failed, it is entirely possible that economic development might have been long retarded." The results of the Puritan "victory" were "portentous": nothing less than the transformation of the world. But it is to be observed that although Mr. Dobb assumes this position throughout his book, he nowhere gives any evidence to prove it. As soon as he reaches the "decisive period" of capitalism, he suddenly becomes vague. "The lines of this development," we learn, "are far from clearly drawn"; "the details of this process are far from clear and there is little evidence that bears directly upon it." In fact, not a single piece of documented evidence is produced for what is throughout assumed to be the crucial event in the whole history of European capitalism. And Mr. Hobsbawm is even more summary. He dwells at length upon the economy of Europe at the time of the revolutions. He assumed the "portentous" importance of the Puritan revolution in changing the economy. But of the actual connexion between the two he says not a word.[7]

[6] In, *Past and Present*, no. 5 (May 1954) and no. 6 (Nov. 1954); repr. above, ch. 2–the quotation is at p. 32.

[7] As far as I can see, Mr. Dobb's only arguments of such a connexion are the statements (1) that agricultural capitalists supported the Parliament while old-fashioned "feudal" landlords supported the Crown; (2) that "those sections of the bourgeoisie that had any roots in industry . . . were wholehearted supporters of the parliamentary cause"; and (3) that the industrial towns, particularly the clothing towns, were radical. None of these statements seems to me sufficient. (1) is incorrect: the only evidence given consists in undocumented statements that Oliver Cromwell was an improving agriculturalist (which is untrue: in fact having–in his own words–"wasted his estate", he had declined from a landlord to a tenant farmer), and that "Ireton

Altogether, it seems to me that the Marxist identification of the seventeenth-century revolutions with "bourgeois" "capitalist" revolutions, successful in England, unsuccessful elsewhere, is a mere *a priori* hypothesis. The Marxist see, as we all see, that, at some time between the discovery of America and the Industrial Revolution, the basis was laid for a new "capitalist" form of society. Believing, as a matter of doctrine, that such a change cannot be achieved peacefully but requires a violent "break-through" of a new class, a "bourgeois revolution," they look for such a revolution. Moreover, seeing that the country which led in this process was England, they look for such a revolution in England. And when they find, exactly half-way between these terminal dates, the violent Puritan revolution in England, they cry ευρηκα! Thereupon the other European revolutions fall easily into place as abortive bourgeois revolutions. The hypothesis, once stated, is illustrated by other hypotheses. It has yet to be proved by evidence. And it may be that it rests on entirely false premises. It may be that social changes do not necessarily require violent revolution: that capitalism developed in England (as industrial democracy has done) peacefully, and that the violent Puritan revolution was no more crucial to its history than (say) the fifteenth-century Hussite and Taborite revolutions in Bohemia, to which it bears such obvious resemblances.

If the crisis of the seventeenth century, then, though general in western Europe, is not a merely constitutional crisis, nor a crisis of economic production, what kind of a crisis was it? In this essay I shall suggest that, in so far as it was a general crisis—i.e. ignoring inessential variations from place to place—it was something both wider and vaguer than this: in fact, that it was a crisis in the relations between society and the State. In order to explain this, I shall try to set it against a longer background of time than is sometimes supposed necessary. For general social crises are seldom explicable in terms of mere decades. We would not now seek to explain the communist revolution in Russia against a background merely of the twelve years since 1905, nor the great French Revolution against the background merely of the reign of Louis XVI. For such a purpose, we think it necessary to examine the whole *ancien régime* which came to an end here in 1917, there in 1789. Similarly, if we are to seek an explanation of the general European crisis of the 1640s, we must not confine ourselves to the preceding decade, ascribing all the responsibility (though we must undoubtedly ascribe some) to Archbishop Laud in England or the Count-Duke of Olivares in Spain. We must look, here too, at the whole *ancien régime* which preceded the crisis: the whole form of State and society which we have seen continually expanding, absorbing all shocks, growing more self-assured throughout the sixteenth century, and which, in the mid-seventeenth century, comes to an end: what for convenience we may call the state and society of the European Renaissance.

The Renaissance—how loose and vague is the term! Defining it and dating it has become a major industry among scholars, at international congresses and in learned papers. But let us not be deterred by this. All general terms—*"ancien régime, "* "capitalism," "the Middle Ages"—are loose and vague; but they are nevertheless serviceable if we use them only generally. And in general terms we know well enough

his chief lieutenant was both a country gentleman and a clothier" (for which I know of no evidence at all). In fact some of the most obvious "improving landlords," like the Earl of Newcastle and the Marquis of Worcester, were royalists. (2) is unsubstantiated and, I believe, incorrect; wherever the industrial bourgeoisie has been studied—as in Yorkshire and Wiltshire—it has been found to be divided in its loyalty. (3) is correct, but inconclusive; the radicalism of workers in a depressed industry may well spring from depression, not from "capitalist" interest.

what we mean by the European Renaissance. It is the sudden expansion of our civilization, the excited discovery of world upon world, adventure upon adventure: the progressive enlargement of sensitivity and show which reached its greatest extension in the sixteenth century and which, in the seventeenth century, is no more. Expansion, extension—these are its essential characteristics. For the sixteenth century is not an age of structural change. In technology, in thought, in government, it is the same. In technology, at least after 1520, there are few changes. The expansion of Europe creates greater markets, greater opportunities, but the machinery of production remains basically constant. Similarly, in culture, the great representatives of the European Renaissance are universal but unsystematic. Leonardo, Montaigne, Cervantes, Shakespeare, take life for granted: they adventure, observe, describe, perhaps mock; but they do not analyse, criticize, question. And in government it is the same too. The political structures of Europe are not changed in the sixteenth century: they are stretched to grasp and hold new empires, sometimes vast new empires, vaster than they can contain for long without internal change. Nevertheless, as yet, there is no such change. The Renaissance State—up to and beyond 1600—expands continuously without as yet bursting its old envelope. That envelope is the medieval, aristocratic monarchy, the rule of the Christian prince.

It is a fascinating spectacle, the rise of the princes in sixteenth-century Europe. One after another they spring up, first in Italy and Burgundy, then all over Europe. Their dynasties may be old, and yet their character is new: they are more exotic, more highly coloured than their predecessors. They are versatile, cultivated men, sometimes bizarre, even outrageous: they bewilder us by their lavish tastes, their incredible energy, their ruthlessness and *panache*. Even when they are introverted, bigoted, melancholic, it is on a heroic scale: we think of Charles V solemnly conducting his own funeral at Yuste or Philip II methodically condemning millions of future lives to the treadmill of ceaseless prayer for his own soul. Undoubtedly, in the sixteenth century, the princes are everything. They are tyrants over past and future; they change religion and divine truth by their nod, even in their teens; they are priests and popes, they call themselves gods, as well as kings. And yet we should remember, if we are to understand the crisis at the end of their rule, that their power did not rise up out of nothing. Its extraordinary expansion in the early sixteenth century was not *in vacuo*. Europe had to make room for it. The princes rose at the expense of someone or something, and they brought in their train the means of securing their sudden, usurped new power. In fact, they rose at the expense of the older organs of European civilization, the cities; and they brought with them, as the means of conquest, a new political instrument, "the Renaissance Court."

Not much has been written about the eclipse of the European cities on the eve of the Renaissance; but it is an important phenomenon.[8] For how can we think of the Middle Ages without thinking of the cities, and yet who thinks of them after 1500? In the Middle Ages the free communes of Flanders and Italy had been the founders of Europe's trade and wealth, the centres of its arts and crafts, the financiers of its popes and kings. The German cities had been the means of colonizing and civilizing the barbarous north, the pagan east of Europe. These cities, moreover, had had their own way of life and had imposed upon Europe some of their own methods of government and standards of value. In its earliest form, the Renaissance itself had been a city phenomenon: it had begun in the cities of Italy, Flanders and south Germany before it

---

[8] Fernand Braudel has touched on it in his great work, *La Méditerranée et le Monde Méditerranéen au Temps de Philippe II* (Paris, 1949), pp. 285-91.

was taken over, and changed, by princes and popes. And this early Renaissance had the character of the cities within which it was still contained. Like them it was responsible, orderly, self-controlled. For however great their wealth, however splendid their town halls and hospitals, their churches and squares, there is always, in the cities, a trace of calculation and self-restraint. It is the virtue of civic self-government, however oligarchically controlled: a spirit very different from the outrageous, spendthrift, irresponsible exhibitionism of the princes which was to come.

For between the fifteenth and the sixteenth century the princely suitors came, and one after another the cities succumbed. The rich cities of Flanders gave in to the magnificent dukes of Burgundy, the rich cities of Lombardy and Tuscany to the magnificent princes of Italy. The Baltic cities of the Hanse were absorbed by the kings of Poland or Denmark or ruined themselves by vain resistance. Barcelona yielded to the King of Aragon, Marseilles to the King of France. Even those apparent virgins, Genoa and Augsburg, were really "kept cities," attached by golden strings to the King of Spain and the Emperor. The Doge of Venice himself became a prince, ruling over lesser cities in the *terra ferma*. Only a few, like Geneva, remained obstinate spinsters; and that sour, crabbed city missed the gaiety of the Renaissance. Even the exceptions prove the rule. Accidental princely weakness, or indirect princely patronage, lie behind the new prosperity of Frankfurt, Ragusa, Hamburg, Danzig.

For as a rule surrender was the price of continued prosperity: how else could the cities survive, once the princes had discovered the secret of State? By subduing the Church, extending their jurisdiction, mobilizing the countryside, the princes had created a new apparatus of power, "the Renaissance State," with which they could tax the wealth of the cities, patronize and extend their trade, take over and develop their art and architecture. If the cities hope to thrive now, it must be by new methods. It must not be through independence: those days are past. It must be through monopoly, as the sole grantees of princely trade in these expanding dominions; as Lisbon and Seville throve on the grants of the Kings of Portugal and Spain Or they might thrive as centres of extravagant princely consumption, as royal capitals. For in some of the old cities the victorious princes would establish their new courts: courts which sucked up the wealth of the whole country and rained it down on the city of their residence. Essentially the sixteenth century is an age not of cities but of courts: of capital cities made splendid less by trade than by government. It was not as industrial or commercial cities, but as courts, that Brussels, Paris, Rome, Madrid, Naples, Prague achieve their splendour in the sixteenth century. And the brilliance of these courts is not the discreet, complacent self-advertisement of great merchants out of their calculated profits: it is the carefree magnificence of kings and courtiers, who do not need to count because they do not have to earn.

Of course the cities wriggled at first. Ghent resisted its Burgundian dukes. The old cities of Spain struck back against their foreign King. Florence sought to throw out the Medici. Genoa and Augsburg surrendered only after doubt and strife. But in the end each in turn was overpowered, subdued, and then—if lucky—rewarded with the golden shower which fell not from trade, or at least not directly from trade, but from the Court. And with the cities the old city culture was transformed too. Erasmus, preaching peace and civic justice and denouncing the heedless wars and wasteful magnificence of princes, is a true figure of the first, the city Renaissance, cultivated, pious, rational; but he is swept up in the princely embrace and made a mascot of royal courts, until he flees to die in a free city on the Rhine. Sir Thomas More, whose *Utopia* was a league of virtuous, independent cities, is captured and broken by the splendid, cannibal Court of Henry VIII. Soon after 1500 the age of independent city culture is over. So is the age of careful accountancy. We are in the age of the Field of Cloth-of-Gold, of heroic conquests and impossible visions and successive state bankruptcies: the age of Columbus and Cortés, of Leonardo da Vinci and St. Francis Xavier, each, in his way, like Marlowe's hero, still climbing after knowledge infinite, or, like don Quixote, pursuing unattainable mirages, heedless of mortal limitations. It is the age, also, whose fashionable handbooks were no longer civic nor clerical but were called *The Courtier, The Governour, The Prince, The Institution of a Christian Prince, The Mirror* (or *the Horologe*) *of Princes.*

How was this miracle possible? When we look back at that age, with its incredible audacities, its contemptuous magnificence in speculation and spending, we are amazed that it lasted so long. Why did not European civilization burst in the sixteenth century? And yet not only did it not burst, it continued to expand, absorbing all the time the most fearful strains. The Turks in the east wrenched away the outposts of Europe; Christendom was split asunder by religious revolution and constant war; and yet at the end of the century the kings were more spendthrift, their courts more magnificent than ever. The Court of Spain, once so simple, had been changed to a Burgundian pattern; the Court of England, once so provincial, had become, under Queen Elizabeth, the most elaborate in Europe; and the princes of Italy and Germany, with palaces and libraries, picture-galleries and *Wunderkammer,* philosophers, fools and astrologers, strove to hold their own. As the century wore on, social conscience dwindled, for social change seemed impossibly remote. Was ever an architect more effortlessly aristocratic than Palladio, or a poet than Shakespeare, or a painter than Rubens?

How indeed was it possible? One answer is obvious. The sixteenth century was an age of economic expansion. It was the century when, for the first time, Europe was living on Asia, Africa and America. But there was also another reason. The reason why this expansion was always under the princes, not at their expense, why the princes were always carried upwards, not thrown aside by it, was that the princes had allies who secured their power and kept them firmly in place. For the princes could never have built up their power alone. Whatever weaknesses in society gave them their opportunity, they owed their permanence to the machinery of government which they had created or improved, and to the vested interests which that machinery fostered. This machinery, the means and result of princely triumph, is the Renaissance State, and it is to this that we must now turn: for it was the Renaissance State which, in so much of Europe, first broke or corroded the old power of the cities and then, in its turn, in the seventeenth century, faced its own crisis and dissolved.

We often speak of the Renaissance State. How can we define it? When we come down to facts, we find that it is, at bottom, a great and expanding bureaucracy, a huge system of administrative centralization, staffed by an ever-growing multitude of "courtiers" or "officers." The "officers" are familiar enough to us as a social type. We think of the great Tudor ministers in England, Cardinal Wolsey, Thomas Cromwell, the two Cecils; or of the *letrados* of Spain, Cardinal Ximénez, the two Granvelles, Francisco de los Cobos, Antonio Pérez; and we see their common character: they are formidable administrators, machiavellian diplomats, cultivated patrons of art and letters, magnificent builders of palaces and colleges, greedy collectors of statues and pictures, books and bindings. For of course these men, as royal servants, imitated their masters, in lavishness as in other matters. But what is significant about the sixteenth century is not merely the magnificence of these great 'officers', it is the number—the ever-growing number—of lesser officers who also, on their lesser scale, accepted the standards and copied the tastes of their masters. For all through the century the number of officers was growing. Princes needed them, more and more, to staff their councils and courts, their new special or permanent tribunals which were the means of governing new territories and centralizing the government of old. It was for this reason that the Renaissance Princes and their great ministers founded all those schools and colleges. For it was not to produce scholars, or to advance learning or science, that old colleges were reorganized or new founded by Cardinal Ximénez or Cardinal Wolsey, by Henry VIII of England or John III of Portugal, or Francis I of France. The new learning, it is notorious, grew up outside the colleges and universities, not in them. The function of the new foundations was to satisfy the royal demand for officers—officers to man the new royal bureaucracies—and, at the same time, the public demand for office: office which was the means to wealth and power and the gratification of lavish, competitive tastes.

Thus the power of the Renaissance Princes was not princely power only: it was also the power of thousands of "officers" who also, like their masters, had extravagant tastes and, somehow, the means of gratifying them. And how in fact were they gratified? Did the princes themselves pay their officers enough to sustain such a life? Certainly not. Had that been so, ruin would have come quicker: Cobos and Granvelle alone would have brought Charles V to bankruptcy long before 1556, and Henry VIII would have had to dissolve the monasteries fifteen years earlier to sustain the economic burden of Cardinal Wolsey. The fact is, only a fraction of the cost of the royal bureaucracy fell directly on the Crown:three-quarters of it fell, directly or indirectly, on the country.

Yes, three-quarters: at least three-quarters. For throughout Europe, at this time, the salaries paid to officers of State were small, customary payments whose real value dwindled in times of inflation; the bulk of an officer's gains came from private opportunities to which public office merely opened the door. "For the profits of these two great offices, the Chancellor and the Treasurer," wrote an English bishop, "certainly they were very small if you look to the ancient fees and allowances; for princes heretofore did tie themselves to give but little, that so their officers and servants might more depend upon them for their rewards."[9] What Bishop Goodman said of Jacobean England was true of every European country. Instances could be multiplied indefinitely.[10] Every officer, at every court, in every country, lived by the same system. He was paid a trivial "fee" or salary and, for the rest, made what he could in the field which his office had opened to him. Some of these profits were regarded as perfectly legitimate, for no man could be expected to live on his "fee"

[9] Godfrey Goodman, *The Court of King James I* (London, 1839 edn.), i, p. 279.
[10] On this subject generally see Federico Chabod's essay "Y a-t-il un Etat de al Renaissance?" in *Actes du Colloque sur la Renaissance, Sorbonne, 1956* (Paris, 1958), and also, for Milanese instances, his "Stipendi Nominali e Busta Paga Effettiva dei Funzionari nell' Amministrazione Milanese alla Fine del Cinquecento" in *Miscellanea in Onore di Roberto Cessi II* (Rome, 1958) and "Usi e Abusi nell' Amministrazione dello Stato di Milano a mezzo il 1500" in *Studi Storici in Onore di Gioachino Volpe* (Florence, n.d.). For Naples, see G. Coniglio, *Il Regno di Napoli al Tempo di Carlo V* (Naples, 1951), pp. 11-12, 246, etc. For France see R. Doucet, *Les Institutions de la France au XVIᵉ Siécle* (Paris, 1948), pp. 403 ff; cf. Menna Prestwich,"The Making of Absolute Monarchy, 1559-1683" in *France: Government and Society,* ed. J. M. Wallace-Hadrill and J. McManners (London, 1957). I have given some English instances in *The Gentry, 1540-1640* (Econ. Hist. Rev., Suppl. no. 1, 1953). See also J. E. Neale, "The Elizabethan Political Scene," *Proceedings of the British Academy,* xxiv (1948); K. W. Swart, *The Sale of Offices in the Seventeenth Century* (The Hague, 1949).

alone: it was taken for granted that he would charge a reasonable sum for audiences, favours, signatures, that he would exploit his office to make good bargains, that he would invest public money, while in his hands, on his own account. But of course there were other profits which were generally regarded as "corruption" and therefore improper. Unfortunately the line dividing propriety from impropriety was conventional only: it was therefore invisible, uncertain, floating. It differed from person to person, from place to place. It also differed from time to time. As the sixteenth century passed on, as the cost of living rose, as the pressure of competition sharpened and royal discipline slackened, there was a general decline of standards. The public casuists became more indulgent, the private conscience more elastic, and men began to forget about that conventional, invisible line between "legitimate profits" and "corruption."

Let us consider a few instances which illustrate the system. In England, the Master of the Wards had a "fee" of £133 p.a., but even Lord Burghley, a conscientious administrator, made "infinite gains"—at least £2,000 p.a.—out of its private opportunities, quite apart from its non-financial advantages. His son did far better. The Lord Treasurer's fee was £365 p.a., but in 1635 even Archbishop Laud, a notable stickler for administrative honesty, reckoned that that great officer had "honest advantages" for enriching himself to the tune of over £7,000 p.a. The Archbishop made this calculation because he had been shocked by the much larger sums which recent Lord Treasurers had been making at the expense of king and subject alike. In 1600 the Lord Chancellor's fee was £500 p.a., but in fact the office was known to be "better worth than £3,000, p.a." To Lord Chancellor Ellesmere this did not seem enough, and, like many great men, he sighed that he could not make ends meet. He was thought conscientious: perhaps (like Burghley) he was also hypocritical. At all events, his successors had no such difficulty. "How have the Lord Chancellors lived since," exclaimed Bishop Goodman, "how have they flowed with money, and what great purchases have they made, and what profits and advantages have they had by laying their fingers on purchases! For if my Lord desired the land, no man should dare to buy it out of his hands, and he must have it at his own price; for any bribery or corruption, it is hard to prove it: men do not call others to be witnesses at such actions."[11] All writers of the early seventeenth century agree that the casual profits of office had grown enormously; and these casual profits were multiplied at the expense of the consumer, the "country."

Thus each old office granted, each new office created, meant a new burden on the subject. Royal parsimony made little difference. Our Queen Elizabeth, we all know, was judged very parsimonious: far too parsimonious by her own officers. But she was not praised for her parsimony in her own time. For what in fact did it mean? "We have not many precedents of her liberality," says a contemporary, "nor of any large donatives to particular men. . . .Her rewards consisted chiefly in grants of leases of offices, places of judicature; but for ready money, and in any great sums, she was very sparing."[12] In other words, she gave to her courtiers not cash but the right to exploit their fellow subjects: to Sir Walter Ralegh the right to despoil the bishops of Bath and Wells and Salisbury and to interpose his pocket between the producer and consumer of

[11] See, for the Master of the Wards, J. Hurstfield, "Lord Burghley as Master of the Court of Wards," *Trans. Roy. Hist. Soc.*, 5th ser., xxxi (1949); for the Lord Treasurer, P. Heylin, *Cyprianus Anglicus* (1668), p. 285; for the Lord Chancellor, Goodman, loc. cit.; *Manningham's Diary* (Camden Soc., 1868), p. 19.

[12] Sir R. Naunton, *Fragmenta Regalia* (ed. A. Arber, 1870), p. 18.

tin; to the Earl of Essex the right to lease the monopoly of sweet wines to merchants who would recoup themselves by raising the cost to the consumer. All European sovereigns did likewise. They had no alternative. They had not the ready money, and so, if they were to gratify their servants, reward their favourites, service their loans, they had to raise it a discount or pay excessively in kind. They leased Crown lands at a quarter (or less) of their true value in order that "officers" or "courtiers" could live, as lessees, on the difference. They granted monopolies which brought in to the Crown less than a quarter of what they cost the subject. They collected irrational old taxes, or even irrational new taxes, by imposing, fourfold, irrational burdens on the tax-payers. The King of France obliged his peasants to buy even more salt than they needed, in order to raise his yield from the *gabelle*. We all know what a burden wardship and purveyance became in the reigns of Queen Elizabeth and King James. Both visibly cost the subject four times what they brought to the Crown. Invisibly—that is, beyond that invisible line—they cost far more.[13] Nor was it only the Crown which acted thus. The practice was universal. Great men rewarded their clients in exactly the same way. The Church, which was now everywhere a department of State, was similar. It was burdened with its sinecures: absentee clergy, tithe-eating laity; with its "officers": the swollen number of ecclesiastical officers—"caterpillars of the Commonwealth"—was one of the great complaints against the Anglican Church in the 1630's; with its lessees: Church lands, like Crown lands, were regularly leased at absurd under-rents. It was not only the State, the whole of society was top-heavy.

Moreover, and increasingly as the seventeenth century succeeded to the sixteenth, this multiplication of ever more costly offices outran the needs of State. Originally the need had created the officers; now the officers created the need. All bureaucracies tend to expand. By the process known to us as Parkinson's Law, office-holders tend to create yet more offices beneath them in order to swell their own importance or provide for their friends and kinsmen. But whereas today such inflation is curbed by the needs of the Treasury, in the sixteenth century the needs of the Treasury positively encouraged it. For offices, in the sixteenth century, were not granted freely: they were sold, and—at least in the beginning—the purchase-price went to the Crown. If the Crown could sell more and more offices at higher and higher prices, leaving the officers to be paid by the country, this was an indirect, if also a cumbrous and exasperating way of taxing the country. Consequently, princes were easily tempted to create new offices, and to profit by the competition which forced up the price. As for the purchaser, having paid a high price, he naturally sought to raise his profits still higher, in order to recoup himself, with a decent margin, for his outlay: a decent margin with which an ambitious man might hope, in the end, to build a house like

[13] For the cost of monopolies see W. R. Scott, *The Constitution and Finance of . . . Joint-Stock Companies to 1720*, vol. i (London, 1911). The cost of wardship appears clearly from Mr. Joel Hurstfield's studies. He concludes that "the unofficial profits from fiscal feudalism taken as a whole, were at least three times as high as the official ones": "The Profits of Fiscal Feudalism, 1541-1602," *Econ. Hist. Rev.*, 2nd ser., viii (1955-6), p. 58. Of purveyance, Bacon wrote "There is no pound profit which redoundeth to Your Majesty in this course but induceth and begetteth £3 damage upon your subjects, besides the discontentment" (*Works*, ed. Spedding, iii, p. 185). The truth of this last statement is clearly demonstrated in Miss Allegra Woodworth's excellent study, *Purveyance in the Reign of Queen Elizabeth* (Philadelphia, 1945). For Crown lands, Bacon told King James that, properly administered, they "will yield four for one" (*Works*, iv, p. 328): others put the proportion far higher, sometimes twenty to one. Cf. E. Kerridge, "The Movement of Rent", in *Econ. Hist. Rev.*, 2nd ser., vi (1953-4), pp. 31-32. The Earl of Bedford similarly, in 1641, calculated that in some places the proportion was twenty to one (Woburn Abbey, Duke of Bedford's MSS.).

Hatfield or Knole, entertain royalty to feasts costing thousands, retain and reward an army of clients, plant exotic gardens, and collect *objets d'art* and pictures.

So "the Renaissance State" consisted, at bottom, of an ever-expanding bureaucracy which, though at first a working bureaucracy, had by the end of the sixteenth century become a parasitic bureaucracy; and this ever-expanding bureaucracy was sustained on an equally expanding margin of "waste": waste which lay between the taxes imposed on the subject and the revenue collected by the Crown. Since the Crown could not afford an absolute loss of revenue, it is clear that this expansion of the waste had to be at the expense of society. It is equally clear that it could only be borne if society itself were expanding in wealth and numbers. Fortunately, in the sixteenth century, the European economy was expanding. The trade of Asia, the bullion of Africa and America, was driving the European machine. The expansion may have been uneven; there may have been strains and casualties; but they were the strains of growth, which could be absorbed, individual casualties which could be overlooked. Occasional State bankruptcies clear off old debts: they do not necessarily affect new prosperity. War increases consumption: it does not necessarily consume the sources of wealth. A booming economy can carry many anomalies, many abuses. It could even carry—provided it went on booming—the incredibly wasteful, ornamental, parasitic Renaissance Courts and Churches.

Provided it went on booming. . . . But how long would it boom? Already, by 1590, the cracks are beginning to appear. The strains of the last years of Philip II's wars release everywhere a growing volume of complaint: complaint which is not directed against constitutional faults—against the despotism of kings or the claims of estates—but against this or that aspect or consequence of the growth and cost of a parasitic bureaucracy. For of course, although war has not created the problem, war aggravates it: the more the costs of government are raised, the more the government resorts to those now traditional financial expedients: creation and sale of new offices, sale or long lease, at undervalues, of Crown or Church lands, creation of monopolies, raising of "feudal" taxes: expedients which, on the one hand, multiply the already overgrown bureaucracy and thus the cost to the country, and, on the other hand, further impoverish the Crown.

But if the strains are already obvious in the 1590's, they are, as yet, not fatal: for peace comes first. A few opportune deaths—Philip II in 1598, Queen Elizabeth in 1603—hasten the process, and throughout Europe war after war is wound up. And then, with peace, what relief! The overstrained system is suddenly relaxed, and an era of pleasure and renewed extravagance follows. Was there ever an era of such lavishness as the time between the end of Philip II's wars and the outbreak of the Thirty Years' War, the time when the world was ruled, or at least enjoyed, by Philip III and the Duke of Lerma in Spain, James I and the Duke of Buckingham in England, "The Archdukes" in Flanders, Henry IV and Marie des Médicis in France? It is a world of giddy expenditure, splendid building, gigantic feasts and lavish, evanescent shows. Rubens, when he came to the Duke of Buckingham's England, marvelled at such unexpected magnificence "in a place so remote from Italian elegance." No nation in the world, said a contemporary Englishman, spent as much as we did in building. We built houses, said another, thinking of Hatfield and Audley End, "like Nebuchadnezzar's." All "the old good rules of economy," said a third, had gone packing. But the Spanish ambassador, reporting to his king these costly Jacobean festivals, would only say that no doubt they would seem very impressive "to anyone who had not seen the grandeur and state with which we do such things in Spain"—as well he might, in the days when the Duke of Lerma, the courtier of the almost bankrupt King of Spain, went forth to meet his future queen with 34,000 ducats' worth of jewels on his person, and another 72,000 ducats' worth carried behind him.[14]

Such is the character of the Renaissance Courts in their last Indian summer after the close of the sixteenth century. And even this, of course, is only the conspicuous, still sunlit tip of the iceberg whose sides are hidden from us by intervening oblivion and whose greater base was always, even at the time, submerged. How, we may ask, could it go on? Even in the 1590's, even a far less expensive, more efficient bureaucracy had only been saved by peace: how could this much more outrageous system survive if the long prosperity of the sixteenth century or the saving peace of the seventeenth, should fail?

In fact, in the 1620's they both failed at once. In 1618 a political crisis in Prague had set the European powers in motion, and by 1621 the wars of Philip II had been resumed, bringing in their train new taxes, new offices, new exactions. Meanwhile the European economy, already strained to the limit by the habits of peacetime boom, was suddenly struck by a great depression, the universal "decay of trade" of 1620. Moreover, in those twenty years, a new attitude of mind had been created: created by disgust at that gilded merry-go-round which cost society so much more than it was willing to bear. It was an attitude of hatred: hatred of "the Court" and its courtiers, hatred of princely follies and bureaucratic corruption, hatred of the Renaissance itself: in short, Puritanism.

In England we naturally think of our own form of Puritanism: extreme Protestantism, the continuation, to unbearable lengths, of the half-completed sixteenth-century Reformation. But let us not be deceived by mere local forms. This reaction against the Renaissance Courts and their whole culture and morality was not confined to any one country or religion. Like the thesis, the antithesis also is general. In England there is an Anglican Puritanism, a "Puritanism of the Right." What greater enemy had English Puritanism, as we know it, than Archbishop Laud, the all-powerful prelate who drove it to America till it returned to destroy him? And yet he too illustrates this same reaction. Did English Puritans denounce "the unloveliness of lovelocks," gay clothes, the drinking of toasts? The Archbishop forbade long hair in Oxford, reformed clerical dress, waged war on alehouses. In Roman Catholic countries it was the same. Did the English Puritans first denounce, then close the London theatres? In Spain—even the Spain of Lope de Vega—*pragmática* after *pragmática* denounced stage-plays. In France the Jansenist Pascal disliked them hardly less. In Bavaria there was a Catholic prudery, and a police enforcement of it, as disagreeable as the worst form of English Puritanism. There was the same war against luxury too. In 1624 Philip IV of Spain cut down his household, published sumptuary laws, and banished the ruff—that symbol of sartorial magnificence—from Spain by decree, from Europe by example. In France, Cardinal Richelieu was doing likewise. It was a sudden war, almost a crusade, against the old Renaissance extravagance. In Flanders, Rubens would find himself surviving his old Court patrons and would turn to country landscapes. Literature reflects the same change. Of Castiglione's famous manual, *The Courtier,* at least sixty editions or translations were published between 1528 and 1619; after the latter date, for a whole century, none.

In the 1620s Puritanism—this general mood of Puritanism—triumphs in Europe.

[14] *Corespondencia Oficial de . . . Gondomar* (Madrid, 1944), iii, p. 232. P. Mantuano, *Casamientos de España y Francia* (Madrid, 1618), pp. 124-5, quoted in Agustín Gonzales de Amezúa, *Lope de Vega en sus Cartas* (Madrid, 1935), i, pp. 70-71.

Those years, we may say, mark the end of the Renaissance. The playtime is over. The sense of social responsibility, which had held its place within the Renaissance Courts of the sixteenth century—we think of the paternalism of the Tudors, the "collectivism" of Philip II—had been driven out in the early seventeenth century, and now it had returned, and with a vengeance. War and depression had made the change emphatic, even startling. We look at the world in one year, and there we see Lerma and Buckingham and Marie des Médicis. We look again, and they have all gone. Lerma has fallen and saved himself by becoming a Roman cardinal; Buckingham is assassinated; Marie des Médicis has fled abroad. In their stead we find grimmer, greater, more resolute figures: the Count Duke of Olivares, whose swollen, glowering face almost bursts from Velázquez's canvases; Strafford and Laud, that relentless pair, the prophets of Thorough in Church and State; Cardinal Richelieu, the iron-willed invalid who ruled and re-made France. In literature too it is the same. The fashion has changed. After Shakespeare, Cervantes, Montaigne, those universal spirits, with their scepticism, their acceptance of the world as it is, we are suddenly in a new age: an age here of ideological revolt, Milton's "jubilee and resurrection of Church and State," there of conservative pessimism, cynicism and disillusion, of John Donne and Sir Thomas Browne, of Quevedo and the Spanish Baroque: for the baroque age, as Mr. Gerald Brenan says, "—one cannot say it too often—was a tight, contracted age, turned in on itself and lacking self-confidence and faith in the future."[15]

Such was the mood of general, non-doctrinal, moral Puritanism which, in the 1620s, launched its attack—here from within, there from without—on the Renaissance Courts. There are differences of incidence, of course, differences of personality from place to place, and these differences could be crucial—who can say what would have happened if Archbishop Laud had really been, as Sir Thomas Roe thought, "the Richelieu of England"? There were also differences in society itself. But if we look closely we see that the burden on society is the same even if the shoulders which creak under it are different. For instance, in England the cost of the Court fell most heavily on the gentry: they were the tax-paying class: wardships, purveyance and all the indirect taxes which were multiplied by the early Stuarts fell heaviest on them. On the other hand in France the *noblesse* was exempt from taxation, and the *taille* and *gabelle*, which were multiplied by the early Bourbons, fell heaviest on the peasants. No doubt English landlords could pass some of their burdens on to their tenants. No doubt impoverishment of French peasants diminished the rents of their landlords. But the difference is still significant. It was a commonplace in England, where "the asinine peasants of France," with their "wooden shoes and canvas breeches" were regularly contrasted with our own, more prosperous yeomen. It is illustrated by the ultimate result: in England, when revolution came, it was a great revolution, led and controlled by the gentry; in France, there were, every year for the same twenty years, revolts—little but serious revolts—of the peasants. Nevertheless, if the rebels were different, the general grievance against which they rebelled—the character and cost of the State—was the same.

For wherever we look, this is the burden of all complaints. From 1620 to 1640 this is the cry of the country, the problem of the Courts. We can hear the cry from the back-benches of the English parliaments in the 1620s. We can see the problem in Bacon's great essays, written between 1620 and 1625, on "Sedition and Troubles" and "The True Greatness of Kingdoms." We hear the cry in Spain in the protests of the

---

[15] Gerald Brenan, *The Literature of the Spanish People* (Cambridge, 1951), p. 272.

Cortes, see the problem in the pamphlets of the *arbitristas,* in Fernández Navarrete's *Conservación de Monarquías* with its wonderful analysis of the social ills of Spain, and in Olivares's long memorandum to Philip IV, outlining his new programme for the country,[16] both written in the 1620s. We see it in France, above all, in the *Testament Politique* of Richelieu, written in 1629 and the early 1630's, the period when governments everywhere were facing these problems, or trying to face them, before it was too late. And these demands, these problems, are not constitutional, they are not concerned with monarchy or republic, Crown or Parliament. Nor are they economic: they are not concerned with methods of production. Essentially they are demands for emancipation from the burden of centralization; for reduction of fees; reduction of useless, expensive offices, including—even in Spain—clerical offices; abolition of the sale of offices ("for whosoever doth farm or buy offices doth bind himself to be an extortioner," and "they which buy dear must sell dear"); abolition of heredity of offices; abolition of those wasteful, indirect taxes which yield so little to the Crown but on whose superabundant "waste" the ever-expanding fringe of the Court is fed.

Thus the tension between Court and country grew, and the "revolutionary situation" of the 1620s and 1630s developed. But revolutionary situations do not necessarily lead to revolutions—nor (we may add) are violent revolutions necessary in order to create new forms of production or society. Society is an organic body, far tougher, far more resilient, than its morbid anatomists often suppose; the frontiers between opposing classes are always confused by a complex tissue of interests;[17] and if a country is to pass from a revolutionary situation to a revolution, a whole series of political events and political errors must intervene. Therefore if we are to carry this study further, from crisis to revolution, we must take account of these intervening events and errors: events and errors which, by definition, must vary from place to place, and whose variation will explain, in part, the difference between the revolutions in those different places.

Perhaps we can see the problem best if we consider the means of avoiding revolution. If the Renaissance Courts were to survive, it was clear that at least one of two things must be done. On the one hand the parasitic bureaucracies must be cut down; on the other hand the working bureaucracy must be related to the economic capacity of the country. The first programme was one of administrative, the second of economic reform. The first was easy enough to define—any country gentleman could put it in two words—but difficult to carry out: it meant the reduction of a parasitic, but living and powerful class; and although this can be done without revolution, as it was done in nineteenth-century England—one only has to read the *Extraordinary Black Book* of 1831 to see the huge parasitic fringe which had grown again around the eighteenth-century Court—it is at best a delicate and difficult operation. The second was far more difficult to define: it meant the discovery, or re-discovery, of an economic system. Nevertheless, such a definition was not beyond the wit of seventeenth-century thinkers, and in fact several thinkers did point out, clearly enough, the kind of economic system which was required.

What was that system? It was not a "capitalist" system—or at least, if it was capitalist, there was nothing new about it. It did not entail revolution or a change in method of production or in the class structure. Nor was it advocated by revolutionary

---

[16] Published in Valladares, *Semanario Erudito,* vol. xi (Madrid, 1788). (I owe this reference to Mr. J. H. Elliott.)

[17] e.g. in this instance, the interpenetration of 'bourgeoisie' and office-holders, which paralysed the Spanish cortes, the French parlements and even the English parliament.

thinkers: in general, those who advocated it were conservative men who wished for little or no political change. And in fact the economic programme which they advocated, though applied to modern conditions, looked back for its example. For what they advocated was simply the application to the new, centralized monarchies of the old, well-tried policy of the medieval communes which those monarchies had eclipsed: mercantilism.

For what had been the policy of the medieval cities? It had been a policy of national economy—within the limits of the city-State. The city had seen itself at once as a political and as an economic unit. Its legislation had been based on its trading requirements. It had controlled the price of food and labour, limited imports in the interest of its own manufactures, encouraged the essential methods of trade—fishing and shipbuilding, freedom from internal tolls—invested its profits not in conspicuous waste or pursuit of glory, or wars merely of plunder, but in the rational conquest of markets and the needs of national economy: in technical education, municipal betterment, poor relief. In short, the city had recognized that its life must be related to its means of livelihood. In the sixteenth-century eclipse of the cities, in their transformation into overgrown, overpopulated capitals, centres merely of exchange and consumption, much of this old civic wisdom had been forgotten. Now, in the seventeenth-century eclipse of the spendthrift Renaissance Courts, it was being remembered. The economists wished to go farther: to re-apply it.

Of course, they would re-apply it in changed circumstances, to different national forms. The princes, it was agreed, had done their work: it could not be reversed. The new nation-states had come to stay. But, said the Reformers, having come, let them now apply to their different conditions the old good rules of the cities. Let them not merely pare down the parasitic fringe that had grown around them, but also relate their power, in a positive sense, to economic aims. Let them favour a gospel of work instead of aristocratic, or pseudo-aristocratic *hidalguía*. Let them protect industry, guarantee food-supplies, remove internal tolls, develop productive wealth. Let them rationalize finance and bring down the apparatus of Church and State to a juster proportion. To reverse the Parkinson's law of bureaucracy, let them reduce the hatcheries which turned out the superfluous bureaucrats: grammar schools in England, colleges in France, monasteries and theological seminaries in Spain. Instead, let them build up local elementary education: skilled workers at the base of society now seemed more important than those unemployable university graduates, hungry for office, whom the new Renaissance foundations were turning out. "Of grammar-schools," declared that great intellectual, Sir Francis Bacon, "there are too many"; and he and his followers advocated a change in the type of education or the diversion of funds to elementary schools. Of colleges, declared the founder of the French Academy, Cardinal Richelieu, there are too many: the commerce of letters would banish absolutely that of merchandise "which crowns states with riches" and ruin agriculture "the true nursing-mother of peoples." Of monasteries, declared the Catholic Council of Castile in 1619, there are too many, and it prayed that the Pope be asked to authorize their reduction, for although the monastic state is no doubt, for the individual, the most perfect, "for the public it is very damaging and prejudicial." So, in country after country, the protest was raised. It was the backswing of the great educational impulse of the Renaissance and Reformation, the great religious impulse of the Counter-Reformation.[18]

[18] For Bacon's proposal see his *Works,* ed. Spedding, iv, pp. 249 ff; for Richelieu, his

To cut down the oppressive, costly sinecures of Church and State, and to revert, *mutatis mutandis,* to the old mercantilist policy of the cities, based on the economic interest of society—such were the two essential methods of avoiding revolution in the seventeenth century. How far were either of them adopted in the states of western Europe? The answer, I think, is instructive. If we look at those states in turn, we may see, in the extent to which either or both of these policies were adopted or rejected, some partial explanation of the different forms which the general crisis took in each of them.

In Spain neither policy was adopted. In spite of the *arbitristas,* in spite of the wisdom of influential statesmen, including the greatest of Spanish ambassadors, Gondomar, whose letters show him a perfect mercantilist,[19] in spite of the Council of Castile, in spite even of Philip IV and Olivares, the system remained basically unchanged. Whatever projects of reform he may once have entertained, whatever beginnings of reform or paper-reforms he may even have carried out,[20] Olivares, like Richelieu, soon surrendered to necessity and the fact of war. On the other hand Spain—that is, Castile—lacked the organs of effective protest. The middle class was weak and penetrated by office-holders; the old Cortes towns had been suppressed in their last rising against the Burgundian state; and the Cortes of Castile were now an aristocratic body which hardly sought to do more than demur. In spite of constant demands for reduction and disendowment, the wealth and number of churches and monasteries constantly grew; so did Court offices and the sale of offices. In 1621—the first year of crisis and reforming zeal—the number of royal officers had been fixed by law. In 1646 the Cortes of Castile pointed to the factual consequences: instead of one president and three councillors of the Treasury, there were now three presidents and eleven councillors; instead of three *contadores* and a *fiscal,* there were now fourteen *contadores;* instead of four councillors at war there were now more than forty; and all these, salaried or unsalaried (for their salaries, their 'fees', were anyway trifles), had entertainment, expenses, lodgings, privileges and perquisites at the expense of the subject.[21] The weight of this burden might have been redistributed a little within the country, but it had certainly not been reduced.[22] Nor had the Spanish economy been enabled to bear it. For meanwhile the national wealth of Spain had not increased: it had diminished. The voices of the mercantilists were stifled. The trade of Spain was taken over almost entirely by foreigners. The vitality of the country was crushed beneath the dead weight of an unreformed *ancien régime.* It was not till the next century that a new generation of *arbitristas*—philosophers inspired by English and French examples—would again have the strength and spirit to urge on a new dynasty

*Testament Politique* (ed. Louis André, Paris, 1947), pp. 204-5; for Spain the *Consulta del Consejo Supremo de Castilla,* published in P. Fernández Navarrete, *Conservación de Monarquías* (Madrid, 1947, Biblioteca de Autores Españoles, vol. xxv), p. 450.
[19] See, in particular, Pascual Gayangos, *Cinco Cartas Politico-Literarias de D. Diego Sarmiento, Conde de Gondomar* (Madrid, 1869), *Sociedad de Bibliófilos,* vol. iv.
[20] For a summary of these reforms, see H. Bérindoague, *Le Mercantilisme en Espagne* (Bordeaux, 1929), pp. 85-104.
[21] *Consulta* of the Cortes of Castile, 18 Aug. 1646, printed in Alonso Núñez de Castro, *Libro Historio-Político, Solo Madrid es Corte,* 2nd edn. (Madrid, 1669), pp. 84 ff. This whole book, written by the royal chronicler and first published in 1658, illustrates the process I am describing.
[22] For the factual (though not legal) redistribution of fiscal burdens in Spain under Philip IV, see the interesting article of A. Domínguez Ortiz, "La desigualdad contributiva en Castilla en el siglo XVIII," *Anuario de Historia del Derecho Español,* 1952.

the same reforms which had clearly but vainly been demanded in the days of Philip III and Philip IV.[23]

Very different was the position in the emancipated northern Netherlands. For the northern Netherlands was the first European country to reject the Renaissance Court, and the Court they rejected was their own court, the greatest, most lavish court of all, the Burgundian Court which had moved and made itself so fatally permanent in Spain. The revolt of the Netherlands in the sixteenth century was not, of course, a direct revolt of society against the Court. That is not how revolutions break out. But in the course of the long struggle the Court itself, in those provinces which freed themselves, was a casualty. There the whole apparatus of the Burgundian Court simply dissolved under the stress of war. So did the Burgundian Church, that huge, corrupt department of State which Philip II unskilfully sought to reform and whose abuses the great patrons of revolt, in the beginning, were seeking to preserve. Whatever the causes or motives of the revolution, the United Provinces emerged from it incidentally disembarrassed of that top-heavy system whose pressure, a generation later, would create a revolutionary situation in other countries. Consequently, in those provinces, there was no such revolutionary situation. The new Court of the Princes of Orange might develop some of the characteristics of the old Court, but only some: and as it started lean, it could better afford a little additional fat. There were crises no doubt in seventeenth century Holland—the crises of 1618, of 1650, of 1672: but they were political crises, comparable with our crisis not of 1640 but of 1688; and they were surgically solved for the same reason: the social problem was no longer acute: the top-heavy apparatus of the State had been purged: society beneath was sound.

Moreover, if accident rather than design had rid the United Provinces of the Renaissance State, policy had also achieved there the other, economic reform of which I have written. It was not that there was a "bourgeois" or "capitalist" revolution in Holland.[24] Dutch industry was relatively insignificant. But the new rulers of Holland, seeking the means of guarding their hard-won freedom, set out to imitate the fortune and the methods of those older mercantile communities which had preserved their independence through centuries by rationally combining commercial wealth and maritime power. By adopting the techniques of Italy, welcoming the émigré experts of Antwerp, and following the old good rules of Venetian policy, Amsterdam became, in the seventeenth century, the new Venice of the north. The economic originality of seventeenth-century Holland consisted in showing that, even after the victory and reign of the Renaissance Princes, whom they alone had driven out, the mercantilism of the cities was not dead: it could be revived.

Midway between completely unreformed Spain and completely reformed Holland lies what is perhaps the most interesting of all examples, Bourbon France. For France, in the seventeenth century, was certainly not immune from the general crisis, and in

---

[23] For these *arbitristas* of the eighteenth century see M. Jean Sarrailh's excellent work, *L'Espagne eclairée* (Paris, 1954): which does not, however, bring out the extent to which Ward, Jovellanos, Campomanes, etc., were repeating the programme of the early seventeenth-century Spanish mercantilists.

[24] That the economy of the United Provinces was not a new, revolutionary form of capitalism, but a return to the system of the medieval Italian cities is argued by Mr. Jelle C. Riemersma in his article "Calvinism and Capitalism in Holland, 1550-1650", *Explorations in Entrepreneurial History*, i (1), p. 8, and is admitted even by Marxists like Mr. Dobb and Mr. Hobsbawm, who calls the Dutch economy "a feudal business economy" (*Past and Present*, no. 6, 1954, repr. above at p. 42).

the Frondes it had a revolution, if a relatively small revolution. The result was, as in Spain, a victory for the monarchy. Triumphant over its critics and adversaries, the monarchy of the *ancien régime* survived in France, and survived for another century and a half. On the other hand the French monarchy of Louis XIV was not like the Spanish monarchy of Philip IV and Charles V. It was not economically parasitic. Industry, commerce, science flourished and grew in France, in spite of the "failure" of the "bourgeois revolution," no less than in England, in spite of its "success." To all appearances, in 1670, in the age of Colbert, absolutism and the *ancien régime* were perfectly compatible with commercial and industrial growth and power.

And indeed, why not? For what had hindered such growth in the past, what had caused the crisis in society, was not the form of government, but its abuses; and though these abuses might be removed by revolution, or might fall as incidental casualties of a revolution, their removal did not necessarily require revolution. There was always the way of reform. It is not necessary to burn down the house in order to have roast pig. And although France (like Holland) had had a fire in the sixteenth century, in which some of its burden of waste matter had been incidentally consumed, it did also, in the years thereafter, achieve some measure of reform. The fire, indeed, had prepared the ground. The French civil wars of the sixteenth century, if they had done much harm, had also done some good. They had burnt up the overgrown patronage of the great nobles and reduced the patronage of the Court to the patronage of the King. Henry IV, like the Prince of Orange, like Charles II of England after him, found himself at his accession disembarrassed of much ancient parasitism: he could therefore afford to indulge a little new. And on this basis, this *tabula partim rasa,* he was able to achieve certain administrative changes. The *Paulette,* the law of 1604 which systematized the sale of offices, did at least regulate the abuses which it has often, and wrongly, been accused of creating. Sully, by his *économies royales,* did keep down the waste around the throne. And Richelieu, in the 1630s not only meditated a complete mercantilist policy for France, but also, even in the midst of war, succeeded—as Laud and Olivares, whether in peace or war, did not—in regulating that most expensive, most uncontrollable of all departments, the royal household.[25] Thanks to these changes, the *ancien régime* in France was repaired and strengthened. The changes may not have been radical, but they were enough. Richelieu and Mazarin no doubt had other advantages in their successful struggle to maintain the French *ancien régime* in the era of the Huguenot revolt and the Frondes. They had an army absolutely under royal control; they had taxes whose increase fell not on gentry, assembled and vocal in parliament, but on scattered, inarticulate peasants; and they had their own political genius. But they had also an apparatus of state which had already undergone some salutary reform: a State which, in the mind of Richelieu and in the hands of his disciple Colbert, could become a mercantilist State, rationally organized for both profit and power.

Finally there is England. In England the Crown had not the same political power as in France or Spain, and the taxes fell on the gentry, powerful in their counties and in parliament. In England therefore, it was doubly important that the problem be faced and solved. How far was it in fact faced? To answer this question let us look in turn at the two sides of the problem, administrative and economic.

[25] For Richelieu's mercantilism see H. Hauser, *La Pensée et l'Action Economique du cardinal de Richelieu* (Paris, 1944). For his reform of the royal household, see M. R. Mousnier's article in vol. i of *Histoire de France,* ed. M. Reinhard (Paris, 1955). (I owe this reference to Mr. J. P. Cooper.)

In the sixteenth century the apparatus of the English State had neither suffered nor benefited from any such destructive accident as had befallen Holland or France. The Renaissance Court of the Tudors, whose parsimony under Elizabeth had been so unreal and whose magnificence and ceremony had so impressed foreign visitors, survived intact into the new century, when its cost and show were magnified beyond all measure by King James and his favourites. Already in 1604 Francis Bacon warned the new King of the danger. The Court, he said, was like a nettle: its root, the Crown itself, was "without venom or malignity," but it sustained leaves "venomous and stinging where they touch."[26] Two years later, King James's greatest minister, Robert Cecil, Earl of Salisbury, apprehended revolution against the same burden of the Court; and in 1608, on becoming Lord Treasurer, he applied all his energies to a large and imaginative solution of the whole problem. He sought to rationalize the farming of taxes and the leasing of Crown lands, to reform the royal household, liberate agriculture from feudal restrictions, and abolish archaic dues in exchange for other forms of income whose full yield, or something like it, instead of a mere fraction, would come to the Crown. In 1610 Salisbury staked his political career on this great programme of reorganization. But he failed to carry it through. The "courtiers," the "officers" who lived on the "waste," mobilized opposition, and the King, listening to them, and thinking "not what he got but what he might get" out of the old, wasteful, irritant sources of revenue, refused to surrender them. Within two years of his failure, Salisbury died, out of favour with the King, completely unlamented, even insulted by the whole Court which he had sought to reform and, by reform, to save.[27]

After Salisbury, other reformers occasionally took up the cause. The most brilliant was Francis Bacon. He had been an enemy of Salisbury, but once Salisbury was dead he sang the same tune. He diagnosed the evil—no man, perhaps, diagnosed it so completely in all its forms and ultimate consequences—but he could do nothing to cure it except by royal permission, which was refused, and he was overthrown. After his fall, in the years of the great depression, even the Court took alarm, and a new reformer seemed to have obtained that permission. This was Lionel Cranfield, Earl of Middlesex, who set out to carry through some at least of Salisbury's proposals. But permission, if granted, was soon, and conspicuously withdrawn. Cranfield, like Bacon, was ruined by Court-faction, led from above by the royal favourite, the Duke of Buckingham, the universal manager and profiteer of all those marketable offices, benefices, sinecures, monopolies, patents, perquisites and titles which together constituted the nourishment of the Court. Thus when Buckingham was murdered and Strafford and Laud, the "Puritans of the right," came to power, they inherited from him an utterly unreformed Court.[28]

[26] Francis Bacon, *Works* (ed. Spedding), iii, p. 183.

[27] Public justice has never been done to Salisbury's programme of reform in 1608-12, although the "Great Contract," which was only part of it, is well-known. The evidence of it is scattered among the official papers of the time. Of contemporaries, only Sir Walter Cope and Sir William Sanderson, both of whom had been employed in it, sought to make it known and understood, but neither Cope's *Apology for the Late Lord Treasurer* (which was given to the King in MS.) nor Sanderson's *Aulicus Coquinariae* was published at the time. Bishop Goodman and Sir Henry Wotton also appreciated it, but also did not publish their appreciation. See L. Pearsall Smith, *Life and Letters of Sir Henry Wotton* (London, 1907), vol. ii; Goodman, op. cit., i, pp. 36-42, 487-9.

[28] Bacon's projects are scattered through his writings which Spedding collected. One only has to compare his various proposals for reform of the court, the law, education, the Church, the Crown estates, etc., with the demands of the radical party in the 1640s, to see the truth of Gardiner's statement (in *Dict. Nat. Biog.*, s. v. Bacon) that his programme, if carried out, might

Did they do anything to reform it? Ostensibly they did. "The face of the court," as Mrs. Hutchinson wrote, "was changed." King Charles was outwardly frugal compared with his father: but such frugality, as we have seen in the case of Queen Elizabeth, was relatively insignificant. Laud and Strafford waged war on the corruption of the Court, whenever they perceived it; but they left the basic system untouched. Whenever we study that system we find that, in their time, its cost had not been reduced: it had grown. The greatest of Court feasts in Buckingham's days had been his own entertainment of the King in 1626, which had cost £4,000; the Earl of Newcastle, in 1634, went up to £15,000. An office which was sold for £5,000 in 1624 fetched £15,000 in 1640. Wardships, which had brought in £25,000 to the Crown when Salisbury had sought to abolish them in 1610, were made to yield £95,000 in 1640. And the proportion that ran to waste was no smaller. For every £100 which reached the Crown, at least £400 was taken from the subject. As Clarendon says, 'The envy and reproach came to the King, the profit to other men.'

Thus in 1640 the English Court, like the Spanish, was still unreformed. But what of the English economy? Here the parallel no longer holds. For in England there was not that absolute divorce between Crown and *arbitristas* that was so obvious in Spain. The early Stuart governments did not ignore matters of trade. They listened to the City of London. By their financial methods, whether deliberately or not, they encouraged the formation of capital, its investment in industry. There were limits of course to what they did: they did not satisfy the systematic mercantilist theorists; they paid less attention to the base of society than to its summit. Nevertheless, in many respects, they favoured or at least allowed a mercantilist policy. They sought to naturalize industrial processes; they sought to protect supplies of essential raw-materials; they sought to monopolize the herring-fisheries; they protected navigation; they preferred peace abroad and looked to their moat. The years of their rule saw the growth of English capitalism, sponsored by them, on a scale unknown before. Unfortunately such growth entailed dislocation, claimed victims; and when political crisis increased the dislocation and multiplied the victims, the stiff and weakened structure of government could no longer contain the mutinous forces which it had provoked.

For in 1640 the leaders of the Long Parliament did not seek—they did not need to seek—to reverse the economic policy of the Crown. They sought one thing only: to repair the administration. The Earl of Bedford as Lord Treasurer, John Pym as Chancellor of the Exchequer, intended to resume the frustrated work of Salisbury: to abolish monopolies, wardships, prerogative taxes, cut down the "waste," and establish the Stuart Court on a more rational, less costly basis. Having done this, they would have continued the mercantilist policy of the Crown, perhaps extending it by redistribution of resources, rationalization of labour, at the base of society. They would have done for the English monarchy what Colbert would do for the French. All they required was that the English monarchy, like the French, would allow them to do it.

For of course monarchy itself was no obstacle. It is absurd to say that such a policy was impossible without revolution. It was no more impossible in 1641 than it had been in the days of Salisbury and Cranfield. We cannot assume that merely human obstacles—the irresponsibility of a Buckingham or a Charles I, the reckless obscurantism of a Strafford—are inherent historical necessities. But in fact these

have prevented the revolution. For Cranfield's work see R. H. Tawney, *Business and Politics under James I* (London, 1958).

human obstacles did intervene. Had James I or Charles I had the intelligence of Queen Elizabeth or the docility of Louis XIII, the English *ancien régime* might have adapted itself to the new circumstances as peacefully in the seventeenth century as it would in the nineteenth. It was because it remained, administratively and economically as well as aesthetically, "the last Renaissance Court in Europe," that it ran into ultimate disaster: that the rational reformers were swept aside, that more radical men came forward and mobilized yet more radical passions than even they could control, and that in the end, amid the sacking of palaces, the shivering of statues and stained-glass windows, the screech of saws in ruined organ-lofts, this last of the great Renaissance Courts was mopped up, the royal aesthete was murdered, his spendid pictures were knocked down and sold, even the soaring gothic cathedrals were offered up for scrap.

So, in the 1640s, in war and revolution, the most obstinate and yet, given the political structure of England, the frailest of the Renaissance monarchies went down. It did not go down before a new "bourgeois" revolution. It did not even go down before an old "mercantilist" revolution. Its enemies were not the "bourgeoisie"—that bourgeoisie who, as a Puritan preacher complained, "for a little trading and profit" would have had Christ, the Puritan soldiers, crucified and "this great Barabbas of Windsor", the King, set free.[29] Nor were they the mercantilists. The ablest politicians among the Puritan rebels did indeed, once the republic was set up, adopt an aggressive mercantilist policy; but in this they simply resumed the old policy of the Crown and, on that account, were promptly attacked and overthrown by the same enemies, who accused them of betraying the revolution.[30] No, the triumphant enemies of the English Court were simply "the country": that indeterminate, unpolitical, but highly sensitive miscellany of men who had mutinied not against the monarchy (they had long clung to monarchist beliefs) nor against economic archaism (it was they who were the archaists), but against the vast, oppressive, ever-extending apparatus of parasitic bureaucracy which had grown up around the throne and above the economy of England. These men were not politicians or economists, and when the Court had foundered under their blows, they soon found that they could neither govern nor prosper. In the end they addicated. The old dynasty was restored, its new mercantilist policy resumed. But the restoration was not complete. The old abuses, which had already dissolved in war and revolution, were not restored, and, having gone, were easily legislated out of existence. In 1661 Salisbury's "Great Contract," Bedford's excise, were at last achieved. The old prerogative courts—whose offence had been not so much their policy as their existence—were not revived. Charles II began his reign free at last from the inherited lumber of the Renaissance Court.

Such, as it seems to me, was "the general crisis of the seventeenth century." It was a crisis not of the constitution nor of the system of production, but of the State, or rather, of the relation of the State to society. Different countries found their way out of that crisis in different ways. In Spain the *ancien régime* survived: but it survived only as a disastrous, immobile burden on an impoverished country. Elsewhere, in Holland, France and England, the crisis marked the end of an era: the jettison of a

---

[29] The preacher was Hugh Peters, as quoted in *State Trials*, v (1), pp. 129-30.

[30] Those who regard the whole revolution as a bourgeois revolution on the strength of the mercantile policy of the Rump between 1651 and 1653 might well reflect (1) that this policy, of peace with Spain, navigation acts, and rivalry with Holland over fishery and trade, had been the policy of Charles I in the 1630s, and (2) that it was repudiated, emphatically and effectively, by those who had brought the revolution to a "successful" issue—the Puritan Army—and only revived at the Restoration of the monarchy.

top-heavy super-structure, the return to responsible, mercantilist policy. For by the seventeenth century the Renaissance Courts had grown so great, had consumed so much in "waste," and had sent their multiplying suckers so deep into the body of society, that they could only flourish for a limited time, and in a time, too, of expanding general prosperity. When that prosperity failed, the monstrous parasite was bound to falter. In this sense, the depression of the 1620s is perhaps no less important, as a historical turning-point, than the depression of 1929: though a temporary economic failure, it marked a lasting political change. At all events, the princely Courts recognized it as their crisis. Some of them sought to reform themselves, to take physic and reduce their bulk. Their doctors pointed the way: it was then that the old city States, and particularly Venice, though now in decadence, became the admired model, first of Holland, then of England. And yet, asked the patient, was such reform possible, or even safe? Could a monarchy really be adapted to a pattern which so far had been dangerously republican? Is any political operation more difficult than the self-reduction of an established, powerful, privileged bureaucracy? In fact, the change was nowhere achieved without something of revolution. If it was limited in France, and Holland, that was partly because some of the combustible rubbish had already, in a previous revolution, been consumed. It was also because there had been some partial reform. In England there had been no such previous revolution, no such partial reform. There was also, under the early Stuarts, a fatal lack of political skill: instead of the genius of Richelieu, the suppleness of Mazarin, there was the irresponsibility of Buckingham, the violence of Strafford, the undeviating universal pedantry of Land. In England therefore the storm of the mid-century, which blew throughout Europe, struck the most brittle, most overgrown, most rigid Court of all and brought it violently down.

# TREVOR-ROPER'S "GENERAL CRISIS"

Symposium*

*Roland Mousnier, J. H. Elliott, and H. R. Trevor-Roper*

*I: Roland Mousnier*

It is a great pleasure to read Professor H. R. Trevor-Roper's brilliant essay, so sparkling with intelligence. To reduce his rich and luxuriant elaborations to a few dry propositions is to run the risk of distorting his ideas. But in a brief comment, the risk must be taken. According to Trevor-Roper, between 1640 and 1660 Europe witnessed a series of political revolutions. Whether successful or not, they mark a watershed: on the one side is the Renaissance and on the other the Age of Enlightenment. Indeed these revolutions are themselves the apogee of a prolonged crisis in the structure of society. The Renaissance State, with its Court and its bureaucratic apparatus of officials remunerated in part by their own hands, laid too heavy a burden on society. This burden became unbearable during the economic recession of the seventeenth

* From no. 18 (1960). Because of shortage of space, not all the contributions to the original Symposium are reprinted here.

century, when different social groups tried to throw it off through revolt and revolution. The *Stände* rose against the Court. The Court not only tried to quell the rebellions, but also to suppress their cause by adjusting through mercantilism the levies of the bureaucrats to the resources of the country.

Let us examine the validity of these suggestions in the case of France.

Now Trevor-Roper has grasped a vital point: that there was a general crisis in the seventeenth century. I have discussed this crisis in various books and articles published since 1945; and as far back as 1953, I devoted the second part (208 pages) of the fourth volume of the *Histoire Générale des Civilisations* (3rd edn., Paris, 1961) to the European crisis of the seventeenth century.

How far is it true that the revolts of the seventeenth century and the revolution of the Fronde can be interpreted in France as a rising of the country against the Court and against the bureaucratic apparatus of the State? It is clear that the office-holders provoked discontent. Throughout the troubles, nobles and bourgeois complained of the pullulation of office-holders and of the way they drained the public revenues. But they complained just as loudly of the excessive price of offices and the difficulty of acquiring them. They regarded offices as an evil, but strove to lay hands on one. However it must be pointed out that the office-holders helped to provoke the revolts and also played an outstanding part in the attempted revolution of the Fronde. And this seems to me to go directly against the theory of Trevor-Roper.

The part played in the Fronde by the Parlements and by certain groups of office-holders is already well known.[1] In a recent article[2] and more lately I have analysed the movements of peasant revolt, so numerous in France, from about 1625 until the Fronde and beyond. Broadly speaking, this is what seems to have happened in most cases: the landlords, whether gentry or royal officials or municipal magistrates, incited the peasants not to pay the *tailles* or the numerous new taxes imposed by the Government, because if the peasants paid these royal taxes they would be unable to pay their feudal dues or their rents, and also because it was a lord's duty to protect his peasants; the peasants then violently drove off the bailiffs with their warrants or the agents of the tax-farmers; the Government sent *commissaires* to obtain payment; officials and gentry stirred up the peasantry; gentry joined together to help their peasants to resist; in the towns, the royal officials and the *échevins* provoked risings among the urban population to help the peasants by paralysing the movements of the royal *commissaires*; then, as happened with the *Croquants* of Villefranche-de-Rouergue in 1643 and with other movements, the peasants sent some of their men into the towns; or the royal officials made the peasants come from their *seigneuries* and make up bands or companies of insurgents, as in Paris during the Fronde, in Aix and elsewhere; or sometimes the peasants themselves seized a town. Thus in most cases we do not find a revolt of the country against an oppressive public service, but the revolt of a public service which considered itself oppressed and which dragged in its wake those social groups over which the structure of society gave it influence. Is not this exactly the opposite of what Trevor-Roper thinks?

What did the office-holders complain of? *That they contributed too much to the*

---

[1] R. Mousnier, "Recherches sur les Syndicats d'officiers pendant la Fronde. Trésoriers généraux de France et Elus dans la Révolution," *XVIIe Siècle* (Bulletin de la Société de'Etude du XVIIe Siècle), no. 42 (1959); "Quelques raisons de la Fronde. Les Causes des journées révolutionnaires parisiennes de 1648," ibid., no. 2 (1949).

[2] R. Mousnier, "Recherches sur les soulèvements populaires en France avant la Fronde," *Revue d'histoire moderne et contemporaine*, v (1958).

*expenses of the State*; that they were being deprived of their power. It is a theoretical concept to think of this bureaucratic structure of office-holders in terms of pure gain. Sometimes the King made new offices so that existing office-holders would have to buy them up in order to keep away eventual competitors, or would have to pay for their suppression. Sometimes the King decreed an increase in the salaries and fees of officials, but only in return for a cash sum which constituted the capital of which these benefits were merely the interest. The officials often had to borrow the money at interest from others, in which case the whole operation merely turned them into intermediaries in the movement of money, without any personal benefit accruing.[3] Moreover after 1640 the King gradually reduced the salaries and many of the fees of his officials, who now were only getting a minute interest or none at all, in return for a capital investment which was immobilized, or lost. The *Elus*, who were finance officers, alleged in 1648 that they had paid over 200 million *livres* since 1624, including 60 million paid since 1640 "for confirmation of an imaginary right or grant of a fictitious increment".[4] The officials considered themselves robbed.

On the other hand, in the throes of the Thirty Years' War the Government found their administrative routine too slow. It accused them of favouring in the assessment of taxes their lessees and sharecroppers and those of their relatives, associates and friends, and of causing deficiencies by shifting the burden on to others. The Government farmed out to *traitants* or *partisans*, not only the *aides*, but also the direct taxes such as the *tailles*. It handed over to *commissaires*, of whom the most important were the *intendants*, not only the supervision of officials, but also often the execution of their duties.[5] At the same time, when dealing with corporate bodies of officials the royal Government increasingly ignored the *remontrances* which traditionally they were in duty bound to present to the King for the better ordering of the service. Wounded in their honour, their prestige and their interests, the officials revolted. Are Trevor-Roper's views really in keeping with these facts?

Can one say that this bureaucratic apparatus of officers imposed an unbearable burden on the country? Trevor-Roper should have distinguished more clearly between the great officers of the Crown and the courtiers, some of whom became very rich thanks to the privileges of their offices or their relations with tax-farmers, and those officials who were not of the Court but who nevertheless held a high rank in society and exercised important functions: members of the sovereign courts (Parlements, *Chambres des Comptes, Cours des Aides, Grand Conseil*); officials of the *Présidiaux*, the *baillages* and the *senéchaussées; Trésoriers Généraux de France, Elus*, etc. In spite of what Trevor-Roper believes, these officials were on the whole men of simple tastes, who had nothing to do with the opulent way of life of princes and a handful of great courtiers. Plain practitioners learned in the law and in the rules of their profession, rarely humanists and with little interest in the arts, save perhaps at the third generation,[6] they made their money less as office-holders than as landowners and

---

[3] R. Mousnier, *La Vénalité des Offices en France sous Henri IV et Louis XIII* (Rouen, 1945). See pp. 365-86.

[4] See n. 1.

[5] R. Mousnier, "Etat et commissaire. Recherches sur la création des Intendants des provinces (1634-1648)," *Forschungen zu Staat und Verfassung: Festgabe für Fritz Hartung* (Berlin, 1958).

[6] See " 'Serviteurs du Roi.' Quelques aspects de la fonction publique dans la société française du XVIIe siècle" (Etudes sous la direction de R. Mousnier), *XVIIe Siècle, nos. 42-43 (1959).*

feudal lords, as money-lenders and creditors of peasants and artisans. Their salaries and fees, the fortunes built up by the courtiers, could have upset the balance neither of the budget nor of society. In seventeenth-century France the expenses of the Court never represented more than a small fraction of the expenses of the State. The same applies to the salaries and fees of the office-holders. The sums levied by officials in the form of judicial bribes, fees, *taxes de finances*, do not strike me as affecting more than a modest part of the resources of the King's subjects. The great expenses of the State, the heavy burdens on the unprivileged were those of the army and of war, pay, munitions and billeting for the troops. It would therefore be necessary to prove that these huge armies, those long wars, were merely of interest to the Court, and not to the nation, and this would be a difficult task.

Would it be possible, however, to say that in fact this opposition on the part of the office-holders was an aspect of the struggle of the country against the Court? On the one hand there were the officials, owners of their offices, irremovable, given security of tenure by the *Paulette*, landowners and often feudal lords in the district where they practised, linked with many local families, themselves with local roots, convinced that if office demanded fidelity to the King, it required them equally faithfully to serve justice and protect the rights of the King's subjects; they were thus simultaneously notables representing the districts and provinces in their dealings with the King, and instruments of the royal will. On the other hand there were the *commissaires* used by his Council, his Household, his Court. It is not then a struggle of officials against the Court rather than (as in Trevor-Roper's view) of the country against the Court and its bureaucratic apparatus?

But one cannot simplify things in this way. The royal *commissaires* came from the same social stratum as the royal officials. A *maître des requêtes* was also an official. Before becoming one he might have been *conseiller au Parlement*. Many *conseillers d'Etat* came from the sovereign courts. The King's *commissaire* would have been powerless in the provinces if he had not always found among the officials, judges to help him pass judgement, finance officers to help him with their technical skill, and in the country barristers to act as Public Prosecutors. Nor must we forget that it is at Court that the worst revolts occurred. It was when magnates such as Monsieur, the King's brother, or Condé, a prince of the blood royal, withdrew from the Court and rallied their supporters, that provincial risings took a particularly serious turn. Is it not a little artificial to oppose the Court and the rest of the country? Trevor-Roper could obviously answer that what matters is not so much the origins of the *commissaires* and those who helped them as their obedience to the will of the King, in his Council, in his Court.

But what did all their followers want? Monsieur and Condé wanted to turn absolute monarchy to their own ends. They wanted an aristocratic monarchy, not a *Ständestaat*. Other princes and other magnates dreamed of a quasi-independence in their provinces and in their *seigneuries*, of a return to the French institutions of the time of Hugh Capet "and better still if possible." They were followed by many feudal lords, many towns, many provinces, who looked back with regret to their days of autonomy or independence, and feared their increasing subjection. As contemporaries saw very clearly, in most of France it was undoubtedly a struggle of feudal elements against the State.[7] It was less an opposition between the country and the Court, than

[7] R. Mousnier, "Comment les Français voyaient la Constitution," ibid., nos. 25-26 (1955).

between what remained feudal in society and what was new, *étatique*, progressive, "modern" in the King's Council and its dependent organs.[8] Since the time of Henry IV, it was lawyers and no longer landed gentry who formed the majority in the King's Council. If we ask to what extent the Council was part of the Court we raise yet another question: to what extent had society ceased to be feudal and become penetrated by commercial capitalism?[9] This brings us back again to the economic aspect of the problem.

It is doubtful whether one can say that mercantilism represented an attempt to adapt the capacity of the country to support the burdens imposed by the bureaucratic apparatus of officials. Mercantilism was first and foremost a weapon in the struggle against the foreigner, a tool of war and of foreign policy. Already a royal tendency in the days of Louis XI, it became doctrine under Chancellor Duprat in the reign of Francis I. It was taken up once more by the States General of 1576 during the great inflation in the latter half of the wars of religion. In the seventeenth century, Laffemas, Richelieu, Colbert saw it as a means of ensuring French hegemony. The great economic recession of the seventeenth century made it more necessary, without it appearing to be any more closely tied to internal politics.

Nor does it seem that the revolts and the revolutionary attempt of the Fronde mark any sort of watershed in France. Political and social problems are not essentially different before and after. In their nature, they do not seem to change. All that happened was that, for a while, the King was the victor. By the end of the century a process of social change was under way, but this had no connection with the revolts and revolutions of the mid-century. The wars of religion of 1572–98 were certainly of greater importance for France. For those conflicts represent a revolt against the office-holders on the part of those social groups who were thwarted of office, such as barristers, doctors, *procureurs fiscaux*, etc. The victory of Henry IV was, in part, a victory of those in office.[10] It is perhaps to the wars of religion that Trevor-Roper's ideas would best apply.

He appreciates, though perhaps without attaching sufficient importance to it, the strain imposed by the Thirty Years' War, coinciding as it did with the great economic recession of the century. It is a pity that he pays no attention to the increase, during the seventeenth century, in the number of bad harvests, of subsistence crises, of famines, of plagues, which killed off artisans and peasants, and begot a long series of cumulative economic crises. They were so numerous in the seventeenth century that some historians have thought to ascribe them to a change in the climate, which is improbable.[11] After the plague of 1629–30 two thirds of the kingdom was in a state of endemic economic and social distress. In these circumstances it is understandable that the struggle between royal taxes and feudal dues should have worsened, that peasants and artisans should have been more willing to listen to incitements to rid themselves of the agents of the tax-farmers, or the bailiffs with their warrants. A

---

[8] R. Mousnier, "Le Conseil du Roi, de la mort de Henri IV au gouvernement personnel de Louis XIV," *Etudes d'Histoire moderne et contemporaine* (publ. by "La Société d'histoire moderne"), i (1947).

[9] R. Mousnier, "L'Opposition politique bourgeoise à la fin du XVIᵉ siècle et au debut du XVIIᵉ. L'Oeuvre de Louis Turquet de Mayerne," *Revue Historique*, ccxiii (1955).

[10] Henri Drouot, *Mayenne et la Bourgogne, Etude sur la Ligue* (1587-96) (Thèse de Lettres, Sorbonne, 1937), 2 vols.

[11] E. Leroy-Ladurie, "Climat et récoltes aux XVIIᵉ et XVIIIᵉ siècles," *Annales E.S.C.*, xvᵉ année (1960).

number of revolts coincide with price rises due to subsistence crises.[12] Trevor-Roper would do well to look into these matters.

Trevor-Roper is aware that the use of the word "crisis" for the seventeenth century would be less justified if we considered only its political and social aspects. A great crisis of ideas and feeling, a revolution in the manner of thinking and of understanding the Universe, almost an intellectual mutation took place at that time in Europe. It marks the end of Aristotelianism, the triumph of quantitative rationalism, of the notion of mathematical function, of experimental rationalism, with Descartes, the *Mécanistes* and Newton; it is present in the "Catholic Renaissance" and the mystical movement, in all that the words classical and baroque signify, in the growth of witchcraft, and in so many other aspects which would need to be studied, if we really want to talk of the crisis of the seventeenth century. None of these matters is totally divorced from politics. Is it pure chance that in France the kings were "classical" in taste, while the rebel princes favoured the *libertins* and the baroque?

If we stick strictly to Trevor-Roper's brief, his point of departure is a sound one: the political crisis of the seventeenth century represents a crisis in the relations between the State and society. His attempt at synthesis seems to me to rest on inadequate analysis, but there is considerable merit in having presented the problem as a whole. What emerges is the necessity, which I pointed to in 1958,[13] of studying afresh the revolts and revolutions in seventeenth-century Europe, through a rigorous social analysis of these movements, which in turn implies a study in depth of social structures, and methodical comparisons with the social structures and the revolts of the preceding and following centuries.

## II: J. H. Elliott

In his dazzling and ingenious interpretation of the crisis of the seventeenth century, Professor Trevor-Roper calls it "not merely a constitutional crisis, nor a crisis of economic production" but "a crisis in the relations between society and the State." In the context, the point is well worth making, but it does not take us very much farther, for what revolution does not represent a "crisis in the relations between society and the State"? The real problem is to discover what caused the divorce between the two, and it is in Trevor-Roper's answer to this problem that the main interest of his interpretation lies. The clue, he suggests, is to be found in the expansion and the wastefulness of a parasitic State apparatus; in the size and cost of the Court.

It may be suspected that Trevor-Roper's placing of the problem of the Court at the centre of the revolutionary crisis was originally inspired by his inquiries into the origins of the English Civil War. Can the idea be satisfactorily carried across the Channel and still retain such validity as it may have for England? Can it, for instance, help the historian of seventeenth-century Spain to understand the Catalan and Portuguese revolutions—for presumably the object of the exercise is to make these and other revolutions comprehensible? "These days are days of shaking," and even if Catalonia and Portugal virtually disappear from the scene after the first page, we hope by the last to have a better understanding of the seismic movements that shook them.

---

[12] R. Mousnier, "Etudes sur la population de la France au XVIIe siècle," *XVIIe Siècle,* no. 16 (1952).
[13] See n. 2.

Trevor-Roper's thesis, applied to Spain, would seem to be that the Court and the State apparatus had become grossly top-heavy by the end of Philip III's reign; that Olivares tried, but failed to introduce the reforms of the *arbitristas*; that (from this point the stages of the argument have to be reconstructed by reference to France, England and the United Provinces) as the result of his failure, "the tension between Court and country grew, and the 'revolutionary situation' of the 1620s and 1630s developed"; and that the "revolutionary situation" failed to develop into actual revolution in Castile because it lacked the organs of effective protest, but did lead to revolution in Catalonia and Portugal, presumably because they did possess such organs.

If this summary represents his argument correctly, it raises two important questions. First, how far did the Court and the State apparatus absorb the royal revenues and divert the national wealth into unproductive channels? Second, how far is the problem of an unreformed Court really the "cry of the country" from 1620 to 1640, and in particular the cry of the Catalans and the Portuguese?

The first of these questions—as to the real cost of the Court to the country—is virtually unanswerable and is likely to remain so, for, as Trevor-Roper points out, we see only the sun-lit tip of the submerged iceberg. Even in the ostentatious reign of Philip III, however, this is rather less impressive than one might have imagined. If we take the year 1608 as being reasonably representative for the reign of Philip III, we find that ordinary expenditure for the first ten months of the year is expected to be rather over 7 million ducats.[14] Of these 7 million, some 1½ are reserved for miscellaneous expenses and the payment of interest on the Crown's outstanding debts, and another 1½ for the expenses of the Court and the salaries of officials. What happens to the remaining 4 million ducats? They are all devoted to military and naval expenditure.

It is, I think, the proportion of revenues devoted to military purposes—even in the "peaceful" reign of Philip III—rather than to the expenses of Court and government, which is likely to strike anyone who looks at the papers of the Council of Finance. It is, of course, true that real expenditure on the Court always exceeded the anticipated expenditure, since Philip III bestowed an enormous number of pensions and *mercedes* which do not appear in the budget figures. Between 1 January 1619 and 1 December 1620, for instance, he gave away something like 400,000 ducats in pensions and *ayudas de costa*, besides many other unrecorded gifts.[15] Yet military expenditure was just as likely as Court expenditure to outrun the estimated provisions, as the Council of Finance was always lamenting.

If the visible cost of Court and government is well under half, and often nearer a quarter, the cost of military and naval preparations, what of the relative *invisible* costs to the national economy? In discussing the burden of the Court, Trevor-Roper is presumably thinking in particular of the diversion of national resources away from economically productive channels into the stagnant backwater of office in Church and State. Here we are hampered by the lack of any adequate study of the sale of offices in Spain, but from Mr. K. W. Swart's comparative study of the sale of offices in the seventeenth century, it would seem that offices in Spain were not created and sold on quite the same scale as in France, and that there was a good deal less willingness to buy.[16] My own feeling is that, to explain the diversion of money away from

---

[14] A(rchivo) G(eneral de) S(imancas) Hacienda (leg(ajo). 345-475 f. 405. *Relación* 22 Dec. 1607.
[15] AGS Hacienda leg. 414-573 *Relación de . . . mercedes (1621).*
[16] K. W. Swart, *Sale of Offices in the Seventeenth Century* (The Hague, 1949), chap. 2.

economically productive fields of investment, we must look not so much to the sale of offices as to the crippling difficulties that attended industrial development and commercial expansion in Castile, and to the growth of the highly elaborate system of *censos* and *juros* which, unlike trade and industry, provided a safe form of investment and assured rates of interest. In fact, we are driven back again to the appallingly expensive foreign policy of the sixteenth-century rulers of Spain—a foreign policy which led to heavy taxes falling on the most productive members of the community, and to the creation of a vast national debt, in which it was easy and profitable to invest.

Naturally, nobody would dispute the enormous weight of a top-heavy bureaucracy on Castile. This is one of the most frequent complaints of the Spanish *arbitristas*. But we must also remember the burden imposed by Castile's military commitments. One of the principal reasons for the depopulation of Castilian villages must be sought in the activities of the recruiting sergeant and the quartermaster, and I should hesitate to put the scourge of billeting below the plague of officers among the many misfortunes that dogged seventeenth-century societies.

In spite of its intolerable burdens, Castile did not revolt. Trevor-Roper attributes this, with a good deal of justice, to the lack of "effective organs of protest" in Castile. But let us now turn to the two parts of the peninsula which *did* revolt—Catalonia and Portugal. How far was the "general grievance against which they rebelled" the "character and cost of the State"? Catalans who visited Madrid in the reign of Philip III had no illusions about the "character" of the State, and wrote home the most devastating accounts of the extravagance and corruption of life at Court. The Catalans could well afford to be critical of the ways of the Court, since they themselves were excluded from all the delights traditionally associated with living in the royal presence. This ambivalent attitude—half hatred, half jealousy—fits well enough into Trevor–Roper's general framework. But it is difficult to see that the Catalans or the Portuguese had any real cause for complaint about the *cost* of the State, at least to themselves. *They* did not pay for Castile's large bureaucracy or for the lavish Court festivities. They did not even pay for the cost of their own defence, for (like the English gentry?) they were not over-taxed but under-taxed—at least in relation to Castile. Between 1599 and 1640 the King received from the Catalan Cortes one subsidy of 1 million ducats, and no other taxes except ecclesiastical dues and a number of minor taxes which did not even suffice to cover the costs of the small viceregal administration in the Principality. Castile, over the same forty years, was paying over 6 million ducats *a year* to the Crown in secular taxes alone. Nor was money raised in Catalonia by the sale of offices, for the Crown could neither create nor sell offices in the Principality. As a result, the royal administration in Catalonia consisted of only a handful of officials, and there simply did not exist a vast parasitic bureaucracy like the one that lay so heavy on Castile.

We have, then, revolutions in two provinces which admittedly possess effective organs of protest, but which—since the cost of Court and bureaucracy is hardly any concern of theirs—do not seem, on the Trevor-Roper principle, to have much to protest about. Why, then, do they revolt? For the answer to this, we must look primarily to the policies of Olivares. Trevor-Roper rightly points to the "puritanical" character of Olivares's reforming movement in the 1620s—his anxiety to curb the extravagance of the Court, and cut down on the multitude of *mercedes* and offices so lavishly bestowed by the profligate régime that preceded his own. Yet the problem of the Court, serious as it was, can hardly be considered the Conde Duque's principal anxiety. His real problem was the high cost of war. With the expiry of the truce with the Dutch in 1621, the annual provision for the Flanders Army was raised from 1½ to 3½ million ducats, and the sum earmarked for the Atlantic fleet went up to 1 million,[17] And this was only the beginning. It was primarily the needs of defence and the cost of war which imposed on Olivares the urgent need for reform; and this reform necessarily entailed much more than tinkering with the Court or reducing the number of offices in Castile. It demanded a radical reorganization of the fiscal system within the Spanish Monarchy.

It does not, therefore, seem to me that, even if Olivares had succeeded in doing what Richelieu did in the way of household reform, he would have gone very far towards solving his fundamental problem—that of defence (a problem, incidentally, in which the shortage of manpower was to loom as large as the shortage of money). It was his determination to solve this problem which led him to devise schemes for the more effective exploitation of the resources of the Crown of Aragon and Portugal, and these schemes eventually brought him into conflict with the Catalans and the Portuguese. No doubt the knowledge that the Court was still spending lavishly on *fiestas* strengthened their resolve to refuse payment, but I do not believe that "the character and cost of the State," in the sense used by Tevor-Roper, figured very prominently in their calculations. At the time of their revolutions, the apparatus of the State still lay lightly on them, and such money as had been squeezed out of them was being used, not to subsidize the Court, but to improve the very inadequate defences of their own territory. Their principal purpose in rebelling was to escape the imminent threat to their national identities and to their economic resources implied in the Conde Duque's demands that they should play a fuller part in the war.

While, then, Trevor-Roper has performed a valuable service in drawing attention to the size and cost of the State apparatus, this seems to be of use mainly in explaining the troubles of the part of Spain which did *not* rebel—Castile. And even here it is very doubtful whether it should be allowed to occupy the centre of the stage, for Court extravagance and the inflation of the bureaucracy would hardly seem to rank in the same class among the causes of Castile's decline as the burden imposed on the Castilian economy and Castilian society by a century of Habsburg wars. Indeed, the proliferation of offices is best regarded, alongside the rise of taxation of the development of *juros*, as one among the many natural consequences of that intolerable burden. To say simply that "war aggravates" the problem of the growth of a parasitic bureaucracy is surely rather a remarkable understatement. Admittedly, "the sixteenth-century wars had led to no such revolutions" but they had bequeathed a terrible inheritance to the seventeenth-century; and, on top of this, seventeenth-century wars were fought on a very different scale. Philip II's army consisted of perhaps 40,000 men, while Philip IV's was probably at least twice as large. This new scale of warfare created problems of an entirely new magnitude and order for the rulers of seventeenth-century States. It placed an additional enormous burden on economies already subjected to heavy strain.

How was the strain to be eased? By relating the State's life, as Trevor-Roper says, to its means of livelihood. This meant a programme of austerity and of "puritanical" reforms; it meant more rational economic policies. But it also meant extending the power of the King over his subjects, in order to draw on the resources of provinces and of social classes hitherto under-taxed or exempt. This was the acid test that faced seventeenth-century ministers. Richelieu may perhaps have met with rather more success than Olivares in his household reforms, but can this really have made any

[17] AGS Hacienda leg. 414-573 f. 303 *Consulta,* 10 Dec. 1621.

significant difference to the relative fortunes of France and Spain? The most obvious difference stems from the fact that Olivares's fiscal demands provoked revolution first. Otherwise, it is the similarities, not the differences, that impress. Both Richelieu and Olivares came to power with the best intentions of putting their own house in order; these intentions were frustrated by the exigencies of war; both were compelled by the cost of the war effort to tighten their grip on the resources of their States, and, in so doing, *they unwittingly precipitated revolutions.* This, I believe is the real moral of the story. The reforming movement of the 1620s, so far from showing the way of escape from revolution, in fact hastened its approach, because real reform included a fiscal, constitutional and social reorganization so radical that it inevitably brought the power of the Crown into head-on collision with those who had hitherto enjoyed special liberties and immunities. The essential clue to the revolutionary situation of the 1640s is, I suspect, to be found in the determination of governments to exercise fuller control over their States without yet having the administrative means or fiscal resources to ensure obedience to their will; and that determination sprang in the first instance from something which could not be gainsaid and brooked no delay—the imperious demands of war.

### III: H. R. Trevor-Roper

In some ways, in my essay, I have doubtless sacrificed clarity to brevity. Let me try to reverse the process by some further explanations. First, let me make it clear that by the words "office" and "Court" I have never meant only the offices directly under the Crown, or the Court in its narrow sense, as the group of metropolitan officials and the courtiers around the sovereign. By "office" I mean all the offices, metropolitan and local, which formed the bureaucratic machine of government, including offices in the law and the State-Church; and by "Court" I mean the sum of such offices. Consequently any reform of the system was not merely "household reform," it was social reform. Secondly, when writing of the cost to society of such offices, I am not referring merely to the cost paid by the Crown out of taxes but to the whole cost of maintaining this apparatus, the greater part of which fell not on the Crown but directly upon the country. I think that I may have made this latter point more clearly than the former, but it may be that I did not make either of them clearly enough. If they are made, a significant change in emphasis follows. For instance, it could be argued that in England in the 1630s the cost of the Court, in the narrow sense of the word, was reduced; but in the wider sense, in which I used it, I believe that it can be shown to have risen.

The same distinction must be made in Spain. Mr. Elliott quotes Mr. K. W. Swart's view that offices were not created and sold in Spain on the same scale as in France. This may be so—although until someone gives as much attention so Spain as M. Mousnier has done to France, I would prefer to suspend judgement. But even if it is so, is creation and sale by the Crown a sufficient criterion, and does Mr. Swart use "office" in the same wide sense as I do? I believe that it is a good rule that the foot knows where the shoe pinches, and the literature of complaint shows every sign of multiplication of office in the reigns of Philip III and Philip IV. These offices may not all have been sold by the Crown, but if they (or their reversions, which was perhaps more usual in Spain) were sold from person to person, the effect upon society would be the same. So in 1619 Philip III was urged to abolish, as a burden to society, the 100 *receptores* created six years earlier, even though that should mean repaying the price at which they had bought their offices. In 1622 Philip IV, in his brief reforming period, declared that since an excessive number of offices is pernicious in the State ("most of them being sold, and the officers having to make up the price they have paid"), and since a great number of *escribanos* is prejudicial to society ("and the number at present is excessive, and grows daily") the number of *alguaciles, procuradores,* and *escribanos* in Castile must be reduced to one-third, and recruitment must be discouraged by various means. Such demands are regular in Spain; they are repeated in the submissions of the Cortes, the *consultas* of the Councils, the programmes of the *arbitristas,* the letters of statesmen; they were officially granted in the famous *Capítulos de Reformación* of 1623; but their constant repetition thereafter shows how ineffective were the measures taken to satisfy them.[18]

Moreover, whatever the case of lay offices, it is certain that offices in the Church grew enormously. Socially, superfluous idle monks and friars had exactly the same effect as superfluous, parasitic officials, and in this sector Spain probably suffered more than France. Philip III and the Duke of Lerma were praised by devout writers for their foundations and privileges (Lerma alone founded eleven monasteries as well as other *obras pias*), and those years were praised as a revival of "the golden age of St. Jerome"; and yet all the time Philip III and Philip IV were being repeatedly begged to reduce these foundations, which contained many persons "rather fleeing from necessity to the delights of indolence than moved by devotion." Thus, using "office" in the wide sense, as I have used it, it does not seem to me that Spain was less burdened than other western monarchies. As Gondomar wrote to Philip III, the monarchy was imperilled by "two powerful enemies: first, all the princes of the world, and secondly, all us officers and courtiers who serve your Majesty (*todos los ministros y criados que servimos a V. Magd.*)[19]

The point about the Church as a department of State is important and I regret that I did not express myself more fully. It seems to me that in the sixteenth and seventeenth centuries the Church should be regarded, sociologically, as an element in the bureaucratic structure. The Reformation movement, Catholic as well as Protestant, was in many respects a revolt against the papal "court" in the widest sense: the indecent, costly, and infinitely multiplied personnel, mainly of the regular orders, which had overgrown the working episcopal and parish structure. One only has to read the records of the Council of Trent to see this: the exclusion of the Protestants from that assembly merely shows that, socially, Catholic demands were identical. The difference is that, in Catholic countries, such demands were ultimately defeated: the "Catholic Reform" may have been a moral and spiritual reform, but structurally it was a positive aggravation. On the other hand this aggravated clerical bureaucracy could also, if it were reanimated, be made socially palliative, and this is what happened in Catholic countries after the Counter-Reformation. The new orders then created may on the one hand have doubled and trebled the burden of 'the Court' upon society, but, on the other hand, by evangelization, they reconciled society to the burden which they increased. They also physically strengthened the Court. It was partly for this

---

[18] Archivo Histórico Español, *Colección de Documentos Inéditos para la Historia de España y de sus Indias,* vol. v (Madrid, 1932), pp. 28, 381, etc. *Actas de las Cortes de Castilla,* vol. xxii, pp. 434, etc.

[19] *Correspondencia Oficial de D. Diego Sarmiento de Acuña, Conde de Gondomar,* ed. A. Ballesteros y Beretta (*Documentos Inéditos para la Historia de España*), vol. ii (Madrid, 1943), p. 146.

reason, I suspect, that in the Mediterranean countries the Court was able to survive and stifle the forces of change, so that Queen Henrietta Maria could regard Popery, and Italian princes could regard the Jesuits, as the sole internal preservative of monarchy. It was partly for this reason, also, that I described the English Court as the most "brittle" of all. There the oppressive class of "courtiers," "monopolists," lawyers who composed "the Court" lacked the massive support of the preaching orders. The English friars, the lecturers, were on the other side. Hence, in part, the relative fragility of the English Court. It lacked the costly, but also effective outworks which the Counter-Reformation was able to build up around the Catholic thrones.

I agree with Mr. Elliott that the final strain, perhaps even the greatest strain, was war. But can one separate the impact and burden of war from the form of the society which sustains it? In the arguments in the Spanish Council of State before 1621, those who advocated a renewal of war against the Netherlands regularly appealed to a social fact: the fact that whereas the Dutch had constantly gained strength and wealth throughout the years of peace, the Spanish economy, even in peace, had as constantly declined; and this decline, they a !mitted, was due to social, structural reasons. War to these men was an expedient—a desperate, and as it proved, a fatal expedient—to remedy a disease which was already perceptible in peacetime. Although clearly there are many factors to consider, I would still prefer to say that in the monarchies of western Europe there was a structural crisis which was general, although the transition from structural crisis to revolution, which is not natural or inevitable but *requires* the intervention of a political event, was effected here by war, there without it.

Moreover, there is a further point to be made about war and structure. Since my article was published, the late J. Vicens Vives published the communication he proposed to make to the Eleventh International Historical Congress at Stockholm.[20] In this he argued that the European Renaissance monarchies, as I have defined them, were created by and for the necessities of war. In other words, it was in order to make war and survive the burden of war, that they developed their peculiar social structure. But if this is so, and if war in fact imposed too great a strain upon them, then it follows not that war was an unexpected burden to them, but that their social structure was inadequate within their own terms of reference. And if war created the burden of the Renaissance Courts, equally it developed and overdeveloped that burden. M. Mousnier, in his great work *La Vénalité des Offices sous Henri IV et Louis XIII,* has shown how the French Government, again and again, considered reform of that venality of office which was the basic mechanism of the monarchy, but on each occasion, faced by the threat of war, postponed its projects and, instead of reforming, positively strengthened the system. Richelieu at first (like Olivares in Spain) sought to combine war and reform, but in the end (again like Olivares) sacrificed reform to war. Marillac would have sacrificed war to reform. In both countries, we may say that war not only created but extended the system, until not war but its own weight overwhelmed it.

At one point I evidently over-simplified my argument, and I regret that, in the cause of brevity, I omitted two paragraphs which would perhaps have clarified it. This passage concerned the point, or rather the social area, within which the opposite pressures of "Court" and "country" met. By excessive economy I have here exposed myself, as I believe, to misunderstanding by M. Mousnier. He points out that in many cases, and particularly in the French Fronde, the antithesis of Court *v.* country is not

[20] J. Vicens Vives, "Estructura administrativa estatal en los siglos XVI y XVII," *XIᵉ Congrès International des Sciences Historiques* (Stockholm, 1960), Rapports iv.

at all clear, and seems to ask me in which category, "Court" or "country," I place the French Parlements. But this is precisely what cannot be done. If Court and country were absolutely separable, then, I submit, there would not have been a social crisis. Social crises are caused not by the clear-cut opposition of mutually exclusive interests but by the tug-of-war of opposite interests *within one body*. Figuratively, they are to be represented not by a clean split, but by an untidy inward crumbling: the result of complex pressures on a complex body. And this complexity is caused by the complexity of human iterests. "Court" and "country" in the seventeenth century, like bureaucrats and tax-payers, or producers and consumers today, constantly overlap. A man feels himself part of the "country," a taxpayer, in one respect, and then discovers that, in another hitherto forgotten respect, he too is of "the Court," dependent on taxes. The history of all revolutions is full of such painful discoveries, leading occasionally to painful apostasies. Sometimes they prevent revolution from breaking out; sometimes, when it has broken out, they entangle its course, making it bloody and indecisive: instead of performing a neat, surgical operation upon society, men find themselves hacking blindly among unpredicted organs. It is not only in the Fronde that one sees this. The English Parliament, which represented many of the grievances of the country, consisted also of "officials" with a vested interest in the system against which they complained. Even the Spanish Cortes were similarly divided; the representatives of the towns might be mere functionaries, "courtiers," aristocrats, but they did also, at times, represent "country" grievances. The spokesmen of a society in crisis represent not its separate compartments, but its inmost contradictions.

M. Mousnier remarks that the general crisis of the seventeenth century was a crisis of ideas as well as of structure. Of course I agree with him. But to embark on this topic would be another task and any summary might prove grossly simplified. So I will only say that whereas I believe that experimental science, mysticism and the witch-craze can all be related to the social and structural revolution, I do not believe that they can be equated with any single social force or party in that revolution. I believe that here too they are to be related rather to the formation or disintegration of the Church-State than to any particular interest which contributed to either process. I believe that the sociologists who (for instance) equate experimental science with Puritan opposition are guilty of over-simplification only a little less gross than those who equate the witch-cult with Protestantism. I hope I may some time say something on this subject, but not here.

Finally, a point made by Mr. Elliott. I quoted contemporaries to illustrate the sense of universal revolution, and those contemporaries included, in their catalogues, Catalonia and Portugal. But I did not myself pursue the cases of Catalonia and Portugal because I do not consider them to be comparable. In Catalonia and Portugal local separatism and particular forces exploited the weakness of Castile; but it is the structural weakness of the Castilian Crown, not the forces which exploited it, which is relevant to my analysis. A better comparison is between Catalonia and Portugal on the one hand and Scotland on the other: Scotland, which I also omitted, as largely irrelevant, from my analysis.

For of course no one would suggest that the crisis of society in the seventeenth century was *only* a social crisis: many other stresses were involved in it. In particular there was the stress of "provincial" opposition, caused by the federal structure of the great monarchies. In response, no doubt, to social or economic pressures, the Kings of Spain, France, England all sought to impose the bureaucratic system, which had been established in their greater kingdoms, upon the different societies of those lesser realms which their ancestors had ruled as independent kingdoms but which were now without resident princely Courts. In consequence they provoked risings which the very absence of a local Court and local patronage made it more difficult to suppress, and to which the historic national identity of the revolting provinces gave an added ideological strength. The revolt of the Netherlands had been such a revolt in the sixteenth century; the revolts of Béarn, Scotland, Catalonia and Portugal illustrate the similar but greater pressures of the period in which I have placed "the general crisis of the seventeenth century."

# 8 / The Industrial Revolution: Misery or Well-Being for the Working Classes?

As much if not more than any of the topics reviewed in this volume, the Industrial Revolution has lent itself to differences of interpretation between historians. They have disagreed, for example, over the extent to which it was caused by—or, as also has been argued, the extent to which it caused—such changes as occurred in technology, agriculture, commerce, population and consumer demand, the concentration of capital, and forms of entrepreneurship during the eighteenth and first half of the nineteenth centuries. Also the conventionally ascribed time limits of the Industrial Revolution, from 1760 (accession of King George III) to 1830 or 1850, have been frequently repudiated to the point where some historians speak of an earlier "industrial revolution" in England from the middle of the sixteenth to the middle of the seventeenth centuries,[1] while others ignore the concept of an "industrial revolution" altogether.[2]

But taking precedence in interest over the differences just mentioned has been the debate over whether the living standard of the English worker improved or deteriorated from roughly 1760 to 1830 or later. The verdict of earlier scholars working in the field, Arnold Toynbee in the 1870's and later the Webbs and the Hammonds, was that it did deteriorate. The coming of industrialism brought a "bleak age," where misery was the lot of most workers—a somber and unrelieved description of the times still perpetuated in some history textbooks.[3]

As R. M. Hartwell points out in the first selection, the Toynbee-Webb-Hammond verdict went "relatively unchallenged" until J. H. Clapham published the first volume of *An Economic History of Modern Britain* in 1926. In the preface to this volume, Clapham wrote:

Again, the legend that everything was getting worse for the working man, down to some unspecified date between the drafting of the People's Charter and the Great Exhibition dies hard. The fact that after the price fall of 1820-1, the purchasing power of wages in general—not—of course—of everyone's wages—was definitely greater than it had been just before the revolutionary and Napoleonic wars, fits so ill with the

---

[1] Most notably J. U. Nef, "The Progress of Technology and the Growth of Large-Scale Industry in Great Britain, 1540-1640," *The Economic History Review*, Vol. V (1934), pp. 3-24.

[2] Most notably J. H. Clapham, *An Economic History of Modern Britain*, Vol. I, *The Early Railway Age*, 1820-1850 (Cambridge: The University Press, 1926) where he never uses the term.

[3] See Eric E. Lampard, *Industrial Revolution, Interpretations and Perspectives* (Washington, D. C.: Service Center for Teachers of History, 1957), pp. 5-8.

tradition that it is very seldom mentioned, the work of statisticians on wages and prices being constantly ignored by social historians.[4]

In the ensuing decades Clapham's "optimistic" point of view seemed to have won the day. Then in the early 1960's younger English historians such as E. J. Hobsbawm and E. P. Thompson began to publish work which contributed to a revival of the "classical school" or "pessimistic" position of the older Toynbee-Webb-Hammond interpretation.

Especially noteworthy is Thompson's *The Making of the English Working Class* from which the second selection below is taken. Thompson concedes that the Hammonds were "too willing to moralize history" but he insists that they, unlike the "optimists," had "a sense of the whole process—the whole political and social context" of the Industrial Revolution. For them and for Thompson, the "political *counterrevolution* of 1792-1832" was even more important in the experience of the working class than the population explosion and the technological Industrial Revolution. This political climate permitted and justified what Thompson calls "the truly catastrophic nature of the Industrial Revolution."

Much of his book is devoted to the "grievances felt by working people as to changes in the character of capitalist exploitation." Thompson takes these grievances seriously and accords them a large place in the "making" of the English working class. In addition, however, he attempts an "objective," quantitative critique of the "optimist" case. Here it is apparent that gaps and uncertainties in the statistics can lead honest historians to quite contradictory conclusions.

[4] J. H. Clapham, *An Economic History of Modern Britain,* Vol. I, *The Early Railway Age* (Cambridge: The University Press, 1926), p. vii.

# INTERPRETATIONS OF THE INDUSTRIAL REVOLUTION IN ENGLAND: A METHODOLOGICAL INQUIRY*

**R. M. Hartwell**

*I*

Perhaps the most important methodological problem in the writing of history is to discover why different historians, on the basis of the same or similar evidence, often have markedly different interpretations of a particular historical event. Why, for example, in a world in which there is almost unquestioned belief, even by Marxist historians, that industrialization is the grand remedy for the economic and social ills of poor and underdeveloped countries, do some historians, and especially the Marxists, still argue about the goods or ills bestowed on the worker by the first great experiment in industrialization, the industrial revolution in England? The expected economic dividend of modern industrialization is undoubtedly a higher standard of living, and the occasional opponents of such development base their opposition not on this indisputable material advance but on the "moral risk" involved in the transformation of life by industrialization.[1] The historians, however, while concerned also with this possible moral risk, are not all certain that the industrial revolution in England *before* 1850 did cause the average standard of living of the worker to rise. This uncertainty might be resolved by finding out what actually happened, but in the meantime interpretations differ, and have differed, on the basis of some evidence, of much confusion, and of differing value judgments. It is the specific aim of this article to give a history of the interpretations of the industrial revolution, and to explain them.

Today, in spite of weighty opposition, the thesis "that everything was getting worse for the working man, down to some date between the drafting of the People's Charter and the Great Exhibition"[2] strongly persists, mainly because of the continuing influence of a distinguished group of social historians and *social critics*, especially those gifted wife-husband writers, the Webbs and the Hammonds. Their interpretation has been well expressed by Sidney Webb: "If the Chartists in 1837 had called for a comparison of their time with 1787, and had obtained a fair account of the actual social life of the working man at the two periods, it is almost certain that they would have recorded a positive decline in the standard of life of large classes of the population."[3] And their influence is best attested by the continuing popularity of

---

* This essay had its origin in an address, given jointly by the author and A. G. L. Shaw of Sydney University, at the inaugural meeting of the Sydney Historians' Group in 1953. It owes much, therefore, to discussion with Shaw. Although many books and articles are cited, the essay does not claim to be bibliographically comprehensive.

[1] See G. Freyre, "Morals and Social Change," *Transactions of the Third World Congress of Sociology* (8 vols.; London: International Sociological Association, 1956), I, 20-33.

[2] J. H. Clapham, *An Economic History of Modern Britain* (3 vols.; Cambridge, England: Cambridge University Press, 1926), I, vii.

[3] S. Webb, *Labour in the Longest Reign* (Fabian Tract No. 75; London: The Fabian Society, 1897), p. 2.

those historical best sellers on the condition of life of the English worker between 1760 and 1832 by J. L. and B. Hammond that have dominated modern interpretation, both popular and scholarly, of the industrial revolution.[4]

The Hammonds gave the worst possible interpretation of early industrialization. "The history of England at this time," they wrote, "reads like the history of civil war. . . . Surely never since the days when populations were sold into slavery did a fate more sweeping overtake a people than the fate that covered the hills and valleys of Lancashire and the West Riding with the factory towns that were to introduce a new social type for the world to follow." Economic and social decline was the main conclusion that the Hammonds derived from their study of village, town, and skilled laborers:[5]

Amid the great distress that followed Waterloo, it was a commonplace of statesmen like Castlereagh and Canning that England was the only happy country in the world. . . . That class has left bright and ample records of its life . . . it has left dim and meagre records of the disinherited peasants that are the shadow of its wealth; of the exiled labourers that are the shadow of its pleasures; of the villages sinking into poverty and crime and shame that are the shadow of its power and its pride.

In their preoccupation with the debit side of the industrial revolution, however, the Webbs and Hammonds were only expanding in greater detail the traditional view held by most English economic historians before J. H. Clapham. In particular Arnold Toynbee's *Lectures on the Industrial Revolution in England*, published in 1884, stimulated interest in the industrial revolution, and by dramatically emphasizing its unfortunate consequences influenced all subsequent writers. Toynbee wrote:[6]

These were dark patches even in [Adam Smith's] age, but we now approach a darker period—a period as disastrous and as terrible as any through which a nation ever passed; disastrous and terrible, because, side by side with a great increase of wealth was seen an enormous increase of pauperism; and production on a vast scale, the result of free competition, led to a rapid alienation of classes and to the degradation of a large body of producers.

These conclusions were strengthened by the combined support of those distinguished historians, J. E. Thorold Rogers and W. Cunningham. Thorold Rogers'

[4] *The Village Labourer, 1760-1832* (London: Longmans, Green & Co., 1911); *The Town Labourer, 1760-1832* (London: Longmans, Green & Co., 1917); *The Skilled Labourer, 1760-1832* (London: Longmans, Green & Co., 1919); *The Rise of Modern Industry* (London: Methuen, 1925); *The Age of the Chartists* (London: Longmans, Green & Co., 1930); *The Bleak Age* (London: Longmans, Green & Co., 1934); and *Lord Shaftesbury* (London: Constable, 1923). The popularity of these books can be judged from the number of reprints; thus, *The Village Labourer* was first published in 1911, reprinted in 1912, 1913, 1919, 1920, 1924, 1927, 1932, 1936, and 1948; *The Town Labourer*, which was first printed in 1917, had four new impressions by the end of 1920. Very few history books in the twentieth century have sold so well.
[5] *The Skilled Labourer*, pp. 1 and 4; *The Village Labourer* (1948 Guild ed.), II, 136-37. There is a significant difference between the early books and *The Bleak Age* (published in 1934), which admitted that "historians have been apt to draw the life of this time in colours too sombre for the truth," that the explanation of "systematic and widespread discontent . . . must be sought outside the sphere of strictly economic conditions," and that "after the forties there was a slow and gradual improvement in the conditions and temper of social life." (Pelican ed., pp. 15 and 226.) The change in attitude can be seen also in "The Industrial Revolution and Discontent," *The Economic History Review*, II (January 1930), written in response to Clapham's claim that the standard of living improved between 1790 and 1830.
[6] A. Toynbee, *Lectures on the Industrial Revolution in England* (London, 1884), p. 84.

study of prices and wages over many centuries gave his argument impressive authority; and he argued that "in the long run, labour . . . gained by the inventions of Arkwright, of Watt, and of Cartwright, but the process which preceded the gain was accompanied by profound suffering"; and he described the first two decades of the nineteenth century as "the worst time . . . in the whole history of English labour."[7] Cunningham's analysis of the industrial revolution was more sophisticated than those of either Thorold Rogers or Toynbee, and he argued that the sufferings of the period were "the inevitable difficulties of transition," aggravated by the wars, with France and the United States, by fluctuations of trade, and by bad government; while recognizing "the rapid advance of material prosperity," he balanced it against "the terrible suffering which was endured in the period of transition."[8]

With such influential backing the immiserization theory of the industrial revolution was firmly embedded in textbooks and in works of general history. Thus, for example, the much-reprinted *Industry in England* by H. de B. Gibbins affirmed, without the qualifications imposed by Thorold Rogers or Cunningham, that

it must continually be remembered that the condition of the mass of the people in the first half of this [the nineteenth] century was one of deepest depression. . . . The fact has been, that after the introduction of the new industrial system the condition of the working classes rapidly declined; wages were lower, and prices, at least of wheat, were often higher; till at length the lowest depth of poverty was reached about the beginning of the reign of Queen Victoria.[9]

This kind of argument, with varying degrees of qualification, and with the particular help of the Hammonds, remained relatively unchallenged until Clapham published the first volume of his economic history of Britain in 1926. After that the Toynbee-Hammond view still commanded wide support, but there was more talk of stability and less of decline, and more of special reasons why the standard of living failed to rise rather than of general reasons why it fell. Thus, for example, in 1952 E. J. Hamilton wrote that between 1800 and 1852 "real wages of fully employed workers rose, but this was largely offset by chronic and cyclical unemployment";[10] and Colin Clark, that "the first half of the nineteenth century, with all the tremendous changes brought about, only just succeeded in maintaining real income per head constant."[11] It is now probably true that most economic historians favor the Clapham rather than the Toynbee-Hammond thesis, but many textbooks and general works still depend heavily on the Hammonds,[12] and probably for this reason one distinguished economic

---

[7] J. F. Thorold Rogers, *Six Centuries of Work and Wages* (10th ed.; London: Swan Sonnenschein, 1909), pp. 485 and 492.

[8] W. Cunningham, *The Growth of Industry and Commerce in Modern Times* (6th ed.; 3 vols.; Cambridge, England: Cambridge University Press, 1925), III, 668 and 617.

[9] H. de B. Gibbins, *Industry in England: Historical Outlines* (5th ed.; London: Methuen, 1907), p. 421.

[10] E. J. Hamilton, "Prices as a Factor in Business Growth," *The Journal of Economic History*, XII (Fall 1952), 344.

[11] *The Review of Economic Progress*, IV (July 1952), 4.

[12] Thus H. E. Friedlander and J. Oser, *Economic History of Modern Europe* (New York: Prentice-Hall, 1953) describes labor conditions in England before 1870 almost entirely in terms of "social consequences," quoting as authorities the Hammonds, the Webbs, the Coles, M. Beer, E. Lipson, W. Page, and G. Slater (p. 154 ff.). See also P. Gregg, *A Social and Economic History of Britain, 1760-1950* (London: Harrap, 1952) and A. Bryant, *The Age of Elegance, 1812-1822* (London: Collins, 1950).

historian not so long ago thought it necessary to take up cudgels on behalf of Clapham.[13]

To describe the more optimistic interpretation of the industrial revolution as the Clapham thesis, however, is to ignore other historians and economists who had the same thesis before Clapham gave it wide circulation. Indeed, Clapham's arguments depended heavily on the work of statisticians on wages and prices, work that he complained had been "constantly ignored by social historians."[14] In particular he depended on research on nineteenth-century wages by A. L. Bowley and G. H. Wood, which appeared in a series of articles between 1895 and 1909, and which remain today the only comprehensive studies of wages that could help to give finality to the problem of discovering what happened to the standard of living between 1800 and 1850.[15] Both Bowley and Wood were cautious in their conclusions, but both agreed that the average standard of living had increased between 1800 and 1850. But these conclusions, even though their publication *preceded* the books of the Hammonds, made little impact on the interpretation of the industrial revolution already popularized by Toynbee.

As might have been expected, the modern reaction to the Toynbee interpretation began in Manchester. In 1920 G. W. Daniels wrote in his *Early English Cotton Industry:*[16]

Frequently, and with much justification, the view is taken of the transition period, particularly of the last decade of the eighteenth and the first decades of the nineteenth centuries, that it was a time of great distress and of social retrogression for a large part of the population, and a considerable stress is laid upon the economic movement as a cause. *A priori* the idea that an economic movement such as we have been considering, which was characterised on the one hand by a greater power of production, and on the other by an expanding economic unity could, of itself, be a cause of widespread distress and of social retrogression is a hard one to accept. However, when the previous position in Lancashire and the effects the economic movement was having upon it are taken into account, there seems no good reason why it should be accepted for this period.

And George Unwin, in his delightful study of Samuel Oldknow published in 1924, added his gentle but persuasive protest. "In spite of all the noble eloquence and sound prophecy of Carlyle," he wrote, "those who know something of both periods may be permitted to doubt whether the twelfth century was any better than the nineteenth. . . . If Carlyle had chanced on the records of Mellor [Oldknow's factory]

[13] T. S. Ashton, "The Standard of Life of the Workers in England, 1790-1830," *The Journal of Economic History,* IX (1949), 38.
[14] Clapham, *Economic History of Modern Britain,* I, 561.
[15] Bowley published in the *Journal of the Statistical Society* (1895, 1898, 1899, and 1902) and in *The Economic Journal* (1895, 1896); G. H. Wood's researchers were summarized in two articles, "The Course of Average Wages between 1790 and 1860," *The Economic Journal,* IX (1899) and "Real Wages and the Standard of Comfort since 1850," *Journal of the Statistical Society,* LXXII (1909). Bowley's researches are summarized in *Wages in the United Kingdom in the nineteenth century* (Cambridge, England: Cambridge University Press, 1900) and *Wages and Income in the United Kingdom since 1860* (Cambridge, England: Cambridge University Press, 1937).
[16] G. W. Daniels, *The Early English Cotton Industry* (Manchester: Manchester University Press, 1920), pp. 145-146. Daniels went on to argue, pp. 147-148, that the distress of the period was caused by the Napoleonic Wars, which "distorted" economic development and "thwarted" social development.

as well as on Jocelyn's Chronicle he might have struck a juster balance between Past and Present."[17]

Then came authoritative backing from Cambridge. In 1926 J. H. Clapham prefaced the first volume of his massive *Economic History of Modern Britain* with a general attack on legends in history, and a particular attack on the legend that the average standard of living was declining between 1800 and 1850. "For every class of urban or industrial worker about which information is available," he wrote, "except—a grave exception—such dying trades as common hand-loom cotton weaving, wages had risen markedly during the intervening sixty years [since 1790]. For fortunate classes, such as London bricklayers or compositors, they had risen well over 40 per cent, and for urban and industrial workers in the mass, perhaps about 40 per cent."[18]

Clapham's reminder to economic historians (like his equally famous reminder to the economists of the "arid formalism" of contemporary economic theory),[19] together with the authority of his scholarship, certainly marked a turning point in modern interpretation of the industrial revolution. Thereafter the attacks on the Toynbee-Hammond thesis were frequent and forceful. In the same year W. H. Hutt produced a most damaging attack on the Hammonds' use of sources, taking the particular case of their dependence on the notoriously rigged Sadler's Committee of 1832. Hutt concluded that there had been "a general tendency to exaggerate the 'evils' which characterised the factory system before the abandonment of laissez-faire."[20] And in 1928 T. E. Gregory argued that a generation of students of English economic history had been misled, and that the historian, by becoming "Social Philosopher" had made economic history "an instrument of condemnation of that Past which it is his primary object to understand." "The England of Toynbee and the Hammonds," he concluded, "is not the England of Tooke and Newmarch."[21]

In 1930 Ivy Pinchbeck, with her attention focused particularly on women in industry, wrote: "Although the workers did not participate to the extent they might have done in the advantages arising from the use of machinery, yet even so, for the majority of workers the factory meant higher wages, better food and clothing and an improved standard of living. This was especially so in the case of women."[22] And in 1931 Mrs. D. George generalized: "In most parts of the world industrialism has meant an advance in material civilisation, a rise in the standard of living, an improved status, and greater political power for the humbler classes; it has bettered health, lengthened life, lessened laborious toil and brought with it greater leisure."[23]

If this was intended to describe what happened in England between 1800 and 1850, it could be argued that the reaction had gone too far. Moreover, the effect on the general economic historian was confusion rather than enlightenment: thus one

[17] George Unwin *et al.*, *Samuel Oldknow and the Arkwrights* (Manchester: Manchester University Press, 1924), pp. 241-242.

[18] *Ibid.*, p. 561.

[19] "Of Empty Economic Boxes," *The Economic Journal*, XXXII (1922).

[20] W. H. Hutt, "The Factory System of the Early Nineteenth Century," *Economica*, VI (1926), 93. Compare with Appendix VIII to Vol. VI of T. Tooke and W. Newmarch, *A History of Prices . . . 1792-1856* (6 vols.; London, 1838-1857), which shows the beneficial effects of the Factory Acts.

[21] T. E. Gregory, *An Introduction to Tooke and Newmarch's "A History of Prices and of the State of the Circulation from 1792 to 1856"* (London: King, 1928), pp. 119-120.

[22] Ivy Pinchbeck, *Women Workers and the Industrial Revolution* (London: Routledge, 1930), p. 311.

[23] D. George, *England in Transition* (London: Routledge, 1931; and Pelican edition, 1953), p. 144.

economic historian in 1931, after quoting the views of both the Hammonds and Clapham, concluded that the time was "not yet ripe for dogmatic pronouncements on the subject."[24] It was to convince those in doubt and in error, presumably, that T. S. Ashton produced his justly famous articles of 1948 and 1949.[25] As a direct consequence of Ashton's articles, the "controversy," which had been relatively quiescent, was renewed. Yet it is important to notice that the argument since then has been rather one-sided, and to describe as a controversy what have really been essays in agreement is perhaps misleading.[26] Moreover, this agreement has been strengthened by a revaluation of the role of the business man in the industrial revolution and an attack on the naïve idea of exploitation.[27] Indeed, it might have been claimed that Ashton had settled the problem once and for all, had not warning recently been given by E. J. Hobsbawm that it will still need "vastly stronger evidence than has so far been adduced" to discredit the Hammonds' view.[28]

Dr. Hobsbawm's recent assurance that the controversy is not yet dead is comforting to those who feel that finality of conclusion is difficult, if not impossible, in history. But he is quite wrong when he describes the controversy as a social phenomenon of the last thirty years, claiming that until Clapham attacked it, "the classical view" (that is, the Marx-Toynbee-Hammond–Hobsbawm view) was held by "enquirers and historians of all political views" and that it represented "the consensus of informed and intelligent contemporaries, a majority of whom, as even critics admit, took the dark view."[29] This is nonsense. In fact, the controversy about the social costs and economic gains of the industrial revolution is as old as the revolution itself, and perhaps its most acrimonious phase occurred while the first important changes in industry were taking place, before 1850.

Of the contemporary critics of industrialization none were more vocal than the great literary figures of the day, with the important exception of Macaulay. The literary opposition to the industrial revolution, indeed, continued into the Victorian era: Wordsworth, Shelley, Coleridge, Southey, Peacock, Hood, Carlyle, Kingsley, the Brontës, Mrs. Gaskell, Dickens, Disraeli, Arnold, and Ruskin were all severe critics of "the factory system" and, to a greater or lesser degree, praisers of the past. They, even more than Cobbett, were responsible for the contrast of past and present and for the particular legend of "the golden age" of the eighteenth century. They set up the ideal standard of an imagined past and decried everything modern by contrast. In this way, for example, Carlyle greatly impressed Arnole Toynbee because he gave "the most tender and pathetic picture of the Past, the most unsparing indictment of the Present."[30] Although in the late eighteenth century furnaces at factories in rural

---

[24] A. Redford, *The Economic History of England, 1760-1860* (London: Longmans, Green & Co., 1931), p. 65.

[25] T. S. Ashton, "The Standard of Life of the Workers in England, 1790-1830," *The Journal of Economic History,* IX (Fall 1949); "Some Statistics of the Industrial Revolution in Britain," *Manchester Statistical Society* (January 14, 1948).

[26] See F. A. Hayek, *Capitalism and the Historians* (London: Routledge, 1954), and W. H. Chaloner, *The Hungry Forties* ("Aids for Teachers Series," No. 1; published by *The Historical Association;* London, 1957).

[27] See "The Moral History of U.S. Business" and "What Historians Teach About Business," *Fortune,* December 1949 and April 1952; also W. Woodruff, "History and the Businessman," *The Business History Review,* XXX (1956).

[28] E. J. Hobsbawm, "The British Standard of Living, 1790-1850,"*The Economic History Review,* X (August 1957), 61.

[29] *Ibid.,* p. 46.

[30] Toynbee, *The Industrial Revolution,* p. 193.

settings were welcomed as examples of "the sublime," the nineteenth century brought with it "an age of despair."[31] Burke saw the essential qualities of the sublime in the *"vastness* and *power"* and the *"obscurity"* of the engines and forges of Coalbrook Dale; Wordsworth saw the factory as a temple

where is offered up
to Gain, the master idol of the realm
Perpetual sacrifice.[32]

The reactions of Wordsworth and other writers of the day were partly aesthetic and romantic, partly moral and humanitarian, and partly political; they objected to the ugliness and squalor of the urban-industrial as compared with the rural-agricultural life; they objected also to its motivating spirit and to the "oppression" it brought with it. There is no better example of an uncompromising critic of industrialization than Southey, who declared that "the immediate and home effect of the manufacturing system ... is to produce physical and moral evil, in proportion to the wealth which it creates."[33] Or take Coleridge, who wrote that "the tillers of the land [are] paid by poor rates, and the remainder of the population [are] mechanised into engines for the manufactory of new rich men;—yes, the machinery of the wealth of the nation [is] made up of the wretchedness, disease, and depravity of those who should constitute the strength of the nation."[34] But such critics wrote with more feeling than science; and more formal social analysis and greater documentation was produced by a host of less well-known writers like J. Fielden, C. Wing, J. P. Kay, S. Kydd, T. Thackrah, and R. Oastler, and the early socialist theorists, J. F. Bray, W. Thompson, and F. Engels.[35] Engels, for example, combined *par excellence* a sentimental regard for the past and a condemnation of the present, claiming that before industrialization "the workers vegetated throughout a passably comfortable existence, leading a righteous and peaceful life in all piety and probity; and their material position was far better than that of their successors."[36]

But, as with the modern controversy, for every contemporary that criticized, there

[31] F. D. Klingender, *Art and the Industrial Revolution* (London: Royle, 1947), p. 71 ff.
[32] *Ibid.,* p. 74; and *The Excursion,* Books VIII and IX.
[33] T. Southey, *Sir Thomas More: or Colloquies on the Progress and Prospects of Civilization* (2 vols.; London, 1829), I, 197.
[34] S. T. Coleridge, *The Constitution of Church and State* (London, 1829), pp. 66-67.
[35] J. Fielden, *The Curse of the Factory System* (London, 1836); C. Wing, *The Evils of the Factory System Demonstrated by Parliamentary Evidence* (London, 1837); J. P. Kay, *The Moral and Physical Condition of the Working Classes Employed in the Cotton Manufacture in Manchester* (London, 1832); S. Kydd, *The History of the Factory Movement* (London, 1857); C. T. Thackrah, *The Effects of Arts, Trades and Professions ... on Health and Longevity* (London, 1831); for R. Oastler, see C. Driver, *Tory Radical, the Life of Richard Oastler* (New York: Oxford University Press, 1946); J. F. Bray, *Labour's Wrongs and Labour's Remedy* (Leeds, 1839); W. Thompson, *An Enquiry into the Principles of the Distribution of Wealth Most Considerate to Human Happiness* (London, 1850); and F. Engels, *The Condition of the Working Class in England in 1844* (London, 1845).
[36] Engels, *The Condition of the Working Class* (1950 ed.), p. 2. Engels' book has had more influence on English interpretations of the industrial revolution than Marx's *Capital,* but there has *never* been an influential English Marxist historian of the industrial revolution. The traditional English denigrators have been Tory Radicals or Fabian Socialists, the first stimulated by opposition to Whig progress, the second by direct observation of English industrial conditions rather than by Continental theorizing. Nevertheless, Engels' book, which became a Socialist classic, was read by Toynbee, the Webbs, and the Hammonds, who consistently overvalued it as history;

was one that praised. Perhaps the most spirited defense of industrialization ever written was by Macaulay in 1830:[37]

The labouring classes of this island, though they have their grievances and distresses, some produced by their own improvidence, some by the errors of their rulers, are on the whole better off as to physical comforts than the inhabitants of any equally extensive district of the old world. For this very reason, suffering is more acutely felt and more loudly bewailed here than elsewhere .... We must confess ourselves unable to find any satisfactory record of any great nation, past or present, in which the working classes have been in a more comfortable situation than in England during the last thirty years .... The serving man, the artisan, and the husbandman, have a more copious and palatable supply of food, better clothing, and better furniture .... Yet is the country poorer than in 1790? We firmly believe that, in spite of all the misgovernment of her rulers, she has been almost constantly becoming richer and richer. Now and then there has been a stoppage, now and then a short retrogression; but as to the general tendency there can be no doubt. A single breaker may recede; but the tide is evidently coming in.

If Macaulay matched Southey and Coleridge in eloquence and feeling, G. R. Porter and T. Tooke matched Engels with massive research and statistics.[38] Thus Porter concluded in 1847 that "although at certain seasons all those who live by daily wages must have suffered privations, yet with some exceptions their condition has, in the course of the years, much ameliorated.[39] And even some contemporary critics of industrialization admitted that, with the exception of the hand-loom weavers, wages were "more than amply sufficient to supply all that is wanted even for liberal support."[40]

It was after 1850, however, that increasing support was given to the view that the condition of labor had improved and was still improving. W. R. Greg's essay on "England As It Is" in *The Edinburgh Review*, for example, complained of the "disposition to decry the present and exalt the past," and argued for an "undeniable improvement of our population as a whole."[41] Samuel Smiles in 1861 wrote that the English artisan was better off than at any former period: "the process has been one of solid and steady improvement .... The more closely, indeed, that the vaunted 'good old times' of the labouring classes are investigated, the more clearly will it appear that they were times of hard work and small pay, of dear food and scanty clothing, of defective means of education and wretched household accommodation."[42] "The progress—that is, the material progress—of the working classes of this country during the last half century," declared J. Ward in 1868, "has, however, been remarkable.

but see the introduction to a new edition by W. O. Henderson and W. H. Chaloner (Oxford: Blackwell, 1958), which has a realistic reappraisal, and an unflattering one, of Engels as a historian.
    [37] T. B. Macaulay, "Southey's Colloquies," *Edinburgh Review* (January 1830); reprinted in all standard editions of Macaulay's essays, e.g., Longmans Popular edition (London, 1902), pp. 119-121.
    [38] G. R. Porter, *The Progress of a Nation* (London, 1847) and Tooke and Newmarch, *A History of Prices.*
    [39] Porter, *ibid.,* p. 459; *cf.* Tooke and Newmarch, *A History of Prices,* II, 70-71. Porter excepted the "hand-loom weavers, and others following analogous employments, conducted in the dwellings of the workmen."
    [40] P. Gaskell, *The Manufacturing Population of England* (London, 1833), p. 161; see also Kay, *The Moral and Physical Condition of the Working Classes,* pp. 26-27. Both Gaskell and Kay argued for "moral decline."
    [41] W. R. Greg, *Essays on Political and Social Science* (2 vols.; London, 1853), I, 321, 343.
    [42] S. Smiles, *Workmen's Earnings, Strikes and Savings* (London, 1861), pp. 12, 13, 17.

History furnishes no such parallel, to whatever age or country we refer."[43] Such claims were given an enduring documented form in 1884—in the same year as Toynbee's *The Industrial Revolution* appeared—by the publication of Robert Giffen's presidential address of the Statistical Society, *The Progress of the Working Class in the Last Half Century*.[44] Giffen, referring to the years 1840 to 1880, concluded that improved living standards were reflected in lower mortality, better education, diminished crime and pauperism, and increased savings.[45] But while Giffen was writing, the Fabians were preparing their first attacks on English institutions and society, attacks that influenced a generation of historians, and quieted the old controversy until Clapham's dogmatic attack in 1926.

*II*

For every firm judgment about the industrial revolution in England, then, there has been an equally firm contrary judgment. Can these differences be explained? Have they arisen merely because of the difficulty of drawing up a neat historical balance sheet of a complex event like the industrial revolution, which affected a whole society over half a century? Indeed, the bulk and diversity of the evidence have resulted in such varied and conflicting studies that any consideration of the industrial revolution as a whole has been driven inevitably from simple to complex interpretations.

Moreover, history is all things to all men; and the selection of evidence in accordance with some abstract principle, and the abridgement of evidence in accordance with an implicit principle of selection, have imposed different patterns on the facts and "proved" different interpretations of what happened. Are the historians, then—because of the complexity of the industrial revolution, because of the bulk and diversity of the evidence, and because of differences in personal bias—talking rather of different things, asking and answering different questions, not really disagreeing (except on values) but engaging in meaningless arguments? Certainly the problem of the sources and integrity in their use must be taken into account in considering the historians of the industrial revolution; for although there is room enough for objective disagreement on the basis of the evidence, the historians have been, too often, either believers in progress (for example, Manchester liberals), or social critics (for example, Fabian socialists), each with a tendency to "abuse" the evidence in favor of particular beliefs.

This political bias in interpretation has had three main phases: in the first and contemporary phase the argument was between Whig and Tory, a reflection of the shift in economic and political power that was occurring between 1800 and 1850, with Whig praising economic and political change and Tory decrying it. In the second phase the conflict was between progressives—and by this time both Liberal and Conservative viewed the nineteenth century as one of massive and continuous progress—and distributionists, especially the Fabians, who condemned the organization and ethos of capitalism and who wished to change it. In the third and modern phase the Fabian

[43] J. Ward, *Workmen and Wages at Home and Abroad* (London, 1868), p. 224. See also G. Nichols, *A History of the English Poor Law* (new edition by H. G. Willink; 3 vols.; London: King, 1904), II, 46; J. M. Ludlow and L. Jones, *Progress of the Working Class, 1832-1867* (London, 1867), p. 297; T. Brassey, *On Work and Wages* (London, 1873), p. 126; L. Levi, *Wages and Earnings of the Working Classes* (London, 1867), p. 128; J. S. Jeans, *England's Supremacy* (London, 1885), Ch. 1.
[44] Published as a threepenny pamphlet in 1884; later included in *Economic Inquiries and Studies* (2 vols.; London: Bell, 1904), I, 382-423.
[45] *Ibid.*, p. 28.

attack has been reinforced by the Marxists, who accept the dogma of Engels as expanded by Marx and who argue that capitalism both in its evolution and present form must be evil, and therefore that whereas the industrial revolution in England did harm to the worker, the economic growth of the U.S.S.R. has benefited him.

"Private opinion, and private passions," Eden wrote in 1797 on the subject of *The State of the Poor*, "will, in spite of us all, too often interfere, and bias and influence the most honest and intelligent minds, in their judgment respecting even matters of fact."[46] But few historians heeded his warning. To Macaulay, for example, there could be no questioning of the beneficial effect on economic progress of economic liberalism. "It is not by the intermeddling of Mr. Southey's idol, the omniscient and omnipotent State," he wrote, "but by the prudence and energy of the people, that England has hitherto been carried forward in civilization; and it is to the same prudence and the same energy that we now look with comfort and good hope."[47] To the Hammonds, however, economic progress was vitiated by inequitable distribution and consequent social division; the industrial revolution had produced a social system that "in its extreme form ... made the mass of the people the cannon-fodder of industry" and whose persistence showed "what humanity must lose if it makes a god of industrial power."[48] So strong were the Hammonds' feelings, for example, that they used Sadler's 1832 report on factory children as "a classical document ... one of the main sources of our knowledge of the conditions of factory life of the times," in spite of the fact that it included evidence *only* of Sadler's supporters and that it was refuted to an important extent by subequent reports of 1833 and 1834.[49] When beliefs are strong, the historian can be blind to what he does not believe or does not want to believe; and although it is difficult to suspect any historian of consciously ignoring or suppressing evidence or of falsifying or inventing it, the fact remains that history has long been used as "a weapon in party strife" and has been made "to serve every conceivable theory or temperamental peculiarity."[50] Thus much of the conflict of opinion on the industrial revolution arises from bias, from passionately held views about values and how they are affected by social change.

There have always been historians who gloomily regarded social change as retrogression, and others who hopefully regarded it as progress. The optimists, with their belief in continuous though fluctuating progress, have predominated since 1800,[51] especially in political history, where the Whig interpretation was for so long unchallenged.[52] It is indeed curious that a Tory-Radical interpretation of the industrial revolution—as advanced by contemporaries like Southey and Oastler and later by the Hammonds and Webbs—had widest allegiance at the same time as the Whig version of political history was most widely acclaimed; and that more recently, when the Whig political interpretation has been under increasing attack, the traditional Whig attitude towards the industrial revolution has been gaining favor.

The original disagreement lay in differing attitudes to the main and obvious social effect of industrialization: the breaking up of the old social units and social

[46] F. M. Eden, *The State of the Poor* (3 vols.; London, 1797), I, ii.
[47] Macaulay, *op. cit.*, p. 122.
[48] J. L. and B. Hammond, *The Town Labourer*, p. vi.
[49] Hutt, *op. cit.*, pp. 78-93.
[50] P. Geyl, *Use and Abuse of History* (New Haven: Yale University Press, 1955), pp. 10 and 75.
[51] See M. Ginsburg, *The Idea of Progress* (London: Methuen, 1953).
[52] See H. Butterfield, *The Whig Interpretation of History* (London, Bell, 1931), esp. pp. 45-46.

relationships. Whereas some argued that the result was harmful, with deleterious effects on morals, health, happiness, and income, others claimed that industrialism freed men from the old bondages of soil and weather, of a constrictive social system, and gave them opportunities for a larger and richer way of life. In particular, the pessimists argued that industrialization was a threat to morals and values. "The great mischief of the present system," N. Scatcherd wrote in 1830, "is that it has completely broken the tie . . . between parent and child . . . . The tie of authority thus broken–the tie of duty and affection is of small account. The servant is now the master–the child now the lodger only."[53]

But this process was often seen as emancipation, especially by women, for there is little doubt that the industrial revolution commenced the social revolution in the status of women. Later in the century Miss Foley claimed, for example, that the factory and workshop

... take the girl out of "the home," cribbed, cabined, and confined as to space, light, air, ideas and companionship, mould her in habits of punctuality, obedience, promptness, handiness, "gumption," and sustained attention and effort, spur her on to work well, bring out her capacities for comradeship and social action, and train her in self-respect, self-reliance and courage.[54]

Guest, the historian of the cotton industry, had argued similarly that the factory worker was "sharpened and improved by constant communication," and "from being only a few degrees above their cattle in the scale of intellect they became Political Citizens."[55] But Parson Bull of Yorkshire, attacking what Guest had praised, complained that the workers were "more addicted to the study of politics, than of the Bible."[56]

Complicating the issue was the pessimistic argument that industrialization loosened morals. "Factories," declared Whitaker, "are the hot-beds of early immorality, premature marriage, and unnatural population,"[57] But such accusations were based on "the theoretical deduction, that where a large number of both sexes were thrown together, immorality must of necessity exist."[58] They linked, moreover, in the period before 1850, with the Malthusian fears of overpopulation. In any case the evidence both on the religion and morals of the working classes was so varied as to be capable of alternative interpretation. The Factory Commission Report of 1833 stated:[59]

In respect of morals, we find that though the statements and depositions of the different witnesses that have been examined are to a considerable degree conflicting, yet there is no evidence to show that vice and immorality are more prevalent among the people, considered as a class, than amongst any other portion of the community in the same station and with the same limited means of information.

---

[53] N. Scatcherd, *The History of Morley* (Leeds, 1830), pp. 88-89.

[54] *The Economic Journal*, IV (1894), 187, reviewing "Royal Commission on Labour. The Employment of Women" (London, 1893); quoted by Pinchbeck, *op. cit.*, p. 308.

[55] R. Guest, *A Compendious History of the Cotton Manufacture* (Manchester, 1823), p. 37.

[56] *Parliamentary Papers*, 1840, XXIII, 568; *cf. Parliamentary Papers*, 1834, X, 419, with J. Makin saying that "the writings of Carlyle and Taylor and other infidels are more read than the Bible, or any other Book."

[57] Scatcherd, *op. cit.*, p. 88.

[58] W. Smith, *The History and Antiquities of Morley* (London, 1876), pp. 212-213.

[59] *Parliamentary Papers*, 1833, XX, 32.

As with morals, so with religion: Chapman declared in 1840 that "the attendance of the weavers at some place of worship is very general. Around Leeds the . . . numerous chapels . . . are usually filled."[60] Guest wrote, indeed, that the weavers "showed as much zeal and ardour in favour of the new Religion, as their predecessors had previously shown at the Reformation."[61] But Parson Bull and others of the established church were as much concerned with the *type* of religion as with the *lack* of it. Similarly, some of the complaint about the character of the workers stemmed from disapproval of their consumption of "luxuries"—for example, imported foodstuffs and printed cottons—and of the increasing social independence, with higher wages and combinations, of at least the skilled artisans.

The pessimists recognized, therefore, in what they considered to be lack of discipline, immorality, and political and religious radicalism, dangerous tendencies that threatened old interests and old values. They were right about the threat, but whether the new society was less moral than the old is still an open question. Nevertheless, a conviction of moral decline has persisted, so that there are many today, like Ortega y Gasset, who have claimed that the most important effect of the industrial revolution was to leave Europe without a moral code.[62]

Obviously there was little chance of agreement about the industrial revolution when the interpreters were (and are) separated by such absolute convictions about values. Even on the narrower problem of defining economic progress—as against the broader problem of comparing ways of life—there has been little agreement. G. T. Jones, for example, claimed that "the direct measurement of social progress" was impossible, while Colin Clark declares that "comparisons of economic welfare between one community and another, one economic group and another, and between one time and another, are the very framework of economic science."[63] But the problem of comparing "the satisfaction derived from a diet that includes bread, potatoes, tea, sugar and meat with that derived from a diet consisting mainly of oatmeal, milk, cheese and beer" (the problem as seen by T. S. Ashton)[64] has not been reduced, and probably cannot be, to objective quantitative measurement; so that, as in comparing rural with urban living, the answers given have depended on value-judgments about which disagreement has been certain.

Yet not all disagreement has arisen in this way. Another important source of misunderstanding has been the particular character of the parliamentary reports on which the historians of the industrial revolution have, of necessity, relied so much. These reports are "a class of evidence which suffers from the fact that it is concerned largely with calamities and distress."[65] While they chronicled the ills of society, often in morbid detail, they provided only incidental evidence of progress. Too often, therefore, the historian has found evidence only (or mainly) of the abnormal, of the worst, of the most dramatic aspects of society and the economy. Again, without discounting the strong element of compassion in the motives of those who stress the ills of society, the historian has too often been attracted by the sad spectacle of man's

---

[60] *Parliamentary Papers,* 1840, XXIII, 543.

[61] Guest, *op. cit.,* p. 43.

[62] *Cf.* H. Belloc, *The Servile State* (London: Foulis, 1912).

[63] G. T. Jones, *Increasing Return* (Cambridge, England: Cambridge University Press, 1933), p. 1; C. Clark, *The Conditions of Economic Progress* (2nd ed.; London: Macmillan, 1951), p. 16.

[64] T. S. Ashton, *op. cit.,* 33.

[65] D. George, *London Life in the Eighteenth Century* (London: Kegan Paul, 1925), p. viii.

inhumanity to man. It is indeed, for most of us, easier, more interesting, and emotionally more satisfying to worry about man's wickedness and suffering than to contemplate his achievements. Misery, vice, and cruelty invariably fascinate, while virtue often bores.[66] Moreover, having looked at suffering and evil and, in consequence, having laid the blame and sought a remedy, our conscience is eased and our indignation allayed. But as Butterfield points out, "It is not clear that moral indignation is not a dispersion of one's energies to the great confusion of one's judgment."[67] For these various reasons the working and living conditions of the most depressed industrial and domestic workers were examined and documented as of no other group of people, and so much was found out about them that the weight of evidence was itself a bias when comparisons were made with other groups about whom knowledge was more scanty. It led, for example, to the generalization that because, in many instances, conditions were very bad, they could not have been worse and therefore must once have been better.

Perhaps the most important source of conflict in interpretation has arisen because different historians have been referring to different people and different time periods and have been making comparisons that are inappropriate and generalizations that are invalid. It is quite unrealistic, for example, to talk about the workers as though they were a homogenous group. This was pointed out by Place in 1834:[68]

If the character and conduct of the working-people are to be taken from reviews, magazines, pamphlets, newspapers, reports of the two Houses of Parliament and the Factory Commissioners, we shall find them all jumbled together as the "lower orders," the most skilled and the most prudent workmen, with the most ignorant and most imprudent labourers and paupers, though the difference is great indeed, and indeed in many cases will scarce admit of comparison.

Thus any account of the hand-loom weavers after 1830 is bound to be depressing, and any generalization about their sufferings not necessarily applicable to the whole of the laboring population.[69] Nevertheless, statements about the poorest workmen and about the worst living and working conditions have been used, without proper qualification, as though they were generally applicable. The example of the Hammonds' improper use of the 1832 Sadler report has already been quoted; their description of "The State of the Towns" in *The Bleak Age* can be critized similarly for its concentration on extremes and for its ignoring of the contrary evidence to be found even in the sources they used.[70] Once differences between groups of workers are admitted, however, their significance can be examined; in particular, a comparison can be made between the

---

[66] Thus, for example, Lionel Trilling says of Zola that he gives the reader "the strange pleasure we habitually derive from the indictment of human kind." *Observer*, August 18, 1957.

[67] Butterfield, *op. cit.*, p. 1.

[68] Quoted by D. George, *England in Transition*, p. 210. Compare W. T. Thornton's statement in *Over-Population and Its Remedy* (London, 1846), p. 10:

"The labouring population has . . . been spoken of as if it formed only one class, but it is really divided into several, among which the rates of remuneration are far from being uniform; . . . so that, in order to represent with perfect fidelity the state of the labouring population, it would be necessary to describe each class separately."

[69] The writers who thought that the working classes were "progressing" between 1800 and 1850 nevertheless excepted the hand-loom weavers; thus Porter, McCullock, and Ure.

[70] *The Bleak Age*, Ch. 5.

wages and working conditions of the workers in the old as against the new industries. Mrs. Gilboy has shown, for example, how wage differentials between north and south and between town and country provided the stimulus for labor migration into the growing industrial areas of the eighteenth century;[71] Redford's study of labor migration between 1800 and 1850 showed how the same forces operated during the industrial revolution.[72] Similarly, Miss Pinchbeck has argued that the advances made by the factory worker between 1800 and 1850 can be seen only when the conditions of other workers at the same period are also considered:[73]

Among lacemakers, straw plaiters, glovemakers, frame-work knitters, nailmakers and other domestic workers, women and children were still working in overcrowded insanitary cottages for long hours each day; few of them, in spite of unremitting toil, could even earn a living wage, and they were powerless to resist payments in truck, petty exactions and such tyrannies as might be imposed by the greed or dishonesty of the middleman.

Historians have not been careful to make quite clear either the people to whom they were referring or the period of time they were considering. There has been little disagreement that *in the long run* the general standard of living rose; few would dispute, for example, that the worker was better off in 1900 than he was in 1800. Disagreement, when other confusion is eliminated, centers on the date at which the standard of living *began* to rise, and on whether the improvement was preceded by a period when working and living conditions actually deteriorated. Certainly much of the criticism of the period 1800 to 1850 is based on assumptions about the eighteenth century, and since the perennial themes of "the good old days" and "a golden age in the past"– often unexamined premises–seem characteristic of all ages, it is important to know whether the eighteenth century provided a higher standard of living for the English worker than the nineteenth. This is the most relevant comparison; it is of little use to place the standard of living in 1800 to 1850 against that of the mid-twentieth century.

Any study of the eighteenth century reveals the existence of many of the "evils" that have been associated more or less exclusively with the industrial revolution. To be sure, careful accounts of eighteenth-century wages by F. M. Eden in 1797 and by E. W. Gilboy in 1934 show that wages had increased during the century. Eden believed that "not only the aggregate body of the nation must have advanced to wealth and independence, but that portion of the community, which consists of those who are emphatically called the labouring classes, must have considerably bettered its condition in the course of the . . . century."[74] Yet to say, as with the nineteenth century, that conditions were improving is not inconsistent with the claim tht conditions were very bad. Everything we know of the workers of the eighteenth century, especially the urban workers, indicates indeed that conditions were very bad. Hogarth's *Gin Lane,* for example, depicts living conditions similar to those revealed in the reports of the Health of Towns Commission in the 1840's. The Webbs were at least as shocked by the eighteenth as by the nineteenth century; for their study of local government in the eighteenth century they collected evidence which they described as

[71] E. W. Gilboy, *Wages in Eighteenth Century England* (Cambridge, Mass.: Harvard University Press, 1934).
[72] A. Redford, *Labour Migration in England, 1800-1850* (Manchester: Manchester University Press, 1926).
[73] Pinchbeck, *op. cit.,* p. 308.
[74] Eden, *op. cit.,* 404.

"a horrifying mass of sensual and sordid delinquency." It was a century, they believed, of "private licentiousness" and "public disorder," with too much drinking and gambling and increasing sensuality. The London fairs, they wrote, "were orgies of drunkenness, sensual immorality and disorder."[75] Colquhoun, describing London at the end of the eighteenth century, declared: "Poverty is no where to be found cloathed, in so great a degree, with the garb and emblems of extremist misery and wretchedness, as in London."[76] Given the fact that contemporary observers like Francis Place and subsequent writers like the Webbs and Mrs. George believe that conditions began to improve *after* 1800,[77] it would be hazardous to argue that they deteriorated without more detailed investigation of the eighteenth century. The evidence indicates at least that conditions then were certainly bad and might well have been worse than in the early nineteenth century.[78]

### III

The differences in interpretation of the industrial revolution can be explained, but can they be resolved? Why, particularly, do historians today tend to favor the Macaulay-Clapham rather than the Toynbee-Hammond interpretation? The modern approval of the industrial revolution arises partly from an interest in economic growth and a consequent understanding of, and sympathy for, a period of dramatic and successful growth. The major economic problem of the modern world—as it was with the world of the industrial revolution—is to increase production faster than population. The industrialization of England was the successful solution to this problem, and is therefore more admired than criticized.

Yet approval stems also from a growing conviction, based both on a change in values and on more adequate research, that the English worker did in fact benefit from the industrial revolution. Three things in particular have conduced to this belief: consideration of estimates of national income and wealth, of production indexes, of wage and price series, of consumption trends, and of social indexes—*all* of which indicate an *unambiguous* increase in the average standard of life; *a priori* skepticism, on the basis of the modern theory of economic development, that economic progress over a long period could make the rich richer and the poor poorer; and an increasing awareness of the mistakes, confusions, and delusions of the opponents of progress.

Other factors have reinforced this conviction. There has been, for example, a revaluation of the importance (and character) of the entrepreneur, coupled with a general loss of appeal of the Fabian-Socialist preoccupation with the problems of distribution and their championship of the industrial proletariate. Moreover, in any age of many and massive inhumanities, the sustained capacity for indignation at the spectacle of children in factories and women in mines has been lost: the facts and fictions that roused the humane passion of the Hammonds tend to leave the modern reader, well disciplined by familiarity with concentration camps, comparatively unmoved.

---

[75] Ruth Atkins, "Report on the Webb Local Government Collection in the London School of Economics and Political Science" (unpublished, in Miss Atkins' possession, University of Technology, Sydney).

[76] P. Colquhoun, *A Treatise on the Police of the Metropolis* (London, 1796), p. 33.

[77] See in particular D. George, *op. cit.,* for numerous references to Place; also Atkins' "Report." It would seem that the Webbs were somewhat inconsistent on this point.

[78] This indicates, perhaps, a latent controversy to stimulate future Hammonds and Claphams.

Nevertheless, the controversy that has now excited historians for a century and a half can hardly be over. The present quietness is surely not permanent, being the result not only of better research, but also of temporary doctrinal unanimity among the historians. If Hobsbawm does not return to the attack of the now acceptable Whig interpretation of the industrial revolution, some other historian certainly will, either now or in the future. However, unambiguous the evidence showing that there was an increasing standard of life between 1800 and 1850, other criteria of progress will be used to demonstrate deterioration. So long as there are varieties of beliefs about values, the controversy will remain alive; and, after all, this is a good thing. History can only survive in a society where there are no "approved" values, and where all interpretations are subjected to continuous skepticism and investigation.

The conclusion? It is quite obvious that interpretations of the industrial revolution in England have not depended entirely on unbiased analysis of the evidence; to an important extent they have resulted from particular attitudes towards social, economic, and political change. Disagreement has stemmed as much from differing opinions as from differing facts. The whole controversy, indeed, was brilliantly satirized by Thomas Love Peacock in *Headlong Hall*, written in 1815, when he contrasted the views of "Mr. Foster, the perfectabilian; Mr. Escot, the deteriorationist; [and] Mr. Jenkinson, the statu-quo-ite":

[Mr. Foster] held forth with great energy on the subject of roads and railways, canals and tunnels, manufacturers and machinery; "In short," said he, "every thing we look on attests the progress of mankind in all the arts of life, and demonstrates their gradual advancement towards a state of unlimited perfection." Mr. Escot . . . here took up the thread of the discourse, observing, that the proposition just advanced seemed to him perfectly contrary to the true state of the case: "for," said he, "those improvements, as you call them, appear to me only so many links in the great chain of corruption, which will soon fetter the whole human race in irreparable slavery and incurable wretchedness . . . . " "Your opinions," said Mr. Jenkinson . . . "seem to differ *toto coelo*. I have often debated the matter in my own mind, *pro* and *con*, and have at length arrived at this conclusion,—that there is not in the human race a tendency either to moral perfectability or deterioration; but that the quantities of each are so exactly balanced by their reciprocal results, that the species, with respect to the sum of good and evil, knowledge and ignorance, happiness and misery, remains exactly and perpetually *in statu quo.*"

# THE ENGLISH WORKING CLASS

### E. P. Thompson

. . .If the character and conduct of the working-people are to be taken from reviews, magazines, pamphlets, newspapers, reports of the two Houses of Parliament and the Factory Commissioners, we shall find them all jumbled together as the "lower orders," the most skilled and the most prudent workman, with the most ignorant and imprudent labourers and paupers, though the difference is great indeed, and indeed in many cases will scarce admit of comparison.[1]

---

[1] Cit. M. D. George, *London Life in the 18th Century* (1930). p. 210.

Place is, of course, right: the Sunderland sailor, the Irish navy, the Jewish costermonger, the inmate of an East Anglian village workhouse, the compositor on *The Times*—all might be seen by their "betters" as belonging to the "lower classes" while they themselves might scarcely understand each others' dialect.

Nevertheless, when every caution has been made, the outstanding fact of the period between 1790 and 1830 is the formation of "the working class." This is revealed, first, in the growth of class-consciousness: the consciousness of an identity of interests as between all these diverse groups of working people and as against the interests of other classes. And, second, in the growth of corresponding forms of political and industrial organisation. By 1832 there were strongly-based and self-conscious working-class institutions—trade unions, friendly societies, educational and religious movements, political organisations, periodicals—working-class intellectual traditions, working-class community-patterns, and a working-class structure of feeling.

The making of the working class is a fact of political and cultural, as much as of economic, history. It was not the spontaneous generation of the factory-system. Nor should we think of an external force—the "industrial revolution"—working upon some nondescript undifferentiated raw material of humanity, and turning it out at the other end as a "fresh race of beings." The changing productive relations and working conditions of the Industrial Revolution were imposed, not upon raw material, but upon the free-born Englishman—and the free-born Englishman as Paine had left him or as the Methodists had moulded him. The factory hand or stockinger was also the inheritor of Bunyan, of remembered village rights, of notions of equality before the law, of craft traditions. He was the object of massive religious indoctrination and the creator of new political traditions. The working class made itself as much as it was made.

To see the working class in this way is to defend a "classical" view of the period against the prevalent mood of contemporary schools of economic history and sociology. For the territory of the Industrial Revolution, which was first staked out and surveyed by Marx, Arnold Toynbee, the Webbs and the Hammonds, now resembles an academic battlefield. At point after point, the familiar "catastrophic" view of the period has been disputed. Where it was customary to see the period as one of economic disequilibrium, intense misery and exploitation, political repression and heroic popular agitation, attention is now directed to the rate of economic growth (and the difficulties of "take-off" into self-sustaining technological reproduction). The enclosure movement is now noted, less for its harshness in displacing the village poor, than for its success in feeding a rapidly growing population. The hardships of the period are seen as being due to the dislocations consequent upon the Wars, faulty communications, immature banking and exchange, uncertain markets, and the trade-cycle, rather than to exploitation or cut-throat competition. Popular unrest is seen as consequent upon the unavoidable coincidence of high wheat prices and trade depressions, and explicable in terms of an elementary "social tension" chart derived from these data.[2] In general, it is suggested that the position of the industrial worker in 1840 was better in most ways than that of the domestic worker of 1790. The Industrial Revolution was an age, not of catastrophe or acute class-conflict and class oppression, but of improvement.[3]

[2] See W. W. Rostow, *British Economy in the Nineteenth Century* (1948), esp. pp. 122-5.
[3] Some of the views outlined here are to be found, implicitly or explicitly, in T. S. Ashton, *Industrial Revolution* (1948) and A. Radford, *The Economic History of England* (2nd edn. 1960). A sociological variant is developed by N. J. Smelser, *Social Change in the Industrial*

The classical catastrophic orthodoxy has been replaced by a new anti-catastrophic orthodoxy, which is most clearly distinguished by its empirical caution and, among its most notable exponents (Sir John Clapham, Dr. Dorothy George, Professor Ashton) by an astringent criticism of the looseness of certain writers of the older school. The studies of the new orthodoxy have enriched historical scholarship, and have qualified and revised in important respects the work of the classical school. But as the new orthodoxy is now, in its turn, growing old and entrenched in most of the academic centres, so it becomes open to challenge in its turn. And the successors of the great empiricists too often exhibit a moral complacency, a narrowness of reference, and an insufficient familiarity with the actual movements of the working people of the time. They are more aware of the orthodox empiricist postures than of the changes in social relationship and in cultural modes which the Industrial Revolution entailed. What has been lost is a sense of the whole process—the whole political and social context of the period. What arose as valuable qualifications have passed by imperceptible stages to new generalisations (which the evidence can rarely sustain) and from generalisations to a ruling attitude.

The empiricist orthodoxy is often defined in terms of a running critique of the work of J. L. and Barbara Hammond. It is true that the Hammonds showed themselves too willing to moralise history, and to arrange their materials too much in terms of "outraged emotion".[4] There are many points at which their work has been faulted or qualified in the light of subsequent research, and we intend to propose others. But a defence of the Hammonds need not only be rested upon the fact that their volumes on the labourers, with their copious quotation and wide reference, will long remain among the most important source-books for this period. We can also say that they displayed throughout their narrative an understanding of the political context within which the Industrial Revolution took place. To the student examining the ledgers of one cotton-mill, the Napoleonic Wars appear only as an abnormal influence affecting foreign markets and fluctuating demand. The Hammonds could never have forgotten for one moment that it was also a war against Jacobinism. "The history of England at the time discussed in these pages reads like a history of civil war." This is the opening of the introductory chapter of *The Skilled Labourer.* And in the conclusion to *The Town Labourer,* among other comments of indifferent value, there is an insight which throws the whole period into sudden relief:

At the time when half Europe was intoxicated and the other half terrified by the new magic of the word citizen, the English nation was in the hands of men who regarded the idea of citizenship as a challenge to their religion and their civilisation; who deliberately sought to make the inequalities of life the basis of the state, and to emphasise and perpetuate the position of the workpeople as a subject class. Hence it happened that the French Revolution has divided the people of France less than the Industrial Revolution has divided the people of England. . .

"Hence it happened . . . ." The judgment may be questioned. And yet it is in this insight—that the revolution which did *not* happen in England was fully as devastating, and in some features more divisive, than that which did happen in France—that we find a clue to the truly catastrophic nature of the period. Throughout this time there

*Revolution* (1959), and a knockabout popularisation is in John Vaizey, *Success Story* (W.E.A., n.d.).
[4] See E. E. Lampard, op. cit., p. 7.

are three, and not two, great influences simultaneously at work. There is the tremendous increase in population (in Great Britain, from 10.5 millions in 1801 to 18.1 millions in 1841, with the greatest rate of increase between 1811-21). There is the Industrial Revolution, in its technological aspects. And there is the political *counter*-revolution, from 1792-1832.

In the end, it is the political context as much as the steam-engine, which had most influence upon the shaping consciousness and institutions of the working class. The forces making for political reform in the late 18th century—Wilkes, the city merchants, the Middlesex small gentry, the "mob"—or Wyvill, and the small gentry and yeomen, clothiers, cutlers, and tradesmen—were on the eve of gaining at least some piecemeal victories in the 1790s: Pitt had been cast for the role of reforming Prime Minister. Had events taken their "natural" course we might expect there to have been some show-down long before 1832, between the oligarchy of land and commerce and the manufacturers and petty gentry, with working people in the tail of the middle-class agitation. And even in 1792, when manufacturers and professional men were prominent in the reform movement, this was still the balance of forces. But, after the success of *Rights of Man,* the radicalisation and terror of the French Revolution, and the onset of Pitt's repression, it was the plebeian Corresponding Society which alone stood up against the counter-revolutionary wars. And these plebeian groups, small as they were in 1796, did nevertheless make up an "underground" tradition which ran through to the end of the Wars. Alarmed at the French example, and in the patriotic fervour of war, the aristocracy and the manufacturers made common cause. The English *ancien régime* received a new lease of life, not only in national affairs, but also in the perpetuation of the antique corporations which misgoverned the swelling industrial towns. In return, the manufacturers received important concessions: and notably the abrogation or repeal of "paternalist" legislation covering apprenticeship, wage-regulation, or conditions in industry. The aristocracy were interested in repressing the Jacobin "conspiracies" of the people, the manufacturers were interested in defeating their "conspiracies" to increase wages: the Combination Acts served both purposes.

Thus working people were forced into political and social *apartheid* during the Wars (which, incidentally, they also had to fight). It is true that this was not altogether new. What was new was that it was coincident with a French Revolution: with growing self-consciousness and wider aspirations (for the "liberty tree" had been planted from the Thames to the Tyne): with a rise in population, in which the sheer sense of numbers, in London and in the industrial districts, became more impressive from year to year (and as numbers grew, so deference to master, magistrate, or parson was likely to lessen): and with more intensive or more transparent forms of economic exploitation. More intensive in agriculture and in the old domestic industries: more transparent in the new factories and perhaps in mining. In agriculture the years between 1760 and 1820 are the years of wholesale enclosure, in which, in village after village, common rights are lost, and the landless and—in the south—pauperised labourer is left to support the tenant-farmer, the landowner, and the tithes of the Church. In the domestic industries, from 1800 onwards, the tendency is widespread for small masters to give way to larger employers (whether manufacturers or middlemen) and for the majority of weavers, stockingers, or nail-makers to become wage-earning outworkers with more or less precarious employment. In the mills and in many mining areas these are the years of the employment of children (and of women underground); and the large-scale enterprise, the factory-system with its new discipline, the mill communities—where the manufacturer not only made riches out of the labour of the "hands" but could be *seen* to make riches in one generation—all contributed to the transparency of the process of exploitation and to the social and cultural cohesion of the exploited.

We can now see something of the truly catastrophic nature of the Industrial Revolution; as well as some of the reasons why the English working class took form in these years. The people were subjected simultaneously to an intensification of two intolerable forms of relationship: those of economic exploitation and of political oppression. Relations between employer and labourer were becoming both harsher and less personal; and while it is true that this increased the potential freedom of the worker, since the hired farm servant or the journeyman in domestic industry was (in Toynbee's words) "halted half-way between the position of the serf and the position of the citizen," this "freedom" meant that he felt his *un*freedom more. But at each point where he sought to resist exploitation, he was met by the forces of employer or State, and commonly of both.

For most working people the crucial experience of the Industrial Revolution was felt in terms of changes in the nature and intensity of exploitation. Nor is this some anachronistic notion, imposed upon the evidence. We may describe some parts of the exploitive process as they appeared to one remarkable cotton operative in 1818—the year in which Marx was born. The account—an Address to the public of strike-bound Manchester by "A Journeyman Cotton Spinner"—commences by describing the employers and the workers as "two distinct classes of persons":

"First, then, as to the employers: with very few exceptions, they are a set of men who have sprung from the cotton-shop without education or address, except so much as they have acquired by their intercourse with the little world of merchants on the exchange at Manchester; but to counterbalance that deficiency, they give you enough of appearances by an ostentatious display of elegant mansions, equipages, liveries, parks, hunters, hounds, &c. which they take care to shew off to the merchant stranger in the most pompous manner. Indeed their houses are gorgeous palaces, far surpassing in bulk and extent the neat charming retreats you see round London . . . but the chaste observer of the beauties of nature and art combined will observe a woeful deficiency of taste. They bring up their families at the most costly schools, determined to give their offspring a double portion of what they were so deficient in themselves. Thus with scarcely a second idea in their heads, they are literally petty monarchs, absolute and despotic, in their own particular districts; and to support all this, their whole time is occupied in contriving how to get the greatest quantity of work turned off with the least expence. . . . In short, I will venture to say, without fear of contradiction, that there is a greater distance observed between the master there and the spinner, than there is between the first merchant in London and his lowest servant or the lowest artisan. Indeed there is no comparison. I know it to be a fact, that the greater part of the master spinners are anxious to keep wages low for the purpose of keeping the spinners indigent and spiritless . . . as for the purpose of taking the surplus to their own pockets.

"The master spinners are a class of men unlike all other master tradesmen in the kingdom. They are ignorant, proud, and tyrannical. What then must be the men or rather beings who are the instruments of such masters? Why, they have been for a series of years, with their wives and their families, patience itself—bondmen and bondwomen to their cruel taskmasters. It is in vain to insult our common understandings with the observation that such men are free; that the law protects the rich and poor alike, and that a spinner can leave his master if he does not like the wages. True; so he can: but where must he go? why to another, to be sure. Well: he goes; he is asked where did you work last: 'did he discharge you?' 'No; we could not agree about wages.' 'Well I shall not employ you or anyone who leaves his master in that manner.' Why is this? Because there is an abominable *combination existing amongst the masters,* first established at Stockport in 1802, and it has since become so general, as to embrace all the great masters for a circuit of many miles round Manchester, though not the little masters: they are excluded. They are the most obnoxious beings to the great ones that can be imagined. . . . When the combination first took place, one of their first articles was, that no master should take on a man until he had first ascertained whether his last master had discharged him. What then is the man to do? If he goes to the parish, that grave of all independence, he is there told—'We shall not relieve you; if you dispute with your master, and don't support your family, we will send you to prison'; so that the man is bound, by a combination of circumstances, to submit to his master. He cannot travel and get work in any town like a shoe-maker, joiner, or taylor; he is confined to the district.

"The workmen in general are an inoffensive, unassuming, set of well-informed men, though how they acquire their information is almost a mystery to me. They are docile and tractable, if not goaded too much; but this is not to be wondered at, when we consider that they are trained to work from six years old, from five in a morning to eight and nine at night. Let one of the advocates for obedience to his master take his stand in an avenue leading to a factory a little before five o'clock in the morning, and observe the squalid appearance of the little infants and their parents taken from their beds at so early an hour in all kinds of weather; let him examine the miserable pittance of food, chiefly composed of water gruel and oatcake broken into it, a little salt, and sometimes coloured with a little milk, together with a few potatoes, and a bit of bacon or fat for dinner; would a London mechanic eat this? There they are, (and if late a few minutes, a quarter of a day is stopped in wages) locked up until night in rooms heated above the hottest days we have had this summer, and allowed no time, except three-quarters of an hour at dinner in the whole day: whatever they eat at any other time must be as they are at work. The negro slave in the West Indies, if he works under a scorching sun, has probably a little breeze of air sometimes to fan him: he has a space of ground, and time allowed to cultivate it. The English spinner slave has no enjoyment of the open atmosphere and breezes of heaven. Locked up in factories eight stories high, he has no relaxation till the ponderous engine stops, and then he goes home to get refreshed for the next day; no time for sweet association with his family; they are all alike fatigued and exhausted. This is no over-drawn picture: it is literally true. I ask again, would the mechanics in the South of England submit to this?

"When the spinning of cotton was in its infancy, and before those terrible machines for superseding the necessity of human labour, called steam engines, came into use, there were a great number of what were then called *little masters;* men who with a small capital, could procure a few machines, and employ a few hands, men and boys (say to twenty or thirty), the produce of whose labour was all taken to Manchester central mart, and put into the hands of brokers. . . . The brokers sold it to the merchants, by which means the master spinner was enabled to stay at home and work and attend to his workmen. The cotton was then always given out in its raw state from the bale to the wives of the spinners at home, when they heat and cleansed it ready for the spinners in the factory. By this they could earn eight, ten, or twelve shillings a week, and cook and attend to their families. But none are thus employed now; for all the cotton is broke up by a machine, turned by the steam engine, called a devil: so that the spinners' wives have no employment, except they go to work in the factory all day at what can be done by children for a few shillings, four or five per week. If a man then could not agree with his master, he left him, and could get employed elsewhere. A few years, however, changed the face of things. Steam engines came into use, to purchase which, and to erect buildings sufficient to contain them and six or seven hundred hands, required a great capital. The engine power produced a more marketable (though not a better) article than the little master could at the same price. The consequence was their ruin in a short time; and the overgrown capitalists triumphed in their fall; for they were the only obstacle that stood between them and the complete controul of the workmen.

"Various disputes then originated between the workmen and masters as to the fineness of the work, the workmen being paid according to the number of hanks or yards of thread he produced from a given quantity of cotton, which was always to be proved by the overlooker, whose interest made it imperative on him to lean to his master, and call the material coarser than it was. If the workman would not submit *he must summon his employer before a magistrate;* the whole of the acting magistrates in that district, with the exception of two worthy clergymen, being gentlemen who have sprung from the *same* source with the master cotton spinners. The employer generally contented himself with sending his overlooker to answer any such summons, thinking it beneath him to meet his servant. The magistrate's decision was generally in favour of the master, though on the statement of the overlooker only. The workman dared not appeal to the sessions on account of the expense. . . .

"These evils to the men have arisen from that dreadful monopoly which exists in those districts where wealth and power are got into the hands of the few, who, in the pride of their hearts, think themselves the lords of the universe."[5]

This reading of the facts, in its remarkable cogency, is as much an *ex parte* statement as is the "political economy" of Lord Brougham. But the "Journeyman Cotton Spinner" was describing facts of a different order. We need not concern ourselves with the soundness of all his judgements. What his address does is to itemise one after another the grievances felt by working people as to changes in the character of capitalist exploitation: the rise of a master-class without traditional authority or obligations: the growing distance between master and man: the transparency of the exploitation at the source of their new wealth and power: the loss of status and above all of independence for the worker, his reduction to total dependence on the master's instruments of production: the partiality of the law: the disruption of the traditional family economy: the discipline, monotony, hours and conditions of work: loss of leisure and amenities: the reduction of the man to the status of an "instrument."

That working people felt these grievances at all—and felt them passionately—is itself a sufficient fact to merit our attention. And it reminds us forcibly that some of the most bitter conflicts of these years turned on issues which are not encompassed by cost-of-living series. The issues which provoked the most intensity of feeling were very often ones in which such values as traditional customs, "justice," "independence," security, or family-economy were at stake, rather than straight-forward "bread-and-butter" issues. The early years of the 1830s are aflame with agitations which turned on issues in which wages were of secondary importance; by the potters, against the Truck System; by the textile workers, for the 10-Hour Bill; by the building workers, for

[5] *Black Dwarf,* 30 September 1818.

co-operative direct action; by all groups of workers, for the right to join trade unions. The great strike in the north-east coalfield in 1831 turned on security of employment, "tommy shops," child labour.

The exploitive relationship is more than the sum of grievances and mutual antagonisms. It is a relationship which can be seen to take distinct forms in different historical contexts, forms which are related to corresponding forms of ownership and State power. The classic exploitive relationship of the Industrial Revolution is depersonalised, in the sense that no lingering obligations of mutuality—of paternalism or deference, or of the interests of "the Trade"—are admitted. There is no whisper of the "just" price, or of a wage justified in relation to social or moral sanctions, as opposed to the operation of free market forces. Antagonism is accepted as intrinsic to the relations of production. Managerial or supervisory functions demand the repression of all attributes except those which further the expropriation of the maximum surplus value from labour. This is the political economy which Marx anatomised in *Das Kapital.* The worker has become an "instrument," or an entry among other items of cost.

In fact, no complex industrial enterprise could be conducted according to such a philosophy. The need for industrial peace, for a stable labour-force, and for a body of skilled and experienced workers, necessitated the modification of managerial techniques—and, indeed, the growth of new forms of paternalism—in the cotton-mills by the 1830s. But in the overstocked outwork industries, where there was always a sufficiency of unorganised "hands" competing for employment, these considerations did not operate. Here, as old customs were eroded, and old paternalism was set aside, the exploitive relationship emerged supreme.

This does not mean that we can lay all the "blame" for each hardship of the Industrial Revolution upon "the masters" or upon *laissez faire.* The process of industrialisation must, in any conceivable social context, entail suffering and the destruction of older and valued ways of life. Much recent research has thrown light upon the particular difficulties of the British experience; the hazards of markets; the manifold commercial and financial consequences of the Wars; the post-war deflation; movements in the terms of trade; and the exceptional stresses resulting from the population "explosion." Moreover, 20th-century preoccupations have made us aware of the overarching problems of economic growth. It can be argued that Britain in the Industrial Revolution was encountering the problems of "take-off"; heavy long-term investment—canals, mills, railways, foundries, mines, utilities—was at the expense of current consumption; the generations of workers between 1790 and 1840 sacrificed some, or all, of their prospects of increased consumption to the future.[6]

These arguments all deserve close attention. For example, studies of the fluctuations in the demand of the South American market, or of the crisis in country banking, may tell us much about the reasons for the growth or retardation of particular industries. The objection to the reigning academic orthodoxy is not to empirical studies *per se,* but to the fragmentation of our comprehension of the full historical process. First, the empiricist segregates certain events from this process and examines them in isolation. Since the conditions which gave rise to these events are assumed, they appear not only as explicable in their own terms but as inevitable. The Wars had to be paid for out of heavy taxation; they accelerated growth in this way and retarded it in that. Since this

---

[6] See S. Pollard, "Investment. Consumption, and the Industrial Revolution," *Econ. Hist. Review,* 2nd Series, XI (1958), pp. 215-26.

can be shown, it is also implied that this was *necessarily* so. But thousands of Englishmen at the time agreed with Thomas Bewick's condemnation of "this superlatively wicked war".[7] The unequal burden of taxation, fund-holders who profited from the National Debt, paper-money—these were not accepted as given data by many contemporaries, but were the staple of intensive Radical agitation.

But there is a second stage, where the empiricist may put these fragmentary studies back together again, constructing a model of the historical process made up from a multiplicity of interlocking inevitabilities, a piecemeal processional. In the scrutiny of credit facilities or of the terms of trade, where each event is explicable and appears also as a self-sufficient cause of other events, we arrive at a *post facto* determinism. The dimension of human agency is lost, and the context of class relations is forgotten.

It is perfectly true that what the empiricist points to was there. The Orders in Council had in 1811 brought certain trades almost to a standstill; rising timber prices after the Wars inflated the costs of building; a passing change of fashion (lace for ribbon) might silence the looms of Coventry; the power-loom competed with the hand-loom. But even these open-faced facts, with their frank credentials, deserve to be questioned. Whose Council, why the Orders? Who profited most from corners in scarce timber? Why should looms remain idle when tens of thousands of country girls fancied ribbons but could not afford to buy? By what social alchemy did inventions for saving labour become engines of immiseration? The raw fact—a bad harvest—may seem to be beyond human election. But the way that fact worked its way out was in terms of a particular complex of human relationships: law, ownership, power. When we encounter some sonorous phrase such as "the strong ebb and flow of the trade cycle" we must be put on our guard. For behind this trade cycle there is a structure of social relations, fostering some sorts of expropriation (rent, interest, and profit) and outlawing others (theft, feudal dues), legitimising some types of conflict (competition, armed warfare) and inhibiting others (trades unionism, bread riots, popular political organisation)—a structure which may appear, in the eyes of the future, to be both barbarous and ephemeral.

It might be unnecessary to raise these large questions, since the historian cannot always be questioning the credentials of the society which he studies. But all these questions were, in fact, raised by contemporaries: not only by men of the upper classes (Shelley, Cobbett, Owen, Peacock, Thompson, Hodgskin, Carlyle) but by thousands of articulate working men. Not the political institutions alone, but the social and economic structure of industrial capitalism, were brought into question by their spokesmen. To the facts of orthodox political economy they opposed their own facts and their own arithmetic. Thus as early as 1817 the Leicester framework-knitters put forward, in a series of resolutions, an under-consumption theory of capitalist crisis:

> That in proportion as the Reduction of Wages makes the great Body of the People poor and wretched, in the same proportion must the consumption of our manufactures be lessened.
>
> That if liberal Wages were given to the Mechanics in general throughout the Country, the Home Consumption of our Manufactures would be immediately more than doubled, and consequently every hand would soon find full employment.
>
> That to Reduce the Wage of the Mechanic of this Country so low that he cannot live

---

[7] T. Bewick, *Memoir* (1961 edn.), p. 151.

by his labour, in order to undersell Foreign Manufacturers in a Foreign Market, is to gain one customer abroad, and lose two at home. . . .[8]

If those in employment worked shorter hours, and if child labour were to be restricted, there would be more work for hand-workers and the unemployed could employ themselves and exchange the products of their labour directly—short-circuiting the vagaries of the capitalist market—goods would be cheaper and labour better-rewarded. To the rhetoric of the free market they opposed the language of the "new moral order." It is because alternative and irreconcilable views of human order—one based on mutuality, the other on competition—confronted each other between 1815 and 1850 that the historian today still feels the need to take sides.

It is scarcely possible to write the history of popular agitations in these years unless we make at least the imaginative effort to understand how such a man as the "Journeyman Cotton Spinner" read the evidence. He spoke of the "masters," not as an aggregate of individuals, but as a class. As such, "they" denied him political rights. If there was a trade recession, "they" cut his wages. If trade improved, he had to fight "them" and their state to obtain any share in the improvement. If food was plentiful, "they" profited from it. If it was scarce, some of "them" profited more. "They" conspired, not in this or that fact alone, but in the essential exploitive relationship within which all the facts were validated. Certainly there were market fluctuations, bad harvests, and the rest; but the experience of intensified exploitation was constant, whereas these other causes of hardship were variable. The latter bore upon working people, not directly, but through the refraction of a particular system of ownership and power which distributed the gains and losses with gross partiality.

These larger considerations have been, for some years, overlaid by the academic exercise (through which all students must march and counter-march) known as the "standard-of-living controversy." Did the living standards of the bulk of the people rise or fall between 1780 and 1830—or 1800 and 1850?[9] To understand the significance of the argument, we must look briefly at its development.

The debate on values is as old as the Industrial Revolution. The controversy on the standard-of-living is more recent. The ideological *muddle* is more recent still. We may start at one of the more lucid points of the controversy. Sir John Clapham, in his Preface to the first edition of his *Economic History of Modern Britain* (1926) wrote:

The legend that everything was getting worse for the working man, down to some unspecified date between the drafting of the People's Charter and the Great Exhibition [1837 and 1851: E.P.T.], dies hard. The fact that, after the price fall of 1820-1, the purchasing power of wages in general—not, of course, of everyone's wages—was definitely greater than it had been just before the revolutionary and Napoleonic wars, fits so ill with the tradition that it is very seldom mentioned, the work of statisticians on wages and prices being constantly ignored by social historians.

To this, J. L. Hammond offered a reply in the *Economic History Review* (1930) of two kinds: first, he criticised Clapham's statistics of agricultural earnings. These had

---

[8] H. O. 42.160. See also Hammonds, *The Town Labourer*, p. 303.

[9] The futility of one part of this discussion is shown by the fact that if different datum-lines are taken, different answers may come up. 1780-1830 favours the "pessimists"; 1800-1850 favours the "optimists."

been based on totting up the country averages, and then dividing them by the number of counties in order to reach a national average; whereas the population in the low wage-earning counties of the south was more numerous than that of the high wage-earning counties (where agricultural earnings were inflated by the proximity of industry) so that Hammond was able to show that the "national average" concealed the fact that 60 per cent of the labouring population was in counties where wages were below the "average" figure. The second part of his reply consisted in a switch to discussions of value (happiness) in his most cloudy and unsatisfactory manner. The first part of this reply Clapham, in his Preface to his second edition (1930), accepted; the second part he met with dry caution ("a curve in words", "higher matters") but nevertheless acknowledged: "I agree most profoundly . . . that statistics of material well-being can never measure a people's happiness." Moreover, he asserted that when he had criticised the view that "everything was getting worse"—"I did not mean that everything was getting better. I only meant that recent historians have too often . . . stressed the worsenings and slurred over or ignored the betterings." The Hammonds, for their part, in a late revision of *The Bleak Age* (1947 edition), made their own peace: "statisticians tell us that . . . they are satisfied that earnings increased and that most men and women were less poor when this discontent was loud and active than they were when the eighteenth century was beginning to grow old in a silence like that of autumn. The evidence, of course, is scanty, and its interpretation not too simple, but this general view is probably more or less correct." The explanation for discontent "must be sought outside the sphere of strictly economic conditions."

So far, so good. The most fertile—but loose—social historians of the period had encountered the astringent criticism of a notable empiricist; and in the result both sides had given ground. And, despite the heat which has subsequently been generated, the actual divergence between the hard economic conclusions of the protagonists is slight. If no serious scholar is now willing to argue that everything was getting worse, no serious scholar will argue that everything was getting better. Both Dr. Hobsbawm (a "pessimist") and Professor Ashton (an "optimist") agree that real wages declined during the Napoleonic Wars and in their immediate aftermath. Dr. Hobsbawm will not vouch for any marked general rise in the standard-of-living until the mid-1840s; whereas Professor Ashton notes a "more genial" economic climate after 1821—a "marked upward movement broken only by the slumps of 1825-6 and 1831"; and in view of increasing imports of tea, coffee, sugar, etc., "it is difficult to believe that the workers had no share in the gain." On the other hand his own table of prices in the Oldham and Manchester districts show that "in 1831 the standard diet of the poor can hardly have cost much less than in 1791," while he offers no corresponding wagetables. His conclusion is to suggest two main groups within the working class—"a large class raised well above the level of mere subsistence" and "masses of unskilled or poorly skilled workers—seasonally employed agricultural workers and hand-loom weavers in particular—whose incomes were almost wholly absorbed in paying for the bare necessaries of life." "My *guess* would be that the number of those who were able to share in the benefits of economic progress was larger than the number of those who were shut out from these benefits and that it was steadily growing."[10]

In fact, so far as the period 1790-1830 goes, there is very little in it. The condition

[10] My italics. T. S. Ashton, "The Standard of Life of the Workers in England, 1790-1830", in *Capitalism and the Historians* (ed. F. A. Hayek), pp. 127 ff.; E. J. Hobsbawm, "The British Standard of Living. 1790-1850", *Economic History Review*, X, August 1957.

of the majority was bad in 1790: it remained bad in 1830 (and forty years is a long time) but there is some disagreement as to the size of the relative groups within the working class. And matters are little clearer in the next decade. There were undoubted increases in real wages among organised workers during the burst of trade union activity between 1832-4: but the period of good trade between 1833 and 1837 was accompanied by the smashing of the trade unions by the concerted efforts of Government, magistrates, and employers; while 1837-42 are depression years. So that it is indeed at "some unspecified date between the drafting of the People's Charter and the Great Exhibition" that the tide begins to turn; let us say, with the railway boom in 1843. Moreover, even in the mid-40s the plight of very large groups of workers remains desperate, while the railway crash led to the depression years of 1847-8. This does not look very much like a "success story"; in half a century of the fullest development of industrialism, the standard-of-living still remained—for very large but indeterminate groups—at the point of subsistence.

This is not, however, the impression given in much contemporary writing. For, just as an earlier generation of historians who were also social reformers (Thorold Rogers, Arnold Toynbee, the Hammonds) allowed their sympathy with the poor to lead on occasions to a confusion of history with ideology, so we find that the sympathies of some economic historians today for the capitalist entrepreneur have led to a confusion of history and apologetics.[11] The point of transition was marked by the publication, in 1954, of a symposium on *Capitalism and the Historians,* edited by Professor F. A. Hayek, itself the work of a group of specialists "who for some years have been meeting regularly to discuss the problems of the preservation of a free society against the totalitarian threat." Since this group of international specialists regarded "a free society" as by definition a capitalist society, the effects of such an admixture of economic theory and special pleading were deplorable; and not least in the work of one of the contributors, Professor Ashton, whose cautious findings of 1949 are now transmuted—without further evidence—into the flat statement that "generally it is now agreed that for the majority the gain in real wages was substantial."[12] It is at this stage that the controversy degenerated into a muddle. And despite more recent attempts to rescue it for scholarship,[13] in many respects it is as a muddle of assertion and special pleading that the controversy remains.

The controversy falls into two parts. There is, first, the very real difficulty of constructing wage-series, price-series, and statistical indices from the abundant but patchy evidence. We shall examine some of the difficulties in interpreting such evidence when we come to the artisans. But at this point a further series of difficulties begins, since the term "standard" leads us from data amenable to statistical

---

[11] Lest the reader should judge the historian too harshly, we may record Sir John Clapham's explanation as to the way in which this selective principle may order the evidence. "It is very easy to do this unawares. Thirty years ago I read and marked Arthur Young's *Travels in France,* and taught from the marked passages. Five years ago I went through it again, to find that whenever Young spoke of a wretched Frenchman I had marked him, but that many of his references to happy or prosperous Frenchmen remained unmarked." One suspects that for ten or fifteen years most economic historians have been busy marking up the happy and prosperous evidence in the text.

[12] T. S. Ashton, "The Treatment of Capitalism by Historians," in *Capitalism and the Historians,* p. 41. Professor Ashton's essay on "The Standard of Life of the Workers in England" originally appeared in the *Journal of Economic History,* 1949.

[13] The most constructive appraisal of the controversy is in A. J. Taylor's "Progress and Poverty in Britain, 1780-1850." *History,* February, 1960.

measurement (wages or articles of consumption) to those satisfactions which are sometimes described by statisticans as "imponderables." From food we are led to homes, from homes to health, from health to family life, and thence to leisure, work-discipline, education and play, intensity of labour, and so on. From standard-of-life we pass to way-of-life. But the two are not the same. The first is a measurement of quantities: the second a description (and sometimes an evaluation) of qualities. Where statistical evidence is appropriate to the first, we must rely largely upon "literary evidence" as to the second. A major source of confusion arises from the drawing of conclusions as to one from evidence appropriate only to the other. It is at times as if statisticians have been arguing: "the indices reveal an increased *per capita* consumption of tea, sugar, meat and soap, *therefore* the working class was happier," while social historians have replied: "the literary sources show that people were unhappy, *therefore* their standard-of-living must have deteriorated."

This is to simplify. But simple points must be made. It is quite possible for statistical averages and human experiences to run in opposite directions. A *per capita* increase in quantitative factors may take place at the same time as a great qualitative disturbance in people's way of life, traditional relationships, and sanctions. People may consume more goods and become less happy or less free at the same time. Next to the agricultural workers the largest single group of working people during the whole period of the Industrial Revolution were the domestic servants. Very many of them were household servants, living-in with the employing family, sharing cramped quarters, working excessive hours, for a few shillings' reward. Nevertheless, we may confidently list them among the more favoured groups whose standards (or consumption of food and dress) improved on average slightly during the Industrial Revolution. But the hand-loom weaver and his wife, on the edge of starvation, still regarded their status as being superior to that of a "flunkey." Or again, we might cite those trades, such as coal-mining, in which real wages advanced between 1790 and 1840, but at the cost of longer hours and a greater intensity of labour, so that the breadwinner was "worn out" before the age of forty. In statistical terms, this reveals an upward curve. To the families concerned it might feel like immiseration.

Thus it is perfectly possible to maintain two propositions which, on a casual view, appear to be contradictory. Over the period 1790-1840 there was a slight improvement in average material standards. Over the same period there was intensified exploitation, greater insecurity, and increasing human misery. By 1840 most people were "better off" than their forerunners had been fifty years before, but they had suffered and continued to suffer this slight improvement as a catastrophic experience. In order to explore this experience, out of which the political and cultural expression of working-class consciousness arose, we shall do these things. First, we shall examine the changing life-experience of three groups of workers: the field labourers, the urban artisans, and the hand-loom weavers.[14] Second, we shall discuss some of the less "ponderable" elements in the people's standard-of-life. Third, we shall discuss the inner compulsions of the industrial way of life, and the bearing upon them of Methodism. Finally, we shall examine some of the elements in the new working-class communities.

[14] These groups have been selected because their experience seems most to colour the social consciousness of the working class in the first half of the century. The miners and metal-workers do not make their influence fully felt until later in the century. The other key group—the cotton-spinners—are the subject of an admirable study in the Hammonds, *The Skilled Labourer*.

* * *

## Standards and Experiences

### i. Goods

The controversy as to living standards during the Industrial Revolution has perhaps been of most value when it has passed from the somewhat unreal pursuit of the wage-rates of hypothetical average workers and directed attention to articles of consumption: food, clothing, homes: and, beyond these, health and mortality. Many of the points at issue are complex, and all that can be attempted here is to offer comments upon a continuing discussion. When we consider measurable quantities, it seems clear that over the years 1790-1840 the national product was increasing more rapidly than the population. But it is exceedingly difficult to assess how this product was distributed. Even if we leave other considerations aside (how much of this increase was exported owing to unfavourable terms of trade? how much went in capital investment rather than articles of personal consumption?) it is not easy to discover what share of this increase went to different sections of the population.

The debate as to the people's diet during the Industrial Revolution turns mainly upon cereals, meat, potatoes, beer, sugar and tea. It is probable that *per capita* consumption of wheat declined from late 18th-century levels throughout the first four decades of the 19th century. Mr. Salaman, the historian of the potato, has given a convincing blow by blow account of the "battle of the loaf," by which landowners, farmers, parsons, manufacturers, and the Government itself sought to drive labourers from a wheaten to a potato diet. The critical year was 1795. Thereafter war-time necessity took second place to the arguments as to the benefits of reducing the poor to a cheap basic diet. The rise in potato acreage during the Wars cannot be attributed to wheat shortage alone: "some deficiency there was, but unequal division between the different classes of society consequent on inflated prices was a far more potent factor . . . ." The great majority of the English people, even in the north, had turned over from coarser cereals to wheat by 1790; and the white loaf was regarded jealously as a symbol of their status. The southern rural labourer refused to abandon his diet of bread and cheese, even when near the point of starvation; and for nearly fifty years a regular dietary class-war took place, with potatoes encroaching on bread in the south, and with oatmeal and potatoes encroaching in the north. Indeed, Mr. Salaman finds in the potato a social stabiliser even more effective than Halévy found in Methodism:

> . . . the use of the potato . . . did, in fact, enable the workers to survive on the lowest possible wage. It may be that in this way the potato prolonged and encouraged, for another hundred years, the impoverishment and degradation of the English masses; but what was the alternative, surely nothing but bloody revolution. That England escaped such a violent upheaval in the early decades of the nineteenth century . . . must in large measure be placed to the credit of the potato.[15]

Nutritional experts now advise us that the potato is full of virtue, and certainly whenever standards rose sufficiently for the potato to be an *added* item, giving variety to the diet, it was a gain. But the substitution of potatoes for bread or oatmeal was felt

[15] R. N. Salaman, *The History and Social Influence of the Potato* (Cambridge, 1949), esp. pp. 480, 495, 506, 541-2. J. C. Drummond and A. Wilbraham, the historians of *The Englishman's Food* (1939), also see this as a period of decline.

to be a degradation. The Irish immigrants with their potato diet (Ebenezer Elliott called them, "Erin's root-fed hordes") were seen as eloquent testimony, and very many Englishmen agreed with Cobbett that the poor were victims of a conspiracy to reduce them to the Irish level. Throughout the Industrial Revolution the price of bread (and of oatmeal) was the first index of living standards, in the estimation of the people. When the Corn Laws were passed in 1815, the Houses of Parliament had to be defended from the populace by troops. "NO CORN LAWS" was prominent among the banners at Peterloo, and remained so (especially in Lancashire) until the anti-Corn Law agitation of the 1840s.

Meat, like wheat, involved feelings of status over and above its dietary value. The Roast Beef of Old England was the artisan's pride and the aspiration of the labourer. Once again, *per capita* consumption probably fell between 1790 and 1840, but the figures are in dispute. The argument turns mainly upon the number and weight of beasts killed in London slaughterhouses. But even if these figures are established, we still cannot be sure as to which sections of the people ate the meat, and in what proportions. Certainly, meat should be a sensitive indicator of material standards, since it was one of the first items upon which any increase in real wages will have been spent. The seasonal workers did not plan their consumption meticulously over fifty-two Sunday dinners, but, rather, spent their money when in full work and took what chance offered for the rest of the year. "In the long fine days of summer," Henry Mayhew was told,

. . . the little daughter of a working brickmaker used to order chops and other choice dainties of a butcher, saying, "Please, sir, father don't care for the price just a-now; but he must have his chops good; line-chops, sir, and tender, please—'cause he's a brickmaker." In the winter, it was, "O please, sir, here's a fourpenny bit, and you must send father something cheap. He don't care what it is, so long as it's cheap. It's winter, and he hasn't no work, sir—'cause he's a brickmaker." [16]

Londoners tended to have higher standards of expectation than labourers in the provinces. In the depth of the 1812 depression, it was the impression of an observer that the London poor fared better than those of the north and the west:

The Poor of the Metropolis, notwithstanding the enormous price of the necessaries of life, are really living comparatively in comfort. The humblest labourer here frequently gets meat (flesh meat) and always bread and cheese, with beer of some sort, for his meals, but a West Country peasant can obtain for his family no such food. [17]

There was, of course, a variety of inferior "meats" on sale: red herrings and bloaters, cow-heel, sheep's trotters, pig's ear, fagots, tripe and black pudding. The country weavers of Lancashire despised town food, and preferred "summat at's deed ov a knife"—a phrase which indicates both the survival of their own direct pig-keeping economy and their suspicion that town meat was diseased—if forced to eat in town "every mouthful went down among painful speculations as to what the quadruped was when alive, and what particular reason it had for departing this life". [18] It was not a new thing for town dwellers to be exposed to impure or adulterated food; but as the proportion of urban workers grew, so the exposure became worse. [19]

[16] Mayhew, op. cit., II, p. 368.
[17] E. Waugh, *Lancashire Sketches*, pp. 128-9.
[18] *Examiner*, 16 August 1812.
[19] See J. Burnett, "History of Food Adulteration in Great Britain in the 19th Century," *Bulletin of Inst. of Historical Research*, 1959, pp. 104-7.

There is no doubt that *per capita* beer consumption went down between 1800 and 1830, and no doubt that *per capita* consumption of tea and of sugar went up; while between 1820 and 1840 there was a marked increase in the consumption of gin and whiskey. Once again, this is a cultural as well as dietetic matter. Beer was regarded—by agricultural workers, coalwhippers, miners—as essential for any heavy labour (to 'put back the sweat") and in parts of the north beer was synonymous with "drink." The home-brewing of small ale was so essential to the household economy that "if a young woman can bake oatcake and brew well, it is thought she will make a good wife": while "some Methodist class-leaders say they could not lead their classes without getting a 'mugpot' of drink."[20] The decline was directly attributed to the malt tax—a tax so unpopular that some contemporaries regarded it as being an incitemen. to revolution. Remove the malt tax, one clerical magistrate in Hampshire argued in 1816, and the labourer—

... would go cheerfully to his daily employ, perform it with manly vigour and content, and become attached to his house, his family, and, *above all,* his country, which allows him to share, in common with his superiors, in a plain wholesome beverage, which a poor man looks up to, more, indeed, than to any thing that could possibly be granted them by a British Parliament."[21]

The additional duty upon strong beer led to widespread evasion: and "hush-shops" sprang up, like that in which Samuel Bamford was nearly murdered as a suspected exciseman until he was recognised by one of the drinkers as a *bona fide* radical "on the run."

The effect of the taxes was undoubtedly to reduce greatly the amount of home-brewing and home-drinking; and, equally, to make drinking less of a part of normal diet and more of an extra-mural activity. (In 1830 the duty on strong beer was repealed and the Beer Act was passed, and within five years 35,000 beer-shops sprang up as if out of the ground.) The increase in tea-drinking was, in part, a replacement of beer and, perhaps also, of milk; and, once again, many contemporaries—with Cobbett well to the fore—saw in this evidence of deterioration. Tea was seen as a poor substitute, and (with the increased consumption of spirits) as an indication of the need for stimulants caused by excessive hours of labour on an inadequate diet. But by 1830 tea was regarded as a necessity: families that were too poor to buy it begged once-used tea-leaves from neighbours, or even simulated its colour by pouring boiling water over a burnt crust.[22]

All in all, it is an unremarkable record. In fifty years of the Industrial Revolution the working-class share of the national product had almost certainly fallen relative to the share of the property-owning and professional classes. The "average" working man remained very close to subsistence level at a time when he was surrounded by the evidence of the increase of national wealth, much of it transparently the product of his own labour, and passing, by equally transparent means, into the hands of his employers. In psychological terms, this felt very much like a decline in standards. His own share in the "benefits of economic progress" consisted of more potatoes, a few articles of cotton clothing for his family, soap and candles, some tea and sugar, and a great many articles in the *Economic History Review.*

[20] J. Lawson, op. cit., pp. 8, 10.
[21] *Agricultural State of the Kingdom* (1816), p. 95.
[22] For an indication of some of the points at issue here, see the articles on the standard-of-living by T. S. Ashton, R. M. Hartwell, E. Hobsbawm, and A. J. Taylor cited above.

## ii. Homes

The evidence as to the urban environment is little easier to interpret. There were farm labourers at the end of the 18th century who lived with their families in one-roomed hovels, damp and below ground-level: such conditions were rarer fifty years later. Despite all that can be said as to the unplanned jerry-building and profiteering that went on in the growing industrial towns, the houses themselves were better than those to which many immigrants from the countryside had been accustomed. But as the new industrial towns grew old, so problems of water supply, sanitation, over-crowding, and of the use of homes for industrial occupations, multiplied, until we arrive at the appalling conditions revealed by the housing and sanitary enquiries of the 1840s. It is true that conditions in rural villages or weaving hamlets may have been quite as bad as conditions in Preston or Leeds. But the size of the problem was certainly worse in the great towns, and the mulitplication of bad conditions facilitated the spread of epidemics.

Moreover, conditions in the great towns were—and were *felt* to be—more actively offensive and inconvenient. Water from the village well, rising next to the graveyard, might be impure: but at least the villagers did not have to rise in the night and queue for a turn at the only stand-pipe serving several streets, nor did they have to pay for it. The industrial town-dweller often could not escape the stench of industrial refuse and of open sewers, and his children played among the garbage and Privy middens. Some of the evidence, after all, remains with us in the industrial landscape of the north and of the Midlands today.

This deterioration of the urban environment strikes us today, as it struck many contemporaries, as one of the most disastrous of the consequences of the Industrial Revolution, whether viewed in aesthetic terms, in terms of community amenities, or in terms of sanitation and density of population. Moreover, it took place most markedly in some of the "high-wage" areas where "optimistic" evidence as to improving standards is most well based. Common sense would suggest that we must take both kinds of evidence together; but in fact various arguments in mitigation have been offered. Examples have been found of improving mill-owners who attended to the housing conditions of their employees. These may well lead us to think better of human nature; but they do no more than touch the fringe of the general problem, just as the admirable charity hospitals probably affected mortality rates by only a decimal point. Moreover, most of the serious experiments in model communities (New Lanark apart) date from after 1840—or from after public opinion was aroused by the enquiries into the Sanitary Conditions of the Working Classes (1842) and the Health of Towns (1844), and alerted by the cholera epidemics of 1831 and 1848. Such experiments as ante-date 1840, like that of the Ashworths at Turton, were in self-sufficient mill villages.

It is also suggested that worsening conditions may be somehow discounted because they were no one's fault—and least of all the fault of the "capitalist." No villain can be found who answers to the name of "Jerry." Some of the worst building was undertaken by small jobbers or speculative small tradesmen or even self-employed building workers. A Sheffield investigator allocated blame between the landowner, the petty capitalist (who offered loans at a high rate of interest), and petty building speculators "who could command only a few hundred pounds," and some of whom "actually cannot write their names."[23] Prices were kept high by duties on Baltic timber,

[23] G. C. Holland, *The Vital Statistics of Sheffield* (1843), pp. 56-8.

bricks, tiles, slates; and Professor Ashton is able to give an absolute discharge to all the accused: "it was emphatically not the machine, not the Industrial Revolution, not even the speculative bricklayer or carpenter that was at fault."[24] All this may be true: it is notorious that working-class housing provides illustrations of the proverb as to every flea having "lesser fleas to bite 'em." In the 1820s, when many Lancashire weavers went on rent-strike, it was said that some owners of cottage property were thrown on the poor-rate. In the slums of the great towns publicans and small shopkeepers were among those often quoted as owners of the worst "folds" or human warrens of crumbling mortar. But none of this mitigates the actual conditions by one jot; nor can debate as to the proper allocation of responsibility exonerate a process by which some men were enabled to prey upon other's necessities.

A more valuable qualification is that which stresses the degree to which, in some of the older towns, improvements in paving, lighting, sewering and slum clearance may be dated to the 18th century. But, in the often-cited example of London, it is by no means clear whether improvements in the centre of the City extended to the East End and dockside districts, or how far they were maintained during the Wars. Thus the sanitary reformer, Dr. Southwood Smith, reported of London in 1839:

> While systematic efforts, on a large scale, have been made to widen the streets . . . to extend and perfect the drainage and sewerage . . . in the places in which the wealthier classes reside, nothing whatever has been done to improve the condition of the districts inhabited by the poor.[25]

Conditions in the East End were so noisome that doctors and parish officers risked their lives in the course of their duties. Moreover, as the Hammonds pointed out, it was in the boom towns of the Industrial Revolution that the worst conditions were to be found: "what London suffered [in the Commercial Revolution] Lancashire suffered at the end of the eighteenth and at the beginning of the nineteenth century.[26] Sheffield, an old and comparatively prosperous town with a high proportion of skilled artisans, almost certainly—despite the jerry-builders—saw an improvement in housing conditions in the first half of the 19th century, with an average, in 1840, of five persons per house, most artisans renting a family cottage on their own, with one day room and two sleeping rooms. It was in the textile districts, and in the towns most exposed to Irish immigrations—Liverpool, Manchester, Leeds, Preston, Bolton, Bradford—that the most atrocious evidence of deterioration—dense overcrowding, cellar-dwellings, unspeakable filth—is to be found.[27]

Finally, it is suggested, with tedious repetition, that the slums, the stinking rivers, the spoliation of nature, and the architectural horrors may all be forgiven because all happened so fast, so haphazardly, under intense population pressure, without premeditation and without prior experience. "It was ignorance rather than avarice that was often the cause of misery."[28] As a matter of fact, it was demonstrably both; and

[24] *Capitalism and the Historians*, pp. 43-51.
[25] *Fifth Annual Report of the Poor Law Commissioners* (1839), p. 170. See also *Fourth Report* (1838), Appendix A, No. 1.
[26] See M. D. George, *London Life in the Eighteenth Century*, Ch. II; *England in Transition* (Penguin edn.), p. 72; Hammond, *The Town Labourer*, Ch. III and Preface to 2nd edition; Dr. R. Willan, "Observations on Disease in London," *Medical and Physical Journal* 1800, p. 299.
[27] G. C. Holland, op. cit., p. 46 *et passim*. An excellent account of the working man's urban environment in mid-century Leeds is in J. F. C. Harrison, *Learning and Living* (1961), pp. 7-20.
[28] R. M. Hartwell, op. cit., p. 413.

it is by no means evident that the one is a more amiable characteristic than the other. The argument is valid only up to a point—to the point in most great towns, in the 1830s or 1840s, when doctors and sanitary reformers, Benthamites and Chartists, fought repeated battles for improvement against the inertia of property-owners and the demagoguey of "cheap government" rate-payers. By this time the working people were virtually segregated in their stinking enclaves, and the middle-classes demonstrated their real opinions of the industrial towns by getting as far out of them as equestrian transport made convenient. Even in comparatively well-built Sheffield,

All classes, save the artisan and the needy shopkeeper, are attracted by country comfort and retirement. The attorney—the manufacturer—the grocer—the draper—the shoemaker and the tailor, fix their commanding residences on some beautiful site. . . . . .

Of sixty-six Sheffield attorneys in 1841, forty-one lived in the country, and ten of the remaining twenty-five were newcomers to the town. In Manchester the poor in their courts and cellars lived,

. . . hidden from the view of the higher ranks by piles of stores, mills, warehouses, and manufacturing establishments, less known to their wealthy neighbours—who reside chiefly in the open spaces of Cheetham, Broughton, and Chorlton—than the inhabitants of New Zealand or Kamtschatka.

"The rich lose sight of the poor, or only recognise them when attention is forced to their existence by their appearance as vagrants, mendicants, or delinquents." "We have improved on the proverb, 'One half of the world does not know how the other half lives,' changing it into 'One half of the world *does not care* how the other half lives.' Ardwick knows less about Ancoats than it does about China. . . ."[29]

Certainly, the unprecedented rate of population growth, and of concentration in industrial areas, would have created major problems in any known society, and most of all in a society whose *rationale* was to be found in profit-seeking and hostility to planning. We should see these as the problems of industrialism, aggravated by the predatory drives of *laissez faire* capitalism. But, however the problems are defined, the definitions are no more than different ways of describing, or interpreting, the same events. And no survey of the industrial heartlands, between 1800 and 1840, can overlook the evidence of visual devastation and deprivation of amenities. The century which rebuilt Bath was not, after all, devoid of aesthetic sensibility nor ignorant of civic responsibility. The first stages of the Industrial Revolution witnessed a decline in both; or, at the very least, a drastic lesson that these values were not to be extended to working people. However appalling the conditions of the poor may have been in large towns before 1750, nevertheless the town in earlier centuries usually embodied some civic values and architectural graces, some balance between occupations, marketing and manufacture, some sense of variety. The "Coketowns" were perhaps the first towns of above 10,000 inhabitants ever to be dedicated so single-mindedly to work and to "fact."

*  *  *

*iv. Childhood*

We have touched already on child labour: but it deserves further examination. In one

29 G. C. Holland, op. cit., p. 51; W. Cooke Taylor, *Notes of a Tour in the Manufacturing Districts of Lancashire* (1842), pp. 12-13, 160.

sense it is curious that the question can be admitted as controversial: there was a drastic increase in the intensity of expolitation of child labour between 1780 and 1840, and every historian acquainted with the sources knows that this is so. This was true in the mines, both in inefficient small-scale pits where the roadways were sometimes so narrow that children could most easily pass through them; and in several larger coalfields, where—as the coal face drew further away from the shaft—children were in demand as "hurryers" and to operate the ventilation ports. In the mills, the child and juvenile labour force grew yearly; and in several of the outworker or "dishonourable" trades the hours of labour became longer and the work more intense. What, then, is left in dispute?

But "optimists" have, since the time of the Hammonds, surrounded the question with so many qualifications that one might almost suspect a conspiracy to explain child labour away. There was "nothing new" about it; conditions were as bad in the "old" industries as in the new: much of the evidence is partisan and exaggerated: things were already improving before the outcry of the 1830s was made: the operatives themselves were the worst offenders in the treatment of children: the outcry came from "interested" parties—landowners hostile to the manufacturers, or adult trade unionists wanting limitation of hours for themselves—or from middle-class intellectuals who knew nothing about it: or (paradoxically) the whole question reveals, not the hardship and insensitivity, but the growing humanity of the employing classes. Few questions have been so lost to history by a liberal admixture of special pleading and ideology.

Child labour was not new. The child was an intrinsic part of the agricultural and industrial economy before 1780, and remained so until rescued by the school. Certain occupations—climbing boys or ship's boys—were probably worse than all but the worst conditions in the early mills: an orphan "apprenticed" by the parish to a Peter Grimes or to a drunken collier at a small "day-hole" might be subject to cruelty in an isolation even more terrifying.[30] But it is wrong to generalise from such extreme examples as to prevalent attitudes before the Industrial Revolution; and, anyway, one of the points of the story of Peter Grimes is his ostracism by the women of the fishing community, and the guilt which drives him towards his grave.

The most prevalent form of child labour was in the home or within the family economy. Children who were scarcely toddlers might be set to work, fetching and carrying. One of Crompton's sons recollected being put to work "soon after I was able to walk":

My mother used to bat the cotton on a wire riddle. It was then put into a deep brown mug with a strong ley of soap suds. My mother then tucked up my petticoats about my waist, and put me into the tub to tread upon the cotton at the bottom. . . . This process was continued until the mug became so full that I could no longer safely stand in it, when a chair was placed besides it, and I held on to the back. . . .

Another son recollected "being placed, when seven years of age, upon a stool to spread cotton upon a breaker preparatory to spinning, an elder brother turning the wheel to put the machine in motion".[31] Next came the winding of bobbins: and, when ten or eleven, spinning or—if the legs were long enough to reach the treadles—a

[30] See M. D. George, *London Life in the Eighteenth Century*, Ch. V.
[31] G. F. French, *Life of Samuel Crompton* (1859), pp. 58-9, 72; see also B. Brierly, *Home Memories* (Manchester, 1886), p. 19.

turn in the loom. So deeply-rooted was child labour in the textile industries that these were often held up to the envy of labourers in other occupations where children could not find employment and add to the family earnings; while the early hand-loom "factories" in the woollen industry met with opposition on the grounds that they would lead to child unemployment. If the factory system were to prevail, declared one witness in 1806,

... it will call all the poor labouring men away from their habitations and their homes into Factories, and there ... they will not have the help and the advantage from their families which they have had at home. Supposing I was a parent and had four or five or six children, and one of them was 14, another 12, another 10; if I was working with my family at home, I could give them employment, one to wind bobbins, another to work at the loom and another at the jenny; but if I go to the Factory they will not allow me to take these boys, but I must leave them to the wide world to perish. ...[32]

By contemporary standards this was arduous, even brutal. In all homes girls were occupied about the baking, brewing, cleaning and chores. In agriculture, children— often ill-clothed—would work in all weathers in the fields or about the farm. But, when compared with the factory system, there are important qualifications. There was some variety of employment (and monotony is peculiarly cruel to the child). In normal circumstances, work would be intermittent: it would follow a cycle of tasks, and even regular jobs like winding bobbins would not be required all day unless in special circumstances (such as one or two children serving two weavers). No infant had to tread cotton in a tub for eight hours a day and for a six-day week. In short, we may suppose a graduated introduction to work, with some relation to the child's capacities and age, interspersed with running messages, blackberrying, fuel-gathering or play. Above all, the work was within the family economy and under parental care. It is true that parental attitudes to children were exceptionally severe in the 18th century. But no case has been made out for a general sadism or lack of love.

This interpretation is validated by two other circumstances: the persistence, in the 18th century, of games, dances and sports which would have been scarcely possible if children had been confined for factory hours: and the resistance of the hand workers to sending their children into the early mills, which was one cause for the employment in them of pauper apprentices. But it was not the factory only—nor, perhaps, mainly—which led to the intensification of child labour between 1780 and 1830. It was, first, the fact of specialisation itself, the increasing differentiation of economic roles, and the break-up of the family economy. And, second, the breakdown of late 18th-century hamanitarianism; and the counter-revolutionary climate of the Wars, which nourished the arid dogmatisms of the employing class.

We shall return to the second point. As to the first, nearly all the vices known to the 18th century were perpetuated in the early decades of the 19th, but in an intensified form. As Dickens knew, Peter Grimes was as likely to be found in early Victorian London as in Georgian Aldeburgh. The reports of the Children's Employment Commissions of 1842 showed new-model Boards of Guardians, in Staffordshire, Lancashire and Yorkshire, still getting rid of pauper boys of six, seven and eight, by apprenticing them to colliers, with a guinea thrown in "for clothes." The boys were "wholly in the power of the butties" and received not a penny of pay; one boy in Halifax who was beaten by his master and had coals thrown at him ran away, slept in

[32] *Committee of the Woollen Trade* (1806), p. 49.

disused workings, and ate "for a long time the candles that I found in the pits that the colliers left overnight."[33] The mixture of terror and of fatalism of the children comes through in the laconic reports. An eight-year-old girl, employed for thirteen hours a "day," to open and close traps: "I have to trap without a light, and I'm scared. . . .Sometimes I sing when I've light, but not in the dark; I dare not sing then." Or seventeen-year-old Patience Kershaw, who discussed the merits of different employments:

. . . the bald place upon my head is made by thrusting the corves; my legs have never swelled, but sisters' did when they went to mill: I hurry the corves a mile and more under ground and back; they weigh 8 cwt. . . .the getters that I work for are naked except their caps . . . sometimes they beat me, if I am not quick enough. . . . .I would rather work in mill than in coalpit.[34]

This is no more than the worst 18th-century conditions multiplied. But specialisation and economic differentiation led to children outside the factories being given special tasks, at piece-rates which demanded monotonous application for ten, twelve or more hours. We have already noted the card-setting village of Cleckheaton, where "little toddling things of four years old . . . were kept hour after hour at the monotonous task of thrusting the wires into cards with their tiny fingers until their little heads were dazed, their eyes red and sore, and the feebler ones grew bent and crooked." This might still be done at home, and the evidence suggests that sweated child labour of this sort was if anything increasing throughout the early decades of the century in most outwork industries, in rural industries (straw-plaiting, lace), and in the dishonourable trades.[35] The crime of the factory system was to inherit the worst features of the domestic system in a context which had none of the domestic compensations: "it systematized child labour, pauper and free, and exploited it with persistent brutality . . . ."[36] In the home, the child's conditions will have varied according to the temper of parents or of master; and to some degree his work will have been scaled according to his ability. In the mill, the machinery dictated environment, discipline, speed and regularity of work and working hours, for the delicate and the strong alike.

We do not have to rehearse the long and miserable chronicle of the child in the mill, from the early pauper apprentice mills to the factory agitation of the 1830s and 1840s. But, since comforting notions are now abroad as to the "exaggerated" stories of contemporaries and of historians, we should discuss some of the qualifications. Most of them are to be found in a provocative, almost light-hearted, article published by Professor Hutt in 1926. A spoonful of lemon-juice is sometimes good for the system, but we cannot live on lemon-juice for ever. This slight, scarcely documented, and often directly misleading article, has appeared in footnotes until this day and has been republished in *Capitalism and the Historians*.[37] Nearly every point which it makes was anticipated and met in the arguments of the 10 Hour advocates; and notably in John Fielden's restrained and well-documented *The Curse of the Factory*

[33] *Children's Employment Commission. Mines* (1842), p. 43.
[34] Ibid., pp. 71, 80.
[35] It is to be noted that some of the worst examples in Marx's *Capital* are taken from the Children's Employment Commission of the 1860's.
[36] H. L. Beales, *The Industrial Revolution* (1928), p. 60.
[37] W. H. Hutt, "The Factory System of the Early Nineteenth Century", *Economica*, March 1926.

*System* (1836) whose republication would be a more useful service to scholarship.

It would be tedious to go over all the points. It is true that some of the worst atrocities were inflicted upon pauper apprentices at the end of the 18th century, and that the parish apprenticeship system gave way increasingly to "free" labour in the 19th. It is true—and it is heartening to know—that some employers, like Samuel Oldknow and the Gregs, provided fairly decent conditions for their apprentices. It is true that some reformers dug up the worst cases, and quoted them many years after the event. But it is by no means true that this provides evidence as to the extinction of the same abuses in the 1830s. (The reformers often encountered the greatest difficulty in securing sworn evidence of contemporary abuses, for the simple reason that the workers were in fear of losing their employment.) It is true that Peel's two Acts, of 1802 and 1819, indicate both a stirring of humanity and an attempt on the part of some of the larger masters to enforce regulation upon their smaller or most unscrupulous rivals. It is true also that there was a general improvement in conditions in Manchester, Stockport and environs by 1830. But this improvement did not extend to remoter areas or country districts nor outside the cotton industry. And since the first three decades of the 19th century see a great expansion in country mills, as well as the introduction of the full factory system to worsted-spinning, and its expansion in silk and flax, the gains of Manchester are offset by the abuses of Bradford, Halifax, Macclesfield, and the Lancashire uplands.

It is true—and a point which is frequently cited—that the evidence brought before Sadler's Committee of 1832 was partisan; and that historians such as the Hammonds, and Hutchins and Harrison (but not Fielden or Engels), may be criticised for drawing upon it too uncritically. With Oastler's help, Short-Time Committees of the workers organised the collection of evidence—notably from the West Riding—for presentation to this Committee; its Chairman, Michael Sadler, was the leading parliamentary champion of the 10 Hour Bill; and its evidence was published before any evidence had been taken from the employers. But it does not follow that the evidence before Sadler's Committee can therefore be assumed to be untrue. In fact, anyone who reads the bulk of the evidence will find that it has an authenticity which compels belief, although care must be taken to discriminate between witnesses, and to note the differences between some of the worst conditions in small mills in smaller centres (for example, Keighley and Dewsbury) as compared with conditions in the larger mills in the great cotton towns. There is no basis for Professor Hutt's assertions that the Factory Commission appointed—on the master's insistence—in the following year provided "effective answers to nearly all the charges made before [Sadler's] committee"; nor that the charges of systematic cruelty to children were "shown to have been entirely without foundation"; nor that "such deliberate cruelties as did exist were practised on children by the operatives themselves, against the will and against the knowledge of the masters." Much of the evidence before the Commission tends towards different conclusions. Moreover, where the evidence conflicts, one is at a loss to follow the logic by which we are asked to give unhesitating preference to that adduced by the masters (and their over-lookers) as against that of their employees.[38]

Those who, like Professors Hutt and Smelser, exalt the evidence of the Factory Commission (1833) as opposed to that of Sadler's Committee, are guilty of the same error as that of which the Hammonds are accused. Rightly or wrongly, Oastler and the

---

[38] *Capitalism and the Historians,* pp. 165-6. Professor Hutt even repeats the *canaille* of the masters and of Dr. Ure, such as the baseless charge that John Doherty had been convicted of a "gross assault" on a woman.

Short-Time Committees regarded the appointment of this Commission as a deliberate measure of procrastination, and the Commissioners as instruments of the employers. As a matter of policy they refused to give evidence before them. The movements of the Assistant Commissioners in the factory districts were closely watched. They were criticised for dining and wining with the mill-owners and for spending only a derisory portion of their time in inspection. It was noted that mills were specially whitewashed and cleansed, and under-age children removed from sight, before their visits. The workers contented themselves with mounting hostile demonstrations.[39] The reports of the Commissioners were subjected to as much criticism from the workers' side as that of Sadler's Committee received from the employers.

"I was requested by one of my neighbours," declared one of Sadler's witnesses,

> . . . to recommend the Committee to come to Leeds Bridge at half past five o'clock in the morning, while the poor factory children are passing, and they would then get more evidence in one hour there than they will in seven years examination. I have seen some children running down to the mill crying, with a bit of bread in their hand, and that is all they may have till twelve o'clock at noon: crying for fear of being too late.

Even if we leave the stories of sadistic overlookers aside, there was then commenced a day, for multitudes of children, which did not end until seven or eight o'clock; and in the last hours of which children were crying or falling asleep on their feet, their hands bleeding from the friction of the yarn in "piecing," even their parents cuffing them to keep them awake, while the overlookers patrolled with the strap. In the country mills dependent upon water-power, night work or days of fourteen and sixteen hours were common when they were "thronged." If Professor Hutt does not regard this as "systematic cruelty," humane mill-owners like Fielden and Wood were in no doubt.

Nor are there any mysteries as to the attitude of the adult workers, many of whom were the parents or relatives of the children. As Professor Smelser has shown,[40] there is a sense in which the family economy of the domestic system was perpetuated in the factory. The child's earnings were an essential component of the family wage. In many cases, although probably not in the majority, the adult spinner or worker might be kin to the child working for him. The demand for the limitation of adult, as well as child, hours was necessitated by the fact that they worked at a common process; if children's hours only were limited, nothing could prevent evasion, or the working of children in double relays (thus lengthening the adult working-day). Only the actual stoppage of the mill machinery could guarantee limitation. If the adults also stood to benefit by shorter hours, this does not mean that they were indifferent to humane considerations nor does it justify the offensive suggestion that the great pilgrimages and demonstrations on behalf of the factory child in the 1830s were hypocritical.

It is perfectly true that the parents not only needed their children's earnings, but expected them to work. But while a few of the operatives were brutal even to their own children, the evidence suggests that the factory community expected certain standards of humanity to be observed. A spinner in the Dewsbury area, noted for his evil-temper and for striking children with the billy-roller, "could not get any one to work for him in the whole town, and he went to another place . . . ." Stories of

---

[39] See *The Voice of the West Riding*, 1 June 1833: "The men of Leeds—the working classes—have nobly done their duty. They have indignantly refused to co-operate with a set of men who, if they had the least spark of honesty amongst them, would have let the Tyrannical Factory Lords do their own dirty work. . . ." Also ibid., 15 and 22 June 1833 and Driver, op. cit., Ch. XIX.
[40] N. J. Smelser, op. cit., esp. Chs. IX and X.

parents who visited vengeance upon operatives who maltreated their children are not uncommon. Thus a witness before Sadler's Committee described how, when he was a child, he was beaten by the slubber. "One of the young men who served the carder went out and found my mother":

She came in . . . and inquired of me what instrument it was I was beaten with, but I durst not do it; some of the by-standers pointed out the instrument . . . and she seized it . . . and beat it about the fellow's head, and gave him one or two black eyes.[41]

This assorts ill with loose statements sometimes made as to the general indifference of the parents. The evidence of both Reports suggests that it was the discipline of the machinery itself, lavishly supplemented by the driving of overlookers or (in small mills) of the masters, which was the source of cruelty. To say that practices common to whole industries were continued "against the will and against the knowledge of the masters" does not require refutation. Many parents certainly connived at the employment of their own children under the legal age enacted in 1819 and 1833. It is to the credit of men like Doherty and of the Short-Time Committees that they campaigned imperiously amongst the operatives against such evils, encouraging dignity among the degraded and explaining the value of education to the uneducated. The Factory Movement also involved many thousands who were not factory operatives: the weavers who wished to "muzzle the monster steam": parents displaced from the mills by juveniles, and supported by their children's earnings. Gaskell saw (in 1833) that the workers' discontent arose less from simple wage issues than from—

. . . the separation of families, breaking up of households, the disruption of all those ties which link man's heart to the better portion of his nature,—viz. his instincts and social affections. . . .[42]

The Factory Movement, in its early stages, represented less a growth of middle-class humanitarianism than an affirmation of human rights by the workers themselves.

In fact, few arguments are so specious as that which proposes that because unlimited child labour was tolerated in the 18th century but, in its new and more intense forms, became less tolerable by the 1830s, this is another sign of the growing humanitarianism of "the age". Professor Hayek has referred to "this awakening of social conscience," to this—

. . . increasing awareness of facts which before had passed unnoticed. . . . Economic suffering both became more conspicuous and seemed less justified, because general wealth was increasing faster than ever before.

Professor Ashton has offered a variant of this argument. The Royal Commissions and parliamentary committees of inquiry of the early 19th century—

. . . are one of the glories of the early Victorian age. They signalized a quickening of social conscience, a sensitiveness to distress, that had not been evident in any other period or any other country.

And he has shown unaccustomed strength of feeling in his defence of the parliamentary investigators:

[41] Against such stories we have to set the appalling accounts of sadism, employed by adult operatives themselves upon pauper apprentices, during the period of the Wars. See J. Brown, *Memoir of Robert Blincoe* (Manchester, 1832), pp. 40-1.

[42] P. Gaskell, *The Manufacturing Population of England*, p. 7.

. . . a generation that had the enterprise and industry to assemble the facts, the honesty to reveal them, and the energy to set about the task of reform has been held up to obloquy as the author, not of the Blue Books, but of the evils themselves.[43]

Blue Books in the early 19th century served many purposes, but reform comes low on the list. Parliamentary investigations took place as a routine response to petitions; as a means of "handling and channelling" discontent, procrastinating, or fobbing off ill-behaved M.P.s; or purely from an excess of utilitarian officiousness. Ireland's decline through misery after misery to the seemingly inevitable climax of the Great Famine was accompanied by the absence of any important measure of alleviation—and by an average of five parliamentary enquiries per year.[44] The hand-loom weavers and framework-knitters were duly enquired into as they starved. Eight enquiries in ten years preceded the establishment of the police. (The fact that action resulted in the latter, but not in the former, cases is instructive.) Mr. Gradgrind was most certainly out and about after 1815, but as Dickens knew perfectly well he stood not for an "awakening of social conscience" or "sensitiveness to distress" but for efficiency, cheap centralised government, *laissez faire*, and sound "political economy."

The Blue Books (at least until we came to the great sanitary enquiries) were not the product of "an age" or the fruit of "a generation," but a battle-ground in which reformers and obstructionists fought; and in which humanitarian causes, as often as not, were buried. As for the upper classes, what we see in the 1830s is not a new "awakening of conscience" but the almost volcanic irruption, in different places and people, of a social conscience quiescent throughout the Napoleonic Wars. This conscience is certainly evident in the second half of the 18th century. The campaign to protect the climbing-boys, in which Hanway took a part, reached the statute book, against little opposition, in 1788. Every abuse returned during the Wars, and attempts to secure new legislative protection in their aftermath met direct opposition, and were thrown out in the Lords—for, if boys had been dispensed with, their Lordships might have had to make alterations to their chimneys.[45] All Howard's honourable work on behalf of prisoners left little lasting impression, as conditions reverted after his death. We have noted already how the infection of class hatred and fear corrupted the humanitarian conscience. It is true that Peel's Act of 1802 stands out against this darkness; but its operation was confined to pauper apprentices, and it was less a precedent for new legislation than an attempt to extend customary apprenticeship safeguards in a new context. What is more important—and was more disastrous for the factory child—was the atrophy of the conscience of the country gentry, the only men who had the authority or the traditional duty to protect the poor.

Nothing more confirms this atrophy, and the profound moral alienation of classes, than the manner of the real "awakening" when it came. Scores of gentlemen and professional men, who gave some support to humanitarian causes in the 1830s and 1840s, appear to have been living in the 1820s in the midst of populous manufacturing districts, oblivious to abuses a few hundred yards from their gates. Richard Oastler himself lived on the edge of Huddersfield, but it was not until the Bradford manufacturer, John Wood, *told* him about child labour that he noticed it. When girls

---

[43] *Capitalism and the Historians*, pp. 18-19, 35-6.
[44] See E. Strauss, *Irish Nationalism and British Democracy* (1951), p. 80: and Mr. Strauss's comment—"Ignorance of the facts was not one of the causes of Irish misery during the nineteenth century."
[45] See J. L. and B. Hammond, *The Town Labourer*, pp. 176-93.

were brought half-naked out of pits, the local luminaries seem to have been genuinely astonished:

> Mr. Holroyd, solicitor, and Mr. Brook, surgeon, practising in Stainland, were present, who confessed that, although living within a few miles, they could not have believed that such a system of unchristian cruelty could have existed.[46]

We forget how long abuses can continue "unknown" until they are articulated: how people can look at misery and not notice it, until misery itself rebels. In the eyes of the rich between 1790 and 1830 factory children were "busy," "industrious," "useful"; they were kept out of their parks and orchards, and they were cheap. If qualms arose, they could generally be silenced by religious scruples: as one honourable Member remarked, of the climbing-boys in 1819, "the boys generally employed in this profession were not the children of poor persons, but the children of rich men, begotten in an improper manner."[47] This showed a fine sense of moral propriety, as well as a complete absence of class bias.

But the conscience of "the rich" in this period is full of complexity. The argument that the impassioned "Tory" attacks, in the 1830s, upon the abuses of industrialism, voiced by such men as Sadler, Shaftesbury, Oastler, Disraeli, were little more than the revenge of the landowning interest upon the manufacturers and their Anti-Corn Law League makes some sense in "party political" terms. It is true that they revealed deep sources of resentment and insecurity among traditionalists before the innovations and the growing power of the moneyed middle class. But even a hasty reading of *Sybil*, of the Hammond's Life of Shaftesbury or of Cecil Driver's impressive life of Oastler will reveal the shallowness of any judgement limited to these terms. We seem to be witnesses to a cultural mutation: or, as in the case of 18th-century constitutionalism, to a seemingly hollow and conventional rhetoric which took fire, in individual minds, as a deliberate and passionate belief.

\* \* \*

On the other hand, while the virtual unanimity of complicity on the part of official Nonconformity exposed it to the biblical attacks of Bull and Oastler, as well as of Short-Time Committee operatives (some of whom had first learned their texts in the mill-owners' own Sunday schools), it should by no means be supposed that the Established Church was working unitedly and without remission on the children's behalf. Indeed, we have it from Shaftesbury himself—who would surely have given credit to the Church if it were due—that with the notable exception of Bull the Anglican clergy as "a body . . . will do nothing".[48]

The claim, then, as to a general "awakening of conscience" is misleading. What it does is to belittle the veritable fury of compassion which moved the few score northern professional men who took up the cause of the children; the violence of the opposition to them, which drove them on occasions into near-revolutionary courses; and—as humanitarian historians have tended to do—it underestimates the part played in the agitation over twenty and more strenuous years, by such men as John Doherty and the workers' own Short-Time Committees. More recently, one writer has surveyed the issue with that air of boredom appropriate to the capacious conscience of the

---

[46] *Children's Employment Commission. Mines* (1842), p. 80.
[47] Cited in *The Town Labourer*, p. 190.
[48] E. Hodder, *Life of Shaftesbury* (1887 edn.), pp. 175, 378.

Nuclear Age. The modern reader, he says, "well disciplined by familiarity with concentration camps" is left "comparatively unmoved" by the spectacle of child labour.[49] We may be allowed to reaffirm a more traditional view: that the exploitation of little children, on this scale and with this intensity, was one of the most shameful events in our history.

[49] R. M. Hartwell, "Interpretations of the Industrial Revolution in England," *Journal of Econ. Hist.*, XIX, 2, June 1959.

# THE AGE OF STATE BUILDING

# 9 / Reason of State: The Legacy of Machiavelli

In 1924, in *Die Idee der Staatsräson in der neueren Geschichte,* the late Friedrich Meinecke gave a historical formulation of reason of state (*raison d'état*) based on a study of certain political philosophers from the sixteenth through the nineteenth centuries. Numerous German editions and an English translation in 1957 attest to the endurance of Meinecke's now classic formulation.

For Meinecke, reason of state is "the fundamental principle of national conduct, the State's first law of motion." The state is "an organic structure whose full power can only be maintained by allowing it in some way to continue growing; and reason of state indicates both the path and the goal for such a growth."[1]

Although Meinecke finds that reason of state operated in classical antiquity and that medieval Christendom "moved continuously toward a new center of Will concentrated in the State,"[2] he sees reason of state first revealed as a fully developed idea in the writings of Machiavelli. It is, in fact, so fully revealed that in Meinecke's study subsequent elaborations of the idea are often judged on the extent to which they represent an understanding or misreading of Machiavelli.

With Machiavelli, the State becomes the highest good and law; in the person of its rulers, it must be able to do whatever it wants, provided it is for the good of the whole community and not just for the personal aggrandizement of the ruler. This Meinecke calls Machiavelli's "ancient heathen idealism of the State." But the other side of the coin is "the ancient heathen realism of his statecraft."[3] Necessity of state may clash with the traditional morality, in which case the former must prevail, a position graphically described in certain passages of *The Prince* and one which the Church and other detractors of Machiavelli were quick to seize on. But as Meinecke puts it, "what was publicly condemned was secretly acted on," and he regrets that it was Machiavelli's realism rather than his idealism that influenced historical life.[4]

At all events, for better or worse, with Machiavelli we have a rationale for the absolute monarchy of a Louis XIV and, as some scholars would maintain, the nationalisms and imperialisms of the nineteenth century or even certain aspects of present-day statecraft. In the first selection that follows, Meinecke explains Machiavelli's uniqueness—the revolutionary nature of his thought and "the historical power of his work." Also, because Meinecke believes reason of state is an operative force in history, he takes care to analyze that ethical side of Machiavelli's writings which is often neglected or misunderstood.

---

[1] Friedrich Meinecke, *Machiavellism, The Doctrine of Raison d'Etat and Its Place in Modern History* (trans. Douglas Scott) (New Haven, Conn.: Yale University Press, 1957), p. 1.
[2] *Ibid.,* pp. 26-27.
[3] *Ibid.,* p. 45.
[4] *Ibid.,* pp. 44-45.

Carl Friedrich, political scientist and historian, has praised Meinecke's classic,[5] but in the second selection below, he presents an analysis of Machiavelli's thought which questions Meinecke's assertion, found in the first selection, that Machiavelli was the first to understand the real nature of reason of state. The second selection is a chapter from Friedrich's *Constitutional Reason of State: The Survival of the Constitutional Order.* In the preface to this book, Friedrich has noted that Meinecke paid "scant attention" to the *"rational* basis" of the idea of reason of state and to "that aspect of it which we are particularly concerned with here: reason of state in its application to the government of law, the constitutional order, in short 'constitutional reason of state' or more precisely 'reason of the constitutional state.' "[6]

[5] C. J. Friedrich, *Constitutional Reason of State: The Survival of the Constitutional Order* (Providence, R. I.: Brown University Press, 1957), pp. 120 ff.
[6] *Ibid.,* p. vii.

# MACHIAVELLI

Friedrich Meinecke

\* \* \*

It was a historical necessity that the man, with whom the history of the idea of *raison d'état* in the modern Western world begins and from whom Machiavellism takes its name, had to be a heathen; he had to be a man to whom the fear of hell was unknown, and who on the contrary could set about his life-work of analysing the essence of *raison d'état* with all the naïvety of the ancient world.

Niccolò Machiavelli was the first to do this. We are concerned here with the thing itself, not with the name for it, which he still did not possess. Machiavelli had not yet compressed his thoughts on *raison d'état* into a single slogan. Fond as he was of forceful and meaningful catch-words (coining many himself), he did not always feel the need to express in words the supreme ideas which filled him; if, that is, the thing itself seemed to him self-evident, if it filled him completely. For example, critics have noticed that he fails to express any opinion about the real final purpose of the State, and they have mistakenly deduced from this that he did not reflect on the subject.[1] But, as we shall soon see, his whole life was bound up with a definite supreme purpose of the State. And in the same way his whole political way of thought is nothing else but a continual process of thinking about *raison d'état*.

Machiavelli's system of thought was brought into being by an absolutely special and sublime, and at the same time extraordinary, conjunction of events: the coinciding of a political collapse with a spiritual and intellectual renaissance. In the fifteenth century Italy enjoyed national independence, and was, in the pregnant words of Machiavelli (*Principe*, ch. 20), *in un certo modo bilanciata* by the system of five States which kept each other within bounds: Naples, the Papal States, Florence, Milan and Venice. There was growing up in Italy, fostered by all the realistic elements in Renaissance culture and directly promoted by the arrangement (which was just coming into fashion) of having permanent embassies, a form of statecraft which was carried on according to fixed and definite rules. This statecraft culminated in the principle of *divide et impera*, it taught that everything ought to be considered with a view to its usefulness, it surmounted all religious and moral limitations in a naïvely playful manner, but itself functioned by means of relatively simple and mechanical operations and thought-processes.[2] Only the catastrophes which overtook Italy after 1494, with the invasion by the French and the Spanish, the decline of Neapolitan and Milanese independence, the precipitate change in the form of government in Florence, and most of all the collective impact of foreign countries on the entire Apennine peninsula—only these

---

[1] Heyer, *Der Machiavellismus*, 1918, p. 29; *cf.* also A. Schmidt, *N. Machiavelli und die allgemeine Staatslehre der Gegenwart*, 1907, p. 104.

[2] How the new calculating and rational spirit also arose simultaneously in economic life, particularly in the two mercantile states Venice and Florence, is shown by L. Brentano, *Die Anfänge des modernen Kapitalismus*, 1916.

catastrophes succeeded in maturing the spirit of politics to that point of passionate strength, depth and acuteness, which is revealed in Machiavelli. As a secretary and diplomat of the Florentine Republic until the year 1512, he learnt everything that Italian statecraft had achieved up to that time, and he was also beginning already to shape his own original thoughts on the subject. What caused them to pour out suddenly after 1512 was the crushing fate which overtook both him and the republic in that year. As a member of the party which had been overthrown and was being temporarily persecuted, Machiavelli, in order to re-establish himself, was forced to seek the favour of the new rulers, the Medicis, who were once more in power. Thus a conflict arose between his own personal and egotistical interests, and the ideals of republican freedom and the city-state which he had held up to now. It is indeed the greatness of Machiavelli that he strove now to settle this conflict, and bring it to a final issue. Against the obscure and not particularly attractive background of his own naïve and unscrupulous egoism, there came into being the new and masterly reflections on the relation between republic and monarchy, and about a new national mission of monarchy; it was in a context of all this that the whole essence of *raison d'état,* compounded of mingled ingredients both pure and impure, both lofty and hateful, achieved a ruthless expression. He had reached his fortieth year—the age at which productive scientific minds often give of their best—when after 1513 he wrote the little book about the prince and the *Discorsi sopra la prima deca di Tito Livio.*

A spiritual and intellectual renaissance must also, as we said, have been a formative influence. Machiavelli did not by any means absorb the whole of the Renaissance movement. He did not share its religious needs, or its urge towards speculative philosophy; and, although unconsciously steeped and bathed in its aesthetic spirit, he still did not value its artistic attempts particularly highly. His passionate interest was the State, the analysis and computation of its different forms, functions and conditions for existence; and thus it was that the specifically rational, empirical and calculating element in Italian Renaissance culture reached its peak in him. But a mere cool consideration of questions of political power would not have signified any complete spiritual and intellectual renewal. The faith and energy necessary to sustain it, and out of which the ideal of a rebirth could grow, were, so far as Machiavelli shared in them, of ancient origin. The spirit of antiquity was certainly not signalized in him (as it was in so many humanists of the Renaissance) by a merely learned and literary regeneration, with the bloodless rhetorical inspiration of a schoolmaster. Often his enthusiasm for the heroes and thinkers of antiquity shows a somewhat classicist lack of independence and judgment. But in the main the element of antiquity in him rose anew out of the tradition and hereditary feeling, which in Italy had never been entirely lost. In spite of his outward respect for the Church and for Christianity (frequently mingled with irony and criticism), and in spite of the undeniable influence which the Christian view had on him, Machiavelli was at heart a heathen, who levelled at Christianity the familiar and serious reproach (Disc., II, 2) of having made men humble, unmanly and feeble. With a romantic longing he gazed towards the strength, grandeur and beauty of life in antiquity, and towards the ideals of its *mondana gloria.* He wanted to bring back once again that united strength of sense and intellect in the natural genuine man, where *grandezza dell'animo* and *fortezza del corpo* combined together to create heroism. He broke then, with the dualistic and onesidedly spiritualizing ethic of Christianity, which depreciated the natural impulses of the senses. Although indeed he retained some of its structural ideas about the difference between good and evil, he strove principally for a new naturalistic ethic which would follow the dictates of nature impartially and resolutely. For whoever follows these dictates (as he said once) can find no fault in carrying on lighthearted amorous affairs in the midst of serious business—even Nature is full of change and contradiction.[3]

This kind of naturalism can easily lead to a harmless and unreflecting multiplicity in the question of human values. But (in spite of the offering which he gladly brought to the altar of Venus) Machiavelli concentrated all his real and supreme values in what he called *virtù*. This concept is exceedingly rich in meaning, and although it was taken over from the tradition of antiquity and humanism, it had been felt and elaborated in a quite individual manner; ethical qualities were certainly embraced in it, but it was fundamentally intended to portray something dynamic, which Nature had implanted in Man—heroism and the strength for great political and warlike achievements, and first and foremost, perhaps, strength for the founding and preservation of flourishing States, particularly republics.[4] For in the republics, of which Rome in its great republican period seemed to him an ideal example, he saw the conditions most favourable for the generation of *virtù*. It therefore embraced the civic virtues and those of the ruling class; it embraced a readiness to devote oneself to the common good, as well as the wisdom, energy and ambition of the great founders and rulers of States. But the *virtù* which the founder and ruler of a State had to possess counted for Machiavelli as *virtù* of a higher order. For in his opinion this kind of *virtù* was able, by means of appropriate "regulations," to distil out of the thoroughly bad and wretched material of average specimens of humanity the other kind of *virtù* in the sense of civic virtue; to a certain extent the latter was *virtù* of a secondary quality, and could only be durable if it was rooted in a people whose spirit was naturally fresh and unspoilt. This separation of *virtù* into two types, one original and the other derived, is of exceptional significance for a complete understanding of the political aims of Machiavelli. For it shows that he was a long way from believing uncritically in the natural and imperishable virtue of a republican citizen, and that he viewed even the republic more from above, from the standpoint of the rulers, than from underneath, from the standpoint of broad-based democracy. He appreciated the proverb, which was popular in his time, that *in piazza* your opinions were not the same as they were *in palazzo* (Disc., II, 47). His republican ideal therefore contained a strain of monarchism, in so far as he believed that even republics could not come into existence without the help of great individual ruling personalities and organizers. He had learnt from Polybius the theory that the fortunes of every State are repeated in a cycle, and that the golden age of a republic is bound to be followed by its decline and fall. And so he saw that, in order to restore the necessary quantum of *virtù* which a republic had lost by sinking to such a low point, and thus raise up the State once again, there was only one means to be adopted; namely, that the creative *virtù* of one individual, of one *mano regia,* one *podestà quasi regia* (Disc., I, 18 and 55), should take the State in hand and revive it. Indeed he went so far as to believe that for republics which were completely corrupt and no longer capable of regeneration, monarchy was the only possible form of government. Thus his concept of *virtù* formed a close link between republican and monarchical tendencies, and, after the collapse of the Florentine Republic, enabled him without inconsistency to set his hopes on the rule of the

---

[3] To Vettori, 31st Jan. 1515. *Lettere di Mach. ed. Alvisi.*
[4] CF. the work of E. W. Mayers mentioned by me, *Machiavellis Geschichtsauffassung und sein Begriff virtù,* 1912.

Medicis, and to write for them the Book of the Prince. In the same way it made it possible for him immediately afterwards to take up again in the *Discorsi* the strain of republicanism, and to weigh republic and monarchy against one another.

Moreover his own special ethic of *virtù*—a product of the joyous worldly spirit of the Renaissance—begins now to throw light on the relation in which he stands to the ordinary Christian, and so-called genuine, morality; this relationship has been the cause of much dispute and a continual subject of reproof to Machiavelli. We have already remarked that he retained the basic Christian views on the difference between good and evil. When he advocated evil actions, he never denied them the epithet evil or attempted any hypocritical concealment. Nor did he dare to embody direct traits of morally wicked behaviour in his ideal of *virtù*. In Chapter 8 of the *Principe*, which deals with Agathocles, he says that to murder one's co-citizens, to betray one's friends, to be lacking in loyalty, piety and religion, cannot deserve the name of *virtù*; these things can achieve mastery, but not glory. And yet in Agathocles, who behaved in this way, he recognized at the same time a real *virtù* and *grandezza dell'animo*, i.e. great virtues of a ruler. The ethical sphere of his *virtù* therefore lay in juxtaposition to the usual moral sphere like a kind of world of its own; but for him it was the higher world, so it could be permitted to trespass and encroach on the moral world in order to achieve its aims. These encroachments and infringements, these "sins" in the Christian sense, never ceased to be judged by him as immoral, and did not indeed constitute *virtù* itself—but they could in the last resort (as we shall soon see more clearly) arise out of *virtù.*

Let us first look more closely at his theory of *virtù*, and at the striking mixture of pessimism and idealism, of mechanistic and vitalistic elements, which go to compose it. In the *Discorsi* (I, 4), he says that of their own accord men will never do anything good, unless they are driven to it by some "necessity." Hunger and poverty, he goes on, make men industrious, and laws make them good. The penalties imposed on any infringement of the laws lead on towards a recognition of justice. For him, therefore, moral goodness and justice were produced and could be produced by the constraining power of the State. How high his opinion was of the State, and how little he thought of individual human beings! But this rigid positivist causal nexus was relaxed through the medium of *virtù*, and by a belief in the creative powers of great men, who, through their own *virtù* and the wise regulations which they made, were able to raise up the average level of humanity to a new, secondary form of *virtù.* Then too it was another mechanistic and fatalistic belief of his that, since the world always remained the same and all things were repeated in a cycle, *virtù* did not exist in the world in unlimited supply, but was passed round in the world continually, and now this, now that people was privileged to possess it. This was echoed by Hegel three hundred years later when, in his theory about the "dominant peoples of world history" (who are entrusted by the World Spirit from time to time with the task of directing its affairs in the world), he made the fatalistic element part of a sublime philosophy of progress and ascent. Machiavelli however contented himself with stating resignedly that only in ancient times did it happen that a single nation was blessed with a preponderance of this *virtù*; in modern times it was divided up amongst a number of nations. This brings out very clearly the similarity and the difference between the centuries. Surrounded by the collapse of the political world in which they lived, both thinkers cast longing eyes on the representatives of strength and efficiency in world history—Hegel with an optimistic belief in progress, the result of the century of the Enlightenment, Machiavelli with the old belief in the everlasting similarity of historical life, a belief which had always been fostered by the Christian disdain for this world and which the vital energy of the Renaissance had not been able to break down. But this vital energy was still strong enough not to lose courage even amid the collapse and in the face of the contempt of humanity, and strong enough to watch out for fresh *virtù*. For the development and creation of *virtù* was for Machiavelli the ideal, and completely self-evident, purpose of the State. To raise his own nation by means of *virtù* from the low point to which it had sunk, and to regenerate the State, if this was still possible (he continually wavered between doubting this and believing it), became his life interest. But this new political idealism was not indeed burdened with the serious problematical element which was inherent in the character of *raison d'état*. This brings us nearer to our real task.

It was certainly impossible, once the moral and religious bond had been severed which held together the mediaeval Christian ideal of life, to set up immediately a new worldly system of ideals which would have the same inner unity and compactness. For, to minds freshly released from the restraints of the Middle Ages, so many provinces of life were not opened up simultaneously that it was not possible at once to find a distinctive point of view, from which the secularized world could be grasped and comprehended once again as harmonious unity. One made discoveries, first in one place, then in another; one devoted oneself enthusiastically and often quite wholeheartedly to the discovery of the moment and became so completely taken up with it, that one had no opportunity to examine the contradictions and discrepancies between the experiences one had newly acquired and the human values which had held up till now. Machiavelli possessed this one-sided passion for discovery to an extraordinary degree. He threw himself on his particular aim of the moment in such a way that occasionally all he himself had previously thought and said was entirely forgotten. In a quite undaunted, now and then almost fanatical manner, he deduced the most extreme, and sometimes the most terrible consequences from the truths which he had found, without ever testing their reaction on other beliefs he held. In the course of his experimental discoveries he was also fond of changing his standpoint, and identifying himself for the moment with widely different interests in the political struggle, so that for each interested party, whether it be a prince or an enemy of princes, he could devise some powerful remedy, some *medicina forte* (and wherever possible a *regola generale*). His occasional recipes, then, should often be taken as having a certain degree of relativity. And these tendencies of his should be kept firmly in view.

The most serious discrepancy in his system of thought—a discrepancy which he never succeeded in eliminating and which he never even tried to eliminate—lay between the newly discovered ethical sphere of *virtù*, and of the State animated by *virtù*, on the one hand, and the old sphere of religion and morality on the other. This *virtù* of Machiavelli was originally a natural and dynamic idea, which (not altogether unhappily) contained a certain quality of barbarity (*ferocia*); he now considered that it ought not to remain a mere unregulated natural force (which would have been in accordance with the spirit of the Renaissance) but that it ought to be raised into a *virtù ordinata*, into a rationally and purposively directed code of values for rulers and citizens. The *virtù ordinata* naturally set a high value on religion and morality, on account of the influence they exerted towards maintaining the State. In particular, Machiavelli spoke out very forcibly on the subject of the indispensability of religion (Disc., I, 11 and 12); at any rate, he was strongly in favour of a religion which would make men courageous and proud. He once named "religion, laws, military affairs" together in one breath, as the three fundamental pillars of the State. But, in the process, religion and morality fell from the status of intrinsic values, and became nothing more than means towards the goal of a State animated by *virtù.* It was this that led him on to make the double-edged recommendation, which resounded so fearsomely down the centuries to come, inciting statesmen to an irreligious and at the same time dishonest scepticism: the advice that even a religion tinged with error and deception ought to be supported, and the wiser one was, the more one would do it (Disc., I, 12). Whoever thought like this was, from a religious point of view, completely adrift. What final certainty and sure foundation was there left in life, if even an unbelieved and false religion could count as valuable, and when moral goodness was seen as being a product of fear and custom? In this godless world of Nature man was left alone with only himself and the powers Nature had given him, to carry on the fight against all the fateful forces wielded by this same Nature. And this was exactly what Machiavelli conceived his own situation to be.

It is striking and forceful to observe how he strove to rise superior to it. On the one side *fortuna,* on the other *virtù*—this was how he interpreted it. Many people today (he says in ch. 25 of the *Principe*), in the face of the various blows of Fate and unsuspected revolutions we have experienced, are now of the opinion that all wisdom is entirely unavailing against the action of Fate, and that we must just let it do what it likes with us. He admits that even he himself has occasionally felt like this, when in a gloomy mood. But he considered it would be lacking in *virtù* to surrender to the feeling. One must rouse oneself and build canals and dams against the torrent of Fate, and then one will be able to keep it within bounds. Only half our actions are governed by Fortune; the other half, or almost half, is left to us. "Where men have not much *virtù,* then *fortuna* shows its strength clearly enough. And because it is full of change, so there are numerous changes in republics and states. And these will always go on changing, until sooner or later there will come a man who so loves antiquity, that he will regulate *fortuna;* then it will not be able to show every twenty-four hours how much it is capable of accomplishing" (Disc., II, 30). *Fortuna* has got to be beaten and bruised like a woman one wants to possess, and boldness and barbarity will always be more successful there than coldness. But this boldness has got to be united with great cunning and calculation, for each situation of fate demands a method specially suited for dealing with it. He began to meditate very deeply on just this particular problem, for it showed up very clearly both the powers and the limitations of *virtù,* and of humanity altogether. The individual agent cannot escape the nature he is born with. He acts in such and such a way because this nature requires it. Hence it arises that, according to the disposition of Fate, this same method which his character dictates will turn out well one day, and badly the next (Disc., III, 9). An insight of this kind could lead back to fatalism. But the effect on him of all these doubts and impulses was like the bending of a taut-strung bow. He let fly his arrows with all the more force.

Enemies learn to use each other's weapons. *Virtù* has the task of forcing back *fortuna. Fortuna* is malicious, so *virtù* must also be malicious, when there is no other way open. This expresses quite plainly the real spiritual origin of Machiavellism: the infamous doctrine that, in national behaviour, even unclean methods are justified, when it is a question of winning or of keeping the power which is necessary for the State. It is the picture of Man, stripped of all transcendent good qualities, left alone on the battlefield to face the daemonic forces of Nature, who now feels himself possessed too of a daemonic natural strength and returns blow for blow. In Machiavelli's opinion, *virtù* had a perfectly genuine right to take up any weapon, for the purpose of mastering Fortune. One can easily see that this doctrine, which appeared so dualistic on the outside, had really sprung from the background of a naïve Monism, which made all the powers of life into forces of Nature. It now became a presupposition for the discovery which Machiavelli had made about the essence of *raison d'état*.

But in order to make this discovery, yet another theory was needed—one which he thought out and applied just as clearly and consistently as he did the theory of the struggle between *virtù* and *fortuna*. This was the theory of *necessità*. *Virtù, fortuna* and *necessità* are three words which keep on sounding again and again throughout his writings with a kind of brazen ring. These words, and perhaps also the refrain of the *armi proprie* (which sums up the demands he made on the State in the way of military matters and power politics), show his ability to condense the wealth of his experience and thought, and how the rich edifice of his mind rested on a few, quite simple, but solid pillars. For him *virtù* and *necessità* were related in a way very similar to that in which, in modern philosophy, the sphere of values is related to the sphere of causal connection; i.e. where the causal connection provides the means and possibility of realizing the values. If *virtù* was the vital power of men, a power which created and maintained States, and gave them sense and meaning, then *necessità* was the causal pressure, the means of bringing the sluggish masses into the form required by *virtù*. We have already heard how he traced back the origin of morality to "necessity." We have discussed fully (so he says in the *Discorsi*, III, 12) how useful *necessità* is for human actions, and to what glory it can lead on. And (as several moral philosophers have written) the hands and speech of Man—which are the two principal tools for his ennoblement—would never have functioned completely, and human achievments would never have reached their present high level, if they had not been pushed to it by *necessità*. The old military commanders recognized the *virtù di tal necessità* and used it to instil into their soldiers the dogged spirit of combat, when they planned to put them in a situation where they would *have* to fight. Come with me, a Volscian leader shouts to the soldiers round him, in Livy (4, 28), *virtute pares, quae ultimum ac maximum telum est, necessitate superiores estis*. These were words to warm Machiavelli's heart. The more *necessità* there is, he insists in the *Discorsi*, I, 1, the more *virtù* there will be also, and *necessità* can bring us to many things, which reason is not strong enough to drive us to (Disc., I, 1). And alongside the conception of *virtù ordinata* he placed the equally characteristic conception of *necessità ordinata dalle leggi* (Disc., I, 1) as engendering first-class human material for the State. Thus it is always a question of following the natural forces of life, but also at the same time of regulating them by means of reason. If one were to adopt for a moment the unlovely nomenclature of "—isms," one could call his system a triad of naturalism, voluntarism and rationalism. But without his belief (rooted in universal history) in the positive *blessing* of *necessità*, without the real warmth which he gave it, he would never have come to proclaim with such determination and conviction that which one can call the *curse* of *necessità*, of necessity of State.

One more trait of his personality must have contributed: namely, the quite unconventional and at the same time radical nature of his thought, which never shrank back before any abyss. Certainly his contemporaries too had long learnt never to shrink back before any moral abyss, and to wade quite cheerfully through any filth. For if it had not been for the general stultifying of moral feeling in life, and without the examples offered by the Papacy from the time of Sixtus IV and Alexander VI, with his frightful son Cesar Borgia, Machiavelli would never have had the milieu required for his new ideas about the use of immoral methods in politics. They were indeed not new as regards content; but they were new in the sense that he dared to express them, and to combine them into a system which embraced a universal outlook. For up till now theory had only limped after practice. The selfsame humanists who, like Pontanus at the court of Naples, saw clearly all the dark side of the new statecraft, were indeed prepared to permit cunning and deception when it was for the good of the community; but after that they fell back once more on the formal pattern of the figure of the Prince, filled in with classic phrases.[5] If I am to offer something really useful, says Machiavelli, it seems to me more suitable to follow the real truth of things, rather than the imaginary picture one has of them. Many people have imagined for themselves republics and principalities, the like of which one has never seen or even thought possible; for the difference between what one actually does and what one ought to do is so great that whoever, in considering how people ought to live, omits to consider how they behave is riding for a fall. That is to say, the man who makes it a rule in all circumstances to perform nothing but good actions is bound to go under amongst so many who are evil. Therefore it is "necessary" for a prince, if he is to maintain his position, to learn also how not to be good, and then to utilize or not utilize this knowledge, as *necessità* prescribes.

It is worthy of notice that Machiavelli did not introduce near the beginning of his essay on the Prince this new principle of method—a principle which was to break fresh ground for so many centuries, and which was so purely empirical and so completely free from presuppositions. He does not bring it in till much further on, in Chapter 15. For he himself underwent development during the course of his work on the book. Chapter 15 belongs (as we have tried to prove elsewhere[6]), not to the original conception of the *Principe*, but rather to an extension of it which probably came soon afterwards. Henceforth he always exercised the new principle, which was closely akin to the aesthetic honesty and directness of Florentine art. Then, when he was in the full spate of work, he suddenly became conscious that he was treading new paths. It was the climax of his life, and at the same time also a turning point for the history of European thought. And in this matter history of thought touched very closely upon the history of nations; they were both struck by the *same* electric shock. Even if the statesmen themselves learnt nothing new from it, the very fact that it was *being taught* was still new. For it was not until after it had been grasped as a principle that the historical tendencies achieved their full power of impact, and reached the stage when they could be called ideas.

But the initial application of the new scientific method, and its effect on historical life, were frightful and shattering. A prince must also learn how not to be good—this was the requirement of *necessità,* by which all human life was governed and constrained. But it was quite another matter to decide whether, on the one hand, the moral law should be broken only in the practice of politics, or whether, on the other hand, it was permissible to justify (as from now on became possible, and in fact more and more tended to happen) such an infringement by the plea of an unavoidable "necessity." In the first instance the moral law itself had, in its sanctity as a supra-empirical necessity, remained entirely unimpaired. But now this supra-empirical necessity was broken down by an empirical necessity; the force of evil was fighting for

[5] Benoist, *L'Etat italien avant Machiavell. Revue des Deux Mondes,* 1st May 1907, p. 182; *cf.*
   [6] *Klassiker der Politik Bd. 8, Machiavelli, Der Fürst,* and so on, Introduction, pp. 32 ff. I was not convinced by Chabod's counter-arguments in *"Archivum Romanicum."*

a place alongside that of good, and was making out that it was, if not an actual power of good, then at least an indispensable means for obtaining a certain kind of goodness. The forces of sin, which had been basically subdued by the Christian ethic, now won what was fundamentally a partial victory; the devil forced his way into the kingdom of God. There now began that dualism under which modern culture has to suffer: that opposition between supra-empirical and empirical, between absolute and relative standards of value. It was now possible for the modern State, following its own inmost vital impulse, to free itself from all the spiritual fetters that had constrained it; it was possible for it, as an independent power acknowledging no authority outside this world, to effect the admirable accomplishments of rational organization, which would have been unthinkable in the Middle Ages, but were now due to increase from century to century. But it already contained the poison of an inner contradiction, from the very moment it began its ascent. On the one hand religion, morality and law were all absolutely indispensable to it as a foundation for its existence; on the other hand, it started off with the definite intention of injuring these whenever the needs of national self-preservation would require it. But surely (it will be asked) Machiavelli must have felt this contradiction, and the serious consequences it was bound to have?

He was not able to feel it, for the reason that his cast-iron theory of *necessità* concealed it from him, or because (as he believed, at least) the theory of *necessità* resolved the contradiction. The same force which impelled princes to refrain from being good under certain circumstances, also impelled men to behave morally; for it is only from necessity that men perform good actions (*Principe*, ch. 23). Necessity was therefore the spear which at the same time both wounded and healed. It was the causal mechanism which, provided that *virtù* existed in the State, saw to it that the necessary morality and religion were present, and that any failings in that respect were made good. Thus the theory of the struggle between *virtù* and *fortuna*, and the theory of *necessità*, worked together very closely to justify the prince in the use of underhand measures, and to prevent this from being harmful in his opinion.

For all the time Machiavelli held firmly to the absolute validity of religion, morality and law. Even in the most evil and notorious chapter of the *Principe*, Chapter 18, which justifies breach of contract, and declares that a prince (and especially a new prince), for the purpose of maintaining the State, "is often obliged (*necessitato*) to act without loyalty, without mercy, without humanity, and without religion"—even in this chapter he still emphasizes that a prince, when he *can*, should not leave the path of morality, but only that he should, in case of necessity (when *necessitato*), also know how to tread the path of evil. Bad indeed was the infamous advice which he gives here: that it is not necessary for the prince to possess all the good moral qualities of loyalty, sincerity, and so on, but that he must always appear to have them, because the former case, in which they would always be exercised, would be harmful, but the latter case where he appeared to have them would be useful. With this he helped to make any hypocritical scoundrel secure on a throne. It would throughout have been perfectly in keeping with his purposes and with the main line of his thought, to demand from the prince himself a certain inner moral restraint, even if it were united with the power to take upon himself, in a case of necessity of State, the entire conflict between State-interest and individual morality, and thus make a tragic sacrifice. But perhaps this kind of solution to the problem (one which Frederick the Great was to give later on) was still entirely alien to the intellectual climate of the period and to Machiavelli's own way of thought. The ability to think in terms of inner conflicts, violations and tragic problems, presupposes a more modern and sophisticated mentality, which perhaps only began with Shakespeare. It was in the spirit of the time to delight in tracing precise and rectilinear paths; and in opposition to the straight path of Christian morality Machiavelli laid down another path, just as straight in its own way, a path which was directed exclusively towards the goal of what was useful for the State. He then proceeded, with a pleasure which was characteristic of him, to draw from it the most extreme consequences.

But was it then, one cannot help challenging him once more—was it then really the well-being of the State which he had in mind when he wrote the *Principe?* Or was it merely a breviary for the Medicis, whose favour he needed and to whom he dedicated the book, in order to found for himself a new principality by recommending the methods of the frightful Cesar Borgia? We have tried to prove elsewhere[7] that this interpretation is much too narrow. The personal and contemporary political motives which induced him to write the book are undeniable; but from far back there also entered in his entire philosophy of the State, and also his longing to see Italy freed from the Barbarians. Cesar Borgia, with his rational exercise of cruelty and bad faith, must certainly have offered a model for the practical methods of power politics in the situation as it then existed. But the ideal and supreme pattern for the new princes in Italy must have been the great national liberators and founders of States, such as Moses and Cyrus, Theseus and Romulus. The whole book from beginning to end, even including the last chapter (which is sometimes erroneously taken to be an appendix and not an integral part of the book), grew up out of one uniform and fundamental conception, and is built up on the great theme of the struggle between *virtù* and *fortuna.*

It is certainly true that, as regards its technical chapters, the *Principe* can easily arouse the feeling the Machiavelli is only watching out for the personal advantage of the prince. In this respect Machiavelli yielded to his passion for one-sided emphasis and excessive subtlety in dealing with the *thema probandum* of the moment. But if his work is taken together with the *Discorsi* and the other writings and treated as a whole, then this impression entirely disappears. One sees clearly what is the real central idea in Machiavelli's life: namely, the regeneration of a fallen people by means of the *virtù* of a tyrant, and by means of the levering power of all the measures dictated by *necessità.*

This is what is peculiar to Machiavelli, and at the same time constitutes the historical power of his work—the fact that he, the first person to discover the real nature of *raison d'état,* did actually succeed in taking the measure of all the heights and depths to which it led on. He knew its depths, which lead down to the bestial element in Man—"thus it is necessary for a prince, that he should have a proper understanding of how to make use of the brute as well as the man" (*Principe*, ch. 18). He could in the process, as we already saw, when drawn on by his deep-rooted passion for analysis, sink much more deeply into the filth of bestiality than was strictly necessary in order to make a proper use of that bestiality. He knew also that a case of necessity of State (where perhaps a republic which is threatened by dangerous neighbours might be obliged to adopt a policy of conquest) did not represent merely a simple factual necessity, but contained in addition certain elements of power-drive and power-appetite—"molestation by others will give rise to the desire and necessity for conquering" (*la voglia e la necessità dello acquistare,* Disc., II, 19).[8] But he despised a

---

[7] *Ibid.*, Vol. 8.
[8] *Cf.* also *Principe*, Ch. 3: *E cosa veramente molto naturale et ordinaria desiderare di acquistare, e sempre quando li uomini lo fanno che possano, saranno laudati e non biasimati.*

mere insensible greed for power, the *brutta cupidità di regnare* (Disc., III, 8), and he always returned once more to the utilitarian middle way of *raison d'état*. Keep your head clear, he advised, so that you only wish for what is attainable; do not become presumptuous after victory, but, if you have a stronger opponent, take care to make peace at an opportune moment (Disc., II, 27). Nor should you exasperate an enemy with threats or insult him in words; threats make him more cautious, while insults will increase his hatred (Disc., II, 26). To draw hatred on oneself without getting any benefit from it is indiscreet and unwise (Disc., III, 23). Under no circumstances should a system of government be built up on a permanent hatred amongst the people. It would be better even to provoke an attack from the nobles, because there are only a few of them, and they can therefore be more easily subdued; but even here he advocated a rationally balanced procedure, "to refrain from reducing the nobles to despair and to satisfy the people" (Princ., ch. 19).

Political utilitarianism was also at the same time a policy of relativity. Nowadays, he taught, it is necessary to pay attention to the subject peoples, because the peoples are of more significance than the armies. The Roman emperors, on the other hand, had to accommodate themselves to the soldiers rather than the people, because the soldiers could do more at that time than the people could (Princ., ch. 19). Fortified castles may be useful or not, according to the state of the times; but not to be hated by one's people is better than any fortified castle (Princ., ch. 20). But each thing always has concealed in it some special evil that is peculiar to it (Disc., III, 11); therefore whenever one is acting in accordance with *raison d'état*, one must always be conscious of the spheres of uncertainty of change, and of two-fold consequences, in which it works. "No State ought to think that it can adopt a course which is absolutely secure, but it ought to reflect rather that all are doubtful; because it is in the order of things, that one can never avoid an evil without running into another one. Wisdom therefore consists in distinguishing between different qualities of evil, and in accepting the lesser evil as a good" (Princ., ch. 21).

As we have already seen, he adopted a relativist view, when considering the various forms which the State could take. The contrast between the monarchist bias in the *Principe* and the republican tinge of the *Discorsi* is only apparent. The quantity of *virtù*, which existed in a people, was the factor that decided whether a monarchy or a republic was the more suitable. So it was only consistent that, for his disjointed times, he demanded a monarchical despot and took this to be a necessity of State. The fact that the thing he was asking for might cut both ways was perfectly clear to him; he knew quite well that the tool of monarchical power, which with supreme art he was putting into the hands of the prince, could be misused in the interests of a purely personal greed for power. One can undersand why he does not proceed to treat this problem in the *Principe*. But in the *Discorsi* he gives it quite openly as his really sincere opinion, that only in a republic can it be ensured that public good will take precedence of private advantage, and thus make it possible for the State to achieve greatness (Disc., II, 2). With the passionate exaggeration into which he sometimes fell, he was capable of laying down, with reference to a city-state ruled by a prince, the following proposition: that what the prince did for his own advantage, would in most cases injure the State, and that what he did for the benefit of the State, would injure him.[9] Yet immediately afterwards he went on to modify his own crude conception, and

[9] His reference for this is to Xenophon's treatise *De tyrannide*—it is (as shown by Ellinger, *Antike Quellen der Staatslehre Machiavellis, Zeitschr. f.d. ges. Staatswissenschaften Bd.* 44, 40) the dialogue *Hieron*, which has been ascribed to Xenophon.

contrasted the barbaric type of oriental ruler with the pattern of the Western prince; in that, if the latter be of a normal human stamp, then he will have a uniform paternal love for the cities which come under his care, and he will leave their old constitutional arrangements undisturbed. It is also in the essence of Machiavellian *raison d'état*, as one can see, that with regard to the inner life of the State it should still wish to behave in a relatively conservative and considerate manner.[10] But ruthless acts of interference, when they were necessary to protect power against direct threats, were not thereby excluded. Certainly there also appeared on the horizon of his political imagination the wish-fantasy of a great regenerator of fallen States, "who, either through his own *virtù*, or by means of the *virtù* of a regulation" (i.e. of a general reform), would breathe new life into these States. The practical needs and possibilities of his time, however (and he generally based his calculations on these), did not go beyond the suppression of actual resistance inside the State, i.e. did not go beyond a rational and at the same time thorough opposition, by direct and indirect means, to all conspiracies. The aims of the later type of absolutism, with its levelling tendencies, were still completely foreign both to himself and to his time. Machiavellism had certainly opened up the road which led to them, but they themselves had not yet come in sight. It is for this reason that we see no signs in Machiavelli of *raison d'état* taking precedence over statute law, which in the seventeenth century (as we shall see presently) was to constitute the principal importance of *raison d'état*. On the contrary a fundamental respect for the existing laws was part of the very essence of his rational autocracy. "It is well that princes should know that, in the very hour when they begin to break the laws, and disturb old arrangements and customs under which men have long lived, in that hour they begin to lose the State" (Disc., III, 5).

All this shows that he moved on the ethical heights of a *raison d'état* which within the limits of his time could only have limited aims indeed, but which was capable of a vital consciousness of the good of the community, the *bene comune* of the whole people. And ultimately he was even capable of rising to the highest ethical feeling which is possible for action prompted by *raison d'état;* this sacrifice consists in taking on oneself personal disgrace and shame, if only it offers a means of saving the Fatherland. Occasionally he would express it in the very same breath with his prosaic utiliarianism: "It will always be difficult to win the masses over to such conclusions as these, which appear to indicate cowardice and defeat, but do in reality signify salvation and gain" (Disc., I, 53). But the heights and depths of his *raison d'état* are united in the most powerful manner by that phrase, which is to be found at the end of his *Discorsi* (III,41), and which must surely have sounded in the ears of a certain great German statesman during the First World War: that one may save the Fatherland even *con ignominia.* "When it is a question of saving the Fatherland, one should not stop for a moment to consider whether something is lawful or unlawful, gentle or cruel, laudable or shameful; but, putting aside every other consideration, one ought to follow out to the end whatever resolve will save the life of the State and preserve its freedom."

\* \* \*

[10] *Cf.* the advice in Ch. 3 of the *Principe:* "In newly conquered countries with the same language, the laws and taxes ought not to be changed."

# MACHIAVELLI: THE STATE AS A WORK OF ART AND ITS RATIONALITY

## C. J. Friedrich

In his justly celebrated study of reason of state, Friedrich Meinecke started with a chapter on Machiavelli. He frankly admitted that Machiavelli had not used the term, but he still felt that Machiavelli was the first who "thought through" the true nature and essence of reason of state. He furthermore felt that this was a historical necessity, because this could only have been done by a "pagan who did not know the terrors of hell, but approached his lifework with the naïveté of classical antiquity." Our view is quite at variance with this position. Meinecke himself points out that classical antiquity never grasped the problem in its true nature, because the ancient Greeks and Romans considered the state the highest value in life, and therefore ethics and political ethics "coincided." While this is only true in general terms, it is correct to say that political practice usually conformed to amoral patterns of expediency. The famous discussion between the Athenians and Melians to which we have already referred brings this out. But it is equally clear—and Meinecke fails to mention it—that Thucydides not only realized that the Athenians' bald enunciation of the doctrine that "Might makes right" shocked the Greek world, but also that this shock hurt the Athenians in later dealings with other Greeks and therefore probably contributed to their defeat.[1] Still and all, the main point is that Machiavelli broadly accepted the view of classical antiquity, namely that the state is the highest value. He was thereby precluded from seeing the issue of the clash between a transcendent morality and the requirements of security and survival of the political order in its more dramatic form. Meinecke himself remarks that Christendom, through the mouth of St. Augustine, passed the final judgment upon the outlook of classical antiquity in stating that *remota justitutia quid sunt regna nisi magna latrocinia,*[2] that is to say that without justice, states (kingdoms) are nothing but great bands of robbers. The Middle Ages lived facing this injunction, and in theory at least, all government was seen as strictly subordinated to law, not only the law of nature, but also customary law on a comprehensive scale. Yet that medieval world had passed from the stage of Italian politics long before Machiavelli came to consider the matter. More especially in the turbulent factionalism of Florence the actions of government were certainly not ruled by any scrupulous regard for law, whether customary or natural. And it is against this background of a cynical condottiere politics that Machiavelli's reflections must, it is

---

[1] *Cf.* John H. Finley, Jr., *Thucydides* (1942) pp. 103-104 and 208 ff., and David Grene, *Man in his Pride* (1950) esp. pp. 56 ff.

[2] It might be mentioned in passing that the phrase *remota justitutia* permits of several interpretations, depending upon whether one takes it to mean if, when, *or* since justice is absent; it should also be borne in mind that the phrase speaks of *regna* and not of *civitates.* The matter has been in heated dispute between the learned; men like Figgis, McIlwain and the Carlyles having taken markedly divergent views. But whichever way interpreted, there can be no doubt that St. Augustine insisted upon the transcendent morals which his concept of justice implied, oriented as it was toward God and the love which the just man will bear him.

generally agreed, be projected. If that is done, it becomes immediately clear that his views are inspired by a deep-felt desire to substitute a higher value for the rampant egoism of the times. Not that Machiavelli was the romantic nationalist, such as Fichte, Hegel and others in the nineteenth century saw fit to describe him. But he was indeed a true Renaissance thinker in that he wished to bring about a rebirth of that spirit of classical antiquity which was manifest in Athenian, Spartan and Roman patriotism. And like other works of the Renaissance, his version was not a mere copy, but was a vitally altered and reformed philosophy of politics: the state is seen as a work of art, rather than as the framework of education for virtue.[3]

This vital alteration and moulding is reflected in his central conception of *virtù*. *Virtù* which is often very misleadingly rendered as "virtue" is in point of fact meant as an antithesis to much that the word virtue implies: its Christian as indeed its Platonic and Judaic connotation.[4] But does this mean that *virtù* is wholly devoid of moral implications? Does it imply a *virtù* from which all notion of virtue is excluded, and stress is laid upon force and force alone? Some have argued that Machiavelli's conception of *virtù* might be summed up in the qualities of a successful highway robber or brigand chief.[5] Actually *virtù* is nowhere definitively defined by Machiavelli. It is a concept which was quite current in fifteenth-century Italy.[6] It is a complex and somewhat dialectical concept in which the Christian notions survive through their kinship with Stoic views which lie embedded in the Roman *virtus*. But Meinecke is right when he suggests[7] that the concept has a flavor peculiar to Machiavelli. This probably results from his pre-occupation with the state as a work of art. *Virtù* thus involves manliness, which means courage and prowess, but also self-discipline and steadfastness. *Virtù* means a willingness to fight, but also a willingness to sacrifice oneself for the *patria*. It means a determination to succeed but also a recognition of the civic obligation to serve. In short, *virtù* is, like the Roman *virtus* and the Greek *areté*,[8] the congeries of qualities required of the citizen of a constitutional republic such as Athens or Rome in classical antiquity; its nearest modern equivalent is excellence. It appears from time to time in exceptional degree in an outstanding individual, a hero who possesses the capacity for great political and military achievements. It is then that a state is founded or reformed. Thus *virtù* is the kind of

---

[3] This point has been developed by J. H. Whitfield, *Machiavelli* (1947), in a chapter entitled "The Anatomy of Virtue," basing his analysis upon F. Ercole's *La Politica di Machiavelli* (1926), but our own position differs somewhat in seeking positively to identify the grounds of Machiavelli's moral position. *Cf.* also R. de Mattei, "Fortuna e Virtù del Machiavelli al Lottino" in *Archivio di Storia della Filosofia Italiana,* VII (1938) Fasc. IV.
[4] Among the large number of studies on Machiavelli, one might mention, besides the works noted below, the following: Ettore Janni, *Machiavelli* (1927) (English ed. 1930); H. Butterfield, *The Statecraft of Machiavelli* (1940, 1949); Leonhard von Muzalt, *Machiavelli's Staatsgedanke* (1945); Leonard Olschki, *Machiavelli, the Scientist* (1945); Roberto Ridolfi, *Vita di Niccolò Machiavelli* (1954).
[5] Jacques Maritain, *La Fin du Machiavélisme* (1941); G. Toffanin, *Machiavelli e il Tacitismo* (1921) and *Il Cinquecento* (1929).
[6] See Ida Wyss, *Virtù und Fortuna bei Boiardo und Ariost* (1931) and E. E. Cassirer, *Individuum und Kosmos in der Philosophie der Renaissance* (1927).
[7] Meinecke, *Machiavellism, The Doctrine of Raison d'Etat and Its Place in Modern History* (1957), p. 39 f. Meinecke largely follows the study of his pupil E. W. Mayer, *Machiavelli's Geschichtsauffassung und sein Begriff Virtù* (1912) which Whitfield does not seem to have come across.
[8] On the *areté* concept, see Werner Jaeger, *Paideia–A Study of Greek Culture* (1934–1944). Jaeger in this renowned study shows the central position of *areté* in the Greek system of values.

excellence needed in the citizen of a republic and in the ruler and leader as well. In monarchies it is primarily needed in the ruler. But for Machiavelli the focus of interest was that higher *virtù* which characterizes the founder and builder of a state, the man of heroic stature who creates that most extraordinary of all human creations or works of art: a political order. Through such an order the conditions for an ordered and disciplined civic life, a *virtù ordinata,* are created, and thereby both fortune and necessity are mastered.

If the state is thus seen as a work of art, the human beings involved in its creation, as well as other material circumstances and relations are seen in analogy to the clay in the sculptor's hand, to the wood and stone of the architect. They have their material qualities and these qualities are given. Machiavelli sees them as *necessità,* something to be reckoned with and mastered. This notion of a necessity, of laws of nature which must be obeyed by him who would succeed, give the statesman-artist an opportunity for moulding his human material. Machiavelli speaks recurrently of the *necessità ordinata dalle leggi.* Here, too, he is the reviver of classical notions: for the lawgiven in Greek and Roman antiquity, the *nomethetes* of Plato and the *Rector Republicae* of Cicero are employing the laws to make men virtuous.[9]

But the world of politics is for Machiavelli not only compounded of *virtù* struggling with *necessità,* of human excellence building a political order in terms of the needs and requirements of such an order and of the obstacles that environment presents, but there must also be recognized the contingent intervention of good or bad luck. *Fortuna,* a Renaissance concept as current as *virtù,* is seen as wholly unpredictable and fortuitous. Machiavelli says that *fortuna* is a woman, and that therefore it is well to be impetuous when dealing with her. "It is necessary, if you wish to master her, to conquer her by force; and it can be seen that she lets herself be overcome by the bold rather than by those who proceed coldly." And in keeping with the views of the time, and presumably his own amatory experiences, he adds: "and therefore, like a woman, she is always a friend to the young, because they are less cautious, fiercer, and master her with greater audacity."[10] About half man's actions are governed by this unpredictable goddess, but the other half man can control, and in Machiavelli's opinion, the less wisdom and valor men possess, the greater is the role of fortune. States will thereforefluctuate less if a ruler or leader is ready to master fortune. They will continue to fluctuate "until some ruler shall arise who is so great an admirer of antiquity as to be able to govern such states so that Fortune may not have occasion, with every revolution of the sun, to display her influence and power."

It is evident that among these three ideas of *virtù, fortuna* and *necessità* which Machiavelli employs as a central frame of reference for his interpretation of politics, *necessità* is the most novel, though some discussions of *necessità* antedate Machiavelli. But it is this stress upon the harsh realities, the requirements of power and the bitterly felt needs of politics which distinguishes Machiavelli's approach to politics from the preceding medieval and humanist thought. For the stress here, as well as in classical antiquity's philosophers, had been upon what ought to be; in Machiavelli it is upon

---

[9] See *Discorsi*, I, 1 and 6 and II, Introduction as illustrative. Compare in this connection H. Butterfield's *The Statecraft of Machiavelli* (1941), which strikes a sane balance between those who would misinterpret Machiavelli as a perverter of all morals and a glorifier of violence *per se* and those others who would overlook the decisive challenge to all transcendent moral ideals, that is to say, transcending the political order, which Machiavelli's views imply.

[10] See *Prince*, XXV (at end). The role of fortune as discussed in the *Discourses* is well stated in II, 30 (at end) and in III, 9 (at end).

what is. Many of his most shocking remarks, such as the pointed *rebus sic stantibus* doctrine concerning treaties in the eighteenth chapter of *The Prince,* are rooted in this necessity which according to an old adage "knows no law." No law, that is, of a normative kind; political life is ruled by the "laws of necessity."[11] And therefore it behooves the practitioner of the art of politics to study these laws with cold detachment and to act accordingly. The Roman admonition *politica est res dura,*[12] politics is a hard matter, forms the heart of this doctrine.

This doctrine of necessity is the core of Machiavelli's much praised and much abused "scientism" (*Prince* XV). His works are replete with rigidly factual, existential judgments and of prudential advice based upon them such as "a prince therefore should be slow in undertaking any enterprise upon the representations of exiles, for he will generally gain nothing by it but shame and serious injury." Presumably what holds for a prince, holds for a republic as well. There is no need for dwelling upon this point, often disputed in terms which are derived from present-day aspirations in the social sciences, especially when seen in relation to public policy,[13] for basically Machiavelli's approach to the question is in terms of a naïve empiricism which would derive its material from casual observation, unchecked reports and uncritical reading of the writers of classical antiquity (*Disc.* I, 6). The results were, as has often been pointed out, most deplorably unscientific: his belief in a citizen army, at a time when there impended a revolution in the military field toward professional armies, his fallacious assessment of the political chances of Cesare Borgia, his recourse to the city state of classical antiquity in a period of rising national territorial states, his notion of the state as a construct, a willful creation rather than the result of forces associated with the growth of national communities and new economic forms, his altogether striking disregard of economic factors—these are only a few of the numerous illustrations for the highly unscientific nature of his alleged scientism. But the impulse was nonetheless there. Machiavelli wanted to understand the world as it actually is, he was certain that success in politics depends upon such understanding and he tried as best he could to make some progress in that direction.[14]

But the very cast of his thought kept him from "discovering" the problem of the reason of state. Reason of state as a doctrine merely constitutes, as we have said, a particular species of the generic class of behavior or conduct which is rationalized in terms of the means required to achieve a given end. It is incorrect to make an absolute

---

[11] I am reminded here of an incident which is said to have occurred at the commencement of the more radical phase of the English revolution. When some MPs protested at the doors of parliament house against being excluded by Pride's Purge, crying "By what law? By what law?" the sergeant-at-arms replied: "By the law of necessity."

[12] The doctrine is related to the rising emphasis on calculation and accounting in business and statistics, the *Rechenhaftigkeit* which Burckhardt, in *The Culture of the Renaissance,* stressed.

[13] See the volume edited by Daniel Lerner and Harold D. Lasswell, *The Policy Sciences* (1952), and the author's review article: "Is Public Policy a Science? " in *Public Policy,* Vol. IV (1953).

[14] This point has recently been stressed by Leonardo Olschki, *Machiavelli, The Scientist* (1945), but Olschki overestimates both the novelty and the success of Machiavelli. He overlooks the extent to which the type of question which he claims to be wholly novel had been dealt with by Aristotle and Polybius, *inter alias.* Nor is it clear why he should on the one hand say that Machiavelli is not an empiricist, yet on the other stress that he was essentially basing his conclusion on practical observation, rather than classical and humanist learning. It would seem that Felix Gilbert's approach,—which Olschki rejects,—is sounder, as put forward in "The Humanist Concept of the Prince" in *The Journal of Modern History,* XI, (1939). See also A. H. Gilbert, *Machiavelli's Prince and its Forerunners* (1938).

dichotomy, as the school of Max Weber and others tend to do, between this kind of rationality which Weber called *"zweckrational"* and the other kind which reasons about values or ends which Weber called *"wertrational."* The reason is that means and ends cannot be thus kept in two wholly separate and mutually exclusive boxes. Not only can means become ends, and ends means, as Weber recognized, but in many cases the one is so definitely implied in the other that they cannot be thought about as apart from each other. Machiavelli's approach offers a good illustration for this aspect of the matter, in that his view of the state (when he means the government or the political order by it) invests the state with such paramount value that it becomes the source of all other values. The state is for Machiavelli the supreme and all-inclusive good and therefore no genuine good can be found outside the state. As a result, Machiavelli sees no need for "justifying" the means which are required for building and maintaining a state. The state's security and survival are *"hors de discussion."* Consequently, we might say that it is self-justifying as any absolute value is (for that is presumably what absolute means). It is, in this connection, interesting to note that some of the passages in which Machiavelli is said to have expounded the infamous doctrine that the end justifies the means—an interpretation which is so general that it has led translators to impute it to Machiavelli when the plain purport of the words is quite different —actually merely state that men tend to behave in such a way as to achieve their ends. Thus the passage at the end of chapter eighteen of *The Prince* which is customarily translated as "the end justifies the means" says in the original that *attioni degli uomini . . . si guarda al fine,* an entirely reasonable proposition. For Machiavelli, in short, the problem of reason of state does not exist in its more pointed and typical form, because the necessity of acting in accordance with the state's requirements needs no justification.[15]

For those who later in the century came to expound the doctrine of the reason of state, more especially Giovanni Botero, who is credited with inventing the term,[16] the problem presented itself how such conduct as would rationally be required for the survival and security of the state might be "justified" within the context of Christian morality. For only those who had abandoned once again the idea that the political order is the source of all true value, and had through reformation or counter-reformation been re-confirmed in their belief in a transcendental source of moral judgments, were confronted with the problem of "justification." Reason of state in this perspective is the doctrine by which organizational requirements are fitted into the value system of Christian morals. But it is defined by Botero as the knowledge of the means which are suited to found a state, to maintain it and to enlarge it.[17]

When seen in this perspective, the position of Machiavelli can be further illuminated by

[15] In his learned commentary on Machiavelli's *Discourses,* Leslie J. Walker discusses the matter in a contrary sense, although he agrees that the doctrine that the end justifies the means has no place in *The Prince.* He cites, however, *Discourses* I, 9, 3 in support of the contention that Machiavelli espouses the doctrine here. But what does Machiavelli say? "Conviene bene, che, accusandolo il fatto, lo effetto lo scusi; e quando sia buono . . . sempre lo scuserà." But excusing is not justifying, but almost the opposite. See *The Discourses of Niccolò Machiavelli* (1950), pp. 118 ff. Machiavelli is here talking of "racconciare," or mending, of reforming a system. Significantly, and in keeping with his general outlook, he goes on to comment on the danger, in a monarchy, of a successor using the power he has inherited *ambiziosamente* rather than *virtuosamente.*

[16] See *Della Ragion di Stato* (1589) and in Latin *De Ratione Status* (1666) *passim.* Meinecke says nicely concerning Botero that his doctrine "represents a richly ornamented Jesuit church, developed out of the Renaissance style" which satisfied the friends of Spain and the Holy See as well as the admirers of the Republic of Venice.

[17] *Cf.* our definition above Ch. I, p. 4, for contrast.

considering finally the question of the role of religion, as seen by Machiavelli. Many have either assumed or argued from certain well-known passages that Machiavelli is a "pagan" in the sense that religion has purely heuristic value for him. Machiavelli might, from this viewpoint, have agreed with Marx that religion is the opium of the people. In point of fact, Machiavelli displays a very marked interest in religion. He notes at the outset in the *Discourses* that the greatness of Rome was due to her religious tradition, and he puts the founders of a religion at the very top of human beings. Indeed, he phrases the latter thought in such a way that one can become doubtful about the position of Machiavelli regarding the supreme value of the State. At the beginning of chapter X he writes:

> Of all men who have been eulogized, those deserve it most who have been the authors and founders of religions; next come such as have established republics and kingdoms. . .On the contrary, those are doomed to infamy and universal execration who have destroyed religions, who have overturned republics and kingdoms. . .

Not only is it difficult to believe that the man who wrote these passages desired for himself the title of a destroyer of the Christian religion, but one is obliged to wonder whether religion is not, after all, assigned a superior rank in the scale of values and whether transcendental morals is not thereby reenthroned. But this passage speaks actually of public opinion, not of Machiavelli's. And Machiavelli thereafter does not concern himself further with the problems of religion which he would have done, if religion embodied what to him was the primary value. Quite on the contrary, he discusses both the religion of the Romans and contemporary events in such terms as to suggest that the value of religion itself is due to its vital importance for a well-ordered state. Machiavelli might well have written the royalist slogan "no bishop, no king," but he would still have thought that it was the maintenance of the kingdom that was the primary consideration. Religion is an instrument, albeit a very important one:

> Princes and republics who wish to maintain themselves free from corruption must above all things preserve the purity of all religious observances, and treat them with proper reverence; for there is no greater indication of the ruin of a country than to see religion contemned.

> *—Discourses* I, 12.

The Protestant perspective on reason of state (to be discussed in the next chapter) may serve to open up a dimension of Machiavelli's thought which links him to the constitutional theorists with whose thought on survival and security we are primarily concerned. But more important unquestionably is the Roman Republican tradition. For to the extent that Machiavelli is inclined to look upon the Roman Republic as the ideal state which a hero embodying *virtù* might expect to realize, he is bound to find himself, as he recurrently does, confronted with a conflict between the type of virtue which the Romans, and more especially the Stoics, were stressing and the requirements which the state's security and survival posit. In a very interesting passage in the *Discourses* (I, 10) Machiavelli indicates this problem in commenting upon Caesar:

> Nor let anyone be deceived by the glory of that Caesar who has been so much celebrated by writers; for those who praised him were corrupted by his fortune, and frightened by the long duration of the empire that was maintained under his name, *and which did not permit writers to speak of him with freedom.* . . . .Caesar is as much

more to be condemned, as he who commits an evil deed is more guilty than he who merely has the evil intention ... Let him also note how much more praise those emperors merited who. . .conformed to the laws like good princes, than those who took the opposite course. . . (Italics mine.)

In elaborating upon this theme, Machiavelli shows clearly that he not only recognized a moral element in the qualities of excellence to be demanded of a prince, but that he attributed survival value to it; for these emperors, he says, did not need legions to defend them, "because they were protected by their own good conduct, the good will of the people and the love of the senate." The Neros, on the other hand, being criminals, were not even protected by all the armies in the world. It seems highly significant that Machiavelli speaks here of criminals, *scellerati*, and that he elaborates on this theme in terms specifically of *sicurtà*, security. He relates this contrast to the statistics about assassination and notes that wicked princes more frequently die by violence. It is clear from such passages as these that virtue in the higher moral sense is recognized by Machiavelli as a genuine achievement, and of real value. Yet such virtue must not be allowed to interfere with the work of the architect who builds or maintains or rebuilds a state. The normativity of the moral norms finds its boundary in the requirements of what the artist builder needs for his work. Here it would seem that nothing is wrong, except what is inexpedient, what will not work. Just as the builder will fashion his materials to suit his purpose, so the statesman, the founder, lawgiver and builder of a state will handle his human material on strictly operational grounds, that is to say, with strict regard to success. Since the state is man's greatest, noblest, most magnificent work, since the state requires man's most creative art, the artist engaged in this enterprise will act with strict regard to the end: *attioni degli uomini si guarda al fine.*

But Machiavelli does not stop at this general point, but recognizes the problems of security and survival of the constitutional order. He grasps the dangers to such an order itself which result from this problem. And how could it have been otherwise, considering his experiences in Florence and his close study of the Roman constitution?[18] But in spite of his sharp criticism of the abuse of the institution of the dictatorship by Marius, Sulla and more especially Caesar, Machiavelli has nothing better to suggest than such a constitutional dictatorship. In two chapters of the *Discourses,* he addresses himself to the proposition that "the authority of the dictatorship has always proved beneficial to Rome, and never injurious."[19] He specifically rejects those writers who "have blamed the Romans who first introduced the practice of creating dictators as being calculated in time to lead to despotism in Rome." Such a view is in his opinion the result of superficial study; "neither the name nor the rank of the dictator subjected Rome to servitude, but the authority which citizens usurped to perpetuate themselves in the government." If this title had not been available, then another one would have served; for "power can easily take a name, but a name cannot give power" (*perchè e'sono le forze che facilmente*

---

[18] On Machiavelli's environment, the most interesting recent study, and a remarkable one, indeed, is Rudolf von Albertini, *Das Florentinische Staatsbewusstein im Übergang von der Republik zum Prinzipat* (1955), especially pp. 15-90. See also the newest detailed biography of Machiavelli by Roberto Ridolfi, *Vita di Niccolò Machiavelli* (1954), *passim.* Felix Gilbert's "Bernardo Rucellai and the Orti Oricellari" in *Journal of the Warburg and Courtauld Institute*, X (1949), is very valuable on Machiavelli's relations to the "Republicans."

[19] *Discourses,* I, 34 and 35.

*s'acquistano i nomi, non i nomi le forza*). What really caused the trouble was the usurpation and the fact that the attachment to the constitutional order had become so weak as to make such an usurpation possible; for whenever the dictator was appointed "according to public law" he benefited the republic. He gives several reasons for this. First, the constitutional dictator was appointed for a limited term only. Secondly, the power of a dictator was restricted to removing a particular emergency. Thirdly, the dictator could not alter the constitutional order itself, abolish existing institutions (*ordini*) or create new ones. Fourthly, the appointment of the dictator was precisely circumscribed by the constitution itself (and besides the Roman method was a very wise one, he thought). When these conditions were fulfilled, and as long as "the Roman people were not yet corrupted"—a vital condition, indeed!—the institution of the dictatorship was beneficial. Machiavelli goes so far as to claim that this institution was among those essential to Rome's greatness. Without it, Rome would with difficulty have escaped extraordinary emergencies; he mentions the slowness with which regular constitutional arrangements work because of the division of power among several bodies. As a parallel, Machiavelli suggests the emergency powers of the Venetian Council of Ten. If a republic lacks some such system, it will either have to disregard the constitutional order or perish. And it is essential that in a well-ordered system there be no need for recourse to extraordinary (that is to say extraconstitutional) measures: for such measures are apt to create a pernicious precedent. Further to buttress his argument, he contrasts the *dictator's* office with that of the *Decemvirs,* and he shows how the latter, appointed for longer periods and with undefined powers, were able to convert a conferred authority into an usurped one which make them "tyrants." The dictators, clearly confined to dealing with a particular situation in a limited period and under the supervision of the established constitutional authorities could not do that.[20]

All in all, we find Machiavelli clearly aware of the problem, in its more general connotation, and content to advocate the Roman solution for it, namely a constitutional dictatorship. This sort of approach does not, of course, help with the creeping paralysis of what Machiavelli considered simply "corruption." This to him was a "natural" process, beyond the power of man to cope with.

If it were our purpose to explore the general development of the idea of reason of state, one would now want to turn to Giovanni Botero, who perhaps invented and certainly popularized the term, and who as we said above, sought to "justify" such reason of state within the context of Christian morals. But since we are here principally concerned with those writers who were "constitutionalists" and as such believed in a government of laws and not of men, we must leave these predominantly absolutist trends aside. We may, however, be justified in adding a few comments on the large number of Italian writers who, following Botero, developed the doctrine of reason of state in its various dimensions.[21]

In the course of their protracted discussions, reason of state gradually came

---

[20] For the application of these reflections to contemporary constitutional systems, see C. J. Friedrich, *Constitutional Government and Democracy* (1941 and 1950), last chapter, and the literature cited there. See also below Ch. VII.

[21] Extracts from some of these writers were offered by B. Croce and S. Caramella, *Politici et Moralisti del Seicento—Strada—Zuccolo—Settala—Accetto—Brignole Sale—Malvezzi* (1930); these and others have been the subject of numerous papers (see note 26 at end) by Rudolfo de Mattei, by far the most learned student of this literature in Italian. I owe to Professor Mattei's remarkable private collection the opportunity of consulting quite a few of these works.

to be identified with politics, because all the problems of politics have a bearing upon reason of state. Reason of state comprises all that is worth knowing about the state, that is to say, politics.[22] At the same time, the concept lost all its peculiar poignancy in such propositions as that it is not to be distinguished from civil prudence. "True reason of state is not different from civil prudence . . . it is not unconnected with moral virtue, nor with religion . . . it is the true rule of government . . . "Indeed man is born to it.[23]

In some of these writers, the idea that every form of government has its proper "reason of state" comes to the fore which later plays a role in the work of Harrington and more particularly Montesquieu. "To act in accordance with reason of state does not mean anything else but acting in conformity with the essence and form of that state which man has decided either to preserve or to establish . . . all reason of state revolves around the knowledge of the means . . . which are opportune for ordering or preserving a particular kind of constitution of the republic whatever it may be."[24] In him as well as other writers of this school, a strongly utilitarian aspect of reason of state arguments is noticeable, foreshadowing Hobbes, Hume and Bentham. This utilitarianism has, of course, Stoic and medieval roots. In any case, once reason of state is recognized as the rational means for maintaining a constitutional order, the road is opened toward a specific republican constitutional reason of state. It would be too much to expect such a development in these sixteenth- and seventeenth-century Italians. Suffice it to note that they were much concerned to show that a constitutional democracy such as Athens had its brutal side. Time and again it is pointed out that ostracism in such a state might be a rational means for preserving the political order. Nor is this their preoccupation to be wondered at when one remembers that after all Machiavelli's deeper attachment was to such a constitutional order, and hence his effort to discover rules of rational conduct were more particularly focused

[22] Mattei cites Cardinal de Luca as follows: "Questa parola *Politica* è sinonima, e dinota l'istesso che *la Ragione di Stato*, posciaché la parola 'ragione' abbraccia tutto quello che di giusto e di ragionevole dalle leggi Divina, naturale, delle genti, positiva e di convenienza si dispone ovvero si richiede anche tra privati . . ." Giovanni Battista de Luca, *Il Principe Cristiano Pratico* (1680) pp. 66-7 as cited in R. de Mattei, "La Posizione Dottrinale del Botero e le Recenti Interpretazioni Critiche" in *Bollettino della Società per gli Studi Storici, Archeologici ed Artistici nella Provincia di Cuneo* (1954) pp. 29 ff. and 49.

[23] Federigo Bonaventura (1555-1602), *Della Ragion di Stato e della Prudenza Politica* (1601; 1623), Preface. He as well as Ludovico Settala (1555-1633) and many others follow Botero in trying to distinguish between a "good" and a "bad" reason of state, depending on whether the prince is good or a tyrant. This leads to the paradoxical position that a good man may more justifiably do bad things than a bad one.

[24] Ludovico Zuccolo (1568?-1630?), *Considerazioni Politiche e Morali sopra Cento Oracoli d'Illustria Personaggi Antichi* (1623), esp. Oracolo XI, pp. 54-73. The passage is found in Croce's reprint, pp. 27-8. A similar distinction was developed by Scipione Chiaramonte (da Ossena), who in his treatise on reason of state (printed 1635) elaborates the differentiations, distinguishing ten meanings of *ragione* and two of *stato* (the land and people or the rulers and form of government). He obviously is making a sort of digest of earlier views, pointing out the contradictions in speaking of reason of state as good or bad, concluding that it is both good and bad, true and apparent. He finally differentiates six kinds of *ragion di stato*. Chiaramonte also clearly sets down the fact that one cannot contrast law and reason of state by assigning to the former the determinate rules. "Io nego non aver la ragion di stato materia determinata et regola determinata." When things change, other rules apply, but *ragion di stato* consists of very definite rules. At times, these may even take the form of law, "ma non sempre è legge: perchè ella è anco fallenza di legge, oltre che non ogni regola di ragion di stato sarà espressamente commandata dalla legge." Here the thought of Chiaramonte comes close to that of English writers on the prerogative. See pp. 82 f. below.

on such a state's survival. But as we have seen, Machiavelli did not elaborate an institutional or behavioral model as a solution to this problem.[25]

In conclusion, it is fair to say that Machiavelli and the Machiavellians and anti-Machiavellians had, in laying bare the hard core of how to conduct governmental affairs rationally and in accordance with scientific knowledge and understanding, touched upon the problem of an immanent conflict, an antinomy involved in the security and survival requirements of a republican (that is to say, a constitutional) government. But the introduction of the problem of a conflict between it and the transcendental norms of an ethic derived from a revealed religion had soon obscured the true nature of this issue, even though Machiavelli himself had vaguely seen and dimly perceived it.[26]

It required a more favorable institutional setting, and an extended process of constitutional development for these issues to crystallize into at least partial answers.

[25] Very interesting specific suggestions can be gleaned from Rudolf von Albertini's *Das Florentinische Staatsbewusstsein im Übergang von der Republik zum Principat* (1955), where the institutional setting of Machiavelli's thought is presented.

[26] The most penetrating guide to all this mass of literature is contained in a series of articles, published by Rudolfo de Mattei, under the general title of "Il Problema della 'Ragion di Stato' nel Seicento" in *Rivista Internazionale di Filosofia del Diritto*, 1949, 187-210; 1950, 25-38; 1951, 333-356, and 705-723; 1952, 1-19; 1953, 445-461; 1954, 370-384 and 369-383, dealing successively with (1) general problems, (2) origins, (3) Botero, (4) objections and corrections, (5) Zuccolo, (6) Ammirato, (7) prudence, (8) complete denials, and (9) Jus publicum. It is to be hoped that Professor de Mattei will be able to pull these fine studies together into a book on the problem of reason of state in sixteenth-century Italy. I should like to add the following studies by Mattei: L'idea Democratica e Contrattualista negli Scrittori Politici Italiani del Seicento" in *Rivista Storica Italiana*, LX (1948), pp. 1-51; "La Teoria dello 'Stato Misto' nel Dottrinarismo del Seicento" in *Rivista di Studi Politici Internazionali* (1948), pp. 406-436, and "Politica e Morale prima di Machiavelli" in *Giornale Critico della Filosofia Italiana* (1950), pp. 56-67.

# 10 / Louis XIV: Despot or State-Builder?

In textbooks or other histories, there is no understimating the importance of the reign of Louis XIV. In one form or another, they give it the dignity of an "age" in which other monarchs are most often represented as satellites of the "Sun King" at Versailles, and France is described as the leader of Europe not only in the magnificence of her court, but in statecraft, diplomacy, warfare, and the arts.

However, in the history of a reign which was founded on divine right absolutism and which lasted more than half a century there is room for differences of interpretation. Absolute monarchy by its nature raises the question of depotism. And the wars, religious persecutions, and attendant fiscal troubles which occupied so large a part of Louis's reign force the historian to ask whether these canceled out the positive achievements of the reign or whether, at the very least, they did not help pave the way for the ultimate collapse of the Old Regime in the French Revolution.

In the first of the selections below, an English historian, David Ogg, takes a critical view of Louis XIV's rule, calling it "irresponsible" and Louis "capricious." He also shows how Louis violated the fundamental law of the kingdom of France. Although Ogg does not use the word *despot,* it can be argued that it applies to the picture he draws of Louis.

The second selection presents the view of Roland Mousnier, the latest in the long line of French historians who have interested themselves in Louis XIV. He gives us a novel and interesting interpretation of Louis's power, which he finds both "autocratic" and "revolutionary." Mousnier prefers to concentrate on the positive aspects of Louis's statecraft and claims tha absolutism answered a demand for stability. He concludes that Louis "brought the class struggle to a point of equilibrium between the two classes which assured his personal power, and which maintained unity, order, and hierarchy in the Government and the State."

In the third selection, Mousnier offers some observations on absolutism and despotism, which while they go beyond Louis's reign, show the limits within which he ruled. They should help the reader decide whether the charge of despotism against Louis XIV is justified or not.

# LOUIS XIV: THE RULER OF FRANCE

**David Ogg**

Louis caused a record to be drawn up of the main principles which inspired his policy. The *Historical Memoirs,* written specially for the guidance of his son, the Dauphin, were compiled by editors under his supervision, probably in the years 1666–9; for this reason they take rank in the literature wherein kings expound the mysteries of their craft. It is true that the editors do not indulge in those flights of humour or irony which make Frederick the Great so readable; nor did they command that erudition, sacred and profane, which give such weight to the statements of James I of England; but nevertheless, the Memoirs authorized by Louis are remarkable for frankness and clarity, and they throw some light on his general principles of government.

God is defined as "a superior power, of which our royal power is a part." Kings are "absolute sovereigns, having full disposition of the goods of their subjects, both lay and clerical." Kingship is described as an exacting profession, perhaps the most strenuous of all careers; because it requires continual application to business, personal study of the minutest details, and a power of subordinating one's feelings to the interests of the State. For example, a king may have his love affairs, but these must be kept in their place; they must not interfere with the daily routine; the harem and the cabinet must be kept quite distinct. The true king combines two things—a man, subject to passion and error; and a living embodiment of the State, a bloodless personality which, like a corporation, knows nothing of sin or regret, and must function every day with the same inevitable regularity. Hence, a transcendental morality and intelligence, distinct from those of the ordinary individual. One instance of this transcendental morality is provided; how he kept his word with the Dutch when he went to their aid in 1666, and how Spain was so touched with this evidence of good faith that her government entrusted him with the personal safety of Margaret, his wife's half-sister, when she went from Madrid to Vienna in order to marry the Emperor Leopold. It is not a very clear illustration of either moral conduct or its reward; but it was the example chosen by Louis. Another virtue he couples with good faith—moderation. In illustration of this he cites the concessions which he made at the Treaty of Aix-la-Chapelle, and how these helped to establish confidence among neighbouring states. Here, again, he informs the Dauphin he had his reward; for the Emperor thereupon signed the secret treaty of partition with him. This illustration is weakened by the fact that the partition was made before and not after the Treaty of Aix-la-Chapelle; but the moral lesson is the same nevertheless. Louis would not, however, push scruple to extremes. There are occasions when, in the interests of the State, the king must violate his faith. This is specially true of treaties, which are full of compliments and assurances of eternal friendship; but nobody takes these seriously; for they are merely diplomatic embroidery; and hence there may justifiably be secret infractions of such obligations; indeed "everyone expects that there should." These are among the most noteworthy of the principles formulated by Louis XIV for the guidance of his son.

"Holding as it were the place of God we seem to participate in his knowledge." This is the keynote of Louis's policy. Inspiring his industry and application was this implicit faith in the divine intention of his kingship. It was not an unusual nor, at that time, an unreasonable claim; for its appeal was directed to the instinct for worship innate in man, and it attributed the origin of sovereignty to a source less artificial than the social contract; the exceptional thing was that Louis acted on this principle with a consistency and conviction without parallel in history. It is because of this sense of high purpose that he has so often been contrasted with idle or dissolute kings, and assigned such exalted place in the annals of monarchy.

Louis's rule may be considered briefly according as it concerned the Court, the Church and the Nation.

Ever mindful of the Fronde, Louis completed the atrophy of the French nobility. This he did at the great palace of Versailles, the most enduring monument of the reign. Here, on sandy wastes he constructed architectural triumphs which, better than anything else, attest the monarch's love for spaciousness and lavishness. Though commenced in 1669, the palace was not finally completed until 1710, and throughout these years thousands of men were actively engaged in excavations and building. A chapel in marble and porphyry; avenues and parks decorated with fountains and statues; orangeries, woods and immense vistas; all these took shape under the direction of a king who loved to superintend every detail of this magnificent memorial. Not the least magnificent thing at Versailles was the King himself; there alone was his natural setting, its quiet greys and greens providing the best background for the flaming scarlet of the King's shoes and the tossing ostrich plumes of his hat. Bright flowers and tuneful sounds were among the few things that he loved passionately; nor did he spare any effort to procure an abundance of both; for even when conducting a campaign his thoughts were always of his palace and its gardens; and when he could not have his carnations or tulips he had his violins and hautboys. In the royal chapel mass was sung by a choir of select voices; dinner was taken to the accompaniment of the twenty-five violins known as the Grand Band, and another cohort of skilled instrumentalists officiated at fêtes and hunts. Music was an essential part of the routine of the Court. The Italian Lulli, supervisor of the King's music, made opera so popular in France that even the nobility were allowed to take part in it without incurring social stigma; most of the librettos were supplied by Quinault; and except for the absence of humour and the more recondite harmonies, the partnership of these two had the national importance which attached to that of Gilbert with Sullivan. The florid genius of Lulli accorded well with the monarch's taste; and in *Roland,* one of the best-known of these operas, was depicted the triumph of glory over every other passion, including even love.

At Versailles, in surroundings of almost barbaric splendour, were the Whitehall and the Monte Carlo of France. Here Louis read the despatches of his ambassadors, or penned his diplomatic memoranda, or received the envoys of foreign states; here also the nobility paid obsequious service of an oriental exactitude to a new Jehovah who functioned with such invariable regularity that it was possible to tell the time by observing his acts; or they exchanged fortunes at the card tables, which came out with the candles. At Versailles men lost their money and women their honour; but always in artistic surroundings; for there were canvases of heroic proportion in the Grand Gallery; there were frequent performances of the comedies of Molière or the tragedies of Racine; and if one were insensitive to these things, there were yet the furniture and the tapestry to compel admiration. There was a profusion of gilt and colour; of contrast between the small noisome apartments in which the courtiers slept and the great public chambers in which the King held state; but it was exotic, and was no place for the natural frankness and wit of the French people. It remained the residence of the French monarchy until 1789; in 1830 Louis Philippe made it a national museum.

The Queen took little part in this public life. Her place was at first taken by Mademoiselle de la Vallière, one of the maids of honour to the duchess of Orlèans, by whom Louis had two children; in 1667 she was succeeded by another maid-of-honour, Madame de Montespan; of whose children three survived. These five natural children were all legitimized, and so were given a contingent right of succession to the French throne. In 1684, one year after the death of Maria Theresa, Louis married the nurse of one of these children—Madame de Maintenon, widow of the poet Scarron; but the bride was not accorded the status of Queen. She was in a class quite different from that of the women in whom Louis had hitherto taken pleasure; for she had refinement and a sympathetic understanding, and she influenced her royal consort by her qualities of mind and character. It is difficult to prove that she exercised a restraining influence on Louis; indeed it is more likely that she deepened and hardened her husband's piety, and created in him a greater solicitude for his spiritual welfare, soon to be reflected in his attitude to heretics; but of Madame de Maintenon's charm there can be no doubt; and in these lines which Ahasuerus addresses to Esther, it is certain that Racine depicted the royal consort:

Je ne trouve qu'en vous je ne sais quelle grâce
Qui me charme toujours et jamais ne me lasse.
De l'aimable vertu doux et puissant attraits!
Tout réspire en Esther l'innocence et la paix;
Du chagrin le plus noir elle écarte les ombres
Et fait des jours sereins de mes jours les plus sombres.

Of the other personages in the royal entourage there was the Dauphin, born in 1661, Louis's only son by Maria Theresa. His education was conducted by Bossuet, and special editions of the classics were produced for his use; he died in 1711, after an unobstrusive life. Another personage who was completely overshadowed by the monarch was Louis's younger brother, the duke of Orléans, who, on his death in 1701, was succeeded by his son, afterwards famous as Regent. The youngest generation was represented by the three sons of the Dauphin, namely, the dukes of Burgundy, Anjou and Berry; of whom the first died in 1712, leaving an infant son, who was afterwards king as Louis XV, while the second became king of Spain by the will of Charles II. The duke of Berry died in 1714. Thus narrowly was the succession maintained in the legitimate Bourbon line. Louis admitted neither his son nor brother to his state councils.

Versailles helped to bestow on France an eminence in the arts of peace such as she already possessed in the arts of war. It was in this respect that Louis's rule had most beneficent results. However much his policy may have injured France and Europe, he made Versailles the symbol of his race; of a France universal and omnipotent; typified not by the strutting cock, but by the flaming sun; always tempered nevertheless by the embellishments and refinements of an artistically-minded race. The numerous imitations were tributes to the pre-eminence of his Court. All this helped to strengthen national consciousness, and to create for it a rallying point; more, indeed than any other king Louis had this *flair* for publicity and propaganda, and round him revolved a whole planetary system, every world illuminated and energized by the sun at the centre. It was sometimes difficult to determine whether this portion of the universe was inspired by an intelligent purpose; had Louis himself been asked, he would probably have answered that its motive was Glory, a personal transcendence, which raised the whole nation on its wing. But his successors had neither the assiduity nor the money for a successful maintenance of his tradition.

* * *

Increasing zeal for orthodoxy was reflected in Louis's attitude to the Huguenots, as the French Protestants were named. These had at first been an independent community, a state within a state; their political and religious independence guaranteed by the Edict of Nantes (1598), the avowed object of which was to win them over by clemency and the example of their orthodox brethren. After the seige of La Rochelle, Richelieu was obliged to destroy their political separatism; but by the Peace of Alais (1629) their religious independence was preserved; it is important therefore that by Louis XIV's reign the Huguenots had ceased to be a political danger; on the contrary, they were specially distinguished by two things—loyalty and industry. They provided good soldiers and officials; many of them were capitalist employers or rich merchants; they were among the most contented and enterprising of French society. It is true that they still adhered to their religion; and although the Edict of Nantes remained the guarantee of that religion, the government was still awaiting the fruits of the clemency which had inspired that Edict. Now, nothing is easier than to stultify a law by a mean or niggling interpretation of its clauses. Louis XIV was naturally unwilling to violate a fundamental law; but he had no difficulty in securing such a rigid enforcement of everything not explicitly authorized by the Edict as to make it valueless. He may have been encouraged to adopt this attitude by the belief that many Huguenots had in fact gone back to the old faith, and that only the wicked and recalcitrant remained to be coerced; and it is certain that, among the French bishops and clergy he found ardent supporters of his ideal, that of a France absolutely uniform in religion; an ideal common in the preceding century, but now becoming somewhat out of date.

So, with increasing pressure the position of the Huguenots was made more and more untenable. After 1666 their lives were subjected to strict inquisition; they were deprived of offices; many of their chapels were pulled down; their children were "converted" before their parents' eyes; and for the voluntary conversion of adults payments were made from a special fund. A steadily increasing number left the country; petitions to the monarch were tried in vain. In 1684 an inspired Assembly of the French Clergy petitioned that, as the Edict was not being properly observed, it should be withdrawn; this was done in October, 1685, by the famous Revocation, which proclaimed that, as the Edict had already served its purpose, it could therefore be dispensed with. It was not the intention of Louis's Government to expel the Huguenots; rather, the object was to retain them in France, and so guarantee their enforced Catholicism; consequently, those who were caught attempting to leave France were sent to the living death of the galleys; while from those who remained was extracted abjuration of their Protestantism by the methods then commonly employed in "well-conditioned" states—by dragoons. Nevertheless, a large number succeeded in making their escape to England, Holland, Switzerland, and Brandenburg, where their influence was soon experienced, because most of them were highly skilled, and they introduced improved methods of weaving and finishing textiles; they also supplied many men of integrity and ability for State service in their adopted countries. No economic history of these countries can ignore the advantages which they secured by the influx of Huguenots.

The results for France were not so fortunate. Economically, the Revocation meant the ruin of Colbert's enterprises, because the Protestants had played the leading part in these; their faith was also that of many of the foreign workmen and capitalists introduced into France in order to teach new crafts. These men were not expelled, but nevertheless they left the country, taking their capital with them. Louis never realized how disastrous was the Revocation for the industries of his country; and, although his correspondence with ambassadors shows that attempts were made to bring back some of the refugees by force or fraud, he eventually came to the conclusion that they were a good riddance; a view confirmed by Bossuet, who publicly asserted that, by the Revocation, the reign of Jesus Christ was brought within sight. There was still another effect. Among the exiles were many men of talent, some of whom recorded their experiences; these may or may not have been exaggerated, but they served to incite European opinion against Louis, and their published records of atrocities provided an illustration of what the King meant by peaceable conversion to the true faith. The lesson was not lost on England, where James II was gradually feeling his way to the restoration of Catholicism.

*   *   *

The rule of Louis, like that of the Stuarts, was based on what was then the strongest of foundations—divine right. This was less a concerted theory of government than a sentiment, and a sentiment may be more potent and more enduring than a syllogism. It was possibly more widely diffused than in England, as it was not confined to Clergy and Court; it was also more intense, amounting to a passion. The reign of Louis XIV served to strengthen it; but as he had no serious illnesses, and as no attempt was made to assassinate him, it is not possible to cite actual proofs of its strength, which would have been most clearly manifested had the life of the King been threatened in either of these ways. But for the reign of his successor it is possible to apply such a test. In 1744 Louis XV was seriously ill at Metz, and the number of masses for his safety recorded and paid for in Notre Dame was about 6,000; thirteen years later, after Damiens's attempt at assassination, the number dropped to 600; in April, 1774, during his last illness the number was 3. This is perhaps the most eloquent commentary on the tremendous prestige created for the monarchy by Louis XIV, and the steady decline of that prestige in the reign of his great-grandson. In England, the collapse of divine right was sudden and complete; in France, it gradually faded away in the fierce light of scepticism and disillusionment.

It was characteristic of *Le Grand Siècle* that what was pre-eminently a human and devotional sentiment was reduced to the formalism and challenge of a code. This was done by Bossuet in his *Politique tirée des propres paroles de l'écriture sainte,* wherein he expounded this thesis: that, as the absolute rule of divinely appointed kings was the normal characteristic of the Israelitish history depicted in the Old Testament, this must be the polity best adapted for the modern Christian state. As a corollary, criticism of the divine-right prerogative was identified with blasphemy. This was a perfectly valid conclusion so long as the literal inspiration of each book of the Bible was indisputable, and provided it was permissible to detach from its context any passage of Holy Writ and urge it as an infallible rule. It was long before either of these axioms was impugned; but the process had already begun, and was being carried far by the researches of the scientists into the forces of nature. As the older, biblical doctrine refused to yield an inch, and as philosophy and science came to discard all the preconceptions which hitherto had been accepted without question, there were brought into antithesis two entirely distinct worlds of thought; the one clinging to tradition and authority, the other determined to sacrifice all that hitherto had been considered fundamental. This antithesis can be detected throughout the course of the eighteenth century; its continued existence helped to increase the artificiality and instability characteristic of the Ancien Régime.

The view that Louis's rule was popular with the mass of the French people receives some confirmation from the character of the revolts; for not one of these was against the monarchy. The most serious, because the hostilities were prolonged, was that of the Protestants in the Cevennes, who, especially in the years 1702-5, maintained a guerrilla warfare in the mountains against the dragoons, and proved a match for the troops led by Villars. In spite of numerous executions, the Protestant faith survived among the Camisards, as well as in Dauphiné and in many parts of Languedoc; but the French Protestants were monarchists, and there was no scheme of political opposition behind their resistance to the royal troops. The same is true of the risings caused by taxation. Of these, the most noteworthy were that of the territory of Boulogne (1662) against a tax enforced in lieu of the enforced billeting of troops; that of the Landes in 1664 against the imposition of the *gabelle* on a province hitherto exempt; that of Bordeaux (1675) against new taxes on tobacco and stamped paper. These last taxes were the occasion of a serious rising in Brittany in 1675. The offices of the tax-collectors in Rennes were demolished, and there was fighting in the streets between the rebels and the troops of Militia brought in by the Governor; elsewhere in the province the movement assumed the form of a peasants' revolt against the feudal rights still enforced by the seigneurs. For a few days it seemed that nobility and tax-collectors alike might perish in this mutiny of a whole province. But order was restored by royal troops, and those peasants who fell into the hands of the soldiers were either killed outright or reserved for the gibbet or wheel. More numerous were the victims in those households where soldiers were billeted; and thus was extinguished this seventeenth-century Jacquerie.

France's almost complete acquiescence in the rule of Louis was most notably manifested by the absence of national opposition to the King's violations of fundamental law. It was not known what laws were fundamental; but it was generally assumed that religion, property and the succession carried with them certain sacrosanct rights. In regard to each of these Louis showed that law was exactly coterminous with his will. By the Revocation of the Edict of Nantes he violated one of the most solemn commitments of the French monarchy; in 1692 he threatened the security of property by an edict declaring his superior and universal lordship over all territory in the kingdom, and demanding one year's revenue from landowners; in 1714 he promulgated a decree which qualified his illegitimate children for the succession, thereby impugning the legitimist element in the divine-right theory itself. Thus Louis was capricious where other men might have experienced scruple.

Nevertheless, there was not complete unanimity in this devotion of France to the principle of irresponsible rule. Fénelon taught his royal pupil the duke of Burgundy that the king was made for the people, not the people for the king; and La Bruyère hinted vaguely that the responsibilities undertaken by Louis may have been too much for one man:

If it is too great a responsibility to have charge of a family; if it is enough to be accountable for oneself; what must be the crushing weight of a kingdom? Is a king sufficiently rewarded by the pleasure derived from absolute power, or by the genuflections of his courtiers? I think of the devious and dangerous ways which a king is sometimes obliged to follow in order to ensure public safety; I pass over the desperate but necessary expedients which he often employs for a good end; I know that it is his duty to answer to God for the happiness of his people; and I ask myself; would I be king?[1]

This doubt was expressed less directly in the writings of the great engineer and general Vauban, who died in retirement and disgrace; for his *Dime Royale* (1707), in which he advocated a single tax, equitably assessed, caused such offence to the monarch that its circulation was forbidden, and a copy was burned by the common hangman. Like Fénelon and Racine he sacrificed Louis's approval by the expression of independent opinion. In his few leisure moments Vauban committed to paper his observations on the political and economic conditions of France; and his extensive travels, together with his remarkable powers of observation, give a special value to these opinions; indeed, his writings outline a complete scheme of reform which, had it been capable of adoption, might have saved his country from revolution. These opinions cover a remarkable range of subject. Thus he was against the taking of outlying forts, and would have preferred to base the defence of the eastern and north-eastern frontier on the pivots of Strasbourg, Luxemburg and Mons. He would have reorganized the army on a scheme of modified conscription, in which the unmarried were to be taken in preference to the married, and allowance was made for special cases of hardship. For the colonies in the west he advocated a constructive policy—the monastic foundations to be withdrawn from Canada; the privileged trading companies to be abolished; the English, he contended, ought to be bought out from their parts of St. Kitts, and Canada should be secured against them by an organized scheme of national defence. He emphasized the strategic advantages possessed by the French in North America, and how valuable was their control of the great rivers; but he noted that none of Louis's wars had injured either of the maritime powers, and he prophesied that one day Canada would fall to English or Dutch.

In regard to religious and political questions he showed a similar enlightenment. Like the Englishman, Sir William Petty (1623-87), he believed in the value of statistics, and was the first Frenchman not only to think that there was a science of statistics, but that it was an essential preliminary to efficient government. He was opposed to the Revocation of the Edict of Nantes and the attempts to convert Huguenots; "force," he wrote, "will never make a true Catholic." He deplored also the abuses to which continued warfare gave rise; namely, the intensification of poverty; the dishonest profits of army contractors; the rise to wealth and power of the unscrupulous; the inequality of sacrifice—death, disablement or starvation for one, and a fortune or a title for another. As with war, so with government. The system on which the French monarchy rested he thought corrupt; and in his *Dime Royale* he used the word *gangrene* to describe the body politic; to this inherent corruption he attributed the fact that, by the later wars of Louis, one-tenth of the population was reduced to beggary, and one-half of the remainder was scarcely able to subsist. These were daring

---

[1] La Bruyère, *Du Souverain*.

assertions from a man in the employment of Louis XIV; he was perfectly loyal, but he spoke his mind. He hinted not obscurely that Versailles was directly responsible for the miseries endured by France, and even suggested that the whole administration had come to be controlled in the interests of women and courtiers. Equally daring was his plea for reform of the prisons; long before Beccaria and Howard he directed attention to this, one of the sombre underworlds which underlay the tinsel and finery of the Ancien Régime. The King, he thought, should himself visit the prisons once a year in order to see things for himself; only thus would he realize the horrors concealed by their walls.

Such were the main proposals of Vauban. They serve to suggest that the most effective critic of Louis's policy and administration was the man to whom most of the military successes of the reign were due.

# LOUIS XIV AS STATE BUILDER

### Roland Mousnier

Absolutism was desired by the masses who believed that they would find their salvation in concentrating all power in the hands of one man, incarnating the kingdom, a living symbol of the order and unity they desired. Everyone wished to recognize God's image in the King: "you are God on earth . . ."[1] In addition, many people shared the old humanistic dream: the King must be a Hero, a lover of glory, as in antiquity, a patron of the arts, as was Augustus, a protector of the Church, as was Constantine, and a legislator in the image of Justinian, but he must have "a predeliction for the arts of war," since "the attribute of conqueror was considered the highest and most noble of titles" by all his contemporaries.

As God's lieutenant, the King is sovereign. "The sovereign Prince makes the law, he is consequently above the law." He can do what he pleases. It follows that Kings "by nature have the right to dispose fully and freely of all property, secular as well as ecclesiastic, in order to use it as a wise steward would, that is, according to the needs of the State." The public good was more important than the right to property. As a result the Church was subject to the sovereign and owed him an account of the property which had been given to it "for the good of the kingdom." It followed that "Just as the sovereign power of the Prince is a ray emanating from the omnipotence of God, so the power of public servants is a fragment derived from the absolute power of the Prince . . ." The comparison with the Sun was a natural one, and Louis XIV, *Nec pluribus impar,* was simply underlining an old monarchical symbol.

But, as God's representative on earth, the King must be Providence incarnate. He must bring about the reign of justice, "that precious trust which God has handed over to Kings as a means of sharing his wisdom and power." He must make all the professions and callings in society as perfect as possible, because "each has its purpose, which the others would find it hard to do without. . . . This is why, far from showing contempt for any of these callings, or praising some more highly than others, we must take care to bring all of them, if possible, to the greatest degree of perfection of which

---

[1] This and following quotes unidentified by the author are from the writings of contemporary observers or servants of the monarchy. [Editor's note.]

they are capable." This was the ideal of a society where essential labor was controlled and the professions gained their position in the hierarchy according to the needs of man. Finally the King must protect the weak, he must "grant to the peoples who are our subjects the same tokens of paternal love which we receive from God each day," he must "have no greater care than to protect the weakest against the oppression of the strongest and to ease the misery of those in greatest need." Louis XIV lived these ideas, but Henry IV almost as much as he and Louis XIII to a hardly lesser degree than Henry had each wished to be Hero, Sovereign, and Providence.

Depending on the period, the King exercised power in two different ways. If he was not very able, as in the case of Louis XIII, or too young, as was true of Louis XIV betwen 1643 and 1661, a ministerial regime was established. A prime minister, such as Cardinal Richelieu or Cardinal Mazarin in France, or the Duke of Olivares in Spain, and so on, governed in the name of the King and was accountable to him. In the case of a King such as Louis XIII, this was no mere formality: "The few square feet of the King's private chamber are harder for me to conquer than all the battlefields of Europe."

But in those days of dependence and patronage, the minister's behavior began to resemble that of a "mayor of the palace" under the Merovingian Kings. He surrounded the King with his men, awarded all the important posts to his followers, and created his own dynasty. His relatives became marshals, generals of the galleys, dukes and peers, and he married his nieces to princes of the blood. He even owned, as Richelieu did, garrison towns such as Brouage, and Le Havre, which he could bequeath to his heirs, and, finally, he possessed his own troops: infantry regiments and regiments of noblemen. The King gradually found himself abandoned by his officers, who were joining his ministers; he could see that a day might come when he would find himself alone and powerless, facing his minister who had the best swordsmen in the Kingdom under his command, and that he would be able to exact obedience from his subjects only with the help of the minister and his men. The death of the prime minister was always a relief for the King.

Thus, Louis XIV, building a theory out of that which Henry IV had known instinctively, resolved that he would be his own prime minister, that he would be alone in understanding the over-all management of State affairs, and that he alone would be indispensable. The King was therefore compelled to lead an increasingly bureaucratic life, organized for maximum efficiency. "Though 300 leagues away, if one were equipped with a calendar and a watch, one could tell exactly what he was doing." He found it necessary to isolate himself, at Versailles, in a palace and in a city which had been built for the work of the King as much as for his pleasure and for display. Some have believed this bureaucratic life was modeled after Spain, whereas, in fact, it appeared wherever absolutism was evolving. It was born of necessity.

During the period of the great prime ministers, the organization of government and of society was being stabilized. But the development of the governing bodies gave power to dangerous people, the most important nobles and the prime minister. Louis XIV began a regression which would result in giving free rein to the royal will. During the period of the great ministries, power in government was still dependent on family ties, on high birth, on titles, and on the office held. The *Conseil d'en Haut* consisted of members of the royal family, princes of the blood, dukes and peers, the Chancellor, and the Minister of Finance. Ministers held an office, granted to them through letters patent, into which they "settled," and of which they took "possession." Louis XIV was bringing about a revolution. He kept out of the *Conseil d'en Haut* all those who might claim political power because of their birth, title, or office. He first removed his mother, his brother, and the princes of the blood; the government was no longer in the hands of a family, it had become truly personal. The Chancellor, the prelates, the great nobles, and finally the great civil servants were all weeded out of the *Conseil*. All the secretaries of State did not become ministers. To be a minister ceased to be a permanent calling. Letters patent and commissions no longer existed. One became a minister on the day the King had one summoned by his bailiff; one ceased to be a minister on the day there was no call from the bailiff. At certain times the King discussed affairs of State with those it suited him to consult, but no one, beside the King, had the right to govern. All power was centered in the person of the King.

During the period of the great ministries an important effort had been made to develop an agent of royal authority, that is, the *Conseil*. New sections, such as the *Conseil des Dépêches pour l'Intérieur*, and the *Conseil de Conscience*, were added. The political section, the *Conseil des Affaires* or *Conseil d'en Haut*, the administrative sections, *Conseil des Finances*, *Conseil d'État et des Finances*, and *Conseil Privé*, had become more specialized and there was a new and better allotment of functions. Louis XIV, on the contrary, distrusted the *Conseils*. Since he could not dispense with them, he tried to limit them to routine functions. He preferred to work alone, with each of his secretaries of State in turn and with the Comptroller General of Finances. He made all the important decisions, and the decisions were brought only *pro forma* before the *Conseils*, or their approval was dispensed with entirely. Thousands of the *Conseil's* edicts were signed "by command" of a secretary of State, or of the Chancellor, without ever having passed through the *Conseil d'en Haut*, the *Conseil des Dépêches*, or the *Conseil Royal des Finances*.

The King looked upon his ministers and his secretaries of State with suspicion. He reinstated the division of responsibilities, and he tried to assign blocks of work dealing with a variety of problems, so that no specialist would ever be in a position to thwart his wishes. He would set his deputies one against another, he would excite them, divide them, and inflame their mutual jealousy; he saw a guarantee of his power in the antagonism between men such as Colbert and Le Tellier.

Both before and after becoming his own prime minister, Louis XIV's problem was not only to make his subjects obey him, but it was also to make his own administrative officers, who had become independent thanks to the venal nature of their functions, submit to his authority. He must retain the full exercise of legal and judicial power, and complete control of the "police" and of the administration.

To accomplish these ends, the King used *lettres de cachet* to convey his wishes directly to individuals and to the administrative bodies. Through *lettres de cachet*, the King imprisoned his subjects, sent them to the Bastille, or exiled them; at their families' request, he would, by writing a *lettre de cachet*, directly chastise a son or spouse accused of misconduct; he used these *lettres* to anticipate opposition and to punish rebellion against the regime and conspiracy with the enemy, without having to resort to a trial. When the King himself had spoken, there was no recourse but to bow down to his authority, the legal source of justice.

The King, more and more, employed commissioners named by him, whom he could dismiss at will. Moreover, the *conseillers d'État* of the administrative *Conseils* were also commissioners. During the period of the ministries, the King had elevated the *Conseils* to the rank of highest administrative body in the kingdom, with authority over the "sovereign" Courts even in the absence of the King. Beginning in 1632, the *Conseils* could nullify and revoke any decrees, including those of the *Parlements*, which opposed the ordinances of the King, or which ran counter to royal authority, to public interest, or to the rights of the crown. The *Conseils* removed public affairs to their jurisdiction, passed judgment on them, and dispossessed the sovereign Courts of their function. Under Louis XIV, the authority of the *Conseils* was maintained, if only as a useful fiction; in fact, the decrees of the *Conseils* were often issued directly by the King or his closest assistants, the secretaries of State and the Comptroller of Finances.

During both periods, the King asserted authority (which in principle was expressed through the *Conseils*) over the sovereign Courts. In 1641, Louis XIII solemnly reserved to himself the right of cognizance of all affairs of State. He limited the Courts to two objections before the recording of financial decrees, and he eliminated their right to make objections to decrees, concerned with matters of State, after they were recorded. Again, Louis XIV affirmed his sole jurisdiction over affairs of State; in 1673, he compelled the sovereign Courts to record edicts immediately, and in their original form; their objections would be heard only once, and after the edicts were recorded. The Courts preferred to give a simple opinion; they thus found themselves excluded from making general policy and from debating constitutional questions. The King was confirmed in his authority in political matters, in his complete legislative powers, and consequently, in his power to levy taxes and to use the revenue therefrom at his own discretion. The King could ask Commissions, made up of administrators personally devoted to him, to draft laws (the Civil Statute of 1667, the Criminal Statute of 1670, and Statute on Commerce of 1673) to which the King conferred legal validity without finding it necessary to record them, to consult those in offical positions, or require participation of the administrative bodies. The drafting of these laws indicated a clear trend toward unity and equality, a truly revolutionary achievement.

The King also created Commissions of the *Conseil* in order to try a case or enforce an edict; such Commissions as the Court of Justice of the Arsenal, which met in 1631, and the Commission which tried the Governors of La Capelle and Le Châtelet after the Peace of Corbie, were not merely empowered to make investigations, they could also pass sentence.

The King employed Army intendants, and intendants of Justice, of Police and of Finance. They were primarily inspectors, whose functions were to supervise the King's subjects and those holding public office and to report to the *Conseil*. The *Conseil* then could either decide the case by issuing a decree, or delegate to the intendants the power to make decisions and the power to judge and to rule by means of ordinances. The intendants could thus be present at the Governor's *Conseil* and express their opinions, they could preside at the Law Courts and make justice conform with the ordinances. They were to determine whether public servants were fulfilling their responsibilities, and if not, the intendants could put them under suspension; it was also their duty to hear the complaints of the King's subjects and make sure that their cases were brought before a judge. The intendants presided over the town Assemblies, supervised elections, audited the books of the corporations and the guilds, and in general insured that orders and regulations were enforced; a rough draft of an administrative guardianship had been sketched out. And again, the intendants supervised the collecting of taxes and presided over the financial offices; in this realm they also looked after the enforcement of ordinances and regulations. However, they only possessed complete and discretionary powers and the authority of final judgement in two cases: first, in case of embezzlement and extortion on the part of civil servants, and second, in the event of illegal assemblies, rebellions, riots, or the raising of armed troops.

The intendant was a very adaptable tool of royal power. In time of war or of internal crisis, the *Conseil* could extend the intendants' powers indefinitely until they took over all the functions of civil servants and government officials, leaving to those officials nothing but a useless title. At such times the intendants and their deputies constituted an administration of commissioners alongside that of the regular officials. However, the Royal Government, Richelieu and Colbert, considered these periods as exceptional, and the measures taken to be an unfortunate necessity. In peacetime, the King tried to limit the intendants, who were always trying to extend their powers, to the role of inspectors. He forbade them to substitute themselves for public servants, and he prescribed that they should only supervise; if the public servants did their work badly, the *Conseil* was to be notified, but the intendants had to await its permission in order to remedy the situation.

The King made use of a political police consisting of intendants and of spies and agents scattered everywhere. In Paris members of this police included the Governor of the Bastille, the lieutenant in charge of criminal affairs, and after 1667, the lieutenant-general of police, La Reynie. Whether one was a duke or a lackey, a word out of turn was enough to send one to the Bastille. The intendants and the *Conseil* built up cases of *lèse-majesté* on the flimsiest of evidence. Judgements were made simply on the basis of presumptions; for Richelieu, Louis XIII, and Louis XIV claimed that, where conspiracy was concerned, it was almost impossible to have absolute proof, and that one must not wait for the worst to happen. Rather than relying on trials, the King, by issuing a *lettre de cachet*, would have recourse to preventive imprisonment of indefinite duration. A standing army of mercenaries, who were paid regularly and kept under strict discipline, assured the execution of the Royal orders.

Louis XIV insisted on placing in all the important offices, such as ministries, secretaries of State, Comptroller-General, and so on, only those totally "devoted" to him. He chose men who would be able to perform personal services; men such as Colbert, who was willing to transmit messages to the King's favorites and welcome his adulterous children into the world when the Royal mistresses gave birth. He made use of feudal loyalties, but he wanted to be their sole beneficiary. He wished to achieve absolutism by creating a personal bond between every Frenchman and the King, just as a vassal is linked to his lord. He wanted to be the sole and universal lord, or at least the universal patron. "All eyes are focused on him and on him alone; it is to him alone that all pleas are directed; he alone receives all manifestations of respect; on him alone are all expectations focused; one seeks nothing, one hears nothing, one does nothing without recourse to him alone." All ties of feeling and shared concerns converged upon the King, who thus incarnated the wishes and the hopes of all his subjects. In this way, just as much as through the exercise of personal might, the King concentrated the power of the State in himself. The unification of the State was completed in his person, thus preparing his subjects, by the use of very old sentiments, to understand the abstract concept of a State. Through the medium of medieval survivals, Louis XIV was paving the way for the modern State. The King prepared the way by setting one class against another and by encouraging the rise of the bourgeoisie on the social ladder. As the century progressed, the King picked an ever-increasing number of his ministers, advisers and intendants from the ranks of the magisterial and legal bourgeoisie. These were his own men, "whose origins were totally and completely plebeian," but who had been "exalted above the highest rank." The King ennobled men such as Le Tellier and Colbert; they became Marquis and Lords known by the name of their lands: Louvois, Barbezieux, Croissy and Torcy. He created ministerial dynasties, and "bourgeois" blood lines whose power he pitted against that of the families and dynasties of the nobility. In 1695, the head-tax roll included the ministers of State among those belonging to the first class, and the Chancellor and the Comptroller-General of Finances were given a rank equal to that of the princes of the blood. In the administrative divisions of the *Conseil d'État* the percentage of its members belonging to the magisterial and legal professions was growing. The regulation of 1673 determined that, of the 30 members of the *Conseil,* 24 should be drawn from the ranks of the magisterial and legal bourgeoisie, three from the Church, and three from the nobility. And, moreover, it was not even necessary for the last three to belong to the old nobility; the ennobled son of a magistrate was eligible. The dukes and peers who were members, by right, of the *Conseil Privé* were gradually being replaced. The regulations of 1673 omit them entirely. The *Conseillers d'État* received titles of nobility which their sons could inherit, they and their wives were received at Court and they were allowed to pay their respects to the King. They owned fiefs and became lords, their sons often becoming officers in the King's regiments for a period of time before serving in his administration. The King thus systematically promoted the members of the legal and magisterial class who were devoted to his service: he created a new nobility of magistrates. More and more, it was through serving the sovereign, who represents the State, that one reached a high rank in society.

The nobles grumbled. They despised these "bourgeois"; Saint-Simon was to snarl: "It was the most abjectly bourgeois reign." The nobility was suffering from the levelling of society encouraged by a State which cut down all opposition. The prisons were filled with eminent prisoners: the Count de Cramaing, Marshal de Bassompierre, and Baradas, one of the favorites of Louis XIII. On the other hand, the kings tried to procure honors and a livelihood for the nobles. Governorships were set aside for them, as were most of the high posts in the army; younger sons were given preference in the hierarchy of the Church. The kings pressed them into their personal service, instilled in them a spirit of subordination, and little by little turned them into civil servants. Louis XIV achieved the organization of the Court, and, at St. Germain, at Fontainebleau, and at Versailles, he surrounded himself with the most important and powerful members of the nobility. He completed their ruin by making them constantly alternate between the burdensome and expensive life of the army camps and the stately life of the court. He was not loath to use war as a means of conferring fame and glory upon the nobility; his gifts of pensions, doweries and church property indebted them to him. Mme. de Sévigné was to say, like a faithful dog: "As one pays him court, one might find oneself receiving crumbs from his table." But Louis XIV gave the nobility a psychological alibi for its weakness. In a series of splendid and brilliant festivals, the King would appear in the costume of a God from Olympus, his courtiers representing Heroes or the lesser deities; the nobles could thus sublimate the failure of their dreams of real power and grandeur in this imitation of the life of the Olympians. They felt elevated above the run of common humanity, and though they had to obey, at least they were obeying the "Lord Jupiter," and God-King. Through etiquette, they became accustomed to seeing the King as a divine being. The men would bare their heads in front of the King's bed, and the women would genuflect, as they did in Church before the High Altar. At the *lever,* the princes of the blood fought for the right of helping the King put on his shirt. An elaborate ritual, accompanied by many obeisances controlled the *lever,* the *coucher,* and the meals of the King; in fact, his whole life. A courtier expressed this perfectly when he exclaimed at the funeral of Louis XIV: "If the King could die, anything could happen."

The Court and its etiquette were no longer copied after Spain's, but they were dictated by the state of society and the nature of things.

The King thus divided the different offices in the State between two classes, reserving the most important ones for the lesser class, the bourgeoisie. By deliberately promoting its fortunes and making it as important as the nobility, originally the stronger of the two, the King brought the class struggle to a point of equilibrium between the two classes which assured his personal power, and which maintained unity, order, and hierarchy in the Government and the State. But, without specifically wishing to change the structure of society, and perhaps compelled by crises and wars, the King also had achieved an equalizing and a levelling of the classes through the total submission and complete obedience which he demanded of all who served the State. In the reign of Louis XIV, the power of the King had thus become both autocratic and revolutionary.

# SOME REFLECTIONS ON ABSOLUTISM AND DESPOTISM

### Roland Mousnier

Even today two apparent errors are frequently made. Some historians simply establish an equation between absolutism on the one hand and despotism, tyranny and even totalitarianism on the other.[1] Certain others adopt as a definition of absolutism the extreme position of certain theorists who push ideas to their logical limits. Agreeing with Machiavelli and Hobbes, they recognize as absolutism only such cases in which the King possesses the right to legislate without reference to an eternal law or a code of ideal principles, without the intervention of any authority outside of the state, and without restriction from any person or constitutional body within the state.[2] Is it then surprising that "Absolute Monarchy" should vanish? Is it surprising that P. R. Doolin should seek another term to describe the French *Ancien Régime* during the seventeenth and eighteenth centuries?[3]

I believe that we should accept as definitions of true absolutism only those made by contemporary commentators observing the functioning of their own governments. The Elizabethan writer James Morice, in speaking of the English Government asks us to "Behold the *Sovereigne Authoritie* of one, an *absolute Prince,* rulinge and reigninge, yet *guided* and *directed* by Principles and precepts of Reason, which wee terme the lawe. No Spartane Kinge, or Venetian Duke, but *free from accompt and cohercion* of

---

[1] V. L. Carsten, "The Resistance of Cleves and Mark to the Despotic Policy of the Great Elector," *English Historical Review,* LXVI (1951), pp. 219-241; "The Great Elector and the Foundation of the Hohenzollern Despotism," *ibid.,* LXV (1950), pp. 175-202; A. L. Rowse, *The England of Elizabeth: The Structure of Society,* 1951, p. 261; M. A. Judson, *The Crisis of the Constitution,* 1949, p. 47. See also p. 107: Under Charles I,"There were no secret police, no intendants, no Bastille, and no *lettres de cachet."* Thus "the government was royal . . . but for the greater part it could not be called tyrannical or arbitrary." In Judson's opinion, the French government, which had all these institutions from Louis XIII on, was tyrannical.

[2] P. V. Baumer, *The Early Tudor Theory of Kingship,* 1940, pp. 5-6, notes 5-6. He goes so far as to write "there where there is a fundamental law, there can be no absolute monarchy."

[3] P. R. Doolin, *The Fronde,* Harvard Historical Studies, XXIX, 1935, pp. xi-xiii.

anye, equall or Superior; yet firmilie bound to the Common Wealth by the faithful Oathe of a Christian Prince, bearinge alone the sharpe sworde of Justice and Correction, yet tempered with mercy and compassion; requiring Taxe and Tribute of the people, yet not carelesse, *nor without common assent.*

"Wee agayne the subjects of this Kingdome are borne and brought upp in due obedience, but far from Servitude and bondage, subject to lawfull aucthoritye and enjoying by lymitts of lawe and Justice oure liefs, lands, goods and liberties in great peace and security.[4] Is it a mistake or a misuse of language that leads James Morice to describe as absolute a Prince whose will is limited by his oath and by the law?

Is it political expedience alone that prompted the King's advocate general, Omer Talon, one of the king's men addressing his master who was holding the *lit de justice* of January 15, 1648: "You are, Sire, our *Sovereign Lord;* your majesty's might comes from on high, and need account, after God, only to conscience . . ." and during the sessions of July 31st: "Sovereigns, in conducting affairs of State, act through God's inspirations and with the spiritual strength and knowledge that God imparts to them; *it is not the place of their subjects to question them nor to ask them to account for their actions.*" Later in the same address, Talon reminded the King that it is necessary to observe the laws of the Kingdom, to respect the rights of his subjects and also the dictates of religion and justice, and to have his laws endorsed by a free vote in *Parlement.*[5] Is there not a contradiction between these limits to royal sovereignty and the claim that this supreme authority is unlimited? Between this absolutism and these checks and balances?

Did not the French jurist Loyseau know what he was saying when, in describing the state of affairs in the France of his day, he declared, "Sovereignty is the form which gives Being to the State . . . in monarchies, it belongs to the King . . . But, it resides in *absolute power,* that is to say, in every way complete and total . . . However . . . there are three kinds of laws which limit *the Sovereign's power* without affecting sovereignty. To wit, the laws of God, since a Prince is no less sovereign for being subject to God; the rules of non-positive and natural justice, since it is of the essence of public stewardship that it be exercised not arbitrarily but justly; and finally, the fundamental laws of the State, since the Prince must use his sovereignty in accord with its true nature and within the framework and conditions in which it is established" (1609?).[6]

These texts, then, describe as absolute and sovereign, powers which we logically consider as limited. It is pertinent to take a close look at this discrepancy.

If we consider France, from the beginning of the sixteenth century to the second half of the eighteenth, we observe that in practice Frenchmen in favor of absolute monarchy agree on a number of propositions.[7] Since we seek to understand what the concept of absolutism was, we need not concern ourselves with its opponents: the Monarchomaques, the Huguenots abroad, and such rank feudalists as Fénelon and so on.[8]

---

[4] *A remembrance of Certain Matters Concerning the Clergie and Their Jurisdiction,* 1593, cited by Judson, *op. cit.,* pp. 61-62.

[5] Omer Talon, *Mémoires* (éd. Michaud-Pougoulat), pp. 209-212 and 259-260.

[6] Ch. Loyseau, *Des Seigneuries,* Ch. 2, Nos. 1-9.

[7] *Cf.* Doolin, *op. cit.,* W. F. Church, *Constitutional Thought in Sixteenth Century France,* Harvard Historical Studies, XLVII, 1941; R. von Albertini, *Das politische Denken in Frankreich zur Zeit Richelieus,* Marburg, Simon Verlag, 1951; R. Mousnier, "Comment les Français voyaient la France," *XVIIème siècle, Bulletin de la Société d'Etude du XVIIème siècle,* Nos. 25-26 (1955).

[8] *Cf.* R. Mousnier, "L'opposition politique bourgeoise à la fin du XVème et au début du

The absolutists believed that France possessed an unwritten constitution, which was derived from the vital needs of the body politic, whose head was the King and whose members were his subjects. This constitution stood above the will of the King. It determined the form of the State which is the juridical personification of the Nation, a moral being, an ideal and permanent retainer of sovereignty, and therefore all powerful. It determined the forms of government, a monarchy in which succession is established through the male line, by order of primogeniture, and in which the King exercises all power, concentrating in his person all the prerogatives of the State.

The unwritten constitution limited the power of the State and of the King. In the first place, the government could not change its form because of the Salic law, a fundamental law, unwritten, as old as France, and taken from nature itself—an instinct graven upon the heart. This law was imposed upon the King; he could not change it. Moreover, his rights and his authority were derived from the "law of the land" which had established them. The fundamental law was superior to the King. The State was superior to the King. This was a constitutional law, older and greater than ordinary laws, to be respected by the legislative power which could neither repeal nor modify it. Thus, the absolutist constitution was "rigid." It was the opposite, in this respect, of the English constitution, which was "flexible" and did not differentiate between constitutional laws and ordinary laws. The English Parliament (the King, the House of Lords and the House of Commons) could pass laws pertaining to the Constitution, as well as any other matter as long as it respected the common law and the rights of its subjects. The King of France could not.

Next, the unwritten absolutist constitution forced the King to respect the natural right of the French people to liberty and property. The French considered themselves free, and they made a careful distinction between absolutism and despotism. The absolute King was bound to respect the person and property of his subjects. Monarchies, such as Turkey and Russia, which the French believed did not possess these guarantees, seemed to them barbarous, unnatural and unworthy of Christian Princes.

Finally, the unwritten constitution imposed upon the King, who had taken the Coronation oath, the respect of God's Commandments. The King was anointed, was crowned and was God's representative on earth. But, as a result, it was his duty to treat his subjects with the goodness and justice of God.

Therefore, what the French called absolute monarchy, was a monarchy limited by divine law and by natural law. But it was absolute, in the sense that, though limited, it was not controlled. And, in the interest of public safety, the King was granted unlimited power. The King was no longer bound to respect any limit in cases which threatened the body politic (wars, revolts, crises). At such time *lettres de cachet,* the Bastille, *intendants,* seizures and confiscations were considered legitimate. It is true that under such circumstances individual rights and liberties are suspended even in free societies with democratic governments. The monarchy was also absolute because the State, incarnate in the person of the King, no longer shared the attributes of sovereignty with the nobility, with the towns, or with the guilds; and because these individuals and bodies no longer had the right to legislate, to name officers, to raise troops, to wage war, to make peace, or to conclude a truce, to contract alliances, to

XVIIème siècle. Louis Turquet de Mayerne," *Revue Historique* (January-March 1955); G. L. Dodge, *The Political Theory of the Huguenots of the Dispersion,* 1947; R. Mousnier, "Les idées politiques de Fénelon," *XVIIème siècle. Bulletin de la Société d'Etude du XVIIème siècle,* Nos. 12-14 (1952).

render justice and lastly to mint money or to levy taxes. *Absolute monarchy* is a term which means the opposite of feudal dispersion. But it does not mean despotism and tyranny. Moreover, the Constitution was unwritten, the product of many obscure and contradictory precedents and of powerful, but vague and hidden, feelings rather than clear and distinct ideas: Thus there was room in it for diverse tendencies. The King and his counselors tended to concentrate more sovereignty in the person of the King—to give him even greater power. They were aiming to concentrate further the State in the person of the monarch. The concern for the independence of the Nation, and the necessity of freeing France from all subjection to the Pope or the Emperor—which had led to the proclamation of the King's sovereignty as early as the thirteenth century[9]—were used to further this aim. This principle of sovereignty would in effect have led to despotism if carried to its logical conclusion. The old, popular notion of royal sanctity[10] which, under the influence of the Renaissance, had been revived by the humanists in the guise of the Hero-King, and Sun-King, was channeled in this direction. Above all was stressed the necessity of developing to the utmost the might of the Kingdom in order to conquer in war and unite and put into working order a complete hierarchy of Lords, Orders and Guilds, each with their rights and privileges. Accordingly, the tendency toward Royalism gained around. But never did the Kings, including Louis XIV, ever forget the constitutional limits of their powers.

What does the saying, attributed to Louis XIV, *"L'État, c'est moi"* signify? Pamphleteers such as the remarkable anonymous author of *Sighs of an Enslaved France,* have reproached him for substituting his personal interests for those of the State. In reality this was not so. Moreover, Louis XIV made a very clear distinction between himself and the State. On his deathbed he said: "I am going, but the State will always remain." And these words are as authentic as the others are doubtful. I cannot possibly agree with those who wrongly compare the formula attributed to Louis XIV, *"L'État, c'est moi,"* with that credited to Frederick II, *"Moi, c'est l'État."*[11] To their way of thinking, Louis XIV would have sacrificed the State to his own personal and dynastic interests, whereas Frederick II would have sacrificed himself to the State. In fact, the maxim attributed to Louis XIV has exactly the same meaning as the one credited to Frederick II, as witnessed by the remarks of Louis XIV on the business of being King (1679). "When one's concern is the State, one works for oneself. What is good for the one glorifies the other." And the formula credited to Frederick II is not new, as his line in the *Essay on the Forms of Government* (1777) demonstrates: "The Sovereign represents the State; he and his people constitute one body." This is a very old concept.

Beginning in 1673, the *Parlements* no longer opposed Louis XIV. But the Edict of 1673 did not differ in character from that of 1641. It did not abolish the right of remonstrance. During the war in Holland, it regulated this right in order to prevent the *Parlement* from obstructing and opposing urgent fiscal edicts. The Edict of 1673 was a wartime measure and in no way an innovation. But France, from 1673 to 1715, was always at war or on a war footing. Let us also note that at the time Louis XIV abolished the *Ministériat,* when he began to govern only with his State secretaries, and

[9] W. Ullman, "The Development of the Medieval Idea of Sovereignty," *English Historical Review,* LXIV (1949), pp. 1-33.

[10] M. Bloch, *Les Rois thaumaturges,* Strasbourg, 1924.

[11] F. Hartung, "L'État, c'est moi," *Historische Zeitschrift,* 169 (1949), pp. 1-31.

when he centered the State in his person,[12] he was answering the prayers of the most ardent *Frondeurs.*

Neither did Louis XV in any way repudiate the unwritten Constitution, when, on April 8, 1755, in answer to the remonstrances of the *Parlement* of Paris he declared that "it is only in the person of the King that the universality, the plentitude, and the indivisibility of authority reside," and that the King is "the sole legislator in his Kingdom,"[13] or when at the famous sitting of the *Flagellation,* on March 3, 1766, he said: "In my person alone does sovereign power reside . . . to me alone does legislative power, independent and undivided, belong . . ." This had always been the consensus of opinion, at least since the end of the fifteenth century, and it went along very well, in point of fact, if not of logic, with the necessity for *Parlement* to give final form and validity to the ordinances of the King.[14] Louis XV did not really take any new steps until he transformed the *Parlement* of Paris in 1771, an action which was to free his administration and the State from the bodies which formed the Kingdom, and which started the French Revolution. Even then, the *Parlement,* weakened and transformed as it was, retained the function of registering edicts.

An opposite tendency to that of the Monarch and his counselors was to increase the limits to the power of the King by making some of his subjects share in the exercise of power. The Princes of the Blood Royal declared themselves born counselors of the State, and they believed that the King could not govern without their advice. The *Parlements* claimed to be the descendants of the old *Cour-le-Roi* and of the *États Généraux,* and also to be the representatives of the French people. By virtue of this, they claimed the right to ratify, by freely exercising their votes, the declarations and edicts of the King, and thus to participate in the exercise of legislative power and the imposition of taxes. Some went very far, inasmuch as they invoked the theory of social contract, and inasmuch as Chassereuz in the sixteenth century, and Le Coigneux in the seventeenth, gave the word *absolute* a different meaning, making a distinction between the *ordinary* power of the King, which was very limited, and his *absolute* power, which he might exercise only in case of urgent necessity and through which on his own authority he could legislate and levy taxes. But, at the same time, most authorities proclaimed, as the ultimate truth, all the rest of the Constitution, and in particular the concentration of sovereignty in the person of the King. From the *Parlement* of Francis I, which rejected the *Concordat,*[15] to the *Parlement* of Louis XV, which intended to judge the Duc d'Aiguillon,[16] in spite of the King, there is little difference in the idea of absolute monarchy. The differences are in the relationship between the social classes: these are the differences which made *Parlement* at the time of the *Fronde* more revolutionary than it was conceived to be.[17]

[12] *Cf.* R. Mousnier, "Les XVIème siècles. Les progès de la civilisation européenne et le déclin de l'Orient (1492-1715)," in *Histoire générale des civilisations,* IV, 1954.
[13] Flammeront et Tourneux, *Remontrances du Parlement de Paris,* II, pp. 184-188.
[14] E. Maugis, *Histoire du Parlement de Paris,* I, pp. 517-547.
[15] R. Doucet, *Étude sur le gouvernement de François Ier dans ses rapports avec le Parlement de Paris,* 1921-1926.
[16] J. Flammeront, *Le Chancelier Maupeou et les Parlements,* 1883.
[17] R. Mousnier, "Quelques raisons de la Fronde. Les causes des journées révolutionnaires parisiennes de 1648," *XVIIème siècle. Bulletin de la Société d'Étude du XVIIème siècle, No. 2* (1949).

# 11 / The Origins of the English Civil War: Socio-Economic Crisis or a Conflict of "Faith and Freedom"

The importance of the English civil war (1640-1660) in British, western, and world history can be measured readily by the quantity of historical writings it continues to generate. As one historian noted, there are three "orthodox" schools of interpretation—a Tory, a Whig (or Liberal), and a religious (Anglican versus Puritan).[1] In addition, there are several varieties of Marxist views.

Was the English civil war a "great rebellion" against the legally constituted authority of King, Court, and Church by self-seeking groups of gentlemen who misled the common man? Was it the justifiable outburst of liberty-loving Englishmen against the threat of continentally inspired absolutism—a form of rule thoroughly deviating from English political practices? Was it a war between an established religion and a dissenting sect? Or, was the civil war the inevitable confrontation of synamic, modern entrepreneurs (urban and rural) against the dead hand of arrogant, parasitic feudal landowners? These and other questions direct our attention to the complex problem of understanding the origins of the conflict.

In the last three decades, the question of origins has produced a rather bitter controversy wherein the idea of class conflict plays a central role. In 1941, the late R. H. Tawney published an article in the *Economic History Review* entitled "The Rise of the Gentry, 1558-1640." There he described a rural bourgeoisie, the gentry, rising in wealth and influence at the expense of a declining feudal aristocracy. When the former took over the government in 1640, they were simply effecting the political confirmation of economic and social changes. In 1953, also in the *Economic History Review,* H. R. Trevor-Roper in "The Gentry, 1540-1660" attacked the statistical evidence on which Tawney's idea of a rising gentry was based and went on to posit a declining "mere gentry" in desperate but, by 1640, successful rebellion against the Court. It is impossible here to refer to the ideas and men who entered the discussion which turned essentially on the question of what was happening to landowners and ruling elites in country and town.[2] The contribution of J. H. Hexter's "Storm over the Gentry" to the scholarly fray shifted the arguments from the general economic framework in which they were couched to a more spiritual and intellectual base.

The first selection here is an excerpt from Hexter's review essay of Lawrence Stone's *Crisis of the Aristocracy,1558-1641* (Oxford University Press, 1965). Stone's massive and learned study of the changing status of peerage and gentry over one century emphasized socio-economic factors along with sociological concepts of class and elite

---

[1] Christopher Hill, *The English Revolution, 1640* (3rd ed.; London: Lawrence & Wishart, 1955), pp. 6-13.
[2] For a bibliography of the controversy, see J. H. Hexter, *Reappraisals in History* (Evanston, Ill. and Chicago: Northwestern University Press, 1961), pp. 149-152.

behaviour. Hexter's discussion points the reader toward the need to understand the primary role that ideology—"faith and freedom"—played in the denouement of the English civil war. For Hexter, emphasis on materialistic interpretations obscures the guiding power of ideas.

Professor Stone's brief response to Hexter's thorough review constitutes the second selection in this section. Here, Stone rejoins that he prefers his own interpretation of his data but admits that probably neither of them have a total corner on the "truth."

After going through the materials presented in this section, the reader is advised to refer back to Chapter 7 for additional perspective on the question of the midseventeenth-century English upheaval.

# THE ENGLISH ARISTOCRACY, ITS CRISES AND
# THE ENGLISH REVOLUTION, 1558-1660

**J. H. Hexter**

"A landmark in the historical landscape"*–The Economist*; "A major contribution . . . an impressive achievement, which must in future put all historians in his debt"*–The Listener*; "A remarkable achievement . . . an outstanding study of a very real and great value"*–History;* "A mammoth and marvellous book"–American *Historical Review*; "Immense value"*–English Historical Review*; "A model"*–Journal of Economic History*; "A major historical contribution . . . a magisterial and seminal work"*–Journal of Modern History*; "A brilliant and original contribution"*–New York Review of Books*; "Social history at its absolute best"*–Past and Present.*

Such was the chorus of critical encomium that greeted the publication of Lawrence Stone's *Crisis of the Aristocracy, 1558-1641*. Despite the chorus Stone could hardly have helped being disappointed at the actual reviews. One or two were almost as fatuous as they were brief. Others, sensible within their limits, were still too short. This seems to have been the fault of editors, so intimidated by the pejorative sense of the term "discrimination" that they refuse to discriminate between a work worth more than twenty pages and one worth less than twenty words, performing their editorial duties in the matter of book reviews with a sort of timorous and lunatic egalitarianism. Moreover, in considering Stone's work, many of the reviewers hastily plunged into what has come to be called "the gentry controversy" or "the storm over the gentry," and some became almost totally immersed in it.[1] This tendency is unfortunate because so much of what Stone wrote stands on a base quite independent of its ultimate relation to that area of high historiographic turbulence and deserves attention simply on its own merits. Only three reviewers were given anywhere near enough space to do justice to the most important work on the period from the accession of Elizabeth I to the Great Rebellion written in the past quarter century or longer. In consequence of the ancient rancor of unappeased academic feuds and out of a certain condescension among economic historians, two of the three spent most of their time carping, sometimes justly, sometimes trivially, at Stone's inferences from a small cluster of his statistics. The exception to all these strictures—and it is a notable exception—is G. E. Aylmer's thoughtful and perceptive review in *Past and Present.*[2]

The intent, then, in what follows is somewhat to redress a corporate injustice by historians to a great piece of history writing; and this requires a doing of justice, a rendering to Stone's book of what is clearly its due, and at the same time a making explicit of several reservations, doubts, and questions. Why then is *The Crisis of the*

---

[1] Esp. John Kenyon, "Decline and Fall," *New York Review of Books,* July 7, 1966, pp. 23-24; D. C. Coleman, "The 'Gentry' Controversy and the Aristocracy in Crisis, 1558-1641," *History,* LI (1966), 165-74.
[2] G. E. Aylmer, *Past and Present,* No. 32 (1965), 113-25; see also the briefer, skillful review by Edward Miller, "The Elizabethan and Early Stuart Peerage," *Historical Journal,* IX (1966), 133-36.

*Aristocracy* "an original contribution" "a seminal work," "a milestone," "a landmark," and a great monument?

If one is to find an answer to this question, the first step is to ask what substantively the book seeks to do. Mainly it seeks to cope with three questions:

1. What was the way of life of the English aristocracy between about the middle of the sixteenth and the middle of the seventeenth century? What was the "total environment of [this] *élite*,"[3] and in what respects and to what extent did it change between about 1558 and about 1641?
2. What was the economic condition of the English peers during this period? What ups and downs did they suffer individually and collectively—how high up, how far down, and when?
3. How did it come about that in the early seventeenth century the leadership of concerted opposition to the actions of the ruler, exercised by English peers and magnates in the Middle Ages, fell to men about one step down on the social pyramid—the parliamentary gentry and lawyers?[4]

Stone's heart is so set on finding answers to the second and third questions that he refers to the answer to the first as a "secondary object." In doing so he greatly undervalues his most remarkable achievement. It is no depreciation of his very serious effort to answer all three questions to say that in his handling of the first question, he is most successful. Some of what he says on the second and third questions may be subject to qualification, and he defines the answer to the third question in a way that in part puts that answer out of his reach.[5] His reconstruction of the patterns of life of a social group, "the aristocracy," over a period of almost a hundred years, however, is surely not surpassed in the historical literature of any country in the world.[6]

\* \* \*

III

The third question that Stone seeks to cope with is how it came about that in the early seventeenth century the leadership of concerted opposition to the actions of the ruler, exercised by English peers and magnates in the Middle Ages, fell to men about one

---

[3] Lawrence Stone, *The Crisis of the Aristocracy, 1558-1641* (Oxford, 1965), p. 7.

[4] The key words here are "concerted opposition to the actions of the ruler." This phrase is intended to eliminate localized and uncoordinated revolts of peasants and other social groups. What is being pointed at is not so much the Civil War itself but the activities both in Parliament and in the country during the preceding twenty-one years, which along with the actions of James I, Charles I, and their officials and courtiers were constitutive of the situation from which the Civil War resulted. My three-point analysis of *Crisis of the Aristocracy* diverges slightly from Stone's own two-point analysis to make possible what I believe to be a more satisfactory account of what he has done. *Ibid.*, pp. 7-8.

[5] See below, pp. 70-71.

[6] It is touched by one small bias that readers might keep in mind. In his category of "The aristocracy" Stone includes the rich gentry, some five hundred families in 1640, as well as the peerage. Much of his nonquantitative data, however, centers around the court and courtiers, and almost all of his quantitative data have to do only with the peerage. Proportionately the peerage was more heavily represented at court than the upper gentry were. Thus 25 per cent of the peerage held office between 1625 and 1642 as against 12 per cent of the knights. G. E. Aylmer, *The King's Servants* (London, 1961), p. 324. Since, however, peerage is hereditary, a considerable number of

step down on the social pyramid—the parliamentary gentry and lawyers. It reveals another historiographic stratum of *The Crisis of the Aristocracy*. One can only guess when Stone's view of his task began to change. Perhaps between 1953 and 1958, for it was then that other scholars proposed views on the genesis of the English Revolution, divergent from and irreconcilable with the ones that had started him on his long journey through the aristocracy. However that may be, one suspects his debt to others was limited and that he mainly propelled himself into a change of opinion as his research turned up more and more data. Most likely his energy, his integrity to his evidence, and his impatience wearied him of whittling his findings down to fit the exiguous dimensions of his initial hypothesis, "that the difficulties of the sixteenth- and seventeenth-century aristocracy were at bottom financial." He ceased to believe that a financial crisis "was the sole, or even necessarily the prime, cause of their troubles."[7] Having arrived at this crucial point, he never looked back until he reached the conclusion of the concluding chapter in his big book: the crisis of the aristocracy was a crisis of prestige, the causes of which were

manifold . . . They include the decline in the wealth of the peers relative to that of the gentry; the shrinkage of their territorial possessions, in both absolute and relative terms; the decay of their military power in men, arms, castles, and will to resist; the granting of titles of honour for cash not merit, in too great numbers, and to too unworthy persons; the change in their attitude towards the tenantry from suppliers of manpower to suppliers of rent; the undermining of their electoral influence due to the rise of deeply felt political and religious issues; the increasing preference for extravagant living in the city instead of hospitable living in the countryside; the spread throughout the propertied classes of a bookish education, acquired at school and university, and the demand by the State for an administrative *élite* of proved competence, irrespective of the claims of rank; the pervasive influence of the rise of individualism, the Calvinist belief in a spiritual hierarchy of the Elect, and the Puritan exaltation of the private conscience, which affected attitudes toward hierarchy and obedience in secular society; and finally the growing psychological breach between Court and Country in attitudes, real or supposed, towards constitutional theory, methods and scale of taxation, forms of worship, aesthetic tastes, financial probity, and sexual morality.[8]

Even beyond this he came to recognize that

Particular crises arising from particular events, personalities, and policies, the ineptitude of James, the corruption of Buckingham, the obstinacy of Strafford, Laud, and Charles; the rise of puritanism, the growth of a sense of constitutionalism, the development of improved procedural techniques by the house of Commons . . . together . . .still provide the best guide to the issues which divided men one from another when civil war broke out in 1642.[9]

The movement of historical thought during a quarter of a century in the direction of sophistication and maturity implied in these long sentences may best be gauged by

peers were too young to be courtiers, thus increasing the disproportion. Therefore, the available evidence and Stone's book provide a less distorted image of the peers' way of life than of the five hundred gentry families, except for the comparatively small proportion of the latter who were also courtiers.

    [7] *Ibid.*, p. 6.
    [8] *Ibid.*, pp. 748-49.
    [9] *Ibid.*, p. 10.

repeating here the sweet simplicities of 1940. In "the English Revolution of 1640-1660 . . .an old order that was essentially feudal was destroyed by violence, a new capitalist social order created in its place."[10] As both a symptom and an exemplar of this movement, *The Crisis of the Aristocracy* is indeed a "landmark in the historical landscape," a monument to what can be achieved by historians when they break the bonds of a sterile and stifling orthodoxy and accept both the intellectual delights and the intellectual risks that such an emancipation offers to and imposes upon them.

Sharply to change directions in mid-flight to a book is a hard maneuver; the path of one's earlier trajectory almost inevitably leaves traces on one's final course; evidence gathered with one view of the past in mind does not readily accommodate itself to an altered view; and a reasonable economy with the expenditure of one's own life does not warrant a return trip through the record. In his pursuit of an understanding of the subordinate role of the peerage in the events that precipitated the upheaval of the 1640s, Stone made such a shift in mid-flight. This happened when he decided that the financial difficulties of the peers were secondary to a crisis of prestige and confidence in dragging them down. Under the circumstances it is hardly remarkable that he did not completely succeed in reorienting his work; it is remarkable that he succeeded so well. Insofar as he was able to deal with that crisis under the rubrics of power, education, and the inflation of honors, he could hardly have done better. A few of the traits of the age of crisis Stone came to understand well but in some degree too late. His earlier momentum deflected him from adequately conveying their importance, an importance which his shift in direction had enabled him adequately to grasp. His way of organizing his book (and his thoughts) diffuses attention from those traits rather than directing it to them. The problem is one of focus not, except in one particular, of omission. The three traits of the age that escape rather than capture the attention they deserve are the court-country tension and the impact of Puritanism, with which Stone deals diffusely, and the position of the lay peers as the preponderant element in the House of Lords, with which he does not deal at all.[11] What follows is an attempt, mainly in the light of evidence that Stone himself provides, to force these matters into the center of attention, rather than to permit them to flicker on the periphery.

Almost casually Stone himself makes the main point: *"The peerage in 1615 still retained its full dignity and respect."*[12] If this is so, then with respect to the crisis in the prestige of the aristocracy and of confidence in it, the hinge date is after 1615.[13]

---

[10] Hill, *English Revolution,* p. 9. This is not to argue that it is *impossible* to reduce Stone's complexities to the early simplicities. It is to suggest that those who wish to reduce the "explanation" of the English Revolution *in this or any other way* to a simplicist pattern address themselves to those complexities and not merely prescind from them on the grounds that they are unimportant. The practice of deciding in advance on meta-historical grounds and without consideration of the record of the past what is important and what is not is itself now hopelessly passé and (hopefully) past.

[11] The following observations are based on a fairly extensive, if desultory, reading in sources and secondary works on the period. In almost every detail the observations themselves require direct confimration from a systematic study of the sources.

[12] Stone, *Crisis,* p. 103. My italics.

[13] Most of the data for the following paragraphs are drawn from *ibid.,* ch. iii, "The Inflation of Honours"; App. III, p. 755; App. VIII, C, p. 761; App. XXIX and XXX, p. 789. Only *creations* from Buckingham's own accession to the peerage to the end of 1628 are counted as "Buckingham peers." The choice may be faulted on several points: 1) Buckingham's accession to favor antedates by two or three years his promotion to the peerage, leaving some peers in no man's land between Somerset's fall and Buckingham's creation. Actually, however, there are only four

But as a result of his youthful prepossessions Stone must have oriented much of his statistical investigation to the financial crisis of the peers around 1602. Despite his own later reorientation he retains that statistical bench mark in some tabulations where the issue is not financial condition but prestige, and also where the interplay of finance and prestige renders advisable the intrusion of an additional tabulation from about 1618 to 1628. Although Stone's statistics never systematically single out that decade, the figures for the inflation of honors clearly mark it for special attention. James's creation of almost a thousand knights at his accession was rather hasty, but it would not have been catastrophic had replacement been held to the annual rate of about fifty, to which it fell between 1606 and 1615, while the King's early errors slowly went down the drain of mortality. The doubling of the rate of creations from 1616 to 1625, coupled with the introjection of the baronetage, obliterated the chance for healthy attrition. And in the succeeding decade the new honor of baronet, kept well in bounds to 1618, went the way of the old one of knight, when almost two hundred new creations swamped the initial group of about one hundred. As for the peerage itself, between the promotion of Buckingham in 1618 and 1628, the number of peers almost doubled. For the mathematics of prestige and confidence, it is this cohort about which statistics would be especially welcome. In only a few of Stone's tabulations, however, can it be isolated from the whole set of creations between 1603 and 1641. With respect to marriage the group can be sorted out. It then appears that in contrast to the almost complete absence of such alliances among more ancient peerage families, by 1630 this later lot had fourteen marriages of mercantile heiresses to their credit (or discredit) either before or after their creation.

The failure to draw a line around about 1618 causes most difficulty in dealing with the economic viability of the peers, for here it is most clear that the creations of the first decade of James's reign should be treated in the main as long overdue grants of honor to Elizabethan families of means and mark—Cecil, Sydney, Egerton, Petre, Spencer, Cavendish, Stanhope, Arundell. Statistically this appropriate transfer of the dividing line would sharply increase the average and aggregate manorial holdings that Stone assigns to the "old peers" and sharply set off the narrow territorial base of the creations of the Buckingham ascendancy.[14] A comparison of their respective rental incomes in 1641 indicates the difference in landholding between the two groups of peers.[15] In 1641 the average income of peers whose families entered the peerage before 1613 was 5.1 on Stone's I-to-VIII scale. The average of those who entered in

such peers. *Ibid.,* App. V, p. 757. 2) It does not include *promotions within* the peerage during the Buckingham era. It may be argued, however, that while these promotions may have resulted in the embitterment of relations within the peerage, as far as impact on the country gentry is concerned, the major harm was done only by promotion to the peerage, since it was that promotion which exalted the status and precedence of those who received it over baronets and/or knights. 3) The list is extended beyond Buckingham's death to the end of 1628 on the grounds the Duke's influence here reached from beyond the grave, and that the braking process on creations does not become evident until 1629 at the earliest. *Ibid.*

[14] The figures as Stone gives them already mark a sharp distinction between the landed position of the "old" and "new" peerage in 1641, the former with an average of thirty-four manors apiece, the latter with twenty apiece, the former with proportionally twice as many families as the latter holding forty or more manors. *Ibid.,* App. XI, p. 764. With the creations of 1603-13 added to their number, the first group would almost certainly appear with double the average manorial holding of the peers created during the Buckingham ascendancy and with four times as many holders of forty or more manors among an approximately equal number of peers.

[15] Stone's data for 1641 are based mainly on royalist compounding papers. This should minimize *relative* error among considerable samples of peers. One cannot discount the likelihood

1618-28 was 6.2. This would mean an average gross rental of about £4000 for the peers of the Buckingham era as against £6400 for peers whose families entered the peerage before 1613; or in relative terms, on the average the Buckingham peers had just about five eighths of the income enjoyed by those of earlier vintage. By 1641 the peers created during the Duke's ascendancy had had between a quarter of a century and about half that time to augment their landholdings. Given the tendency of the aristocracy to transform other assets into acres, the shortness of so many Buckingham peers in landed wealth in 1641 suggests that they comprised a more than ordinary number of lean cattle.

The value of the above statistical exercise in terms of a prestige analysis depends in the first place on the contemporary social visibility of the groups examined. In this context the utility of Stone's statistics based on the grouping of peerage families as ante- or post-1602 is doubtful, because it is doubtful whether many contemporaries saw them in that chronological framework. By way of contrast the Buckingham peers began to attain an unenviable visibility shortly after the Villiers succeeded to full favor. That visibility increased throughout the favorite's life and may not have been wholly dimmed in the period of Charles I's personal rule. This is what gives point to the above calculation. Average income, however, is not a trait socially visible to contemporaries, and for prestige analysis the visibility of the trait quantified is important. For such analysis both the number and proportion of peers meagerly endowed with land is of special interest; in a conspicuously landed aristocracy such a meager endowment confers a negative distinction. In the group of peerage families surviving to 1641, there were more land-short peers among the creations of the ten-year Buckingham period than among all the families whose peerages antedated 1613, eighteen as against fourteen. Moreover, the land-short peers made up less than a quarter of the pre-1613 group as against more than two fifths of the Buckingham peers. Finally, there is the question of the "fit" of the especially visible subgroups of poor Buckingham peers and poor pre-1613 peers into the structure of the community. With respect to the pre-1613 peers this could hardly have been much of a problem; all but one of the families in the group had been poor before 1602, all but five before 1558. By the second quarter of the seventeenth century, their straitened circumstances should have become assimilated bits of the local social landscape, rather like venerable ivy-clad ruins. It was otherwise with the Buckingham peers, and if they lived in the country, they were trebly conspicuous: their promotions were new; the circumstances of their promotions were often questionable or simply scandalous; and in terms of talent, service, and wealth their claims to local precedence over the upper country gentry were exiguous or nonexistent. Yet their new titles automatically conferred such precedence on them. To that same upper gentry, which five times in the 1620s and twice again in 1640 gathered for meetings of Parliament, some of the poor Buckingham peers were unduly visible in the country; some of the poor and some of the rich ones, who did not make themselves visible locally, were only too visible in London, where they swarmed after or peddled the favors of a discredited court.

The mention of favor and court leads to one last statistical point. If Stone's figures are even approximately correct, the channels of large-scale favor open to English peers, scandalously broad after the accession of James, became even more scandalously

---

that men took a chance on understating the value of land for the release of which they had to pay a mulct proportional to its worth, but there is no reason to suppose that there was a marked differential in mendacity quotient as between the peers created up to 1613 and those created from 1618 through 1628.

narrow twelve years later and remained so for about another twelve. During that relatively short time the Duke of Buckingham may have been the beneficiary of offices and rewards equal to those enjoyed by the entire Elizabethan peerage throughout the whole of the Queen's forty-five-year reign.[16] In James's last days the young lover of the doting, doddering homosexual King took all, and he continued to take all for four years more as favorite of James's son and successor. Whoever else received more than scraps of reward at court enjoyed them at the hands and the behest of the Duke of Buckingham. For the English peerage this produced a dilemma not resolvable and a disaster not retrievable at the time or in the years that followed Buckingham's assassination. It transformed the diffuse difficulties of the peers into an insoluble crisis of prestige and confidence in the aristocracy. What gave form to the crisis that precipitated itself around Buckingham was a complex interplay among Puritanism, the tension between court and country, and the political position of the House of Lords. By the time he finished his great study, Lawrence Stone knew this, but like the fox he knew many things. Like hedgehogs, observant contemporary Englishmen knew scarcely more than this one big thing and often did not precisely formulate what they knew, but nevertheless they knew it very well.

Better to understand what happened and its impact on the aristocracy, one needs to examine a process of change within the social matrix of the early modern English ruling class. A no doubt oversimplified analysis may help bring into sharp focus relations between court and country, peerage and gentry, on which Stone's study casts abundant light, but light that in consequence of his chosen structure of presentation is intermittent and diffused. The components of the matrix are court peers, country peers, country gentry, court gentry, thus:[17]

|  | PEERS | GENTRY |
|---|---|---|
| COURT | court peers | court gentry |
| COUNTRY | country peers | country gentry |

In terms of *legal status* throughout the period, the line of division between peers and gentry is at each moment distinct. From the moment he enters the peerage, a man is legally distinguishable from a gentleman of whatever lower degree. So sharp a division does not necessarily separate court and country as *spheres of activity and influence.* Some peers and some of the gentry can be active both at court and in the country and have influence in both places. This social matrix may be thought of not only as a matrix of honors and a matrix of activity and influence but also as a *communications network* through which circulate and are exchanged the views and outlook of each group. In the country gentry section, however, this communications network has one peculiarity that requires special attention. That sector differs from the others in its internal structure. It is composed of the hierarchies of *local* eminence in the separate

[16] *Ibid.*, App. XIX, C, p. 775.
[17] The model suggested derives from the one which Robert Walcott found necessary in order to make some sense of English politics from the 1670s to the accession of the Hanoverian dynasty. Robert Walcott, *English Politics in the Early Eighteenth Century* (Oxford, 1956), pp. 155-58.

counties of England and Wales. The politically effective country gentry are those who stand high in at least one country hierarchy.[18] It is only this group—by Stone's estimate some five hundred men at any given time between 1558 and 1641—that is here relevant. With respect to this group of country gentry, questions arise not only about their communication with the other three components of the social matrix but with respect to intercommunication among the hierarchies across county boundaries.

Given this general structure, what follows is an attempt somewhat schematically to describe the functioning of the system that it defines at two points in time forty years apart—the late 1580s, when Elizabeth stood at the peak of her popularity, and the late 1620s. In the 1580s the line of honor between the upper gentry and the peerage had rarely been crossed in the thirty years since the Queen's accession. In that whole time by creation, restoration, and resumption there had been only fifteen accessions to the peerage in all, on the average of one every two years, and there had been but one accession in the past fifteen years. At the center among the court group there was little correlation between peerage on the one hand and power and prestige on the other. For years advancement in power and office had not brought a title to any of the court gentry, nor did possession of a title warrant expectation of official advancement. Within the framework of a deferential system, possession of peerage honors created no presumption at all as to influence on policy. The Catholicism or incompetence or relative poverty that discouraged a considerable number of peers from seeking place at a court which often demanded inputs of expenditure in excess of its outputs of rewards consigned them to "the idiocy of rural life." On the other hand, for the upper gentry places at court commensurate in power and prestige with their local authority, dignity, and "worship" were too few to attract more than a small cluster. Seen from the other direction, however, the proportion of court peers and court gentry who actively participated in the affairs of the local county hierarchies seems to have been considerable. The high place in that hierarchy legally due to the court peers by virtue of their mere titles was also practically theirs by virtue of a continuing interest in county affairs, an interest re-enforced by the appointment of some of them to the recently instituted county office of lord lieutenant. And the restrictive policy that had closed promotion to peerage to the court gentry ensured that the more eminent among them would command wealth and prestige sufficient to entitle them to a high and unchallenged position in one county hierarchy or another.

This pattern determined the directions of flow of communication. At court it flowed freely between and within gentry and peerage. And because of the local activity of court gentry and court peers alike, there was a considerable flow of effective communication between the local gentry hierarchies and the court. On the other hand, the intercommunication between the local hierarchies seems to have been relatively slight. The one institutionalized structure encouraging such communication was Parliament, where members of those hierarchies gathered in a general assembly. But meetings of Parliament under Elizabeth were both rare and brief, rarer and briefer than in the reigns of her sister, of her brother, or, after 1529, of her father. And for whatever reason, the upper country gentry does not seem to have developed a highly effective and extra-legal network of communication among the county hierarchies.[19]

18 I know of no effort to discover whether and in what number members of the upper country gentry stood high in more than one such hierarchy; I have only a vague and unverified impression that such men were few, and that even those who had estates in more than one county concentrated their struggle for influence and pre-eminence in one county only.

19 No study has been made of the role of the more or less pure country peers in local

The central switchboard, so to speak, of the lines linking the county hierarchies was at court. Because the court gentry and the court peers maintained ready and continuous communication between court and country, they retained their leadership in Parliament. This leadership was only occasionally and not very effectively challenged by a few members of the country gentry. The efforts of this cluster of men were indeed often, and not necessarily by design, frustrated by the readiness of some of the court peers and gentry to assume a mediatorial rather than an intransigent posture as between current royal policy and country misgivings about it, misgivings which they sometimes shared in part.

The set of relations among those who ruled England, just described, was remarkably effective in maintaining conditions of internal repose. It was also capable of absorbing the impact of Puritanism in its current form and state of development. For more than a decade before 1588, the program of the Puritan ministers had aimed at the substitution of Presbyterianism for episcopal government in the church, at revision of the liturgy to eliminate "Popish" elements, at congregational power over church discipline, and at an extension and better performance of preaching of the Word. Unsuccessful maneuvers to achieve the first three goals had absorbed a large part of the energy and talent of the Puritan ministry. Those goals had elicited some support from peers and gentry both at court and in the country. But in face of the Queen's intransigent opposition, they had not evoked enough enthusiasm from a large enough group anywhere to polarize the governing classes along the lines set by religious issues.

While the Puritan ministry was frustrated in its ecclesiological, liturgical, and disciplinary designs, Puritan gentry and peers were not cut off from positions of honor and power either in the country or at court. On the contrary, the Queen's long-time favorite, the Earl of Leicester, her principal Secretary of State, Sir Francis Walsingham, and a very considerable number of court peers and gentry acted as protectors and advocates for the Puritans. Indeed in Parliament itself, where Puritan country gentry found an occasional opportunity to press for one item or another of the program of the Puritan ministry, they often received open support from highly placed peers and gentlemen of the court. This open court-country alliance of Puritans did not budge the Queen's effective resistance to Puritan demands; on the other hand, it did not reduce the zeal of the court Puritans for the royal service or result in the withdrawal of royal favor from them or in any concerted action against them by the Queen and the supporters of her ecclesiastical policy. The result was that Puritanism had a diffusive rather than a polarizing impact on the English governing class and did not jeopardize its relatively easy and smooth functioning. Under the circumstances of the 1580s religious divergence did not exacerbate the tendency of court and country to polarize into two cultures incompatible and at loggerheads with each other, unable either to communicate effectively across the gulf between them or to unite their energies in a joint enterprise. The viability of the peculiar social pattern just examined was fully vindicated by effective coordination of the ruling class in court and country at the time of the Armada crisis.[20]

The passage of forty years witnessed noteworthy changes in the patterns of

affairs. It is evident that a peer like Robert Rich, 2nd Earl of Warwick, exercised large if not paramount power in Essex. To the south in Kent, however, affairs seem to have been in control of a gentry oligarchy, and just to the north the gentry dynasty of the Barnardistons with Sir Nathaniel as its head dominated Suffolk.

[20] The contrast between the situation of France and England in this respect merges in stark and dramatic vividness from the pages of Garrett Mattingly, *The Armada* (Boston, 1959).

relations within the social matrix of the ruling class. Increase in the number of peers and especially increased readiness to reward service in high court office with peerages automatically enhanced the power of the court peers. This dual process correlatively and inevitably diminished the importance and power at court of the court gentry. The diminution of their power at court weakened their position within the county hierarchies. With neither the wealth nor the prestige that four decades earlier their eminence at court had afforded them in the country, they tended to withdraw from activities in which they no longer could hope to receive the respect and "worship" that their predecessors had enjoyed. This decline in status and power became markedly evident in the incapacity of the court gentry to lead that assembly of the upper country gentry, the House of Commons. In the county hierarchies the influence of the court peers did not expand proportionally to the shrinkage of the influence of the court gentry there; if anything, to the contrary. The inflation of peerage honors created a fatal dichotomy between legal right of precedence on the one hand and respect, worship, and effective power in the actual workings of the county hierarchies on the other. The latter increasingly went to those who actually did the work—the more assiduous deputy-lieutenants and justices of the peace, painstaking in their attendance at musters, quarter sessions, and petty sessions. Neither court peers nor country peers exercised much control over these rulers of the countryside, whose power and influence depended on local estimates of merit and worth that increasingly diverged from the canon for advancement at court.

By 1628 communication between the country gentry and the court, which forty years earlier had proceeded smoothly, was hopelessly snarled. No analysis of the sort favored by Stone can quite do justice to the circumstances that raised the misunderstanding and cross-purposes between the court on one side and the country gentry on the other to the crisis level, where what one regarded as communication the other deemed irrelevant and intolerable noise. Month by month, year by year, for a quarter of a century, while alienation from the country and contempt for the tastes and modes of both perception and valuation current there increased at court, misgiving, doubt, distrust, and detestation of almost everything that began in and emanated from the court rose among the country gentry. The accentuation of mutual distrust started with the accession of James or perhaps a little before.[21] It was more intense in 1615 than it had been in 1603. With the accession of Buckingham, aside from one brief, adventitious respite of good will that followed the breakdown of negotiations for the Spanish match in 1624, the force of the flood of anger grew. At the dissolution of Parliament in 1629, it culminated in a sort of collective rage of mutual frustration and bitterness. Such a process can best be presented not in analytical but in narrative form. The story itself becomes the explanation of the series of events it recounts. Only when one follows those events in chronological sequence does one acquire a sense of the cumulative fury that was creating the situation of the later 1620s when the court and country hierarchies no longer adequately understood what the other was saying, because in matters of the utmost importance to both they had practically ceased to speak the same language.

The breakdown of understanding between the court and the local gentry hierarchies coincided with and was in fact the occasion for a most significant development of intercommunication among the local hierarchies of country gentry. By

[21] Some of the debates in the later Elizabethan Parliaments over issues not specifically related to religion suggest the earlier date. So does the extraordinary and rapid response of the House of Commons, beginning on the very first day of James's first Parliament, evoked by the case *Goodwin vs. Fortescue.*

1628 that communication had markedly increased in quantity and improved in quality. The improvement in quality was assisted by the improvement and intensification of the education of the upper gentry. In the universities and at the Inns of Court, more of them received a training that was both longer and better suited to their needs than it had been. The improvement was also a function of an improved information network. Pitifully meager no doubt by present-day standards, the growing volume of newsletters flowing from London to the country provided the county hierarchies of the 1620s with a larger body of shared information (and misinformation) about current events in the great world than their predecessors of the 1580s received. The increase in volume of intercommunication among the county hierarchies was itself a consequence of their better education and better information; men communicate more when they know more to communicate about. Above all, however, the impulse to create means of intercommunication among the country gentry across county lines derived from the common sense of a need for it. The need was the result of the divergence of outlook, opinion, and judgment between the court and the upper country gentry on an ever broader range of issues. Obligingly, though under some duress, the court itself nurtured in the leaders of the counties an awareness of how fully they shared common views on major matters and provided them with opportunities for communication unparalleled in Elizabeth's reign. In the five Parliaments that James and Charles summoned between 1621 and 1628, the greater country gentry from all over England met and worked together, day in and day out, in the House of Commons. There they unconsciously constructed a collective representation of a common enemy, the court, which temporarily obliterated all the latent divergencies in their own views.

These circumstances did not make the country gentry Puritan; about 1628 some were Puritans, some were not. To identify some country gentry who clearly were Puritan at the time is not hard; to identify many who clearly were not is more difficult unless they enthusiastically took part in or supported Archbishop Laud's measures of ecclesiastical policy; and such men were few. The transformation in Puritanism itself is what makes it hard to define the boundary zone between Puritan and mere (anti-Laudian) Protestant in the late 1620s.

Like its antecedent in this matter, Christian humanism, Puritanism slowly re-educated the English landed classes and reoriented and inflated their expectations both of themselves and of others. This reorientation touched many aspects of human existence. It especially touched public life. Puritanism did not create the idea of such a life; some such notion had begun to re-emerge in the Middle Ages and received further specification during the Renaissance. But for many Puritanism gave a new and special poignancy to their conception of the purpose of public life. It set the goal of that life very high, no less than the *regnum Christi*, the kingdom of God on earth, where His will should be done. With so exalted an end, Puritanism made very severe demands on those who took part in ruling the English commonwealth, the Elect Nation of God, the cynosure of the faithful everywhere, "as a City on a Hill." There office should be precatory rather than predatory, for prayer not for prey, a dedication rather than an exploitation.

The spread of this sense of the nature of public life was slow and sporadic.[22] The propagation of the Puritan view of the right quality of life, even the effective and

[22] Its earliest embryonic expression in England was perhaps pre-Reformation. There are elements of it, at least, in Thomas More's *Utopia*, with the appropriate Christian overtones but, of course, without the emotional charge generated by the conflict with Popery, and without the special rhetoric that that conflict engendered.

detailed formulation of that view, were the consequences of a paradox. They owed much to Elizabeth and James I who opposed, frustrated, and defeated the Puritans in the arena of ecclesiastical politics. From the 1570s to the first decade of the seventeenth century, the Puritans tried to impose their ecclesiological and liturgical views on the English Church by exerting pressure at court indirectly through Parliament and directly through friends in the Queen's Council and near her person. Their successive defeats gradually diverted the energies of many Puritans from the divisive issues of the one right government and form of worship for the church. Puritans were also deprived of access to the responsibilities and ambiguities of power and, from the late sixteenth century on, turned their main effort toward the ministry and molding of conscience. In this range of activity the central authorities failed effectively to restrain the spiritual brotherhood from propagating a version of the gospel increasingly in conflict with the ethical outlook of the court.

With declining hope of access to power through the court and an increasingly well-defined opposition to the way of life, the ethic, the ordering of values characteristic of the court, the Puritan ministry zealously sought a welcome for its message among leaders of the county hierarchies who dominated life in the country. By that time the spiritual brotherhood of godly ministers in England was no longer so overtly or intensely committed as it had been to a program that required a remodeling of the whole ecclesiastical structure and therefore the support of the authority of the Crown. In 1641 that ministry again turned its attention directly to the divisive problems of church government. In the interval between the successful repression of the Presbyterian movement by Elizabeth and Archbishop Whitgift and its re-emergence in the early days of the Long Parliament, the principal concerns of the godly clergy had become the effective ministry of the Word, the cultivation and sensitizing of Christian consciences, and propaganda against the Popish resurgence at home and abroad, preoccupations which the Puritans shared with a very large segment of the country gentry. These shared preoccupations make it hard for us at three centuries' distance to identify lay Puritans and may have made it hard at the time for some men to be clear in their own minds whether they were Puritan or not. The new direction of thrust of Puritan thought and action after political defeat by Elizabeth thus encouraged the symbiosis between Puritanism and the country gentry and afforded to the Puritan laity opportunities for leadership in the country that they had lost at court.

The favorable circumstances, partly accidental, partly the fruit of policy, that in the 1580s enabled the court so to manage the Puritans as to enjoy the benefits of their energy and intelligence without having to suffer their domination, ceased to exist. By the 1620s the Puritans for practical purposes were out of court in fact and in hope. They had no place to turn but to the country and primarily to the country gentry. Beyond all other issues uniting the country gentry and dividing them from the court in the 1620s was the one that had bound court and country together in the 1580s – the posture of the Elect Nation in its relation to a beleaguered international Protestantism on the Continent and in the face of a victoriously resurgent Popery. In the present context, discussion of the shortcomings of the views current among the country gentry on such complex matters, of the inadequacy of their understanding, of the irrationality of their response is irrelevant. Whether under the circumstances any policy that the Government attempted to follow could have succeeded, whether the country gentry had the faintest notion of viable alternatives to the succession of cul-de-sacs into which James and Charles plunged, does not matter. What does matter is that everything the Stuarts tried failed and that, as the decade passed, responsibility for failure rested ever more clearly on the Duke of Buckingham. And all this concurred in time with the suspicion that he was responsible for most of the doings at court that annoyed, alarmed, and shocked the country gentry, and with his evident responsibility for many of them. The diffuse but fervent international Protestantism of the larger and richer part of the country gentry had at its hard core the zeal of the Puritan gentry. The anguished cry "Avenge, O Lord, Thy slaughtered Saints!" was wrung from a Puritan heart at a later time, but some of the emotion it reflects — pity for the continental Protestant victims and hatred for their Popish tormentors — was common to the Puritan clergy, the Puritan gentry, and the mere Protestant gentry of the country of the 1620s. And in the 1620s that emotion was powerfully magnified by impotent rage at the paralysis of English policy and by hysterical dread of the inroads of Popery at home, especially at court. Men who a couple decades earlier would not have much troubled themselves to act in behalf of the ministers ejected for resistance to the canons of 1604 had little patience with attacks on preachers whose offense was zeal in denouncing doings that they themselves deplored, doings which in appearance and often in fact were generated and consummated at court.

How much of the Puritan ethic forced its way into the hearts of the country gentry by the way of a widely shared concern for the perils of Protestantism is hard to know and hard to find out; but it is scarcely an accident that Richard Baxter, who was well enough aware that he was a dissenter after 1660, did not know that he was a Puritan before the 1640s. It is at least likely that involvement in the care and feeding of zealous preachers of the Word absorbed into the Puritan lay fellowship a part of the gentry which had hitherto stood outside it. It also provided new means and new motives for intercommunication of the gentry hierarchies. Favorite preachers among the lecturers established lines of communication between the gentry of different counties; so too did the need to protect them from harassment directed from the court. Finally, bonds of friendship, reinforced by a shared religious outlook originating in the several Puritan-dominated colleges at Oxford and Cambridge, carried over among the Puritan gentry after college days. The seeds for the dense growth of interrelations among the Puritans in the country, so easy to discern in the 1630s, were sown some decades earlier and matured very fast in the favorable climate of the 1620s. Puritanism, then, advanced the consolidation of the country gentry, broadened the "credibility gap" that isolated the court from the country, and itensified the nationwide crisis of the 1620s.

Supposing the foregoing description of the transformation of the political scene in about four decades to be reasonably accurate, adequately to document it would require years of work in published sources, national and local archives, and private muniments. An early study of mine sought to lay bare the intricate links of cousinship that, regardless of county lines, bound several Puritan "families" of cousins and clients into a sort of Mafia of saints.[23] A letter from a devout dowager to Sir Simonds D'Ewes about her step-grandson, Sir Nathaniel Barnardiston, the leading gentleman and leading Puritan in Suffolk, further illustrates the transvaluation of values that took place in the days of the early Stuarts:

Let me desire you further this bearer Mr. Burrell, the late and to my sence the yet minister of Wratting, if Sir Nathan:B:bee as I hope he is earnest to have him restored

[23] J. H. Hexter, *The Reign of King Pym* (Cambridge, Mass., 1942), pp. 84-88.

as well to liuing as libertye. You may out of your interest in him and respect towards him in direct tearmes let him know that he will suffer much in the opinion of his country neighbors here in these parts, many looke upon the success of this business, and surely as this man speed Sir Nath wilbe censured if it be not fully evidenced to them that he desired and indevoured to have him restored to both. The name of Barnardiston is and ever shalbe precious to me: and if any of that name, especially the Luster of the house, should undergoe justly any tart censure or insurre an harde conceit amongst his neighbors, and those of the best ranke according to Gods account, it would even much devert me, in these my declining dayes. Therefore at my intreatie be verie earnest about this desire of myne, and of this I am confident: that the work will be acceptable to god, and bring much comfort to your own conscience, which that it may doe shalbe the earnest desire.[24]

What survives of older days and older ways in Lady Anne's letter is the intense concern for "the name of Barnardiston" and "the luster of the house." This depends on the place of the head of the house, Sir Nathaniel, in the county hierarchy. That place ultimately depends on "the opinion of his country neighbors." That opinion itself, however, is no longer to be won by any of the marks of favor that the court can lavish on a country man. On the contrary, it is to be won by an act of quiet but manifest subversion, in which Sir Nathaniel restores to his living a Puritan minister displaced by the clerical faction favored at court. And finally beyond court favor, the older complex measure of earthly status in the country — an amalgam based on broad acres, a loyal tenantry, riches, and ancient lineage — is made yet more intricate by dependence on the approval of a rather special reference group, a new kind of hierarchy, *those of best rank according to God's account*, an account not wholly accessible short of Judgment Day.

The crisis of aristocracy was in part a correlate of this broader crisis which caught the peerage in a cross fire from which there was no escape. In the first place, the polarization between the court and the country gentry destroyed the capacity of the peers corporately and individually to play the mediatorial role in which they were cast by Elizabethan policy. There was no way for them to harmonize the signals of discontent and disaffection that came up to them from the country with the demands for unquestioning trust and compliance that came down to them from the court. What was true of their activity was equally true of their mode of life. It had been hard enough to maintain a viable pattern of behavior appropriate to both court and country in the sixteenth century before the demands of the two so completely diverged. In the 1620s it was almost impossible. No peer who maintained the style of life at court under Charles I that the Earl of Leicester did under Elizabeth could have gained and retained leadership of the Puritan-country "coalition." The Puritan-country ideal of zeal, sobriety, austerity, and indifference to earthly rewards was not congenial to the court; even less so were its practice of sanctimony and plain speaking and its distaste for ceremony. The courtier's ideal of grace, urbanity, and cultivated hedonism was not

[24] BM, Anne Barnardiston to Sir Simonds D'Ewes, Jan. 1641, Harl. MSS, 384, fol. 27. This document came to my attention through Kenneth Shipps. I hope and expect that Shipps's doctoral dissertation on the relations between the clergy and laity in early Stuart East Anglia will firm up or blow up some of the framework above outlined. Meantime, I thank him for permission to publish this letter.

congenial to the Puritan-infested county hierarchies; even less so were its practice of and, worse, its tolerance of idleness, display, flattery, gambling, fornication, adultery, and sodomy. These ancient sports were surely not unknown in the country, but there they carried penalties in terms of power or at least exacted that hypocrisy which is vice's tribute to virtue. At the very time when court and country demands on the aristocracy so sharply diverged, the inflation of peerage from 1618 to 1628 injected into that body a large increment of members without much inclination to the country ideal or practice. Their aptitudes such as they were seemed to lie in the direction of the court ideal and especially of court practice.

What has been said helps to provide an answer to the third problem posed early in this study: why did the members of the upper gentry rather than of the peerage assume the positions of leadership in "the general crisis of the seventeenth century, 1618-1641" in England? There were of course, perforce or by choice a considerable number of country peers. Some, however, were disqualified for leadership by religion; they were overt or crypto-Catholics, and their religious attachment opposed them to the partly Puritan and wholly anti-Catholic leadership of the upper gentry. Many of the rest were too insignificant to cut much of a local figure. But worst of all, it may be suspected, most of them were too stupid. Inheritance of title is not a very satisfactory predictor of political talent, certainly not to be compared to ability, energy, and dedication to duty and to acquisition of power. These latter traits, not merely wealth and legal status, inherited or granted by court favor, were required of those who worked their way up or held on to their places in the highly competitive, quasimeritocracies of the counties. Not only were the peers pulled apart by the divergence of expectations between court and country analyzed above; they were also trapped by the rising demand for competence on the country side, as the need for experience, knowledge, ability, and aptitude for countermaneuver against court policy increased. In this crisis situation, in comparison with the upper country gentry, the peers who cast in with them were relatively deficient in talent, training, experience, and number. In this situation they found their place beside rather than above, as collaborators with rather than leaders of, the disaffected gentry.

So much emerges by refining and slightly altering the focus on data, almost all of which can be found in *The Crisis of the Aristocracy*. But at the very outset of his book, by declining to consider the peers as a corporate body, members of the House of Lords, Stone separates the crisis from the political collapse of the House. On purely historical grounds the procedure is hard to justify;[25] it is like putting asunder whom, if not God, at least English public law had long since joined. It was a joining that surely affected the positions of the peers individually as well as collectively between 1559 and 1641, for after all an important element in the prestige and the power of every individual peer was the prestige and power of the corporate body of which he was a proud member. And in the general crisis that took shape from 1618 on, that corporate body had a lot going against it. Specifically, it ran athwart the statistics and mathematics of the peerage in Parliament. The details of those statistics would require close, almost daily, examination as the crisis moved from one issue to another in Parliament, which after all was where much of the action was or at least where it ended up being. However, a simple and rough computation at an arbitrary date about 1641 makes the gross outlines evident enough. It goes like this:

[25] Stone could well justify it on other grounds: that enough—or fourteen years' work—is enough. I would heartily agree.

150   total peers *ca.* 1641
76   majority of peers

minus $\left\{ \begin{array}{l} 26 \\ 20 \end{array} \right.$  bishops   Catholic peers $\left. \begin{array}{l} \\ \end{array} \right\}$ safe for the King

leaving      30   non-Catholic lay peers required for court majority

i.e.       24% of total lay peers (124) required for court majority (30 ÷ 124 = 24%)

It is possible, of course, that the country gentry who led the House of Commons never made so crude a computation. But in parliamentary matters they were anything but stupid men; if they did not make it, it is because of its crudity not because of their excessive moral sensibility or of defective political awareness and intelligence. Some such calculation clearly preceded the bill to exclude bishops from the upper house in 1641. It would be a little surprising if the leading members of the House of Commons did not explicitly or intuitively strike a series of trial balances substantially rather like the one above on issue after issue in the Parliaments from 1621 on.[26] For them the House of Lords, like a lady of easy virtue, was often in demand, usually available, but never wholly to be trusted.

A theory which treated the peers in Parliament as an aristocracy holding the balance of the constitution between monarchy (the king) and democracy (the House of Commons) had been propounded in Elizabeth's day. It vanished under the early Stuarts.[27] James I and Charles I were disinclined to regard their own powers in a light so unflatteringly secular and potentially restrictive. And although they had no theory of their own that would break the deadlock that had developed between them and the court, the Puritan-country political calculators had no inclination to a theory that awarded to the peers, who sat in Parliament solely by virtue of birth, of royal caprice, or of flat cash payment, a voice as authoritative as that which the Commons claimed as representatives of the communities of England and held as a result of the superior intelligence of their leaders. In effect, from the 1620s to 1642 the peerage ran into a kind of situation that recurred in 1827-32 and 1906-11; in their corporate capacity they did not appear as a body that did nothing in particular and did it very well, but as a body peculiarly constituted in existing circumstances to do something in particular and do it badly. The addition of this political element to the others that Stone deals with either definitely or diffusely increases the intelligibility of the crisis of the aristocracy.

It also calls attention to one of the most annoying perplexities of the period—the ultimate revival of the prestige of the aristocracy. At the Restoration the peerage regained political effectiveness after a decline and fall lasting four decades or more.

[26] That politically passive busybody, John Chamberlain, was already counting the votes of the bishops in the Addled Parliament of 1614. There are subsequent intimations of awareness in the House of Commons of the influence of the court "bloc" in the House of Lords, and in crucial matters it was clear that the bishops provided the court with the controlling votes in the upper house in the Short Parliament. C. H. Firth, *The House of Lords during the Civil War* (London, 1910), pp. 36, 48, 66.

[27] As late as 1607, with surprising docility, the House of Commons swallowed without protest the Earl of Northampton's view that only the upper house was institutionally qualified to deal with "matters of state" such as foreign affairs. As representatives of purely local interests, he alleged, the House of Commons was institutionally disqualified, regardless of any accidental qualifications of some of its members in such matters. *Ibid.,* pp. 34-35.

The gradual absorption into the pattern of political orthodoxy of that theory of mixed government by King, Lords, and Commons to which both court and country were inhospitable under the early Stuarts was a symptom of this revival. This first perplexity is simply a part of a still broader perplexity that has afflicted many historians of the period, a certain uneasiness about the English Revolution when viewed as one of the series of great revolutions in the Western World—the Reformation, the English, the American, the French, and the Russian Revolution. On analysis this uneasiness seems to have two components, one historiographic or mythographic, the other more strictly historical. The historiographic grounds for uneasiness are so well documented as to be scarcely arguable. In the patterns in which whole peoples think of their past, 1517, 1776, 1789, and 1917 appear to have an uneradicable place in the collective memory. However historians nowadays or hereafter may evaluate their actual consequences, men very soon afterwards thought of the events of those years as inaugurating a new era, a *novus ordo saeclorum,* and have continued so to think of them to this day. No such thing happened in the English case. If historians today tried to settle on a common date—1628? 1640? 1649? 1688?—inaugurating the new era in English history, they would be as hard put as if they tried to dislodge those other dates—1517, 1776, 1789, 1917—from their time-hallowed places. In at least one clear sense in which the Reformation, the American Revolution, the French Revolution, and the Russian may be said to have made it, the English Revolution did not make it at all.

The failure of the English people as a whole or any large number of them to enshrine in their hearts the English Revolution of the mid-seventeenth century drove historians who believed it really was a revolution anyhow to an anxious search for plausible grounds for their conviction. Most of the search was conducted during a time span ill-starred in two respects. First, there was little consensus among historians on what to count as a revolution; yet they suffered from the illusion, at once uncomfortable and unwarranted, that the term was useless unless they could discover or define what a revolution "really" was. Since to discern a common essence in the Neolithic Revolution, the Industrial Revolution, the Scientific Revolution, the French Revolution of 1789, and the Revolution of 1830 in the Netherlands requires hallucinatory gifts not granted most historians, the search was on the whole unsuccessful. Second, the search coincided with a growing conviction that to count as a "real" revolution, any lapse of a relatively stable human community into long internecine war involving the disruption, displacement, or alteration of the prime center of accepted authority had to be a social revolution.

Instead of clarifying counsel, this somewhat gratuitous stipulation confused it. It committed historians to the view that all major or big or real revolutions were brought about by and in the interest of particular social classes. By means and as a consequence of each such revolution, the victorious revolutionary class wholly or in part achieved its conscious (or semiconscious) social ends.[28] Its ends always encompassed the increase of its own political and economic power in the community and, as a condition of that increase, the overthrow, subjection, exploitation, and expropriation of other classes. Unfortunately this model makes something less than a perfect fit on any of the revolutions it is supposedly designed for, and on none worse than the English

---

[28] Consequences *inverse* to the intention of the revolutionaries should not count, for example, bureaucratization in Soviet Russia, Bonapartism in nineteenth-century France, or the increased secularization of politics in England after 1660. They may have been in part consequences of what the revolutionaries did; they were not at all what the revolutionaries wanted.

Revolution, on which it hangs in disarray like an ill-designed, ill-cut sack. Historians who have tried to cope with this unhappy situation have not had much luck. The more they work at the problem, the more it appears that the notion that the English Revolution, 1640-60, was not in the foregoing sense a social revolution has something going for it, and that historians who want it the other way have a good bit going against them.

Nothing else is going as badly against them as the actual outcome of the English Revolution *vis-à-vis* the aristocracy. From pretty far back that class seemed destined to be overthrown, expropriated, and suppressed—both the immediate and the ultimate victim of the upheaval. Even before the revolution its prestige and social status had grown shaky. The imperatives that governed the decisions and actions of much of the aristocracy had become irrelevant and even repugnant to other social classes, particularly to those a step or two down the social pyramid.[29] Because so many aristocrats ended as allies and supporters of the Crown, once the revolution broke out, their property was sequestrated, decimated, and in some instances confiscated outright. The large packet of political authority and power once theirs as members of the House of Lords got whittled down in practice until 1649, when it too was wholly confiscated. Finally, all these changes took place over a relatively short time span at the behest of the leaders of the revolution or with their consent and in pursuit of what they deemed their proper purposes. For historians the trouble with the English Revolution is that none of these changes lasts or leaves an indelible impress on the social order.

What makes the English Revolution suspect as a social revolution is the restoration of the peerage economically, politically, socially, and ideologically after 1660. For this is what happened, and what Stone says happened, for which he will earn less than golden opinions from those whose presuppositions require them to believe otherwise. Since, by the criteria of social revolution proposed above, the peers seemed to be marked out to be the losers, the main thrust of history writing from the 1920s to the 1950s was to force them to play the role in which historians cast them. As it actually happened, the peers, who should have been the victims, were the victors. Some peerage families loyal, but not too loyal, to King Charles indeed suffered both during the Interregnum and after from the cost incurred in meeting payment for compounding for the return of their estates to their possession before 1660. Other changes—more flexible mortgage arrangements improvements in the terms of credit, stricter estate settlements—however, improved their situation. Economically the peerage still comprised England's greatest landlords. In a society in which land remained the surest route of access to political consequence, the peers' collective share of landed income appears to have been greater in 1688 than in 1601.[30] After the Restoration individual peers learned better how to use their wealth for political purposes. The day of connectional and interest politics was dawning, when the management of family parliamentary interests combined with access to a share of crown patronage was the key to power, a key that peers inclined to politics were long to manipulate with great success. The high noon of "the Whig oligarchy" was not far off. The political viability of the peers as individuals was complemented by that of the peerage in its

---

[29] For the notion of the fabric of imperatives, see J. H. Hexter, "The Loom of Language and the Fabric of Imperatives: The Case *Il Principe* and *Utopia*," *A.H.R.,* LXIX (1964), 945-68.

[30] The worst that can be said for the estimates of Thomas Wilson (1601) and Gregory King (1688) is that they provide no ground for believing otherwise. The estimates are given in Stone, *Crisis,* App. XII, p. 767.

constitutional embodiment in the House of Lords. The reinstitution of that House after its aboliton during the Interregnum was complete and integral. It was accompanied by the gradual but almost universal acceptance of the theory of mixed government which conferred on the House of Lords the function of "balancing" the constitution, of preventing it from drifting too far in the direction of "mere monarchy" embodied in the king or "mere democracy" embodied in the House of Commons. Finally, the old social hierarchy of deference and place re-established itself. Alexander Pope's celebration of the Great Chain of Being in the Age of Newton was perhaps less grand than Shakespeare's in the Age of Gloriana; nevertheless, it fitted the temper of that later age better. So did the formulations of the contemporary pretensions of the peers to their due place in the social hierarchy (at the top), which was put in civil rather than theological terms. And so in the outcome of the English Revolution, the lordly victims were victors.

One victor in the revolution at least was its victim. The habits of thought associated with it no doubt continued to form the characters of many Englishmen, but at the Restoration Puritanism had lost its power to define the expectations of the politically effective classes. After 1660 not many Englishmen in a position to exert strong political pressure brought it to bear in the service of the aspirations once evoked by conceptions like the Elect Nation, the Holy Commonwealth, the Rule of the Saints, and the New Jerusalem. The moral climate of politics had undergone an abrupt change, becoming in the process considerably less rigorous. In twenty years of power the Saints had failed and failed and failed again to construct viable foundations for the Government of England, and as a major political force Puritanism itself was buried in the rubble of their failures. They had proved unable to rise to the level of their own demands, and so in the interest of a workable civil order, the expectations of their rulers that the Puritans had entertained and taught others to entertain had to be scaled down.[31] One effect of this reduction of expectations was to relieve the peers of some of the impossible demands for austerity of political conduct and dedication to selfless ends that they failed to meet before 1640. Such an austerity and dedication, unrelated or potentially adverse to their individual and corporate interests, are extremely rare in the members of any group and are scarcely to be dreamed of in a group created by the principles of selection governing the English peerage.

After 1660 the peers were also relieved of the second impossible demand that faced them from the 1620s to the 1640s, a demand for levels and kinds of competence quite beyond their reach, though well within the reach of the combined talents of the upper gentry and great lawyers, the group from which the bulk of the House of Commons was chosen. By the quite intelligible deficiency and default of the peerage, this group had been left to meet and did meet the central crisis of the age, the crisis of the constitution. Again this crisis abated somewhat at the Restoration and yet more at the Revolution of 1688, and with it abated the almost continuous demand for high skill as well as for Puritanical fervor that the crisis had evoked before 1640. Once the upheavals subsided, the House of Lords could get along quite comfortably "with no pretence of intellectual eminence or scholarship sublime." In addition to the powers of adaptation that the peerage displayed, to which Stone does full justice, it was this double lowering of expectation and demand that brought the English aristocracy out of the turbulence of the early seventeenth century and the catastrophes of its middle

---

[31] The trajectory of expectations could probably be traced with reasonable accuracy by a study of the successive terms of political settlements proposed or deemed acceptable by the various Puritan groups, excepting only small clusters of apocalyptic chiliasts.

decades into the quieter waters beyond. The accommodation was after all mutual—an adaptation of the aristocracy to a changing society, but also an adaptation of the demands of that society to what the aristocracy had a capacity to supply.

To say that the English Revolution was not in any clearly intelligible sense a social revolution is not to say that it was trivial. An eruption that kept England in turmoil for twenty years cannot be thus casually written off. Beyond that, it did settle, perhaps more effectively than its surviving leaders thought when the Restoration came, several important political issues that were in doubt as late as 1640. How completely it settled them was not altogether evident until the foolish younger son of the revolution's most eminent victim stumbled into an attempt to alter the terms of settlement. To his loss James II learned how firmly fixed were the boundaries to the authority and power of the king of England.

With respect to the problems that the term "revolution" poses for historical discourse, a contemplation of the result of the crisis of the English aristocracy in the seventeenth century is most instructive. It suggests that the term sometimes may be sensibly applied to upheavals which did not permanently alter the distribution of wealth, the control of the means of production, or the structure of society, and which only modified but did not subvert the prior organization and distribution of political power. In the general upheaval in England between 1640 and 1660, one can discern a religious revolution that first succeeded and then collapsed, the Puritan Revolution; a political revolution that succeeded and then collapsed, the republican revolution; and a potential socio-political revolution that flared up briefly but did not succeed, the Leveller movement. To deny that those twenty years were an era of revolution would seem to entail an excessive austerity in the use of the term, or to impose gratuitously the rather unreasonable restrictive covenant that only revolutions that were ultimately successful shall count as revolutions, which leaves one with no term to apply to the many revolutions that have not succeeded. It is even more arbitrarily restrictive to apply the term only to those upheavals the consequences of which were permanent drastic alterations in the structure and the functioning of society. And it is an act of desperation to bend and twist the evidence in order tightly to bind such upheavals to major long-run social changes to which at best they were linked casually and tangentially. In the case of the English Revolution, some scholars have engaged in such distortions in order to force that revolution to fit a simplicist model of the over-all development of Western or world civilization. The motive is intelligible, but the result is rarely commendable.

Equally intelligible but even less commendable is the peculiar psychological quirk that causes some historians to identify their own achievement with the magnitude or success or "importance" in the past of the events and affairs that engage their attention. There is after all no evidence whatever that merely by choosing a "big subject," a historian adds a cubit to his stature. Nor is there evidence that for the understanding of the past the investigation of failure is less rewarding than the exploration of success. The measure of a historian is not the importance in the past of what he chooses to write about, but the importance of what he writes about it, which is a very different thing. Of this the book here so closely scrutinized is the best proof. It may be hard or impossible to evaluate the over-all importance in the past of two crises, both of relatively brief duration, in the affairs of some of the 382 men that constitute the English peerage from 1558 to 1641. That a history written about those men seen in the framework of those crises can be important indeed, Lawrence Stone has demonstrated beyond reasonable doubt. He has done so in the most convincing way possible—by writing about them one of the most important historical works of the past quarter-century—"a milestone," "a landmark," a monument.


# POSTSCRIPT TO EIGHT HUNDRED AND FORTY-ONE PAGES

### Lawrence Stone

It would be churlish indeed for an author to carp at a review of his book so expansively generous in scale and in tone, so perceptive in understanding his purpose, and so ingenious in employing his data to suggest new hypotheses. These remarks are strictly confined to a critique of the last section of the article by J. H. Hexter, in which he puts forward his own theory to explain the English Civil War and Revolution.

Hexter argues that the basic political polarity of the early seventeenth century was that of court against country, both regarded as "spheres of activity and influence." In the late Elizabethan period their spheres interlocked in such a way as to defuse tension. The court embraced peers and gentry, Anglicans and Puritans, hawks and doves and was therefore able to handle the first assault of Presbyterianism, the financial crisis of the aristocracy, and the political strains of an eighteen-year war. By the 1620s, however, the spheres were revolving independently, and tension was building up between them. Peers were becoming increasingly identified with and dependent upon the court, and gentry were being excluded; a narrow and intolerant high Anglicanism was extruding all Puritans from positions of authority or influence at court and driving them back into the country; and the Government was obstinately pursuing an intensely unpopular and unsuccessful foreign policy. To alter the metaphor, in the 1580s the court acted as the central switchboard for the lines of communication between the forty-odd county hierarchies; by the 1620s the central switchboard was out of action, and new lines were being developed laterally between the hierarchies which short-circuited it.

Secondly, Hexter argues that the most explosive political force of the seventeenth century was Puritanism, and it was the failure of the court to handle the Puritan problem which was the cause of its downfall. It was Puritanism which created the lines of communication between the county hierarchies, and Puritanism which set up a rival ideological hierarchy which threatened the old social and political patterns of authority in both court and country. "Puritanism, then, advanced the consolidation of the country gentry, broadened the 'credibility gap' that isolated the court from the country, and intensified the nationwide crisis of the 1620s."

There is obviously much truth in all this, and Hexter's brilliant formulation enables historians to see connections and understand trends which were only dimly perceived before. In my book I talked about the importance of the court/country split in religious, political, social, and cultural terms, the growing concentration of the peers on the court, the fatal role of the Duke of Buckingham, and the corrosive influence of Puritanism on the hierarchic view of secular society as then established, but I failed to spell out the linkages between these phenomena. Hexter has helped to identify the problem more clearly and to spell out the chronology of the political crisis.

But my reservations concerning this part of Hexter's hypothesis are twofold. First, I am deeply suspicious of any mono-causal theory of history as no doubt Hexter is, but I think that he here places far too much of the burden of explanation on the already overloaded shoulders of Puritanism. No religious ideology—particularly one as amorphous as Puritanism—exists in a social vacuum, as Hexter knows very well, and therefore it cannot be conscripted to serve as a self-sufficient intellectual *deus ex machina* with which to explain a major revolution. Puritanism itself needs explanation, and that explanation must be social, political, and institutional as well as intellectual. Furthermore, the spread of Puritanism among the gentry and the consequences of it hypothesized by Hexter have still to be proved, as he himself admits. Local studies, like that of Alan M. Everitt for Kent, suggest that that influence was limited to a minority of the gentry, although a critically important minority. No one—not even the Marxists—can or does deny today that Puritanism was a *necessary* cause of the English Revolution, without which it would not have taken place. It was the ideology of Puritanism which gave the parliamentary opposition that sense of moral conviction of their own rectitude which drove them to defy the King even by force of arms. But was it by itself a *sufficient* cause? Even if it were a factor in its own right, one of those disembodied ideas floating in historical space which some intellectual historians love to toy with, even if it could be proved that its influence was as pervasive as Hexter suggests, it still would not by itself be a sufficient cause for the English Revolution. The long-drawn financial crisis of the state, the relative economic and status decline of the aristocracy, the erosion of respect for a monarchy which favored men like Buckingham, Archbishop Laud, Sir Thomas Wentworth, and Sir Francis Windebank, the financial, administrative, and moral condition of the Anglican Church, the rise of literacy and grammar school and university education, the permeation of the governing classes with the constitutional ideas of the common lawyers, the tension between the petty bourgeois in the towns and the monopolistic merchant elites—all these and many more are factors which would have to be included in any overarching framework of explanation for the English Revolution. Even if it could be proved that Puritanism played the part Hexter ascribes to it, even if it is assumed to be a closed system without causes running back deeply into society, to concentrate upon a single factor, important though it was, is to fly in the face of all that scholars have learned about human nature and the historical process.

The second hypothesis advanced by Hexter is that the English Revolution cannot have had deep social causes because it did not have deep social consequences. As he rightly points out, the monarchy and the Anglican Church were restored, the importance of the aristocracy in society and politics actually grew, and the hierarchical principle in church and state was reaffirmed. This is all true enough, and indeed I have long been arguing publicly that of the so-called "Great Revolutions," the English was the least revolutionary of all in terms of accomplished social change.

But this does not mean that it did not have profound social causes, nor that it did not have profoundly revolutionary aspirations. Neither the Levellers, nor the Independents, nor the Harringtonians can be brushed aside; the (temporary) abolition of Anglican Church, House of Lords, and monarchy is an historic fact. Hexter has, I believe, fallen for the theory of intended consequences, the notion that in history things turn out the way the actors intended them to. Nothing is further from the truth, as the most casual reflection on contemporary events readily proves. Everything we know about events in the past, whether it is the Statute of Artificers or the Second Reform Bill, tells the same story. To deduce from what happened in the end to what was meant to happen, and from what was meant to happen to the causes of what happened to begin with, is to adopt an unacceptable historical procedure. For one thing, it ignores the extremely complex dynamics of revolution and reaction in which chance accidents of historical personality and catastrophe often determine the final outcome, a methodological point which Hexter has himself stressed in another place.

To sum up. I agree—and I said so in my book—that in some ways the basic polarity of English society was court and country; I agree—and I said so in my book—that Puritanism was a powerful corrosive of traditional social values; I agree—and I said so in my book—that the social consquences of the English Revolution were very small. But I reject any attempt to make court and country into the *only* polarity, to elevate Puritanism into a sufficient instead of a necessary cause, and to deduce historical causes from historical consequences. Thanks to Hexter's powerful article I can now see things that I did not see before. But I do not believe that either of us has the whole truth by the tail.


# POSTSCRIPT TO AN AWFULLY LONG REVIEW

### J. H. Hexter

Two careful readings of Lawrence Stone's "Postscript to Eight Hundred and Forty-one Pages"[1] did not relieve me of an uneasy sense of puzzlement. Even second time around the "Postscript" still seemed to be not quite relevant to the section of my article on "The English Aristocracy, Its Crises, and the English Revolution, 1558-1660" to which it purported to address itself.[2] Somehow Stone seemed either to misunderstand or to misconstrue all my main intentions. If he did so, there are at least two possible explanations for the misconstrual.

First, quite understandably, Stone may have been just plain weary of the whole subject (the title of his reply somehow suggests this), so that he had not given his full attention to what I was saying. Or second, my indications of purpose may have been unduly opaque or ambiguous. After further careful scrutiny of both Stone's postscript and my article, I am inclined to suspect that a bit of both is involved, but a bit more of inattention on Stone's part than of opacity on mine. In any case, here is an attempt to straighten out any confusion as to what I was up to that may remain either in Stone's mind or in the minds of the readers of my article.

Stone ascribes to me the view that "the English Revolution cannot have had deep social causes because it did not have deep social consequences" and then suggests that I have "fallen for the theory of intended consequences, the notion that in history things turn out the way the actors intended them to."[3] Although I am not at all sure about how one identifies "deep social causes," and find that the phrase lacks the scientific precision which both Stone and I admire so much, I surely did not advance the view that Stone attributes to me. And certainly no man who has lived half a

---

[1] Lawrence Stone, "Postscript to Eight Hundred and Forty-one Pages," *J.B.S.*, VIII (1968), 79-82 (hereafter cited as Stone, "Postscript").

[2] J. H. Hexter, "The English Aristocracy, Its Crises, and the English Revolution, 1558-1660," *ibid.*, VIII (1968), 22-78 (hereafter cited as Hexter, "Aristocracy").

[3] Stone, "Postscript," p. 81.

century and is not daft could seriously believe that "in history things turn out the way the actors intended them to," a notion daily refuted by everyman's experience, as he trips on the curbstone, gets caught out in a rainstorm, hits his thumb rather than the nail, or is caught *in flagrante delicto.*

Seeking carefully for any remark of mine that may have so misled Stone as to my opinion, I encountered the sentence, "To say that the English Revolution was not *in any clearly intelligible sense* a social revolution is not to say that it was trivial."[4] This statement was a piece of carelessness on my part. Given time, I could think of a large number of senses in which the English Revolution might be called a social revolution and that each of these would be intelligible, though not perhaps very sensible or useful. The phrase ought to be amended to read, "The English Revolution was not, *in the sense previously specified,* a social revolution." The sense previously specified is that social revolutions are those

brought about by and in the interest of particular social classes. By means and as a consequence of each such revolution, the victorious revolutionary class wholly or in part achieves its conscious (or semiconscious) social ends. Its ends always encompass the increase of its own political and economic power in the community and, as a condition of that increase, the overthrow, subjection, exploitation, and expropriation of other classes.[5]

Given that definition of social revolution, Stone and I are clearly in agreement that the English Revolution was not one. It looks, however, as if Stone thinks that I actually subscribe to this conception of the English Revolution and seek to impose it on others. Since I do not do so, do not say I do so, and rather clearly indicate that I do not do so, some of my perplexity at Stone's misunderstanding remains.

Second, Stone expressed a deep suspicion of "any monocausal theory of history" and suggests that while I share his view, I fell misguidedly and inadvertently into the monocausal heresy by hinting that Puritanism was not only "a necessary cause of the English Revolution . . . but . . . a sufficient cause."[6] In this, he unfortunately mistakes the purpose of my discussion of Puritanism and the court-country dichotomy under the early Stuarts. I do not for a moment entertain (as Stone appears to) the naive belief that historians can possibly elicit the necessary and sufficient causes for so enormous a constellation of events as the English Revolution. Nor do I believe that it is necessary for them to do so in order to stay in business. On the contrary I consider the whole notion of necessary and sufficient cause an indigestible morsel of philosophy which historians have swallowed. It has given them undue and unnecessary discomfort, and since they cannot assimilate it, they had better regurgitate it.

I had hoped that I made clear the intention of that part of my essay which concerns Puritanism and the court-country, peerage-gentry matrix. That intention was to "bring into sharp focus the relation between court and country, peerage and gentry, on which Stone's study casts . . . light that in consequence of *his chosen structure of presentation* is intermittent and diffused."[7] The purpose of this shift of focus, then, was not to elicit necessary and sufficient causes but, far more modestly, "better to understand what happened" after 1615 when, to quote Stone, "the peerage still

---

[4] Hexter, "Aristocracy," pp. 76-77.

[5] *Ibid.,* p. 73.

[6] Stone, "Postscript," p. 80.

[7] Hexter, "Aristocracy," p. 58. Italics added here.

retained its full dignity and respect."[8] What did happen, as Stone has so well demonstrated, was a crisis of confidence in the aristocracy. In this matter it is possible not only to discover what Stone misunderstood in my essay, but to discern how he happened to misunderstand it. He thinks that the point I tried to make was historical; actually my aim was historiographic. Or more precisely, he believes I was speaking to the substance of the past when I intended to speak only to the strategy of historical discourse. I merely meant to suggest that if one arrays some of his data and a few other scraps of evidence around Puritanism and the court-country, peerage-gentry matrix, patterns present, yet blurred and latent, in his treatment emerge sharply, and that the enhanced visibility of these patterns renders more intelligible that crisis of confidence in the English peerage which is one line of access to a fuller understanding of the civil conflagration that erupted in 1642. If, as Stone so generously remarks, "thanks to Hexter's . . . article I can now see things that I did not see before,"[9] for him I did exactly what I set out to do.

Perhaps these specific misunderstandings result from a more general misunderstanding of the entire section of the article to which Stone gives his attention. It was by no means my aim to "put forward [my] own theory to explain the English Civil War and Revolution."[10] I am on the whole averse to the view that satisfactory historical explanations normally take the form of what scientists usually mean by the terms "theory" and "hypothesis," and I certainly reject the apocalyptic view that Stone, or I, or any other historian is about to provide a final explanation of the English Civil War and Revolution. This reasonably modest outlook has some merits, if only in the way of spiritual comfort for our craft. If final explanations are very unlikely, all of us can at least look forward to the continuing intellectual employment of offering provisional ones, although obviously the "irrelevance" for the Now Generation of anything prior to the Vietnam War is about to reduce us all to technological unemployment.

[8] Lawrence Stone, *The Crisis of the Aristocracy, 1558-1641* (Oxford, 1965), p. 103.
[9] Stone, "Postscript," p. 82.
[10] *Ibid.*, p. 79.

# 12 / Politics in the Reign of King George III: The Controversy Around Sir Lewis Namier's History

The Whig interpretation of history, according to Herbert Butterfield, one of its most celebrated critics is, the result of a "tendency in many historians to write on the side of Protestants and Whigs, to praise revolutions provided they have been successful, to emphasize certain principles of progress in the past and to produce a story which is the ratification if not the glorification of the present."[1] Putting the words *protestant* and *whig* in lower case and reading them broadly, Butterfield's definition covers the largest part of important historical writing in Europe and America during the second half of the nineteenth and the first decade of the twentieth centuries.

It was from this broader definition that, in 1931, Professor Butterfield first attacked Whig history in his now classic *The Whig Interpretation of History* and showed its shortcomings in the treatment of such diverse topics as the Dark Ages, Luther, and Napoleon. Since then, Whig history has stood securely condemned as a history that passed moral judgments on preceding ages in terms of its own, which was an age confident in political and social progress and the triumph of representative government.

If controversy is a yardstick, it develops that nowhere has Whig history been more guilty of this charge and consequently, it may be argued, more influential than in its treatment of the reign of George III. The reason for this is not hard to see. The reign of George III was a transitional era of "mixed government," when the cabinet's role as an executive arm of the government was not defined, when ministerial responsibility or party discipline did not exist, and when the monarch's prerogative extended to the selection of his ministers. Yet under the first two Georges, the cabinet had accumulated authority, and the monarchs had regularly chosen their ministers from the "Whig" majority in Parliament. Thus when George III attempted to revive the royal prerogative and rule without party, he could appear to the Whig historian as moving athwart progress or even as subverting the Constitution.

In the second half of the nineteenth century, inspired by monarchs who reigned but did not rule and by a developed party system in a Parliament that was considered an example for the rest of the world, such magisterial British scholars as Erskine May (*Constitutional History of England*, 1861), William E. H. Lecky (*History of England in the Eighteenth Century*, 1882), and G. O. Trevelyan (*Early History of Charles James*

---

[1] H. Butterfield, *The Whig Interpretation of History* (London: George Bell & Sons, Ltd., 1931), p. v.

*Fox,* 1880) all propagated, with varying degrees of emphasis, the Whig interpretation of the reign of George III. With Harold Temperley (*Cambridge Modern History,* 1909) and D. A. Winstanley (*Personal and Party Government in the Reign of George III,* 1912), revisionism began.

The job of totally destroying the Whig interpretation fell, however, to a later generation of historians. Starting in 1929 and continuing to the present, it has been the work of the late Sir Lewis Namier and his followers. Using more of a social science approach than most British historians had been previously prepared to accept in this area, they have analyzed what they call "the structure of politics" in the eighteenth century through investigation of the actions, origins, and connections of *all* members of Parliament at a given period. From this exhaustive research, among other things, has come the virtual obliteration of the ideology and party labels so central to the Whig interpretation of George III's reign.

Professor Butterfield, although not a member of this group, has also made a contribution to the destruction of the Whig myth with a work of solid scholarship (*George III, Lord North and the People,* 1949), and in a more recent book (*George III and the Historians,* 1957) he may be said to have delivered it a *coup de grâce* via the historiographical essay at which he is so adept. In the final section of the latter work, however, he turned to an extensive attack on Professor Namier and the "Namier School" and launched the liveliest debate current in British historical circles. Although Butterfield has accused the Namierites of formulating a "Whig fallacy turned inside out,"[2] and the debate has turned on the meaning of "party," "cabinet," and "King's friends," it remains essentially a methodological one.

The selections that follow will enable the reader to judge the debate's dimensions. In the first, Professor Namier writes briefly and engagingly of his research techniques and aims. The second selection contains the gist of the Butterfield attack on Namier. In the third, Professor Price, an American scholar, analyzes Namier's work, and the Butterfield attack and suggests why the debate may well continue.

---

[2] Herbert Butterfield, *George III and the Historians* (London: Collins Publishers, 1957), p. 295.

# THE BIOGRAPHY OF ORDINARY MEN

**Sir Lewis Namier**

Study-circles of working men, when asked what subject they would like to take, almost invariably answer with a request for "economic history." Political history, they reason, is about kings and statesmen and wars, while they want to learn about "the likes" of themselves—as all the other classes and professions did before them. But how much of that desire is satisfied by stories about the enclosures, the spinning-jenny, the Poor Law, the Factory Acts or the Free Trade controversy? Students are landed once more in the sphere of legislative enactments and of Government measures; for these are "documented" and can be easily dished up, whereas the tale of those ordinary men and women about whom they want to know is buried in casual remarks, in crevices of unknown texts—pins in haystacks. In the correspondence of the upper classes remarks occasionally occur which throw a flood of light on the life and condition of "the lower orders," but will anyone ever collect and blend them into a picture? Why, even a history of the rank and file of what may best be described as "the political nation" is seldom attempted; biographies of famous men still hold the field, though hero-worship is no longer the creed of the writers. But, then, a biography has well-defined limits, a natural sequence and an established practice, and can be compiled by an individual writer in a reasonably short time; nor is it attempted unless materials are ready to hand. Lastly, the public is accustomed to read biographies, and so they continue to be produced.

In biographies, as in plays, the central figures act and speak, the others being mere dummies in the background, "citizens," "soldiers," and so on. In most cases the biographer does not profess an exclusive interest in the psychology of his "hero" and would not deny the importance of the men who surround him; and yet they remain a dark, dumb, nameless crowd. We have written about Parliamentary leaders and great administrators, and more or less ignored those whom they led and with or through whom they had to do their work, the individual Members of Parliament, the Civil Servants, and so on. We have written about changes in methods of production, the rise of modern finance, trade statistics, but very seldom about the men behind these developments, the merchants who turned manufacturers or bankers, the landowners who became mining adventurers, and so on. Now the heroes of biography are often approached in a sceptical, would-be humorous, depreciatory manner, and this is the main tangible expression of the doubt which besets the writers as to whether these men truly deserve the prominence they receive. The outstanding figures are reduced to ordinary dimensions, but continue to fill the picture, mainly because information about them can be easily obtained. Still, what can one expect from the lonely student, not given even the most elementary help (e.g., of a secretary or an assistant to do for him some of the more mechanical work) or the necessary leisure for his researches, as usually he is compelled to earn his living by teaching? Is he to attempt to cross an ocean in a boat of the most primitive construction? Our interests and requirements have changed and broadened, we want to know about the life of crowds, to hear

310

symphonies and not arias, and then a single virtuoso is invited to perform them. Occasionally we take refuge in collective works, and fondly expect "fifty men to make a centipede"; more often than not, these attempts at joint and yet individual work end in failure. Historical research to this day remains unorganized, and the historian is expected to make his own instruments or do without them; and so with wooden ploughs we continue to draw lonely furrows, most successfully when we strike sand.

The biography of the ordinary man cannot be profitably attempted unless one writes the history of a crowd. It would not pay to go through hundreds of volumes of manuscripts and many thousands of books merely to fish out some twenty documents or passages about one man. Proper returns cannot be obtained from the work except by following up many threads, by establishing the average and selecting the typical. The student has to get acquainted with the lives of thousands of individuals, with an entire ant-heap, see its files stretch out in various directions, understand how they are connected and correlated, watch the individual ants, and yet never forget the ant-heap. An interesting piece of research into economic history could be done by studying the lives of the members of any great trading company in the seventeenth and eighteenth centuries, or, say, of the directing personnel of the East India House. But most of all there is that marvellous microcosmos of English social and political life, that extraordinary club, the House of Commons. For centuries it has been the goal of English manhood, and besides those who found seats in it on the strength of a tradition or of a quasi-hereditary right, there were in every House many scores of men, for whom its membership set the crown (and often the coronet) on achievements and success in other walks of life. Generals, admirals, and pro-consuls entered it, business men who had made their fortunes and now aspired to social advancement, Civil Servants, lawyers and political wire-pullers who tried to raise their professional status, and so on. The rise of "interests" and classes can be traced through the personnel of the House of Commons, the forms of English gregarious existence can be studied, the social structure of England is reflected in it, the presence or decay of independent political life in boroughs and counties can be watched in their representation. When the sons of peers or leading country gentlemen begin to invade the representation of boroughs, it is clear that Parliament is becoming the governing body; when the brewers, clothiers and iron-masters start acquiring seats in the House, it is obvious that fortunes are being made in these branches of trade, and that the early capitalists have made their appearance; by the number of West Indians in the House one can measure the prosperity of the "sugar islands"; when many families of country gentlemen, who for generations had sat in it, withdraw from the House of Commons, one can guess that agricultural rents are falling—on a careful inquiry it will be found that the coming in of American wheat has wrought a greater change in the composition of the British House of Commons than the first two Reform Acts. From the "circular letter," the whip which in the eighteenth century was sent to Government Members at the opening of the session, one can learn a good deal about political groupings; about 1750, independent country gentlemen sitting "in their own right" received it usually from the leader of the House, relatives or retainers of politically prominent peers through them, members of professional groups through their chiefs (naval officers through the First Lord of the Admiralty, lawyers through the Lord Chancellor, Government contractors and financiers through the Secretary to the Treasury, and so on), and lastly, in one or two cases, territorial managers made their appearance.

We have discussed kings and statesmen and wars, and when desirous to show our appreciation of "progress"—institutions, inventions and "reforms." But how much do we know about the real political life of the country, even about that body which before the eyes of the nation has for centuries shaped its joint existence? How much do we know about the Members of the Long Parliament, or about the changes which came over the House between the accession of George III and the voting of the First Reform Act? When did local citizens disappear from the representation of most small provincial boroughs? When did rich City merchants begin to plant themselves out on them? When did provincial business men of the new type start entering the House in considerable numbers? When did national politics become the dominant issue in elections? When and how have parties got the upper hand over individual candidates? When was the loyalty of the average elector transferred from organic constituencies to party organizations? In the eighteenth century as many excuses had to be made for "disturbing the peace" of a county or borough as in our time for starting a war, and every candidate in an election contest naturally tried to prove that it was not he who was the aggressor, but that his opponent, by an inexcusable disregard of his "just pretensions," had forced a contest on him, in which he himself confidently relied on the fairness of his neighbours to secure his victory. The idea that constituencies should be contested for the political education of the electorate was as alien to the eighteenth century as would be to us a proposal that the summer manoeuvres of our army should take the form of a three-days' battle with that of some other nation. Even about the middle of the nineteenth century, in a good many constituencies the local issues still predominated, and, e.g., the Radicals could form an almost separate body in the House without producing any considerable number of triangular contests, for the battle was not fought on a national scale. Without underrating the value of work on what is called the political history of the British nation, one might wish that at least a start should be made with a history of the British "political nation." And a biographical history of the House of Commons, covering the seven centuries of its existence, could well supply the spade-work for such a new venture along lines consonant with the general change in our outlook and interests.

Parliamentary histories based on the biographies of Members have been attempted for various counties, and much of this work has been done by real scholars. Useful as these books undoubtedly are, they suffer from the following of "vertical" lines—what has Adam Fitz-Richard, returned for Liverpool in 1295, in common with some big merchant of the eighteenth century, or with George Canning who represented Liverpool 1812-23? By taking counties or single constituencies, one can study, for example, the degree of heredity in their representation, but one touches merely the outskirts of political life, and cannot properly follow up the personal connections even of the Members in question, for these extended in most cases far beyond the borders of their constituency or county. Much better results could be reached by doing the work "horizontally"—an attempt of that kind seems to have been planned by Mr. Pink, one of the greatest antiquaries of our time, who collected biographical material about the Members of the Long Parliament, but died without having published anything on the subject. The student of Parliamentary biography whose work is limited to one period, but extends over the entire country, can do what is impossible for those working on vertical lines—he can plunge into the mass of manuscript and printed material extant for his period and obtain from it a living picture of the men. Still, no such study of one single period can fully realize its aim unless similar studies, on the same plan, are available for other periods; only by comparison can we gauge movement and correctly define its nature.

In short, the task cannot be undertaken by individual researchers, working independently of each other. It has to be organized on a national scale, given national standing, and financed from national resources. A central organization is required, an editorial board composed of experts and working under the auspices of a Parliamentary Committee, co-operating with various county organizations, with bodies such as the editors of *The Complete Peerage,* with scholars working on the biographies of members of universities, colleges or schools, with other experts specializing in cognate subjects. *A Dictionary of Parliamentary Biography* should be compiled, but based on periods, and not on the alphabet. The entity and individuality of consecutive Houses have to be clearly preserved, for the pageant of history must not be arranged under capital letters, like the luggage on the pier at Liverpool. The value of such work executed on a sufficiently large scale and according to the highest standards of scholarship could hardly be exaggerated. It would be a *Who's Who* of politics and social life throughout the ages, the most indispensable reference book for everyone engaged on English political history and for every editor of historical manuscripts—and it would save us from having to do the same work over and over again, often without sufficient means or knowledge. But of equal or perhaps even greater importance would be the attempt inherent in that work to organize historical research, and last, but not least, the training which the work would give to younger collaborators. It is difficult to imagine a better preparation for history work on any given period than a study of the lives of the men of that time, in the course of which a proper knowledge of the available materials would naturally be acquired.

# GEORGE III AND THE NAMIER SCHOOL

**Herbert Butterfield**

## Narrative History and Structural Analysis

We must not exaggerate the revolution produced by the new methods.[1] Some of the good things which we are now told about the workings of eighteenth-century politics were available to discerning politicians who were living at the time. Such things had leaked into the literary evidence, and they had passed into historiography by another route. The plan of compiling the lives of all members of parliament is going to provide historians with a piece of apparatus that will be invaluable during an indefinite future. But whether scientific methods (statistical procedures and devices of correlation) can be applied to the resulting materials—whether these will produce more valuable conclusions about the politics of a period than were available to a contemporary statesman with a good nose—is not yet very clear.

It is necessary that we should not magnify too greatly even the importance of the study of "structure." It still has to be admitted (and the members of the Namier school seem anxious sometimes to remind us of the fact) that through a sense of responsibility or an attachment to principle, men in the eighteenth century might break with their party or act against what appeared to be their immediate personal interest on occasion. There were in any case many independent members of parliament who, though they might normally support the government, would be prepared to vote

[1] Those of Sir Lewis Namier and his collaborators. [Editors' note.]

as their judgment dictated; so that the course of debate, the influence of popular passion, or the existence of a national crisis, would be calculated to affect their conduct. In such cases, which by their very nature are likely to be significant, the politics of George III's reign could not be regarded as responding to structure or as explicable solely in terms of structure. And where the votes of many people are affected—as in the case of Dunning's famous motion on 6th April, 1780—it is necessary to resort to the ordinary method of the narrative historian, who puts the microscope on the episode as such, and even studies very carefully (so far as the evidence is available) the course of the parliamentary debate itself. It would in fact be true to say that the whole policy of stressing the significance of the independent members (or bringing out the pivotal importance that these may have, as Dr. Owen has recently done in *The Rise of the Pelhams*) automatically increases the propriety of the older type of narrative method, and even the analysis of parliamentary debates. This is being neglected by the new school, and for this reason we hear too much about structure and vested interests, and too little about those higher political considerations which clearly enter the case at these important points in the story, and which help to turn the study of history into a political education. In fact, it is just here that, over and above the irrationalities of the world, the social pressures and the sheer play of forces, there moves something of rational purpose, something of the conscious calculations of reasoning and reasonable men. And surely the fault of the Whig historians was that, though they would give long rambling *résumés* of parliamentary debates, they did not treat these on an analytical method. On crucial occasions they assumed in too facile a manner that the votes on one side of the question were given automatically—that is to say were the mere effect of vested interests involved, the mere counterpart of "the structure of politics." If it is important to study parliamentary elections, individual members of parliament and the various constituencies, we today can hardly neglect the activities of the two houses and even the analysis of parliamentary debates.

We are in an analogous position when we are told that the French Revolution cannot be explained merely by general causes—merely by the operation of a standing system of historical necessity. And that is why it is so significant when Professor Labrousse—the supreme student of the economic correlations that can be made—insists so strongly that the Revolution emerges from the clash of personalities, the play of fear and passion, the interaction of purposes and cross-purposes, with the intervention sometimes of sheer mischance. At this stage in the argument the analysis of mere conditions, or of structure as such, loses that unique importance which some people like to give it; and much may hang on the things that human beings chose to do in regions of conduct where they could easily be imagined to have made a different choice. For the sake of historical explanation itself we must watch human beings deliberating and choosing their conduct; and we must examine the story of what happens between people, we must examine the considerations upon which men make their decisions. All this is a vindication of the older kind of political history, which did not overlook the part played also by conditions, though in all things it may have been less precise and microscopic than twentieth-century scholarship manages to be. That Professor Labrousse should have realised the position in respect of the French Revolution is remarkable, since his own peculiar studies might easily have led him to the opposite conclusion. But one of the theses of the Namier school is the authenticity of the independent member of the House Of Commons and the pivotal importance he was capable of having. It means that, over and above the structure of politics, we must have a political history that is set out in narrative form—an account of adult human beings, taking a hand in their fates and fortunes, pulling at the story in the direction they want to carry it, and making decisions of their own. We must have the kind of story in which (no matter how much we know about the structure of politics and the conditions of the time) we can never quite guess, at any given moment, what is going to happen next.

All this should be considered in its bearings on the conception of an over-all history of the reign of George III. The older writers, who are now taunted and condemned, were above all things narrative historians. The relevant question to ask before they are summarily dismissed, and before the earlier historiography of the subject is thrown into the waste-paper basket, is the question how the new kind of analysis affects the shape of the previously accepted story. It is not permissible to imagine that the England of 1760 is unique in the sense that just here, and just at this particular date, the study of "structure" must replace other forms of history. To people who have studied the Glorious Revolution, the Hanoverian Succession, the policy of Walpole and the role of William Pitt in the Seven Years' War, we cannot say that after the accession of George III mere story-telling must be over and done with—that just here the "narrative" method has been rendered obsolete. In any case the world cannot afford to sacrifice the kind of history which broadened a man's political outlook—the history which dealt with politics and statesmanship and the march of great events. It is curious that there has never been a more desperate cry from the teaching profession than the demand in recent years for light and help in respect of the interpretation of the reign of George III.

Perhaps the ideal kind of history is the kind in which a story is given and events are presented in motion, but the story is re-told so to speak "in depth," so that it acquires a new dimension; it is both structure and narrative combined. This has been achieved on occasion by scholars and writers; and here, where history is both a story and a study, one may gain a profounder insight into both the ways of men and the processes of time. For the rational purposes and the conscious intentions of human beings on the one hand, and the historical process, with its systems of necessity and ironies of circumstance on the other hand—these two together are the weft and warp of the fabric of human destiny. They are the ingredients of that history which in one aspect men make for themselves and which in another aspect they suffer, as they see it being manufactured over their heads.

In this present study we are primarily concerned with the things which affect the interpretation of what might be called the ordinary narrative history of the reign of George III.

## The Occupational Disease of the Historians of Structure

Sir Lewis Namier tells us that *England in the Age of the American Revolution,* which his collaborators are fortunately to continue in a considerable series of volumes, sets out to provide "the chronological narrative of political events." But in his own original volume, as well as in the recent addition to the series by Mr. Brooke, it seems to be assumed that such narrative need be little more than the "structure of politics" extended in time and turned into a sequence. We are given a story which becomes silent or curiously neglectful as it touches the very things that governments and parliaments exist to do. There is little interest in the work of ministers within their departments; in the springs of policy and the origins of important decisions; in the actual content of the political controversies of the time; in the attitude of the public to measures and men; and in the thrust and counter-thrust of parliamentary debate. Nothing is added to the story of British policy in respect of the American colonies, and even of Townshend's disastrous intervention in this field, though the title of the whole series might have created a certain degree of expectancy here. These problems are dealt with only as they touch the fundamental theme of the whole work; and since the fundamental theme, even in this narrative side of the history, concerns rather the interplay of factions and the manipulative side of politics, even the topics that belong to statesmanship tend to be reduced to just such terms as these. We must not imagine that this is the only way in which a history of this particular period can be reconstructed. We must not imagine that what is being supplied is really "the history of the reign of George III."

Such tendencies are calculated to raise the question whether the new form of structural analysis is not capable of producing in the practitioners of the craft its own kind of occupational disease. Within the field with which the volumes are explicitly concerned, it would appear that the anatomising method may have its defects, unless it is complemented by the activity of a sympathetic—even a synthesising—mind. In the two volumes of narrative which have so far appeared, it is remarkable to see how often the things which are most clearly true are by no means new, and how often the points of interpretation which are novel and paradoxical are inadequately demonstrated. One may have misgivings about the selectivity in the use of sources, and about the processes of inference which are brought to bear upon the evidence. In any case there are certain points which must always be borne in mind by those who, in reading the writings of this school, mean not to suspend their critical awareness.

There may seem to be something unanswerable in the thesis that the Labour party opposed the Suez adventure because it was their business to defeat the Conservatives. And some people feel that it would be too much of a coincidence if we accepted the members of that party as also sincerely attached to the ideals of the United Nations. It is possible, therefore, to describe the activities of such an opposition on such an occasion in terms of interests; and when we are in a certain mood we may find it even satisfactory to discount, or quite explain away, all the evidence of higher purpose and rational discussion which may appear amongst the papers or the speeches of the men in question. In reality, however, the egotisms of human beings do in every age of history find subtle and complicated ways of combining with higher purposes, though the mode of combination may well be different in every generation. It seems to be true that the Whig historians will tend to assess the virtues of the Rockinghamites by their ideals, but that still they may be content to measure the followers of Lord North only by their interests—a procedure which is not improved if the opponents of the Whigs merely reverse the formula. Antagonistic political parties must be examined from both points of view, and even individual people may require very sympathetic treatment from the historian. John Wilson Croker could pretend to demonstrate how powerful a motor behind the actions and the writings of Horace Walpole was his selfish concern for his sinecures. Croker could also show in a moving passage, however, the genuineness of certain aspects of Horace Walpole's Whiggism, and the wisdom of his opposition to the conflict with the American colonies. How easy it is for the historian to rest his mind in the first of these demonstrations, and to close his eyes to the fact that the second may be at least of equal significance!

It is not clear that the Namier method possesses the kind of receiving-set that is capable of catching all the relevant wave-lengths. At a certain level, recognition is given to the fact that, particularly on critical occasions, politicians think of their country and have regard to the public cause. Men do not support the government merely because they enjoy profits and places; and corruption itself is not sufficient to bind the House of Commons when a serious issue has been raised. Even in Ireland, where the corruption was more notorious than in Great Britain, it was explicitly realised in the reign of George III that "the occasional favours of government" could not be relied on to secure the vote of the House of Commons against the interest of the country or the passions of an awakened people. On this point the Lord Lieutenant, the Earl of Buckinghamshire, for example, once expressed himself in a most insistent manner. Precisely where the issues were more than the routine ones (in which "party discipline" might operate effectively) political conduct was not unlikely to have its reference to the things that men were thinking on public questions. Let it be remembered (though there are people who forget the point) that this was true of the regular opposition as well as the customary supporters of government. As Winstanley put it, in a remarkable sentence: "It is too often overlooked that if George III was fighting for a principle, so were his opponents." Human beings are the carriers of ideas as well as the repositories of vested interests. And political history requires the over-all narrative—the account of policies, legislative projects, diplomacy, wars, and so on—for it is about such things as these that the practitioners of politics are apt to have ideas. And for these reasons it is never sufficient to study even eighteenth-century politics with too exclusive a concentration on the manipulative side or the play of faction. Horace Walpole in the eighteenth century and Croker in the nineteenth knew the quality of faction. They did not even need historical imagination for its understanding, since they had been in a position to learn the "feel" of it practically at first hand. Like the polemical literature of the early 1760's, however, they recognised also that there were important political and constitutional issues to discuss.

Because the Whig historians took ideological pretensions too much at their face value, the modern school tend to drain the intellectual content out of the things that politicians do. The *dramatis personae* are portrayed without that outer framework of ideas and purposes which affects political conduct, and which statesmen and monarchs—even a George III—could scarcely unload from their minds if they tried. This framework of ideas and conscious purposes may appear only in partial glimpses—though it certainly does appear—in the correspondence of political personages who generally write to one another rather to discuss detailed decisions and day-to-day moves. The parts of the correspondence which are here in question are the ones which the new writers are apt to neglect or to slur over. These are the things, however, which give some coherence to political history and rescue it from mere atomisation; and one may despise them over-much if one is too intent on delving into structure and self-interests, or even into the darkness of man's unconscious mind. There is a danger that the study of the under-side of the piece of embroidery will be puffed and exalted, and turned into an end in itself. Even U.N.O. today would provide a sorry picture if we examined it from the point of view of the "structure of politics," leaving the other dimensions of the story out of account.

There is a way of studying history which atomises everything, especially if one slurs over the very kind of evidence which gives intellectual content to the things that politicians do. There is a form of fundamental analysis, excellent in itself, which—for lack of obvious safeguards—can lead to the erosion of the avowed political purposes that give meaning as well as cohesion to the events of history. It may seem paradoxical, but it can be true, that there is danger in an attempt to write history merely from the kind of documentation that might be called "bed-rock." A man who wished to write the history of my College, and tried to confine himself to the documents in the College Treasury, might too easily imagine that we were a body concerned only with the administration of money, buildings and other property. If he would go outside and consult some forms of evidence that he might regard as inferior—discussions in the *University Reporter* and the *Cambridge Review,* for example, or the essays of Sir Adolphus William Ward—he would discover that men in Cambridge have a real interest in education too. And this analogy illustrates another of the errors of the Namier school.

### *The Occupational Disease of the Research Student*

In one of the most interesting and brilliant and important passages in his *England in the Age of the American Revolution* (pp. 147-149) Sir Lewis Namier attacks the tendency to overrate "the importance of the conscious will and purpose in individuals." He asks us to "to ascertain and recognise the deeper irrelevancies and incoherence of human actions, which are not so much directed by reason, as invested by it *ex post facto* with the appearances of logic and rationality." He insists that "when watched at close quarters, the actions of men are in no way correlated in weight and value to the results they produce." We must see history, therefore, as a thing which "started in ridiculous beginnings, while small men did things both infinitely smaller and infinitely greater than they knew." All this doctrine is particularly applied to those events immediately after the accession of George III which for nearly two centuries now have been the object of so much discussion and political controversy. In a sentence that is meant to carry particular significance, we are therefore told that "History of infinite weight was to be made in the absurd beginnings of [this] reign."

Certainly there is an important truth in all this exposition; and a realisation of the importance of the truth is possibly an essential step towards the achievement of historical understanding. The truth has genuine relevance, moreover, for the student of these early years of the reign of George III. Historians once imagined that Pitt fell in 1761 because the King and his favourite, Bute, had determined to drive him out of office. It is easy to imagine in this way that the things which happened were things which George III and Bute had resolved to bring about. Even from the earliest times, there had been men, however, who were not deceived by the optical illusion; and from the closing decades of the nineteenth century it was being shown once again that Bute had not in fact conspired to bring about the resignation of Pitt. When Winstanley, nearly fifty years ago, explained that this resignation had not been "part of the original programme of the court," he, too, had called attention to the paradox in the historical process. He, too, had written with some justification: "Events had shaped themselves in a way that had not been foreseen."

There is truth in the view, then; but we must remember that if we carry the idea of Sir Lewis Namier to an extreme, it is difficult to see why the study of history—a history so woven out of chances and ironies of circumstance—should be considered an important matter for anybody. Like Professor Isaiah Berlin, one may see history as only a succession of chances or conjunctures—but, if so, there is nothing to study, there are no correlations to be made between events, and in fact there is only a rope of sand, a series of non-sequiturs which one can do nothing but narrate. Just as one can be too doctrinaire even in one's anti-doctrinairism, one may be too wilful in one's emphasis on the wilfulness of history and the caprice of time.

All political narrative becomes more complicated—more trickily entangled with chance and change—when seen under the microscope. Young research students are even apt to be disillusioned with their work, and too contemptuous of the subject of it, when they study the policy of even a first-class statesman at close quarters, and see the untidiness of the result. The thing which, when telescoped into abridged history, appears as a mighty act of volition, may be broken by research into a multitude of little pieces, the statesman appearing not to know what he wants, and showing an apparent readiness to drift with wind and tide. In spite of all this, the political practitioner, even if he is only a George III, does possess a framework of ideas and purposes which affect his actions and modify the course of things. They may seem to be checked or side-tracked, they may even seem to be contradicted entirely, as one watches the man in his day-to-day conduct of business. But it is the optical illusion or the occupational disease of the research student to imagine that only the details matter, and that the details are all of equal value—that the statesman has no cohesive purpose but is merely a bundle of contradictions—and that everything is under the rule of chance, under the play of absurdly little chances—history reducing itself at the finish to an irony of circumstance.

George III himself is the first to suffer from the new method and from the theory that history issues from absurdly small and irrelevant beginnings. But all parties—the court, the Rockinghamites and the followers of John Wilkes—can be reduced to the same uninspiring level if this method and this view of history are pressed too far. A century ago Ranke dealt with the question of the uniqueness of each event, each conjuncture in history, and the way the historian must take pleasure in detail as such. But he saw that history also was not without its "inner connectedness"; and, indeed, that one could not write history if one did not see the possibility of grouping the details into coherent shapes, and if one did not possess also an eye for generalities.

# PARTY, PURPOSE, AND PATTERN: SIR LEWIS NAMIER AND HIS CRITICS

**Jacob M. Price**

The recent death of Professor Sir Lewis Namier (19 August 1960) provides an occasion to assess, albeit most tentatively, if not the man (I did not know him well), then at least his contribution to the writing of English history.[1] The need for such an assessment is a little ironic, for Sir Lewis, for all his renown, has left a somewhat indistinct after-image among historians in this country. Ever since the appearance in 1929 of his great work on the *Structure of Politics at the Accession of*

---

[1] This paper is concerned primarily with the methodological aspects of Sir Lewis Namier's work. For a discussion of some specific problems in interpreting English eighteenth-century history, see W. R. Fryer, "The Study of British Politics Between the Revolution and the Reform Act," *Renaissance and Modern Studies,* I (1957) 91-114.

*George III*,[2] his name has been a fixture in bibliographies and in the knowingness of knowing graduate student and cannier undergraduate. Yet few in this country have read his work through—that is, his monumental works on eighteenth century politics on which most of the *estime* of his *succès d'estime* has been built. Many more are familiar with the lectures, reviews and critical works on modern German and diplomatic history to which he devoted much of his productive effort between 1933 and 1953.[3] Though these last are works of some importance, the ultimate reputation of Namier as a scholar must rest on his eighteenth century work—in fact upon his publications of 1929 and 1930. It is this work and some of the methodological questions it raises which are under discussion here.

\* \* \*

Sir Lewis's two chief works are *The Structure of Politics at the Accession of George III* (1929) and *England in the Age of the American Revolution:* Vol. I (London, 1930). The latter title is confusing; it might better have been the *Operation of Politics in the Age of the American Revolution,* in contrast to the earlier structural volume. It was conceived as the first instalment of a larger work going from 1760 to 1784; as volume one, it carried the narrative only through 1762. After its appearance, Namier's energies were absorbed increasingly by his teaching duties at Manchester, and his writing on modern German and diplomatic history.[4] Only well after the fall of Hitler and his own retirement from Manchester in 1953, did Sir Lewis revive the old project, but now in the form of a collaborative venture. Separate periods within the larger scheme were "put out" to collaborators of his. This plan produced during 1956–1958 the meticulous and sophisticated volumes of John Brooke on Chatham's ministry, 1766–1768,[5] and Ian Christie on the last years of North's government, 1780–1782.[6] Death cut short Sir Lewis's announced intention of prefacing the new collaborative series with an introductory volume of his own.

Casual critics frequently refer to Sir Lewis's "interpretation" of the eighteenth century. Far more fundamental is his method. This is, first of all, characterized by the utmost intellectual rigor. Within human limits, he read nothing into his documents that was not there and missed little that was there; he trained his students to do as much. At the same time, close reading, perception, fierce industry and an inspired imagination in envisaging relationships which further research could verify enabled him to recreate a political world with striking clarity, life-giving detail and verisimilitude, leaving us an impressive triumph of intellectual discipline over preconception and anachronism.

Closely allied to this rigor is a clear understanding of and focus on what one is doing. Sir Lewis and his followers know what they are doing and what they are not doing: they are not conjuring up the spirit of an age or giving their impressions of a society in

---

2 2 Vols. (London, 1929); 2nd ed., 1 Vol. (London, 1957).

3 Including: *Conflicts: Studies in Contemporary History* (London, 1942); *1848: The Revolution of the Intellectuals* (London, 1944); *Facing East* (London, 1947); *Diplomatic Prelude, 1938-1939* (London, 1948); *Europe in Decay; A Study in Disintegration, 1936-1940* (London, 1950); *In the Nazi Era* (London, 1952); *Vanished Supremacies: Essays on European History, 1812-1912, (Collected Essays,*I) (London, 1958).

4 See note 3.

5 *The Chatham Administration 1766-1768* (London, 1956).

6 *The End of North's Ministry 1780-1782* (London, 1958).

toto, or recreating the thought of an age or tracing down constitutional precedents; they are analyzing and describing the locus and transmission of power, through the observable phenomenon, political behavior. The reader is shown the system as a whole, but he is also taken down on his knees into the tall grass and given a large glass to watch the little creatures scurry about their business. What people in power and in politics say is interesting and sometimes significant; what they do is usually more important. Rhetoric may well be only rhetoric; "reasons" analyzed too frequently prove but rationalizations.

To bring this rigor and focus to bear most fruitfully on the topic at hand, Namier had to perfect the most thorough research technique. By the standards he established, all previous and much subsequent historical writing on the eighteenth century is thin gruel indeed. He did not only search out with great industry the papers of numerous major *and* minor political figures. The most novel part of his research technique was his development of what may be called collective biography. For the first time in modern British historiography, a professional historian had shown how to utilize the vast amount of miscellaneous information which local historians, genealogists, antiquarians, and so on, had been publishing for several centuries. Such material has been mocked as dross; Sir Lewis showed that it could also be mined for gold. On the one hand, its use enables the historian to recreate the tangled fabric of kinship and interest which bound men together in the politics of the midcentury. On the other hand, it enabled him to tackle the problem of the social structure of the House of Commons. It was now possible to dispel a lot of nonsense and talk meaningfully of just how many country gentlemen, sons of nobility, service officers, placemen, merchants, and nabobs there were in the house.[7]

The Namier school is at its most characteristic and its most nearly unique in its use of quantitative technique. As such it is closer to modern social science methodology than any other branch of British historiography. Yet its critics are all too frequently inclined to pooh-pooh quantification as the mere counting of heads, an occupation suitable for second-class minds that lack the "imagination" to do anything better. Such criticism is distressing. Is it not at bottom a rather disturbing form of anti-intellectualism, parading beneath the banner of no matter what irrelevant aesthetic?Too many performances confirm the suspicion that relatively few historians know how to use numbers rigorously. Though it may be easy "to count heads," few who have not tried it can quite appreciate the difficulty of finding the heads to count, or the imaginative, sympathetic sense of an age needed to know which heads to bother looking for to count—or what the heads totalled mean.

Actually, it is the perfection of these biographical and quantitative research techniques that has enabled Namier and his followers to make their most valuable contributions: analyzing the social structure of the House of Commons, the motives or behavior patterns that drew men into the house, the electoral structure of the varying constituencies,[8] the relative importance of the differing types of influence that might be manifest at elections, the behavior patterns of groups of differing social and electoral background once in the house, and so on. For the first time, scholars knew what to do with division lists. By contrast, the simple narrative passages of the group, though marked by their usual rigor and perception, are much less epoch-making or

---

[7] For example, one of the myths exploded by Sir Lewis was Horace Walpole's tale of the supposed new influx of East India nabobs into Commons in the election of 1761. *Structure of Politics,* 2nd ed., 158, 170-172.

[8] This was by no means original with Namier.

even novel. The careful use of correspondence belongs to a much older tradition of western historical writing, particularly developed in our own day by diplomatic historians.

Frequent reference to "Sir Lewis Namier and his followers" suggests the present difficulty of disentangling the man from the movement. Recent critics in a spirit of fun or venom have been increasingly inclined to speak of "the Namier school" or even "Namier Incorporated"—"the most powerfully organized squadron in our historical world at the present time"[9]—a vast intellectual steam-engine that threatens to consume all the energies of historical research in its own wish-drive for self perpetuation. Actually, until fairly recently, Sir Lewis had relatively few published followers of any sort. In the twenty years following the publication of the *Structure of Politics,* there was little to show except the ingenious editing of Mr. Sedgwick,[10] an article by Professor Walcott,[11] and rather remotely the work of Professor Barnes on the younger Pitt.[12] The master like St. Simeon sat alone on his high column. Explanations are not hard to find: the work was simply too difficult and too exacting to attract many graduate students in a hurry; neither the period nor the class was in vogue (the art market for English eighteenth century portraits collapsed in the 1930's); nor was the rigorous, skeptical, inductive cast of Sir Lewis's mind and work in harmony with the easy ideologising of the 1930's.

Of recent years, the situation has improved. Several independent scholars of standing have been identified in the professions's mind with the "Namier school" though they can hardly be classed as disciples. The late Professor Richard Pares, though methodologically an outsider, conveyed to a wide audience in an individual manner much of the "Namierite" way of looking at the constitution.[13] Even more significant is the work of the Principal of Lady Margaret Hall whose distinguished work on the political history of the East India Company is the most important methodological and conceptual addition to the orthodox Namier canon.[14] In it, Dr. Sutherland shows how the study of a type of institution neglected by Sir Lewis himself could be approached with his and analogous methods and produce results important in themselves while adding a new dimension to the "Namierite" view of the political world. Hers was followed by the "imprimatur" works of Brooke and Christie already mentioned[15] and the more independent works of Owen[16] on the 1740's and Walcott[17] on Queen Anne's time. (Of late there has been a falling off again and the future is not bright, at least for studies within the eighteenth century.)

All this still makes a pretty short catalog, hardly imposing enough to constitute that

---

[9] Herbert Butterfield, *George III and the Historians,* 1st ed. (London, 1957), 10; 2nd ed. (New York, 1959), 10.

[10] Romney Sedgwick, ed., *Letters from George III to Lord Bute, 1756-1766* (London, 1939).

[11] Robert Walcott, Jr., "English party politics (1688-1714)" in *Essays in Modern English History in Honor of Wilbur Cortez Abbott* (Cambridge, Mass., 1941), 81-131.

[12] Donald Grove Barnes, *George III and William Pitt, 1783-1806* (Stanford, 1939). Although Professor Barnes is not interested in structural analysis to the degree characteristic of the Namier school, he works within the Namier tradition (or methodological and interpretive mode) and extends it chronologically in a most significant way.

[13] *King George III and the Politicians* (Oxford, 1953).

[14] Lucy Stuart Sutherland, *The East India Company in Eighteenth-Century Politics* (Oxford, 1952).

[15] See above, notes 5 and 6.

[16] John B. Owen, *The Rise of the Pelhams* (London, 1957).

[17] Robert Walcott, *English Politics in the Early Eighteenth Century* (Oxford, 1956).

"most powerfully organized squadron" that seems to threaten some. Over the years, however, a number of historians working in periods outside Sir Lewis's interest have employed his or analogous methods. The Long Parliament has received full analytic treatment in the Namier mode from Brunton and Pennington[18] at Sir Lewis's own Manchester and from Dean Keeler[19] in this country. In the nineteenth century there has been the most significant work of Norman Gash on party politics in the age of Peel[20] and of H. J. Hanham in that of Disraeli[21] Of much longer standing and greater extent, however, has been the even more independent work of Sir John Neale and his own school on the reign of Elizabeth.[22]

There have also been institutional developments reflecting "Namierite" influence. Even in the 1930's it was evident to some that the most original and perhaps important part of Sir Lewis's and similar work[23] was the biographical-statistical element; and that this was by and large too laborious and too demanding a type of work to be undertaken usefully by even the best trained of individuals. There is simply too much social waste involved in separate scholars' attempting to assemble such material individually for their separate projects. Such research, like that which went into the *Dictionary of National Biography* or even the *O.E.D.*, might more efficiently be undertaken as a group project and suitably financed. In the 1930's a private foundation was organized by the late Colonel Wedgwood and others to compile a multi-volume biographical dictionary of every person who sat in Commons since the Middle Ages. The difficulties were underestimated. By the war, only one not entirely satisfactory volume had appeared,[24] and after the war the project had to be suspended for lack of funds. In the 1950's, however, the project was revived by the promise of a government grant of several hundred thousand pounds spread out over twenty or so years. When one recollects the rarity in any country of government grants for historical research, one may surmise the origin of some of the cries against that "most powerfully organized of squadrons." In actuality, though, the annual grants now received may be too small to attract, train and retain a staff of sufficient expertise to carry out a project of such scope and technical difficulties. Thus, even though policy calls for working on only a few volumes (defined chronologically) at one time, the central staff, with its quite limited resources, has not attempted to do all the work even on these volumes. Wherever possible, the unpaid services have been recruited of independent historians, local specialists, genealogists or just enthusiastic amateurs.

[18] Douglas Brunton and Donald H. Pennington, *Members of the Long Parliament* (London, 1954).

[19] Mary Frear Keeler, *The Long Parliament, 1640-1641: A Biographical Study of Its Members (Memoirs of the American Philosophical Society,* XXXVI) (Philadelphia, 1954).

[20] *Politics in the Age of Peel: A Study in the Technique of Parliamentary Representation, 1830-1850* (London, 1953).

[21] *Elections and Party Management: Politics in the Time of Disraeli and Gladstone* (London, 1959).

[22] Including: *The Elizabethan House of Commons* (London, 1949); *Elizabeth I and Her Parliaments,* 2 vols. (London, 1953-1957).

[23] E.g., work like Charles A. Beard's *An Economic Interpretation of the Constitution of the United States* (New York, 1913). Few have noticed how closely the work of Beard and his critics (e.g., Forrest McDonald, *We the People: The Economic Origins of the Constitution* (Chicago, 1958) anticipate and parallel what English critics sometimes regard as the peculiarly "Namierite" technique of collective biography. Although "results" have sometimes led to controversy, in general quantitative technique would seem to be much more generally accepted and frequently used among historians of the United States than among historians of England.

[24] Josiah Clement Wedgwood, *et al., History of Parlicment . . . 1439-1509* (London, 1936).

The volumes of the new *History of Parliament* when they appear will consist primarily of short biographies of every member of the House of Commons in the years covered. However, they will not simply be a *D.N.B.* of less important people. This biographical material will be processed statistically, and the introductory volume to each part will contain tabular representations of the social and political composition of the House broken down in all meaningful categories practicable. There will also, presumably, be analyses of selected divisions. When and if completed, this series will provide historians with a major statistical and analytical tool of extraordinary value, unique in English historiography. With his *History of Parliament* at his elbow, the future political historian will have all the dirty work done, the composition of each House, the significance of each election, the meaning of many divisions all neatly laid out in statistical tables for those that can read statistical tables. A casual glance at the biographical section will enable him to speak knowingly of the long connection of the This's of That with Tother borough, and of the rather involved genealogical connection of Placeman X to Boroughmonger Y's mother-in-law. Then indeed will the "imagination" be able to play blissfully over carefully nurtured lawns, protected by wise statistical hedges from ever going too far astray.

With such a prospect of downhill bliss before him, one would think that even the laziest historian could get out a faint huzza. Such has unfortunately not been the case. Ever since the rebirth of the *History of Parliament* project, the grumbles have been getting louder. With the appearance of the "imprimatur" works of Brooke and Christie and the related efforts of Walcott and Owen, the brickbats started flying, sometimes on the seeming principle: "Banzai for the tenders; keep away from the battleship!"

What has been the basis of this dissatisfaction? Long before the recent critics started, anyone who read Sir Lewis realized, without getting too far into his volumes, that his canvas, though richly detailed, brightly illuminated and remarkably alive, depicted nevertheless only a small corner of historical reality. To Sir Lewis, the House of Commons was the essence, the epitome, the microcosm of the political nation:

Small boys play at kings and soldiers, or at riders, engine-drivers, chauffeurs and airmen—the material expression of that fancy varies with methods of locomotion. But for several centuries the dream of English youth and manhood of the nation-forming class has remained unchanged; it has been fixed and focused on the House of Commons, a modified, socialized arena for battle, drive and dominion.[25]

To this arena, to the adjacent hippodrome of the Lords, and to their front office—the ministry—he devoted all his attention. The rest of the political nation was neglected, except at election times; the administrative apparatus almost totally ignored, except insofar as it offered places, sinecures and contracts with which political influence might be built. "Namierites" are not interested in the extensive body of legislation that passed through parliament each year with routine government support or without controversy or with controversy that did not involve the government. Only the rare division that became a party issue and might challenge the government has attracted their investigatory zeal.

This is particularly unfortunate in the case of the administrative apparatus for it tends to obscure the ways in which policy could then as now originate from below and merely pass through the hands of the "responsible" minister. This in turn leads to an

[25] *Structure of Politics*, p. 1.

under-emphasis of the political weight of towns and nonpolitical businessmen. This bourgeois influence was usually exerted in the first instance through the administrative apparatus and only in desperate cases carried to the level of parliament or cabinet. Then too, by neglecting the administrative side of a minister's place, one tends to underemphasize that great stumbling block in forming so many ministries—the extraordinarily limited number of "men of business" among politicians who could in fact fill a technically demanding office like Chancellor of the Exchequer.

To most of this, however, an honest judge must answer "True, but irrelevant." The "Namierites" are monograph writers and a monograph writer need never apologize for his calling. To dig deep one must circumscribe the breadth of one's diggings. The river Platte is a mile wide at its mouth and how many inches deep. There are mightier torrents than the Platte within much more confined banks, and there are greater historians than H. G. Wells. The "Namierites" are concerned with a very difficult problem: the locus, structure and transmission of power in politics. To handle it adequately, they must concentrate their attention and the attention of the reader. There are plenty of books on military, naval, diplomatic, economic, social, ecclesiastical and intellectual history; one need not expect to find everything in every book, least of all in one by Sir Lewis.

Any author may then defend himself fairly well on charges of scope and coverage by replying, usually with the weight of reason on his side, "You're looking for a book I never intended to write." The more important criticism of method cannot be so easily side-stepped. Although methodological doubts about the Namierites have been raised in passing reviews from time to time, we have had to wait for Professor Herbert Butterfield's recent *George III and the Historians*[26] for a full-scale critique. His work is at once the fullest treatment and most intemperate attack upon Sir Lewis and his "school," their methods, their presuppositions and their results. The present discussion of the remaining problems posed by Namierite methodology will therefore be organized around the chief points suggested by a reading of Butterfield.

The Master of Peterhouse's new work stands rather interesting comparison with his earlier (1931) well-known work on the *Whig Interpretation of History*.[27] In the earlier work, a tour de force of intellectual legerdemain, without mentioning specific historians, Butterfield drew a composite picture of the Whig historical mind at work, distorting all that came its way. Each line of that elegant essay strikes true somewhere, yet the composite end product is only a caricature; it doesn't even fit Froude. In his new book, Butterfield devotes two-thirds of his attention to slaying some more Whig historians—the guiltiest being Erskine May, the biggest being Lecky—for not being kind enough to George III. In doing this, however, he uses a most peculiar technique: instead of the uncitable archetype of his earlier work, he now treats specific historians individually and cites from them liberally. Yet in evaluating each one, he does not consider his subject's over-all interpretation of George III, or of the first 23 years of his reign, but instead confines his investigation and comparisons to the opening years of the reign and to a limited number of rather eccentrically selected topics: the superficial personality of George III (i.e., in Sunday School rather than Freudian terms), his "intentions" on ascending the throne, the influences of his mother, the influence of Bute after his resignation. Needless to say, these are not the most ultimately important issues in the reign of George III. But had Butterfield used other

[26] See note 9.
[27] (London, 1931.)

more important issues (e.g., George III's concept of ministerial responsibility and proper lines of authority, or the way he made up his mind on key issues, and so on), he might have obtained different results. The strength of the Whig historians generally lay in their broad synthetic vision, their ability to unify and explain; their chief weakness lay in anachronism, their tendency to read results back into origins, their assumption of a greater logic and purposiveness in historical figures and events than they in fact possessed. All this can be much more dramatically "highlighted" in the Whigs by concentrating on their treatment of the pre-history of the misfortunes of George III's reign than on the misfortunes themselves.

When in the last third of his book, Butterfield comes to the "Namier school," he reverses his techniques once more. Direct quotation and citation become once more almost as rare as in the *Whig Interpretation.* We hear relatively little of Sir Lewis, Brooke, or Christie, but high priest and acolyte are once again rendered indistinguishable beneath the anonymous hoods of an impersonal sect. Only, the abominable heresy of this new sect is not whiggish historicism but historical anti-whiggery. For, paradoxically, the Butterfield who is so unrelenting with the Whig historians has a rather warm place in his heart for some actual Whigs themselves.

His concentration on what historians "say about" George III or the Whigs epitomizes one side of Butterfield's approach: as Richard Pares observed, he seems not so much interested in history as in historiography.[28] That is, he seems not so much interested in what George III or "the Whigs" did, as in what later historians have to say about what they did or, better still, said. He attaches great importance to which historian first suggested an interpretation, regardless of whether such a suggestion arose from anything more than a lucky, healthy hunch. By contrast, the most rigorous scholarly examination of a problem gains little grace in his treasury if its reported results are not entirely novel. His concentration on priority of interpretation as the major criterion of historiographical evaluation would seem to leave Butterfield a bit indifferent to the rival claims of research methodology, the true glory of the "Namierites."

Yet we should not make too much out of the convenient distinction between "interpretation" and "methodology" as *alternative* measuring sticks for the historiographical critic. So many apparent distinctions (structure/analysis, interest/ideology) break down at the test. This more general one is no exception. The construction of an historical interpretation of the sort that would merit professional consideration today cannot be an intellectual process totally distinct from the intellectual processes we call research methodology. Or, phrased somewhat differently, both interpretation and research of necessity proceed within modes of operation (methodologies) that overlap, that indeed have much in common. If, for a relevant example, research in a given area demands a certain range of semantic rigor, then interpretation within that said area must employ the same degree of rigor. It is on just such technical questions that Butterfield and the "Namierites" seem farthest apart. If for them interpretation is but a function of research, for him interpretation would seem to have a life and style of its own. Thus, while they demand the utmost verbal attention from their readers, he seems no more interested in semantic rigor than in any other of the niceties of their methodology. We read him in vain for those fine

28 Richard Pares, "Round the Georgian Mulberry Bush," *New Statesman,* LIV, (23 November 1957), 698-699.

distinctions between actual institutions and the words used to describe them so basic in understanding their work.

Thus far, the reader not immediately familiar with Namier or Butterfield may wonder what blood or passion could ever have resided in all these empty boxes. Before proceeding to their more macrocosmic differences, it would be well to narrow the focus for a few pages and examine in microcosm some specific misunderstandings that arise between them because of such seeming semantic trivia as "the nice distinctions between actual institutions and the words used to describe them." *Party* will do quite nicely for a start—a workaday term everyone uses in writing about eighteenth century politics, though not always with the care it deserves. The recent volume in the *Oxford History of England*,[29] for example, hardly mentions party in its analytical chapters. We are told that Whig and Tory meant little in 1760, but no mention is made of the lesser, more meaningful groups, nor how governments of the day built working majorities out of the farraginous materials of the House of Commons. Yet is is precisely here that some of the "Namierites'" most important work has been done—and here that the semantic distance between them and their critics is often the widest.

* * *

Sir Lewis and his school do not necessarily stop on every page to announce in what sense they are now using the word *party* or *faction* or *connection*. The agile reader, however, alert to the danger of being deceived by the appearances of words, can catch the distinctions without too much trouble. On the other hand, in reading Butterfield's critique of the "Namierites," the present writer has been unable to detect that sense of semantic rigor necessary for a full appreciation of the "Namierites" at their most characteristic. There seems to be little difference for the Master of Peterhouse between party as a body of sentiment and party as a form of organization; or between the lowly amorphous level of organization observable in the ordinary connection and the higher level of a meaningful party disciplined enough to vote and resign as ordered. Thus, he refuses to understand Brooke when Brooke scrupulously confines his use of "party" to the last, most rigorous sense. Thus, when Brooke says that the Rockingham party was born in the Rockingham administration, he does not mean that the connections which made it up did not antedate it, or that the self-identity of its members with sentimental Whiggery, however defined, did not antedate it, but that its disciplined internal cohesion only dated from its time in office.[30]

Party thus is not something to be once analyzed and tagged and thereafter regarded as a constant; it is an extremely dynamic and elusive phenomenon requiring constant re-analysis lest the narrative historian fall into anachronism. For the historian of party, both analysis and narrative are wheels perpetually engaged, perpetually in motion. It is therefore particularly unfortunate that, in one of his unguarded forays into the field of methodology, Butterfield should posit the antagonism of analysis and narrative and accuse the "Namierites" of concentrating on structural analysis to the detriment of narrative.[31] This immediately raises two questions: (one) is the postulated dichotomy meaningful? and (two) are the "Namierites" guilty? The first question needs no

29 J. Steven Watson, *The Reign of George III* (Oxford, 1960).
30 Brooke, *Chatham Administration,* Ch. 6; Butterfield, *George III and the Historians,* 1st ed., 219-223, 2nd ed., 222-226 (substantially altered).
31 Butterfield, *op. cit.,* 1st ed., 204-207; 2nd ed., 202-205.

belaboring. Few serious historians today could regard analysis and narrative as anything more than the static and dynamic phases of the single process of historical reconstruction. As such they are complementary, rather than antagonistic. That his dichotomy is rather shaky, Butterfield himself seems to admit: thus he half concedes that it is all right for a narrative historian to analyze a division, though too much structural analysis is somehow unhealthy. This avoids the question of how a narrative historian is to analyze a division meaningfully if he has not previously analyzed the structure of the House.[32]

As for the second question, Butterfield is not alone in his tendency to view the "Namier school" as simply structural or static analysts when in fact all of them seriously attempt to describe process. It is perhaps a misunderstanding of the title of Sir Lewis's most famous book, the *Structure of Politics* that has encouraged the inference that "the Namier approach" leads primarily to static analysis. Actually, Namier is not important simply as a static analyst. Previous writers from Porritt to Laprade[33] had analyzed much of the electoral system, and many before him had catalogued the factions in the parliaments of the 1760's. Namier of course carried all this further, and his breakdown of the House of Commons by degree of independence or affiliation as well as by class, interest, and so on, was unprecedented. But he went beyond nose counting to dynamic analysis. As an outsider, he could ask questions of the obvious. Everyone knows the Duke of Wellington's maxim that "the king's government must be carried on" In the eighteenth century, the business of government was government, i.e., administration: preserve order, collect taxes and get through each year's parliamentary session the routine bills necessary for the business of the year. Compared to such technically "urgent" tasks, "reform" or any other technically nonpressing legislation took very low priority indeed. Now it did not appear at all obvious to Sir Lewis that members of parliament should support the government of the day in all the routine but technically necessary legislation of the year. If they did so, there must have been reasons. Hence, his dynamic view of parliamentary government as a continuous, ongoing process of ministry-and-majority building, requiring constant attention to negate the effects of attrition and indifference, each major defection having to be balanced by an equivalent accretion of strength.

* * *

But were issues necessarily tactical? Let us turn back from the process of government-making to the simpler phenomenon of "party." The farther a party moved from the status of a simple or natural connection, the more self-justification it might require. At any given time, any really significant party had views on any number of issues. The historian can dig under the rhetoric, as Brooke does, and find inconsistency in these views; or he can rake through the rhetoric to discern an essential consistency. Consistency, however, is not the most important question one can ask about a party and its professions. More fundamental is the functional relationship of party and

---

[32] *Ibid.*, 1st ed. 205; 2nd ed., 203. Professor Butterfield is not clear. It is possible that in commending the historian who "puts the microscope on the event" (i.e., the vote on Dunning's resolution), etc., he is not suggesting the analysis of divisions.

[33] Edward and Annie Gertrude Porritt, *The Unreformed House of Commons,* 2 vols. (Cambridge, 1903-1909); William Thomas Laprade, ed., *Parliamentary Papers of John Robinson, 1774-1784* (Royal Historical Society, Camden 2nd ser., XXXIII) (London, 1922).

program. Looking now not just at mid-eighteenth-century parties as described by Namier but at party and program generally, one might ask: which comes first, the party or its program? Does program (conceived either as idea or as objective social need) exist first either logically-inherently or chronologically, creating party as its means towards realization; or does party have an ultimate institutional-operational logic of its own, independent of its momentary program, itself utilizing program for its own self-perpetuating ends? These questions are not unconnected with the separate question of the purposiveness and self-awareness of individual activity.

The general tendency of "Namierite" history has been to treat program operationally and tactically. No party is formed around an issue and successful parties rarely let themselves become too wedded to issues. Circumstance created the American issue for the Rockinghams; but they would have existed as a party in any event. Such an approach has led to the frequent complaint, most commonly from the left, that Sir Lewis was really an arch-Tory in the Hume sense of one skeptical of the independent role of either ideas or logic in directing human behavior. Of course, by this formulation, Marx would also be an arch-Tory. To this charge, Namier more than once pleaded guilty: he was skeptical. Unfortunately, those who raise the issue seem unwilling to formulate it and argue it on a general philosophic or even historical-methodological level. They prefer to treat the question as some peculiar vice of Sir Lewis's. At the same time, they shy away from arguing the question in the specific context of any particular situation when evidence might legitimately be called for. Instead, they prefer to leave the issue hovering somewhere above the level of evidence, somewhere below the level of philosophy.

In Butterfield's hands, this issue becomes one more brick to throw at structural analysis, through the assumption of an inherent antipathy between such analysis and a due appreciation of ideology. By a rather obscure, not to say obscurantist, rule, he would have it that to investigate the ties of interest, dependency, consanguinity, proximity, friendship, and so on, that encouraged men to act together in politics is to deny any role at all to ideology as a determinant of men's political action.[34] But Butterfield cannot seriously suggest that the historian must choose between ideas and social analysis. Ideas do not exist in a void. Professor Caroline Robbins[35] is not the first to point out that ideas are frequently transmitted within the structures of families and connections whose analysis tells us much about the diffusion of those ideas. Nor must the effectiveness of ideas be measured only by impressions or by literary evidence. Structural and operational analysis can help measure the observable effectiveness of ideology. Under structural analysis, some connections reveal individuals whose affiliation to the group is professedly ideological and, for want of contrary evidence, may be assumed to be genuinely so, as well as individuals whose motivation is so obscure that it may well be assumed to be ideological. We are reminded of some of the types who followed the elder Pitt. That we do not find more such types tells us much about the times; but we cannot blame that paucity on structural analysis any more than a company's insolvency can be blamed on the accountant who discovered it. Operational analysis is equally useful in measuring some of the observable effects of ideology. We noted above that the ongoing process of government building required good House of Commons men on the government bench to attract the independent and uncommitted. Part of this ability to attract may well have lain in the ability of the frontbencher to personify an ideology or at least to

---

[34] Butterfield, *op. cit.*, 1st ed., 208-212; 2nd ed., 206-210.
[35] *The Eighteenth-Century Commonwealthman* (Cambridge, Mass., 1959).

manipulate symbols. But when Butterfield says the historian should spend less time analyzing the structure of the house and more time analyzing the contents of debates, he may be going too far, even taking a methodologically retrograde step. After all, if the managers could predict the results of the division days in advance, the contents of the debate may not have been all that important.

Closely allied to the problem of *ideology* is that of *rationality*. To Sir Lewis, "masses act but are supposed to reason." That is, historians can readily and with some certainty reconstruct a wide range of "deeds" but are too ready to pre-suppose behind them a rational consciousness, which may or may not have been there, but which they cannot verify with equal certainty. Acts and even words then are best first studied naked and only clothed with rationality after appropriate evidence has been gathered and evaluated. In analyzing individual behavior, Sir Lewis was more than careful, he was a frank irrationalist in the respectable tradition from Hume to Freud and Pareto. To Butterfield, all this is deeply offensive. Not only would he by contrast seem to be a psychological rationalist, but, by some obscure process, he seems to link "irrationalist" views of human behavior with the profession of structural and interest analysis.[36] (That is, historians who specialize in analyzing structure must believe in the "irrationality" of political behavior.) Against all which, he protests that "over and above the irrationalities of the world, the social pressures and the sheer play of forces [whatever that may mean] there moves something of rational purpose, something of the conscious calculations of reasoning and reasonable men." In a specific instance, he assumes that if one can show that a significant proportion of the Commons were independent, unpledged or unpredictable in their voting behavior, this is *evidence* that their voting was regulated by the rational or "higher political considerations" brought forth in the debate (what others might call rhetoric or cant).[37] The inference then is that the M.P. who, out of a conscious calculation of his own interest, or out of his appreciation of the general issues at stake in the existing political situation, attached himself to a particular party or faction and voted regularly with it was somehow acting less rationally than the unattached M.P. who entered the House uncommitted and let his vote be swayed by the excitement and passions of the debate. This is a surprisingly flattering view both of the content of eighteenth-century debates and of the intellectual and moral discernment of the unattached backbencher.

Though the most irrational of men can be highly deliberate, Butterfield tends further to link, *rationality* and *purposiveness,* the latter of which he also sees unjustly deflated by structural analysis.[38] As an irrationalist, Sir Lewis naturally ascribed relatively little weight to the subsequent or even immediate declarations of purpose in persons whose actions or whose personalities cast doubt on such rationalizations. This is made brilliantly clear in his exemplary essay on the personality of George III.[39] To Butterfield, by contrast, using judgments that must be theological in root, such psychology in effect dehumanizes man, or in theological terms deprives him of his free will. Thus, thrusting psychology and Namier aside, Butterfield insists that "the political practitioner, even if he is only George III, does possess a framework of ideas and purposes which affect his actions."[40] Presumably by "affect," Butterfield means "direct"; otherwise the sentence would be meaningless. This *a priori* postulacy of

[36] Butterfield, *op. cit.,* 1st ed., 211-213; 2nd ed., 209-211.

[37] *Ibid.,* 1st ed., 205; 2nd ed., 203.

[38] *Ibid.,* 1st ed., 214-215, 298; 2nd ed., 212-213.

[39] "King George III: A Study of Personality," *Personalities and Powers* (London, 1955), 39-58.

[40] As in note 38.

"ideas and purposes" (in tandem) represents Butterfield's *system* at its most characteristic: insofar as these ideas and purposes are held to have an existence independent of the situation (including values, loyalties, and so on) of the "practitioner" as revealed by structural analysis, this postulacy may also be held to mark another point of most significant divergence between this critic and the "Namierites." For Butterfield starts where many historians would be happy to end.

Historical methodology is not just a matter of semantics and psychology; it may also be a matter of philosophy. Butterfield uses the word "purpose" not simply in the individual psychological sense, but also in another or "higher" sense, to suggest the transcendant framework or pattern within which events take place. By contrast, Sir Lewis is lumped together with Sir Isaiah Berlin among those who see history "only as a succession of chances or conjunctures." To Butterfield, the pattern or whole has a validity that transcends the details that make it up and "it is the optical illusion or the occupational disease of the research student to imagine that only the details matter."[41] From his vantage point above mere details, the generalizing historian can then see "those higher political considerations which ... help to turn the study of history into a political education."[42] Yet, one wonders in what mind these higher political considerations are to be understood to reside. Surely not in the mind of the actors—unless we are to take this too *a priori*. Surely not in the mind alone of the historian, for Butterfield is no relativist. But where? The reader must regret the modesty (or archness) which has led Butterfield to keep his teleological cards so close to his chest. An unwary reader of his book might easily have lost his way and come away under the misapprehension that it was some nice point of research methodology or quite specific problem of historical interpretation that most separated Sir Lewis and his principal critic. It would have been rather simpler all around if he had spelled out his specific historistic or determinist premises and started from there—instead of assuming that the reader knew everything, or nothing, about them.[43]

To return, in concluding, to simple history, many students seem confused by the seeming inconsistency of positions in the triangle Namier-Butterfield-Whig historians. Shouldn't the caustic Butterfield of the *Whig Interpretation* really be a Namierite by necessary conviction? Why then is he not only so anti-Namier but so enraged by, for example, Brooke's rather skeptical treatment of the Rockinghams? Is then the Butterfield of the *Whig Interpretation* the only Butterfield? If not, who are the other Butterfields? It was noted above that the strength of the Whig historians generally lay in their broad synthetic vision and their ability to unify and explain, while their chief weaknesses lay, *inter alia*, in their tendency to read results back into origins and in their assumption of a greater logic and purposiveness in historical figures and events than they in fact possessed. By such criteria, do not the other Butterfields—the political educator, the rational behaviorist, the defender of the "higher" purposes of party and of history—go far to adding up to Butterfield "the Whig historian," a Butterfield for whom Rockingham and Fox still sit on Olympus? Sometimes, all the Butterfields come pouring out in a single sentence, deeply revelatory of the Whiggery of his attitudes towards Whigs and Namierites alike:

Those of us who have been enemies of the Whig interpretation all our lives, and have deplored the injustice done to George III, will not necessarily follow a form of

---

41 *Ibid.*
42 *Ibid.*, 1st ed., 205; 2nd ed., 203.
43 *Cf.* his *Christianity and History* (London, 1949), esp. Ch. I, V.

historiography which lacks the breadth to comprise the higher purposes of the Rockinghamites—an historiography which seems to reduce the programme of this party to a mere device of eighteenth-century faction.[44]

Value systems do not surrender easily. For the past seventy-five years, English historiography has been struggling to disengage itself from an older and not unworthy literary-moralistic tradition and to re-establish itself on firm professional (if not necessarily scientific) foundations. The newer discipline has required a considerable self-discipline in its practitioners; its victory has been noticeably less complete in the modern than in the medieval field precisely because so many of the issues and value conflicts of more modern history (even as far back as the sixteenth century) are still very much alive today. Thus the modern historian must, even while intruding his imagination to the mind of the age he is studying, take care to free his judgment (as far as is possible) from the unconscious value judgments of both that *and* his own age. This can be an emotionally wrenching experience. In the long run, the significance of the work of Sir Lewis Namier and his followers lies in their thus wrenching loose the study of a small but significant period of history from the emotional grip of such symbols as George III, the Declaration of Independence, Charles James Fox and Edmund Burke. Such wrenching is rarely a clean job; this particular operation has left behind its full share of value residues and psychic wounds. Memorial gardens do not grow on those battlefields yet. For decades to come, both pre-Namierite examination papers and pre-Namierite books will undoubtedly continue to be written.

[44] Butterfield, *op. cit.*, 1st ed., 273, 2nd ed., 274.

# THE AGE OF
# REVOLUTION

# 13 / Towards the Origins of Modern Revolutions: Crowds, Millenarianism, Populism

The essence of modern European history is change. But the *idea* of change, indeed of *revolution*, a fundamental and sudden alteration in political, social, and economic institutions, becomes generally popular only in the course of the late eighteenth and early nineteenth centuries.

Before the era of modern revolutions—American, French, and Russian—certain patterns of dissent had already developed. Even then, mass dissent had become a serious question. Prior to 1850 (later in some places), organized workers and political parties were not the source of this dissent. "Messianic" religious movements, more or less amorphous "crowds," and several forms of "populism" were the common vehicles of malcontent.

Vittorio Lanternari, author of *The Religions of the Oppressed*,[1] insists on the importance of the religious impulse in the early stages of revolutionary movements. The first selection is a general discussion of the nature and causes of *messianism* which he defines as "a collective movement of escape from the present and of expectation of salvation promoted by a prophet-founder." Its aim is "a renewal of the world which will be realized in an eschatological perspective as a return to a primordial and paradisiacal age."

In the second selection, the British historian Eric Hobsbawm takes up the problem of messianism (millenarianism) and other primitive forms of social agitation in the context of "Western and Southern Europe, and especially Italy, since the French Revolution." A major contention of Professor Hobsbawm is that under certain circumstances millenial movements can develop into wholly modern social movements. Noteworthy are Lanternari's and Hobsbawm's differences on the relationship of messianism to the Judeo-Christian Tradition.

Another British historian, George Rudé, is a leading scholar of a second form of early social protest—the pre-industrial crowd. In the third selection, Rudé defines the crowd as he has studied it in France and England from the 1730's to the 1840's. Leading problems of his work include an assessment of the importance of economic versus political reasons for the gathering of crowds, and an evaluation of the degree of success of such movements. Failures or not, Rudé regards these early struggles "as the forerunners of later movements whose results and successes have been both significant and enduring."

In May 1967, a conference on the problem of "populism" was held at the London School of Economics and Political Science. The symposium demonstrates that this important form of "primitive" radicalism is even harder to define and analyze than

[1] New York: Alfred A. Knopf, 1963.

messianism or the nature of crowds. Certainly it is no less important. Professor Peter Worsley remarked to his distinguished colleagues that "populism was the biggest growth industry. It led everywhere." There are Russian and North American populisms. Latin American, African, and Asian populisms. There are right wing and left wing, rural and urban populisms. Some have suggested that the "New Left" of the 1960's is merely a revival of populism. The fourth selection contains the conclusions of the symposium. Appropriately it ends with a general definition of populism. Some readers may prefer to begin there.

# MESSIANISM: ITS HISTORICAL ORIGIN AND MORPHOLOGY

Vittorio Lanternari

The Western tradition, of Jewish and Christian origin, has so deeply and univocally influenced our ideas on religious phenomena that it might seem improper to speak of messianism in a sense which intentionally transcends the Judeo-Christian religious tradition. Recently an ethnologist, experienced in the prophetism of primitive peoples, pointed out to us that the term "messianism" cannot correctly be applied to religious phenomena that are not in some way linked to the original cultural milieu which the very term is etymologically rooted ("Messiah" from the Jewish *māshīah* = "the annointed" [of God], i.e., the "chosen"). The same scholar said that there is no true messianism without a personal savior.[1] In this regard, we must note in the first place that in its origin the Jewish term had such a generic and, so to speak, extra-messianic meaning (from a Christian point of view) that it was used to designate at the same time a high priest or a Jewish monarch, inasmuch as they were endowed with a high dignity, and even a pagan foreigner like the Persian Cyrus who gave back freedom to the captive Jews in Babylon.

It is true that the term could also be applied to that person announced and expected from among the Israelites, and who, according to many prophetic texts, was to bring the Golden Era, one of freedom, peace, harmony, and justice. But only as a result of the later religious tradition, that is, only in the Christian Hellenic tradition (John 1:41, and never before the Book of Enoch, the word "messiah" was circumscribed and identified with the historic person of the expected "savior" ("anointed," *christós*), interpreted as the renewer of the world. The same word designated also previously (Pss. 89:39, 52; 84:10) the whole people, Israel, or the Patriarchs (Pss. 105:15; I Chron. 16:22).

The term "messiah," therefore, has a history, having changed its meaning in the course of time from a generic to a restricted and individual one.[2] The identification Messiah-Jesus is sanctioned in the Western world by a tradition of two thousand years, but in the light of the history of the word and from the viewpoint of a comparative history of religions, it seems scientifically correct to broaden the meaning of this word "messianism" so that we may include in it a series of manifestations which are homogeneous in their function. Needless to say, there remains an obligation to note not only the similarities but also the concrete differences among the different types of "messianic" manifestations. Besides, the same messianic complex which originated in Judaism and was confirmed in Christianity, with the figure of a future savior, was neither born from nothing nor was the fruit of a sudden and miraculous intuition of this or that prophet; on the contrary, it shows profound and distant roots that reach down deep to the Mosaic level and presumably further back since Mosaism itself is a new synthesis of more ancient elements.[3] Be that as it may, the message of the Jewish

---

[1] G. Guariglia, *Prophetismus und Heilserwartungsbewegungen als völkerkundliches und religionsgeschichtliches Problem* (Horn-Wien, 1959), pp. 26-27, 33. The date of publication is fictitious; the book actually came out in 1960.

[2] J. Klausner, *The Messianic Idea in Israel* (London, 1956), pp. 7-12.

prophets is related to a theme of messianic expectation already contained in the archaic Mosaic message (Deut. 18:15–22). They elaborate this message again in forms which are appropriate to the new exigencies of liberation whether they call the Messiah "Servant of God" (Isa. 35, 42), "Lord of Justice" (Jer. 13:5–8), "Son of Man" (Ezek. 10:33, 42, 33), Chief of Armies" (Dan. 9:23–27), etc.

Therefore, as a working hypothesis it seems to us that we should use the term "messiah" to designate any being, singular or plural, more or less anthropomorphic, expected by a community as the future savior in a religious context.

Now is seems legitimate to us, in the general picture of the history of religions, to raise the problem whether the messianic attitude is connatural, peculiar, and exclusive to the Jewish-Christian-Islamic stream (in the order: Moses and the prophets, Apocalypse, Mahdism), or rather whether this attitude has counterparts in heterogeneous religions of primitive background, independently of Western influence.

Another great messianic stream is already present in some historic religions, among the most advanced, Zoroastrianism and Buddhism. In Zoroastrianism the coming of Saosyant, the future savior, is awaited for the decisive struggle against the god of evil, Angramaniu, and the final triumph of good. From this idea, interwoven with the Indo-Iranian theories of the progressive decadence of the cosmic ages until the beginning of a new cycle of time, there evolved within popular Buddhism the idea of the future Buddha, Maitreya, who is to descend one day upon earth after evil will have filled the world, to reestablish the kingdom of good.[4]

As one can see, the expectation of a supernatural being who will come or return at the end of a whole cycle of human existence to open a new era of freedom is shared by other religions outside the Jewish-Christian-Islamic tradition. In any case, it is interesting to note at this point that the messianic expectation is present within religious movements of salvation like Zoroastrianism, Buddhism, Mosaism, Jewish prophetism of the Exile, and Christianity, and that these movements, like other ones, arose from time to time as an answer to a real need for renewal and catharsis, resulting from a state of oppression, anxiety, tension, and conflict at a collective and social level.[5]

But in order to come nearer to the basic problem, it will be better to ask once again: outside the "great historic religions" what are the concrete forms in which a correspondent or at least an embryonic messianic attitude is manifested? And so: on what cultural and social ground does messianism thrive to such an extent as to constitute true and proper "movements" of expectation of salvation?

In this regard it will be useful to refer to one of the newest and most meaningful chapters of the modern history of religions: that which deals with the prophetic movements of freedom and salvation called nativistic or revivalistic, millenaristic, or movements of messianic expectation, etc. Morphological and comparative synthesis

---

[3] Concerning Mosaism as a synthesis of archaic components of pastoral and agricultural origin, see V. Lanternari, *La grande festa* (Milan, 1959), pp. 448-51.

[4] E. Abegg, *Der Messiasglauben in Indien und Iran* (Berlin-Leipzig, 1928).

[5] For the birth of Zoroastrianism in relation to the conflict between two heterogeneous and contrasting cultural trends, see Lanternari, *op. cit.*, p. 448. Concerning the rising of Buddhism and of Christianity in relation to the conflict between priesthood and state on the one hand and popular religious needs on the other, see my remarks in *Nuovi Argomenti*, XLII-XLIII (1960), 100-101. The Jewish prophetism of the time before the Exile (Amos, Isaiah, etc.) should be seen in relation to the disasters afflicting the Jewish people at that time (political and religious schism, fall of the kingdom of Samaria) and to those easily forseeable because of hostilities on the part of the neighboring peoples, and of Babylonian supremacy. Finally, the prophets of the Exile act in a time of catastrophe and collective desperation. In any case, the prophets interpret a need for liberation from present or imminent evils which can be historically identified and determined.

has hardly begun in the abundant literature concerning the prophetic movements at the ethnological level, not to mention the prophetic movements of the modern and cultured milieu.

*  *  *

In synthesis, the phenomena of the return of the culture-hero, of the supreme being, and of the spirits of the dead are various manifestations of a true religion of return. The religion of return manifests itself in very different forms which may in turn depend on the cultural context, on different religious traditions, and on different prophetic personalities. But the religion of return is the essential kernel of messianism as such. Through it the era of salvation appears mythically as the reinstatement of the age of the origins. *We can therefore say that any prophetic movement has its messianic aspect, because in it a salvation is expected which will be brought by mythical beings or events, whatever they might be.* We said "mythical beings or events." In fact, besides the examples we have mentioned above and in which we find one or more demiurges of the world's rebirth (culture-hero, supreme being, spirits of the dead), there are instances in which the religion of return assumes even more different and original forms: it appears as the expectation of a particular and concrete event, namely, the reinstatement of a certain *ancient historical situation no longer existing or present.* There is no expectation for the return of mythical beings, whatever they may be, but of an historic age far remote in time and in the collective experience, an age which has become a myth and has been projected into the future. It will be the heavenly age of liberation and salvation.

Among the many manifestations of this kind is the recent movement of Ras Tafari among the Negroes of Jamaica. Its prophetic nucleus is based on the expectation of a massive "return" of the Negroes to Africa, to the faraway original land where centuries ago their ancestors had been captured by the white slave merchants. Ras Tafari, the Negus of Ethiopia, is mythologized as the hero liberator, the exemplary defender of Negro independence against the oppression of the whites. According to the followers of this movement, Ras Tafari will be the liberator and the founder of the era which is the object of the messianic expectation of the Negroes.

As one can see, the messianic idea of a "return to Africa" is based on concrete historical experience though these latter have been tinged with mythical conceptions. In brief, the identification of Ethiopia with Africa, of Haile Selassie with the Negro Messiah, and of Africa itself with the heavenly kingdom of salvation—all these are mythical remoldings of definite events and historical experiences. This shows how myths are created *ex novo,* under the impulse of vital experiences which have become particularly urgent and dramatic. Other religious forms of the "return to Africa" are expressed in the Negro Afro-American cults of Central and South America (Voodoo in Haiti, Candomble of Bahia, Xango, etc.). In these cults we see a symbolic "return to Africa" through the renewal of the original mythical African rites. Thus find adequate expression the desires of the Negroes for religious and cultural autonomy.[6]

The return to a distant historical age now lost was announced and promoted in the movement of the prophet Santos Atahuallpa in Peru in the eighteenth century (Campa culture). Santos preached, as a remedy for all evils, the restoration of the empire of the Incas against the Spanish domination; he introduced himself as the last descendant of

---

[6] V. Lanternari, *Movimenti religiosi di libertà* . . ., chap. iii, B (movements of Ras Tafari and Afro-American cults).

the Incas. On the other hand, in the neo-Brazilian prophetic movements studied by M. I. deQueiroz (movements of Contestado-Canudos, Joazeiro) the founders advocated the restoration of the monarchy and the abolition of the Brazilian Republic. To make this utopian dream come true, the prophets did not hesitate to take to arms and actively rebel against the regime in power.[7] Finally, the Burkhanian prophetic movement, which arose among the Altaic peoples in 1904, advocated the reinstatement of the ancient and fallen empire of the Mongols as a way to salvation. The founder, Chot Chelpan, announced the imminent return of Oirot Khan, leader of the Altaic Turks, who was to restore the ancient Khanate of Oirot and to set the people free from tzarist domination.[8]

In the instance just mentioned a return is announced, on a messianic and mythical ground, of statuses which the local history offers as a pattern of an "age of the origins" or, what is essentially the same, of a heavenly age. In this regard it should not be forgotten that the fundamental nucleus of the Mosaic prophetism is constituted by a program of "return" to the lost land of Zion, and that also the prophets of the captivity pursue a similar religious idea, that is, the return to a historical condition anterior to that of their time. We cannot therefore hold to the culture-hero as the irreplaceable nucleus of the prophetic movements without disregarding the infinite variability of the prophetic formations and of the "religion of return." This latter takes different forms according to themes which in turn originate from myths (culture-hero, supreme being, spirits of the dead) or from history (return to Africa, to the empire of the Incas, to the monarchy, to the empire of the Mongols, even to Zion). In all these instances we have many spontaneous religious remoldings, whether of myths or history, according to the various demands for renewal.

In fact, the transition from history to myth is imperceptible and almost continuous in primitive cultures. Not only past history is subject to the process of being mythologized; present history is also subject to the same process. Thus contemporary prophets and founders become protagonists of a millenarian expectation: they are expected to return to earth, to bring the desired salvation, and to redeem men from evil. Such is the case of André Matsua, the Congolese revolutionary leader who after he died became precisely the mythical protagonist of a millenarian expectation. And this also is the case of Macandal, the national hero of the Haitian independence: according to the popular belief his spirit escaped from the flames of the stake at which he was burned alive. In the prophetic movements of Java there was the messianic expectation of the "Prince of Justice," Ratuadil. Until recent times (twentieth century) the expectation among the Indonesians of the return of Prince Diponegoro, the Javanese hero, was very popular.[9] Alexander Bedward, the founder of Bedwardism in Jamaica, is yet another exponent of this "religion of return" based on the mythical expectation of real persons. In fact, he himself announced his coming ascension into heaven and his subsequent return as the redeemer of the Negroes. In the modern popular religion of Brazil there is the instance of the prophets, João-Maria and Padre Cicero, who founded the prophetic movements mentioned above and who are faithfully expected to return and restore the kingdom of peace and justice. Also the great current of Mahdist movements in Africa and in Asia express with recurring cycles the same expectation of a reinstatement of ancient conditions. Even the "Negro Christ," so widely worshiped in the prophetic religions of black Africa, represents the messianic reincarnations, projected into the future, of various prophets who really lived once and who are now

[7] *Ibid.*, chap. iii, C, d.
[8] *Ibid.*, chap. vi.
[9] *Ibid.*

expected to return as liberators. When Isaiah Shembe, the founder of Zionism in South Africa, died, the rumor was spread that he would rise again.[10] The same rumor was circulated when Kanakuk, the prophet of the Kickapoos, died in an epidemic of smallpox; some of his followers remained with his body in confident expectation until they also died, stricken by the epidemic.[11]

When Simon Kimbangu, the founder of the prophetic movement of liberation in the Congo, died, the Congolese believed explicitly that he would be born again. At the same time, some members of the Salvation Army arrived in the country and they were regarded as reincarnations of the great Simon: the letter $S$ which they wore on their uniforms was considered to be the initial letter of the name Simon.[12]

These are, as one can see, reinterpretations in a messianic sense of persons who really once belonged to history. What was history imperceptibly becomes myth.

But the contrary is also true, that is, that *myth definitely tends toward history*. We would be unable to understand the meaning and the function of the prophetic movements in general were we to underestimate either the historical causes that gave birth to them or the most immediate and dramatic developments they underwent on the religious, social, and political ground. It is easy to misunderstand the historical value of these movements if one fails to consider that following the prophetic movements, movements of liberation arise, often of a revolutionary nature, new separatist and dissident churches are born, new sanctuaries and religious centers are founded of a definitely autonomous character, new "holy cities" are born as a result of the prophetic preaching, modeled on the biblical pattern (e.g., the Zionistic movement in South Africa, that of the Mormons, and the neo-Brazilian movements). Such initiatives and institutions are certainly of a religious nature, but they are at the same time affirmations of a cultural autonomy. They are also expressions of a social and political revolution and represent an active need for autonomy and freedom from oppression.

The "religion of return" is thus articulated between two poles dialectically opposed: myth and history. History is transformed into myth; and myth gives meaning to history.

Retrospectively, the religion of return reinterprets the myths of the origins, as a realization of the *eschaton* and a renewal of the world. The various programs of freedom and salvation advocated by the prophets are undoubtedly based on the pattern of the myth and appear as a return to the origins. But in reality the rising of messianism and of the mythical "return to the origins" is determined by cultural and environmental factors, and by the cultural, social, and political clash with oppressive powers and institutions.

What is the functional and historical significance of this "religion of return"?

The return to the origins is the affirmation of a need for escape from the present situation, always one of risk and crisis. But, on the religious ground, the abolition of the present can only take the form of a return to the primordial time. In fact, the religious time, by its static character, is distinct from the profane duration inasmuch as it is without dimensions in the past and without any future perspective in a historical sense. The only past which can be the object of a religious experience belongs definitely to the *primordia,* to the origins. It is a mythical past, prototypical and outside of history. The future also, in a religious sense, is a messianic and eschatological future, mythical and beyond history.

[10] B. Sundkler, *Bantu Prophets in South Africa* (London, 1948), pp. 111, 126.
[11] Mooney, *op. cit.,* pp. 692-700.
[12] Anderson, *op. cit.,* pp. 126-35.

In this regard, the return to a primordial past, as stated by all prophetic movements, is the only possible escape from an unhappy present, and the only accessible form for a renewal of life in a *religious* sense.

On the other hand, the expectation of a future time in which freedom, happiness, and salvation will be realized against all sufferings gradually develops into a millenarian myth which is the only possible religious solution to the need of evading an unbearable present. The fact is that religious experience tends by its very nature to escape the dimensions of history and the level of civil initiative, and this especially in a society where the priesthood is insufficiently organized. In the collective unconsciousness there is an expectation of an event which is imminent and, at the same time, remote, and which is regarded as dreadful on account of its revolutionary nature.

Thus the escape from a painful present is made mythical in a primordial past and in an eschatological future; in such mythical forms the religious program which reshapes the world in a satisfactory way finds expression.

In fact, every prophetic movement has a revolutionary program meant to renew and reform things: in brief, an anticosmic program against the established order. In it is expressed not only a mythical need or a mere nostalgia for a past mythical age,[13] there is also a historical dynamism in the prophetic movements which should not be forgotten. The patterns of the age of origins and perfection, proposed in the messianic myths, have value inasmuch as they are as many programs of transformation, and inasmuch as they are capable of nourishing the hope for renewal, and still more, they are in themselves a beginning of rebirth. In conclusion, the most important fact in the prophetic movements is that they contain in themselves a renewal of the religious as well as cultural, social, and political life, and that this renewal takes place as an answer to existential needs which through history have grown within the developing culture. For the followers of these movements the creative future is more important than the nostalgic past, because such movements are in reality new syntheses and in any case in disagreement with the actual tradition. Thus the religion of return appears in history as a *creative religion of renewal.*

What we have said so far, in a "phenomenological" perspective, concerning the prophetic movements at an ethnological level, their millenarian myths, the expectation of salvation and the needs of regeneration expressed in them, holds, no doubt, in the same measure as regards the prophetic movements of great historic religions, and particularly Mosaism, the Jewish prophetism of the Exile, and Christianity itself. In such forms they have given a new life to a religious nucleus which was already present

---

[13] Mircea Eliade, the great historian of religions, has recently expressed his evaluation of the millenaristic movements of primitive civilizations ("Dimensions religieuses du renouvellement cosmique," *Eranos Jahrbuch,* 1960, pp. 241-75). Eliade stresses the general character of renewal of these religious manifestations and of the cosmogonic implications of the eschatological and millenaristic myths and of the rituals that are contained in the same religious manifestations. According to Eliade, these religious phenomena are to be placed in the larger and multiform picture of the religious manifestations of renewal, such as the traditional New Year festivals, initiation rites, rites for the instauration of kings, and other ritual manifestations of primitive and ancient religions. The comparison which Eliade makes between the millenaristic cults of primitive civilizations and the many other mythical and ritual manifestations we just mentioned shows in clear light the fundamental analogies of form and meaning among these various religious phenomena, but neglects the differences which are connected with each cultural formation and its existential situation. The "yearning for Paradise" is, according to Eliade, the fundamental idea of the myths and rites of renewal.

in the "pagan" religions, that is, myths and rites of expectation of salvation.[14] In fact, beyond the peculiarities due to the different cultural and historical context in which each movement arises, a genetic nucleus can be recognized, common to all of them, even in the most backward religions. In this sense we believe that there is an uninterrupted continuity of development between the so-called primitive religions and the great historic religions, including Christianity. So that if one examines them carefully and without prejudice, one can recognize in them the various ritual and mythical complexes of ancient origin which have been taken again, elaborated, and transformed according to the various cultural and historical developments and to the different and ever renewed religious and cultural demands.

In reality, if we now consider again the objection made by the ethnologist we mentioned at the beginning of this paper aganist our intent of unifying, for a phenomenological and comparative purpose, under a common "messianic" denominator various phenomena taken from the most diverse cultural levels, including the ethnological field, we can see that the preoccupation underlying such an objection is of a subjective, theological nature. Such preoccupation shows, we believe, a dangerous and hidden anti-historical tendency. The danger is that the author, moved solely by an extrascientific concern, may state as a postulate a fundamental difference between religious phenomena which are however historically linked among themselves through a true continuity. In fact, the dichotomy that our author puts between authentic and unauthentic "messianism" is equivalent to the old and outmoded distinction between *Naturvölker* and *Kulturvölker*. Any phenomenology must needs proceed by comparison, and the first step in history is precisely comparison. It is true that after having detected the similarities among various phenomena history must also acknowledge their differences and peculiarities, but we shall deal with this problem a little later.[15]

Now from a merely historical point of view the problem of the so-called authenticity or non-authenticity of a religious inspiration seems to us meaningless. The essential problem is rather that of identifying, by comparing the many messianic movements,

[14] The first author to recognize, from a methodological point of view, the expectation of salvation as the central nucleus of the prophetic movements is Guariglia *(op. cit.).*

[15] This "diversity between *authentic* messianism and all other movements in which there are messianic tendencies only" *(Verschiedenheit zwischen echtem Messianismus und allen jenen anderen Bewegungen, die nur tendenziell messianisch sind)* is affirmed in Guariglia, *op. cit.,* pp. 26, 33. The author assumes as the essential element of any "true messianic" movement, the presence of a personal messiah who summarizes in himself the entire destiny (the "history") of mankind. With that there could be no disagreement. But it is obvious that the culture-hero, the supreme being, and the dead who are expected to return in the movements of salvation of the "primitive" peoples express exactly the "destiny" and "history" of these peoples, as these latter understand and desire it. And therefore it is impossible to state, on this basis, that the messianism of the "great civilizations" *(Hochkulturen)* is *different* from the "religion of expectation" *(Heilserwartungsglaube)* of the "primitive" peoples.

The other difference, according to Guariglia, between "true" messianism and movements of primitive peoples is the role of "mediation" *(Vermittlung)* the messiah holds between men and "God." But this should imply that a "true" messianism can exist only in monotheistic religions, and it would be an evident presupposition (cf. *ibid.,* p. 22).

Finally, as far as the "historicity" of the person of the messiah is concerned (Guariglia holds that the messiah must be a "historical" person; cf. p. 26), we have shown above that history and myth are constantly interwoven in the movements of salvation, so that mythical persons are believed and expected to return among men in reality ("historically"), and, vice versa, historical persons are mythologized as persons who will come back to life and bring to men the expected paradise.

their social, cultural, and historical origins: whether they announce the return of the dead or of a culture-hero or someone else, or, finally, of the person of a divine man. A second problem is that of distinguishing according to a progressive historical development the different levels of messianism in relation to the different cultural phases reflected in each of the levels.

In conclusion, our historico-religious comparison enables us, at this point, to identify what appears to be the constant morphological and historical nucleus of messianism: *A messianic movement is, in general, a collective movement of escape from the present and of expectation of salvation, promoted by a prophet-founder, following a mystico-ecstatic inspiration: a movement which intends to start a renewal of the world which will be realized in an eschatological perspective as a return to a primordial and paradisiacal age.* In reality, mystico-ecstatic inspirations are peculiar to all prophet-founders, both in primitive religions and in the great historical religions: from Kimbangu to Wowoka, John Wilson, Handsome Lake, Te-Ua, etc. They are fundamental experiences based on one or more visions, trances, or "dreams," etc. From a phenomenological point of view they are entirely equivalent to phenomena with which we are more familiar, such as the "enlightenment" of Buddha, the "apocalypse" of St. John, the "revelation" of Moses or Jesus.

As far as the historical development of messianism is concerned, it is entirely to be referred to the degree of social and cultural development of the different communities. Among religious cultures of a more archaic type, with a social structure scarcely differentiated, the "messiah" assumes more or less impersonal and anonymous forms, like the culture-hero, the supreme being, or the dead. At this cultural level his function is also undifferentiated because he is (or they are, when there is an anonymous multiplicity, as in the case of the dead) merely endowed with the generic magico-creative power attributed to him by the original myth. In the polytheistic religions the "messiah" is identified with a "divine person" well defined in its form and differentiated in its function: that is the case among the Polynesians where Lono, the god of agriculture, disappears but will return, bringing prosperity. The polytheistic cultures have an agricultural structure and a society with a definite hierarchy. Progressing from polytheistic civilizations, it is possible to speak of a "messiah" identified in an anthropomorphic sense and, at the same time, as a divine person. An ulterior development can be seen in Jewish messianism (Mosaism). In it the necessity to affirm a pure monotheism over the popular polytheistic tendency of Canaanean (agricultural) origin results in a theological re-evaluation and reinterpretation of the Jewish history as a *praeparatio* for an *eschaton* (final time) when the Kingdom of God is to be realized: peace, harmony, and justice for men, and full and sincere worship for God beyond any anti-polytheistic controversy. The peculiar character, however, of the first Jewish messianism is not so much the human-divine person of the messiah as rather its monotheistic component and the messianic and theological reinterpretation of history.[16] Still it is substantially a "national" history. Only through the prophets of the Exile is the ulterior development of messianism realized in a definite universalistic direction. However, it should not be forgotten that such a universalistic development

---

[16] See Klausner, *op. cit., passim,* where the author systematically distinguishes between a redemption through a messiah and a "redemption without a human redeemer" (p. 8); on the other hand, he also distinguishes between a "messianic expectation," vaguely conceived (p. 9) which is the "positive element in the message of the prophets" (p. 21) and the proper "belief in the messiah, in which the political part goes arm in arm with the ethical part, and the nationalistic with the universalistic" (p. 10).

of the entire Jewish religion, forerunner of the Christian universalism, was the historical result of the dramatic experiences the Jewish people had undergone in its massive deportation, in the clash with great powers chaotically engaged in the pursuit of their particularistic interests. From this revolutionary experience and through the prophets, the consciousness of a new mission grew among the "chosen people." The prophets showed the way of salvation in a universalism in which all peoples would be accepted without discrimination. Christianity took again the universalistic idea of the prophets of the Exile and elaborated it again in function of a new religious, cultural, and social crisis. The original national theme is still, however, recognizable: the messiah, whose advent was realized and whose return is expected at the end of time, is "of the root of Isai," that is, of David's family. At the same time, however, Christian messianism faced a new crisis: the moral, intellectual, and individual crisis of a decaying culture afflicted with the problem of its own survival. To solve this crisis Christian messianism offered the way to transcendent salvation. That is really "transcendence"—the peculiar, highest, and unmistakable character of Christian messianism.

Such are, in synthesis, the historical and concrete developments of messianism from its embryonic germs at an ethnological level to its most advanced and complex manifestations. Finally we should also answer the question we posed above: on what historical, social, and cultural ground does messianism thrive and give birth to genuine movements of salvation? On the basis of most ample documentation we may state that the announcement of an imminent "savior" or of a complex of beings and events expected to bring prosperity always accompanies and follows situations of extreme distress, crisis, and existential precariousness. Such situations have their origins in disastrous events such as detribalization, conquest of a country, destruction of cultures (on the part of the whites), collective deportations or catastrophes, etc; in conflicts against institutions or oppressive groups on the part of rival powers; in clashes among cultures of different levels; and other causes of collective danger which have developed in time.

We have said above that there is an unbroken continuity from the "little" prophets of Africa, America, Oceania, and colonial and semicolonial Asia to the great universal prophets, Moses, Isaiah, and Jesus. All have interpreted in a genuine, spontaneous, and daring way the needs of societies fallen into a state of serious precariousness and have pointed out to their followers a new way to salvation.


# ARCHAIC FORMS OF SOCIAL AGITATION

### E. J. Hobsbawm


## Introduction

This essay consists of studies on the following subjects, all of which can be described as "primitive" or "archaic" forms of social agitation: banditry of the Robin Hood type, rural secret societies, various peasant revolutionary movements of the millenarian sort, pre-industrial urban "mobs" and their riots, some labour religious sects and the use of ritual in early labour and revolutionary organizations. I have supplemented my accounts with "case-papers" which illustrate the thoughts and assumptions of the people who took part in such movements as are here described, preferably in their own words. In the main, the field covered is Western and Southern Europe and especially Italy, since the French Revolution. The curious reader may simply read this book as a description of some social phenomena which are interesting, and surprisingly little known, having provoked only a rather sparse literature in English. However, the purpose of this book is analytical as well as descriptive—indeed, it contains no facts unfamiliar to the expert in these subjects—and it may therefore be as well to explain what it is trying to do.

The history of social movements is generally treated in two separate divisions. We know something about the ancient and medieval ones: slave revolts, social heresies and sects, peasant risings, and the like. To say that we possess a "history" of them is perhaps misleading, for in the past they have been treated largely as a series of episodes, punctuating the general story of humanity, though historians have disagreed on their importance in the historical process and still debate their precise relationship to it. So far as modern times are concerned such agitations have been regarded by all, except anthropologists who are obliged to deal with pre-capitalist or imperfectly capitalist societies, simply as "forerunners" or odd survivals. On the other hand "modern" social movements, that is to say those of Western Europe from the later 18th century, and those of increasingly large sectors of the world in subsequent periods, have normally been treated according to a long-established and reasonably sound scheme. For obvious reasons the historians have concentrated on labour and socialist movements, and such other movements as have been fitted into the socialist framework. These are commonly regarded as having their "primitive" stages—journeymen's societies and Luddism, Radicalism, Jacobinism and Utopian Socialisms—and eventually as developing towards a modern pattern which varies from one country to the next but has considerable general application. Thus labour movements develop certain forms of trade union and co-operative organization, certain types of political organization such as mass parties, and certain types of programme and ideology, such as secularist Socialism.

The subjects of this book fit into neither category. At first sight they belong to the first division. At any rate nobody would be surprised to encounter Vardarelli and bodies such as *Mafia,* or millenarian movements, in the European Middle Ages. But the point about them is that they do *not* occur in the Middle Ages, but in the 19th and 20th centuries, and indeed the past 150 years have produced them in abnormally large numbers, for reasons discussed in the text. Nor can they be simply written off as marginal or unimportant phenomena, though older historians have often tended to do so, partly out of rationalist and "modernist" bias, partly because, as I hope to show, the political allegiance and character of such movements is often underdetermined, ambiguous or even ostensibly "conservative," partly because historians, being mainly educated and townsmen, have until recently simply not made sufficient effort to understand people who are unlike themselves. For, with the exception of the ritual brotherhoods of the Carbonaro type, all the phenomena studied in this book belong to the world of people who neither write nor read many books—often because they are illiterate—, who are rarely known by name to anybody except their friends, and then often only by nickname, who are normally inarticulate, and rarely understood even when they express themselves. Moreover, they are *pre-political* people who have not yet found, or only begun to find, a specific language in which to express their aspirations about the world. Though their movements are thus in many respects blind and groping, by the standards of modern ones, they are neither unimportant nor marginal. Men and women such as those with whom this book deals form the large majority in many, perhaps in most, countries even today, and their acquisition of political consciousness has made our century the most revolutionary in history. For this reason the study of their movements is not merely curious, or interesting, or moving for anyone who cares about the fate of men, but also of practical importance.

The men and women with whom this book is concerned differ from Englishmen in that they have not been born into the world of capitalism as a Tyneside engineer, with four generations of trade unionism at his back, has been born into it. They come into it as first-generation immigrants, or what is even more catastrophic, it comes to them from outside, insidiously by the operation of economic forces which they do not understand and over which they have no control, or brazenly by conquest, revolutions and fundamental changes of law whose consequences they may not understand, even when they have helped to bring them about. They do not as yet grow with or into modern society: they are broken into it, or more rarely—as in the case of the gangster middle class of Sicily—they break into it. Their problem is how to adapt themselves to its life and struggles, and the subject of this book is the process of adaptation (or failure to adapt) as expressed in their archaic social movements.

However, words like "primitive" and "archaic" should not mislead us. The movements discussed in this book all have considerable historical evolution behind them, for they belong to a world which has long known the State (i.e. soldiers and policemen, prisons, tax-collectors, perhaps civil servants), class differentiation and exploitation, by landlords, merchants and the like, and even cities. The bonds of kinship or tribal solidarity which—whether or not combined with territorial links[1] —are the key to what are normally thought of as "primitive" societies, persist. But though they are still of considerable importance, they are no longer a man's primary defence against the vagaries of his social environment. The distinction between these two phases of "primitive" social movements cannot be hard and fast, but should, I think, be made. The problems to which it gives rise are not discussed in this book, but may be illustrated fairly briefly, by eamamples taken from the history of social banditry.

This confronts us with two extreme types of the "outlaw." At one extreme we have the classical blood-vengeance outlaw of, say, Corsica, who was *not* a social brigand fighting the rich to help the poor, but a man who fought with and for his kin (including its rich) against another kin (including its poor). At the other extreme we have the classical Robin Hood who was and is essentially a peasant rebelling against landlords, usurers, and other representatives of what Thomas More called the "conspiracy of the rich." Between the two stretches a chain of historical evolution which it is not my purpose to uncover in detail. Thus all members of the kinship community, including the outlaws, may consider themselves as enemies of the exploiting foreigners who attempt to impose their rule on them. All may consider themselves as collectively "the poor" as against, let us say, the wealthy inhabitants of the plains which they raid. Both these situations, which have in them the germs of social movements as we understand them, may be discerned in the past in the Sardinian highlands, which Dr. Cagnetta has studied. The coming of the modern economy (whether or not it is combined with foreign conquest) may, and indeed probably will, disrupt the social balance of the kinship society, by turning some kins

[1] I do not propose to enter into the discussion revived in I. Schapera, *Government and Politics in Tribal Societies* (London 1956).

into "rich" families and others into "poor," or by disrupting the kin itself. The traditional system of blood-vengeance outlawry may—and indeed probably will—"get out of hand" and produce a multiplicity of unusually murderous feuds and embittered outlaws, into which an element of class struggle begins to enter. This phase has also been documented and partly analysed for the Sardinian highlands, notably for the period between, say, the later 1880s and the end of the First World War. Other things remaining equal, they may eventually lead to a society in which the class conflicts are dominant, though the future Robin Hood may still—as often in Calabria—take to the hills for personal reasons which are similar to those which drove the classical Corsican into outlawry, notably blood-vengeance. The final result of this evolution may be the classical "social bandit" who takes to outlawry through some brush with the State or the ruling class—e.g. a quarrel with a feudal retainer—and who is simply a rather primitive form of peasant rebel. This, broadly speaking, is the point at which the analysis of the present book begins, though it may cast an occasional glance backwards. The "pre-history" of the movements here discussed, is left aside. However, readers should be warned of its existence, especially if they are inclined to apply the observations and conclusions of this book to primitive social agitations which still show its traces. It is not my intention to encourage careless generalization. Millenarian movements such as those of Andalusian peasants no doubt have something in common with, let us say, Melanesian cargo cults; the labour sects of North Rhodesian copper-miners have something in common with those of Durham coal-miners. But it must never be forgotten that the differences may also be great, and that the present essay provides no adequate guide to them.

The first set of social movements discussed in this book is overwhelmingly rural, at least in the Western and Southern Europe of the 19th and 20th centuries, though there is no *a priori* reason why they should be confined to peasants. (Indeed, *Mafia* had some of its strongest roots among the sulphur-miners in Sicily before they turned Socialist; but then, miners are a peculiarly archaic body of workers.) They are treated in order of increasing ambition. *Social banditry*, a universal and virtually unchanging phenomenon, is little more than endemic peasant protest against oppression and poverty: a cry for vengeance on the rich and the oppressors, a vague dream of some curb upon them, a righting of individual wrongs. Its ambitions are modest: a traditional world in which men are justly dealt with, not a new and perfect world. It becomes epidemic rather than endemic when a peasant society which knows of no better means of self-defence is in a condition of abnormal tension and disruption. Social banditry has next to no organization or ideology, and is totally inadaptable to modern social movements. Its most highly developed forms, which skirt national guerilla warfare, are rare and, by themselves, ineffective.

*Mafia* and similar phenomena (Chapter II) are best regarded as a somewhat more complex development of social banditry. They are comparable to it, insofar as their organization and ideology are normally rudimentary, insofar as they are fundamentally "reformist" rather than revolutionary—except, once again, when they take some of the forms of collective resistance to the invasion of the "new" society—and insofar as they are also endemic, but sometimes epidemic. Like social banditry it is almost impossible for them to adapt to or to be absorbed by modern social movements. On the other hand *Mafias* are both more permanent and more powerful, since they are less a series of individual revolts and more of an institutionalized system of a law outside the official law. In extreme cases they may amount to a virtual parallel or subsidiary system of law and power to that of the official rulers.

Being extremely archaic, and indeed pre-political, banditry and *Mafia* are difficult to classify in modern political terms. They can be and are used by various classes, and indeed sometimes, as in the case of *Mafia,* become primarily the instruments of the men of power or of aspirations to power, and consequently cease to be in any sense movements of social protest.

The various *millenarian* movements with which I deal—the Lazzarettists in Tuscany (Chapter III), Andalusian and Sicilian peasant movements (Chapters IV and V)—differ from banditry and *Mafia* because they are revolutionary and not reformist, and because, for this reason, they are more easily modernized or absorbed into modern social movements. The interesting problem here is, how and how far this modernization takes place. I suggest that it does not take place, or takes place only very slowly and incompletely, if the matter is left to the peasants themselves. It takes place most completely and successfully, if the millenarian movement is fitted into a framework of organization, theory and programme which comes to the peasants from outside. This is illustrated by the contrast between the Andalusian village anarchists and the Sicilian village Socialists and Communists; the former converted to a theory which virtually told the peasants that their spontaneous and archaic form of social agitation was good and adequate, the latter converted to a theory which transformed it.

The second set of studies deals essentially with urban or industrial movements. It is naturally much less ambitious, for most of the main tradition of urban or working-class agitations has been deliberately left aside. There is, obviously, still a great deal to be said about the primitive and even the developed stages of labour and socialist agitations—for instance about the utopian stages of socialism—but the object of this book is not so much to supplement or to revalue a story which is already reasonably well known in outline, but to attract attention to certain topics which have been very little studied and are still largely unknown. Hence we are here dealing with phenomena which may be much more correctly described as marginal.

The study of the *"mob"* (Chapter VI) deals with what is perhaps the urban equivalent to social banditry, the most primitive and pre-political of the movements of the urban poor, particularly in certain kinds of large pre-industrial cities. The mob is a particularly difficult phenomenon to analyse in lucid terms. Nearly the only certain thing about it is that its activity always was directed against the rich, even when also directed against someone else such as foreigners, and that it possessed no firm or lasting political or ideological allegiance except perhaps to its city or its symbols. Normally it may be regarded as reformist, insofar as it rarely if ever conceived of the construction of a new order of society, as distinct from the correction of abnormalities and injustices in a traditional old order. However, it was perfectly capable of mobilizing behind leaders who were revolutionaries, though perhaps not fully grasping the implications of their revolutionism, and, being urban and collective, was familiar with the concept of the "seizure of power." Consequently it is far from easy to answer the question of its adaptability to modern conditions. As it tended to disappear in the modern type of industrial city, the question very often answers itself, for an organized industrial working class operates on quite different lines. Where it did not disappear the question ought perhaps to be rephrased as follows: at what stage did the mob, when operating under ostensibly political slogans, cease to attach itself to traditional ones ("Church and King") and attach itself to modern ones, Jacobin, Socialist or the like? And how far was it capable of permanent absorption into the modern movements to which it attached itself? I am inclined to think that it was and is fundamentally rather inadaptable, as indeed one might expect.

The *Labour Sects* (Chapter VII) represent a more clearly transitional phenomenon between the old and new: proletarian organizations and aspirations of a sort expressed through traditional religious ideology. The phenomenon is exceptional in its developed form, and indeed largely confined to the British Isles, for elsewhere in Western and Southern Europe the industrial working class emerged from the beginning as a de-christianized group, except where it was Roman Catholic, a religion which lends itself much less well than Protestantism to this peculiar adaptation. Even in Britain it may be regarded as a phenomenon of archaic industrialism. Though there is no *a priori* reason why religious labour movements should not be revolutionary, and they have sometimes been so, there are some ideological and more sociological reasons why labour sects should have a bias towards reformism. Certainly labour sectarianism, though as a body fairly readily adaptable to moderate modern labour movements, has been somewhat resistant to adaptation to revolutionary ones, even when it continued to provide a breeding-ground for individual revolutionaries. However, this generalization is perhaps unduly based on British experience, that is to say on the history of a country in which revolutionary labour movements have been abnormally weak for the past century.

The last study, of *ritual in social movements* (Chapter VIII), is difficult to classify at all. It has been included chiefly because the peculiar ritualization of so many movements of this kind in the period between the late 18th and the middle of the 19th century is so patently primitive or archaic in the commonly accepted meaning of the word, that it could hardly be left out. But it belongs essentially to the history of the main stream of modern social movements which runs from Jacobinism to modern Socialism and Communism, and from the early craft journeymen's societies to modern trade unionism. The trade unionist side of it is fairly simple. I merely attempt to describe the character and function of the early rituals, which have since gradually faded away as the movement has become more "modern". The study of the revolutionary ritual brotherhood is more anomalous, for while all the other phenomena described in this book belong to the labouring poor, this is, at least in its initial stages, essentially a movement of people belonging to the middle and upper classes. It belongs to this story because modern forms of revolutionary organization among the poor may be traced by lineal descent to it, at least in part.

These observations naturally do not exhaust the problem of how primitive social movements "adapt" to modern conditions, let alone the wider problem of which this one is a part. As I have already observed, certain types of primitive social protest have not been considered at all here. No attempt has been made to analyse the analogous or equivalent movements which have occurred and are occurring in the overwhelming bulk of the world which lies outside the narrow geographical area surveyed here—and the non-European world has produced primitive social movements in much greater profusion and variety than Southwestern Europe. Even within the chosen area, certain kinds of movement have been only glanced at. For instance, I have said little about the pre-history of what may be loosely called "national" movements, at least insofar as they are mass movements, although elements of the phenomena discussed here may enter into them. *Mafia,* for instance, may at a certain stage of its evolution be regarded as a very young embryo of a subsequent national movement. On the whole I have confined myself to the pre-history of modern labour and peasant movements. All the subjects surveyed in this book occur, broadly speaking, in the period since the French Revolution, and deal fundamentally with the adaptation of popular agitations to a modern capitalist economy. The temptation to point to analogies from earlier European history or from other types of movement, has been great, but I have attempted to resist it in the hope of avoiding irrelevant and possibly distracting arguments.

These limitations are not to be defended. A full comparative study and analysis of archaic social movements is badly needed, but I do not think that it can yet be undertaken, at least here. The state of our knowledge does not permit it yet. For our knowledge about even the best-documented of the movements in this book is capricious, and our ignorance of them vast. Very often what is remembered or observed about archaic movements of this kind is only that small corner of them which has, by some accident, been uncovered in the law-courts, or by journalists in search of sensation, or by some student with an eye for "off-beat" matters. Our map of them, even in Western Europe, is as uncharted as that of the world in the period before proper cartography. Sometimes, as in social banditry, the phenomena are so standardized that this does not matter greatly for the purposes of a short survey. At other times the mere task of extracting a coherent, ordered and rational account from a mass of doubtful and mutually contradictory facts, is almost overwhelming. The chapters on *Mafia* and Ritual, for instance, can at best claim to be coherent. Whether the interpretations and explanations given are also true, is much harder to verify than in the case of, let us say, the social bandits. The student of *Mafias* has hardly more than a single reasonably attested phenomenon on which to base his views. Even for Sicily his material is extremely poor, except perhaps for one specific period of *Mafia's* development, and even for that his sources rely largely on rumour or "common knowledge." Moreover, what material there is, is often contradictory, even when it has the air of common sense and does not consist of the sort of sensational gossip which this type of subject attracts, as pears attract wasps. Any historian who spoke with confidence, let alone finality, under such conditions, would be a fool.

This book is therefore tentative and incomplete, and pretends to be no more. It is open to criticism by all those on whose preserves it poaches, not only for poaching but in some cases for clumsy poaching. It is also open to the criticism of all who think a single and thorough monograph better than a set of necessarily cursory sketches. There is only one answer to such objections. It is high time that movements of the kind discussed in this book were seriously considered not simply as an unconnected series of individual curiosities, as footnotes to history, but as a phenomenon of general importance and considerable weight in modern history. What Antonio Gramsci said of the South Italian peasants in the 1920's applies to a great many groups and areas in the modern world. They are "in perpetual ferment but, as a mass, incapable of providing a centralized expression for their aspirations and their needs." That ferment, the inchoate strivings after an effective expression of these aspirations, and the possible ways in which both may evolve, are the subject of this book. I know of no other student in this country who has so far attempted to consider several of such movements together as a sort of "pre-historic" stage of social agitation. Perhaps this attempt to do so is mistaken or premature. On the other hand, perhaps someone ought to make a start, even at the risk of making a false start.

*NOTE:* This may be the place for a note clarifying some terms frequently used in this study. It would be pedantic to define all those which lend themselves to misinterpretation. My usage of such terms as "feudal" may be open to criticism from medievalists, but since the argument of the text is not disturbed by the substitution of another term, or its omission, it is hardly necessary to explain or defend it. On the other hand the argument does in part rest on the acceptance of the distinction between "revolutionary" and "reformist" social movements. It is therefore desirable to say something about these terms.

The principle is quite clear. Reformists accept the general framework of an institution or social arrangement, but consider it capable of improvement or, where abuses have crept in, reform; revolutionaries insist that it must be fundamentally transformed, or replaced. Reformists seek to improve and alter the monarchy, or to reform the House of Lords; revolutionaries believe that nothing useful is to be done with either institution except to abolish them. Reformists wish to create a society in which policemen will not be arbitrary and judges at the mercy of landlords and merchants; revolutionaries, though also in sympathy with these aims, a society in which there will be no policemen and judges in the present sense, let alone landlords and merchants. For the sake of convenience the terms are used to describe movements which have views about the entire social order, rather than about particular institutions within it. The distinction is old. It was made, in effect, by Joachim of Fiore (1145-1202), the millenarian whom Norman Cohn has plausibly called the inventor of the most influential prophetic system known to Europe before the appearance of Marxism. He distinguished between the reign of *justice* or *law,* which is essentially the equitable regulation of social relations in an imperfect society, and the reign of *freedom,* which is the perfect society. It is important to remember that the two were in no sense the same, though one might be a necessary preliminary stage on the road to the other.

The point of this distinction is that reformist and revolutionary movements will naturally tend to behave differently, and to develop different organization, strategy, tactics, etc. It is therefore important, when studying a social movement, to know to which of the two groups it belongs.

This is by no means easy, except in extreme cases and for short periods of time, though this is no reason for abandoning the distinction. Nobody will deny the revolutionary aspirations of millenarian movements which reject the existing world to the point of refusing to sow, to reap, or even to procreate until it has ended, or the reformist character of, say, the Parliamentary Committee of the British T.U.C. in the later 19th century. But normally the situation is more complex, even when not obfuscated by the reluctance (which is universal in politics) of people to accept accurate descriptions whose implications they do not like; for instance, by the unwillingness of French Radical Socialists to forgo the electoral advantages of a name which conceals the fact that they are neither Radical nor Socialist.

In practice, every man who is not a Dr. Pangloss and every social movement undergoes the pull of both reformism and revolutionism, and with varying strength at different times. Except at the rare moments just preceding or during profound crises and revolutions, the most extreme revolutionaries must also have a policy about the existing world in which they are obliged to live. If they want to make it more tolerable while preparing for revolution, or even if they want to prepare effectively, they must also be reformists, unless they abandon the world altogether by constructing some Communist Zion in the desert or on the prairie, or—like many religious bodies—transfer their hope entirely to the hereafter, merely seeking to traverse this vale of tears uncomplainingly until liberated by death. (In the latter case they cease to be either revolutionaries or reformists and become conservatives.) Conversely, the hope of a really good and perfect society is so powerful, that its ideal haunts even those who have resigned themselves to the impossibility of changing either the "world" or "human nature," and merely hope for lesser reforms and the correction of abuses. Inside the most militant reformist there is often a modest and overawed revolutionist hankering to be let out, though advancing age normally imprisons him more firmly. Given the total absence of the prospect of successful revolution, revolutionaries may turn into *de facto* reformists. In the intoxicating and ecstatic moments of revolution the great surge of human hope may sweep even reformists into the camp of the revolutionaries, though perhaps with some mental reservations. Between these two extremes a wide variety of positions may be occupied.

These complexities do not invalidate the distinction, whose existence can hardly be denied, since (whether they are right or not) there are plainly people and movements regarding themselves as revolutionary or reformist, and acting on revolutionary or reformist assumptions. It has, however, been attacked indirectly, chiefly by those who deny that any revolutionary transformation of society is possible, or to be envisaged by rational human beings, and therefore incapable of understanding what revolutionary movements are at. (Cf. the persistent tendency, first systematized by the positivist criminologists of the later 19th century, to regard them as psycho-pathological phenomena.) This is not the place to discuss these views. The reader of this book is not required to sympathize with revolutionaries, let alone primitive ones. He is merely advised to recognize that they exist, and that there have been at least some revolutions which have profoundly transformed society, though not necessarily in the way planned by revolutionaries, or as utterly and completely and finally as they may have wished. But the recognition that profound and fundamental changes take place in society does not depend on the belief that utopia is realizable.

\* \* \*

## MILLENARIANISM I: LAZZARETTI

Of all the primitive social movements discussed in this book, millenarianism is the one least handicapped by its primitiveness. For the only thing really primitive about it is external. The essence of millenarianism, the hope of a complete and radical change in the world which will be reflected in the millennium, a world shorn of all its present deficiencies, is not confined to primitivism. It is present, almost by definition, in all revolutionary movements of whatever kind, and "millenarian" elements may therefore be discovered by the student in any of them, insofar as they have ideals. This does not mean that therefore *all* revolutionary movements are millennial in the narrower sense of the word, let alone that they are primitive, an assumption which deprives Professor Norman Cohn's book of some of its value.[2] Indeed, it is impossible to make much

[2] *The Search for the Millennium* (1957). This erudite study of many medieval millennial movements is, to my mind, vitiated by a tendency to interpret medieval in terms of modern revolutionary movements and the other way round, a practice which clarifies neither our understanding of the Hussites nor of modern Communism.

sense of modern revolutionary history unless one appreciates the differences between primitive and modern revolutionary movements, in spite of the ideal which they have in common, that of a totally new world.

The typical old-fashioned millenarian movement in Europe has three main characteristics. First, a profound and total rejection of the present, evil world, and a passionate longing for another and better one; in a word, revolutionism. Second, a fairly standardized "ideology" of the chiliastic type as analysed and described by Professor Cohn. The most important ideology of this sort before the rise of modern secular revolutionism, and perhaps the only one, is Judeo-Christian messianism. At all events it seems that classical millenarian movements occur only, or practically only, in countries affected by Judeo-Christian propaganda. This is only natural, for it is difficult to construct a millenarian ideology within a religious tradition which sees the world as a constant flux, or series of cyclical movements, or as a permanently stable thing. What makes millenarians is the idea that the world as it is may—and indeed will—come to an end one day, to be utterly re-made thereafter, a conception which is alien to such religions as Hinduism and Buddhism.[3] It does not follow that the actual beliefs of any millenarian movement will be chiliastic in the strictly Jewish or Christian sense. Third, millenarian movements share a fundamental vagueness about the actual way in which the new society will be brought about.

It is difficult to put this last point more precisely, for such movements range from the purely passive at one extreme, to those which skirt modern revolutionary methods at the other—indeed, as we shall see, to those which merge naturally into modern revolutionary movements. However, it may perhaps be clarified as follows. Modern revolutionary movements have—implicitly or explicitly—certain fairly definite ideas on how the old society is to be replaced by the new, the most crucial of which concerns what we may call the "transfer of power." The old rulers must be toppled from their positions. The "people" (or the revolutionary class or group) must "take over" and then carry out certain measures—the redistribution of land, the nationalization of the means of production, or whatever it may be. In all this the organized effort of the revolutionaries is decisive, and doctrines of organization, strategy and tactics, etc., sometimes very elaborate, are evolved to aid them in their task. The sort of things revolutionaries do is, let us say, to organize a mass demonstration, throw up barricades, march on the town hall, run up the tricolour, proclaim the Republic one and indivisible, appoint a provisional government, and issue a call for a Constituent Assembly. (This, roughly, is the "drill" which so many of them learned from the French Revolution. It is not, of course, the only possible procedure.) But the "pure" millenarian movement operates quite differently, whether because of the inexperience of its members or the narrowness of their horizons, or because of the effect of millenarian ideologies and preconceptions. Its followers are not makers of revolution. They expect it to make itself, by divine revelation, by an announcement from on high, by a miracle—they expect it to happen somehow. The part of the people before the change is to gather together, to prepare itself, to watch the signs of the coming doom, to listen to the prophets who predict the coming of the great day, and perhaps to undertake certain ritual measures against the moment of decision and change, or to purify themselves, shedding the dross of the bad world of the present so as to be able to enter the new world in shining purity. Between the two extremes of the "pure"

---

[3] At least this seems to reflect the consensus of opinion among the specialists who discussed the subject at the Manchester lectures, on which this book is based.

millenarian and the "pure" political revolutionary all manner of intermediate positions are possible. In fact, the millenarian movements discussed here occupy such intermediate positions, the Lazzarettists nearest to one extreme, the Spanish anarchists theoretically much nearer to the other.

When a millenarian movement turns into, or is absorbed by, a modern revolutionary movement, it therefore retains the first of its characteristics. It normally abandons the second at least to some extent, substituting a modern, that is in general a secular, theory of history and revolution: nationalist, socialist, communist, anarchist or of some other type. Lastly it adds a superstructure of modern revolutionary politics to its basic revolutionary spirit: a programme, a doctrine concerning the transfer of power, and above all a system of organization. This is not always easy, but millenarian movements differ from some of the others discussed in this book in opposing no fundamental *structural* obstacles to modernization. At any rate, as we shall see, such movements have been successfully integrated into modern revolutionary ones; just possibly also into modern reformist ones. Their interest for the historian of the 19th and 20th centuries lies in the process by which they are so absorbed, or in the reasons why sometimes they are not. This will be sketched in this and the two subsequent chapters.

It is not always easy to recognize the rational political core within millenarian movements, for their very lack of sophistication and of an effective revolutionary strategy and tactics makes them push the logic of the revolutionary position to the point of absurdity or paradox. They are impractical and utopian. Since they flourish best in periods of extraordinary social ferment and tend to speak the language of apocalyptic religion, the behaviour of their members is often rather odd by normal standards. They are therefore as easily misinterpreted as William Blake, who until quite recently was commonly regarded not as a revolutionary, but simply as an eccentric other-worldly mystic and visionary.[4] When they wish to express their fundamental critique of the existing world, they may, like the millenarian anarchist strikers in Spain, refuse to marry until the new world has been instituted; when they wish to express their rejection of mere palliatives and lesser reforms, they may (again like the Andalusian strikers of the early 20th century) refuse to formulate demands for higher wages or anything else, even when urged to do so by the authorities. When they wish to express their belief that the new world ought to be fundamentally different from the old, they may, like the Sicilian peasants, believe that somehow even the climate can be changed. Their behaviour may be ecstatic to the point where observers describe it in terms of mass hysteria. On the other hand their actual programme may be vague to the point where observers doubt whether they have one. Those who cannot understand what it is that moves them—and even some who do—may be tempted to interpret their behaviour as wholly irrational or pathological, or at best as an instinctive reaction to intolerable conditions.

Without wishing to make it appear more sensible and less extraordinary than it often is, it is advisable for the historian to appreciate the logic, and even the realism—if the word can be used in this context—which moves them, for revolutionary movements are difficult to understand otherwise. It is their peculiarity that those who cannot see what all the bother is about are disabled from saying anything of great value about them, whereas those who do (especially when among primitive social movements)

---

[4] The modern view was pioneered by J. Bronowski, *William Blake, A Man without a Mask* (London 1944 and Pelican Books).

cannot often speak in terms intelligible to the rest. It is especially difficult, but necessary, to understand that utopianism, or "impossibilism" which the most primitive revolutionaries share with all but the most sophisticated, and which makes even very modern ones feel a sense of almost physical pain at the realization that the coming of Socialism will not eliminate *all* grief and sadness, unhappy love-affairs or mourning, and will not solve or make soluble *all* problems; a feeling reflected in the ample literature of revolutionary disillusionment.

First, utopianism is probably a necessary social device for generating the superhuman efforts without which no major revolution is achieved. From the historian's point of view the transformations brought about by the French and Russian Revolutions are astonishing enough, but would the Jacobins have undertaken their task simply to exchange the France of the Abbé Prévost for the France of Balzac, the Bolsheviks to exchange the Russia of Tchekhov for that of Mr. Khrushchev? Probably not. It was essential for them to believe that "the ultimate in human prosperity and liberty will appear after their victories".[5] Obviously they will not, though the result of the revolution may nevertheless be very worth while.

Second, utopianism can become such a social device *because revolutionary movements and revolutions appear to prove that almost no change is beyond their reach.* If the revolutionaries needed proof that "human nature can be changed"—i.e. that no social problem is insoluble—the demonstration of its changes in such movements and at such moments would be quite sufficient:

> This other man had I dreamed
> A drunken vainglorious lout . . .
> Yet I number him in the song;
> He, too, has resigned his part
> In the casual comedy;
> He, too, has been changed in his turn,
> Transformed utterly;
> A terrible beauty is born.

It is this consciousness of *utter* change, not as an aspiration but as a fact—at least a temporary fact—which informs Yeats' poem on the Easter Rising, and tolls, like a bell, at the end of his stanzas: All changed, changed utterly. A terrible beauty is born. Liberty, equality, and above all fraternity may become real for the moment in those stages of the great social revolutions which revolutionaries who live through them describe in the terms normally reserved for romantic love: "bliss was it in that dawn to be alive, but to be young was very Heaven." Revolutionaries not only set themselves a standard of morality higher than that of any except saints, but at such moments actually carry it into practice, even when it involves considerable technical difficulty, as in the relation between the sexes.[6] Theirs is at such times a miniature version of the

---

[5] M. Djilas, *The New Class* (1957), 32, discusses this point interestingly. This book by a disillusioned revolutionary is valuable for the light it throws on revolutionary psychology, including the author's own, and for very little else.

[6] Djilas, *op. cit.*, 153, "Between men and women in the movement, a clean, modest and warm relationship is fostered: a relationship in which comradely care has become sexless passion," etc. Djilas, doubtless with the period of the partisan war in mind, also stresses the historical moment ("on the eve of the battle for power") when "it is difficult to separate words from deeds"), but also notes, perceptively, that "these are the morals of a sect."

ideal society, in which all men are brothers and sacrifice all for the common good without abandoning their individuality. If this is possible within their movement, why not everywhere?

As for the masses of those who do not belong to the revolutionary élite, the mere fact of becoming revolutionary and of recognizing the "power of the people" seems so miraculous that anything else seems equally possible. An observer of the Sicilian Fasci has correctly noted this logic: if a sudden vast mass movement could be stamped out of the ground, if thousands could be shaken out of the lethargy and defeatism of centuries by a single speech, how could men doubt that great and world-overturning events would soon come to pass? Men *had* been utterly changed and were being visibly transformed. Noble men who in their lives followed the dictates of the good society—poverty, brotherliness, saintliness, or whatever else they were—could be observed working among them even by the unregenerate, and provided further proof of the reality of the ideal. We shall see the political importance of these local revolutionary apostles among the Andalusian village anarchists, but every observer of modern revolutionary movements is aware of it in almost all of them, and of the pressure upon the revolutionary élite to live up to the role of moral exemplars: not to earn more or live better, to work harder, to be "pure," to sacrifice their private happiness (as happiness is interpreted in the old society) in full public view. When normal modes of behaviour creep in again—for instance, after the triumph of a new revolutionary régime—men will not conclude that the changes for which they long are impracticable for long periods or outside exclusive groups of abnormally devoted men and women, but that there has been "backsliding" or "betrayal." For the possibility, the reality, of the ideal relationship between human beings has been proved in practice, and what can be more conclusive than that?

The problems facing millenarian movements are or look simple in the intoxicating periods of their growth and advance. They are correspondingly difficult in those which follow revolutions or risings.

Since none of the movements discussed in this book have so far been on the winning side, the question what happens when they discover that their victory does not in fact solve *all* human problems does not greatly concern us. Their defeat does, for it faces them with the problem of maintaining revolutionism as a permanent force. The only millenarian movements which avoid this are the completely suicidal ones, for the death of all their members makes it academic.[7] Normally defeat soon produces a body of doctrine to explain why the millennium has not come and the old world can therefore expect to go on for a while. The signs of imminent doom were not read right or some other mistake has been made. (The Jehovah's Witnesses have quite a large exegetical literature to explain why the failure of the world to end on the date originally predicted does not invalidate the prediction.) To recognize that the old world will continue is to recognize that one must live in it. But how?

Some millenarians, like some revolutionaries, do indeed tacitly drop their revolutionism and turn into *de facto* acceptors of the *status quo*, which is all the easier if the *status quo* becomes more tolerable for the people. Some may even turn into reformist ones, or perhaps discover, now that the ecstasy of the revolutionary period is

---

[7] The best known, but not the only one, of this type was the movement of Antonio the Counsellor in the backwoods of Brazil in 1896-7, which provides the subject of a literary masterpiece, Euclides da Cunha's *Rebellion in the Backlands*. The rebel Zion of Canudos fought literally to the last man. When it was captured, no defender was left alive.

over, and they are no longer swept away by it, that what they wanted really does not require quite so fundamental a transformation as they had imagined. Or, what is more likely, they may withdraw into a passionate inner life of "the movement," or "the sect," leaving the rest of the world to its own devices except for some token assertions of millennial hopes, and perhaps of the millennial programme; for instance pacifism and the refusal to take oaths. Others, however, do not. They may merely retire to wait for the next revolutionary crisis (to use a non-millenarian term) which must surely bring with it the total destruction of the old world and the institution of the new. This is naturally easiest where the economic and social conditions of revolution are endemic, as in Southern Italy, where every political change in the 19th century, irrespective from what quarter it came, automatically produced its ceremonial marches of peasants with drums and banners to occupy the land,[8] or in Andalusia where, as we shall see, millenarian revolutionary waves occurred at roughly ten-year intervals for some sixty or seventy years. Others, as we shall see, retain enough of the old fire to attach themselves to, or to turn into, revolutionary movements of a non-millennial type even after long periods of apparent quiescence.

There, precisely, lies their adaptability. Primitive reformist movements are easily lost in a modern society, if only because the task of securing an equitable regulation of social relations within the existing framework, the creation of tolerable or comfortable conditions here and now, is technically specialized and complicated, and much better done by organizations and movements built to the specifications of modern societies: co-operative marketing organizations are better at the job of giving peasants a fair deal than Robin Hoods. But the fundamental object of social-revolutionary movements remains much more unchanged, though the concrete conditions of the fight for it vary, as may be seen by comparing the passages in which the great utopian or revolutionary writers make their critique of existing societies with those in which they propose specific remedies or reforms. Millenarians can (as we shall see in the chapter on the Sicilian Fasci) readily exchange the primitive costume in which they dress their aspirations for the modern costume of socialist and Communist politics. Conversely, as we have seen, even the least millenarian modern revolutionaries have in them a streak of "impossibilism" which makes them cousins to the Taborites and Anabaptists, a kinship which they have never denied. The junction between the two is therefore readily made, and once made, the primitive movement can be transformed into a modern one.

I propose to discuss three movements of different degrees of millenariansim, and adaptation to modern politics, the Lazzarettists of Southern Tuscany (from c. 1875 onward), the Andalusian village anarchists (from the 1870s to 1936) and the Sicilian peasant movements (from c. 1893 onwards). In the 19th and 20th centuries such movements have been overwhelmingly agrarian, though there is no a priori reason why they should not be urban, and in the past they have sometimes been so. (But urban workers in our period have normally acquired more modern types of revolutionary ideology.) Of the three chosen here, the Lazzarettists are a laboratory specimen of a medieval millenarian heresy surviving in a backward corner of peasant Italy. The second and third are examples of the millenarian characteristics of social movements along an endemically revolutionary peasantry in very poor and backward areas. The anarchists are chiefly interesting in that they show millenarianism wholly divorced from traditional religious forms, and indeed in a militantly atheist and anti-Christian shape. On the other hand they also demonstrate the political weakness of millenarian

---

[8] Cf A. LaCava, "La rivolta calabrese del 1848," in *Arch. Stor. delle Prov. Napoletane,* N. S. XXXI, 1947-9, 445 ff., 540, 552.

movements which are transformed into imperfectly (i.e.ineffectively) revolutionary modern ones. The Sicilian Fasci, though in some senses much less "modern"—for their members only abandoned their traditional ideology very incompletely—enable us to study the absorption of millenarianism into a modern revolutionary movement, the Communist Party, particularly clearly.

It only remains to note that the present account is sketchy and tentative, and that, in spite of considerable temptation, I have avoided all comparisons with the millenarian movements outside Europe which have lately received some very able scholarly attention.[9] My reasons for resisting the temptation are briefly outlined in the Introduction.

*   *   *

We have discussed the causes and nature of peasant millenarianism, and its connexion with modern social movements. It remains to consider its function in peasant movements, for in fact it had a practical function, which may explain why a "millenarian atmosphere" surrounds even many revolutionary movements which are not otherwise given to it. It helped to organize masses of hitherto unorganized people on a national scale, and almost simultaneously.

All social movements expand in jerks: the history of all contains periods of abnormally, often fantastically rapid and easy mobilization of hitherto untouched masses. Almost always such expansion takes the form of contagion: a propagandist arrives in a locality, and within a short time the whole region is affected; someone establishes or re-establishes a union in a disorganized trade, and within weeks members swamp the new organization; a strike breaks out, or perhaps even better, a strike is won, and within days hundreds of factories in contact with the original strikers are also out.[10] Within a village or town such contagion is easy, since men and women are in close personal contact, and in advanced countries news is spread by press, radio and TV, and communications are easy. In backward countries they are slow and patchy. The difficulties of organizing a movement on a national scale are ironically underlined by the Sicilian experience in organizing the first May Day in 1890: had it not been for the nervousness of the authorities who warned local officials of the need to prevent disorder on that day—information which gossip rapidly spread—the local Socialists would often not even have known that the International expected them to demonstrate. But an atmosphere of high exaltation greatly facilitates the spreading of news. It provides teams of men and women who will spread the joyful tidings wherever they can, for at millennial times, as we have seen in Andalusia, everyone becomes a propagandist. "Peasants from Piana and San Giuseppe Iato," wrote a newspaper in Trapani province, "have come here for the harvest, describing the enthusiasm in those parts and inflaming our peasants."[11] It invests even the smallest organizational advance with an aura of invincibility and future triumph, and nothing is more contagious than success. By these means a movement can almost simultaneously mobilize masses over a wide area, and nothing is more important politically than to do this, for six villages developing a movement at the same time make a vastly greater impact, and generate incomparably more political effectiveness than the same villages

[9] E.g. in Peter Worsley's *The Trumpet Shall Sound* (London 1957), a first-rate study of the Pacific "cargo" cults.
    [10] I have discussed some aspects of this discontinuity in "Economic Fluctuations and some Social Movements," in *Econ. Hist. Rev.*, 2d Ser. V, 1, 1952.
    [11] Salvatore Costanza, "I Fasci dei Lavoratori nel Trapanese," in *Movimento Operaio, loc. cit.*, 1028 n.

developing the same sort of movement separately at intervals of, say, a year. Millenarianism, in fact, is not merely a touching survival from an archaic past, but an extremely useful phenomenon, which modern social and political movements can profitably utilize to spread their range of influence, and to imprint the groups of men and women affected by it with their teaching. For, as we have seen, without being imprinted with the right kind of ideas about political organization, strategy and tactics and the right kind of programme, millenarianism inevitably collapses. Alone it can maintain itself at best as an underground current of belief among a sect, as with the Lazzarettians, or as a body of potential leaders and a predisposition to periodic revolt, as in Andalusia. It can be, indeed it will always be, intensely moving to anyone who cares for the fate of man: but, as we have seen, it will certainly be perennially defeated.

However, when harnessed to a modern movement, millenarianism can not only become politically effective, but it may do so without the loss of that zeal, that burning confidence in a new world, and that generosity of emotion which characterizes it even in its most primitive and perverse forms. And no one can read the testimony of such people as the anonymous peasant woman of Piana without hoping that their spirit can be preserved.

# THE CROWD: THE SUBJECT AND ITS PROBLEMS

**George Rudé**

## The Subject and Its Problems

Perhaps no historical phenomenon has been so thoroughly neglected by historians as the crowd. Few would deny that the crowd has, in a rich variety of guises, played a significant part in history. Yet it has, over many years, been considered a subject fit to be studied by the psychologist or the sociologist rather than by the historian. This book is a historian's attempt to do something to redress the balance.

Of course, I have no intention of attempting to deal with the crowd as a whole, and I shall begin by explaining my subject and defining its limits. In the first place, I am assuming the crowd to be what sociologists term a "face-to-face" or "direct contact" group[1] and not any type of collective phenomenon, such as a nation, a clan, caste, political party, village community, social class, the general "public," or any other "collectivity too large to aggregate." This would seem evident enough, had not some writers in the field (and there are eminent names among them) chosen to extend the crowd's boundaries to encompass far wider horizons. Gustave Le Bon, for example, the founding father of modern crowd psychology, being preoccupied with mental states rather than physical phenomena, includes in his crowd not only castes, clans, and classes but electoral "crowds," criminal juries, and parliamentary assemblies.[2] And Dr. Canetti, a newcomer in the field, discusses "the crowd in history" (such is the subheading to one of his chapters) in terms of the various national symbols that he

---

[1] See articles by L. L. Bernard on "Crowd" and "Mob" in *Encyclopaedia of Social Sciences* (15 vols. New York, 1931-5), IV, 612-13; X, 552-4.
[2] Gustave Le Bon, *The Crowd: A Study of the Popular Mind* (English translation, 6th impression, London, 1909), pp. 181 ff.

considers most appropriate to Englishmen, Frenchmen, Dutchmen, Germans, Jews, and Italians.[3]

This, however, can only be a first step in the process of delimitation. Any sort of crowd may, exceptionally, be termed suitable material for history; yet the "historical" crowd is more likely to be found among some of the sociologists' neat categories than among others. I say "more likely" quite deliberately, as we shall see that one type of crowd is liable, by the intrusion of the unexpected or of forces outside itself, to be converted into another. Nevertheless, in general, we may exclude from our present considerations crowds that are casually drawn together, like sight-seers; crowds assembled on purely ceremonial occasions or crowds taking part in religious or academic processions; or "audience" crowds (as they have been termed) who gather in theaters or lecture halls, at baseball matches or bullfights, or who used to witness hangings at Tyburn Fair or in the Place de Grève in Paris. Equally, we should generally exclude those more active, or "expressive" crowds that come together for Mardi Gras, participate in dancing orgies or student "rags," or attend revivalist meetings to hear Billy Graham or Father Divine, as they listened two hundred years ago to George Whitefield and the Wesleys. Certain "escape" or "panic" crowds (again to use the sociologist's jargon) are more likely to fall within our province: such manifestations have sometimes accompanied food riots and runs on banks, and these may be the very stuff of social history. Other outbursts of mass hysteria—from the convulsions around St. Médard's tomb in eighteenth-century Paris or the self-immolating orgies of Russia's Old Believers to the more recent frenzies stirred by Orson Welles' "Martian" broadcast—are fascinating material for the student of crowd psychology, but they may be of only casual interest to the historian. In fact, our main attention will be given to political demonstrations and to what sociologists have termed the "aggressive mob" or the "hostile outburst"[4]—to such activities as strikes, riots, rebellions, insurrections, and revolutions.

Even now, without further limitation, the subject would be far too vast to cover in a single volume. It is not the "crowd in history" in general that I propose to deal with, but the crowd within a limited period and within a limited area. For this purpose, I have chosen the period of the 1730s to 1840s in French and English history: apart from their importance as having seen the great political revolution in France and the industrial revolution in England, they were years of transition leading to the new "industrial" society.

Some may object to so arbitrary a division of what I am calling the "pre-industrial" and the "industrial" ages. Admittedly, my starting point is a somewhat arbitrary one, and the 1730s are chosen as much for convenience as to mark any sudden change in the pattern of social and political development. There is, however, a stronger case, in considering these two countries, for drawing a line somewhere around the 1840s. By then the effects of both the political and industrial revolutions were (earlier in the city and later in the village) transforming old institutions, uprooting the old society, changing old habits and modes of thinking, and imposing new techniques. To name only a few innovations, factory towns, railways, stable trade unions, a labor movement, socialist ideas, and the new Poor Law and police force in England were evidence that a new age was not only in the making but in being.

[3] Elias Canetti, *Crowds and Power* (London, 1962), pp. 169-200.
[4] See R. W. Brown, "Mass Phenomena," in *Handbook of Social Psychology* (2 vols. Cambridge, Mass., 1954), II, 847-58; and N. J. Smelser, *Theory of Collective Behavior* (London, 1962), pp. 222-69.

Such breaks with the past could not fail to leave their mark on the form and content of the crowd's activities; and we may as sharply (or as broadly) distinguish the typical popular disturbance of the new industrial society from that of the "pre-industrial" age as we may distinguish the latter from that of earlier times. In industrial society, the disturbances most prone to be historically significant take the shape of strikes and other labor disputes, or of public mass meetings and demonstrations conducted by political organizations; their objects tend (though by no means always) to be well defined, forward looking, and rational enough, even if only acceptable, in the first instance, to one side in the dispute; and participants tend, except in distinct peasant communities, to be wage earners or industrial workers. Similarly, the "pre-industrial" age has its own type of disturbance whose objects, behavior, forms of actions, and participants are, more or less, peculiar to the times. In our transitional period the typical form of social protest is the food riot, not the strike of the future or the millenarial movement or the peasant *jacquerie* of the past. Those engaging in popular disturbances are sometimes peasants (as in the past), but more often a mixed population of what in England were termed "lower orders" and in France *menu peuple* (or, for a short period in the 1790s, sans-culottes); they appear frequently in itinerant bands, "captained" or "generaled" by men whose personality, style of dress or speech, and momentary assumption of authority mark them out as leaders; they are fired as much by memories of customary rights or a nostalgia for past utopias as by present grievances or hopes of material improvement; and they dispense a rough-and-ready kind of "natural justice" by breaking windows, wrecking machinery, storming markets, burning their enemies of the moment in effigy, firing hayricks, and "pulling down" their houses, farms, fences, mills, or pubs, but rarely by taking lives. The riot, then, is the characteristic and ever-recurring form of popular protest which, on occasion, turns into rebellion or revolution.

It would be ridiculous, of course, to press this general distinction too far. Strikes were frequent enough in the eighteenth and early nineteeth centuries in France and England, particularly after the 1770s; and, on occasion, they assumed forms almost identical with those of more recent times. Londoners demonstrated and signed petitions in St. George's or Copenhagen Fields, and Parisians in the Champ de Mars or Place de Grève, as they might today in Trafalgar Square or Downing Street, around the "Bastille Column" or in the Place de la Concorde. Race riots today are not unlike religious riots of an earlier period. Outbursts of mass hysteria provoked by rumors of Flying Saucers or Martian invaders, recall similar manifestations in the past. Revivalist orgies and the antics of "Holy Rollers" (though little known in present-day Western Europe) are by no means strangers to modern industrial society. Again, in 1914, German bakers' shops in the East End of London were pillaged and wrecked as they might have been in Paris in the Revolution; and mythical Russians with "snow on their boots" were then as much a figment of popular imagination as the dreaded "brigands" of the Great Fear of 1789. And, if we need any further reminder that past or "archaic" forms may spill over into the present, we have but to turn to Dr. Hobsbawm's studies on millenarial, "populist-legitimist," and "Robin-Hood" types of movement in southern Europe today.[5] The overlap between periods is, then, considerable and extends into fields that are as much the concern of the historian as of

---

[5] E. J. Hobsbawm, *Primitive Rebels: Studies in Archaic Forms of Social Movement in the 19th and 20th Centuries* (Manchester, 1959).

the sociologist; yet, in my view, they are not sufficient to invalidate the general distinction that I am seeking to establish.

\*   \*   \*

## Motives and Beliefs

As long as the crowd in history was considered unworthy of serious attention, it was natural that the study of its motives should have been somewhat superficial. Explanations of why the crowd rioted or rebelled have naturally tended to vary with the social attitudes or *values* of the writer. To those to whom the crowd's actions were wholly reprehensible, the crowd would appear to be prompted by the basest motives, by the lure of loot, gold, rape, or the prospect of satisfying other lurking criminal instincts. To those to whom the crowd seemed, on balance, to be an object worthy of sympathy or compassion rather than of reprobation (though this would vary with the occasion), noble ideals, particularly those of sound middle-class and liberal inspiration, would play an important part. To others again, those whom Marx in his day termed the proponents of a "vulgar" materialism, short-term economic factors seemed the most valid explanation of all types of popular unrest, and every disturbance became almost by definition a hunger riot, or *émeute de la faim*.

None of these explanations are wholly without merit, yet all are either superficial or misleading. Why this is so will, I hope, appear in the course of the present chapter. But a preliminary word needs to be said about the first of these interpretations, which, being the most pervasive of the three, calls for a separate comment. Its underlying assumption appears to be that the masses have no worthwhile aspirations of their own and, being naturally venal, can be prodded into activity only by the promise of a reward by outside agents or "conspirators." "In most popular movements," writes Mortimer-Tenaux, a historian of the French Revolutionary Terror, "money plays a greater role than feeling or conviction (*la passion*)"; and Taine and his school offer similar explanations of why the Bastille fell or the French monarchy was overthrown.[6] But such a view, with its evident social bias, was by no means the invention of these writers: on the contrary, it receives ample confirmation from the opinions of contemporary observers. For as long as no serious attempt was made to probe the deeper aspirations of the poor, the periodic outbursts in riot or rebellion were liable to be attributed to the machinations of a political opponent or a "hidden hand."

Such an attitude was shared by all in authority, whether aristocratic or middle class, conservative, liberal, or revolutionary, though the sort of outbreak that might, exceptionally, be condoned would naturally vary from one class or party to the other. Where Sir Robert Walpole, the King's Chief Minister, attributed the riots of 1736 in England to a Jacobite conspiracy and some of his agents spoke darkly of "high church" or "popish priests," Lord Granville, an opposition peer, was willing to ascribe such "tumults" to "oppression." Again, where George III's ministers and their agents hinted that the Gordon Riots might have been instigated by French or American gold, some opposition leaders were inclined to blame the government itself for deliberately fostering riot as a pretext for calling in the army and imposing martial law. Indeed it was common in eighteenth-century England for one party to accuse the other of

---

[6] M. Mortimer-Ternaux, *Histoire de la Terreur* (8 vols. Paris, 1862-81), VIII, 455; H. Taine, *Les origines de la France contemporaine. La Révolution* (3 vols. Paris, 1878), I, 129.

"raising a Mob." In France, Voltaire, being a critic of aristocracy and a friend of Turgot, convinced himself that the grain-rioters of 1775 were in the pay of Turgot's enemies at Court. During the French Revolution, both revolutionary leaders and their royalist or aristocratic opponents were remarkably liberal with such charges when it suited them: Montjoie, a royalist journalist, claimed to have first-hand proof (which proved to have little foundation) that the Réveillon rioters of 1789 had been bribed with *louis d'or;* and Girondins and Jacobins alike were disposed to believe that food rioters like those that invaded Paris grocery shops in February 1793 had been paid by agents of Pitt or the "aristocrats."[7] Thirty or forty years later, such simple explanations had lost much of their force: we have but to read English parliamentary debates on the Luddites and Chartists to appreciate the difference; but, throughout the eighteenth century, the police—the French perhaps more stubbornly than the English—clung to their conviction that the twin agents of riot and rebellion were bribery and "conspiracy."

To illustrate the point, we quote the remarkable cross examination by the Beauvais police of a woolen worker arrested in the market town of Mouy at the time of the corn riots of 1775:

Q. How was it known that there were riots elsewhere?
A. Everybody said so in the market at Mouy.
Q. Did any "strangers" come by who urged the people to riot?
A. He saw none.
Q. What did these "strangers" look like?
A. Repeats that he saw none.
Q. What did they talk about?
A. Repeats that he saw no "strangers."
Q. Did they claim to be bearers of the King's orders and did they produce papers purporting to prove it?
A. Repeats that he saw no "strangers."
Q. Did they give, lend, or promise money?
A. He saw no one offering money.
Q. Did any of them produce mouldy bread . . . to stir up the people?
A. He saw no mouldy bread.
Q. Does he know where and by whom this mouldy bread was baked?
A. Repeats that he saw no mouldy bread.
Q. How was it that the inhabitants of each village assembled on the same day and at the same hour?
A. This was always so on market days.
Q. Had he seen bills posted up or distributed?
A. No.
Q. Were they printed or written by hand?
A. Repeats that he saw none.
Q. Does he know where they were printed?
A. Repeats that he saw none.
Q. Does he recognize the writing on those written by hand?
A. Repeats that he saw none.
Q. Where had they been drinking, with whom, and who paid for the drinks?
A. Repeats that he saw no one.[8]

[7] *The Crowd in the French Revolution* (Oxford, 1959), pp. 191-3.
[8] Archives de l'Oise, B 1584 (my translation).

It is remarkable that such searching and persistent questioning should, in this and other cases, have yielded almost entirely negative results. Occasionally a prisoner or a witness, unlike the prisoner in the present instance, admits to having heard rumors about money having been distributed to provoke disorder; but never once does he appear to have been present at the transaction or to have been personally involved. This is not to argue that such rumors were all equally without foundation, though it strongly suggests that cases of bribery in popular movements were not so frequent as the authorities supposed they were.[9] Nor does it exclude the fact of bribery in other cases, as when gangs of strongarm men were recruited by a man of "quality" to beat up or intimidate a political opponent. Such was the case at the Middlesex election of December 1768, when the Court candidate, Sir William Beauchamp Proctor, hired a band of Irish chairmen—at the rate of 2 guineas a day, it was claimed by their leader—to drive his radical opponent's supporters off the hustings.[10] This was the well-known device of "raising a Mob"; but it has nothing to do with the sort of popular movement we are here discussing.

In any case, such explanations, even where they contain a more solid substance of truth, are grossly over simplified. The crowd may riot because it is hungry or fears to be so, because it has some deep social grievance, because it seeks an immediate reform or the millenium, or because it wants to destroy an enemy or acclaim a "hero"; but it is seldom for any single one of these reasons alone. Of course, it would be ludicrous to reject the simple and obvious answers merely because they are so. Economic motives, for example, may be presumed to be dominant in strikes and food riots, as political issues play a part of varying importance in both radical reform movements and movements directed against radical reform, such as the Priestley riots in Birmingham in 1791. When Cornish tin miners or West Country weavers burn down their employer's house or mill or destroy his machinery in the course of an industrial dispute, we need no particular powers of divination to conclude that, whatever the form of disturbance, it is higher wages that they are after. Similarly, when food rioters threaten bakers, invade markets, and rip open sacks of flour or grain, we may assume that the real purpose is not so much to intimidate or destroy as to bring down the price of food. Again, when Parisians assault and capture the Bastille and Londoners "pull down" Catholic houses and chapels, we must suppose that they intended to do precisely this. In looking for motives we must, therefore, not be so subtle or devious as to ignore the overt or primary intention.

The latter, however, only gives us a clue to the general nature of a disturbance; and here we are not so much concerned with this as with what prompted people, often of different social groups, occupations, and beliefs to take part in the event. Even if the immediate or overt motives leap to the eye, we still have to explore those that lie beneath the surface; and if persons of differing classes or creeds are involved, some may be impelled by one motive and some by another. Motives will, therefore, vary not only between one action and the next but between different groups participating in the same disturbance. Even so, we shall become hopelessly confused if we do not attempt to make some distinction between what we may term dominant and underlying motives or beliefs. Here, for the sake of clarity, it is proposed to divide the former into "economic" and "political" and to consider what part they played, both separately and in association, in the activities of the pre-industrial crowd.

[9] For a fuller discussion of the evidence, see my *The Crowd in the French Revolution*, pp. 191-6.

[10] See my *Wilkes and Liberty* (Oxford, 1962), p. 59.

Let us begin with those disturbances in which economic issues were clearly paramount. Such were food riots (at this time, the most frequent of all), strikes, peasant attacks on châteaux, the destruction of gates and fences, the burning of hayricks and the wrecking of industrial and agricultural machinery. These account, as we have seen, for the vast majority of disturbances in which the pre-industrial crowd in France and England was actively engaged. And in these we must assume (unless we have evidence to the contrary) that the common people of town and countryside were impelled by the urge to maintain or improve living standards, to raise or prevent reductions in wages, to resist encroachments on their holdings in land or their rights of common pasture, to protect their means of livelihood against the threat of new mechanical devices, and, above all, to ensure a constant supply of cheap and plentiful food. Yet bad, even abysmal, economic conditions were not an automatic "trigger" to disturbance. In England, strikes and trade-union activity tended to occur not at moments of deepest trade depression and unemployment, but rather on the upswing of a boom: as in 1792, 1818, 1824, and 1844-6[11] (the year 1768 appears to have been an exception). During the French Revolution, we noted, the most protracted industrial disputes were those of 1791 and 1794, which were years of comparative prosperity; and that when runaway inflation and unemployment set in, as in the winter of 1794-5, strikes came to an end and food riots took over. Food riots, unlike strikes, were the direct product of bad harvests and trade depression, rising prices and shortage of stocks; but they did not necessarily occur at the peak of a cycle of rising prices: we saw rather that they tended, as in the largest disturbances of their kind before 1789—those of 1766 in England and 1775 in France—to arise as the result of a sudden sharp upward movement leading to shortage and panic buying. Again, strikes, food riots, and peasant movements, even when the prevailing issues were purely economic, might take place against a political background that gave them a greater intensity or a new direction. In London in 1768, already existing industrial disputes were touched by the Wilkite political movement: we find striking weavers and coal heavers acclaiming John Wilkes; and, in France in 1789, it seems unlikely that the peasants would have chosen that particular moment to settle accounts with their landlords if the general political conditions had not been what they were.

Conversely, economic motives often impinged on movements that were, in their essence, political. City riots, upon which political issues usually obtruded, frequently took place against a background of rising prices or food shortage: we saw examples from Paris in 1720, 1752, and 1788, and from London in 1736, 1768, and 1794; though here, the Gordon Riots and the later Wilkite disturbances appear to have been exceptions.[12] Similarly, the French revolutions of 1830 and 1848 broke out during periods of food shortage and trade depression; and we have noted the particular part played by the unemployed in Paris in June 1848. The same intrusion of economic issues is evident in English disturbances of the early nineteenth century; Professor Rostow has vividly illustrated the point in his "social tension chart" for the years 1790 to 1850.[13]

On such occasions, the shortage and high price of bread and food appear to have acted as a stimulus to popular participation in movements that were obstensibly concerned with other objects and issues. During the first French Revolution concern

---

[11] E. J. Hobsbawm, "Economic Fluctuations and Some Social Movements since 1800," *Economic History Review,* 2nd series, V, i (1952), 8.

[12] See Chapter 3.

[13] W. W. Rostow, *British Economy of the Nineteenth Century,* (Oxford, 1948), p. 124.

for the price of bread runs like a constant thread through every phase of the struggle of parties and through nearly every one of the great popular *journées*, and accounts, perhaps more than any other factor, for the unity and militancy of the Parisian sans-culottes. The revolutionary crisis of 1789 broke out against a backcloth of steeply rising bread prices: we saw how the peasant movement began with raids on markets, millers, and granaries before turning into a war against the landlord; and the Réveillon rioters, who destroyed the houses of two unpopular manufacturers, also raided food shops and demanded a reduction in the price of bread. In October, the women of the markets who marched to Versailles to fetch the royal family to Paris chanted as they marched (or, at least, so tradition has it), "let us fetch the baker, the baker's wife and the little baker's boy"; and Barnave, in describing the day's proceedings to his *Dauphinois* constituents, wrote that while "the bourgeoisie" were mainly preoccupied with the political issues, "the people" were equally concerned with the shortage of food. The outbreak of war brought further problems: not only bread, but meat, wine, coffee, and sugar began to disappear from the shops, and in Paris food riots preceded or accompanied each one of the political *journées* of 1792 and 1793. In September 1793, as we saw, it was as the direct result of the popular agitation in the markets, streets, and Sections that the National Convention adopted the law of the General Maximum that placed a ceiling on the prices of most necessities. And, after the Jacobins had fallen and the *maximum* had been abandoned, the insurgents of May 1795 wore on their caps and on their blouses the twin slogans, "The Constitution of 1793" and "Bread."[14]

We are certainly not arguing that short-term economic factors eclipsed all others and that all popular movements of this period, even such politically oriented movements as those of the French Revolution, were really food riots in disguise. We saw in an earlier chapter that even before 1789 the political ideas of the *parlements* in Paris and of the Common Council of the City of London played a part in popular disturbance. Mr. Edward Thompson claims that the London crowd of the 1760's and 1770's "had scarcely begun to develop its own organization or leaders" and, that, having little theory distinct from that of its middle-class "managers," was as yet an unreliable instrument of radical policies.[15] This is true enough, and the proof lies in the fact that the same crowd that had shouted for "Wilkes and Liberty" in 1768 was, a dozen years later, directing its energies into channels that were hardly propitious for the radical cause—destroying Catholic houses and chapels. Nevertheless, the political lessons learned were not entirely forgotten, and they revived and were enriched under the impact of the French Revolution. For, both in England and France, the Revolution of 1789, by posing sharply in their multiform aspects the new concepts of the "rights of man" and the "sovereignty of the people," added a new dimension to popular disturbance and gave a new content to the struggle of parties and classes.

Some historians have doubted the depth of the penetration of these political ideas among the common people. Professor Cobban, for example, has questioned the importance of the circulation of a few political slogans, for (he writes) "one knows how easily a crowd can be taught to chant these and how little serious political content they can have."[16] This would be true enough if it were only a matter of mouthing borrowed slogans, though even these were of some importance in mustering popular support for a radical cause: it is surely significant, for example, that even

[14] *The Crowd in the French Revolution*, pp. 201-207.
[15] E. P. Thompson, *The Making of the English Working Class* (London, 1963), pp. 70-71.
[16] A. Cobban, *The Social Interpretation of the French Revolution* (London, 1964), p. 127.

before the Estates General assembled at Versailles on May 5, 1789, Parisian crowds had taken up the rallying cry of *Vive le Tiers État!* and (like Arthur Young's peasants of a few months later)[17] given it a special meaning of their own. And such ideas and slogans were certainly not kept on ice, as it were, for the great political occasions: on the contrary, there is ample evidence that they permeated ever more deeply and widely as the Revolution progressed. Already in August 1789, we find a journeyman gunsmith arrested at Versailles for speaking slightingly of General Lafayette supporting his claim to a fair hearing with an appeal to the "rights of man"; and Malouet, a hostile observer, relates how at this time chairmen at the gates of the National Assembly were eagerly discussing the rights and wrongs of the case for a royal right of "veto." A year later, the democrats of the Cordeliers Club were forming popular clubs and societies through which they began to give systematic instruction to small craftsmen and wage earners in the more advanced revolutionary doctrines; and, in police records, we read of journeymen and domestic servants subscribing to the radical press and even taking out subscriptions to the more exclusive Jacobin Club.[18] Under this impetus, the sans-culottes not only formed political organizations of their own but later, when they dominated the Paris Sections and Commune, began to advance policies and solutions that proved highly embarrassing to their Jacobin allies. And not only that; for, having assimilated their ideas, they gave them a new content that corresponded more with their own interests than with those of their middle-class teachers.[19]

The sans-culotte movement ended, as we have seen, in the final outbreak and disaster of May 1795, and when it reappeared in the 1830's it had acquired a new social content and new battle cries and slogans. As we noted in Chapter 11 it was the advent of the industrial revolution and the growth of a working-class movement in the intervening years that were largely responsible for the transformation. Babeuf had already, during the first of the political revolutions, given a new socialist twist to the ideas of 1789, but he had come too late to find an effective audience among the sans-culottes. It was only after 1830 that his ideas and ideas similar to his evoked a deep response among the clubs and workers' organizations that sprang up in Paris and played so large a part in the events of 1848. What was new now was not only the content of the ideas themselves but the class of men who voiced them. Among those arrested after the June "days" of that year was Antoine Bisgambilia, an obscure and illiterate mechanic (*mécanicien*), who, in a note dictated to the police from La Roquette prison, expressed his political convictions as follows:

> Everybody knows that I don't compromise with my conscience and that, as long as I have breath left in my body, I shall use it for the triumph of the Democratic and Social Republic.[20]

Admittedly, this declaration appears in an isolated document and we should hardly expect to find many others of the kind; but the nature of the June revolt and the large number of those arrested and convicted suggest that such views were shared by many others. What is certain is that, by now, wage earners—railwaymen, building workers, and journeymen of the traditional crafts—were playing a far larger part in political movements than they had in the first revolution, and were even (like the shopkeepers and craftsmen of 1793) voicing political demands of their own.

[17] A. Young, *Travels in France and Italy* (Everyman Library, London, 1915), pp. 172-3.
[18] *The Crowd in the French Revolution*, pp. 196-9.
[19] A. Soboul, *Les sans-culottes parisiens en l'an II* (Paris, 1958), pp. 505-648.
[20] Arch. de la Préfecture de Police, Aa 429, fo. 441.

A similar evolution had taken place in England; and in some respects it had proceeded more rapidly than in France. As England went through no revolution of her own, the new revolutionary ideas of the rights of man and popular sovereignty were largely borrowed from across the Channel. Through the works of Thomas Paine and others, these began, from early in 1792, to circulate among democrats, dissenters, and the master craftsmen, and journeymen of the big cities and industrial towns. This was also the year that Thomas Hardy's London Corresponding Society began to meet at The Bell in Exeter Street, with its membership of small urban tradesmen and artisans: similar in its social composition to those who met in the clubs and committees of revolutionary Paris. Yet, in some of the English societies like that of Sheffield, there appears to have been a larger percentage of "the inferior sort of Manufacturers and Workmen" than in similar bodies in France.[21] To that extent, it may perhaps be claimed that in England the new revolutionary ideas met with a proportionately greater response among wage earners than in France herself. The English societies were, however, short lived, succumbed to early repression, and had little opportunity of making recruits among the newly emerging factory population.

Jacobin ideas survived, however, gradually found a wider audience and, "driven into weaving villages, the shops of the Nottingham framework knitters and the Yorkshire croppers, the Lancashire cotton-mills, were propagated in every phase of rising prices and of hardship."[22] They emerged on the surface again in the freer political atmosphere of the Westminster election of 1807, when the radicals Burdett and Cochrane were borne to victory by the popular vote; and they inspired the Lancashire weavers who were cut down by the Manchester yeomanry at the great parliamentary reform meeting in St. Peter's Fields in August 1819. After this, the Jacobin-radical tradition, enriched by memories of "Peterloo," took on a new form with the advent of the socialist idea propounded by Robert Owen and others. It was such a mixture of ideas that moulded the political thought of men like George Loveless, the trade unionist and Tolpuddle Martyr of 1834, who, some years before Marx, wrote that "nothing will be done to relieve the distress of the working classes, unless they take it into their own hands."[23] And, on a far wider canvas, they were carried forward into the nationwide agitation for the People's Charter, which, as we have seen, both drew its inspiration from the past and looked forward to the future.

It will perhaps not escape the reader that so far we have largely dealt with the "forward-looking" aspects of the crowd's motives for riot and rebellion. If, we may appear to have been arguing, men and women were drawn into such activities, it was either because they were hungry, because they wanted to end a real or imaginary oppression, or to assure themselves of a richer and happier future; or for a mixture of similar reasons. Yet this is only a part of the story. If we limit our attention to factors such as these, how do we account for popular manifestations like the Gordon Riots, millenarial movements, Luddism, or "Church and King," or even for the paradox of the Parisian revolutionary sans-culottes who, as a vanguard of radical democracy, looked forward to the future and, for the solution of their economic ills, looked back to the idyllic conditions of an imaginary past?[24] To make such phenomena

[21] Thompson, *op. cit.,* pp. 149-57.
[22] *Ibid.,* p. 185.
[23] G. Loveless, *The Victims of Whiggery: A Statement of the Persecutions Experienced by the Dorchester Labourers* (London, 1837), p. 23.
[24] See G. Rudé, J. Zacker, Sophie A. Lotte, and A. Soboul, "I Sanculotti: una discussione tra storici marxisti," *Critica Storica,* I, iv (1962), 369-98.

intelligible, we have also to consider some of the underlying motives and traditional myths and beliefs—what crowd psychologists and social scientists have termed "fundamental" or "generalized" beliefs[25]—that played a not inconsiderable part in such disturbances.

To begin with, there is the traditional "leveling" instinct, common to all such occasions, which prompts the poor to seek a degree of elementary social justice at the expense of the rich, *les grands*, and those in authority regardless of whether they are government officials, feudal lords, capitalists, or middle-class revolutionary leaders. It is the common ground on which, beyond the slogans of contending parties, the militant sans-culotte meets the "Church and King" rioter or the peasant in search of his millenium. Even in periods of comparative social peace, we find it in the traditional methods of "self-help" of the rural population, common to both France and England. As hardship presses or as opportunity offers, small farmers and freeholders, peasants and cottagers help themselves to firewood and game at the landlord's or wealthy farmer's expense and, where resistance is offered, assault gamekeepers or burn the farmer's ricks. Such crimes are punished severely at law—in England, progressively so after 1815—but they are not condemned, like murder and common theft, by the rural population. There was a similar elementary form of social protest in the gay abandon with which London crowds, when rioting for Wilkes, smashed the windows of lords and ladies of fashion and painted Wilkes's symbol, the "45", on the soles of the Austrian ambassador's boots. We find it in the London riots against the Corn Law of 1815, when the *Morning Post* reported that

> The mob is particularly enraged against the great parishes of St. Mary-le-Bow, St. George Hanover Square, and St. James, which comprehend the town houses of nearly all the great families of the United Kingdom.[26]

But, up to this time, the "leveling" instinct of the crowd might as readily be harnessed to an anti-radical as to a radical cause. In the Gordon Riots, the crowd's choice of targets showed that they were more concerned to destroy the properties of wealthy Catholics than of Catholics in general; and we find a rioter in Bermondsey telling his victim, who had claimed to be a Protestant: "Protestant or not, no gentleman need be possessed of more than £1,000 a year; that is sufficient for a gentleman to live upon."[27] We have noted a similar motive underlying "Church and King" disturbances: if Jacobins were attacked in the streets of Naples in 1799, it was as much because they rode in carriages as because they were allies of the "atheistical" French; and in Birmingham, Priestley and his associates were picked on not only because they were dissenters or radical reformers, but also because they were manufacturers, magistrates, and men of wealth and status.[28] Similarly, the peasants of the Vendée reacted against revolutionary Paris because, for quite particular reasons, their hatred of the urban bourgeois was greater than their hatred of the local landlord; and Tocqueville, though his sense of history was not as acute as Marx's, showed more than a grain of good sense

---

[25] Thus Le Bon distinguishes between "accidental and passing ideas created by the influences of the moment" and the "fundamental ideas to which the environment, the laws of heredity, and public opinion give a very great stability" (*The Crowd* (London, 1909), p. 68). For "generalized beliefs," see N. Smelser, *Theory of Collective Behavior* (London, 1962), pp. 79-130, 202-203.

[26] Quoted by D. G. Barnes, *A History of the English Corn Laws from 1660 to 1846* (New York, 1961), p. 136.

[27] Old Bailey *Proceedings* (Surrey Special Commission) (London, 1780), p. 11.

[28] See pp. 138-9, 145-6 above.

when he presented the June insurrection as a conflict between the "haves" and the "have-nots," or "a sort of Servile War."[29]

Such an element was, of course, by no means peculiar to the pre-industrial crowd. Of more particular relevance was its antipathy to capitalist innovation. As commercialism and the quest of "improvement" entered the village, common lands were divided and fenced off, turnpikes were erected, and grain was stored in barns and withheld from immediate circulation, while prices were allowed to follow the whims of supply and demand and find their "natural" level. Similarly, as industry developed, labor-saving machinery was introduced into mines and mills, and wages, like prices, found a "natural" level by direct bargaining between the masters and their laborers. Thus, gradually, the old protective legislation against enclosure, engrossing, and forestalling, and the export of grain, and the old laws empowering magistrates to fix prices and wages, were rescinded; and the old notions of the "just" price and "just" wage, imposed by authority or sanctioned by custom, gave way to the new prevailing notions of "natural" wages and prices in a freely competitive market. The transformation was spread over some 150 years and followed a broadly similar course in France and England. In England it started earlier, but in France it received a sharp forward thrust in the 1760's and 1770's and in the legislation of the Revolution. In both countries, the process was largely completed by 1800; yet in both there remained a residue from ancient practices: in France, in the survival of many of the collective traditions of the village; in England, in the Speenhamland System, whereby agricultural wages continued to be subsidized from the parish poor rate until the 1830's.[30]

We have already seen how the small consumers and producers of town and countryside reacted to these innovations. Clinging stubbornly to the old paternalist and protectionist legislation as it was gradually abandoned by their rulers, they appealed to Parliament, to magistrates, and to the King himself to restore or enforce the old regulations: to forbid enclosure, to pull down toll gates, to empower justices to fix prices and wages and to regulate the supply and distribution of bread and flour. During the French Revolution, they went even further and insisted that a general *maximum* be placed on the prices of every article of consumption, thus looking forward to a more highly centralized economy than any of the old laws and statutes had envisaged. Similarly, they denounced farmers and dealers as engrossers or *accapareurs;* and in France, from Louis XV's time, there grew the persistent popular belief that a *pacte de famine* had been deliberately devised to starve the people. In England, we find a similar trend expressed in a handbill distributed at Retford in 1795:

Those Cruall Villions the Millers Bakers etc. Flower Sellers rases Flowe under a Comebination to what price they please on purpose to make an Artificall famine in a Land of plenty.[31]

On occasion, they found allies among an older, or more conservative, generation or those in opposition to government: among magistrates and farmers, or, as in France, in the *parlements* of the Old Regime. Sometimes these allies revived or applied the old methods (we have seen examples from the riots of 1766 and 1775). If not, the people

[29] *The Recollections of Alexis de Tocqueville,* ed. J. P. Mayer (Meridian Books, New York, 1959), p. 150.
[30] See pp. 44, 67 above; and Thompson, *op. cit.,* pp. 67-8.
[31] Quoted by Thompson, *op. cit.,* p. 67.

took the law into their own hands: we noted the outcome in the enclosure riots and food riots of the eighteenth century, the machine breaking of the Luddites and the laborers of 1830, the antics of "Rebecca's daughters" in the early 1840's; and even (though here the object was neither food nor wages) in the depredation of the "No Popery" rioters in London. And such acts, it was believed, far from meriting censure or savage reprisals, were morally justified and performed as a kind of solemn public duty. For if the King, misled by his ministers, "broke his Coronation oath" by allowing relief to Roman Catholics, or magistrates failed to use their powers to apply the old statutes, who but the people could set the matter right? Ned Ludd, from his office in Sherwood Forest, actually claimed the right to break the hosiers' frames under the terms of the charter of the Framework Knitters' Company.[32] The people might also expect to be paid for carrying out such duties: we saw how the "Swing" rioters charged a fee for smashing threshing machines; the Gordon rioters collected money "for the poor Mob"; and the September "massacrers" in Paris exacted their reward in terms of food and drink.

One consequence of all this was to drive a deeper wedge between the riotous crowd that clung to these old customs and the forward-looking, reforming, radical or revolutionary middle class or liberal aristocracy. Wilkes had the good fortune not to have to face this problem, as London and Middlesex were comparatively free from food and enclosure riots; but Voltaire, as we saw, could not fail to conclude that the grain rioters of 1775, who were so patently helping to undermine Turgot's reforms, were in the pay of his political opponents. Gibbon Wakefield, in 1830, managed to evade the issue by assuming that the machine-breaking and rick-burning laborers were only hostile to his enemies, the landlords and Church of England clergy, while sparing the properties of his friends, the farmers. The French middle-class revolutionaries of 1792-4 could have no such illusions: the hostility of the small peasants and sans-culottes to the freedom of trade in grain, bread, meat, and wine helped to drive the Girondins, the most determined advocates of laissez-faire, from power and a year later contributed to the overthrow of their Jacobin successors.[33]

Closely allied to the concern for "justice" was the belief in the King as the protector or "father" of his people. England being a parliamentary monarchy, the tradition there was wearing thin and appeals for protection in such instances as we have listed above were more likely to be addressed to Parliament or to the justices than to the King in person. In countries of absolute monarchy, however, the King was both the symbol and the fount of all justice and legislation, and the belief in his paternal benevolence persisted even through periods of revolution and peasant revolt, when the King's ministers may already have been long discredited and the royal power itself was on the wane. Folk myths abound about the kindly concern for their people of Emperors, Sultans, Tsars, and French Kings from St. Louis to Henri IV and Louis XVI. "Don't fire on us," cry the rebellious Volga peasantry to the general sent to shoot them down, "you are shooting on Alexander Nikoleyevitch, you are shedding the blood of the Tsar."[34] In France, the Bordeaux peasants of 1674 rioted against the salt tax in the name of the King; the grain rioters of 1775 were convinced that they were right to refuse to pay the high prices demanded by farmers, millers, and bakers because, it was firmly believed, the King had ordered that a "just" price be paid; and the peasants of

[32] F. O. Darvall, *Popular Disturbances and Public Order in Regency England* (London, 1934), p. 170.
[33] A. Soboul, *op. cit.*, pp. 1025-1031.
[34] Quoted by E. J. Hobsbawm, *Primitive Rebels* (Manchester, 1959), p. 121.

1789 produced "orders" purporting to come from Louis XVI himself to give legal sanction to their attacks on the landlords' châteaux. Of course, such a paradoxical state of affairs could not last forever: The Revolution was bound, sooner or later, either to reinforce these old notions in terms of "Church and King" (as in the Vendée) or to uproot them altogether. The war, in particular, exposed the King, and not only his ministers, to public condemnation and eventually to the merited charge of treason. It is all the more remarkable, however, that his popularity among the common people should have survived so many crises; and even as late as June 1792 (three years after the Revolution began), the crowd that invaded the Tuileries and forced Louis to toast "the Nation" combined with its vulgar familiarity a residue of reverence. But, after the fall of the monarchy in August, it was not an individual leader, but the National Assembly or the "sacred Mountain" (the Jacobins), that replaced the King as a popular father-figure. So, in the food riots of November 1792 we find the price-fixing peasants and craftsmen of the Beauce invoking the authority not, as the peasants of 1789, of the King but of the newly elected National Convention.[35]

In England, another constantly recurring theme in popular ideology is that of the Englishman's "birthright" or "liberties." The belief that Englishmen were "freeborn" and not "slaves" and did not starve or wear "wooden shoes"—like foreigners in general and Papist foreigners in particular—was deeply ingrained and had been so since the religious and social conflicts of the sixteenth and seventeenth centuries. In the campaign conducted against Walpole's Gin Act of 1736, a circular letter addressed to London distillers declared: "If we are Englishmen let us how that we have English spirits and not tamely submit to the yoak just ready to be fastened about our necks." It is a theme that runs, in one form or another, through all contemporary London riots and is also connected with the prevailing attitude towards crime, of which we have already spoken.[36] It is related, too, to the popular xenophobia or chauvinism with which London crowds, in the eighteenth century, rallied to the cause of bellicose national leaders like the elder Pitt and his City allies and rejected the more pacific overtures of men like Walpole, Bute, and the Dukes of Newcastle and Bedford. Before and during the French wars at the end of the century, it no doubt helped to promote the cause of "Church and King," as reformers like Priestley in Birmingham and Thomas Walker in Manchester were tainted as being friends of the French. Only the Americans, when at war with England, escaped this type of xenophobia. There is no evidence of anti-Americanism among all the other popular prejudices voiced at the time of the Gordon Riots. The reason is perhaps not hard to find; did not the Americans share with the English a common "birthright" and a common concern for "liberty" and the "Protestant cause"?

It was not only a matter of defending existing English "liberties" from foreign attack: there was the other, even greater, problem of restoring them to their "pristine purity" at home. Here, once more, there was a constant appeal to precedent: to the glories of a distant or imaginary past rather than to the prospects opened up by the present. Magna Carta, the Popish Plot, the Bill of Rights, and the "Glorious Constitution" of 1689 were all reminders that these "liberties" had constantly to be fought for against tyranny from within; but one of the most remarkably persistent beliefs of all was that perfect "liberties" had existed under the Saxon Kings and that

---

[35] M. Vovelle, "Les taxations populaires de février-mars et novembre-décembre 1792 dans la Beauce et sur ses confins," *Mémoires et documents*, no. XIII (Paris, 1958), p. 137.

[36] G. Rudé, "The London 'Mob' of the Eighteenth Century," *The Historical Journal*. II, i (1959), 13-14; Thompson, *op. cit.*, 59-61.

these had been filched, together with their lands, from "freeborn" Englishmen by the invading Norman knights under William the Bastard in 1066. This myth of the "Norman Yoke" persisted until Chartist times and was handed down by generations of Levellers, Whigs reared on "revolution principles," London eighteenth-century radicals and democrats nurtured on the more recent doctrines of "popular sovereignty" and the "rights of man." In 1780, that same committee of Westminster reformers whose claims anticipated by half a century the Six Points of the People's Charter demanded the "restitution" of equal representation, annual Parliaments, and universal suffrage, which (it was said) "were substantially enjoyed in the times of the immortal Alfred."[37] A handbill circulated in London in 1793, protesting against the use of "crimping" houses and other oppressive government measures, asks the questions: "Would such atrocious acts have been suffered in the days of Alfred? . . . Did Sydney and Russel bleed for this?"[38] Members of English radical societies in the 1790's wore Saxon dress and organized themselves in divisions based on Saxon *tythings;* and John Frost, the later Chartist leader, was, in 1822, attributing present inequalities in wealth to "the plunder of William the Bastard."[39] Nor were such backward-looking theories peculiar to the British. While Englishmen yearned for Saxon "liberties" and Welshmen called on the Men of Harlech to drive out the "sons of Hengist," Frenchmen of the Revolution sought the "pristine purity" of republican manners and institutions in the days of Ancient Rome.[40]

Millenarial and religious ideas also clearly played a part in popular disturbance. The millenium might assume a secular or a religious form, though (unlike the Wesleyan ideal) it was generally to be realized on earth rather than in heaven. Millenarial fantasies no doubt underlie many of the actions of the poor in the course of the French Revolution; but in none are they so clearly evident as in the sudden upsurge of hope aroused among them by the news that the Estates General should meet in the summer of 1789. The news fostered what French historians since Taine have called *la grande espérance:* the hope that, at last, past promises would be fulfilled and the burdens, particularly the hated *taille,* lifted off the peasants' backs, and that a new golden era would begin. The state of exaltation thus engendered equally produced its corollary, the conviction, once these hopes appeared to be endangered, that their realization was being frustrated by a *complot aristocratique.* This dual phenomenon, it has been argued, does a great deal to explain the almost mystical fervor with which the *menu peuple* pursued their "aristocratic" enemies during the Revolution.[41] Or, as in England, millenarial fantasies might be clothed in the poetic imagery of Blake's "Jerusalem" or the apocalyptic extravagances of a Richard Brothers, whose *Revealed Knowledge of the Prophesies and Times* was published in London in early 1794. This was a time when Jacobin ideas were still making headway among the "lower orders"; and it has been suggested that men like Brothers, who interlaced their talk of "the whore of Babylon" and the "Antichrist" with denunciations of the high and mighty, may have nourished similar political aspirations to those nourished by Tom Paine's *The Rights of Man.*[42] But millenarial ideas, while they might, under certain

[37] Cited by S. Maccoby, *The English Radical Tradition 1763-1914* (London, 1952), p. 36.
[38] Old Bailey *Proceedings* (1794), p. 1327.
[39] C. Hill, "The Norman Yoke," in *Democracy and the Labour Movement,* ed. J. Saville (London, 1954), pp. 11-66; Thompson, *op. cit.,* pp. 84-8, 150; D. Williams, *John Frost: A Study in Chartism* (Cardiff, 1939), p. 50.
[40] French aristocrats before the Revolution had similarly invoked the "liberties" of the "free" Frankish nobles; but this probably played little part in popular mythology.
[41] G. Lefebvre, *Quatre-Vingt-Neuf* (Paris, 1939), pp. 112-14.
[42] Thompson, *op. cit.,* pp. 116-19.

circumstances, stimulate rather than weaken an already existing political movement, might equally act as an antidote to popular militancy or as a consolation for a political defeat. This may have been the case in France after Waterloo and, in England in 1838, in the strange affair of "the battle in Bossenden Wood."[43]

In the latter case, a number of Kentish laborers believed implicitly that their leader, the spurious Sir William Courtenay, was the Messiah. But this is only one guise in which the religious motive may appear in riots. At other times, though overtly proclaimed, it might not be so profound as it was made to appear; or conversely it might lie submerged beneath the surface of events. Of the first kind "No Popery" riots, "High Church" attacks on Methodist or Presbyterian meeting halls and chapels, and urban "Church and King" explosions are obvious examples. Quite apart from their social undercurrents, such movements were never quite what they seemed. We have seen that the ill-assorted slogans "destruction to Presbyterians" and "No Popery" appeared side by side in the Birmingham riots; and one of those sentenced to death for his part in the Gordon Riots said, when questioned: "Damn my eyes, I have no religion; but I have to keep it up for the good of the cause."[44] It is not so much that in such movements the religious element is nonexistent or a mere cloak for other issues (though this was firmly believed by some contemporaries) as that in them religious, social, and political motives are bewilderingly interwoven. Perhaps, in view of their proclaimed purpose to maintain an established Church as part of an established order, we should treat them less as religious movements than as anti-radical political demonstrations.

The case is somewhat different where a dissenting religious tradition serves as an undercurrent rather than as a proclaimed object of disturbance. In London and England's West Country, in particular, religious dissent and popular radicalism had had a long association; and Methodism, even when it professed to stave off riot and lay up its treasures solely in heaven, brought with it a new fervor and moral purpose that, sooner or later, were bound to leave their mark on popular social movements. Such was certainly the case in England and Wales in the disturbances of 1830 and the 1840's: in the "Swing" and Rebecca riots and in the Welsh Chartist movement Protestant nonconformity, both Wesleyan and other, played a part.[45]

Nor must we assume that such secular, rationalist ideas as the "rights of man" and other products of the Enlightenment would, when they gripped the common people, necessarily serve as an antidote to religion. This was no doubt the intention of many rationalist thinkers and middle-class and aristocratic reformers or revolutionaries in England and France in the eighteenth century; and there were moments during the French Revolution when they appeared to have been successful. Certainly, the monopoly and authority of the established Catholic Church were successively undermined and broken—and these were never fully recovered; and Parisian crowds demonstrated to shouts of *A bas la calotte!* ("Down with the priests!") and played a part, at the height of the "de-christianization" movement in the autumn of 1793, in closing down every church in the city. Yet the popular anti-religious (as distinct from the anti-clerical) movement was comparatively short lived; as late as June 1793, Parisians in the revolutionary Faubourg St. Antoine demonstrated for the right to preserve the traditional Corpus Christi procession; and Robespierre himself sought to win further popular support for the Revolutionary Government by launching a

[43] P. G. Rogers, *Battle in Bossenden Wood* (London, 1961). See p. 149 above.
[44] Old Bailey *Proceedings* (1780), pp. 446-52.
[45] See pp. 155, 156 above; and Thompson, *op. cit.*, pp. 350-400.

brand-new religious cult, the Cult of the Supreme Being. This was only the most highly publicized of numerous attempts to effect a fusion between religion and the current political ideas. In many districts, the people took the initiative themselves and the Revolution saw a remarkable upsurge of new religious cults; and solemn ceremonies, accompanied by all the *mystique* of the old religious practices, were dedicated to new local "saints" or to the great popular martyrs of the Revolution, Marat, Chalier, and Lepeletier.[46] Yet once the Revolution was over, such cults appear to have left few traditions; and neither they nor the re-established Catholic Church, nor the religious minority groups, appear to have played any significant part in the revolutions of 1830 and 1848.

The analysis might be carried even further; but to spare the bewildered reader's feelings I propose to stop it here. What we have seen is a rich variety of motives and beliefs, through which economic issues and appeals to customary rights exist side by side with new conceptions of man's place in society and the search for the millenium. Such a medley of seemingly ill-assorted beliefs and aspirations is by no means a feature peculiar to the pre-industrial crowd: it appears as evidently, though with different emphases and variations, in the disturbances of today as it does in those of ancient or medieval times. But through the confusion a certain common pattern peculiar to the age emerges. We shall, however, hardly be aware of it unless we place the riots and rebellions in their historical context and compare those of the early and middle years of the eighteenth century with those of the French Revolution and those that followed later. Even when we do so, we shall not see a steady, gradual disappearance of appeals to custom and millenarial fantasies: these persist, though at times with abated vigor, throughout the period that we are concerned with. But there are significant turning points at which new conceptions enter and, while not eclipsing the old ideas entirely transform them or reduce their relative importance. Such turning points are the revolution of 1789 in France and the growth of independent working-class movements in the 1830's.

Recently, Professor Reinhard Bendix has stressed the contrast between types of popular protest arising in the "pre-democratic" and those arising in the "democratic" period of West European history.[47] The point is an important one, for once the new and essentially forward-looking ideas of the "rights of man" and "popular sovereignty" had gripped the popular imagination, riots and disturbances tended to acquire a new dimension and to assume a stable social-ideological content that they had lacked before. But, equally, emerging industrial society in France and England created an industrial working class, working-class movements, and working-class political ideas. Thus further new ideas and further social forces, unknown in 1789, began to come to the fore: we have seen examples in the French revolution of 1848 and in the Chartist movement in England. These stepping stones are no less significant because many of the old and backward-looking ideas persisted and old forms continued to rub shoulders with the new. Moreover, traditional beliefs might, instead of becoming abandoned, be transformed and adapted to meet new needs; in this sense, there is no radical departure from the old yearning for "protection" in the socialist ideal of a more fully collectivist society.

Thus, gradually, the pattern of popular protest; and the ideas that underlay it, would

---

[46] A. Soboul, "Sentiment religieux et cultes populaires pendant la Révolution: saintes patriotes et martyrs de la liberté," *Archives de sociologie des religions*, July-Dec. 1956, pp. 73-86.
[47] R. Bendix, "The Lower Classes and the 'Democratic Revolution,'" *Industrial Relations*, I, i (Oct. 1961), 91-116.

suffer a sea-change. In 1848, this process was by no means completed; but the new "industrial" crowd, with its richer stock of forward-looking concepts, was already clearly visible on the horizon.

* * *

## The Success and Failure of the Crowd

One final and important question remains. Did all the vigor, heroism, and violence recounted and dissected in these chapters lead to any positive results? In this phase of its history in France and England, what did the crowd achieve? In terms of immediate gains, it must be admitted that it achieved comparatively little. In strikes and wage movements, as long as trade unions were weak and scattered and proscribed, workers could only hope to win short-lived and limited results. The Parisian workers of 1794, who struck work at a time of war and labor shortage, won considerably higher wages, but they were more than swallowed up by the inflation of the following months. The Luddites, though they failed to stop the steam loom, wrung some temporary concessions from the clothiers of Yorkshire and the hosiers of the midlands counties; yet these, too, were withdrawn or eclipsed in the depression that continued long after their riots had been suppressed. In English rural riots, weavers, miners, cottagers, freeholders, and laborers made their social protest for a day or two: they broke down fences, "pulled down" farms or mills, and imposed their price controls on wheat, flour, meat, and butter—until the militia arrived, opened fire, and arrested the "ringleaders," who were hanged, imprisoned, or transported; and "normality" reigned once more. The French grain riots of 1775 thoroughly alarmed the government because of their scope and their threat to the security of the capital; but Turgot mustered a strong military force and brought the rioters to heel, without making the slightest concession to the small consumers whose hardship had provoked them. In fact, of all the many food riots of the period it was probably only those of the French Revolution—particularly those of 1793—that achieved the aims with which they started.

Outside revolutions, urban riots were no more strikingly successful than the rural. In the Gordon Riots, London's "No Popery" crowds held the streets for a week on end; but the Catholic Relief Act, which had prompted them, remained. After the riots of 1791, Priestley felt compelled to leave Birmingham and take refuge in the United States; but this was due as much to the continued hostility of the authorities as to the destructiveness of "Church and King." French city riots, before 1787, were minor explosions and achieved less than the English. And the results of such outbreaks as those at Bristol and Nottingham in 1831 and at Birmingham and in the pottery towns in 1839-42 are impossible to assess because they were part of wider movements: of the Reform Bill agitation in the first case and of Chartism in the second.

But besides its failures the crowd had its indisputable successes. Not only did the Rebecca riots destroy the hated turnpikes, which were not rebuilt, but tolls were reduced in number and County Boards were set up to administer the old unpopular Trusts. "Swing's" successes were less sensational; but, in some districts, the collusion of the farmers ensured that the threshing machines smashed by the laborers were not restored. The Wilkite disturbances in London not only achieved a remarkable series of personal victories for Wilkes himself but contributed substantially to the growth of a mass radical movement in England. Chartism, though a failure at the time, was hardly so in the long run, since five of its Six Points were adopted by a succession of Parliaments over the next hundred years. And, finally, it would be tedious to recount the profound influences exerted on French national life, and beyond France herself, by the revolution of 1789 and, to a lesser degree, by those of 1830 and 1848.

But why should some "hostile outbursts" be successful and others be so patently failures? Of course, in its wider aspects, this question raises a whole host of problems—some social and ideological, others political and administrative—arising both before and after the point of explosion.[48] But, in this short final chapter, we shall be concerned mainly with those arising after the outbreak itself. First, as to the outbreak and the initial "break-through." Here, unless numbers were overwhelming, early success might depend on such factors as a rapid thrust, seizing the initiative, or exploiting the advantages offered by geography. In rural riots, for example, it was comparatively easy to effect an early "breakthrough" before the militia could be summoned or the army mustered. Thus, in 1775, the French grain rioters had been running loose in the markets and villages for a whole week, and had actually entered Versailles and Paris before Turgot was able to summon an armed force adequate to check them. Again, in London in March 1768, crowds celebrating Wilkes's first election victory in Middlesex got off to a good start while the constables were at Brentford, where the election had taken place; and similarly, in the Paris food riots of February 1793, crowds were able to occupy the grocers' shops without opposition because the National Guard was on that day engaged on other duties at Versailles.

At other times, the almost simultaneous outbreak of disturbances over a wide area would make it impossible for even the most astute and determined of police chiefs or military commanders to make an effective disposition of the forces at his disposal. This was certainly the case in the initial stages of the Rebecca and Luddite riots in England; and in April 1848, the Chartist Convention, prompted by Ernest Jones, quite deliberately planned to divert the authorities' attention from London, where the main operation was to take place, by organizing simultaneous demonstrations in the provinces, "so that the myrmidons of power in the country might be kept in check by the brave men there."[49]

Yet, of course, such devices could do no more than win a temporary respite, unless there were other, more solid, reasons for success. And this was so only in one of the cases that I have cited. In London, in 1768, even when the constables returned from their other duties, the forces of law and order were quite inadequate to curb the noisy display of enthusiasm among Wilkes's supporters. In Paris, in February 1793, on the other hand, the return of the National Guard, with the brewer Santerre at its head, brought the riots to a speedy close; and, in the other examples quoted, the authorities only needed time to muster their forces in order to quell disturbance. In 1775, Turgot set two whole armies afoot, the one under the Marquis de Poyanne in the Ile de France and the other under the veteran Duc de Biron in Paris; after which, the riots were over within a week. In England, in the summer of 1812, as we have seen, the Luddites were overawed by an army of 12,000 men, which was larger than any that had previously been called upon to cope with civil disorder.[50] In the main years of Chartist agitation

[48] See N. J. Smelser, *Theory of Collective Behavior* (London, 1962), pp. 261-8, 364-79, for what the author terms the "social control" of tension and disturbance.

[49] Cited by F. C. Mather, *Public Order in the Age of the Chartists* (Manchester, 1959), p. 22.

[50] Before the end of the Gordon Riots of 1780 there were 10,000 troops encamped in the

in England, large forces of regular troops were mustered in the disaffected areas: 10,500 in 1839 and 10,000 in 1842; and in April 1848, to meet the last Chartist threat, nearly 170,000 special constables were enrolled and 7,123 "regulars" and 1,290 armed pensioners were assembled in the capital alone.[51]

Such numbers were impressive; yet, in the final reckoning, it was not so much the numbers in themselves that might prove decisive as the willingness or the ability of the authorities to use them. Much might depend, as we have seen, on the speed and efficiency with which they were assembled, and even more depended on the determination of magistrates, constables, and troops to crush disturbance. In English riots, there were numerous occasions when swift action by justices who commanded respect brought local outbreaks to a speedy close.[52] In June 1848, the troops stationed in London to overawe the Chartists were said to be "so savage that Lord Londonderry told the Duke of Wellington he was sure, if a collision took place, the officers of his regiment would not be able to restrain their men."[53] Even more remarkable, that same month, was the ferocity with which the Parisian Gardes Mobiles, though themselves recruited from young workers and unemployed, mowed down the June insurgents on the barricades. In 1830, it was to a somewhat different social group that the Duke of Wellington appealed in order to break up the "Swing" rioters in Hampshire:

I induced the magistrates [he wrote] to put themselves on horseback, each at the head of his own servants and retainers, grooms, huntsmen, game-keepers, armed with horsewhips, pistols, fowling pieces and what they could get, and to attack in concert, if necessary, or singly, these mobs, disperse them, and take and put in confinement those who could not escape. This was done in a spirited manner, in many instances, and it is astonishing how soon the country was tranquillised and that in the best way, by the activity and spirit of the gentlemen.[54]

Such "spirited" appeals to class might indeed, as in this instance, prove highly effective in mobilizing resistance to disturbance; but there were occasions when the hatreds thus aroused, by alienating or outraging the noncommitted, might rebound on the heads of their sponsors and prove more of a liability than an asset. This was certainly the case with Lafayette and the Parisian National Guard, whose zeal in shooting down unarmed demonstrators in the Champ de Mars in July 1791 stirred passions that were not easily abated. Results similar though not so drastic flowed from the "massacres" of Wilkite supporters in St. George's Fields by the Foot Guards in 1768 and of the Lancashire weavers by the yeomanry at "Peterloo" half a century later.

Yet it was not so much excessive zeal as its direct opposite that was liable to endanger authority and to undermine its defenses. For every vigorous, respected, or over-zealous magistrate in English disturbances, there could usually be found another whose fatuity, arrogance, timidity, or caution would estrange supporters or confuse and paralyze the constables and military commanders at his disposal. Moreover, the antiquated machinery of order, in particular the anomalies surrounding the operation

parks and squares of London (P. de Castro, *The Gordon Riots* (London, 1926), p. 263).

[51] E. Lavisse, ed., *Histoire de France depuis les origines jusqu'à la Révolution* (9 vols. Paris, 1911), IX, 33; F. O. Darvall, *Popular Disturbances and Public Order in Regency England* (London, 1934), pp. 259-60; F. C. Mather, *op. cit.*, pp. 152, 163; M. Hovell, *The Chartist Movement* (London, 1918), p. 290.

[52] See, for example, Darvall, *op. cit.*, pp. 244-5; and Mather, *op. cit.*, pp. 60-61.

[53] Mather, *op. cit.*, p. 180.

[54] Cited by D. Williams, *John Frost* (Cardiff, 1939), pp. 59-60.

of the Riot Act, led to endless confusion; and the Englishman's boasted "right of resistance" to oppression, particularly when the parliamentary opposition chose to exploit it, might almost be construed as a right of rebellion.[55] There were occasions, too, when magistrates (and this applied as much to France as to England) not only were cautious and timid in summoning troops but openly or secretly sympathized with the rioters' cause. Even in the French grain riots of 1775, which were actively repressed, some magistrates, while not openly flouting Turgot's authority, were inclined to meet the rioters half-way. In the Gordon Riots in London, many City magistrates were even more half-hearted in carrying out their duties: being as hostile to Catholic relief as the crowd itself, they virtually condoned their activities until the rioters became a menace not only to Catholic properties but to property as a whole. Such collusion between magistrates and rioters might go even further: in France, in 1788, the *parlements* could hardly be expected to take firm measures against those who rioted on their behalf; and in Birmingham, three years later, there was a strong suspicion that some of the chief instigators of the Priestley riots would be found, if authority felt so disposed, among the magistrates themselves.[56]

But it was only in exceptional circumstances, such as those attending the French "aristocratic revolt" of 1788, that the insubordination or collusion of magistrates could yield more than a temporary advantage to rioters or rebels: generally, it could ensure their complete success only in such limited and negative operations as those undertaken in the name of "Church and King." In the last resort, it was always the army on which authority in both France and England relied to defend itself against popular disturbance; and as long as the army remained substantially loyal any serious threat to the government or the established order was negligible or nonexistent. In theory, it was possible to imagine that vast numbers of civilians, if they had access to weapons and ammunition, might arm themselves and seize power with such speed that the army had time neither to offer resistance nor to become disaffected; but, in fact, this never happened and never has happened since. In England, the army remained stubbornly loyal to King and Parliament throughout this period—though there were moments in 1839 and 1840 when General Napier, who held the northern command, expressed fears that his troops were being infected by Chartist propaganda.[57]

In France, for all the unpopularity of ministers, the army never seriously wavered in its allegiance to the King until the autumn of 1787—so much so that Sébastien Mercier, writing in 1783, thought it was inconceivable that a city as well policed as Paris should ever be exposed to such tumults as London, for lack of such defenses, had suffered during the Gordon Riots.[58] But, of course, as he was soon to discover, it was not just a matter of simple arithmetic: the effectiveness of armies in civil disturbance depended far less on numbers than on their willingness to obey. And this is precisely what the French army, in 1788 and still more in 1789, was not prepared to do. Disaffection started not among the rank and file but among the officers. These, drawn largely from the small provincial *noblesse*, had long-standing grievances concerning their status and opportunities for promotion, and the "aristocratic revolt" provided an admirable occasion to voice them. In Brittany, Dauphiné, and other provinces, they ordered their troops not to fire on demonstrators, refused to arrest rebellious

---

[55] E. Halévy, *A History of the English People in 1815* (3 vols. London, 1937), I, 193-8.
[56] See pp. 29, 59, 94, and 146 above.
[57] Mather, *op. cit.*, pp. 177-81.
[58] L. S. Mercier, *Tableau de Paris* (12 vols. Amsterdam, 1783), VI, 22-5.

magistrates, and generally set their soldiers, who had grievances of their own, an example of disobedience which they were not slow to emulate.

In February, 1789, even before the Revolution had started, Necker advised the King that the army was already too disaffected to be relied on as an instrument for suppressing civil disorder; and from now on it was mainly foreign levies or troops from distant provinces that were brought to Versailles to defend the Court, and later to overawe the capital. In Paris, the Gardes Françaises were loyal enough to shoot down the Réveillon rioters in April; but, by June, they were parading to shouts of *Vive le tiers état!*,and in July they played a crucial part in the capture of the Bastille.[59] After this, a new national army emerged, which proclaimed its allegiance to the nation and the new revolutionary authorites; but it was kept out of Paris, whose defense was entrusted to the National Guard. The Guard, at first solidly *bourgeois,* was effective, as we have seen, in suppressing the demonstration of July 1791; but it gradually became the instrument of the sans-culottes as much of the Assembly; and it was only when the army was called in again, in May 1795, that the long series of popular disturbances that had marked the whole course of the Revolution in Paris was brought to a close.

In 1830 and 1848, the defection of the armed forces was once more decisive in assuring the defeat of the royal government and the success of the revolutionary challenge. Yet the pattern was not the same as that of 1789. The outbreak of 1830 was a short-lived affair and, after three days' street-fighting, Charles X was driven out and Louis Philippe was installed for the next eighteen years. In February 1848, it was the defection of the National Guard in Paris, even more than that of the army (which was passive rather than openly rebellious), that drove Louis Philippe, in his turn, into exile. This time, the popular forces that challenged the authority of the new revolutionary government and Assembly were far stronger and more efficiently organized than they had been in 1789. Yet they were brought to heel not after six years but after a mere four months. This was due partly to the building of railways, which made it possible to summon troops more quickly to the capital; and it was due, perhaps even more, to the loyalty of the bulk of the National Guard and the Mobile Guards, who were the real victors of the June insurrection.

It would seem, then, to be almost a truism that the key factor in determining the outcome of popular rebellion and disturbance is the loyalty or disaffection of the armed forces at the government's disposal. "It is obvious," writes Le Bon, "that revolutions have never taken place, and will never take place, save with the aid of an important faction of the army,"[60] and Professor Crane Brinton is saying much the same when he writes "that it is almost safe to say that no government is likely to be overthrown until it loses the ability to make adequate use of its military and police powers."[61] Such assertions are true enough as far as they go; yet they are not the whole truth and they even tend, when presented in such baldly military terms, to beg the further and more important question of why the army refuses to obey or why the government loses control of its means of defense. Essentially, this is a social and political rather than a military question. For if magistrates condone riots or soldiers fraternize with or refuse to fire on rebels, it is because the ties of class or of political

[59] See my chapter on "The Outbreak of the French Revolution," shortly to appear in *The New Cambridge Modern History,* vol. VIII.

[60] G. Le Bon, *The Psychology of Revolution* (New York, 1913), p. 49; cited by N. Smelser, *Theory of Collective Behavior* (London, 1962), p. 372.

[61] Crane Brinton, *The Anatomy of Revolution* (New York 1960), pp. 266-7.

affiliation are at that moment stronger than allegiance to the established order or government.

We have already seen evidence of this in the actions of the French aristocratic officers in 1788 and of their troops in the following year; and, in February 1848, the National Guard that deserted Louis Philippe clearly showed—in fact, they said so in so many words—that they had, like their fellow tradesmen out of uniform, become infected by the prevailing middle-class demand for political reform. But this could not in itself assure the success of the February revolution: that depended not only on the National Guard but on its cooperation with the middle-class radical journalists and the very different social elements that composed the revolutionary crowd. For social and political reasons, the alliance was short-lived, and in June the popular insurrection failed because it found little or no support among its allies of February. Similarly, in 1789, the great insurrections and popular upheavals of the day were carried through as a joint operation of the sans-culottes—the main elements composing the revolutionary crowd—and a varying combination of middle-class, and even liberal-aristocratic, groups. When this combination of social forces broke down, as it finally broke down in the spring of 1795, the Parisian common people stood no more chance of winning victories by street demonstrations and riots than the small peasants and petty consumers of 1775.

In England, as we have seen, such victories were far less frequent than in France; and England probably stood near to revolution only in 1831, when Irish unrest, rural disturbance, and popular and middle-class excitement over the first Reform Bill combined to bring the country to the brink of civil war. This was not because Methodism or any other religious movement turned men away from earthly strife and thus averted a revolution; but, until the 1840's at least, no insurrectionary movement of the English "lower orders," whether of town or countryside, stood any chance of success without the support of some combination of other social groups. And in England this was rarely forthcoming; when it was, it was too short-lived to yield more than limited results. In the Wilkite movement of the 1760's and 1770's, popular radicalism won some victories; but this was only so as long as the agitation of the crowd in the streets was supported by that of Middlesex freeholders and London craftsmen, shopkeepers, and merchants. Similarly, in the Gordon Riots the crowd could hold the streets just as long as the City magistrates and householders condoned their activities; but once this sanction was withdrawn, the movement had no future. In Birmingham, in 1791, it is doubtful if the "Church and King" crowd would have succeeded in wrecking Priestley's house and driving him out of town without the active or tacit approval of a number of its magistrates. The "daughters of Rebecca" owed their success not to any defection of the military, which was eventually mobilized in sufficient numbers to suppress them, but to the support they enjoyed among the whole farming population—and even, in part, to the willingness of the government to remove the main abuses which had prompted them to riot. The Chartists failed in their immediate aims because their numbers, though considerable, were insufficient to compensate for their lack of middle-class support; and yet, in the long run, most of their Six Points were realized precisely because that support, refused in the 1840's, was forthcoming later.

But, finally, should we judge the crowd's importance in history purely in terms of its record of success or failure? It is indisputable that its impact on events was far more marked in some cases than in others. In this sense, the revolutionary crowds of 1789 and 1848, in respect both of their maturity and their achievement, may justly claim a precedence over those engaged in the more primitive, and often seemingly futile, pursuits of destroying houses in the name of "Church and King," of wrecking toll gates and machinery, or of imposing short-lived price controls in food riots. Such distinctions are valid enough; yet there is a broader sense in which the pre- industrial crowd, irrespective of its immediate failures or successes, marks an important stage in the historical process. As society has changed, so the crowd has changed with it and, in changing, has left its legacy to succeeding generations. As the sans-culotte, small freeholder, and cottager have given way to the factory worker and farm laborer, so the machine wrecker, rick burner, and "Church and King" rioter have given way to the trade unionist, labor militant, and organized consumer of the new industrial society. New wine has certainly on occasion been poured into old bottles; but, in general, it is perhaps not unreasonable to see these earlier, immature, and often crude, trials of strength, even when doomed to failure, as the forerunners of later movements whose results and successes have been both significant and enduring.

## TO DEFINE POPULISM: SYMPOSIUM

**Peter Worsley, Ghiţa Ionescu, Maurice Cranston**

### III. Towards a Definition

*Peter Worsley* remarked that from the way the discussion had progressed one might think that populism was the biggest growth industry. It led everywhere. It was an exploding universe and it would continue to explode sideways unless the problem of conceptualization was tackled. He thought that it was perfectly legitimate to define populism in the broadest terms. But although broad the definition should be precise. Massness, radicalism, orientation to dramatic change, particularly the advent of capitalism, location among the small people, the participatory concept, all these were elements which could be utilized. But it was very difficult with the broad, latitudinarian definition to draw any kind of boundary.

The main division of thought seemed to him to be as follows. First there was the difference between those who emphasized that populism was a strand within socialism and those who would extend the label to cover many kinds of radicalism, including right wing forms of radicalism—Poujadism, Nazism, McCarthyism—and the North-American phenomenon of the entrepreneurial, capitalist farming operation. A second difference arose between those who insisted on the global *Weltanschauung* characteristic of populist ideology and those who saw it as a hotchpotch of synthetic and badly assimilated elements. There was a further division of opinion and analysis between those who would locate populism or identify it specifically as a peasant or rural phenomenon and those who would extend it to embrace various forms of non-rural society.

There were five common elements for which he sensed some general support. There was the reaction to capitalism. Then there was the reaction to externality. There was also massness, at least in aspiration if not in realization. Fourthly there was what was described as the Janus syndrome: populism looked back in order to look forward. Finally it was ideology elaborated usually by the intelligentsia and other elements for or on behalf of the masses.

*Ghiţa Ionescu* was still not sure, at the end of the conference, whether a definition would emerge from it. As the *rapporteur* he thought that a definition was not essential. The discussion, like the play, had been the thing. And in any case, provided an agreement could be broadly reached on what seemed to him to have been the six issues most debated by the conference, a broad and preferably short definition could still be proposed by someone.

One controversial issue was whether populism was primarily an ideology (or ideologies), or a movement (or movements). Personally from what he had heard during these forty-eight hours he thought that the majority was inclined to lean towards the ideological aspect.

But some of the speakers seemed to have meant by this, and that was a second issue, that populism was a sort of recurring mentality, appearing in different historical and geographic contexts as the result of a special social situation, for instance the situation of change faced by a society in which, as Touraine described it, the middle social factors were either missing or too weak.

Thirdly, the element of political persecution-mania was more acute in the political psychology of populism than in many other political psychologies. The political psychology of populism was imbued with the feeling that identifiable or unidentifiable conspiracies were at work, deliberately and tenaciously, against the "people." The basic attitude was one of defence against the unknown outside forces.

As such populism was characterized by a peculiar negativism. Many speakers had stressed that it was *anti*–: anti-capitalistic, anti-urban, as well as xenophobic and very often anti-semitic. It carried with it great doses of blind hatred.

In contrast, and this was the fifth point, it seemed to him that one of the large areas of agreement of the conference was the fact that populism worshipped the people. But which "people"? Surely not the proud *demos* of the Greeks or anything like the *Herrenvolk.* The people the populists worshipped were the meek and the miserable, and the populists worshipped them because they were miserable and because they were persecuted by the conspirators. The fact that they were more often than not embodied in the peasantry was because the peasants were and are, in any underdeveloped societies, the most miserable of the lot—and the more miserable they were the more worshipped should they be.

Finally this recurring mentality disappeared usually by absorption into stronger ideologies or movements. But here he disagreed with those who thought that it could lead only to, or was merely a phase of, socialism. There were three possibilities. In some cases it could lead to socialism. In other cases it led to nationalism. And, as for instance in Eastern Europe at the beginning of the century, it led to peasantism. This third possibility should not be overlooked.

*Maurice Cranston* suggested an approach to the question of definiton more cautious and perhaps more cheerful than Ionescu's. Perhaps a clue could be got from Wittgenstein's later theory of meaning, where it was not so much a matter of looking for some kind of denominator or hard core of meaning, but looking for family resemblance where one gets things which seem to fall into families: *A* resembling *B* and *B* resembling *C,* but all three having nothing in common.

*John Saul* was uneasy about this concentration upon ideologies. It was something which he and others might feel was not legitimate. One of the things which had been raised very clearly was the way in which these ideologies could be used. In some movements there were "people" who really identified with the "people"; in other movements there were people who manipulated these ideas. If one concentrated upon the ideology without situating it, both in terms of the changing society and in terms of the political movements with which it was related, one would not be speaking about populism.

*Hugh Seton-Watson* thought that Ionescu's scheme was a good one to work on but the essence was the ideology: what were the essential features of the populist mentality and the populist ideology. It had to be assumed that it was a genuinely held ideology. Manipulation by others obviously was another dimension and one should keep it distinct.

He wanted to clear away a little dead wood and to single out a few elements which were *not* specific to populism. One was the fact of appealing to the transitional new urban poor. That was true of populism but was not specific to populism. Another point was the presence of the peasants. All revolutions included peasants. The fact that Mao, for instance, appealed to the peasants and used peasants had nothing to do with populism. The third point not specific to populism was the defence of the people against capitalism. Of course, the populists were anti-capitalists, but so were all forms of socialist parties in the early days of socialism, so were the Marxists in the later days and so were the communists in their still later days.

Continuing what Schapiro had said earlier, he thought that it would have been useful to distinguish between *elite* and *elitism*. The element of elite surely entered into populist movements. But the elite did not need to be elitist. The distinction between an elite playing a role and an elite having elitist aims was significant. The *Narodnaya Volya* was elitist in its methods, but not elitist in aim. The fascist parties, on the other hand, were all aiming at an elitist hierarchical society as the end as well as the means.

The last piece of dead wood he wanted to attack was the widespread misuse of the word populism itself in connection with governments in underdeveloped countries for which some respectable label was required. It seemed to him that possibly this had come from use by American social scientists studying underdeveloped countries. They had taken a word from the American experience, derived from an understanding, possibly imperfect at that, of American populism with its peculiar characteristics. They had applied this word particularly to what they found in Africa—something which he thought should more honestly be described as authoritarian nationalist despotism.

*Werner Klatt* thought that the difference between populism and peasantism which Ionescu had mentioned lay in the difference of leadership. In the peasant parties one found men who were actually peasants, or former peasants. The intellectuals who conceived the idea of populism were invariably urban intellectuals.

*F. Venturi* agreed with Seton-Watson that the uprooted peasants who came to the towns did not provide the natural normal basis of a populist movement. Proof could be given from Italy where for instance half of his own town, Turin, was formed of peasants from the south and yet no populist movement was emerging. But the history of Russia made one think that in its particular case the movement of the peasantry led to populism. The peasants not only brought to the urban environment the fact that they were uprooted, but also their own institutions.

*Donald MacRae* wanted to say a little about ideology which was relevant to what

Ionescu had said. His own view was that humanity, perhaps regrettably, had a very limited repertoire of elementary ideas, many of which were extremely old, archaic and primitive. The number of ideas, of themes or items which combined and recombined was limited. He would suggest that ideologies could be formed in the same way as a ballet, with dancers waiting in the wings and reappearing in different costumes, but in perpetual movement of some kind.

*Andrzej Walicki* wanted to propose, for the sake of the model, an ideal type of populism:

First, it was a peasantist oriented socialism, the characteristic feature of which was a combination of backward-looking Utopianism with modern socialism. It meant a combination of modern socialism with an idealization of pre-capitalist relations.

Secondly, it was characteristic of backward countries in confrontation with developed capitalistic countries. This point was very important and it was a bridge between Russian populism and populism in the countries of the third world.

The third point, bound up with the second, was that because populism emerged in backward countries in confrontation with developed capitalist states, the intelligentsia played a very large role in the leadership of the movement and in the formulation of its main ideas. The members of the intelligentsia, being the product of Westernization, felt themselves alienated and put forward the idea of returning to the people who had roots in the soil.

Fourthly, the last feature was the possibility of identifying capitalism with something coming from outside and hence the possibility of combining populist ideas with nationalism, with xenophobia and so on. In the final analysis he agreed with Ionescu that there were three ways out of populism: modern socialism, peasantism and nationalism.

*Donald MacRae* said that he wanted to go back to ideology as a defining point and go through some of the items which might help to bridge something which was genuinely bridgeable, and worth bridging, and that was the Russo-American gap on this point. One should take ideology as the reality and say that a movement is a populist one when the character of its existence, its acts and its propaganda contained a majority of the following elements:

1. The idealization of a *Volk,* and it had to be a particular one, not idealization of *the* people, but of *a* people.
2. Primitivism, meaning that the future was to be an improved archaic past.
3. Statism: the state was justified in its intervention if this was designed to restore society to health.
4. Although it was statist it was even more social: it stressed that society was more important and existed prior to the creation of the state and it was stronger than and embodied more values than the state. The state was the instrument of society.
5. It was personalist: it expressed a belief in man whole and pure.
6. Xenophobia.
7. Hatred of an advanced stage of the division of labour, of advanced social differentiation, occupational differentiation, or multiplication of social roles.
8. Anti-militarism, but not pacifism.
9. Preference for inflation, easy credit, currency reform, rather than economic planning—and against competition.

10. Belief in conspiracy. This went along with the xenophobia, but not all xenophobia was conspirational and not all conspiracy theories were xenophobic.
11. Apocalyptic dreams. These might involve the dreams of a particular populist redeemer, a particular kind of populist hero or a particular sort of Rousseau or "legislator."
12. Belief in spontaneity. The whole man was a spontaneous mass of untutored and immediate virtue.
13. An affiliation with religion. This applied more surely to the Russian than to the American type. The origin in one case was Orthodoxy and in the other American Protestantism.
14. Anti-elitist but inspired often by an elite, and prepared to use an elite in the destruction of an elitist situation.

*S. L. Andreski* thought that the contrast between American and Russian populism was striking. One emanated from the class concerned, the other was engineered by the intelligentsia. One defended the existing and high status of the farmers, while the other strove to improve the condition of the oppressed peasants. One showed a clear commitment to a clear form of political organization, the other vaguely wanted to help the people and to tell them what to do. He suggested that if there was to be a definition which included both, it should be a very general one, something like, "Any movement which strove towards the protection of the interests of the rural population," or something of that sort.

*Isaiah Berlin,* who was the chairman of the last session, proceeded to the final summing-up of the main points made during the discussion, seeking first the common points and then the variations.

"Supposing," he said, "we say that what is common to all populisms everywhere—this cannot be true, but let us try it on—is, first, a vague notion and vague name for it, which is intelligible to everybody here, the notion of *Gemeinschaft*—that is, that famous integral society which everybody talks about, some sort of coherent, integrated society, which is sometimes called *Das Volk*, which has roots in the past, either imaginary or real, which is bound by a sense of fraternity and by a desire for a certain kind of social equality and perhaps liberty—but of the two equality is probably nearer its heart than liberty—and which is opposed to competitive, atomized society, although in the American case it obviously believes in limited competition which is regulated in some so-called natural fashion as against all kinds of unnatural distortions of it."

It is broadly speaking apolitical: that is to say, it is not principally interested in political institutions, although it is prepared to use the state as an instrument for the purpose of producing its ends. But a state organization is not its aim and the state is not its ideal of human association. It believes in society rather than in the state. Moreover all these movements believe in some kind of moral regeneration. I am sure that this is common to them all.

In some sense they are dedicated to producing spontaneous, natural men who have in some way at some time become perverted by something. There must have been a spiritual fall somewhere. Either the fall is in the past or it is threatening—one of the two. Either innocence has been lost and some kind of perversion of men's nature has occurred, or enemies are breeding within or attacking from without. Who the enemies are, we do not need to specify. That will depend upon the specific situation.

The enemy may be capitalism, it may be foreign states which have forms of political, social or economic organization which threaten the spontaneous integral group and the sense of brotherhood which unites them. It still unites them, or once united them, so that one can now resurrect the unity from the past.

Populism certainly does not believe, so far as negative propositions are concerned, in the uniqueness of historical stages in the sense in which, say, most historicists believe that nothing from the past can ever be rescued: that what has happened once has happened once and for all, and, therefore, that there is no way of looking back to the past to try to salve its values. It may believe in the translation of these ancient values into contemporary terms, but it believes these values to be rooted somewhere in the past; they cannot be brand new. I do not think I know of any populism which assumes that man was born in a low undesirable state and that the golden age is somewhere in the future—a novel situation which has never shown any sign of existence in the past. Some degree of past directedness is essential to all populisms.

This seems to me to be one of the roots of American populism—it is one of the causes, for example, of the indignation say, in the relatively undeveloped Middle West, against all kinds of phenomena which its spokesmen regard as hostile—the excessive civilization of the East Coast, its centralized capitalism, Wall Street, the cross of gold, frivolous, polite, smooth forms of insincere behaviour on the part of Harvard or Yale university professors, or smooth members of the State Department, contrasted with the free, spontaneous, natural behaviour of uncorrupted men, cracker-barrel philosophers in the village drug store, from whom simple wisdom flows, uncorrupted by the sophistication of the Eastern cities, the result of some kind of degeneration of a political or of some other kind. This is common to all the populisms: that is, the central belief in an ideal, unbroken man, either in the present or in the past, an ideal type towards which men naturally tend, when no one oppresses or deceives them.

Having established all this very tentatively as common to all these various forms of populism, let me add this. One must again return to the notion of the people. Who the people is will probably vary from place to place. On the whole, it tends to be, as somebody said quite correctly, those who have been left out. It is the have-nots, in some sense. It is peasants in Russia because they are the obvious majority of the deprived: but it might be any group of persons with whom you identify the true people and you identify the true people with them, because the ideology of populism itself springs from the discontented people who feel that they somehow represent the majority of the nation which has been done down by some minority or other. Populism cannot be a consciously minority movement. Whether falsely or truly, it stands for the majority of men, the majority of men who have somehow been damaged.

By whom have they been damaged? They have been damaged by an elite, either economic, political or racial, some kind of secret or open enemy—capitalists, Jews, bureaucrats, etc. Whoever the enemy is, foreign or native, ethnic or social, does not much matter.

One more thing can be said to be true of all populisms. That is, that in some sense it would be true to say that it occurs in societies standing on the edge of modernization—that is to say, threatened by it, or hoping for it; it does not matter which, but in either case uneasily aware of the fact that they cannot stand still; that they will have to take steps towards meeting either the challenge or the danger of modernization, whether at home, on the part of classes or groups in their own country who are pushing towards it, or on the part of persons outside it, whose economic and social development is of such a kind as to threaten them if they do not in some way catch up or create some kind of walls with which to resist them. This seems true of all the varieties of populism.

Then we come to the variations. For example, there is on the one hand the root of socialism and on the other hand the root of peasantism. These are alternative roots, and therefore, alternative species of the same thing. Again, you could probably say that there are certain other variants—for example, elitism. Some forms of populism believe in using elites for the purpose of a non-elitist society and some object to it on the ground that even using elitism as a means leads to elitism in the end.

Some populists believed in an elite, some did not; some believed in it as an instrument, a means to the end, so that to a large extent this was a tactical difference and not a real one. Of course, all these movements and ideologies wished to produce a fraternal, equal society, and not a hierarchical or deferential one. Therefore they must be distinguished from other forms of what might be called romantic archaism or romantic nostalgia for a glorious golden past. There are dreams of a golden past in which men are anything but socially equal or self governed.

Now as to religion. Affiliation to a religion is, I think, a specific property of perhaps some streams of Russian populism—but populism obviously need not be religious. American populism has surely been tinged with Protestantism. But I daresay that if you found some bone dry atheists to be members of a populist movement you would not exclude them on the ground that religious faith was at the heart of such an outlook, that it was at the very least a secularized form of an essentially religious movement.

Then there is the apocalyptic dream and the hero: yes, all populisms, it seems to me, are voluntaristic and anti-necessitarian. They do not accept an inevitable pattern of history. They believe that it is possible by means of a spontaneous gathering of the wills of the good to leap into the new society and create these new men. They all believe this. They do not believe in a historicist time table. They do not believe in necessary stages of historical development which causes this to grow from that, and that to grow inexorably from something else—a predictable ascent up a tremendous historical ladder, the rungs of which are unalterable, which makes it Utopian or impossible to do certain things until the uniquely appropriate stage is duly and inevitably reached. This, after all, is one of the chief differences between every form of Russian populism and every form of Russian social democracy and Russian Marxism.

There is one further point: false populisms. We need not spend too much time on this because I think that on this we have reached general agreement. False populism is the employment of populist ideas for ends other than those which the populists desired. That is to say, their employment by Bonapartists or McCarthyites, or the "Friends of the Russian People," or fascists and so on. This is simply the mobilization of certain popular sentiments—say hostility to capitalism or to foreigners or Jews or hatred of economic organization or of the market society, or of anything you like, for undemocratic ends. The mobilized feeling can be genuine. This pseudo-populism does not necessarily involve cynical employment of tactics of a "double-think" kind. It is clear that some of the demagogues of this type—Poujadists, Greenshirts, social creditors and the like—did in fact sympathize with some populist sentiments, but employed them for the purpose of creating some kind of elitist or socially or racially unequal regime, something totally incompatible with the fundamental faith—if not with fraternity then, at any rate, the passionate egalitarianism—of the real populist movements. That is enough to distinguish, for example, Bonapartism or Greek tyrannies, which were in a certain sense also revolts against the aristocracy, against traditionalism, against hierarchical and deferential systems, from populism proper. This probably applies equally to modern "tyrannoi" like Nasser, or Nkrumah, or Ayub Khan.

It is reasonable to say that, historically speaking, populism like all ideologies is created by ideologists. Ideologists are, on the whole, educated or half educated persons, and educated and half educated persons, particularly in Russia, tended to turn into an intelligentsia for certain historical reasons.

One of the motives of most populist movements is the desire on the part of the creators of populism itself to be re-integrated into the general mass of the people from which they have become divided by their education, by their social position or by their origins.

Therefore, all populisms—I offer this as a general proposition about populism—distinguish between the alienated good and the alienated bad: the alienated good are persons who have become alienated as a result of historical circumstances, but are in a state of contrition. That is to say, they are repentant, they wish to repay their debt to society and re-integrate themselves into the mass of the people. They wonder, like Chernyshevsky, whether they sufficiently express the will of the people because they feel that they are not members of the people. They live at a distance from the masses and, therefore, they are always worried, honourably worried, about whether they are sufficiently penetrated by the spirit with which they wish to be at one.

This is the topic of the debate by Russian populists: do we "go to the people" to tell them what to do, or to learn this from them? What right have we to tell the people what to want? The only populists completely outside this are those who like Tkachov, expressed the greatest possible contempt for the masses and wished to save them against their will; one day no doubt the people will be wise and rational, but we must not listen to what the peasants—stupid, reactionary, dull—say today. This, however, was, before Lenin, a comparatively marginal case.

This kind of populist who has a ferocious contempt for his clients, the kind of doctor who has profound contempt for the character of the patient whom he is going to cure by violent means which the patient will certainly resist, but which will have to be applied to him in some very coercive fashion, is on the whole ideologically nearer to an elitist, fascist, communist, etc. ideology, than he is to what might be called the centre core of populism. But such theorists exist. They exist and they have to be accommodated somewhere on our map. For Lenin, Tkachov was a populist, and his authoritarianism is in part derived from that tradition.

There is one specific populist attribute which may or may not be universal—of that I am not sure. That is the advocacy of a social and economic programme for the single purpose of avoiding the horrors of industrialization and capitalism; it does not entail a passion for integralism, nor the visionary new-mediaevalism of William Morris, it has nothing to do with Morris dancing, or arts and crafts or Ghandi's spinning wheel, or a return to the Middle Ages; it is simply a sober theory of how we are to avoid the horrors of what is happening in the Western world. This is the kind of populism which was professed by sober statisticians and economists towards the end of the 19th century in Russia, who were not necessarily partisans of some kind of *Gemeinschaft*. This was a perfectly rational social doctrine, founded, or at least aspiring to rest, on sober calculation and estimate of the facts: simply a social policy coexisting with other social policies, something which, I should have thought, was probably most prevalent in backward countries as Russia was in the 19th century, or the Balkans, not therefore equally prevalent in the United States and, therefore, representing a particular attribute of a particular populism at a particular time in a particular place.

After further discussion the conference agreed that a short formulation proposed by G. Hall was probably the best general definition of the populist movements. It said:

Populist movements are movements aimed at power for the benefit of the people as a whole which result from the reaction of those, usually intellectuals, alienated from the existing power structure, to the stresses of rapid economic, social, cultural or political change. These movements are characterized by a belief in a return to, or adaptation of, more simple and traditional forms and values emanating from the people, particularly the more archaic sections of the people who are taken to be the repository of virtue.

But everyone also agreed that the subject was much too vast not merely to be contained in one definition, but to be exhausted in one discussion.

# 14 / The Origins of the French Revolution: Three Recent Views

For the French their Revolution is not just a historical episode but a living tradition. It was refought during the revolutions of 1830, 1848, and by the Commune of 1870. And it has been reinvoked during national crises, in political programs, and in public oratory ever since. It is still possible to say that within broad limits, a Frenchman's politics are reflected in his attitude toward the Revolution. If he is of the extreme right he regards it as a calamity or at least unnecessary; if he is of the extreme left he believes it will only be fully realized in a socialist state. In between, moderates, according to their political shading, believe that the Revolution was consummated to a greater or lesser degree during the Third Republic. Under such circumstances, it is not to be expected that historians have remained free from bias in their presentations of the Revolution. The situation has been well described by George Rudé, who has observed:

No period of history has so frequently been rewritten in the light of current preoccupations or been such a repeated battle-ground of conflicting ideologies as the French Revolution. Ever since Edmund Burke, 170 years ago, dipped his pen in vitriol to blast the Revolution in its infancy, generation after generation of Frenchmen, with occasional support from other countries, have joined in the fray and done their bit to disprove the validity of Ranke's contention that history is "what actually happened." The main events of the Revolution—the meetings of the Notables and of the States General, the Constitution of 1791, the fall of the monarchy, the execution of Robespierre, and the rise of Napoleon—have, it is true, been accepted as facts by even the most incredulous and disputatious; but precious little else. What sort of Revolution was it—one of "poverty" or "prosperity"? a *bourgeois* revolution that overthrew feudalism? a national struggle for liberty, democracy, or "eternal Justice"? or, again, a criminal conspiracy against the old social order? What did it achieve? What was its ultimate significance? What sort of men were its leaders, its supporters and its victims? What part was played in it by aristocracy, middle classes, peasants, urban *sans-culottes?* When did it begin? When did it end? What were its most significant landmarks and turning-points? Was there one single French Revolution or were there several? Questions such as these have been asked and variously answered by succeeding generations and "schools" of historians.[1]

The foregoing should indicate the difficulty of surveying in a brief introduction the extensive historiography of the French Revolution.[2] It might be noted here, however,

---

[1] G. Rudé, *Interpretations of the French Revolution* (London: The Historical Association and Routledge and Kegan Paul, 1961), p. 3.
[2] The most up-to-date survey and a useful one is Rudé, *op. cit.* Paul Farmer, *France Reviews Its Revolutionary Origins* (New York: Columbia University Press, 1944), is a more detailed study, particularly of writing done during the Third Republic.

that later histories, with some notable exceptions, have been less influenced by ideology and political circumstances than the classic histories of such nineteenth-century authors as de Tocqueville, Michelet, or Taine. A new era of greater objectivity and more critical scholarship begins with Alphonse Aulard (1849-1928)[3] and his pupil Albert Mathiez (1874-1932),[4] although their bitter quarrel over who was the hero of the Revolution, Danton, or Robespierre, raised nagging doubts as to whether ideological ghosts could be laid low. Of their successor at the Sorbonne, Georges Lefebvre (1874-1959),[5] it has been said, "His writings have been as little subject to controversy as any on the French Revolution can be, and have been generally praised by all schools of thought on the subject."[6]

Schools and controversy continue, but the trend has been to economic and social history and away from political history, which, when it interpreted the Revolution in terms of the aims of political groups or their leaders, provoked the greater controversies. Following the pioneering work of Mathiez and Lefebvre, the present generation of historians of the French Revolution have been more concerned with the role played not by political leaders, but by the different social classes, particularly the long-neglected peasants and urban proletariat, and with the economic pressures which moved them.

The first two selections that follow illustrate this concern. In the first, Albert Soboul, author of a magisterial study of the Parisian *sans-culottes*,[7] analyzes the class structure, the antagonisms between and within classes, and the role of classes before and during the Revolution. In the second, Ernest Labrousse, author of two definitive works on the French economy in the eighteenth century,[8] sees as the primary cause of the outbreak of the Revolution a combination of fiscal policies and an economic crisis which affected all classes of the Third Estate. In the third selection, Jacques Godechot departs from economic and social history to present a brief sketch of a new synthesis which sees the French Revolution as part of a "Revolution of the Western World" lasting from 1763 to 1848.[9]

---

[3] Major works: *Histoire politique de la Révolution Française*, 4 vols. (1901); English trans., *The French Revolution, A Political History* (1910); *Études et leçons sur la Révolution Française*, 9 vols. (1901-1929).

[4] Major works: *La Révolution Française* 3 vols. (1922-1927), English trans., *The French Revolution* (1928); *Autour de Robespierre* (1925), English trans., *The Fall of Robespierre and Other Essays* (1927); *La Vie chère et le mouvement social sous la terreur* (1927).

[5] Major works: *La Révolution Française* (1951); English trans., *The French Revolution*, Vol. I (1962); *Quatre-vingt-neuf* (1939), English trans., *The Coming of the French Revolution* (1947); *Les Paysans du Nord pendant la Révolution Française*, 2 vols. (1924).

[6] R. R. Palmer in Preface to Georges Lefebvre, *The Coming of the French Revolution*, R. R. Palmer (trans.), (Princeton, N. J.: Princeton University Press, 1947), p. vi.

[7] *Les Sans-culottes parisiens en l'An II; mouvement populaire et gouvernement révolutionnaire, 2 Juin 1793-9 thermidor An II* (1958).

[8] *Esquisse du mouvement des prix et des revenus en France au XVIIIᵉ siécle*, 2 vols. (1933); *La Crise de l'économie française á la fin de l'ancien régime et au début de la Révolution* (1944).

[9] A full expression of this synthesis is found in R. R. Palmer, *The Age of the Democratic Revolution. A Political History of Europe and America, 1760-1800* (1959). Palmer and Godechot have cooperated in introducing the concept of an "Atlantic Community" existing in the eighteenth and nineteenth centuries. See *Relazione del X Congresso Internazionale di Scienze Storiche*, Vol. V. pp. 173-239.

# CLASSES AND CLASS STRUGGLES DURING THE FRENCH REVOLUTION

## Albert Soboul

The French Revolution and the English revolutions of the 17th century were the culmination of a long economic and social evolution that made the bourgeoisie the mistress of the world.

This truth, which may pass for a commonplace today, had been proclaimed by the most conscious theoreticians of the bourgeoisie ever since the 19th century. Guizot proved that the characteristic feature of the French, as of English, society, consisted essentially in the fact that between the people and the aristocracy there was a strong bourgeois class which had slowly defined the ideology and then created the leaders of a new society, of which 1789 was the consecration.[1] Tocqueville spoke with "a sort of religious terror" "of this irresistible revolution which has been on the march for so many centuries over every obstacle, and that we still see today advancing in the midst of the ruins it has made."[2] Taine sketched the slow climb of the bourgeoisie in the social scale, at the end of which it could no longer endure inequality.[3] But for all their assurance that the birth and progress of the bourgeoisie had for their ultimate cause the appearance and development of personal wealth, first of commercial and then industrial enterprises, these historians hardly undertook a precise study of the economic origins of the Revolution or of the social classes that had made it.

Jaurès was the first, in his *Histoire socialiste*, to restore to the history of the Revolution its economic and social base, in a vast fresco swept away by eloquence. It still remains a valid monument.[4] It may be that Jaurès' work sins by being schematic. In it the Revolution unfolds all in one piece; its cause was the economic and intellectual power of the bourgeoisie come of age; its result was to enshrine this power in the law. Sagnac, and later Mathiez, went further and brought out the aristocratic reaction which culminated in 1787-88 in what Mathiez designates as "the revolt of the nobility":[5] an expression for their fanatical opposition to any attempt at reform, and for their obstinate refusal to share their pre-eminence with the upper bourgeoisie. Thus was explained the violent nature of the French Revolution, in which the rise of the bourgeoisie was the result, not of gradual evolution, but of a sudden qualitative change.

But the Revolution was not the work of the bourgeoisie alone, even though it alone profited by it. Mathiez, following Jaurès, insists on the rapid disintegration of the

---

[1] *Cf.* in the *Histoire de la Révolution d'Angleterre* the chapter entitled "How the Revolutions of 1648 and 1789 Completed the Work of the Past." See too the preface of 1885 to the *Histoire de la civilisation en France.*

[2] *De la démocratie en Amérique* (1836-1839).

[3] *Cf.* Ch. 3, Book IV, in *Origines de la France contemporaine*, Vol. I, *L'Ancien Régime* (1875).

[4] J. Jaurès, *Histoire socialiste*, Vols. I-IV (1901-1904).

[5] Ph. Sagnac, *La Révolution, 1789-1792* (1929), Vol. I of *Histoire de France Contemporaine*, ed. by Lavisse; A. Mathiez, *La Révolution française* (1922), Vol. I, Ch. 2, "*La revolte nobiliaire.*"

Third Estate and the antagonisms which soon showed up between the various sections of the bourgeoisie and the popular classes; he takes into account the complexity of revolutionary history and the succession of its stages. Since France too at the end of the 18th century was still essentially rural, Georges Lefebvre turned from the Parisian scene and the big cities, which had almost exclusively occupied the attention of historians up to his time, and plunged into the study of peasantry.[6] Before him, peasant action had been thought of as a repercussion of urban movements, as something essentially directed, in accord with the bourgeoisie, against feudalism and the royal power. Georges Lefebvre, on the basis of precise social analyses, showed that within the framework of the bourgeois Revolution there developed a peasant trend with its own autonomous origin, procedures, crises and tendencies.

Georges Lefebvre's work has the value of a proof and an example. Apart from the field in which he broke fresh ground, the social history of the Revolution is still to be written. It is a significant fact that although the bourgeoisie has ruled uncontested for 150 years we have no history of the French bourgeoisie under the Revolution. Apart from some essays, which deal more with ways of thinking than with economic power, and some monographs devoted to a region or a city, a family or a category, we must admit that in this field studies of the Revolution are in a backward state.[7] To be sure we have descriptions of "good society,"[8] but they give us only a picture of customs or a sketch of ideas, whereas what should be made clear are productive relations, revenues and resources. Nor do we have a history of the nobility during the Revolution[9] any more than we do for the bourgeoisie, and still less, of course, one of the popular classes.[10]

The following pages do not pretend, even for a limited sector, to take up this indispensable study; they aim merely at sketching, beyond the basic antagonism of the society of the ancien regime, the complex complementary social antagonisms, which in the last analysis explain the evolution of the class struggles. Not only did the Revolution bring the bourgeoisie to power; in addition, without speaking of the aristocracy, it hastened the evolution, sometimes the destruction, of several categories of the old Third Estate. It permitted the flowering of the bourgeois society which had been in embryo so long.

*I*

The social structure at the end of the 18th century was still strongly marked by the

---

[6] The essential works remain: *Les Paysans du Nord pendant la Révolution française* (1924), *Questions agraires au temps de la Terreur* (1932), *La Grande Peur de 1789* (1932).

[7] Merely as examples: B. Groethuysen, *Origines de l'esprit bourgeois en France* (1927); F. Mireur, *Le Tiers État à Draguignan* (1911); Ch. Pouthas, *Une Famille de bourgeoisie française de Louis XIV à Napoleon* (1931); and six studies relating to the French bourgeoisie in *Assemblée générale de la Commission Centrale et des Comités Départementaux d'histoire économique de la Révolution française* (1942).

[8] L. Ducros, *La Société française au XVIII^e siècle, d'après les mémoires et les correspondances du temps* (1922).

[9] Some indications of the researches to be undertaken will be found in M. Bloch, "Sur le Passé de la noblesse française; quelques jalons de recherche," in *Annales d'Histoire Économique et Sociale,* 1936, Vol. VIII, p. 366.

[10] *Cf.* H. Sée, "Les classes ouvrières et la question sociale à la veille de la Révolution," in *Annales Révolutionnaires,* 1922, Vol. XIV, p. 373.

pre-eminence of the aristocracy, a survival of the days when land, being the only form of wealth, gave its owners every right over those who worked it. Nevertheless, a long evolution had increased the power of personal property, and of the bourgeoisie that held it. Thus faced each other two systems of production and two classes. But history had introduced differentiations into each of them.

The power of the aristocracy was based on landed property and the exercise of the seigneurial powers attached to the land. The economic evolution which brought personal wealth to the forefront, the rise in prices and the corresponding fall in feudal dues, all had produced within the solid ranks of the aristocracy an extreme inequality of fortune and a great diversity in conditions of existence. Above all, and this was the most important element of differentiation, a considerable portion of the landed aristocracy no longer disdained the revenues derived from capitalist enterprise, whether agricultural or industrial. In this way they came closer to the bourgeoisie.

It is obvious today that the French bourgeoisie led the Revolution. The bourgeoisie did not constitute a homogeneous element within the society of the 18th century. Sections of it were integrated into the social economic structure of the ancien régime, and were to disappear with it. Others were the source of the new forms of capitalist production; their development was blocked by the traditional structure of society.

In the first category were commoners who shared in the privileges of the land-holding aristocracy or were part of the apparatus of the state; holders of office which they had bought; *fermiers généraux* [tax-farmers] and stockholders in the priviledged financial companies, "a hybrid social force at the junction of the ancient regime and the new capitalism," according to Jaurès.[11] But part of the capital of the *fermiers généraux* was invested in industrial enterprises. The second category consisted of the commercial and industrial bourgeoisie which was suffocating in the archaic framework of the economy.

The initiators of the new forms of production and exchange, the shipowners, merchants and manufacturers, were increasingly impatient with the impediments a still semi-feudal society placed in the way of their capitalist enterprises. Their importance at the end of the 18th century should not be exaggerated. Capitalism was still essentially commercial. But in the second half of the century great industrial enterprises in the modern sense appear in metallurgy, textiles and chemicals.

The spectacle of this economic activity gave the bourgeoisie an awareness of their class. Sieyès, in his famous pamphlet, defines the Third Estate by the *private* work and the *public* functions it performs. It is all the nation; the nobility can not be part of it, for it consumes "the better part of the product, without having had any share in its creation."[12]

Barnave was much more penetrating. In his *Introduction à la Révolution française*,[13] he asserts that property "influences" institutions, and observes that the institutions created by the landed aristocracy impede and retard the advent of the industrial era. He states that a new distribution of wealth produces a new distribution of power. Just as the possession of lands raised up the aristocracy, so industrial property raises up the power of the people." (Note in passing how the 18th century

---

[11] *Histoire socialiste*, Vol. I, p. 40.
[12] *Qu'est-ce que le Tiers Etat?* (1888), critical edition with an introduction by Edme. Champion, p. 31.
[13] This work was published only in 1843 by Bérenger de la Drome, in Vol. I of Barnave's *Oeuvres*. Jaurès disserts at length on this work in his *Histoire socialiste*, Vol. I, p. 98.

bourgeoisie, like any genuine revolutionary class identifies itself with the nation: Barnave says the *people,* where we mean the *bourgeoisie).* Barnave sharply affirms the antagonism of land and personal property, and of the classes based on them.

The commercial and industrial bourgeoisie, therefore, had a keen sense of economic evolution and of the revolutionary force it represented.

At the end of the 18th century, the mass that works with its hands and produces was designated by the propertied, the aristocrats or the upper bourgeoisie, by the rather disdainful title of *people.* Actually, from those that made up the middle bourgeoisie to the proletariat, to use present-day terms, there were were many nuances and antagonisms. The artisans were linked to the lower classes by their conditions of life and often by their poverty, but nonetheless had their shop, their bit of equipment and the aspect of independent producers. Having journeymen and apprentices below them heightened their bourgeois mentality. But their attachment to the system of petty production and direct sale set them hopelessly at odds with the industrial bourgeoisie. Hence the absence of a definite social ideal among these artisans and shopkeepers. They were to make up the bulk of the sans-culotte movement and to them the bourgeois Revolution was to owe its success.

The journeymen and proletarians (to the extent to which there was a large-scale capitalistic industry) had no class spirit. They were scattered in many small workshops; they were not specialized because of the still limited development of technology, nor concentrated in large factories or industrial districts, and often not too clearly set off from the peasantry. Neither workers nor artisans were able to conceive effective remedies for their wretchedness.

Only the bourgeoisie, by reason of its economic position and its intellectual power, had a coherent program, and it alone was ready to take the lead in the revolutionary action.

The peasant world was at once kept together and torn apart by the same unity and the same contradictions. All the peasantry was under the heavy burden of seigneurial rights, ecclesiastical tithes and royal taxes; that alone was enough to unite it against the feudal aristocracy and the monarchy of the ancien régime. But the shock given to traditional society by the attack of the bourgeoisie was required before the peasantry rushed into the assault. Once the movement had been unleashed, they followed their own aims, which were not always those of the bourgeoisie.

The capitalist movement which renovated industrial production also tended to transform the rural districts, bringing into them elements of differentiation and antagonism. Ever since the middle of the century (and the development of the physiocratic school had been the clear sign of the fact) the application of capital and its characteristic methods to agricultural production, with a view to scientific and intensive cultivation, had obvious repercussions on the state of the peasants in the regions of large-scale farming. At the end of the ancien régime a new class of big farmers, capitalists of agricultural exploitation, developed on a wide scale. In their hands was concentrated more and more the exploitation of the land, if not yet its ownership, while an increased mass of production transformed the traditional market of agricultural products. The traditional antagonism between the peasantry and the landed aristocracy was reinforced in the regions of large-scale farming by the antagonism between agricultural capitalism and a more and more proletarianized peasantry. Lacking land, and deprived of their collective rights as private property and large-scale capitalist farming took hold, the peasants swelled the ranks of a poverty-stricken and unstable rural proletariat, and were as ready to rise against the big farms as against the chateaux.

These conditions of course should not be generalized so as to apply to all France. On the eve of the Revolution, the largest part of the country remained the scene of the traditional petty cultivation. But here too elements of dissociation were at work, the source of future antagonisms. Inequality had come into the rural community, once unified by seigneurial domination. Collective ownership and farming of the common lands, and collective restrictions on private property (prohibition of enclosure, compulsory rotation), customary rights in the fields (common pasture, gleaning and straw) and the woods, all constituted, up to the middle of the 18th century, solid economic bases of the rural community, and cemented its social unity. Even though various levels of life coexisted there, the seigneurial regime and feudal rights gave rise to the basic antagonism of rural France under the ancien régime, that between the rural community and the land-holding aristocracy. In the second half of the 18th century economic evolution brings to the fore in the regions of small-scale farming the class of working proprietors, the "village cocks" on whom day-laborers and small peasants depend for their work, and who take over local administration. They were a prosperous peasantry, a rural bourgeoisie, different from the class of capitalist farmers but already producing for the market to a certain extent, and ready to adopt the new agriculture.

This prosperous peasantry is against the rural community almost as much as it is against the feudal aristocracy, for it aims to free property from all collective and seigneurial rights.[14]

Thus the interplay of social antagonisms in the rural areas became complex and diversified. It could already be seen that the basic conflicts between the peasantry and the landed aristocracy would be supplemented by the latent antagonism between owner peasants and poor peasants, once the landed aristocracy had been cut down.


## II

The real complexity, under a seeming simplicity, of the social structure of the ancien régime, accounts for the vicissitudes of the class struggles under the Revolution.

The essential cause of the Revolution was the power of a bourgeoisie arrived at its maturity and confronted by a decadent aristocracy holding tenaciously to its privileges. The result was the legal enactment of that power. In this sense, the French Revolution, an episode (but the most resounding one) in the general rise of the bourgeoisie, was a single thing; we cannot follow Mathiez, who distinguishes, after the "revolt of the nobility" of 1787-88 and the bourgeois revolution of 1789, a third revolution, democratic and republican, on August 10, 1792, and then a fourth one, May 31-June 2, 1793, leading to a rough sketch of social democracy. August 10 and June 2 were indeed crucial stages in the Revolution; but what we had there was a deepening of the struggle between the bourgeoisie and the aristocracy, marked by the entrance on the stage of the middle and lower classes. The change was not in the nature of the struggle of classes. In 1793 as in 1789 the aim was still to strike down the aristocracy. In this sense we can not speak either of a "change of front" on the

---

[14] On the dissolution of the rural community, see Albert Soboul, "La Communauté rurale à la fin du XVIIIe siècle," in *Le Mois d'ethnographie française*, April 1950.

part of the bourgeoisie after the fall of Robespierre, for after the 9th Thermidor as before it, the essential enemy remained the aristocracy, which did not lay down its arms. The Thermidorians thought they could get along without the alliance with the people. Their calculations proved to be false. Though the partisans of Bonaparte continued to fear the sans-culottes, they feared still more the peril of the aristocracy, and to get rid of it had to resort to military dictatorship. Bonaparte was indeed the soldier of the bourgeois revolution.

Yet, under this essential unity, the Revolution is a complex fact, It had various stages, reflecting the fluctuations forward and backward of the battle against the aristocracy. The Revolution also had various currents which were complementary to the main stream. Without the peasantry and the sans-culottes the bourgeoisie could never have brought down the aristocracy; nonetheless, the sans-culottes and the peasantry pursued goals that were not those of the bourgeoisie.

The revolution was marked by stages, as the struggle of classes became sharper and more complicated. We shall not go over them here, but merely raise some problems, which are organically bound together: the problem of the failure of the compromise policy, the problem of the Girondins' "failure of nerve" when confronted with the necessities of the war, and the problem of the Jacobin dictatorship.

The ruling sections of the bourgeoisie would have accepted a compromise which, in the image of the English revolutions of the 17th century, would have set up over the subdued lower classes the domination of the *notables* and the moneyed class. The aristocracy would have none of it, thus rendering inevitable recourse to the popular masses in order to break its resistance. Only a minority, symbolized by the name of La Fayette, understood that it stood to lose nothing in this compromise; the example of England proved that. Compromise was possible in the spring of 1789; but the monarchy would have had to take the initiative boldly. Its attitude showed instead that it was no longer anything more than the instrument of domination by one class. The decision of Louis XVI at the beginning of July to appeal to the soldier seemed to indicate the end of the nascent bourgeois revolution. The force of the people saved it.

Was compromise still possible after July 14 and the October days? There were those who thought so among the bourgeoisie as well as among the aristocracy, and had plans for bringing it about.[15] But the majority of the nobility, and the aristocratic upper clergy, both refused to accept the initial reforms of the Revolution.

Whether for ambition or lack of political understanding, La Fayette persisted for a longer time. Being a great lord, a "hero of two worlds," he had what was needed to attract the upper bourgeoisie. His policy was, within the framework of constitutional monarchy, to conciliate the landed aristocracy with the industrial and commercial bourgeoisie. He failed because the aristocracy stubbornly resisted. Even more, the disorders due to the persistence of the food crisis, and the agrarian revolts caused by the obligation of redeeming the seigneurial rights, hardened the resistance of the aristocracy. From the summer of 1790 on, the compromise policy was ruined.

Alarmed by the progress of the democrats and by the popular agitation, the upper bourgeoisie tried to put a stop to the Revolution. The passive or disfranchised citizens were excluded from the national guard and collective petitions prohibited. On June 14, 1791, the Loi Le Chapelier proscribed "coalitions" and strikes. The resistance of the aristocracy, however, made this policy impossible. The appeal to foreign

---

[15] *De l'Influence attribuée aux philosophes, aux francs-maçons et aux illuminés sur la Révolution de France* (1801). On Mounier's attempted compromise policy, see Jean Egret, *La Révolution des notables. Mounier et les Monarchiens, 1789* (1950).

intervention, evidenced by the flight of the king on June 21, 1791, showed that class interest made the bourgeoisie prefer to betray the nation rather than yield.

The crisis brought forth from among the bourgeoisie a second and socially different revolutionary generation. It was in part recruited from the cultivated middle bourgeoisie of lawyers and journalists, who were in contact with the commercial bourgeoisie. Their most representative figure was Brissot. This commercial bourgeoisie and the politicians in their service wanted to liquidate the counter-revolution in order to restore the value of the assignats, if business was to thrive. As for war, which the aristocracy wanted in order to bring about an end to the revolution, the commercial bourgeoisie was not against it—had not army orders always been a considerable source of profits? The Girondins, or the party of the commercial bourgeoisie, started the continental war in April 1792, but did not declare war on England until February of the following year. War at sea endangered trade with the islands and the prosperity of the maritime cities.

The continental war served both the economic and the political interests of the Girondin bourgeoisie. It meant carrying to a climax the struggle against the die-hard aristocracy, unmasking it and destroying it beyond the frontiers where it had sought refuge in emigration, intensifying the class struggle on the scale of the European ancien régime.

The war spoiled the calculations of the Girondin bourgeoisie. A new cleavage took its place among the social antagonisms. The Gironde, under the pretext that the war required unity, had already stood warrant for La Fayette and supported Narbonne, the minister of foreign affairs. Here was an anticipatory sketch of that government of notables of which Madame de Stael, Narbonne's mistress, was one of the theoreticians, and which conciliated the interests of that part of the landed aristocracy that had made its peace with the commercial bourgeoisie. The reverses of Spring 1792 made the Gironde realize it needed an alliance with the popular classes to make victory sure. But it showed hesitancy and duplicity. It consented to appeal to the people, on June 20, 1792, only to the extent that the people would keep to the objectives the Gironde assigned them. The Girondine bourgeoisie, unreservedly devoted to economic liberty, was disturbed to see the sans-culottes demand fixed prices on foodstuffs. On August 10, 1792, the monarchy, pillar of the aristocracy and obstacle to an effective policy of national defense, was brushed away by the sans-culottes and the Jacobin middle class. The insurrection of August 10, made without the Gironde, was its death sentence.

The foreign policy of the Girondin bourgeoisie was the logical consequence of this initial attitude toward the people. In order to obtain peace, the Gironde, in fear of the people, was getting ready to drop into a compromise with the aristocracy and the counter-revolution. The upper bourgeoisie also reunited behind it. Once more class interests got the better of the interests of the nation. This is what the historians call modestly the "failure of nerve" of the Gironde. Like the monarchy on August 10, the Girondin bourgeoisie was an obstacle to the national effort and was eliminated by a popular movement disciplined by the petty and middle bourgeoisie. Jaurès has denied the class character of the days of May 31-June 2, 1793.[16] To be sure, if we confine ourselves to the parliamentary aspect of these days, or to the political conflict between the Mountain and the Gironde: both derived from the bourgeoisie (and yet the nuances would have to be noted) and had the same conception of property. But the re-entrance of the sans-culottes into the scene now complicated the interplay of the class struggles. The Girondin Pétion was not mistaken when as early as April 1793, in

[16] *Histoire socialiste*, Vol. IV, p. 1458.

his *Letter to the Parisians,* he sounded the alarm to the bourgeois: "Your property is menaced, and you close your eyes to the danger!"

The internal and external aristocratic menace in 1793-94 required the unity of the Third Estate. The sense of the class struggle was clearer than ever. The energy of the sans-culotte masses was more necessary than ever in this struggle. The Gironde denied itself this aid out of class selfishness, but another section of the bourgeoisie undertook to recruit and discipline the popular ardor in the organization of the revolutionary government and Jacobin dictatorship. This saved the Revolution.

It this coalition, on which the revolutionary government was to rest, the Jacobin middle bourgeoisie that Robespierre incarnated was undoubtedly the leading element, the necessary link between the living forces of the sans-culottes and that section of the bourgeoisie that planned to push the bourgeois revolution to completion. The position did not lack its contradictions and accounted in large measure for the ultimate failure of Robespierre's policy. It was a position that followed from the social condition of that Jacobin middle bourgeoisie that would have to be spelled out by many detailed studies, but was symbolized well by the "cabinet-maker" Duplay, a good Jacobin if there ever was one. He still engaged in the world of labor but got ten to twelve thousand livres of rent from his houses just the same.

The rapid ruin of the revolutionary government is accounted for by the contradictions of the sans-culottes, even more than by the ambiguous position of the Jacobins. But here we touch upon one of those secondary currents of the French Revolution that add to its complexity.

Nothing is clearer than that the sans-culottes fought against the aristocracy first and foremost. July 14 proves that, as well as the ardor of the volunteers. The sans-culottes furnished the bourgeoisie that revolutionary mass that was indispensable for bringing down the old society. For all that, the fact remains that the position of the sans-culottes in the traditional society made them an autonomous element, opposed to the bourgeoisie on many points.[17]

There is thus an autonomous sans-culotte current within the French Revolution, of which the origins would have to be looked for in the deterioration of the conditions of shopkeepers, artisans and workers well before 1789. It is significant that the sans-culottes were set in motion just as much by the foodstuff crises as by the aristocratic plot. The sans-culotte current was autonomous also by virtue of its procedures and organizations, such as general assemblies of the Parisian sections, in which the sans-culottes ruled undisputed in 1793, and people's societies. There was a significant difference between a people's society and the Jacobin Club which the sans-culottes hardly frequented at all. And there was autonomy in certain crises, like the one in early September, 1793, which Mathiez describes as a "Hebertist drive," and which was nothing but a sans-culotte "drive." These days had no strict and precise relationship with the general course of the bourgeois revolution. The sans-culottes demanded fixed prices for foodstuffs and regulation of trade in them, something that the Jacobin bourgeoisie granted only under duress and against its will.

That is where the basic opposition lay between the sans-culottes and the bourgeoisie. The sans-culottes share a pre-capitalist mentality, deeply hostile to the spirit of enterprise that moves the bourgeoisie; the latter demands economic liberty, while the

[17] On the problem of the sans-culottes, see some indications for research in Albert Soboul, *Les Papiers des sections de Paris (1790-an IV), Répertoire sommaire* (1950), p. 6, Introduction.

sans-culottes in September 1793 force upon it price-fixing and controls. Beyond this opposition over the organization of economic life, two conceptions clashed: the bourgeois conception of property as a natural, inalienable, total right, and the sans-culotte conception of a property which was controlled, limited and kept within narrow limits which were precisely the limits of the sans-culottes. On September 2, 1793 the sans-culottes of the section of the Jardin des Plantes demanded of the Convention that an upper limit be set to fortunes, that a single citizen should not own more than one workshop or store.[18] It was a position full of contradiction; but there was contradiction too in the position of the revolutionary government that was based on such dissimilar elements as the Jacobin middle bourgeoisie and the sans-culottes. Once victory over the aristocracy was in sight, the dangerous alliance with the sans-culottes seemed less needful. The bourgeoisie, without changing its front, resumed its freedom of action. The revolutionary government did not survive the ninth of Thermidor.

The ambiguous position of the sans-culottes in the French Revolution explains certain errors of perspective with respect to them. In a recent book Daniel Guérin tried to see the sans-culottes as an advance guard and their attempt of the year II [1793] as an embryonic proletarian revolution: this would confirm the theory of the permanent revolution, according to which the proletarian revolution of the twentieth century was already implicit in the bourgeois revolution of the 18th.[19] Guérin took the sans-culottes for the proletariat. He writes, for example, that the demonstration on September 4, 1793, was specifically *working-class,* adding, without being aware of the distinction, that it contained almost exclusively journeymen. This is to make a proletarian advance guard of what was nothing but a rear guard defending the positions of the traditional economy.

The sans-culottes did not form either a party or a class. There were workers among them, especially journeymen; but there were also shopkeepers and artisans who had some property and petty bourgeois of the liberal professions. What united these men was, beyond their hatred of the aristocracy, their common hostility to the capitalist system of production that threatened to reduce them to the rank of proletarians. Hence their utopian equalitarianism and their desire not to suppress the property that many of them already enjoyed, but to limit it to their own measure. The sans-culottes were at once hostile to capitalism because it tended to push them down into the ranks of the proletariat, and attached to the bourgeois order because they had property or hoped to get it. They demanded price-fixing, but at the same time were attached to the independence of the shop, the artisanate, and the small country holding. On this point they were devotees of economic liberalism. Certainly, on the political plane they were the most advanced democratic element; and this undoubtedly is the source of Daniel Guérin's error of perspective. But on the economic plane their positions were reactionary: they were doomed to decline with all the traditional system of production based on the artisanate and the shop. It is a contradiction that gives the dialectic movement of history all its dramatic quality.

The peasant current is not without analogy with the sans-culotte current in some aspects (especially with respect to the poor peasantry), for it too developed within the

---

[18] *Section des Sans-Culottes. Adresse à la Convention Nationale, 2 septembre 1793,* Bibliothèque Nationale, Lb$^{40}$ 2140.

[19] Daniel Guérin, *La Lutte de classes sous la première République. Bourgeois et "bras nus" (1793-1797)* (1946).

framework of the bourgeois revolution without getting beyond it. Hatred of feudalism linked the peasantry with the bourgeoisie, and its destruction was one of the Revolution's most important reforms.

The peasant current also developed autonomously, without organic connection with the bourgeois revolution. Upon hearing of the fall of the Bastille, the peasants revolted spontaneously and often despite the bourgeoisie which in many localities, in its quality as landowner, took strong repressive measures. The agrarian revolts continued until the total abolition of seigneurial rights in 1793.

The poor peasantry was marked by the same pre-capitalist mentality as the sans-culottes of the cities; it was attached to collective rights and controls; and in the course of the Revolution it was equally opposed to the seigneurs and to the agencies of the capitalist transformation of agriculture. This is proved by the numerous petitions against large farms and for the maintenance of collective rights.[20] The strength of this peasant current was so great that the bourgeoisie had to come to terms. The Revolution, triumphant in other respects, brought about merely a compromise in the rural districts.[21]

### III

If we now try to draw up the balance sheet of the Revolution from the point of view we have taken here, we see how unreal any schematism is. The Revolution destroyed the feudal aristocracy; it still has to be made clear to what extent. At the same time it also ruined those sections of the bourgeoisie that were integrated in one way or another into the society of the ancien régime. The Revolution made certain the triumph of capitalist economy based on economic liberty; in this sense, it hastened the ruin of the social categories that were attached to the traditional system of production. But in the realm of agricultural production, the resistance of the poor peasantry was such that capitalism could not win a definitive victory.

The nobility as a social order disappeared. Distinctions between nobles and commons were done away with. The personal seigneurial rights on which the dependence of the peasants was based were abolished after the night of August 4, 1789. Above all the aristocracy was hit in its economic basis. Other feudal rights were finally terminated by the Convention on June 17, 1793. The Revolution attacked the landed property of the nobility. The former siegneurs had to return the communal lands that they had seized and the property of the émigrés was put on sale in June 1793. As the crisis grew deeper the nobles were gradually excluded from all public positions, civil or military. Exaggeration should be avoided here, however. The nobility was not stripped of its lands altogether nor irrevocably. Only the émigrés had their property confiscated. Many nobles went through the Revolution without great loss and kept their landed properties. Furthermore, fictitious divorces and purchases by straw men enabled some émigrés to save or recover their lands.[22] In this way a certain

[20] There are many such petitions in series $F^{10}$ of the Archives Nationales (papers of the Committees or Commissions on Agriculture of the Revolutionary Assemblies). *Cf.* Georges Lefebvre: *Questions agraires au temps de la Terreur* (1932).
[21] On the whole peasant problem, see the recapitulation of Georges Lefebvre, "La Révolution française et les paysans," in *Cahiers de la Révolution française*, 1934, No. 1.
[22] On what the émigrés were able to recover of their lands, see A. Gain, *La Restauration et les biens des émigrés* (1929).

section of the old aristocracy held on, and during the 19th century merged with the upper bourgeoisie.

The bourgeoisie of the ancien régime shared the fate of the aristocracy in large measure. The bourgeois who lived "nobly" on their income from the land saw their seigneurial dues and rights vanish. Office holders were ruined by the abolition of the sale of offices. The financial upper bourgeoisie received a mortal blow when stock companies and the farming-out of indirect taxes were abolished. It was hard hit too by the disappearance of the Bank of Discount as well as by the resumption of price-fixing and controls. Finally, as a measure of the blows the bourgeois revolution struck at certain sections of the bourgeoisie, we must consider the considerable repercussions of inflation on settled fortunes. The traditional bourgeoisie invested its savings in mortgage loans or the public debt rather than in commercial and industrial enterprises. In 1794, the depreciation of the assignats led debtors to get rid of their mortgage debts at little cost. The consolidation of the perpetual and annuity debts under the Convention, and the two-thirds bankruptcy under the Directory were additional blows. All these facts account for the rallying of the bourgeoisie of the ancien régime to the counter-revolution. It shared the fate of the aristocracy, whose cause it had taken up.

Just as much as the revolutionary bourgeoisie strove for the destruction of the aristocracy, it obstinately sought the ruin of the traditional economic system, which was incompatible with the expansion of capitalist enterprises. After the Ninth of Thermidor, economic liberty was inaugurated triumphantly on the ruins of the sans-culotte movement.

This had grave consequences for the traditional lower classes. The abolition of guilds by the Constituent Assembly might have seemed democratic, but it hurt the interests of the master artisans. Thus, at the same time that the material conditions of social life were being transformed, the structure of the traditional lower classes was changing. All the conditions were now present for a broad development of capitalist economy, which would necessarily transform the sans-culottes into a proletariat. The artisans and journeymen had a foreboding of their fate. The latter knew that machinery would increase the chances of unemployment, the former that capitalist concentration would mean the closing of their workshops and make wage earners of them. The Le Chapelier law of 1791, prohibiting "coalition" and strikes, was an effective means of development for the industrial bourgeoisie.

In the realm of agricultural production, where the resistance of the poor peasantry was more desperate, the bourgeois revolution was less radical in its consequences. It made possible the development of a predominant rural bourgeoisie, but it could not completely destroy the rural community and thereby give free rein to the development of capitalist modes of production.

All the peasantry, whether owners or not, profited by the abolition of seigneurial dues and ecclesiastical tithes. The other agrarian reforms of the Revolution served primarily to strengthen those who were already proprietors. Leaving out the city bourgeoisie, who got into their hands a considerable portion of the national property, the conditions under which it was sold, particularly the auctions, favored the big farmers and the prosperous peasants. The rural bourgeoisie was strengthened and the moat deepened between them and the poor peasantry.[23]

---

[23] Despite some timid attempts in 1793, the bourgeoisie that dominated in the revolutionary assemblies was aware of the need for prohibiting access to ownership for the mass of the peasantry, if industrial enterprises were to be developed. See the report presented to the

But the last-named did not emerge from the Revolution as badly disarmed in the face of the triumphant bourgeoisie as the urban sans-culottes were. The poor peasantry did not get from the revolutionary assemblies the restoration or reinforcement of the traditional rural community, as it had desired. But the bourgeois revolution did not destroy it beyond repair; it did not brutally do away with the communal properties and collective customs that formed its economic basis.[24] Both lasted throughout the 19th century and have not entirely disappeared yet. The law of 1892, still in force, requires the consent of the peasants of the village for the abandonment of common pasture. The rural community has thus survived, going through a slow disintegration.

Here some distinctions are necessary. In the regions of large-scale farming, where the farmers were active agents in the capitalist evolution of agriculture, the rural community broke up rapidly, not by dissociating into antagonistic classes (the big farmers were generally city capitalists who were strangers to the rural community) but by losing its substance, as it were. The poor peasants who were proletarianized were to furnish the labor force needed for capitalist agriculture and big industry. In small-scale farming regions the evolution was slower. The rural community was sapped from within by the antagonism between the rural bourgeoisie and the poor peasantry desperately defending its customary rights to use fields and woods. Thus two forms of economy clashed, one archaic, the other new and asserting the individualism of the capitalist producers. The struggle was covert but bitter, marked during the 19th century by agrarian disorders of the traditional type, the last of them, in 1848-51, being by no means the least violent nor the least typical.[25]

The bourgeois revolution was consequently unable to eradicate the traditional forms of agricultural production. It could only enact a compromise whose full significance can be measured by comparing the development of French and English agriculture. Undoubtedly the bourgeois revolution accelerated the capitalist transformation of agriculture; but that development was considerably slowed up by the maintenance of collective customs and by the subdivision of ownership and cultivation. The autonomy of the small producers was kept up for a long time, giving the political development of France, especially under the Third Republic, some of its characteristic traits. If enclosure and concentration had been imposed in France as they were in England, capitalism might have triumphed as completely in the realm of argicultural production as in that of industrial production. The obstinate resistance of the landed aristocracy to any compromise with the bourgeoisie forced the latter to deal gently with the peasantry, even with the poor peasantry.

If we now consider the class which led the Revolution, and basically profited from it, we note that it has been radically changed. The traditional predominance within it of the settled fortunes has been replaced by that of those who direct production and exchange; the internal equilibrium of the bourgeoisie has been modified. The

Convention the 27 Fructidor year II by Lozeau, deputy of the Charente-Inférieure, "On the Material Impossibility of Making all Frenchmen Landed Proprietors and on the Bad Effects that This Change Would Entail in Any Case." (*Moniteur*, Vol. XXI, p. 748).

[24] Nevertheless, the revolutionary bourgeoisie was aware of the need of doing away with communal property and collective customs for the sake of the progress of capitalist agriculture. See in this connection the report of Lozeau in Messidor year II, "On the Need for Doing Away with Communal Property and on the Principles of Property in a Free Country." (*Bibliothèque Nationale*, $8^0$ Le$_{38}$ 841).

[25] See Albert Soboul, "La Question paysanne en 1848," in *La Pensée*, Nos. 18, 19, and 20; "Les Troubles agraires de 1848," in *1848 et les Révolutions du XIX$^e$ siècle*, 1948, Nos. 180 and 181.

bourgeoisie of the ancien régime was not totally destroyed, since those of its representatives who had not emigrated kept their lands; but it lost its primacy. A new money bourgeoisie appeared in the forefront, made up of industrial leaders, and the directors of commerce and finance. Equipping, arming and supplying the armies, sale of the national property, exploitation of the conquered countries afforded business men new chances for developing their enterprises. Speculation gave rise to immense fortunes. The bourgeoisie renewed itself by incorporating those "nouveaux riches" who set the tone for the "society" of the Directory. True advernturers of capitalist society, they gave new life to the traditional bourgeoisie by their enterprising spirit and their flair for taking chances. On a lower rung of the bourgeois ladder, circumstances had allowed many tradesmen or artisans to rise into the ranks of the bourgeoisie. It was from this middle level that the new dominant class was soon to recruit the public servants and the members of the liberal professions. The traits of the new bourgeoisie hardened during the Napoleonic period that fused these diverse elements.

At the end of this sketch, whose only purpose is to stimulate reflection on the history of the Revolution, several points should be stressed for their educative value.

There are laws of historical development, but they can not be reduced to a mechanical schematism, as some have done by a false application of dialectical materialism. Social classes, even when dominant, are rarely homogeneous; the various sections making them up complicate the interplay of classes in the framework of the general development, sometimes causing autonomous secondary currents, such as the sans-culottes in the bourgeois revolution. Only precise social and economic analysis can account for the place in the class struggle of the various social categories, and disclose the contradictions that may appear between political attitude and an economic position. It will not be forgotten, finally, that as the class struggles develop, they affect and transform the classes engaged in them. The bourgeoisie that profited from the Revolution was no longer the same as the bourgeoisie that started it.

These truths may seem self-evident. They deserve to be recalled nevertheless. History is a dialectical movement. If they are not to deform it by schematization, those who engage in studying it must take into account the complexity that makes its richness, as well as the contradictions that give it its dramatic character.

# THE FISCAL AND ECONOMIC CRISES AT THE END OF THE ANCIEN RÉGIME

### Ernest Labrousse

In many respects, the Revolution certainly appears to have been a revolution of extreme poverty, as Michelet had guessed and contrary to the thesis of Jaurès, which Mathiez was to take up. Not that Jaurès and Mathiez denied the reality and the influence of poverty. But, according to them, it played only a relatively small and occasional role. This might be true if the economic crisis of 1789 were really what it seems at first sight: a simple "crisis of subsistence," which was precipitated by a hailstorm, and to which propitious heavens were to put an end, with the connivance of the "new men" of the National Assembly and the Gallicans on its Ecclesiastical

Committee. Poverty would thus seem to be a kind of meteoroligical incident. The economic collapse of 1788-1790 was unfortunately on another scale. It afflicted all of the French economy, from grain crops and wine to textiles and building—an economy still deeply shaken by the difficulties it was just beginning to overcome and by the cruel blows of 1785. The cyclical crisis of 1789 was doubtless a cause of the Revolution, and, as one would expect, so was the pre-revolutionary economic depression, but to a much higher degree than Jaurès and Mathiez realized. Both crisis and depression had a profound effect on the events of 1789 and 1790. And they were not without influence on institutions, nor did they fail to provoke lasting, sometimes definitive changes in the most important fiscal and social laws. On these grounds they are real causes.

At the immediate source of the Revolution was a financial crisis, itself a consequence of the debts acquired during the war in America. One can say in broad terms—as others have—that without the war in America there would not have been a financial crisis nor a convocation of the Estates General, nor a Revolution—at least not at the time and in the shape in which it broke out. The Revolution, considered as an event, thus is grounded not only in an economic reality having financial consequences but in a recession. Without war—no "American" debt, no massive increase in expenses and no ills to begin with; but with the recession—no resources, no possible increase in returns and no remedies to these ills, or rather very troublesome resorts and remedies. An increase in the important taxes on consumption had to be abandoned after the 10-per-cent increase of 1781. The *brevet de la taille* remained fixed after 1780. The last *vingtième* was imposed in 1782 and discontinued in 1787. The spontaneous increase in revenue from the tax on consumer goods was not sufficient. No doubt the yield from the *aides* increased with the substitution of state control for tax-farming, with the rapid rise in population, and the even more rapid growth of the cities, those great consumers of wine and liquor, and finally with the spread of an economy of trade. The peasant masses, emigrating to the cities, had to pay a tax on the wine they drank in taverns, whereas the wine from their own vineyards, consumed in a closed economy, was tax-exempt. The crisis in wine-growing was itself to increase the *aides,* as it forced the farmer to convert into brandy, which was taxed at a higher rate, sizable quantities of unsold wine. The taxes on consumption held their own or even rose. But the returns would have been very different in an expanding economy of rising prices, which would automatically have increased the revenue from taxes at the wholesale level proportional to prices. This in turn would have induced the farmer to cultivate more land, that is, to multiply the amount of taxable products. And, on the other hand, with an increase in profits, it would have been possible to re-establish the taxes on consumption of 1781 as well as to increase the *brevet de la taille.* To be sure, rewriting history is a strange practice. Let us assume as a hypothesis that at the time of the war in America and in the years following, there existed a state of affairs similar to that at the beginning of the next century, that is, an economy in full expansion: is it so very bold to say that under those circumstances it would have been easier to meet the deficit? or at least that the increase in public returns could easily have served as security for loans to be issued in the future? The Comptroller General would not have had to overcome both the costs of the war and the fast-decreasing revenue from the *taille.* He could have deferred summoning the Assembly of Notables and appealing to the privileged—that is, practically speaking, those people benefiting from rising farm rents, the income from lands which at that time was the only large category of increasing revenue; but these were the very people who obstinately avoided taxation. It would not have been so urgent for the *Ancien Régime* itself to undertake fiscal reforms, namely to survive through self-denial, or to call on the nation to make its Revolution.

The financial consequences of the pre-revolutionary depression and of the revolutionary crisis were therefore very serious. They prevented or made difficult the adjustment of receipts to expenditures. What the State received remained insufficient. But, again because of the depression and the crisis, the amount that a taxpayer had to pay became excessive. The tax rate was not reduced, far from it. Though it remained fixed after 1782, we must remember that it was raised, though moderately, at this date as well as in 1781. It was not so much that the fiscal burden increased, but that those who were obliged to bear it were weaker. The drop in prices brought with it a drop in the volume of business transacted, which itself involved a more than proportionate drop in profits: so much so that the tax, though it might hypothetically remain the same, quickly assumed fantastic dimensions in comparison with a fast-vanishing profit. A universal and automatic "fiscal reaction" aroused the majority of the nation against it.

This relatively little known "fiscal reaction" was itself paralleled by a much better known "seigniorial reaction," a seigniorial reaction, some of whose origins may also be found in the economic difficulties which dominated the reign of Louis XVI. The seigniorial proprietor had hoped to gain, through an increase in the amount of taxes he collected in kind, a compensation for the decline in monetary revenue which had resulted from the fall in prices. And above all the lessees of manorial rights—no doubt the most frequent example—used this method to counteract the effects of the economic decline, when, confident in a rising economy, they had agreed to renew seigniorial leases at a high price. As was true of royal taxes, the seigniorial tax was thus also increasing without regard to profits which were decreasing, at any rate on lands subject to this tax, for example lands subject to the *champart*.

But besides the "seigniorial reaction," as it is usually defined, which perhaps applied only to a small fraction of the lands, another seigniorial reaction, universal and automatic, affected all tenants: whether they paid the *champart* or the *dîme* (in this context, equivalent to seigniorial rights). Those who owed a tax in kind, proportional to the gross product, paid, on this account, a relatively increasing tax because the profit, the net product, had fallen proportionally lower than the total volume of business or gross product. As a result, at a time of economic decline or crisis, the tax proportional to the gross product necessarily became a progressive tax on the net product. Here again the tax-payer felt an added burden, even though the amount he paid remained the same.

The universal and prolonged fiscal reaction and the universal and prolonged seigniorial reaction set the majority of the farmers and cultivators against the monarchical tax and against feudalism, not only at the time of the great economic crisis of 1789, in which these two reactions culminated, but during the preceding ten years. The proletariat was no better off. The day laborer, who was working fewer days and was raising a larger family, also had to pay taxes, which at first increased and then remained constant but in both instances were progressive because these taxes were levied against a declining income. If, as was often the case, the laborer also worked a parcel of land which he might own or rent, his income also had to bear the growing pressure of the seigniorial rights, which had reached their maximum during the crisis of 1789.

Thus, it can also be said that even if the tax remained stable and unchanging, that was enough to make it overwhelming. Open the *cahiers!* See what they have to say about the crisis! Taxes must be blamed. Taxes were responsible for hindering the growth of agriculture and crushing the share-cropper and the farmer. The *aides* must be blamed for ruining the wine-grower by causing underselling which devoured profits. Private taxes or seigniorial rights gave rise to similar complaints. Were not these simply the old complaints? Perhaps. Were they foolish complaints in that they held taxes responsible for the crisis? Certainly. But these complaints were genuine and were justified insofar as they denounced the disproportion between profits and taxes, and between wages and taxes. The provoking increase in royal and seigniorial taxes finally was met by something more than complaints. The offices of the tax-farmers as well as the toll-house gates were put to flames. Grain, collected in kind, was repossessed from the seigniorial granaries. From the farmer to the day laborer, a whole people were in agreement, driven to unite through a common decline in agricultural revenues, and by a joint resistance to the fiscal and seigniorial reaction. The cities joined in crying out against the taxes on food and drink and against the nobles and manorial lords who had monopolized the grain collected in kind. As a result, there occurred not only such events and incidents as the "class war" of 1789 and 1790, but also comparatively lasting laws such as those which abolished the *gabelle* and which transformed and lightened the taxes on food and drink, and finally some permanent laws such as those which abolished the *dîme* and put an end to feudalism.

The financial, fiscal and social consequences of the pre-revolutionary economic difficulties, in themselves, constituted a Revolution. Not *the* Revolution, of course. However, we may conclude that the consequences of these difficulties were even greater, and that the whole younger generation, those who were less than thirty in 1789, and who, from the time they entered economic life, had experienced hardly anything but diminishing profits and growing unemployment, ascribed their difficulties to the regime itself. Their elders, who had lost part of the profits they had accumulated in happier days, or whose salaries remained insufficient, also had the same attitude. Such reactions are not peculiar to this period. One runs into them again sooner or later. It does not matter that a free economy is by definition not a controlled economy: when economic difficulties arise contemporaries ascribe them to the government. It has already been mentioned that taxes were accused of being responsible for the crisis. Taxes are politically instituted: though at first the *taille* and the *aides* were the accused, the Comptroller General, the ministry and the regime were ultimately held responsible. Especially since taxation, as might be guessed, did not appear to those affected as the sole villain. From all sides, there arose the discordant clamor of recriminations. If a depression and a cyclical crisis occurred, it was not only because the fiscal burden was excessive, it was also because expenditures were excessive. The deficit and the ruin of public credit, far from being perceived as consequences, seemed to contemporaries to be causes: causes of the general uncertainty, of the timidity of capital, and of the ruin of the spirit of enterprise. Why was there the prolonged economic contraction, the long period of fall or fluctuation in the price of grain, or the prolonged collapse in the price of wine? Because the State mistakenly discouraged export. There was overproduction; the government could have put a stop to it but abstained from action. Why did it not revive the prohibition against planting new vineyards? Why again was there, in 1789, such a rapid and wild rise in the price of grain? It was conceded that the bad harvest was in part responsible: but the people accused the monopolists and the government, which had allowed too much wheat to leave the country in 1787 and had not allowed enough to enter in

1788. Marat was to denounce Necker, in particular, as a speculator. If agriculture lacked capital, it was not because of the farmer's profit was declining, but because fiscal inequality, exceptions and privileges concentrated the wherewithal of economic activity in the cities. The economic ills were considered political in origin. The remedy was also to be political: a liberal "system of laws"! If industry as well as agriculture languished, it was blamed on foreign protectionism or possibly on French free-trade: it was neither the crisis of 1785 in feed grains, nor the rise in the price of wool, nor the rise in the price of cotton, nor finally the general decline in returns which was considered responsible, but rather the Anglo-French treaty of commerce. And when the growth in population accelerated dangerously, it was blamed on military instituitions and on the militia, which had encouraged marriage by penalizing celibacy. A drumfire of accusations was leveled by all classes against the regime: we shall see that some of them were well founded and that many facts which were considered by the public to be the "causes" of need or poverty had an influence, as contributing factors, on the prolonged French economic crisis. But the public mistook the lesser causes for the essential ones. Thus the atmosphere of discontent, in which the Revolution broke out, spread and thickened. A political crisis arose out of an economic crisis through an enormous error in ascribing causes.

Thus many revolutionary events and some great revolutionary institutions had their beginnings largely in the falling off of profits and wages, in the straitened circumstances of industrialists, artisans and farmers, and in the workers' and day-laborers' poverty. These unfavorable circumstances united the bourgeoisie and the proletariat in joint opposition to the regime. In this respect, and to a much greater degree than Jaurès and Mathiez believed, the Revolution does appear to be a revolution of poverty. As might be guessed, the last part of the 18th century does not explain everything, nor are the last years, years of intercyclical contraction, the only ones affecting institutions. The economic difficulties of the reign of Louis XVI, however great their effect on his contemporaries, nevertheless represent only an episode between the Regency and the Republic. The 18th century remained, on the whole, a century of great economic expansion, of rising capitalist returns, and of advancing bourgeois wealth and power. On this score it prepared the way for the Revolution, a Revolution of prosperity. And one can easily see that a long period of progress had no less an influence on the Revolution than did a relatively short period of economic retreat—no matter how close to events and consequently no matter how dynamic this last period might have been.

In the second part of this introduction, we sketched in an explanation of the century's prosperity, beginning with the phenomenon of rising prices. A rise in prices, as has been stated, generated profits, and in a liberal economy when the natural generation of profits is in process, all is well. This spontaneous functioning of the economy had an important influence on institutionalized procedures. As soon as the economy had begun to run smoothly, the State tended to abstain from action. It relied on the entrepreneur, it abdicated in his favor. There was a decrease in intervention. Under pressure of rising prices and as a result of a prolonged natural expansion in the economy, there slowly evolved, during the second half of the century, new economic statutes which were later ratified by the Revolution. Why laws, when things work without them? Why guilds (that is to say monopolistic institutions which also set quotas) when there is room for everyone and when the prolonged rise in prices shows us that production cannot keep up with the needs of the consumer? To speak of monopolies, quotas or guilds is to speak of a contracted economy, an economy lacking in markets. But the "Economic 18th century" was a time of expanding markets: what better market for French industry than a rising agricultural income or expanding cities? The order of the day was no longer to set quotas and limits but to produce. The open market would give more and better returns than a market limited by a system of privileges. In an economy of spontaneous profit those institutions which protected profit would no longer be needed. The guilds had become an anachronism: moreover, they were an unwholesome and dangerously antisocial anachronism: they limited the hiring of an overpopulous proletariat and kept the workers from being promoted to the rank of artisans. Turgot took up the same line of argument, and later so did those who made the Revolution, Camille Desmoulins among them. If monopolies were anachronisms, so were the subsidies granted to mills and factories and the regulations which were their counterparts: what had condemned the guilds also condemned industry. Put your faith in the artisan! Put your faith in the manufacturer! Put your faith in profit! Everyone will share in this progressive economy which runs by itself. All that is needed is *laisser faire*.

The people showed an equal faith in agricultural profits. The price of wine was rising. Who has the right to reduce production? Why limit the area to be planted? Must this also be regulated? Why should there be restraints and prohibitions? Why should cultivation stop at the common-lands, when the entrepreneurs, attracted by rising prices, want nothing better than to work them? Why should they be forbidden to enclose their lands, when enclosure is essential for the agricultural revolution and heavier yields, and they ask only to produce as much as possible? Why bestow an out-of-date protection upon a poverty-stricken, self-contained peasantry which lived in a closed economy and obtained from the common-lands and *vaine pâture* only draught animals, milk and cheese? The habitual economy, a closed one, could be understood in a society where trade has slowed down. But times had changed. Profits, profits which clear the land and give rise to employment, should be given free rein. The peasant with a small holding would gain more under a free economy and more in wages than he would lose in kind through the disappearance of collective rights. A burgeoning profit is a promise of wages: the change takes place automatically. This is how the optimist Calonne talked. Here again the State must stop its interventions.

Thus royal sovereignty was dismembered. Thus was the separation between the economy and the state created. Thus did the entrepreneurial class—made up alike of nobles, bourgeois and farmers, but under bourgeois leadership—grow both wealthier and more independent. Nevertheless, it continued to solicit favors: a privilege or a subsidy is always helpful, but it did not need them to survive. Prosperity spontaneously gives a guarantee of profit which is worth more than all the guarantees derived from special advantages. Success was no longer dependent on the State. And professional life, in its daily workings, depended on it less and less. Rules and regulations became less important: the comptrollers and the inspectors of manufacture ceased to be feared censors. The entrepreneur, who possessed all the material power inherent in the ever-increasing wealth, was no longer controlled by functionaries. Moreover, the economic renunciation of the monarchy was echoed by a renunciation in social matters: the monarchy relied on the entrepreneurs, not only to run the economy, but also to provide a living for the fastest growing part of the population. The Council of State displayed a growing hostility against the scale of wages approved by the municipal authorities: the entrepreneurs should have free rein. And, above all, it was no longer the concern of the law to provide the hungry multitudes living in the country with a subsistence in kind through a reserve of common-lands and a claim on the lands of the rich. That responsibility now fell upon the entrepreneurs in the cities and in the fields, who must provide for the people's subsistence by employing them. The policy of confidence in profits, which was caused by a prolonged tide of capitalist prosperity, thus had double consequences. At the same time that prosperity liberated the bourgeoisie from governmental control, it made a whole part of the nation dependent upon that very bourgeoisie.

The interruption of this prosperity at the end of the century did not last long enough to modify policy visibly to any extent. It requires time for economic incentives to be taken into account. The rise in profits only began to have an effect on the established order, commencing in 1760, that is, after a very long delay. The drop in prices was not to have any quicker effect. Even if it had possessed that faculty, a policy hostile to economic liberalism would have run counter to the doctrinal positions held during a long period of progress, and counter to the power which the bourgeoisie had acquired during this period. The reversal in economic conditions had no other effect but to irritate the new sovereign and to incite him to complete the work of the century.

## "WORLD REVOLUTION," OR "FRENCH REVOLUTION"

**Jacques Godechot**

It is simply a matter of bad habit, as we remarked in our preface, that one usually speaks of a *French* Revolution. This phrase gives the impression that there developed, at the end of the 18th century, a completely isolated revolution, in no way connected with events which were occurring in the world at the same time. And, until very recently, it is certainly in this way that it was perceived by most of the historians of the "French Revolution." At best, they conceded that the "American Revolution," though also conceived as a separate phenomenon, had a certain influence on the "French Revolution." All the historians of the 19th century, notably the most famous among them: Thiers, Mignet, Michelet, Tocqueville, Edgar Quinet, Taine, shared this view. Again it is true of those historians who are referred to as "scientific" and who were our teachers: Aulard, Mathiez. The *French* Revolution, wrote Mathiez, surprises us "by its irresistible immediacy. . . . It emerged from the ever-deepening divorce between reality and the law, between institutions and *mores* and between the letter and the spirit." But Albert Mathiez does not question whether this divorce is peculiar to France, or whether one finds it as well at the source of the other revolutions that were proliferating at the end of the 18th and the beginning of the 19th century. Indeed, it is outside of France that historians, in examining their own national histories, identified as causes of revolutions in their own countries some that were peculiarly native but also others that were analogous to those of the French Revolution. The Italian historians were the first, apparently, to develop these ideas. During the 19th century and at the beginning of the 20th, most of the historians of the *Risorgimento* linked its origins to the French Revolution, or at any rate to Italy's relative unification under the sceptre of Napoleon. This was the case with Bolton King, with de Crozals and with de Raulich. On the other hand, Ettore Rota, has more recently set the origins of this *Risorgimento* at the beginning of the 18th century and many other contemporary Italian historians believe that the date 1748—that of the Treaty of Aix-la-Chapelle—quite precisely defines the beginning of this great revolution. Thus, it would then seem that the *Risorgimento* is not, at least not exclusively, a result of the French Revolution. Certain of its causes are unique to it, others are undistinguishable from those of the French Revolution. One can conclude that there was an Italian Revolution discrete from the French Revolution, but that both are but aspects of a wider revolution. American historians, in analyzing the causes of the American Revolution, and in comparing them to the causes of the French Revolution, have also concluded that there had been, at the end of the 18th century and at the beginning of the 19th, not only a series of isolated and not very closely related revolutions but a great occidental or Atlantic revolution in which one could recognize an "American phase" and a "French phase." This, at any rate, is the notion of Louis Gottschalk, the eminent authority at the University of Chicago and of R. R. Palmer, the distinguished professor at Princeton University. This viewpoint did not reach France until a few years ago, when the new version of Georges Lefebvre's *Revolution Française* was published in 1951. In this work, the author devotes an important chapter to the world situation at the end of the 18th century. In it he shows that, at least in the western hemisphere, there existed a condition or "climate" of revolution. Moreover, how can we fail to be struck by the succession of revolutions from 1763 to 1848? The Revolution in America between 1763 and 1783, the Revolutions in Geneva from 1766 to 1781, the Revolution in Ireland from 1782 to 1784, the Revolution in the Dutch Republic from 1783 to 1787, the Revolution in Belgium and Liège from 1787 to 1790, and the French Revolution beginning in 1787: this last one spread little by little over most of western Europe, beginning in Belgium and Holland, where the disturbances of 1790 and 1787 had scarcely quieted before they were reawakened; continuing through Germany, Italy and Switzerland; it finally reached Malta and even Poland and distant Egypt. A certain equilibrium seemed to be reached around 1800 with the coming to power of Bonaparte in France and the election of Jefferson in the United States. But the revolution was not over. In Europe, it was Napoleon's army that carried its ferment to Moscow while, beginning in 1810, revolution broke out in all of Spanish America. And these political revolutions were to bring about a profound economic, industrial, agricultural and social revolution. Setting aside the very special case of Poland, one notices that the revolutions we have just mentioned took place in the Americas and in Western Europe, that is, in countries bordering on the Atlantic. Why should we be surprised at this considering that at the end of the 18th century the sea was much more pervious than the land and that goods and ideas traveled across it more quickly? Gold or wheat crossed the ocean more rapidly than they did the continents and they produced quite similar economic conditions on both sides of the Atlantic. Letters and periodicals also passed very quickly from one continent to another: Paris was acquainted with the Declaration of Independence of the United States before it was known in Georgia. There was, then, a great Atlantic revolution, made up of many revolutions in a chain reaction, to use a contemporary expression.

The first link in the chain is represented by the United States, which is between 1763 and 1787, the great hot-bed of revolutionary activity. During this period the American Revolution expanded toward the European shores of the Atlantic. It was in the United States, during the Revolution, that the press began to play an important political role. Moreover, the American War of Independence aroused great interest in

Western Europe. The educated public took an interest in both the protagonists and in the dramatic events of the American Revolution and formed the habit of subscribing to newspapers in order to follow its progress. A political press began to develop in the Netherlands and in Germany. It was in the United States, too, that political clubs and parties proliferated for the first time. As early as 1770, "Committees of Correspondence," actually patriotic clubs, were established in the principal cities of the British colonies in America. Patriotic associations, such as the "Sons of Liberty," were founded to fight against England and to organize the boycott against British merchandise. Following their example, clubs sprang up in Ireland and the Netherlands, two countries with close ties to the United States. Indeed, by this time, many Irish had already emigrated to America, but they had maintained an uninterrupted connection with the mother country. In Holland, contact between the burghers of Amsterdam and their American relatives, who were descended from the founders of New Amsterdam (later New York), had never been broken. The war in America, during which the Dutch Republic allied itself with the United States and France, brought Dutch and Americans even closer. It is not surprising that other nations adopted certain forms of political life in the United States. Under the pressure of circumstances, the Americans, later imitated by the Dutch, the Irish, and then the French, created committees of public safety, demanded oaths of public servants and even private citizens, confiscated and sold the good of *émigrés,* intimidated through the use of violence the adherents of the old regime, printed paper money and established price control.

The American Revolution was not simply a breeding place of revolution acting through the power of example. It swept along with it France, Holland and Spain into a great war against England. That war, through its economic consequences, was in turn to compound the difficulties of Western Europe. In England, the increase in financial levies caused by the conflict brought about the Yorkshire Movement, whose purpose was economic reform and administrative reorganization. In Belgium, the declaration of independence of the province of Flanders uses, in 1789, language identical with that of the American declaration, and the *Act of Union* of 1790 is a literal reproduction of the *Articles of Confederation.*

In France, the expenses of the war brought about a deficit, and we know that it was to meet this deficit—happy deficit! exclaimed the revolutionaries—that the king was forced to convene the *Estates General.* A young American historian, Mr. Forrest MacDonald, has even declared that, after their return to France, the eight thousand soldiers of Rochambeau's army turned into a like number of revolutionary propagandists. After having traced the birthplace of these eight thousand men on a map of France and having compared the resulting map with that of the agrarian uprisings of 1789 to 1792, he was impressed by the correlation, and he concluded, without hesitation that there was a relationship of cause and effect. However, we cannot accept without reservation Mr. Forrest MacDonald's very seductive conclusions. The French soldiers, who were both ignorant of English and whose activities were narrowly circumscribed, could hardly have communicated with the American people. We must look elsewhere for an explanation. The soldiers of the Royal Army were mercenaries who were recruited from the poorest and most depressed provinces in the kingdom, which found it harder than the others to bear the weight of the feudal duties, of the tithe and of the royal taxes. These provinces saw the first and the most violent uprisings. However, it is possible that Mr. MacDonald's interesting hypothesis might not be completely unjustifiable; only further research will permit a final judgment on this score.

Nevertheless, beginning in 1789, the influence of the American Revolution was gradually fading and henceforth we see the spread and the expansion of the French Revolution.

# 15 / Napoleon: "An Argument Without End"

Perhaps no man in modern history has been the subject of so much writing, praising or denouncing him, as Napoleon Bonaparte. The reasons for this are not hard to see. The Napoleonic era, perhaps more than any other, bears the imprint of one man, and few men present such a complex array of talent, ambition, and contradictions as Napoleon.

Also, as with the French Revolution, much of what has been written about him by French historians has been colored by the political passions of their own day. Thus disillusion with the lackluster Bourbon Restoration and the equally unexciting July Monarchy bred a Napoleonic legend of heroic proportions, which did much to bring about the Second Empire. Then, with another Bonaparte on the Imperial throne, French historians were further encouraged to favorable interpretations of the earlier Napoleonic regime. At the same time, growing disillusion with the authoritarian Second Empire fostered such critical studies as Edgar Quinet's *La Révolution* (1865), written from exile in Switzerland, while the Second Empire's debacle in 1870 inspired Taine's highly unfavorable portrait of Napoleon in the fifth volume of *Les Origines de la France contemporaire* (1875-1894).

In spite of Taine's attack, humiliation over the defeat of 1870 and dissatisfaction with the earlier governments of the Third Republic led other historians to look back to the Napoleonic era with admiration. But Napoleon also continued to have his detractors. As the Dutch historian Pieter Geyl shows us in a brilliant historiographical study, *Napoleon, For and Against,* "the argument goes on." In its latest phase, which he dates from 1888 to the present, Geyl finds on one side what he calls the *Académiciens*, historians with literary pretensions who are by inclination pro-Napoleon, and on the other, *Universitaires,* professional historians holding teaching posts, whose inclinations are to be objective but whose judgments, though they differ, are each, in the balance, critical of Napoleon.[1]

In the former group is Louis Madelin, member of the French Academy, whose magisterial sixteen-volume work, *Histoire du consulat et de L'empire,* was completed two years before his death in 1956; in the latter group is the late Georges Lefebvre, who was Professor of the History of the French Revolution at the Sorbonne. His *Napoléon,* first published in 1935, is an authoritative one-volume study of the Napoleonic era. The selections that follow from these works show the contrasting opinions of their authors.

What is the reader to think of them and the controversy over Napoleon in general? The answer, which is appropriate to this concluding series of selections, is perhaps best given by Geyl in an opening statement from *Napoleon, For and Against.* He writes:

[1] This is a generalization, subject, as Geyl says, to "a number of qualifications and restrictions," but it holds remarkably true. See Pieter Geyl, *Napoleon, For and Against* (New Haven, Conn.: Yale University Press, 1949), pp. 160, 351-352, 354.

Truth though for God it may be One, assumes many shapes to men. Thus it is that the analysis of so many conflicting opinions concerning one historical phenomenon is not just a means of whiling away the time, nor need it lead to discouraging conclusions concerning the untrustworthiness of historical study. The study even of contradictory conceptions can be fruitful. Any one thesis or presentation may in itself be unacceptable, and yet, when it is jettisoned, there remains something of value. Its very critics are that much richer. History is indeed an argument without end.[2]

[2] *Ibid.*, p. 16.

# NAPOLEON

**Georges Lefebvre**

## *A Portrait*

What was he like? One cannot draw a full portrait, because his image evolved in a special way, from the studious officer and dreamer of Valence or Auxonne and even from the young general who still held councils of war as on the eve of the Battle of Castiglione; to the Emperor of the later years, drunk with his overruling power and infatuated with his own omniscience. Nevertheless, certain essential traits can be discerned throughout his career; power merely accentuated some and modified others.

Small, with short legs, and well-developed muscles, vigorous and lean at the age of thirty, his body had stamina and responded quickly. The sensitivity and staying power of his nerves were excellent, his reflexes astounding, his capacity for work unlimited; he could sleep at will. There was another side, however; cold damp weather oppressed him and brought on a cough and kidney trouble. Any opposition aroused a terrifying anger. Despite long hot baths, great sobriety, and the moderate though constant use of coffee and tobacco, extreme fatigue sometimes brought on brief spells of weakness which led him to the point of tears. His brain was one of the best that has ever existed. His attention, always on the alert, snatched indefatigably at thoughts and ideas; his memory registered and stored them; his imagination played with them freely. And as if by a secret, steady current, a lasting tension tirelessly invented political and strategic solutions which flashed out in sudden insights, comparable to those of the mathematician and of the poet—most often at night, when he would wake suddenly, with what he himself called "an intellectual spark," "a post-midnight inspiration." When he came to power this cerebral intensity illuminated—through his flashing eyes and the face still flushed—the "Corsican with straight hair." It was this intellectual vitality which made him unsociable not, as Taine would have us believe, the brutishness of a somewhat corrupt condottieri wildly let loose on the world.

He was right when he said of himself, "I am even a fairly good man," and, it is true, he showed himself generous and even friendly to those who could get close to him. Between most men who do their jobs faster so as to abandon themselves to leisure and to distractions, and Napoleon Bonaparte, who was all effort and concentration, there was no common measure nor real communication. The irresistible impulse to action and domination which is called his ambition sprang from his very physical and mental constitution. He understood himself well here too: "They say that I am ambitious, but they are wrong. I am not, or, at least, my ambition is so much a part of my inner self that it cannot be distinguished from it." What more can be said? Napoleon was above all a temperament.

As early as his service at Brienne, a poor foreigner, easily made fun of, eager but timid, he had depended on his self-confidence and scorn of others. By making him an officer, destiny catered remarkably to his instinct to command without resorting to discussion. If as military commander he could inform himself or even take advice, he was in the last resort master of the situation, and the decision was always his. Bonaparte's spontaneous taste for dictatorship became a personal hallmark. In Italy and in Egypt he used it on the level of government. In France he wished to appear a civilian but the stamp (of dictatorship) was indelible. Although he asked the advice of many, he could never tolerate a free opposition; indeed, he was not at ease when faced with a group of men accustomed to discussion. This is why he persecuted men of theory with such a furious hatred. The mob, confused and undisciplined but still to be dreaded, always filled him as much with fear as contempt. It was General Bonaparte who had conquered power, and it was as a general that he used it. Costumes and titles changed nothing.

Nevertheless, beneath his soldier's uniform there were several men, and his power to fascinate derived as much from this diversity as from the variety and brilliance of his gifts. He was consumed by the same appetites as others; there is the Bonaparte of the Year III, wandering about without a penny in his pockets at the celebration of Thermidor, trying to rub elbows with the powerful of that day, the men of money and their beautiful women. He retains to the end something from this time: a certain pleasure in dominating those who had treated him with condescension, a taste for ostentatious magnificence, the concern to advance his family, the clan which had suffered with him. Also certain memorable words reminiscent of the aspiring bourgeois, as for instance on the day of his coronation, "Joseph, if only father could see us now!" He was no less—and much earlier—moved by a nobler urge to know and understand all, which was useful to him but which he gratified without giving it a thought.

As a young officer he was an indefatigable reader, compiler, and writer. It is obvious that if he had not gone to Brienne he could have become a man of letters. As a man of action he remained a man of thought; the man of war would never be happier than when he was in his office surrounded by documents. This characteristic was modified, his thought became practical, and he boasted that he had repudiated "ideology." Nevertheless, he remained a man of the eighteenth century, rationalist and *philosophe*. Far from trusting intuition, he counted on reason, on knowledge, and on systematic method. "I am in the habit of seeing three or four months in advance what I should do and I always expect the worst"; "every operation should be carried out according to a system because nothing succeeds by chance." His insights he regarded as the natural fruit of his patience. He is a classicist in his concept of a monolithic state, all of a piece, following a simple symmetrical plan.

At rare moments, intellectualism manifests itself in him in its most refined form, the ability to look at himself even as he lived his life and to reflect sadly on his own destiny. From Cairo, after learning of Josephine's infidelity, he had written to Joseph, "I need solitude and isolation. Greatness bores me, feeling is dried up, the glory has gone flat. At the age of twenty-nine I have exhausted everything." Walking with Girardin at Ermenonville, he would soon say, "The future will show whether it might not have been better for the people of the world if neither Rousseau nor I had ever lived." When Roederer, inspecting the abandoned Tuileries with him, sighed, "General, this is sad," Bonaparte, First Consul for two months, said, "Yes, like greatness." Thus in a striking paradox, intellectualism itself insinuated the romantic sadness of Chateaubriand and de Vigny into this firm, disciplined mind, but it was never more than a flash of lightning, and he recovered himself immediately.

Everything seemed to lead him toward a realistic policy and indeed, everything, in execution, was realistic down to the smallest detail. As his star was rising he ran the gamut of human passions and learned how to use them: he knew how to exploit self-interest, vanity, jealousy— to the point of dishonesty. He had seen what one could get out of men by exciting their desire for honor and by stirring their imagination. Nor did he overlook that one could subject them by terror. In the accomplishment of the Revolution he had distinguished with a sure eye that which most touched the heart of the nation and that which was useful to his despotism. To win the support of the French people he presented himself at the same time as a man of peace and as a god of war. For this reason he is rated among the great realists of history.

He was only a realist in action, however. There was another side to him, a heroic side, which must have been born in his school days, arising from his desire to dominate a world where he felt himself looked down upon and especially from his desire to match the semi-legendary characters of Plutarch and Corneille. What spurred him most of all was glory. "I live only for posterity. Death is nothing, but to live defeated and without glory is to die every day." His sights were on the masters of the world: Alexander, conqueror of the East, dreaming of conquering the world; Caesar, Augustus, Charlemagne, creators and restorers of the Roman Empire—whose very name implied a universal state. This was not a question of a concrete idea which could serve as a rule, a yard-stick, or measure of a finite political undertaking. These were examples that fired the imagination and lent to action an inexpressible charm. He was less moved by the heroes' accomplishment than by the intellectual ardor to which the accomplishment was a monument. Artist, poet of action, for whom France and mankind were only instruments, he expressed at Saint Helena his feeling about great actions. When remembering the victory of Lodi and the awakening of the conscious will to power, he said magnificently, "I saw the world passing below me as if I were borne on the air." This is why it is futile to search for goal or limits in Napoleon's policies—there are none. To his followers who worried about this he reports that "I always replied that I knew nothing about it," or again, with great seriousness despite the facetious tone, "The position of God the Father? I don't want it—it's a dead end." Here we find again, in psychological form, the dynamic temperament which strikes one at first sight, the romantic Napoleon, a force for which the world is nothing but an opportunity to act boldly. On the other hand realism is recognizable not only in his choice of means but also in that he reckoned on the possible in determining his goals, and if imagination and a taste for grandeur could spur him on, he knew where to stop.

Moreover, if Napoleon escaped from the reality which his mind was so capable of grasping, as Molé has rightly observed, it was not only because of his nature but also because of his background. When he arrived in France he felt himself a foreigner, and, until he had been driven out of Corsica by his fellow citizens in 1791, he remained hostile to the French. Certainly he was sufficiently saturated with French civilization and thinking to feel at home among them; if not he could never have become their master; but he had not had the time to become incorporated into the French community and to assimilate its national traditions to a point where he considered its interest as the ruling or limiting factor of his own actions. Something also remained of the uprooted and of the socially displaced person: neither quite a gentleman nor quite a man of the people, he had served the King and the Revolution without really attaching himself to either. This was one cause of his success, because he thus found himself free to rise above parties and to present himself as the restorer of national unity. Neither in the old regime nor in the new did he follow principles which would hold him to a set norm within given limits. Unlike Richelieu, he had not been bound by a loyalty to the dynasty which would have subordinated his will to his master's interests; neither had he been bound by a civic virtue which would have subordinated his will to the service of a nation.

A self-made soldier, disciple of the *philosophes,* he had hated feudalism, inequality before the law, lack of religious toleration. Seeing in Enlightened Despotism the reconciliation of authority with political and social reform, he made himself the last and most distinguished of the Enlightened Despots. In this sense he was a man of the Revolution. His passionate individualism had never accepted democracy, however, and he had repudiated the great hope of the eighteenth century which animated revolutionary idealism; the hope that mankind would some day be civilized enough to rule itself. Even concern for his own safety failed to bring him to prudence, as it did other men, because in the popular sense of the word he was indifferent to it, dreaming only of heroic and dangerous greatness. There remained the moral restraint, but he did not communicate with other men in this realm. If he understood their passions well and used them skillfully for his own ends, he only held to those passions which allowed him to dominate men, and he disparaged those which lift men to sacrifice themselves—religious belief, civic virtue, love of liberty—because he felt these to be obstacles in his path. It is not that he was not capable of such sentiments, at least in his youth, because they lead easily in the direction of heroic action, but circumstances had oriented him differently and had shut him up in himself. In the splendid and terrible isolation of the will to power, the concept of *mesure,* limit, makes no sense.

The men of theory thought him one of themselves and did not suspect the romantic impulse in him. Perhaps the only way to have confined it would have been to have kept him in a subordinate position in the service of a strong government. In pushing him toward supreme power the men of Brumaire avoided precisely this kind of precaution.

## Bonaparte's Social Policies

The important laws of the year X did not merely extend Napoleon's personal power. They allow us to glimpse certain social conceptions ripening in his thinking. In the *Conseil d'État* he criticized the individualistic society created by the Revolution: men were only "grains of sand," what was needed was "to sow some blocks of granite on the soil of France" to "give direction to the public mind." In plain language it was a question of establishing alliances of interests which would be bound to the government by the expectation of profit and preferments and which in return could assure him of the obedience of the masses because of the influence they exercised upon the wage-earners. That meant reviving the intermediate bodies or corporate groups of the Old Regime while taking precautions so that they could no longer oppose the State's power with their own and degenerate into oligarchies. Bonaparte was artful enough to show that the bourgeoisie could profit from this: the aristocracy was united by reason of blood relationships, upper-class prejudices and the ecclesiastical hierarchy, "whereas *we* are scattered." The Legion of Honor was to "gather together the partisans of the Revolution." But it was he, and he alone, who was to create the social corps; the penal code was to go so far as to make any association of more than twenty persons dependent upon his authorization; thus did all understand that his personal power would become just that much greater.

The assemblies formed one of these social corps, the Legion of Honor another, the electoral colleges still others. The civil servants, whose ranks he enlarged and divided into hierarchical departments, took their place among them—government scholarship-holders were to be their source of talent. On the 19th Germinal in the year XI (April 9, 1803), to work in conjunction with the ministers and the *Conseil d'État*, Bonaparte created 16 under-counselors (that was only the beginning) who were to provide him with a way to recruit for important administrative positions without having to turn, as formerly, to the personnel of the Revolution or the Old Regime. The judges had a place of honor in this system. Being relatively poorly paid, they could only come from the well-to-do bourgeoisie; The Constitution of the year X endowed them with a hierarchy and a professional discipline. The ministerial officers were also brought together into corporations: there had been assemblies of solicitors since the year VIII, and of notaries and official auctioneers since the year IX. The businessmen were not forgotten: the Chambers of Commerce and of Manufactures, the mercantile and financial exchange companies, and the restoration of brokerages were fulfilling not only technical needs, but also a social plan. If it had depended solely on Bonaparte, even the reappearance of professional guilds would have come about.

According to his conception of it at that time the social hierarchy was based on wealth. It couldn't have been otherwise, since he had come to power with the agreement of the bourgeoisie.The men of theory, it is true, had wanted to add ability to wealth in the management of the State by offering instruction at the cost of the nation. But acquired wealth naturally tends to preserve the dominant power for itself and, like the rich, Bonaparte mistrusted "men of ability" as long as they remained poor: they were potential causes of revolutionary discontent. It was thus agreed to use them only in the capacity of technicians, as the former aristocracy and the absolute monarchy had always done. Whenever Bonaparte sets himself up as the representative of the Revolution, it is always in order to limit its importance to the abolition of privileges, the consequence of this being the advent of the bourgeoisie qualified for the franchise. If his despotism be forgotten we realize that the social regime of the year X laid the foundations for the July Monarchy.

The Civil Code was its Bible. Prepared by a committee which had been appointed as early as August 12, 1800, and whose members included Tronchet, Portalis, Bigot, de Préameneu and Malleville, the rough draft of it was made in January 1801. But the conflict between Bonaparte and the assemblies suspended the discussion, which was not resumed until 1803. The Code was officially published on March 21, 1804, under the title "The French Civil Code"; it was later changed to "The Napoleonic Code." Bonaparte's only direct interest in working it out was insofar as it involved the family. Out of personal concern he wanted to strengthen paternal and marital authority, to prevent unacknowledged illegitimate children from inheriting, to reduce the share going to those who were acknowledged, and also to keep the institution of divorce.

Like all Napoleon's work, the Code is twofold in nature. It confirms the disappearance of the feudal aristocracy and adopts the social principles of 1789: personal liberty, equality before the law, separation of Church and State, religious freedom, and freedom of occupational opportunity. It is for these reasons that it appeared in Europe as the symbol of the Revolution, and that it furnished rules necessary for modern society wherever it was introduced. If this characteristic is blurred in our times, a failure to see it in context when the Code was new is to falsify the history of Napoleonic times and misunderstand the extent of French domination. But the Code also confirmed the reaction against the democratic accomplishments of the Republic. Conceived in terms of bourgeois interests, it is above all concerned with the consecration and sanction of the right to property, which was looked upon as natural, anterior to society, absolute and individualistic, and as a guarantee of possession, which is equal to legal ownership. The contracts it regulates deal almost entirely with property, the hiring of labor taking up just two articles. Even the family is considered from this point of view, to a large extent. The meticulous regulations pertaining to the marriage contract turn marriage into a money matter, and if the Code seems greatly interested in family relationships, this is in view of the question of inheritance.

Affairs of possible interest to the State, such as they were conceived by Bonaparte and his jurists, constitute the other element giving direction to the Code. To a certain extent they limit the property owners' rights with regard to subsoil, dispossession for public benefit, and above all the right to make a will. The family is valuable to the State for it constitutes one of those social bodies that discipline individual activity. Paternal authority, weakened by the Revolution, is thus reinforced: the father can have his children imprisoned for six months without interference by judicial authority; he is lord of their property. Similarly, he administers that of his wife and, since conjugal property is held in common, he usually can dispose of it as he likes. But, like all groups, the family can become too powerful from the point of view of the State, and the fact that its cohesive tendencies find their spontaneous source in nature make it just that much stronger—through the family an independent aristocracy could be reconstituted. Therefore it was put under guardianship: the father's right to make a will was limited by the reestablishment of the "legitimate children" formula, and their right to inherit, declared to be a social principle, was subject to regulation by law. From this point of view, the Code was severely criticized by the former nobility and part of the middle class, whose powers were kept limited by a guarantee of the division of inheritances.

Moreover, people who possess nothing are hardly mentioned except to defend their personal liberty by prohibiting the leasing or hiring of labor on a lifetime basis. By proclaiming work to be free and unregulated and citizens equal in the eyes of the law, the Code actually abandons labor to all the dangers of economic competition, just as the Constituent Assembly had wanted to do, and only sees it as a kind of commodity like so many others. It repudiates the idea, proclaimed in 1793, that the citizen has a right to live. In the case of the wage-laborer it even sacrifices the principle of equality before the law, for, in matters of wages, only the employer was taken at his word. Furthermore the State intervenes in the name of its police power, since the poor man, being without property, would otherwise triumph over the Code and frustrate the institution of proceedings against him by his employer to punish his disobedience. The law of 22nd Germinal in the year XI (April 12, 1803) renews the prohibition against coalitions of workers; the decree of the following December 1 obliges the workers to provide themselves with identification papers subject to control by the authorities, and these had to be produced or else it was forbidden to hire the worker.

Thus the Code comes forth as the fruit of the evolution of French society, inasmuch as it had produced the bourgeoisie and brought it to power. The stamp of history is even more apparent in the details of this document, for the Napoleonic jurists borrowed from Domat and Pothier, who had already begun working out systematic codifications; the former of the Roman or written law still used in the south of France, and the latter of customary or common law. They combined this work with that of the Revolution by editing the one and the other so that the Code is a compromise.

The Code's historical character can also be seen in that, for the most part, it deals with questions of real estate, which still remained the principal form of wealth, whereas it is only slightly interested in industrial holdings, business associations, and credit. In short, it is in no sense a work by theorists who would have imposed upon society an abstract system of law which had no relationship to actual reality, and the criticisms of Savigny and other German jurists are totally without foundation. What mainly inspired the latter were aristocratic beliefs of which the Code is a negation.

Public education, as conceived by Bonaparte, is in harmony with his ideas of social organization and the authoritarian nature of his government. It must "form the nation" and it is "the primary responsibility of the government." The law of the 11th Floréal in the year X (May 1, 1802), prepared by Fourcroy, whose project was accepted in place of Chaptal's, judged too ambitious, abandoned popular education to the municipalities, as had been the case under the Old Regime. Bonaparte, like Voltaire before him, as well as many middle-class people of the time, judged that educating the poor had too many drawbacks from a political and social point of view.

His views on the secondary education of his future administrative elite were otherwise. The model was the Prytanée, the former Collège Louis-le-Grand, the only *collège* maintained throughout the Revolution. Under the Directory, boarding-school facilities, which the central schools lacked, were again provided there, and in the year VIII, Lucien Bonaparte, then Minister of the Interior, began the reorganization of the entire secondary school system. Within the area of jurisdiction of each Court of Appeals, a "*lycée*" was to be established at the cost of the State. In addition "secondary schools" were allowed, directed by private interests, but under the authorization and the control of the government. In the year XII the State assumed the right to appoint their teachers. Six thousand four hundred scholarships were designated for the students in the lycées: 2,400 were to go to the sons of officers and civil servants, and the others were reserved for the best students in the secondary schools. To a certain extent these scholarships fulfilled the hopes of the idealists; but in reality, because the poor could not expect to compete for them, they acted as an endowment favoring the civil and military officer class and, in the case of the lower bourgeoisie, a bait which would link it to the upper bourgeoisie and strip it of its most able leaders. Once engaged in the service of the State or in that of the rulers of the economy, the lower bourgeoisie no longer would venture to become a source of revolutionary agitation.

In theory, parochial education did not disappear, although in Paris, at least, the prefect Frochot assumed the right to authorize and supervise it. The Catholic clergy immediately took advantage of this. Bonaparte never put obstacles in their path in connection with elementary education; the teaching monks of the Christian schools reappeared and in the year XII they obtained the establishment of an institute at Lyon. Since Napoleon considered feminine education to be totally unimportant, he immediately authorized the reconstitution of several orders of teaching nuns. But the conflict between the *lycées* and the Catholic secondary schools was not long in coming; it led Napoleon to establish a monopoly.

At the very time he was perpetuating the social domination of the bourgeoisie, however, the First Consul was already showing that he mistrusted it. In the *Conseil d'État,* he spoke harshly of wealth: "You cannot earn a privilege from wealth. A rich man is often a worthless idler. Even a merchant is often rich just by virtue of his skill in overpricing or stealing." He showed himself even less well-disposed toward the financiers. Clearly he was not opposed to all kinds of wealth, but only to mobile wealth, which was exactly what had created the middle class. In the first place it was difficult to lay hold of, either for purposes of taxation or confiscation. Furthermore, it continually gave rise to new individuals who, proud of owing nothing to anyone but themselves and therefore all the more anxious to keep their independence, tended to violate the social framework Bonaparte was endeavoring to set up. As he ascended the steps to the throne he naturally turned his sights toward those monarchical societies where the prince relied upon a landed aristocracy to whom he guaranteed the servitude of the peasants in return. This ideal was not realizable and, at that time, Napoleon was not even thinking of reestablishing a nobility, but, because of these preferences rather than because of the national interest, he was led to favor the counterrevolution. In the months that followed the Constitution of the year X, the characteristic that made the strongest impression on his contemporaries was, indeed, the growth of that tendency.

The application of the Concordat continued. The Papal Legate Caprara, into whose service Emery (fearing the interference of Napoleon) introduced the Abbé Le Surre, showed his desire to restore harmony, and Portalis, without ceasing to manifest an occasional fondness for Gallican traditions, worked hard to satisfy him.

In the course of events, the rebels, or non-jurors, were predominant in the new clergy. Even the bishops who had come in under the Civil Constitution were forced by the government to concede this preeminence to them and indeed, even if it had been otherwise, the number of priests who had taken the oath under the Civil Constitution would have been insufficient to fill all the vacant positions. In the Department of Bas-Rhin, for example, Saurine could only appoint 16 of them, less than 5 per cent of 351 openings, while La Tour d'Auvergne, in the Pas de Calais, and Caffarelli, in the Côtes du Nord, although they were former non-jurors themselves, awarded 12 per cent of the possible positions to those who had taken the oath; the former 78 out of 643 positions, and the latter 43 out of 340. On the other hand, several bishops imposed a formula of submission on those who had taken the oath. This formula constituted a retraction and when the prefects opposed it, the most they could do was to make the final wording less precise. The bishops who had been reconciled were exposed to the insults of their subordinates, and the situation was still worse for the mere priest. Fouché's circulars had insisted on the maintenance of freedom of conscience and pretended, rather impertinently, to treat the bishops like civil servants and even as assistants to the police, inasmuch as they were spiritual gendarmes; but he was out of favor, and Portalis almost always sided against the prefects. The prefects of the Pas de Calais and Bouches du Rhône were finally removed so as to please the bishops. From the year X on, the Organic Articles (of the Concordat) were ignored on many counts. The prelates were accorded their old titles; ecclesiastical dress was seen once more; the ringing of church bells and processions began again without hindrance; the bishops were authorized to speak in the name of "the divine mercy and grace of the Holy See." Portalis refused to make the observance of the Sabbath compulsory although he did not hide the fact that he was in favor of it; he simply believed that custom would soon bring it about. He permitted the reestablishment of marriage bans. Above all, he seconded the efforts of the bishops to assume the right to supervise civil servants. "You are in a better position than anyone else to teach the government about everything which might concern the public welfare," he wrote to Champion de Cicé. Masclet, subprefect of Boulogne, in spite of his mistrust of the clergy, did not refrain from observing to the mayors that even if the clergy remained loyal to their convictions, they would be forced into conformity by the performance of their duties.

The parish priests immediately complained of their wretched state. The peasants accepted them without objection, but many remained indifferent, and no one wanted to pay. Although the Organic Articles had declared religion to be free, they had ordained the division of church offerings between curates and vicars, and these came back into being immediately. The bishops established rates by decree and arrogated to themselves the right to create councils or vestries which would assure the material support of the parishes. Since the parish priests received neither lodging nor salary from their flocks, however, Bonaparte, in the year XI, began to put pressure on the administrative bodies by ordering them to "deliberate" on these subjects; he also restored to the curates the land which had formerly belonged to them and which had not been confiscated by the government.These measures were not very effective. The Empire was soon to increase its acts of generosity to the Church, and the Concordat thus became the point of departure for an evolution which was to prepare the Catholic clergy for the triumphs of the Restoration.

The return of the *émigrés* did not give rise to similar difficulties, but it made a still deeper impression, and it is worth noting that whereas Bonaparte received many formal letters of congratulation upon the occasion of his being appointed Consul for life, he did not receive a single one referring to the amnesty. The latter placed the *émigrés* under police surveillance for ten years, and they could be imprisoned, like others, by a *lettre de cachet.* Therefore they usually were extremely prudent. This did not stop them from playing the part of leaders in the local community nor from trying to get from those who had acquired their lands restitution or a settlement. The people who had acquired land confiscated by the government became alarmed, particularly when on July 23, 1803, Bonaparte ordered an audit of their books. This provoked worried discussions and even some rash actions and gave the impression that the sales might be questionable. If Bonaparte could have decided the question alone, the law of July 17, 1793 (which had annulled without compensation income derived from land which still bore a taint of feudal obligation) might have been revised so as to procure indemnities for the owners and also a revenue for the State Treasury, since many of these rents were included in national property; but he did not dare to go against the opinions of the *Conseil d'État* which declared this law untouchable. Many of the *émigrés* had already rallied to the regime. Ségur was a member of the *Conseil d'État;* Séguier, of the Court of Appeals of Paris and the Duc de Luynes of the Senate. In 1804, M.-J. de Gérando was to become director of the Ministry of the Interior. Bonaparte, on the other hand, married many of his companions at arms to noblewomen, including Junot, Ney, Launes, Augereau, Savary. Some, it is true, preferred the daughters of financiers, for example Duroc and Marmont.

This fusion of old and new became particularly evident at the court of the First Consul, which rapidly took on a look typical of the Old Regime, even more at the Tuileries Palace than at Malmaison. Duroc was already governor of the palace. In November 1802, Josephine received an official title and was given four ladies-in-waiting chosen from the ancient nobility. With this suite, she accompanied Bonaparte to Belgium. Etiquette became constantly more meticulous; Bonaparte himself donned silk stockings and wore the "Regent"[1] on the hilt of his sword. Royal dress, carriages, liveried servants, festivals and opera balls again dazzled the populace. In January of 1803, court mourning was reestablished upon the occasion of the death in Santo Domingo of Leclerc, the husband of Pauline Bonaparte. August 16, 1802, had been designated St. Napoleon's Day, and the republican holidays of July 14 and

---

[1] The "Regent": the famous diamond of the crown of France which was bought in 1717 by Philippe d'Orléans, Regent of France from 1715 to 1723. Its weight is 136 carats. [Editors' note.]

*Vendémiaire* were no longer celebrated by 1804, except perfunctorily. Bonaparte's head appeared on coins minted in 1803.

The fashionable world of the salons eagerly adopted the tone set by the court. This new aristocracy closed its doors to the *nouveaux riches* and the financiers. Bonaparte imposed on it standards unknown to the Old Regime. He had separated Josephine from her former friends, Mme. Tallien and Mme. Hamelin, and restored the fashion of feminine modesty. This severity of manners was only a façade (he allowed himself many indulgences); he cared chiefly about external correctness and moreover was a model of this standard himself. In this respect as in others, the new society was very bourgeois: it repudiated the nonchalance and gracefulness of the eighteenth-century aristocracy through concern with "appearances." That in other areas this evolution was far from being accomplished is clearly shown by the fate of the Legion of Honor. After having violated his own law by making himself master of its council of administration, Bonaparte suspended the designation of members of the Legion. Already this institution, such as he had fashioned it, seemed too closely linked with the memory of the Revolution.

At the close of 1802, so many symptoms could no longer leave any doubt about his real designs. From the point of view of the nation's interest, it is thus the Treaty of Amiens which marks his zenith. The French people wanted peace above all; and Bonaparte had given it to them. They were attached to the social achievements of the Revolution, and Bonaparte had conserved them. Satisfied and proud of their leader, they did not yet have the feeling that he was abusing his power and was aiming at goals contrary to theirs. They did not desire the leader to become king, still less that he create a nobility. But in his heart Bonaparte himself had abandoned the Republic and the ideal of equality. The people, gratified by their success in reaching the natural frontiers, had no desire to go beyond them. But their master, having already crossed them, had made war inevitable. They saw in him only a national hero at the very hour he had ceased to be one.

## A Note on the Imperial Conquests

For his contemporaries and for the earliest historians, the imperial conquests, like the Empire itself, were explained by what they called the "ambition" of Napoleon. Not that this ambition was wholly responsible; opportunities arose, but ambition seized upon them when the national interest would have ordered resisting them. In later years this opinion came to seem an oversimplification to certain observers. Some of these wished to see in Napoleon only the defender of the natural frontiers. They argue that the Republicans had made him Consul and then Emperor to save themselves. This impossible task, legacy of the Revolution, forced him to conquer Europe and finally proved his downfall. In a certain sense these historians only took over the legend that Napoleon's Old Guard had formed of their god and which he himself popularized at St. Helena: Soldier of the Revolution, he had done nothing but defend himself against the kings of the Old Regime.

Others, reluctant to reduce the role of the individual in the course of history and to regard Napoleon as a mere instrument of destiny, persisted in searching in the man himself for the motivating force of his policy and thought they found it in a grand design which makes his policy coherent and unifies it as a whole. According to this line of thought, his objective was to take from England the supremacy of the seas, and his career, at least after the rupture of the Treaty of Amiens, is to be regarded as the final episode of the struggle begun under Louis XIV and is therefore an integral part of the classic tradition of the France of the *Ancien Régime*. Another variation on this theme is that the mirage of the East drew him to the abyss. For those who hold this view, Napoleon was less a Frenchman than a European; they consider that he was aiming for a reconstitution of the Carolingian Empire at first and later the Roman Empire, the οἰχουμένη of western Christian civilization.

Each of these interpretations corresponds to a part of the realty—the reality itself is too great to be contained in any of them. It is true that the men who brought Bonaparte to power wanted to preserve the natural frontiers, and it was tempting to cross them in order to defend them, but it is not true that it was the only or the safest means of protecting them, nor that in extending his conquests Napoleon was thinking only of the interests of the nation. It is true that England had been his constant and stubborn enemy and that in defeating him she had definitely triumphed over France; but if it had been his only aim and he had followed a plan ripened in reflection, his continental policy would have been quite different. Even the blockade, on which so much emphasis is placed, was more a result than a cause of the establishment of the Grand Empire. Nothing would have delighted the new Alexander more than an expedition to Constantinople or toward India, but most of Napoleon's undertakings are related to this dream only by an act of imagination. It is undeniable that he did compare himself to Charlemagne and Caesar and that he attempted to unify the western world politically, but it was not the intellectual desire to recreate the past which spurred him to action. In denouncing the avowed hatred of the Allies for the Soldier of the Revolution, the Napoleonic legend shows an acute perspicacity, and it is surprising that so many historians have overlooked this; but, on the other hand, Napoleon did not confine himself to the defensive.

There is no rational explanation which can make over-all sense of Napoleon's foreign policy; he pursued at the same time ends which, at least at the time, were contradictory. In the final reckoning we must come back to his ambition. His contemporaries, who had before their eyes the theatrical trappings, overdone in their richness and loud in their novelty, the love affairs, the quarrels of a rapacious family, and the thievery of his followers, lowered his ambition—without denying his genius—to the level of the average man's. At a distance, the image stands out less encumbered and reveals its secret: the heroic lure of risk, the magic seduction of dreams, the irresistible drive of temperament.

# NAPOLEON

### Louis Madelin

## *A Portrait*

"Bonaparte is the *finest manifestation of human will*," wrote Schopenhauer, the philosopher of pessimism, after an interview with the youthful Emperor. In fact, perhaps no one has ever shown, to such a degree, so many of the forms of will as Napoleon Bonaparte. *"Impossible* is not a French word" is an expression that has been credited to him. What is certain is that he never applied the word *impossible* to himself. To Molé he said *"Impossible* is a word whose meaning is completely relative. . . . It is the phantom of the humble and the refuge of cowards. *Uttered by one in power, that word, believe me,* is only an admission of impotence!" He was never more sincere. We know that, as a youth, even as a child, against every obstacle, every bond, every "impossibility" he pitted his will. It was used to conquering. "There is no purpose, no ability, and no courage," wrote a foreign ambassador, "that does not break when faced with this *character of iron."* His will power was based on energy. His spirit, save for a few rare occasions, remained intrepid and almost unperturbed, being in this respect different from his brain, which might err. This man was capable of all kinds of bravery. This "skinny mathematician," as his splendid lieutenants of the Army of Italy called him before his great exploits from Toulon to Arcola, was the first to throw himself into the line of fire when all others held back. We will see him in the same role in 1814; and yet he set moral courage much above physical courage. His past experience already permitted him to write in 1802, "There is as much true courage in steadfastly bearing the pains of the soul as in keeping still under the grapeshot of artillery fire." His whole existence will be a unique example of conscious energy, both mental and physical.

"It is characteristic of him not to be able to bear the torments of indecision for long, and it is his wont, once he has chosen a course of action, to sacrifice to it all previous agreements and obligations and to respect neither the principles of justice nor the counsels of prudence which might run counter to it." This was how, as early as the first year of the Consulate, the Minister of Prussia, Lucchesini, judged him; and if, in truth, the diplomat here anticipates the portrait of the future Emperor rather than the present Consul, it is a fact that at all times Napoleon's sense of decision was paralleled by a sense of authority that did not tolerate opposition and shattered all fetters. At the moment when France was waiting for a leader to restore authority, there appeared *the man of authority, par excellence.* "Before the Revolution," he said in the presence of Molé, "authority had fallen to the distaff side, we had an imbecile for a king, he was *hung* [sic], his family was driven away." "A dethroned king," his confidant reports, "was the object of his scorn." Let us remember his attitude toward an insulted Louis XVI when Bonaparte was a young soldier with revolutionary sympathies. At the opening of the Legislative Corps in 1804, he said, *"Weakness in the supreme authority is the most awful calamity that can befall a people."* The young commander-in-chief of the Army of Italy used to boil with impatience when faced with the weakness of the Directory. His letters to the Directors already revealed, and at times were bursting forth with that thirst for authority which, at the very hour, he was satisfying beyond the Alps. To establish "authority" is the primary goal, everything else follows—and mainly order. Napoleon was indeed much too intelligent *to love power for its own sake.* In this respect he never had anything of the tyrant who makes people submit to his desires and whims *for the sole pleasure of making others submit.* Authority would never be more for him than the necessary condition for order, which is the source of all good.

Order was in his blood, in his brain, and in his heart. Henri IV had wished to reestablish order, but his personal habits were disorderly; there was no such contradiction in Napoleon Bonaparte. He was simply extending to the management of a great army, of a great State, and later of a great empire the quality that ruled his mind and his life: *Order.* His minister Chaptal described him as possessing "an orderly mind," but Bonaparte used it first to rule himself. Despite some passing attachments, he showed self-control in his personal life and even more so where the spending of money was concerned, since he believed that it was perhaps in this area that disorder was most dangerous. One of the traits he inherited from his mother, Letizia, was a concern for thrift, which at all times made him save something, whether from his salary of 800 *livres* as a second lieutenant or from his household budget of many millions. Though he was no miser, and some of his expenditures might have seemed extravagant if one did not thoroughly understand his character, he could not tolerate seeing waste and bribery around him. Just as he carefully managed his personal fortune, supervising his lawyer, checking on his purveyors, and calling his stewards to order, he simply transferred to the management of State finances, which were in decline, that same sense of economy which was merely a striking form of his love of order. He in fact told Las Cases that he had kept very little of his savings for himself and that he had bought no landed property, adding, "Everyone has a right to his own ideas; I had a liking for a solid foundation, but I never had a love of property."

Order in financial matters, order everywhere. If we are soon to see him studying the seemingly most trifling subjects—since no more than a Richelieu had he ever acquiesced to *De minimis non curat praetor*—it was because he could not allow a breach against order to go unsanctioned. He wrote to Eugenie, "Be unrelenting with rascals. The uncovering of a disloyal accountant is a victory for the administration." This love of order made him *legalistic*. It is true that he shared the revolutionary fervor, but only in appearance and *pro forma* did he approve of those days of insurrection that were part of the Revolution. Personally he disliked going beyond legal procedure; we know he would have wished to remove all connotations of violence from the *coup d'état* that carried him to power. In fact, the necessity of having the grenadiers throw a few representatives of the people out of the window displeased him very much. He never talked of that unprecedented hour of the 19th Brumaire, and he never celebrated the anniversary of the *coup d'état* which made him ruler; he asked that one forget those few minutes of a revolution which he would have preferred to see carried out through unanimous consent and in a legal manner. At the end of his political life, after Waterloo, he refused the help of the aroused citizens of the *faubourgs* against the Assemblies, because he loathed disorder too much to use their help, even on his own behalf or to save himself. "I would consider myself disgraced," he wrote as early as Vendémiaire, year V, in Italy, "if I allowed political turmoil to ferment in an area under my command."

From this love of order arose his will to organize, to codify, to give a solid base to institutions, to use men in suitable positions, to put each thing and each man in its place. From it arose that talent for administration and the giving of orders which, as in Italy and already in Egypt, dictated the decrees that seemed, in appearance, so far removed from the preoccupations peculiar to an army commander. He would never tolerate an interruption in the normal course of events. He was to say in 1800, in the presence of Roederer, "I wish the ten years of my administration to elapse without having to dismiss a single minister, a single general, or a single Councillor of State." In fact, having been unable in practice to keep such promises, he still found it very hard to discharge a public servant, because continuity remained for him a condition of order, and order must, in every realm, be protected and respected. It must be so even in the realm of appearances, which explains his great concern for deportment and good manners. His letters are full of admonitions on this subject: he would not tolerate a lapse in dignity or behavior from ministers, prefects, generals, bishops, priests, nor even students and singers at the *Opéra*. This intolerance he at times carried over into their private lives and with stronger reason into their working or official lives—because *dignity is only another manifestation of order.*

This concern alone would have been sufficient to make him extremely severe, even if his personality did not already lead him in this direction.

"A king's love is not like a mother's tenderness. Kings must be feared and respected. *The people's love for them is nothing but esteem.*" It was in Roederer's presence that he expressed this thought; and at the Council of State he said, "Nothing is more tyrannical than a government that claims to be paternal." He believed that it is better to forewarn than to repress and that one gives warning only through an inflexible severity, "by examples." He wrote to Fouché (a man who hardly needed such reminders), "The art of the police consists in *punishing severely in order not to punish often.*" And to Barbé-Marbois, *"Best of all is to make an example."* His stay in Egypt had instilled in him a certain contempt for men: "Man, uncivilized, is a beast," and he believed that, unless restrained by severity, civilized man rather quickly reverted to savagery. In the past he had greatly admired Rousseau; he now admitted that the latter was in error. "Man is not good"; he must be forced to respect the law, and especially Frenchmen. "The French people, beginning with the Gauls, have always been the people who most needed to be governed and *consequently to fear those who govern."* But he well knew that this was true everywhere, and when his brother Louis (then king of Holland) wrote that his new subjects were acclaiming his "benevolence," he answered, "My brother, when it is said of a king that he is good, his reign has failed." This sentence would define the Bonaparte of 1800 equally well. But, always intelligent, he admitted that though severity was an essential part of order, justice was its prime condition. "I prefer injustice to disorder"—this phrase is attributed to Goethe. Bonaparte, the Bonaparte of 1800 in any case, does not believe that he must make a choice: the greatest disorder, the source of all disorders, is injustice. Each one must do his duty; if he does, let him be rewarded; if he does not, let him be punished. The thousand *decisions* about individual cases, submitted to him by his ministers and recorded in his *Correspondance,* testify to this lasting concern for order. A sublieutenant had deserted his post, but the minister had added, as a timid plea, "He is not even twenty and is the son of a famous general." Napoleon answered, "This officer must be indicted by a military court and treated in accord with the full strictness of the law. He is a coward." But when a young girl was deprived of her inheritance in favor of a charitable institution he wrote, "Find out why this orphan was despoiled," and he ordered the money returned. It was almost as though the *Chêne de Vincennes*[1] had been planted again. He often, through a spontaneous action, granted pensions and employment to the children of those who, even in preceding regimes. had rendered great services to the State. On the other hand, he could never tolerate irresponsibility; going beyond the mistakes of the little man to those of the great, he searched out those truly responsible. "In my reign," he wrote in the Year XIII, "there will be no immunity before the law." This is because, I repeat, for him order resided essentially in justice, and, for him, justice could not be imagined without severity.

"Hard! even Cruel!" they called him. It is true that, according to a harsh phrase, he "killed them"; but it was in the service of the commonwealth, which itself endures. We will find occasion to describe what kind of work this prodigious regime accomplished in fifteen years. As they labored for a government ceaselessly devoted to its work, administrators, members of the general staff, government officers, civil and military

---

[1] An oak tree in the Forest of Vincennes where Louis IX (Saint Louis), 1226-1270, administered informal justice even for the humblest of his subjects. [Editors' note.]

functionaries—both great and small—all of them bent on their own tasks, soon found themselves totally chained to that government. Meanwhile the whole Nation, spurred on by the government's daily appeals for greater effort, displayed, from the workshops to the fields, an unprecedented activity. It was mainly because, at the very head of this government, a man of iron guided the newly functioning machinery of State with a miraculously firm hand. A man of indefatigable will and of indefatigable intelligence, the young Consul believed that he was superior to his century, but precisely because he had too enlightened a mind, he had no self-conceit. "A man is but a man," as he once said. In addition to the many talents which he possessed to such a high degree, the good fairies seated by the cradle in Ajaccio had given him a final one—the most precious—the capacity to understand men and the ability to "get the most" out of them. It was miraculous that at a time when France was searching for a man who—uniting in his person all the qualities of a great head of State—could raise her from her ruins, there should appear one who possessed such a prodigious combination of aptitudes that he far exceeded the most extravagantly ambitious expectations. Moreover, not only did his character suit the demands of an extraordinary situation, but it happened that his ideas corresponded to those expressing the aspirations of the nation.

### "Blocks of Granite"

The aristocracy was returning; accordingly, the former social order, without being restored, was regaining its adherents. One might have feared that, with the return in two stages of 100,000 members of the Old Regime, who remained hostile to the new society if not to the new government, important support might be given to those who for the preceding two years, though praising the Consulate, had fundamentally remained hostile to the ideas and to the men of the Revolution. But already the First Consul was considering measures calculated to establish this new society solidly, against the return of reaction. He was much impressed by the crumbling of the supporters of the Republic. "Everything has been destroyed," he had said. *"We must rebuild.* There is a government, and there are powers, but all the rest of the Nation, what is it? *Grains of sand. . . . We are scattered, without organization, without unity, without contact.* As long as I am here, I will answer for the Republic, but we must prepare for the future. Do you believe that the Republic is safely established? If so, you would be greatly mistaken. We have the power to create it; but we do not have a Republic, and we will not have one *unless we sow some blocks of granite on the soil of France."*

At the time that he was expressing himself in these striking terms, he was simultaneously organizing, concurrently with the *Concordat* and the restoration of peace, two projects which were to be presented to the Assemblies: one aimed at the establishment of the *Legion of Honor* and the other had as its object the reorganization of *Public Education.* Both were derived from the same concept: *blocks of granite.*

The new educational system had to be organized; it had to be coherent, strong, and subject to an intellectual, moral, and civic discipline which would create, in the near future, the new strata of modern society. But while waiting for the children, who were going to be "set in a new mold," to enter government service, fifteen years would have to go by; meanwhile, should the new society be left without cadres, without common bonds, and without a hierarchy? While working to give education its new statutes, the Consul was at the same time forming the idea of organizing a kind of democratic nobility. Consisting of the most faithful servants of the New France and based—as had, very long ago, been true of the aristocracy—on services rendered to the Nation, it would blot out memories of the old society that the Revolution had destroyed and which the Consul believed should remain destroyed. A *general staff* of 30,000 citizens, grouped in a self-perpetuating *Legion,* would be bound, through its oaths, to the principles of the new regime; but it must not be a simple *grouping* of common interests, such as the wretched oligarchs of the *Directory* might have imagined: it must be given *an ideal.* The Old Regime had possessed one: loyalty to the sovereign by divine right; supporters of the Church had another: loyalty to Christ's doctrine as symbolized in the Pope. What ideal could be given to the new generation, most of whose members no longer felt loyalty to a dynasty and who remained estranged from Christ and the Church? They would be given, as a bond and as a *raison d'être,* the knowledge that throughout his life Napoleon Bonaparte would hold *Honor* to be the greatest of all virtues as well as the mainspring of the soul! The new men would gather together under the banner of *Honor!* It would be the *Legion of Honor,* an element binding society together, but also a sanction given to excellence and to valor in all fields. Article I (the fundamental one) of the projected law stated: "In fulfillment of article 87 of the Constitution concerning *military* awards and in order also to reward *civil* service and virtue, a *Legion of Honor* will be created."

It is difficult for us to understand the incredible "uproar" this project engendered. "It is impossible to explain it properly today," wrote a contemporary thirty years later. I previously stated that the France of *Brumaire* did not retain an ardent attachment for any of the principles of 1789 with the exception of *Equality.* It was on the grounds of *Equality* that the most vehement apprehension was expressed. Indeed, those who, in advance, saw in the Legion of Honor a means for the government, whatever it might be, to master the elite through the bait of high rewards found little support. On that account Bonaparte tried to anticipate criticism: nominations would be made *not by the executive branch* but by a *Great Council,* on which, besides the Consuls, representatives of the Senate, of the Legislative Corps, and of the Tribunate would sit and which itself would elect its "Chancellor." Many people, however, spoke of the revival of an essentially monarchical "order," of gradual steps toward a new monarchy, of a "despotism" upheld by blind supporters. But the protests expressed in the name of Liberty were not as telling as those unleashed in the name of Equality. What offended the survivors of the Revolution—even the moderates—was reestablishing a *differentiation* which, it was said, would lead to the restoration of "a nobility." Thus, once again it was proved that the movement of 1789 had been aimed at a caste, not at a throne. "Down with caste!" The government wished to create a "caste," but it would not be tolerated by the people.

In the Assemblies the opposition, which was thought to have disappeared, was being reconstituted. No one seemed to understand the two aspects of the First Consul's thought, which were in the interests of both the men of the Revolution and of all the French: on the one hand, the security which the association of those believing in the new ideas would give society; on the other hand, the premium given for services to the Nation—civil as well as military—upon which the Consul had insisted in his wonderful appeal to the Council of State. But the Council of State itself was offering resistance: the measure was carried by only four votes. Ten of the old revolutionaries, from Thibaudeau to Réal, notwithstanding their previously great devotion to the work of the Consulate, had voted against it. What would happen in the Tribunate!

In addition, after debate in this assembly had opened, there occurred an unfortunate incident. Lucien Bonaparte, who had been made a member of the Assembly after the *purge,* was very much disliked by most of his colleagues. The ex-president of the *Council of Five Hundred,* who, even more than his brother, had accomplished the *coup d'état* of Brumaire, had, from that day, claimed the right to break up everything. He decided to defend the projected law through preemptory arguments which offended the tribunes. The plan was carried by only 56 votes, against 38 negative votes—an enormous minority in an assembly from which, it was believed, all elements systematically hostile to consular policy had previously been eliminated. In the Legislative Corps, on the 30th of Floréal, the law passed by only 166 votes against 110—mustering 62 votes less than the Concordat. It is true that the Council of State had made a poor choice in the orator entrusted with defending, before the Legislative Corps, the establishment of the *Legion of Honor;* it was Roederer, who informed people would remember that, as a member of the Constituent Assembly, had delivered an impassioned address whose conclusion was that in order to destroy thoroughly the old "feudal sentiment," it was "necessary to *discredit honor.*" Many politicians thus throughout their career carry the burden of an unfortunate utterance.

Many of Bonaparte's own friends, in all three Assemblies, had fought this organization which we consider today one of the most successful produced by these fruitful years. The enemies of the regime gave vent to the sharpest mockery, embroidering on a peculiar yet sincere indignation. Julie Talma, who disliked all consular institutions, made constant allusions to the *Legion of Honor* in her letters to Benjamin Constant, knowing that her friend echoed her feelings. A little later she wrote: "They say that commoners are no longer to fill important positions. The *so-called tribunes* and the *so-called legislators* have decreed a *Legion of Honor;* they have lost the right to take offense. They have proved that they no longer hate *castes or privileges.*"

Bonaparte was not yet prepared to force people and hurry matters. He was to wait two years before promulgating the law (on the 22nd of Messidor, Year XII) and before awarding the 30,000 *crosses, cravats, ribbons,* and *stars* of the new Order, and the prejudice against it was such that many people, at first, were slightly embarrassed to wear these decorations. The royalists thought it a *masquerade:* an English caricature depicts Bonaparte cutting his ribbons out of a Phrygian cap. The caricature was not entirely wrong—according to Bonaparte, the *Legion of Honor* really was a democratic institution, which the friends of the Revolution should have been the last to oppose. It is difficult to understand a republican soldier like Moreau making such fun of the order and, in the guise of parody, awarding to his own cook "the order of the *Saucepan of Honor.*"

In any case the idea had triumphed. The new society had its aristocracy or rather its cadres. One of the *blocks of granite* had been set in the still unstable soil of France.

The new education was to be an even more powerful "block of granite.". . . During one of the debates on education a member of the Convention had exclaimed that one must "get hold of the newborn generation." Bonaparte had exactly the same idea. He considered that the future of the new regime was based on the reorganization of Public Education and the founding of new *collèges* faithful to its principles. But his thoughts were certainly directed to higher objectives. He blushed to see France surprise Europe in the first years of the nineteenth century by the decline of her educational system and scholarship—this after having dominated Europe in the past, and particularly in the last three centuries, through the soundness of her studies and the brilliance of her minds. *"The most important of our institutions is Public Education,"* he was to say to the Council of State. *"Everything depends on it, the present and the future."* As early as 1801 he did not think otherwise.

He admired the old studies and even more the old scholarly disciplines. Right in the middle of the Council of State—composed in great part of *philosophes*—he dared to state: "The Jesuits ... in the State, formed an admirable teaching or rather educational body, unwavering in their methods and their doctrines and possessing a knowledge of men and society which *equipped them to produce fathers, sons, magistrates, political men, and even warriors, rather than scholars."* He added, to calm the fears of his audience: "Doubtless no one would dream of reestablishing them, but *we must try to profit from their experience and try to find again a teaching body possessing their ability."* Moreover, his admiration extended to the Oratorians and in general to those teaching orders which, as he said, "have *left behind them such a great void* in the realm of public education."

He favored classical studies: "We must encourage a great expansion in education, *and young heads must be steeped a little in Greek and Roman studies."* We know, however, that he had felt little relish for ancient languages when he had studied at Brienne. He did not wish to restore the days when the Jesuits made their students speak Latin in "academic" debates or when the Oratorians were able to teach their pupils to perform the tragedies of Sophocles and Euripides in the Greek language. He would be satisfied to see Homer and Virgil, Demosthenes and Cicero, Thucydides and Livy reestablished in a place of honor, but because of his great personal interest in the physical sciences and in the new discoveries, he meant to devote a larger part of the curriculum to the teaching of science than had been the case before 1789. But his main purpose was to reestablish an *academic discipline* which would be strengthened alike by teaching and studying Plutarch as well as Newton.

This academic discipline would prepare the new generation for social discipline and national discipline. Bonaparte was to say, in Molé's presence,"The ethics and the political ideas of the coming generation must no longer be dependent on the news of the day or on circumstances of the moment. We must, first of all, achieve unity, and we must be able to cast a whole generation *in the same mold."* This, as we shall see, was the Emperor's thought in granting the exclusive control of studies to the *Université de France,* which he had founded in 1807. The First Consul may already have held similar ideas, but they did not exclude broader concepts and did not dominate his plans: first of all, in 1801, he meant to foster a new intelligence as well as a new discipline in the "rising" generations. A newspaper article—inspired by him—was to say concerning the restoration of classical studies: *"All children must be exposed to them,"* since "that freedom, inappropriately bestowed on the young, to choose whichever courses please them, to switch from one to another without good reason, and to consult nothing but their whims ... that freedom—given to them in the erroneous belief that they would possess the wisdom and discernment so rare even in maturity—will no longer exist. *The public schools will take up the discipline of the old collèges."* The newspaper added that the new teachers would hereafter devote themselves *entirely* to their teaching, from which they had been diverted by politics. The article was published on the 8th of Floréal, Year X, and discussed the Consular bill which, as the Law of the 10th of Floréal, was to reorganize public education.

The projected bill had at first been debated in the Council of State. The need for it was so obvious that, though the bill was incomplete and embryonic, the Assemblies welcomed it joyfully, and it received a unanimous vote from the Legislative Corps. It was embryonic and incomplete precisely because it was urgent to send bourgeois youth back to the *collèges*. The first Consul had wished to avoid month-long discussions of such great "National Education Plans" as the Assemblies of the Revolution had meant to create but which had accomplished very little. The bill was aimed at the most pressing objective: building up secondary education. *Lycées* were to replace the *Écoles Centrales,* and insofar as possible, there would be one in each departmental capital. A really adequate teaching corps was needed (the *concours d'agrégation* would soon be established and the *École Normale* reinstated). This Corps should be composed, wrote the *Gazette,* of "former teachers whom the Revolution had dispersed and of those who have since followed in their footsteps and, most important, who have maintained the moral caliber required for exercising authority over children." An educational program was set up consisting of the classical languages, French language and literature, history, geography, and elements of the mathematical, physical, and natural sciences. But the main task was to search for and find teachers of unimpeachable morals, who would also be totally devoted to their work as educators. A little later Napoleon stated that he intended to create a teaching corps which, in its complete dedication to education, would emulate the former teaching Orders he so much admired. "They must be wedded to Public Education," he said, "just as their predecessors were wedded to the Church."

In 1802 the *lycées* only numbered 20, but 300 secondary schools—the *collèges*—would soon open. Meanwhile, the State could temporarily look for unexpected help from the newly reestablished private education. The Councillor of State Chaptal was at first responsible for the report on the restoration of Public Education. Indeed it was he who very clearly and eloquently came out in favor of freedom in education and against what he called the "privilege"—we say the "monopoly"—of the State in this area. His report was published in the *Moniteur* of Brumaire, Year IX, and on this account it is likely that he had the approval of the First Consul. No doubt when Chaptal became Minister of the Interior, he had to turn over the preparation of the bill to his colleague Roederer, a man much less inclined to combat "privilege," but the latter was nevertheless finally steered away from giving the State a monopoly of education. Thus, education having temporarily secured its freedom, more than 300 *private* schools were founded and adopted the newly established curriculum. It was enough for the moment, but the Consul was already thinking of building a quite different monument: the *Université de France.* But, precisely because he wished it to be sturdy and of vast dimensions, he intended to give himself time to gather together its various elements. For the present, having made education secure, he expected that 22,000 children would soon fill the *lycées, collèges,* and *primary schools.* He also meant working-class children to receive the new education: 6400 scholarships were created and though, at first, only 3000 were awarded, it was because he wished the choices to be made fairly and only after thorough investigation. The most urgent needs had been met; the Law on Public Education prepared the future, but it was only a rough draft for the edifice which would spring up six years later.

On the 15th of Floréal the First Consul was thus congratulating the Assemblies for having made into law a bill in which the government "had tried to unite the advantages of the old disciplines with the improvements which the progress of knowledge makes one feel are possible." This new "block of granite," which would serve as a solid base for the State as well as the Nation, thus helped counteract the ever-diminishing chaos. One newspaper enthusiastically commented on the end of "this kind of fluctuation which has existed for ten years in the field of education and *was contributing to a lack of stability in the people's mind and soul.*"

It took only a few weeks for the First Consul to make triumphant in the Assemblies all the great measures, which, he believed, would not only pacify the masses for the present but would restore elites in the future. The Concordat became law on the 18th of Germinal; the Amnesty was sanctioned by the *sénatus-consulte* of the 26th of Germinal; and the Legion of Honor was established by the Law of the 30th of Floréal. Meanwhile the bill reorganizing Public Education received an affirmative vote on the 10th of Floréal, and the Treaty of Amiens, establishing general peace, was ratified on the 16th of Floréal by a vote of the Assemblies. There had never been a more fruitful parliamentary session. But the Assemblies did not receive the credit; the people's admiration and gratitude was given to the man who so often had to push through and *impose* on the Assemblies the beneficial laws which would result in the pacification and restoration of the Nation.

Meanwhile, another "block of granite," of even greater importance to France, was soon to come. The Codes were being drafted.

## Epilogue

We must now ask a more general question. Napoleon, at the peak of his power in 1812, had—in less than two years—so precipitously fallen from this summit that he was driven to the unconditional abdication of April 1814. Could he, so to speak, return to life in a permanent form? And, after his fall, could his dynasty and his regime perpetuate themselves without him?

It has been said a thousand times, and with reason, that it is fruitless to rewrite history. But to attempt to illuminate its workings is not forbidden. In the year VIII, Napoleon Bonaparte had lifted France out of anarchy and saved her from the ruin which would have been its inevitable result. He had given the country such sturdy institutions that (probably contrary to his own expectations) they have almost all, from the Napoleonic Code to his administrative system, miraculously survived for a century and a half under a great variety of political regimes. In 15 years, moreover, he added considerably, though at the cost of great hardship, to the inheritance of glory which our nation had gained in ten centuries. Glory is not, as some have claimed, without meaning for a country. Even when great triumphs have ended in the most cruel disasters, the prestige derived from these triumphs is retained by the nation whose valor has been brilliantly displayed to the world through her labors and victories and sometimes even through her courage in defeat. This unequaled prestige has also survived and on many occasions it has given France a matchless strength.

These are reflections which extend beyond my conclusions of today. It is possible that, in a volume supplementing this *Histoire du consulat et de l'empire*, I might come to judge the man and his work in a larger context. And in following Napoleon beyond the grave, I might cite, as the most brilliant justification of his work, the incredible popularity which he still enjoys. But I wish to say today that, in my opinion, the lasting institutions which he gave the country, and the glory which he bestowed on her for so long, are insignificant beside the role he took upon himself in the first years of his government and which he later completely fulfilled. This role, in the words of one of his contemporaries, was that of "the great conciliator of passions," the successful arbitrator of the quarrels which, to a greater degree than ever before were tearing apart the France of the year VIII of the Republic. I have devoted many pages to these quarrels and to the arbitration which, in so few years, put an end to them in a way that seemed truly miraculous to many people. Though he was not a modest man, Napoleon declared, "A man is but a man. Another would have come." Another? What other? All of the unique prestige which his victories had already bestowed upon him in 1799 was needed. But, more important, his unusual combination of superior talents, whose study I have attempted, an⌐ his strength and steadfastness, which apparently no one else possessed, were all necessary to reunite the French people whom the strife and disagreements of ten years of Revolution had deeply divided. The Bourbons, as we know, had almost been recalled as early as 1795, at a time when the nation wished to be rid of a regime forever tainted with the blood of the Terror and which under the Directory was sinking into debauchery. But would the Bourbons, in the year V of the Republic, have been able to accomplish the work Napoleon would take upon himself three years later? When one sees, in 1814, how Louis XVIII found it so difficult to attempt to impose his authority over his friends even fourteen years after internal peace and national reconciliation had been achieved, suppositions are quite unnecessary. For in the aftermath of terrorist excesses, and at a time when the Nation remained greatly disturbed by the heated passions of its citizens, what would the reign of a Bourbon have been like?

In the year VIII Napoleon Bonaparte had been the arbiter which a Bourbon could not be. This, I believe, was the role allotted to him by what some (in his own wor call Destiny, but to which believers give the name of Providence.

His work was almost completed—I have attempted to show this in "The Natio the Reign of the Emperor"—by the year 1812, after which the Empire was to decl. Yes, his work was completed: the two Frances, or rather the ten Frances, so cruel. hostile to each other, were already united and had almost become one. For a time under the Restoration, it seemed as though this work was collapsing, but it had already borne fruit—Louis XVIII must have recognized it, since he personally refused to join some greatly mistaken friends in pursuing the total reaction of which they dreamed. But, this work having been accomplished, the main role of a Napoleon had come to an end. He was not the man—let us admit it—either to create a new monarchical regime o' to establish a "fourth dynasty." He had been responsible for all the concordats and h had based the new France on these agreements between the parties, the churches, ar the different classes. The new France itself would survive, and this would l recognized as early as the second year of the second Restoration.

The man was sailing for St. Helena, but along with the framework of her institutions and his reflected glory, he bequeathed to France the priceless benefit of restored internal peace.